CHRISTIANITY AND MORALS

CHRISTIANITY AND MORALS

By

EDWARD WESTERMARCK

Essay Index Reprint Series

BOOKS FOR LIBRARIES PRESS
FREEPORT, NEW YORK

First Published 1939

Reprinted 1969

STANDARD BOOK NUMBER:

8369-1055-9

LIBRARY OF CONGRESS CATALOG CARD NUMBER:

78-80406

PRINTED IN THE UNITED STATES OF AMERICA

CONTENTS

CHAPTER I

RELIGION AND MORALITY

CHAPTER II

RELIGION AND MORALITY (*concluded*)

CONTENTS

CHAPTER III

THE ETHICS OF JESUS: THEIR RETRIBUTIVE CHARACTER

CHAPTER IV

THE ETHICS OF JESUS: THEIR DISINTERESTEDNESS AND ALTRUISM

CHAPTER V

THE ETHICS OF JESUS (concluded)

CHAPTER VI

THE ETHICS OF PAUL

CHAPTER VII

THEOLOGICAL DOCTRINES BEFORE AUGUSTINE

CHAPTER VIII

LATER THEOLOGICAL DOCTRINES

CONTENTS

CHAPTER IX

ASCETICISM

CHAPTER X

THE SACRAMENTS

CHAPTER XI

CHRISTIANITY AND THE REGARD FOR HUMAN LIFE

CHAPTER XII

CHRISTIANITY AND THE REGARD FOR HUMAN LIFE

(*concluded*)

CHAPTER XIII

CHRISTIANITY AND ECONOMICS

CHAPTER XVII

CHRISTIANITY AND DIVORCE

CHAPTER XVIII

CHRISTIANITY AND IRREGULAR SEX RELATIONS

CONTENTS xiii

CHAPTER XIX

CHRISTIANITY AND THE REGARD FOR THE LOWER ANIMALS

Jesus' sympathy for animals alleged to be as universal as Buddha's, p. 379.—
The regard for them in Buddhism, p. 380 *sq.*—In Brahmanism, p. 380.—
In Jainism, p. 380 *sq.*—In Taoism, p. 381.—In China, p. 381.—In Japan,
p. 381 *sq.*—Its sources, p. 382.—The attitude towards animals in Zoroastrianism, pp. 382–4.—In Islam, p. 384.—In ancient Greece and Rome,
pp. 384–6.—Among the Hebrews, p. 386 *sq.*—In Christianity, pp. 387–9.
—The views of modern philosophers and legislators, p. 390.—Indifference
to animal suffering characteristic of public opinion in Christian Europe up
to quite modern times, p. 390 *sq.*—Laws against cruelty to animals, p. 391.
—Humane feelings towards animals in Europe, pp. 391–3.—The influence
of human thoughtlessness upon the treatment of animals and upon the
moral ideas relating to it, p. 393.

CHAPTER XX

SUMMARY AND CONCLUDING REMARKS, pp. 394–411
INDEX OF PERSONS, pp. 413–22.
INDEX OF SUBJECTS, pp. 423–7.

CHRISTIANITY
AND MORALS

CHRISTIANITY AND MORALS

CHAPTER I

RELIGION AND MORALITY

CHRISTIANITY is in the first place a religion but, as in the case of many other religions, it contains moral aspects closely connected with the purely religious ones.

The term religion has been used in many different senses, and it is therefore necessary that I should define what I mean by it. I take religion in the abstract, so to speak, as distinguished from any concrete[religion, to be a belief in and a regardful attitude towards a supernatural being, on whom man feels himself dependent and to whom he makes an appeal in his worship.] This definition seems to be in agreement with the most common usage of the word. It has been criticised on the ground that it would not apply to genuine Buddhism. But Buddhism was originally a metaphysical and ethical doctrine, which was transformed into a religion when the old gods of Brahmanism came back, when Buddha himself was deified, and Buddhism incorporated most of the local deities and demons of those nations it sought to convert.

The belief in supernatural beings is undoubtedly based on a feeling of uncanniness or mystery. Men distinguish between phenomena that they are familiar with and consequently ascribe to " natural " causes, and other phenomena that seem to them unfamiliar and mysterious and are looked upon as " supernatural," or are supposed to spring from " supernatural " causes. We meet with this distinction among savages as well as civilised races. It may be that in the mind of a savage the natural and supernatural often overlap, that no definite line can be drawn between the phenomena which he refers to one class and those which he refers to the other ; but he certainly sees a difference between events of everyday occurrence or ordinary objects of nature and other events or objects which fill him with a feeling of wonder or mysterious awe. The feeling of mystery and the germ of a distinction between the natural and the supernatural are found even in the lower animal world. The horse fears the whip, but it does not make him shy; on the other hand, he may shy when he sees an umbrella opened before him or a paper moving on the ground. The whip is well known to the horse, whereas the moving paper or the umbrella is strange, uncanny, let us say " supernatural." I had a mule that took no notice of a volley of guns discharged close to her, because she had been in war and was used to the sound, whereas she might take fright when she met a goat or saw an unusually large stone at the side of the road. Dogs and cats are alarmed by an unusual noise or appearance, and remain uneasy till they have by examination satisfied themselves of the nature of its cause.[1] Even a lion is scared by an unexpected sound or the sight of an unfamiliar object;[2] and we are told of a tiger who stood trembling and roaring in a paroxysm of fear when a mouse tied by a string to a stick had been inserted into its cage.[3] Little children are apt to be terrified by the strange and irregular movements of a feather as it glides along the floor or lifts itself into the air.[4]

Supernatural qualities are not only attributed to beings who are able to work wonders at will : the supernatural, like the natural, may also be looked upon in the light of mechanical energy, which discharges itself without the aid of any volitional activity. Such energy is utilised in magic. In religion, man appeals to or worships supernatural beings by natural means, such as prayers, offerings, abstinences and so forth ; in magic, he attempts to influence either natural or supernatural objects or persons by supernatural means which act mechanically and coercively. The religious attitude is in its nature respectful and humble, the magical attitude is domineering and self-assertive. At the root of the difference between religion and magic there is thus a difference in the mental state of the persons who practise them. So far as religion is concerned, this agrees well with the notion so forcibly expressed by Schleiermacher, that the religious feeling is in its essence a feeling of dependence ; whereas the word magician invariably suggests the idea of a person who claims to possess power and to know how to wield

---

[1] C. Lloyd Morgan, *Animal Life and Intelligence* (London, 1890–91), p. 339 ; G. J. Romanes, *Animal Intelligence* (London, 1895), p. 455 *sq.*
[2] Gillmore, quoted by J. H. King, *The Supernatural*, i (London, 1892), p. 80.
[3] Basil Hall, quoted *ibid.* i. 81. See also *ibid.* i. 78 *sqq.* ; T. Vignioli, *Myth and Science* (London, 1882), p. 58 *sqq.*
[4] J. Sully, *Studies of Childhood* (London, 1895), p. 205 *sq.*

it in the magic art. In order to achieve his aim he may make use of spirits, but then he coerces them ; if he tried to gain their assistance by propitiation, his attitude would be religious, not magical.

This view of magic finds support in mediæval conceptions of it. It is true that the theologians mostly attributed the success of magic to demons, who were enticed by men to work marvels ; but the demons were able to do so largely through their superior knowledge of the forces of nature.[1] And besides the marvels worked by spirits, there were others which were produced without their aid, simply by the wonderful virtues inherent in certain objects of nature. To marvels wrought in this manner William of Auvergne applied the term " natural magic."[2] Albertus Magnus likewise associated magic with natural forces and the stars, as well as with demons ;[3] and Thomas Aquinas, though upholding the opinion that magic is due to demons, gives us a glimpse of a different conception of it, according to which magicians were able by personal qualifica-tions, by subtle use of occult natural properties, by rites and ceremonies, and by the art of astrology, either to work wonders directly and immediately or to coerce demons to work wonders for them.[4]

Another view concerning the difference between religion and magic has been expressed by certain writers, from Robertson Smith onwards, who maintain that religion is social in its aim and magic at any rate non-social,[5] or that magic includes " all bad ways, and religion all good ways, of dealing with the supernormal, bad and good as the society concerned judges them."[6] This use of the terms, however, is not in agreement with the most authoritative traditional usage. Besides black magic there is also white magic. Even mediæval theologians distinguished between good and bad magic. William of Auvergne (†1249), whose works present an unexpectedly detailed picture of the magic and superstition of his time, sees no harm whatever in " natural magic," unless it is employed for evil ends ; he observes that the workers of it are called *magi*, because they do great things (*magna agentes*), whereas others,

[1] L. Thorndike, *A History of Magic and Experimental Science*, ii (London, 1923), pp. 343, 973.

[2] *Ibid.* ii. 343.   [3] *Ibid.* ii. 553.   [4] *Ibid.* ii. 604 *sq.*

[5] W. Robertson Smith, *Lectures on the Religion of the Semites* (London, 1894), p. 264 ; É. Durkheim, *Les formes élémentaires de la vie religieuse* (Paris, 1912), p. 60 *sqq.* ; H. Hubert and M. Mauss, ' Esquisse d'une théorie générale de la magie,' in *L'Année sociologique*, vii (Paris, 1904), p. 1 *sqq.*

[6] R. R. Marett, *Anthropology* (London, *s.d.*), p. 209 *sq.*

who work magic by the aid of demons, are to be regarded as evil-doers.[1] Albertus Magnus defends the Magi of the gospel story and tries to exculpate them from the practice of those particular evil, superstitious, and diabolical occult arts which Isidore and others had included in their definitions of magic. " They were not devoted to any of these arts," he says, " but only to magic as it has been described; and this is praise-worthy." He was himself a believer in occult forces and marvels in nature, showed a leaning to the occult sciences, and was called, even by his panegyrists, *magnus in magia* and *in magicis expertus*.[2] In the *Liber aggregationis*, a very popular treatise on magic which has been ascribed to Albertus but is of dubious authenticity, it is said that magical science (*scientia magicalis*) is not evil, since by knowledge of it evil can be avoided and good attained.[3]

Nor does the definition according to which magic includes all bad ways and religion all good ways of dealing with the supernormal seem to me at all suitable for the purpose of scientific classification. It implies, for example, that a prayer to a god for the destruction of an enemy must be classified as religion if it is offered in a cause which is considered just by the community, but as magic if it is disapproved of. When a man makes a girl drink a love-potion in order to gain her favour, it is religion if their union is desirable from the society's point of view, but if he gives the same drink to another man's wife it is magic. The best part of what has been hitherto called imitative or homœopathic magic no longer remains magic at all; if water is poured out for the purpose of producing rain, it is homœopathic magic only in case rain is not wanted by the community, but if it is done during a drought it is religion. The acceptance of the view that the very same practices are religious or magical according as they have social or anti-social ends would overthrow well-established and useful terms and deprive us of the comprehensive, convenient, and in every respect appropriate attribute " magical " for all sorts of supposed impersonal occult or supernatural forces.

In spite of the essential difference between religion and magic they have, nevertheless, been connected with each other in various ways. Owing to the element of mystery which is found in both, magical forces may be personified as spirits or gods, or be transformed into divine attributes or lead to divine injunctions; and magical practices may become genuine acts of religious worship, or acts of worship may become magical

---

[1] Thorndike, *op. cit.* ii. 347.
[2] *Ibid.* ii. 550, 551, 553 *sq.*   [3] *Ibid.* ii. 726.

practices. Numerous instances of such transformations have been given in my book on the *Origin and Development of the Moral Ideas*. For example : the magical forces which give efficacy to curses have been personified as supernatural beings, like the Greek Erinyes of parents,[1] beggars,[2] and guests,[3] and the Roman *divi parentum*,[4] *dii hospitales*,[5] and Terminus ;[6] or they may be transformed into attributes of the chief god, as in the case of Jupiter Terminalis or Ζεὺς ὅριος.[7] The injurious energy attributed to work performed on the seventh day developed into a religious prohibition,[8] and the uncanny feeling experienced in mentioning the name of a supernatural being readily leads to the belief that he feels offended if his name is pronounced.[9] Curses and blessings become prayers ;[10] and on the other hand, prayers become spells which are believed to constrain the gods to whom they are addressed. This appears from the words of many formulas that are used as magical incantations. Assyrian incantations are often dressed in the robe of supplication and end with the formula, " Do so and so, and I shall gladden thine heart and worship thee in humility."[11] Vedic texts which were not originally meant as charms became so afterwards. Incantations are comparatively rare in the Rig-Veda, and seem even to be looked upon as objectionable, but towards the end of the Vedic period the reign of Brahma, the power of prayer, as the supreme god in the Indian pantheon began to dawn.[12] The prayer is imbued with supernatural energy owing to the holiness of the being to whom it is addressed, and its constraining force may then be directed even against the god himself.

But the connection between religion and magic may be still more intimate. I have hitherto spoken of religion in the abstract, as distinguished from any concrete religion. In the popular sense of the word, which certainly must be respected, *a* religion may include many practices which are what I have called magical. In the ancient religions of the East religion

[1] E. Westermarck, *The Origin and Development of the Moral Ideas*, i (London, 1912), p. 623.

[2] *Ibid.* i. 561.   [3] *Ibid.* i. 585.   [4] *Ibid.* i. 624.

[5] *Ibid.* i. 585.   [6] *Ibid.* ii (1917), p. 68.   [7] *Ibid.* ii. 68.

[8] *Ibid.* ii. 286 *sq.*   [9] *Ibid.* ii. 640 *sqq.*

[10] *Ibid.* i. 564 *sq.*, ii. 66–8, 120–3, 658, 686–90, 731.

[11] K. L. Tallqvist, ' Die assyrische Beschwörungsserie maqlû,' in *Acta Societatis Scientiarum Fennicæ*, xx (Helsingfors, 1895), p. 22.

[12] H. Oldenberg, *Die Religion des Veda* (Berlin, 1894), p. 311 *sqq.* ; E. W. Hopkins, *The Religions of India* (London, 1896), p. 149 ; R. Roth, ' Brahma und die Brahmanen,' in *Zeitschrift der Deutschen Morgenländischen Gesellschaft*, i (Leipzig, 1846), pp. 67, 71 ; J. Darmesteter, *Essais orientaux* (Paris, 1883), p. 132.

and magic are indissolubly mixed up together. According to Mohammedan orthodoxy the Arabic words of the Koran work miracles. The Christian sacraments of baptism and the Eucharist are rooted in magical ideas, and the efficacy ascribed to them has always retained a more or less magical character.[1] Although the magical and the strictly religious attitudes differ from each other, they are not irreconcilable, and may therefore very well form parts of one and the same religion ; there is no such thing as *a* magic being opposed to *a* religion. By a religion is generally understood a system of beliefs and rules of behaviour which have reference to, or are considered to be prescribed by, one or several supernatural beings whom the believers call their god or gods—that is, supernatural beings who are the objects of a regular cult and between whom and their worshippers there are established and permanent relationships. If it is admitted that the word " religion " may thus be legitimately used in two different senses, an abstract and a concrete, I think there is little ground left for further controversy as regards the relation between religion and magic.

While the origin of religion may be traced to the feeling of uncanniness and mystery, the moral consciousness has an entirely different foundation. For a discussion not only of the general relations between religion and morality, but also of my particular subject—the relations between Christianity and morals—I find it necessary to give a summary of my views concerning the nature of the moral consciousness, which I have expounded in detail in earlier works.[2] The reader will notice what a fundamental position these views occupy in my arguments.

All moral concepts, which are used as predicates in moral judgments, are ultimately based on one or the other of the two emotions, moral approval and moral disapproval or indignation. Both of them belong to a wider class of emotions, which I have called retributive emotions. Moral disapproval is a kind of resentment, by which I understand a hostile attitude of mind towards a living being (or something taken for a living being) conceived as a cause of inflicted pain ; moral approval is a retributive kindly emotion, that is, a friendly attitude of mind towards such a being conceived as a cause of pleasure. They are related to other kinds of resentment or retributive kindly emotion : moral disapproval to anger and the feeling of revenge, and moral approval to gratitude. But the moral emotions

---

[1] *Infra*, ch. x.

[2] *The Origin and Development of the Moral Ideas*, two volumes (London, 1912, 1917), and *Ethical Relativity* (London, 1932).

differ from those non-moral retributive emotions by being disinterested and, at least within certain limits, impartial. If some one inflicts an injury upon me, or upon a friend of mine, and I feel indignant in consequence, my indignation can be called a moral emotion only if it is felt independently of the fact that it was I or my friend who was hurt ; it must be possible to assume that I should have experienced the same emotion if another similar person in similar circumstances had been subjected to the same treatment. Otherwise my emotion of resentment would have been not moral disapproval, but personal anger. So also, the kindly emotion which I feel for a benefactor can be called moral approval only on condition that it is disinterested and impartial; otherwise it would be personal gratitude.

The origin of retributive emotions may be explained by their usefulness to the species. Resentment, like protective reflex action, from which it has gradually developed, is a means of protection for the animal owing to its tendency to remove a cause of danger. The disposition to experience it may consequently be regarded as an element in the animal's mental constitution that has been acquired through the influence of natural selection in the struggle for existence. And as natural selection accounts for the origin of the disposition to feel resentment, so also it accounts for the origin of the disposition to feel retributive kindly emotion. Both of these emotions are useful to the species : by resentment evils are averted, by retributive kindliness benefits are secured. But retributive kindliness is of much less frequent occurrence in the animal kingdom than resentment. In a very large number of species not even the germ of it is found, and where it occurs it is generally restricted within narrow limits. Anybody may provoke an animal's anger, but only towards certain individuals is it apt to feel retributive kindliness. The limits for this emotion are marked off by the conditions under which altruistic sentiments tend to arise. In its primitive form we find it among animals living in groups, including the small group consisting of mother, or parents, and offspring. The associated animals take pleasure in each other's company, and with this pleasure is intimately connected kindliness towards its cause, the companion himself, who is conceived as a friend. The altruistic sentiment would never have come into existence without such reciprocity of feeling. That there is such an enormous difference between the prevalence of resentment and that of retributive kindly emotion is easily explained by the simple fact that the living in groups is an advantage only to certain species, and that even gregarious animals have many enemies but few friends.

This explanation of the origin of resentment and retributive kindly emotion also holds true of the moral emotions in so far as they are retributive emotions : it accounts for the hostile attitude of moral disapproval towards the cause of pain and for the friendly attitude of moral approval towards the cause of pleasure. But it still remains for us to consider the origin of those elements in the moral emotions by which they are distinguished from other, non-moral, retributive emotions. First, how shall we explain their disinterestedness ?

We have to distinguish between different classes of conditions under which disinterested retributive emotions arise. In the first place, we may feel disinterested resentment, or disinterested retributive kindly emotion, on account of an injury inflicted, or a benefit conferred, upon another individual with whose pain, or pleasure, we sympathise and in whose welfare we take a kindly interest. Our retributive emotions are, of course, always reactions against pain or pleasure felt by ourselves ; this holds good of the moral emotions as well as of anger, revenge, and gratitude. The question to be answered, then, is, Why should we, quite disinterestedly, feel pain calling forth disapproval because our neighbour is hurt, and pleasure calling forth approval because he is benefited ?

That a certain act causes pleasure or pain to the bystander may be due to the close association that exists between these feelings and their outward expressions. The sight of a happy face tends to produce some degree of pleasure in him who sees it ; the sight of bodily signs of suffering tends to produce a feeling of pain. Moreover, sympathetic pain or pleasure may be the result of an association between cause and effect, between the cognition of a certain act or situation and the feeling generally evoked by this act or situation : a blow may cause pain to the spectator before he has witnessed its effect on the victim.

But the sympathetic feeling that results from association alone is not what is popularly called sympathy : it lacks kindliness. Arising merely from the habitual connection of certain cognitions with certain feelings in the experience of the spectator, it is, strictly speaking, not at all concerned with what the other individual *feels*. On the other hand sympathy, in the popular sense of the word, requires the co-operation of the altruistic sentiment or affection, a disposition of mind that is particularly apt to display itself as kindly emotion towards other beings. This sentiment, only, induces us to take a kindly interest in the feelings of our neighbours. It involves a tendency, or willingness, and, when strongly developed, gives rise to an eager desire, to sympathise with their pains and pleasures. But the altruistic sentiment is not merely willingness to sympathise, it is above all a conative disposition to promote the welfare of its object. It is true that sympathetic pain, unaided by kindliness, may induce a person to relieve the suffering of his neighbour, but then he does so, not out of regard to the feeling of the sufferer, but simply to get rid of a painful cognition. The sight of the wounded traveller may perhaps have caused scarcely less pain to the Pharisee than to the good Samaritan ; yet it would have been impossible for the latter to dismiss his pain by going away, since he felt a desire to assist the wounded man, and this desire would have been ungratified if he had not stopped by the way-side.

The co-operation of the altruistic sentiment with sympathy also produces in us disinterested retributive emotions, when the individual towards whom we are kindly disposed is hurt or benefited. In the tendency to feel such emotions, however, there is a great difference between resentment and retributive kindliness. Resentment towards an enemy is itself, as a rule, a much stronger emotion than retributive kindly emotion towards a benefactor. And as for the sympathetic forms of these emotions, it is not surprising that the altruistic sentiment is more readily moved by the sight of pain than by the sight of pleasure, considering that it serves as a means of protection for the species. Moreover, sympathetic retributive kindliness has powerful rivals in the feelings of jealousy and envy, which tend to excite anger also towards him who bestows the benefit on the other individual. As an ancient writer observes, " many suffer with their friends when the friends are in distress, but are envious of them when they prosper." [1] Among the lower animals there seems to be no trace of retributive kindly emotion felt as a result of pleasure taken in kindness shown to another individual. On the other hand, there is sympathetic resentment in consequence of an inflicted injury. A mammalian mother is as hostile to the enemy of her young as to her own enemy. Social animals defend members of their own group, which evidently involves some degree of sympathetic anger. When a young monkey which had been seized by an eagle cried for assistance, " the other members of the troupe, with much uproar, rushed to the rescue, surrounded the eagle, and pulled out so many feathers, that he no longer thought of his prey, but only how to escape." [2] Speaking of a group of chimpanzees in confinement, Professor Köhler says that if one of them was

---

[1] Quoted by L. Schmidt, *Die Ethik der alten Griechen*, i (Berlin, 1882), p. 259.

[2] C. Darwin, *The Descent of Man* (London, 1890), p. 101 *sq.*

attacked before the eyes of the others, great excitement went through the whole group ; and that even the lightest form of punishment, such as pulling the ear of the offender, often stirred single members of the group to much more decisive action.[1] Among domesticated animals sympathetic resentment may be felt even when the individual who is hurt belongs to another species. We are told by a trustworthy authority of a dog at Liverpool who saved a cat from the hands of some young ruffians : he rushed in among the boys, barked furiously at them, terrified them into flight, and carried the cat off in his mouth to his kennel, where he nursed it.[2] The dog who flies at any one who strikes, or even touches, his master is a very familiar instance of sympathetic resentment.

Among a gregarious species of animals the members of a herd are at ease in each other's company, suffer when they are separated, rejoice when they are reunited, and very frequently display affection by defending each other, helping each other in distress and danger, and perform various other services for each other.[3] Among men the members of the same social unit are tied to each other with various bonds of a distinctly human character—the same customs, laws, institutions, magic or religious ceremonies and beliefs, notions of a common descent, and so forth. As men generally are fond of that to which they are used or which is their own, they are also naturally apt to have likings for other individuals whose habits, ideas, and feelings are similar to theirs. Uncivilised peoples are as a rule described as kind towards members of their own community or tribe. Within these limits they are charitable and generous, and their customs relating to mutual aid are often much more stringent than our own ; and this applies even to the very lowest among them.

While disinterested resentment may thus be felt in consequence of an injury inflicted upon another individual as a reaction against sympathetic pain, it may also be directly produced by the cognition of the signs of resentment. In the former case it is really independent of the emotion of the injured individual ; we may feel resentment on his behalf though he himself feels none. In the latter case it is an emotion reflected through the medium of its outward expression in another individual. We are told that among bees, ants, and termites

---

[1] W. Köhler, *The Mentality of Apes* (London, 1927), p. 286 *sq.*

[2] C. Williams, *Dogs and Their Ways* (London, 1863), p. 43.

[3] Darwin, *op. cit.* p. 100 *sqq.* ; P. Kropotkin, *Mutual Aid* (London, 1902), ch. i *sq.* ; F. Alverdes, *Social Life in the Animal World* (London, 1927), p. 133 *sq.*

signs of anger felt by one individual may awaken the whole community to a high pitch of excitement.[1] A group of the captive chimpanzees studied by Köhler might be thrown into a state of blind fury by the angry cries of one of its members, " even when the majority of its members have seen nothing of what caused the first cry, and have no notion of what it is all about." [2] When the yells and shrieks of a street dog-fight are heard, dogs from all sides rush to the spot, each dog being apparently ready to bite any of the others. So, too, in an infuriated crowd of men one gets angry because the other is angry, and often the question Why ? is hardly asked. This form of disinterested resentment is of great importance both as an originator and, especially, as a communicator of moral ideas : it is, in fact, the main foundation of moral tradition. Men are inclined to sympathise with the resentment of persons for whom they feel regard ; hence an act which, though harmless by itself, is forbidden by God and man may be not only professed but actually felt to be wrong. The punishment inflicted by the society, which as a rule is an expression of its moral indignation, may also, by arousing such a feeling, lead to the idea that it deserves to be punished. Children, as everybody knows, grow up with their ideas of right and wrong graduated, to a great extent, according to the temper of the father or mother ; and men are not seldom, as Hobbes said, " like little children, that have no other rule of good and evill manners, but the correction they receive from their Parents and Masters." [3] Any means of expressing resentment may serve as a communicator of the emotion. Besides punishment, language deserves special mention. Moral disapproval may be evoked by the very sounds of words like " murder," " theft," " cowardice," and others, which not merely indicate a certain mode of behaviour but also express the opprobrium attached to it. By the use of some strong word the orator raises the indignation of a sympathetic audience to its pitch.

There is yet a third way in which disinterested resentment may arise. In many cases people feel hostile to a person who inflicts no injury on anybody. There are in the human mind what Bain called " disinterested antipathies," or sentimental aversions, " of which our fellow-beings are the subjects, and on account of which we overlook our own interest as much as in

[1] S. J. Holmes, *The Evolution of Animal Intelligence* (New York, 1911), p. 209.
[2] Köhler, *op. cit.* p. 288.
[3] T. Hobbes, *Leviathan*, i. 11 (Oxford, 1881), p. 76.

displaying our sympathies and affections." [1] Differences of taste, habit, and opinion easily create similar dislikes ; and these, too, have played a prominent part in the moulding of the moral consciousness. The antipathy which is so commonly felt against anything unusual, new, or foreign, may lead to the idea that it is wrong ; and when a certain act which does no harm—apart from the painful impression it makes on the spectator—fills people with disgust or horror, they may feel no less inclined to inflict harm upon the agent than if he had committed an offence against person, property, or good name. Such resentment may also arise from the observation of the feelings of others. As Abraham Tucker said, " we grow to love things we perceive them fond of, and contract aversions from their dislikes." [2]

We have already noticed that sympathy, in the popular sense of the word, may produce not only disinterested resentment but disinterested retributive kindliness as well : when taking a pleasure in the benefit bestowed upon our neighbour we are disposed to look with kindness on the benefactor. Moreover, as resentment may be produced by the cognition of outward signs of resentment in others, so kindly emotion may be produced by the signs of kindliness. Even a dog may be well-disposed towards a stranger when he sees a friend—whether a man or another dog—be friendly to him. Language communicates emotions by terms of praise as well as by terms of condemnation ; and a reward, like a punishment, has some tendency to reproduce the emotion from which it sprang. Finally, men have disinterested likings as they have disinterested dislikes. As an instance of these may be mentioned the common admiration of courage when felt irrespectively of the object for which it is displayed—a feeling which has even elevated it to an independent virtue, and in any case tends to influence the moral verdict.

Having found the origin of disinterested retributive emotions, we have also partly explained the origin of the moral emotions. But, as we have seen, these emotions are not only disinterested, they are also impartial in a wider sense. The possibility of such impartiality, however, is explained by the answer to the more general question, how disinterestedness and a certain degree of impartiality have become characteristics of that particular kind of retributive emotions that we call moral emotions. The solution of this problem is not difficult to find. It lies in the fact that society is the birth-place of the moral

[1] A. Bain, *The Emotions and the Will* (London, 1880), p. 268.
[2] A. Tucker, *The Light of Nature Pursued*, i (London, 1840), p. 154.

consciousness; that the first moral judgments expressed not the private emotions of isolated individuals, but emotions felt by the society at large; that tribal custom was the earliest rule of duty.

Customs are not merely public habits—the habits of a certain circle of men, a racial or national community, a rank or class of society—but they are at the same time rules of conduct. As Cicero observes, the customs of a people " are precepts in themselves." [1] We say that " custom commands " or " custom demands," and even when custom simply allows the commission of a certain class of actions, it implicitly lays down the rule that such actions are not to be interfered with. And the rule of custom is conceived of as a moral rule which decides what is right and wrong. The Greek idea of the customary, τὸ νόμιμον, shows the close connection between morality and custom; and so do the words ἔθος, ἦθος, and ἠθικά, the Latin *mos* and *moralis*, the German *Sitte* and *Sittlichkeit*. Moreover, in early society customs are not only moral rules but the only moral rules ever thought of. The savage strictly complies with the Hegelian command that no man must have a private conscience.

What does it mean that custom is a rule of conduct? It implies that every deviation from custom is apt to call forth public disapproval. In the lower stages of civilisation, especially, custom is a tyrant who binds man in iron fetters, and who threatens the transgressor not only with general disgrace, but often with bodily suffering or even death. In its ethical aspect custom is nothing but a generalisation of emotional tendencies, applied to certain modes of conduct and transmitted from generation to generation. Now if custom is a moral rule, the public disapproval aroused by its transgression may be properly called a moral emotion. Moreover, where all the duties of a man are expressed in the customs of the society to which he belongs, the characteristics of moral disapproval are naturally to be sought for in its connection with custom. Custom is fixed once for all, and admits of no purely individual preferences. It is equally binding for me and for you and for all the other members of the society. A breach of it is equally wrong whether I myself am immediately concerned in the act or not; this involves disinterestedness. So also the condemnation of it is independent of the relationship in which the parties concerned in it stand to me personally; this implies impartiality in a larger sense. And all this holds true whatever be the origin of any particular custom. It may have originated in selfishness

[1] Cicero, *De officiis*, i. 41.

or partiality ; the leading men of the society may at first have prohibited certain acts because they found them disadvantageous to themselves or to the class of people with whom they particularly sympathised.   Where custom is an oppressor of women, this oppression may, in some measure at least, be traced back to the selfishness of the men.   Where custom sanctions slavery, it is certainly not impartial to the slaves.   Yet in one case as in the other custom is assumed to be in the right, irrespectively of one's own station, and the women and the slaves themselves are expected to be of the same opinion.   Such an expectation is by no means a chimera.[1]   Under stable social conditions, largely owing to men's tendency to share the resentment of their superiors, the customs of a society are willingly submitted to and recognised as right by the great majority of its members, whatever be their station.

As public disapproval is the prototype of moral disapproval, so is public approval, expressed in public praise, the prototype of moral approval : it is characterised by the same disinterestedness and impartiality.   But of the two emotions public disapproval, being at the root of custom and leading to the infliction of punishment, is by far the more impressive.   Hence it is not surprising that the term " moral " is etymologically connected with *mos*, which always implies the existence of a social rule the transgression of which evokes public disapproval. Only by analogy has it come to be applied to the emotion of approval as well.

Though moral disapproval and approval have taken their place in the system of human emotions as public emotions felt by the society at large, they have not always remained inseparably connected with the feelings of any special society. The unanimity of opinion that originally characterised the members of the same social unit was disturbed by its advancement in civilisation.   Individuals arose who found fault with the moral ideas prevalent in the community to which they belonged, criticising them on the basis of their own individual feelings.   To deny such individuals the right of speaking in the name of morality true and proper would be to attach to this term a meaning which, in its narrowness, would be utterly different from the established usage of it.   All that is required is that their retributive emotions should possess that disinterestedness and impartiality which have become moral characteristics in connection with custom, but may differ from public approval and disapproval either in intensity or with regard to the facts by which they are evoked.   Indeed, the dissent from

[1] For instances of this see my *Ethical Relativity*, p. 111.

the orthodox views of morality often arises from the conviction that the apparent impartiality of public feelings is an illusion. In the course of progressive civilisation the moral consciousness has tended towards a greater equalisation of rights, towards an expansion of the circle within which the same moral rules are applicable. And this process has been largely due to the example of influential individuals and their efforts to raise public opinion to their own standard of right.

My earlier statement that the predicates of all moral judgments are ultimately based on moral emotions by no means implies that such a judgment affirms the existence of a moral emotion in the mind of the person who utters it : he may do so without feeling any emotion at all. No doubt, to say that a certain act is good or bad may be the mere expression of an emotion felt with regard to it, just as to say that the sun is hot and the weather cold may be the mere expression of a sensation of heat or cold produced by the sun or the weather. But such judgments express subjective facts in terms which strictly speaking have a different meaning. To attribute a quality to something is not the same as to state the existence of a particular emotion or sensation in the mind that perceives it. This, however, does not imply that the term used to denote the quality may not have a subjective origin. I maintain, on the contrary, that the qualities assigned to the subjects of moral judgments really are generalisations derived from approval or disapproval felt with regard to certain modes of conduct, that they are tendencies to feel one or the other of these emotions interpreted as qualities, as dynamic tendencies, in the phenomena which gave rise to the emotion. A similar translation of emotional states into terms of qualities assigned to external phenomena is found in many other cases : something is " fearful " because people fear it, " admirable " because people admire it. When we call an act good or bad, we do not *state* the existence of any emotional tendencies, any more than; when we call a landscape beautiful, we state any characteristics of beauty : we refer the subject of the judgment to a class of phenomena which we are used to call good or bad. But we are used to call them so because they have evoked moral approval in ourselves or in other persons from whom we have learnt the use of those words.

Most people follow a very simple method in judging of an act. Particular modes of conduct have their traditional labels, many of which are learnt with language itself ; and the moral judgment commonly consists simply in labelling the act according to certain obvious characteristics which it presents in common with others belonging to the same group. We hear that some one has appropriated another's property, this is theft, it is wrong ; some one tells an untruth, this is lying, it is wrong ; some one gives money to a needy person, this is charity, it is good ; and so forth.   But when we examine the nature of these acts we find that they are apt to give rise to or, as we may also put it, to become the objects of, certain emotions, either of disapproval or approval, and it is the tendency to feel one or the other of these emotions that has led people to call them bad or good.   Those who first established the use of these and all other moral concepts felt disapproval or approval and expressed in the concepts their tendency to feel such an emotion in the given circumstances.   This is what may be called the intrinsic meaning of the terms.   I do not say that those who use them are aware of this meaning.   We are often unable to tell what is really implied in a concept that we predicate to a certain phenomenon.   When any one is asked what he means by saying that something is or exists, or that something is the cause of something else, I suppose that everybody who is not a philosopher, and even many a philosopher, feels somewhat bewildered. If we want to find out the intrinsic meaning of a term we have to examine the circumstances in which it is used.   And in analysing the predicates of moral judgments, we are guided by the fact that if we ourselves emphatically and truly mean what we say when we pronounce such a judgment, we recognise that we are apt, or at least think we are apt, to feel a moral emotion of either approval or disapproval with regard to that on which the judgment is pronounced.

In order to show that the concepts which are used as predicates in moral judgments are ultimately based upon emotions it is necessary to examine the relations between the concepts and the emotions.   This is a task which has been much neglected by the moralists of the emotional school, from Adam Smith to McDougall, although it is evidently a matter of paramount importance.   I have undertaken it in my earlier works, and shall now only give a brief summary of my views.   The import of the moral concepts is not a topic that requires, for the right understanding of the main subject of my book, as detailed a treatment as the nature of the emotions underlying them.

Moral disapproval has led to the concepts of ought and duty, right and wrong, justice and injustice.   Every " ought "-judgment contains implicitly a prohibition of that which ought *not* to be done.   Nobody would ever have dreamt of laying down a moral rule if the idea of its transgression had not presented itself to his mind.   We may reverse the words of the Apostle and say that where no transgression is, there is no law ;

the law-breaker is, in a way, the law-maker. When Solon was asked why he had specified no punishment for one who had murdered his father, he replied that he supposed it could not occur to any man to commit such a crime.[1] We may certainly applaud him who is faithful to his duty in circumstances where the average man would have felt a strong temptation to yield to a contrary impulse. There is no contradiction in the omission of an act being disapproved of and the performance of it being praised ; but " ought " and " duty " only express the tendency of an act's omission to call forth moral disapproval and say nothing about the consequences of its performance. The tendency in a phenomenon to arouse moral disapproval is directly expressed by the terms " bad " and " wrong."

" Right " is what is in conformity to duty, unless this term is simply used to point out that something is " not wrong." And like the adjective " right " is also the substantive denoting " a right " rooted in the emotion of moral disapproval. To have a right to do a thing is to be allowed to do it, either by positive law, in the case of a legal right, or by the moral law, in the case of a moral right ; in other words, to have a moral right to do a thing implies that it is not wrong to do it. But generally the concept of " a right " means something more than this. From the fact that an act is allowable follows, as a rule, that it ought not to be prevented ; and this character of inviolability is largely included in the very concepts of rights. That a man has a right to live does not merely mean that he commits no wrong by supporting his life, but it chiefly means that it would be wrong of other people to prevent him from living, that it is their duty to refrain from killing him, or even, as the case may be, that it is their duty to help him to live.

Closely connected with the notions of wrongness and rightness are the notions of injustice and justice. " Injustice " implies a violation of some one's right ; " justice," in the strict sense of the term, involves the notion that a duty to somebody, a duty corresponding to a right in him, is fulfilled. But at the same time " injustice " and " justice " are not simply other names for violating or respecting rights. When we style an act " unjust " we emphasise that it is not impartial, when we style an act " just " we point out that an undue preference would have been shown some one by its omission. It is the emphasis laid on the duty of impartiality that gives justice a special prominence in connection with punishments and rewards. A man's rights depend to a great extent upon his actions. Other things being equal, the criminal has not the same rights to

[1] Diogenes Laertius, *Solon*, 10 ; Cicero, *Pro S. Roscio Amerino*, 25.

inviolability as regards reputation, freedom, property, or life as the innocent man ; the miser and the egoist have not the same rights as the benefactor and the philanthropist. On these differences in rights, due to differences in conduct, the terms " just " and " unjust " lay stress ; for in such cases an injustice would have been committed if the rights had been equal. When we say of a criminal that he has been " justly " imprisoned, we point out that he was no victim to undue partiality, as he had forfeited the general right to freedom on account of his crime. When we say of a benefactor that he has been " justly " rewarded, we point out that no favour was partially bestowed upon him in preference to others, as he had acquired the special right of being rewarded. But the " justice " of a punishment or a reward, strictly speaking, involves something more than this ; as we have seen, what is strictly just is always the discharge of a duty corresponding to a right that would have been in a partial manner disregarded by a transgression of the duty. If it is just that a person should be rewarded he ought to be rewarded, and to fulfil this duty is to do him justice. Again, if it is just that a person should be punished he ought to be punished, and his not being punished is an injustice towards all those whose condemnation of the wrong act finds its recognised expression in the punishment, inasmuch as their rightful claim that the criminal should be punished, their right of resisting wrong, is thereby violated in favour of the wrongdoer. Moreover, his not being punished is an injustice towards other criminals, who have been, or who will be, punished for similar acts, in so far as they have a right to demand that no undue preference should be shown anybody whose guilt is equal to theirs. Retributive punishment may admit of a certain latitude as to the retribution. It may be a matter of small concern from the community's point of view whether men are fined or imprisoned for the commission of a certain crime. But justice demands that in equal circumstances all of them should be punished with the same severity, since the crime has equally affected their rights. The emphasis which " injustice " lays on the partiality of a certain mode of conduct always involves a condemnation of that partiality, and is thus a concept that is obviously based on the emotion of moral disapproval. And so is the concept of " justice," whether it involves the notion that an injustice would be committed if a certain duty is not fulfilled, or it is used, more loosely, to denote that a certain course of conduct is " not unjust." But the word " just " may also emphasise the impartiality of an act in a tone of praise. Considering how difficult it may be to be perfectly impartial and give every man his due, especially when one's own interests are concerned, it is only natural that men may be applauded for being just, and, consequently, that to call a person " just " may be to praise him. So also, " justice " is used as the name for a virtue, " the mistress and queen of all virtues." [1] But all this does not imply that an emotion of moral approval enters into the concept of justice as such. It only means that one word is used to express a certain concept, which ultimately derives its import from moral disapproval, and in addition an emotion of approval. That the concept of justice by itself has no reference to the emotion of approval is shown by the fact that it is no praise to say of an act that it is " only just."

From the concepts springing from moral disapproval we shall pass to those springing from moral approval. Foremost among these ranks the concept of goodness. The word " good " is applied to a great variety of objects. But whatever all other good things may have in common, " goodness," in the emphatically moral sense of the word has a characteristic of its own, which makes it widely different from any other " good " : it is a concept rooted in the tendency to feel the emotion of moral approval, it is the general expression for moral praise. The word " virtue," again, is usually applied to denote a disposition of mind characterised by some special kind of goodness. He who is habitually temperate possesses the virtue of temperance, he who is habitually brave the virtue of courage, he who is habitually generous the virtue of generosity. Even when a man is simply said to be " virtuous," this epithet is given him, more or less distinctly, with reference to some kind or kinds of goodness : it may mean that he has many virtues, or that he has much of one. A Supreme Being who is regarded as all-good is not called virtuous.

Like the notions cf goodness and virtue, the " meritorious " derives its origin from the emotion of moral approval ; but while the former merely express a tendency to give rise to such an emotion, the " meritorious " implies that the object to which it refers " merits " praise, that it has a just claim to praise, in other words, that it ought to be recognised as good. This makes the term " meritorious " more emphatic than the term " good," but at the same time it narrows its province in a peculiar way. Just as the expression that something ought to be done implies the idea that it possibly may not be done, so the statement that something is meritorious, in pointing out its goodness, implies

---

[1] Cicero, *De officiis*, iii. 6.

the idea that this goodness may fail to receive due recognition. It would be blasphemous to call the acts of a God who is conceived to be infinitely good " meritorious," since it would suggest a thinkable limitation of his goodness.

CHAPTER II

RELIGION AND MORALITY (*concluded*)

THE gods of uncivilised peoples are to a large extent of a malevolent character, but they are not exclusively so; and though they as a rule take little interest in any kind of human conduct that does not affect their own welfare, some of them are also opposed to acts of ordinary wrongdoing. Among peoples of a higher culture, again, the gods are on the whole benevolent to mankind when duly propitiated. They resent by preference offences committed against themselves personally; but in many cases they at the same time avenge social wrongs of various kinds, act as superintendents of human justice, and are even looked upon as the originators and sustainers of the whole moral order of the world. The gods have thus experienced a gradual change for the better; until at last they are described as ideals of moral perfection, even though, when more closely scrutinised, their goodness and notions of justice are found to differ materially from what is deemed good and just in the case of men.[1]

The malevolence of savage gods is in accordance with the theory that religion is born of fear. The assumed originators of misfortunes were naturally regarded as enemies to be propitiated; while fortunate events, if attracting sufficient attention and appearing sufficiently marvellous to suggest a supernatural cause, were commonly ascribed to beings who were too good to require worship. But growing reflection has a tendency to attribute more amiable qualities to the gods. The religious consciousness of men becomes less exclusively occupied with the hurts they suffer, and comes more and more to reflect upon the benefits they enjoy. The activity of a god which displays itself in a certain phenomenon, or group of phenomena, appears to them on some occasions as a source of evil, but on other occasions as a source of good; hence the god is regarded as partly malevolent, partly benevolent, and in all circumstances as a being who must not be neglected. Moreover, a god who is by nature harmless or good may by proper worship be induced

---

[1] See my book *The Origin and Development of the Moral Ideas*, ii (London, 1917), ch. 1 *sq.*

to assist man in his struggle against evil spirits. The protective function of nature gods becomes particularly important when the god is humanised also with regard to his shape, and consequently more or less dissociated from the natural phenomenon in which he originally manifested himself. Nothing, indeed, seems to have contributed more to the improvement of nature gods than the expansion of their sphere of activity. When supernatural beings can exert their power in the various departments of life, men naturally choose for their gods those among them who with great power combine the greatest benevolence.

×Men have selected their gods according to their usefulness. We have many direct instances of such " supernatural selection." Among the Maori " a mere trifle, or natural casualty, will induce a native (or a whole tribe) to change his Atua." [1]   The negro, when disappointed in some of his speculations, or overtaken by some sad calamity, throws away his fetish, and selects a new one. [2]   When hard-pressed the Samoyed, after having invoked his own deities in vain, addresses himself to the Russian god, promising to become his worshipper if he relieves him from his distress ; and in most cases he is said to be faithful to his promise, though he may still try to keep on good terms with his former gods by occasionally offering them a sacrifice in secret. [3]   North American Indians attribute all their good or bad luck to their Manitou, and " if the Manitou has not been favourable to them, they quit him without any ceremony, and take another." [4] Among many of the Indians of Central America there was a regular and systematic selection of gods. Father Blas Valera says that their gods had annual rotations and were changed each year in accordance with the superstitions of the people. " The old gods were forsaken as infamous, or because they had been of no use, and other gods and demons were elected. . . . Sons when they inherited either accepted or repudiated the gods of their fathers, for they were not allowed to hold their pre-eminence against the will of their heir. Old men worshipped other greater deities, but they likewise dethroned them, and

[1] J. S. Polack, *Manners and Customs of the New Zealanders*, i (London, 1840), p. 233.
[2] J. Leighton Wilson, *Western Africa* (London, 1856), p. 212.
[3] A. Ahlqvist, ' Unter Wogulen und Ostjaken,' in *Acta Societatis Scientiarum Fennicæ*, xiv (Helsingfors, 1885), p. 240. The ancient Scandinavians abandoned their old gods when they found that the Christian God was better able to satisfy their wants (H. Ljungberg, *Den nordiska religionen och kristendomen* [Stockholm and Köpenhamn, 1938], p. 315).
[4] Bossu, *Travels through Louisiana*, i (London, 1771), p. 103 ; J. G. Frazer, *Totemism* (Edinburgh, 1887), p. 55.

set up others in their places when the year was over. . . .
Such were the gods which all the nations of Mexico, Chiapa, and
Guatemala worshipped, as well as those of Vera Paz, and many
other Indians. They thought that the gods selected by themselves were the greatest and most powerful of all the gods." [1]
These are crude instances of a process which in some form or
other must have been an important motive force in religious
evolution by making the gods better suited to meet the wants
of their believers. We find traces of it even in the Old Testament. " Jacob vowed a vow, saying, If God will be with me,
and will keep me in this way that I go, and will give me bread
to eat, and raiment to put on, So that I come again to my
father's house in peace ; then shall the Lord be my God : And
this stone, which I have set for a pillar, shall be God's house :
and of all that thou shalt give me I will surely give the tenth
unto thee." [2] The Hebrews thought of the national religion as
constituted by a covenant rite in which the parties were Yahve
and Abraham,[3] as also by a formal covenant sacrifice at Mount
Sinai, where half of the blood of the sacrificed oxen was sprinkled
on the altar and the other half on the people ; [4] and the idea of
sacrifice establishing a covenant between God and man is also
apparent in the Psalms.[5] Robertson Smith and his followers
have represented the covenant practices as acts of communion,[6]
but similar methods of covenanting, which I have found in
Morocco, have led me to believe that those employed by the
ancient Hebrews in covenanting with the deity aimed at
transferring conditional curses both to the men and to their god.[7]
Such covenanting naturally presupposed a kind of selection.

Men not only select as their gods such supernatural beings
as may be most useful to them in the struggle for life, but also
magnify their good qualities in worshipping them. Praise and
exaggerating eulogy are common in the mouth of a devout
worshipper. In ancient Egypt the god of each petty state was
within it said to be the ruler of the gods, the creator of the world,
the giver of all good things.[8] So also in Chaldea the god of a

[1] Blas Valera, quoted by Garcilasso de la Vega, *First Part of the Royal Commentaries of the Yncas*, i (London, 1869), p. 124 *sq.*
[2] *Genesis* xxviii. 20 *sqq.*   [3] *Ibid.* xv. 8 *sqq.*
[4] *Exodus* xxiv. 4 *sqq.*   [5] *Psalms* l. 5.
[6] W. Robertson Smith, *Lectures on the Religion of the Semites* (London, 1894), lec. ix *sqq.* ; E. S. Hartland, *The Legend of Perseus*, ii (London, 1895), p. 236 ; F. B. Jevons, *An Introduction to the History of Religion* (London, 1896), p. 225.
[7] See my *Ritual and Belief in Morocco*, i (London, 1926), ch. x.
[8] A. Wiedemann, *Religion of the Ancient Egyptians* (London, 1897), p. 11.

town was addressed by its inhabitants with the most exalted epithets, as the master or king of all the gods.[1] The Vedic poets were engrossed in the praise of the particular deity they happened to be invoking, magnifying his attributes to the point of inconsistency.[2] The Hindus say that by praise a person may obtain from the gods whatever he desires.[3] There is a Chinese story that amusingly illustrates this little weakness of so many gods. At the hottest season of the year there was a heavy fall of snow at Soochow. The people, in their consternation, went to the temple of the Great Prince to pray. Then the spirit moved one of them to say : " You now address me as Your Honour. Make it Your Excellency, and, though I am but a lesser deity, it may be well worth your while to do so." Thereupon the people began to use the latter term, and the snow stopped at once.[4] " Every virtue, every excellence," says Hume, " must be ascribed to the divinity, and no exaggeration will be deemed sufficient to reach those perfections with which he is endowed." [5] But though the tendency of the worshipper to extol his god beyond all measure is largely due to the idea that praise or flattery is as pleasant to superhuman as to human ears, it may also be rooted in a sincere will to believe or in genuine veneration. That nations of a higher culture, especially, have a strong faith in the power and benevolence of their gods, is easy to understand when we consider that such peoples have been most successful in their national endeavours. As the Greeks attributed their victory over the Persians to the assistance of Zeus, so the Romans maintained that the grandeur of their city was the work of the gods whom they had propitiated by sacrifices.[6]

The benevolence of a god, however, does not imply that he acts as a moral judge. A friendly god is not generally supposed to bestow his favours gratuitously ; it is therefore not a matter of course that he should meddle with social morality out of sheer kindliness and of his own accord. But by an invocation he may be induced to reward virtue and punish vice.

[1] F. Mürdter and F. Delitzsch, *Geschichte Babyloniens und Assyriens* (Calw and Stuttgart, 1891), p. 24.
[2] A. A. Macdonell, *Vedic Mythology* (Strassburg, 1897), p. 16 *sq.* ; A. Barth, *The Religions of India* (London, 1882), p. 26 ; E. W. Hopkins, *The Religions of India* (London, 1896), p. 139.
[3] W. Ward, *A View of the History, Literature, and Religion of the Hindoos*, ii (London, 1817), p. 69.
[4] H. A. Giles, *Strange Stories from a Chinese Studio*, ii (London, 1880), p. 294.
[5] D. Hume, *Philosophical Works*, iv (London, 1875), p. 353.
[6] Cicero, *De natura deorum*, iii. 2.

The retributive activity of many gods is evidently very closely connected with the blessings and curses of men. In order to actualise their good or evil wishes men appeal to a supernatural being, or simply bring in his name to give their appeal that mystic efficacy which the plain word lacks ; and if this is regularly done in connection with some particular kind of conduct, the idea may grow up that the supernatural being rewards or punishes it even independently of any human invocation. In Morocco the very patron saint of a village is expressly said not to care about the behaviour of its inhabitants outside the precincts of his sanctuary ; yet I found that some particular saints not only resent theft committed at their own shrines, but also punish robbers who merely pass by, either preventing them from proceeding further until they are caught, or making it impossible for them to sell the stolen object, so that they are found out at last. In these cases their hostility to an offence which does not concern them personally is obviously due to the fact that those saints have been so often appealed to in oaths taken by persons suspected of theft that they have at last come to be looked upon as permanent enemies of thieves and guardians of property. At Fez there are certain saints who are said to be so much opposed to wrongdoers that they do not even suffer them to live in the neighbourhood of their shrines, and these saints are exactly those by whom it is considered most dangerous to swear ; hence I assume that they have acquired their remarkable moral sensitiveness just by being such severe avengers of perjury.

Moreover, as I have pointed out before, the magical forces which give efficacy to curses may be personified as supernatural beings or may be transformed into attributes of the chief god. Various departments of social morality have thus come to be placed under the supervision of gods—such as charity, hospitality, the right of property, and the submissiveness of children. Gods are also frequently looked upon as guardians of truth and good faith, which I take to be mainly due to the common practice of confirming a statement or promise by an oath. A god is not only more powerful than ordinary mortals, but may also better know whether the sworn word be true or false ; it is no doubt on account of their superior knowledge that sun or moon or light gods are by preference appealed to in oaths.[1] Owing to its invocation of supernatural sanction, perjury is considered the most heinous of all acts of falsehood, but it has a tendency to make even the ordinary lie or breach of faith a

[1] See *The Origin and Development of the Moral Ideas*, ii. 115, 116, 121 *sq.*

matter of religious concern. If a god is frequently appealed to in oaths, a general hatred of lying and faithlessness may become one of his attributes. There is every reason to believe that a god is not, in the first place, appealed to because he is looked upon as a guardian of veracity and good faith, but that he has come to be looked upon as a guardian of these duties because he has so often been appealed to in connection with them.

Where the oath is an essential element in the judicial proceedings, as it was in the archaic State, the consequence is that the guardianship of gods is extended to the whole sphere of justice. Truth and justice are repeatedly mentioned hand in hand as matters of divine concern, and the same gods as are appealed to in oaths or ordeals are also frequently described as judges of human conduct.[1] Zeus presided over assemblies and trials;[2] according to a law of Solon, the judges of Athens had to swear by him.[3] And the Erinyes, the personifications of oaths and curses, are sometimes represented by poets and philosophers as guardians of right in general.[4]

We have still to consider another set of facts that have tended to make gods moral specialists. In the case of homicide the notion of a persecuting ghost may be replaced by an avenging god. Confusions are common in the world of mystery; doings or functions attributed to one being may be transferred to another. Among some North American Indians, though the revengeful ghost of the murdered man was not lost sight of, the deed was at the same time looked upon as offensive to Wakanda, " the Great Spirit "; no one wished to eat with the murderer; they said : " If we eat with the man whom Wakanda hates for his crime, Wakanda will hate us."[5] In the Chinese books there are numerous instances of persons haunted by the souls of their victims on their death-bed, and in most of these cases the ghosts state expressly that they are avenging themselves with the special authorisation of Heaven.[6] The Greek belief in the Erinyes of a murdered man originated no doubt in the earlier notion of a persecuting ghost, whose anger or curses in later times were personified as an independent spirit.[7] And

---

[1] See The Origin and Development of the Moral Ideas, ii. 115, 116, 121, 122, 686, 687, 699.

[2] L. R. Farnell, The Cults of the Greek States, i (Oxford, 1896), p. 58.

[3] Pollux, Onomasticum, viii. 12. 142.

[4] E. Rohde, Psyche (Freiburg i. B. and Leipzig, 1894), p. 246.

[5] J. Owen Dorsey, ' Omaha Sociology,' in Annual Report of the Bureau of Ethnology, iii (Washington, 1884), p. 369.

[6] J. J. M. de Groot, The Religious System of China, vol. iv, book ii (Leyden, 1901), p. 441.

[7] See C. O. Müller, Dissertations on the Eumenides of Æschylus

the transformation went further still : the Erinyes were represented as the ministers of Zeus, who by punishing the murderer carried out his divine will. Zeus was considered the originator of the rites of purification; at his altar Theseus underwent purification for the shedding of kindred blood.[1] The ritual uncleanness ascribed to a manslayer was thus transformed into spiritual impurity.

It has been said that when men ascribe to their gods a mental constitution similar to their own they *eo ipso* consider them to approve of virtue and disapprove of vice.[2] But this conclusion is certainly not true in general. Malevolent gods cannot be supposed to feel emotions that essentially presuppose altruistic sentiments, and, as already said, an invocation may be required to induce a benevolent god to interfere with the worldly affairs of men. Moreover, where the system of private retaliation prevails, not even the extension of human analogies to the world of supernatural beings would lead to the idea of a god who of his own accord punishes social wrongs. But it is quite probable that such analogies have in some cases made gods guardians of morality at large, especially ancestor gods. These may readily be supposed not only to preserve their old feelings with regard to virtue and vice, but also to take a more active interest in the morals of the living ; and they are notoriously opposed to any deviation from ancient custom. I also admit that the conception of a great or supreme god may perhaps, independently of his origin, involve retributive justice as a natural consequence of his power and benevolence towards his people. Yet it is obvious that even a god like Zeus was more influenced by the invocation of a suppliant than by his sense of justice. Farnell points out that the epithets which designate him as the god to whom those stricken with guilt can appeal are far more in vogue in actual Greek cult than those which attribute to him the function of vengeance and retribution.[3] Hermes was addressed by thieves as their patron.[4] According to the

(London and Cambridge, 1853), p. 155 *sqq.* ; Rohde, *op. cit.* p. 247 ; *idem*, ' Paralipomena,' in *Rheinisches Museum für Philologie*, neue Folge, xv (Frankfurt a. M., 1895), p. 6 *sqq.*

[1] Farnell, *op. cit.* i. 66 *sqq.* ; Rohde, *Psyche*, p. 249 ; *idem*, in *Rheinisches Museum*, neue Folge, xv. 18 ; P. Stengel, *Die griechischen Kultusaltertümer* (München, 1898), p. 140.

[2] Adam Smith, *The Theory of Moral Sentiments* (London, 1887), p. 232 *sq.* ; C. Darwin, *The Descent of Man* (London, 1890), p. 95 ; C. P. Tiele, *Elements of the Science of Religion*, i (Edinburgh and London, 1897), p. 92 *sq.*

[3] Farnell, *op. cit.* i. 66 *sq.*

[4] L. Schmidt, *Die Ethik der alten Griechen*, i (Berlin, 1882), p. 136.

Talmud, " the thief invokes God while he breaks into the house." [1] In Morocco the sultan of all the saints, Mûlai 'Abdlqâder, has the epithet " the patron of liars," and is said to be compelled to assist thieves and liars who invoke him, although he may afterwards punish them for their behaviour. The Italian bandit begs the Virgin herself to bless his endeavours.

ᵡAt the same time we must again remember that men ascribe to their gods not only ordinary human qualities but excellences of various kinds, and among these may also be a strong desire to punish wickedness and to reward virtue.⁺ The gods of mono-theistic religions in particular have such a multitude of the most elevated attributes that it would be astonishing if they had remained unconcerned about the morals of mankind. If flattery or genuine veneration makes the deity all-wise, all-powerful, all-good, they also make him the supreme judge of human conduct. And there is yet another reason for investing him with the moral government of the world. The claims of justice are not fully satisfied on this earth, where it only too often happens that virtue is left unrewarded and vice escapes unpunished, that right succumbs and wrong triumphs ; hence persons with deep moral feelings and a religious or philosophical bent of mind are apt to look for a future adjustment through the intervention of the deity, who alone can repair the evils and injustices of the present. This demand of final retribution is sometimes so strongly developed, that it even leads to the belief in a deity when no other proof of his existence is found convincing. Kant maintained that, since an accurate corres-pondence between happiness and moral worth is not to be expected in a mere course of nature, we postulate a moral and all-powerful Supreme Being who establishes such correspond-ence. Not even Voltaire could rid himself of the notion of a rewarding and avenging deity, whom, if he did not exist, " it would be necessary to invent."

The belief in a god who acts as a guardian of worldly morality undoubtedly gives emphasis to its rules. To the social and legal sanctions a new one is added, which derives particular strength from the supernatural power and knowledge of the deity. The divine avenger can punish those who are beyond the reach of human justice and those whose secret wrongs even escape the censure of their fellow-men. But on the other hand, there are also certain circumstances which detract considerably from the influence of the religious sanction when compared with other sanctions of morality. The supposed punishments and rewards of the future life have the disadvan-

[1] E. Deutsch, *Literary Remains* (London, 1874), p. 57.

tage of being conceived as very remote ; and fear and hope decrease in inverse ratio to the distance of their objects. Men commonly live in the happy illusion that death is far off, even though it is in reality very near, and, therefore, the retribution after death also appears distant and unreal and is comparatively little thought of by the majority of people who believe in it. Moreover, there seems to be time left for penance and repentance. Manzoni himself admitted, in his defence of Roman Catholicism, that many men think it an easy matter to procure that feeling of contrition by which, according to the doctrine of the Church, sins may be cancelled, and therefore encourage themselves in the commission of crime through the facility of pardon. The frequent assumption that the moral law would scarcely command obedience without the belief in retribution beyond the grave is contradicted by an overwhelming array of facts. We hear from trustworthy witnesses that unadulterated savages follow their own rules of morality no less strictly, or perhaps more strictly, than civilised people follow theirs. Nay, it is a common experience that contact with a higher civilisation exercises a deteriorating moral influence upon the conduct of uncultured races, although we may be sure that Christian missionaries do not fail to impart the doctrine of hell to their savage converts.

It has also been noticed that a high degree of religious devotion is frequently accompanied with great laxity of morals. The orientalist Wallin, who had an intimate and extensive knowledge of Mohammedan peoples, often found that those Moslems who attended to their prayers most regularly were the greatest scoundrels.[1] " One of the most remarkable traits in the character of the Copts," says Lane, " is their bigotry " : and at the same time they are represented as " deceitful, faithless, and abandoned to the pursuit of worldly gain, and to indulgence in sensual pleasure." [2] Among two hundred Italian murderers Ferri did not find one who was irreligious ; and Naples, which has (or had ?) the worst record of any European city for crimes against the person, is also the most religious city in Europe.[3] On the other hand, according to Havelock Ellis, " it seems extremely rare to find intelligently irreligious men in prison." [4] Most religions contain an element which

[1] G. A. Wallin, *Reseanteckningar från Orienten åren 1843-1849*, iii (Helsingfors, 1865), p. 166.
[2] E. W. Lane, *An Account of the Manners and Customs of the Modern Egyptians* (London, 1896), p. 551.
[3] Havelock Ellis, *The Criminal* (London, 1895), p. 156.
[4] *Ibid.* p. 159.

constitutes a real peril to the morality of their votaries. They
have introduced a new kind of duties—duties towards gods;
and even where religion has entered into close union with
worldly morality, much greater importance has been attached
to ceremonies or worship or the niceties of belief than to good
behaviour towards fellow-men. People think that they may
make up for lack of the latter by orthodoxy or pious performances. A Christian bishop of the seventh century, who was
canonised by the Church of Rome, described a good Christian
as a man " who comes frequently to church ; who presents the
oblation which is offered to God upon the altar ; who doth
not taste fruits of his own industry until he has consecrated a
part of them to God ; who, when the holy festivals approach,
lives chastely even with his own wife during several days, that
with a safe conscience he may draw near the altar of God ; and
who, in the last place, can repeat the Creed and the Lord's
Prayer." [1]   A scrupulous observance of external ceremonies—
that is all which in this description is required of a good
Christian. Smollett observes in his *Travels into Italy* that it
is held more infamous to transgress the slightest ceremonial
institution of the Church of Rome than to transgress any moral
duty ; that a murderer or adulterer will be easily absolved by
the Church, and even maintain his character in society ; but
that a man who eats a pigeon on a Saturday is abhorred as a
monster of reprobation.[2] Simonde de Sismondi wrote : " The
more regular a vicious man has been in observing the commandments of the Church, the more he feels in his heart that he can
dispense with the observance of that celestial morality to which
he ought to sacrifice his depraved propensities." [3]   And how
many a Protestant does not imagine that by going to
church on Sundays he may sin more freely on the six days
between ?   In reply to Starbuck's question, " What does religion
mean to you ? " a sixty-seven years old business man wrote :
" I find that the most religious and pious people are as a rule
those most lacking in uprightness and morality. The men who
do not go to church or have any religious convictions are the
best. Praying, singing of hymns, and sermonising are pernicious—they teach us to rely on some supernatural power, when

---

[1] W. Robertson, *The History of the Reign of the Emperor Charles V.*,
i (London, 1806), p. 282 *sq.*
[2] Smollett, quoted by Lord Kames, *Sketches of the History of Man*,
iv (Edinburgh, 1788), p. 380.
[3] J. C. L. Simonde de Sismondi, *Histoire des républiques italiennes
du moyen âge*, xvi (Paris, 1826), p. 419.

we ought to rely on ourselves." William James recognises in this man a sufficiently familiar type.[1]

We come at last to a point in which religion, or rather the Christian revelation, is supposed to have exercised a profound influence on moral ideas : it is said to have invested them with objective validity.

All exponents of normative ethics assume that they possess such validity : that the moral values belong to a reality which exists whether there be a mind that perceives it or not, that what is said to be good or bad, right or wrong, cannot be reduced merely to what people think to be good or bad, right or wrong. It makes morality a matter of truth and falsity, and to say that a judgment is true obviously means something different from the statement that it is thought to be true. If a certain course of conduct is objectively right it must be thought to be right by all rational beings who judge truly of the matter and cannot, without error, be judged to be wrong.

Certain philosophers, like Mill and Kant, have adduced rational arguments to prove the objectivity of their first principles and thereby the existence of ethical truths. These have been rejected for good reasons, and the advocates of moral objectivity have generally resorted to a more convenient method of establishing it : they assume that there are self-evident moral principles perceived by intuition. But how can I know if a proposition is really self-evident or only supposed to be so ? In the case of theoretical truths no truth is admitted to have a claim to self-evidence which is not generally accepted as self-evident or axiomatic by all those whose intellect is sufficiently developed to have an opinion on the matter worthy of any consideration at all ; to speak with Sidgwick, the absence of disagreement between experts must be an indispensable negative condition of the certainty of our beliefs.[2] As a matter of fact, however, in the case of moral principles enunciated as self-evident truths disagreement is radical. Some " moral specialists " say it is an axiom that I ought not to prefer my own lesser good to the greater good of another ; whilst others not only deny the self-evidence, but thoroughly disagree with the contents, of this proposition. According to Sidgwick the assertion that pleasure is the only rational ultimate end of action is an object of intuition ; [3] according to Moore, also a professor of moral philosophy,

---

[1] W. James, *The Varieties of Religious Experience* (London, etc., 1903), p. 92.
[2] H. Sidgwick, *The Methods of Ethics* (London, 1913), p. 341 *sq.*
[3] *Ibid.* p. 201.

the untruth of this proposition is self-evident.[1] The latter
finds it self-evident that good cannot be defined ; [2] but others,
who have no smaller claim to the epithet " moral specialists,"
are of the very contrary opinion.   What should we say if two
professors of mathematics quarrelled about the axiom that " if
equals be added to equals the wholes are equal," to which
Sidgwick compares one of his moral axioms ? [3]

But besides rational arguments and intuitive insight that
have been alleged to prove the objectivity of moral judgments
there are also theological arguments.   In spite of all his efforts
to base his own theory on a non-theological basis, Rashdall feels
compelled to admit that, in his opinion, the belief in God is the
logical presupposition of an " objective " or absolute morality.
" A moral ideal," he says, " can exist nowhere and nohow
but in a mind ; an absolute moral ideal can exist only in a
Mind from which all Reality is derived.   Our moral ideal can
only claim objective validity in so far as it can rationally be
regarded as the revelation of a moral ideal externally existing
in the mind of God." [4]   He invalidates, however, in another
place this argument by saying that " the belief in the objectivity
of our moral judgments is a necessary premise for any valid
argument for the belief either in God, if by that be understood
a morally good or perfect Being, or in Immortality." [5]   The
two statements that objective morality presupposes the belief
in God, and that the belief in God presupposes objective morality,
lead combined to the logical conclusion that there is no valid
evidence *either* for the existence of God *or* for the objectivity
of moral judgments.   According to Dean Inge, " Christianity
lifts psychology out of mere subjectivism, and morality out of
mere relativism. . . .   The Christian point of view gives to
conduct an absolute value." [6]   Bishop Bohlin, after a pene-
trating review of the claim to objective validity made by normative moralists, arrives at the conclusion that only a divine
revelation can give morality such validity.[7]

The theological argument in favour of the objective validity
of moral judgments, which is based on belief in an all-good
God who has revealed his will to mankind, contains of course

[1] G. E. Moore, *Principia Ethica* (Cambridge, 1922), pp. 75, 144.
[2] *Ibid.* pp. 6, 8, 148.
[3] Sidgwick, *op. cit.* p. 382 *sq.*
[4] H. Rashdall, *The Theory of Good and Evil*, ii (London, 1924), p. 212.
[5] *Idem, Is Conscience an Emotion ?* (London, 1914), p. 194.
[6] W. R. Inge, *Christian Ethics and Moral Problems* (London, 1932),
p. 44.
[7] T. Bohlin, *Das Grundproblem der Ethik* (Uppsala and Leipzig,
1923), p. 428 *sqq.*

an assumption that cannot be proved scientifically. But even if it could be proved, would that justify the conclusion drawn from it ? Those who maintain that they possess in such a revelation an absolute moral standard and that, consequently, any mode of conduct which is in accordance with it must be objectively right, may be asked what they mean by an all-good God. If God were not supposed to be all-good, we might certainly be induced by prudence to obey his decrees, but they could not lay claim to *moral* validity ; suppose the devil were to take over the government of the world, what influence would that have on the moral values—would it make right wrong and wrong right ? It is only the all-goodness of God that might give his commandments absolute moral validity. But to say that something is good because it is in accordance with the will of an all-good God is to reason in a circle ; if goodness means anything, it must have a meaning which is independent of his will. God is called good or righteous because he is supposed to possess certain qualities that we are used to call so : he is benevolent, he requites virtue and vice, and so forth. For such reasons do we add the attributes goodness and righteousness to his other attributes, which express qualities of an objective character, and by calling him all-good we attribute to him perfect goodness.[1] As a matter of fact, there are also many theologians who consider moral distinctions to be antecedent to the divine commandments. Thomas Aquinas and his school maintain that the right is not right because God wills it, but that God wills it because it is right.

 I have thus arrived at the conclusion that the attempts of philosophers and theologians to prove the objective validity of moral judgments give us no right to accept such validity as a fact. I am now prepared to take a step further and assert that it cannot exist. The reason for this is that in my opinion the predicates of all moral judgments, all moral concepts, are ultimately based on emotions, and that, as is very commonly admitted,[2] no objectivity can come from an emotion. It is of course true or not that we in a given moment have a certain emotion ; but in no other sense can the antithesis

[1] *Cf.* Shaftesbury, *Characteristicks*, ii (London, 1733), p. 49 *sq.* : " Whoever thinks there is a God, and pretends formally to believe that he is just and good, must suppose that there is independently such a thing as justice and injustice, truth and falsehood, right and wrong ; according to which he pronounces that God is just, righteous, and true." A similar remark has been made by C. Stumpf (*Vom ethischen Skeptizismus* [Leipzig, 1909], p. 22) and G. Heymans (*Einführung in die Ethik auf Grundlage der Erfahrung* [Leipzig, 1914], p. 8).

[2] See my book *Ethical Relativity* (London, 1932), p. 60 n.

of true and false be applied to it. The cognition which gives rise to an emotion is of course either true or false ; in the latter case the emotion may be said to be felt " by mistake " —as when a person is frightened by some object in the dark which he takes for a ghost, or is indignant with a person to whom he imputes a wrong that has been committed by somebody else ; but this does not alter the nature of the emotion itself. We may call the emotion of another person " unjustified," if we feel that we ourselves should not have experienced the same emotion had we been in his place, or, as in the case of moral approval or disapproval, if we cannot share his emotion. But to speak, as Brentano does, of " right " and " wrong " emotions, springing from self-evident intuitions and having the same validity as truth and error,[1] is only another futile attempt to objectivise our moral judgments. The same may be said of Nicolai Hartmann's assertions that " the sense of value is not less objective than mathematical insight,"[2] and that the criterion of the genuine and the spurious sense of value " is nothing else than the primary consciousness of value itself," which is also an intuition.[3] But I find in his book no clear criterion of this " primary consciousness of value " as distinguished from any other feeling of value. Very generally the so-called intuitions are nothing but objectivised emotions, or emotional tendencies formulated as judgments, calculated to give moral values an objectivity they do not in reality possess.

Although all moral judgments are ultimately based on emotions, the influence that intellectual factors exercise on such judgments is very great indeed. Emotions are determined by cognitions and differ in nature or strength according as the cognitions differ. This has been a very important cause of the variations of moral judgments : the same course of conduct is differently judged of because different notions are held as to its nature or implications. If a person tells an untruth we are apt to feel indignant ; but if, on due consideration of facts, we find that his motive was benevolent, for instance to save the life of the person to whom it was told, our indignation ceases and may be followed by approval. And, to take another instance, at the lower stages of civilisation there is a considerable lack of discrimination between intentional injuries and accidental ones, and even among ourselves the outward event exercises a

[1] F. Brentano, *Vom Ursprung sittliches Erkenntnis* (Leipzig, 1921), p. 18 *sqq.*
[2] N. Hartmann, *Ethik* (Berlin and Leipzig, 1926), p. 141.
[3] *Ibid.* pp. 55, 105 *sq.*

great influence upon moral estimates.[1] But if it is clearly
realised that a certain event is the result of merely external
circumstances, that it was neither intended by the agent nor
could have been foreseen by him, then there could be no moral
disapproval at all. Such an event could not even call forth a
feeling of revenge. Sudden anger itself cools down when it
appears that the cause of the inflicted pain was a mere accident.
Even a dog distinguishes between being stumbled over and
being kicked.

The variability of moral valuation also depends in a large
measure upon different cognitions arising from different situa-
tions and external conditions of life. We find, for example,
among many peoples the custom of killing or abandoning
parents worn out with age or disease. It prevails among a
large number of savage tribes and occurred formerly among
several Asiatic and European nations, including the Vedic
people and peoples of Teutonic extraction. It is particularly
common among nomadic hunting tribes, owing to the hardships
of life and the inability of decrepit persons to keep up in the
march. In times when the food-supply is insufficient to support
all the members of a community it also seems more reasonable
that the old and useless should have to perish than the young
and vigorous. And among peoples which have reached a
certain degree of wealth and comfort the practice of killing the
old folks, though no longer justified by necessity, may still go

---

[1] We notice this influence even in certain rules and doctrines of
mediæval Christianity. The principle laid down by Augustine (*Sermo
CLXXX*. 2, in Migne, *Patrologiæ cursus*, xxxviii. 973), and adopted by
Canon Law (Gratian, *Decretum*, ii. 22. 2. 3), that " ream linguam non
facit, nisi mens rea," was not always acted upon. Various penitentials
condemned to penance a person who, in giving evidence, swore to the
best of his belief, in case his statement afterwards proved untrue ; and
in other cases also penances were prescribed for mere misfortunes. If
a person killed another by pure accident, he had to do penance—in
ordinary cases, according to most English penitentials, for one year,
according to various continental penitentials, for five or seven years ;
whereas, according to the Penitential of Pseudo-Theodore, he who
accidentally killed his father or mother was to atone his deed with a
penance of fifteen years, and he who accidentally killed his son with a
penance of twelve (see *The Origin and Development of the Moral Ideas*,
i. 230). The Scotists even expressly declared that the external deed
has a moral value of its own, which increases the goodness or badness
of the agent's intention ; and though this doctrine was opposed by
Thomas Aquinas, Bonaventura, Suarez, and other leading theologians,
it was nevertheless admitted by them that, according to the will of
God, certain external deeds entail a certain accidental reward, the
so-called *aureola* (F. A. Göpfert, *Moraltheologie*, i [Paderborn, 1899],
p. 185).

on partly through survival of a custom inherited from harder times, and partly from the humane intent of putting an end to lingering misery. What appears to most of us as an atrocious practice may really be an act of kindness, and is commonly approved of, or even insisted upon, by the old people themselves. Or take the widespread custom of infanticide. Among the lower races custom often decides how many children are to be reared in each family, and not infrequently the majority of infants are destroyed. This wholesale infanticide is also mainly due to the hardships of savage life. Urgent want is frequently represented by our authorities as the main cause of it ; and their statements are corroborated by the conspicuous prevalence of this custom among poor tribes and in islands whose inhabitants are confined to a narrow territory with limited resources. For a similar reason infanticide is or has been a custom among many peoples of a higher civilisation.

The variability of moral judgments further originates in different measures of forethought or knowledge based on experience of the consequences of conduct, and in different beliefs. In almost every branch of conduct we notice the influence which the belief in supernatural forces or beings or in a future state has exercised upon the moral ideas of mankind, and the great diversity of this influence. Religion or superstition has, on the one hand, stigmatised murder and suicide, on the other hand it has commended human sacrifice and certain cases of voluntary self-destruction. It has inculcated humanity and charity, but has also led to cruel persecutions of persons embracing another creed. It has emphasised the duty of truth-speaking, and has itself been a cause of pious fraud. It has promoted cleanly habits and filthiness. It has enjoined labour and abstinence from labour, sobriety and drunkenness, marriage and celibacy, chastity and temple prostitution. It has introduced a great variety of new duties and virtues, quite different from those which are recognised by the moral consciousness when left to itself, but nevertheless in many cases considered more important than any other duties or virtues.

From this motley crowd of influences I shall single out one the result of which has been particularly revolting to the moral feelings of Christians, namely human sacrifice. It is found not only among many savages, but occurred in early times among all Indo-European peoples, the Semites, and the Japanese, and in the New World among the Mayas and the Aztecs, who practised it on an enormous scale. The gods were supposed to be gratified by such offerings—because they had an appetite for human flesh and blood, or because they required attendants, or because they were angry and could only be appeased by the death of him or those who aroused their anger or some representative of the offending community, or—who could exactly tell why ? The principal thing is that people know or believe that on some certain occasion they are in danger of losing their lives ; they attribute this to the designs of a supernatural being ; and by sacrificing a man they hope to avert the danger from themselves by gratifying that being's craving for human life. That this principle mainly underlies the practice of human sacrifice appears from the particular circumstances in which it generally occurs. In such cases it is mostly a matter of public concern, a method of ensuring the lives of many by the death of one or a few—absurd, no doubt, according to our ideas, but not an act of wanton cruelty. When practised for the benefit of the community or in a case of national distress, it is hardly more cruel than to compel thousands of men to suffer death on the battlefield on behalf of their country.

In so far as differences of moral opinions depend on different degrees of reflection, on knowledge or ignorance of specific religious or superstitious beliefs, or on different conditions of life and other external circumstances, they do not clash with that universality which is implied in the notion of the objective validity of moral judgment, as in every kind of truth. But the case is different with some other dissimilarities of moral opinion, which are due to other causes.

When we study the moral rules laid down by the customs of savage peoples we find that they in a very large measure resemble the rules of civilised nations. In every savage community homicide is prohibited by custom, and so is theft. Savages also regard charity as a duty and praise generosity as a virtue, indeed their customs relating to mutual aid are often more exacting than our own ; and many of them are conspicuous for their avoidance of telling lies. But in spite of the great similarity of moral commandments, there is at the same time a difference between the regard for life, property, truth, and the general well-being of a neighbour which displays itself in savage rules of morality and that which is found among ourselves : it has, broadly speaking, only reference to members of the same community or tribe. Among peoples more advanced in civilisation the social unit has grown larger, the nation has taken the place of the tribe, and the circle within which the infliction of injuries is prohibited has extended accordingly. A distinction is still very frequently made between injuries committed against compatriots and harm done to foreigners, but both law and

public opinion may show a very great advance in humanity
with regard to the treatment of the latter. And when we come
to rules laid down by moralists and professedly accepted
by a large portion of civilised mankind, we find such as have
reference to the whole human race. It seems to me obvious
that the dominant cause of this expansion of moral rules has
been the widening of the altruistic sentiment. But this sentiment varies in different individuals both in strength and with
reference to its objects. And this variability will always
prevent the moral rules from being anything like uniform.

The variations of the altruistic sentiment in range and
strength are also responsible for other differences of moral
opinion. Even among ourselves there is no unanimity as to
the dictates of duty in cases where a person's own interests
collide with those of his fellow-men. Sidgwick admitted that
his axiom of " rational benevolence," according to which, other
things being equal, no one must prefer his own lesser good to
the greater good of another, is more rigid than the view of
common sense,[1] and I fail to see that any process of reasoning
or " intuition " could ever harmonise the different views. As
Höffding said, no reasoning can change an egoist into a utilitarian; his position is so far unassailable.[2] While everybody
will agree that some amount of self-sacrifice is a duty in certain
circumstances, the amount and the circumstances can hardly
be fixed in general rules, and on the whole, in cases of conflicting
interests the judgment must to a large extent remain a matter
of private opinion. Kant, that high priest of ethical rationalism,
wrote that it is impossible to assign definite limits how far I
am bound to sacrifice to others a part of my own welfare without
hope of recompense. " This duty, therefore, is only indeterminate; it has a certain latitude within which one may do more or
less without being able to assign its limits definitely." [3]

That moral judgments could not possibly possess that
universality which is characteristic of truth becomes particularly obvious when we consider that their predicates vary not
only in quality but also in quantity. There are no degrees of
truth and falsehood; but there are degrees of goodness and
badness, virtues and merits may be greater or smaller, a duty
may be more or less stringent, and if there are no degrees of
rightness, the reason for it is that right means simply conformity to the rule of duty. These quantitative differences of

---

[1] Sidgwick, op. cit. pp. 9, 13.
[2] H. Höffding, Etik (Köbenhavn and Kristiania, 1913), p. 35.
[3] Kant, Einleitung zur Tugendlehre, 8 (Gesammelte Schriften, vi
[Berlin, 1914]), p. 393.

moral estimates are due to the emotional origin of all moral concepts. Emotions vary indefinitely in strength, and the moral emotions form no exception to this rule. It should be noticed, however, that the quantity of the estimate expressed in a moral predicate is not identical with the intensity of the moral emotion which a certain course of conduct arouses on a particular occasion. We are liable to feel more indignant if an injury is committed before our eyes than if we read about it in a newspaper, and yet we admit that the degree of badness is the same in either case. The comparative quantity of moral estimates is determined by the intensity of the emotions which their objects tend to evoke in exactly similar circumstances.

But in spite of all differences of moral ideas there are most substantial similarities, which are due to the facts that they are all based on moral emotions, and that moral emotions are retributive emotions characterised by disinterestedness and impartiality. I have discussed these facts at a length which may have seemed exorbitant, but which I have found necessary for expressing and justifying my views on Christian morals.

CHAPTER III

THE ETHICS OF JESUS: THEIR RETRIBUTIVE CHARACTER

THE thesis that moral judgments are based on retributive emotions may seem to have been a strange introduction to the discussion of the ethics of the New Testament with their doctrine of love and forgiveness. But I maintain that this thesis is nowhere confirmed more strongly than in the teaching of Jesus as recorded in the three synoptic gospels.

While the Gospel of John is of great value for the history of the teaching of the early Catholic Church and the edifice of Catholic doctrines based on it, it is now very generally admitted to be a comparatively late document which does not give us an authoritative account of the work and teaching of Jesus, but represents a tendentious interpretation of the tradition. The synoptic gospels are founded on a tradition about Jesus which had been preached and taught in the Church either orally or else in small collections capable of expansion.[1] Almost all scholars are now agreed that the short Gospel of Mark, which is earlier than its two companions, has been one of their sources; but that they in addition used also another source, now lost, which has been designated Q. As regards the amount of reliable information which the three gospels contain, it has been pointed out that wherever we can observe the methods of the synoptists we see how little they valued strict accuracy in the reproduction of their authorities, and how fully they felt themselves justified in treating the details with literary freedom.[2] There is no doubt that Jesus never uttered the discourses attributed to him, but that they are artificial compositions of which the most which we can hope is that they employ authentic logia. On closer examination these discourses break up into a number of disjointed sayings or, at best, into small groups of sayings, which appear to be for the most part the work of the primitive community or of the gospel redactors.[3]

[1] M. Dibelius, *A Fresh Approach to the New Testament and Early Christian Literature* (London, 1937), p. 66.
[2] A. Jülicher, *An Introduction to the New Testament* (London, 1904), p. 368.
[3] *Cf.* C. Guignebert, *Jesus* (London, 1935), p. 235.

It is a question whether the tradition, which had only
recollection to sustain it, was sufficiently complete and precise
to enable us to comprehend what Jesus said and meant.
Harnack avers that the synoptics give us a clear idea of Jesus'
teaching in regard both to its main features and to its individual
application.[1] According to Dibelius, " the message of Jesus
has been preserved for us in the first three gospels self-con-
sistently and unspoiled." [2] Professor R. H. Lightfoot, again,
concludes that the gospels yield us little more than a whisper
of the voice of Jesus.[3] Wrede says it should be borne in mind
that only the earliest stratum of the material of the three
gospels existed before the elaboration of the Pauline theology,
and that a considerable part of it came into being alongside or
after that theology, nay even—here and there—under its
influence.[4] In any case the ethics of Jesus are quite distinct :
the principle of divine reward and punishment is the keystone
of his moral teaching, which is thus an expression of retributive
emotions—the basis of all moral judgments.

It should be remembered that moral emotions are *disinterested* retributive emotions. Personal anger and vindictiveness
are strongly condemned by Jesus :

" Ye have heard that it hath been said, An eye for an eye,
and a tooth for a tooth : But I say unto you, That ye resist
not evil : [5] but whosoever shall smite thee on thy right cheek,
turn to him the other also. . . . Ye have heard that it hath
been said, Thou shalt love thy neighbour, and hate thine
enemy. But I say unto you, Love your enemies, bless them
that curse you, do good to them that hate you, and pray
for them which despitefully use you, and persecute you "
(*Matthew* v. 38, 39, 43 *sq.*).

" If ye forgive men their trespasses, your heavenly Father
will also forgive you : But if ye forgive not men their trespasses,
neither will your Father forgive your trespasses " (*ibid*. vi.
14 *sq.*). See also *ibid*. xviii. 34 *sq.*

[1] A. Harnack, *What is Christianity ?* (London and New York, 1904),
p. 32.
[2] Dibelius, *op. cit.* p. 35.
[3] R. H. Lightfoot, *History and Interpretation in the Gospels* (London,
1934), p. 225.
[4] W. Wrede, *Paul* (London, 1907), p. 155.
[5] The Revised Edition has " him who is evil," but also " evil " as
an alternative. J. B. Lightfoot (*On a Fresh Revision of the English
New Testament* [London, 1891], p. 274) thinks that the former rendering is more likely to be the correct one ; and N. Söderblom (*Jesu
bärgspredikan och vår tid* [Stockholm, 1899], pp. 19, 194) insists on
it.

" Then came Peter to him, and said, Lord, how oft shall my brother sin against me, and I forgive him ? till seven times ? Jesus saith unto him, I say not unto thee, Until seven times : but, Until seventy times seven " (*ibid.* xviii. 21 *sq.*).

" When ye stand praying, forgive, if ye have ought against any : that your Father also which is in heaven may forgive you your trespasses. But if ye do not forgive, neither will your Father which is in heaven forgive your trespasses " (*Mark* xi. 25 *sq.*).

" Love your enemies, do good to them which hate you, Bless them that curse you, and pray for them which despitefully use you. And unto him that smiteth thee on the one cheek offer also the other ; and him that taketh away thy cloke forbid not to take thy coat also. Give to every man that asketh of thee ; and of him that taketh away thy goods ask them not again. . . . Love ye your enemies, and do good, and lend, hoping for nothing again ; and your reward shall be great, and ye shall be the children of the Highest. . . . Forgive, and ye shall be forgiven " (*Luke* vi. 27–30, 35, 37).

The injunction of forgiveness, however, is not always unqualified. According to Luke, Jesus said : " If thy brother trespass against thee, rebuke him ; and if he repent, forgive him. And if he trespass against thee seven times in a day, and seven times in a day turn again to thee, saying, I repent ; thou shalt forgive him." [1] He also gave the following injunction : " If thy brother shall trespass against thee, go and tell him his fault between thee and him alone : if he shall hear thee, thou hast gained thy brother. But if he will not hear thee, then take with thee one or two more, that in the mouth of two or three witnesses every word may be established. And if he shall neglect to hear them, tell it unto the church : but if he neglect to hear the church, let him be unto thee as an heathen man and a publican." [2] Moreover, according to some manuscripts and the Authorised Version of the English Bible, Jesus said : " Whosoever is angry with his brother without a cause shall be in danger of the judgment " ; [3] whereas the qualifying clause " without a cause " is lacking in other manuscripts—both the

---

[1] *Luke* xvii. 3 *sq.*

[2] *Matthew* xviii. 15–17.

[3] *Ibid.* v. 22. Adalbert Merx (*Die vier kanonischen Evangelien nach ihrem ältesten bekannten Texte* [Berlin, 1897], p. 231 *sqq.*) has tried to show that this passage belonged to the original text ; and Söderblom (*op. cit.* p. 9) considers his argument convincing. The passage is found in the very early Gothic version (*Die gotische Bibel*, ed. by W. Streitberg [Heidelberg, 1908], p. 2). For this information I am indebted to my friend Professor Hugo Pipping.

Codex Sinaiticus and the *Vaticanus*—and in the *Vulgate*,[1] and has been omitted in the Revised Version of the English Bible. It would of course be absurd to blame a person for expressing moral indignation at an act simply because he himself happens to be the offended party.

✗ The injunctions of forgiveness and kindness to enemies are by no means exclusively Christian tenets. We find them in the Old Testament. " Thou shalt not hate thy brother in thine heart. . . . Thou shalt not avenge, nor bear any grudge against the children of thy people." [2] " Say not thou, I will recompense evil; but wait on the Lord, and he shall save thee." [3] " If thine enemy be hungry, give him bread to eat; and if he be thirsty, give him water to drink : for thou shalt heap coals of fire upon his head, and the Lord shall reward thee." [4] " If thou meet thine enemy's ox or his ass going astray, thou shalt surely bring it back to him again. If thou see the ass of him that hateth thee lying under his burden, and wouldest forbear to help him, thou shalt surely help with him." [5] Sirach says : " Forgive thy neighbour the injury (done to thee), and then, when thou prayest, thy sins will be forgiven." [6] In the apocryphal book ' The Testament of the Twelve Patriarchs,' which is supposed to have been written more than a century before the life and teaching of Jesus, we read : " If a man sin against thee, speak peaceably to him, and in thy soul hold not guile ; and if he repent and confess, forgive him. . . . But if he be shameless and persisteth in his wrongdoing, even so forgive him from the heart, and leave to God the avenging." [7] In the Talmud it is said that " whosoever does not persecute them that persecute him, whosoever takes an offence in silence, he who does good because of love, he who is cheerful under his sufferings—they are the friends of God." [8]

✗ The Koran, while repeating the old rule " an eye for an eye and a tooth for a tooth," [9] at the same time teaches that paradise is " for those who repress their rage, and those who pardon men ; God loves the kind." [10] ✝ Mohammedan tradition puts the

---

[1] As also in the German and Swedish translations.
[2] *Leviticus* xix. 17 *sq.*   [3] *Proverbs* xx. 22.
[4] *Ibid.* xxv. 21 *sq.*   [5] *Exodus* xxiii. 4 *sq.*
[6] *Ecclesiasticus* xxviii. 2.
[7] ' The Testament of Gad,' vi. 3, 7, in R. H. Charles, *The Testaments of the Twelve Patriarchs* (London, 1908), p. 156 *sqq.*
[8] E. Deutsch, *Literary Remains* (London, 1874), p. 58. *Cf.* A. Katz, *Der wahre Talmudjude* (Berlin, 1893), p. 11 *sq.*
[9] *Koran*, ii. 190 : " Whoso transgresses against you, transgress against him like as he transgressed against you."
[10] *Ibid.* iii. 125. *Cf. ibid.* xxiii. 98, xxiv. 22, xli. 34.

following words in the mouth of the Prophet : " Say not, if
people do good to us, we will do good to them, and if people
oppress us, we will oppress them : but resolve that if people do
good to you, you will do good to them, and if they oppress you,
oppress them not again." ¹ Goldziher emphasises Mohammed's opposition to the traditional rule of the Arabs that an
enemy is a proper object of hatred ; ² and Syed Ameer Ali has
collected various passages from the writings of Mohammedan
scholars which prove that, in spite of what has often been said
to the contrary, forgiveness of injuries is by no means foreign
to the spirit of Islam.³ That " the sandal-tree perfumes the
axe that fells it," is a saying in everyday use among the Mohammedans of India.⁴ And Lane often heard Egyptians forgivingly
say, on receiving a blow from an equal : " God bless thee,"
" God requite thee good," " Beat me again." ⁵

× Kindness to enemies was inculcated by Chinese moralists.
" Recompense injury with kindness," says Lao-Tsze.⁶ ⁺ According to Mencius, " a benevolent man does not lay up anger, nor
cherish resentment against his brother, but only regards him
with affection and love." ⁷ In the ' Laws of Manu,' the mythical
Hindu legislator, the following rule is laid down for the twice-
born man : " Against an angry man let him not in return show
anger, let him bless when he is cursed." ⁸ It is said in the
Buddhist ' Dhammapada ' : " Hatred does not cease by hatred
at any time ; hatred ceases by love, this is an old rule. . . .
Among men who hate us we dwell free from hatred. . . . Let
a man overcome anger by love, let him overcome evil by good ;
let him overcome the greedy by liberality, the liar by truth." ⁹

⅄ The principle of forgiveness had also advocates in Greece

¹ S. Lane-Poole, *The Speeches and Table-Talk of the Prophet Moham-
mad* (London, 1882), p. 147.

² I. Goldziher, *Muhammedanische Studien*, i (Leiden, 1896), p. 15 *sqq.*

³ Ameer Ali, *The Ethics of Islâm* (Calcutta, 1893), pp. 7, 26 *sqq.*

⁴ J. J. Pool, *Studies in Mohammedanism* (Westminster, 1892), p. 226.

⁵ E. W. Lane, *An Account of the Manners and Customs of the
Modern Egyptians* (London, 1896), p. 314 *sq.*

⁶ *Tâo Teh King*, ii. 63. 1 ; in *The Sacred Books of the East*, xxxix
(Oxford, 1891). According to *Thâi-Shang*, 4 (*ibid.* xl. [1891]), a bad
man " broods over resentment without ceasing."

⁷ Mencius, v. 1. 3. 2 ; in J. Legge, *The Chinese Classics*, ii (Oxford,
1895).

⁸ *The Laws of Manu*, vi. 48 ; in *The Sacred Books of the East*, xxv
(Oxford, 1886). *Cf. ibid.* viii. 313 ; M. Monier Williams, *Indian Wisdom*
(London, 1893), pp. 444, 446 ; J. Muir, *Additional Moral and Religious
Passages metrically rendered from Sanskrit Writers* (London, 1875), p. 30.

⁹ *Dhammapada*, i. 5, xv. 197, xvii. 223 ; in *The Sacred Books of the
East*, x (Oxford, 1898). *Cf. Jâtaka Tales, Buddhist Birth Stories* (London,
1880), i. 22 ; H. Oldenberg, *Buddha* (London, 1882), p. 298.

and Rome. In one of the Platonic dialogues, Socrates says : " We ought not to retaliate or render evil for evil to any one, whatever evil we may have suffered from him "; though he adds that " this opinion has never been held, and never will be held, by any considerable number of persons." [1] In Stoicism the condemnation of anger and resentment is abundant. " Mankind is born for mutual assistance, anger for mutual ruin." [2] " Anger is a crime of the mind ; . . . it often is even more criminal than the faults with which it is angry." [3] " The truly great mind, which takes a true estimate of its own value, does not revenge an insult because it does not feel it." [4] " We all are bad. . . . There is only one thing which can afford us peace, and that is to agree to forgive one another." [5] " If any one is angry with you, meet his anger by returning benefits for it." [6] " To suppose that we shall become contemptible in the eyes of others unless in some way we inflict an injury on those who first shewed hostility to us, is the character of most ignoble and thoughtless men." [7] " The Cynic loves those who beat him." [8] He is the best and purest " who pardons others as if he sinned himself daily, but avoids sinning as if he never pardoned." [9] " The best way of revenge is not to imitate the injury." [10] " Though we are not just of the same flesh and blood, yet our minds are nearly related, being both extracted from the Deity. . . . Nor can I find it in my heart to hate or to be angry with one of my own nature or family. For we are all made for mutual assistance." [11] " Remember always, when you are angry, that rage is the mark of an unmanly disposition. Mildness and temper are not only more human, but more masculine too." [12] " This is the way to disarm the most insolent, if you continue kind and unmoved under ill usage." [13] Some of these statements breathe rather dignity or pride than kindness ; and Seneca makes the acute remark that " the most contemptuous form of revenge is not to deem one's adversary worth taking vengeance upon." [14] Paul says, as it was said in the Proverbs, that if you feed your enemy when he hungers and give him drink when he thirsts, you will " heap coals of fire on his head." [15]

---

[1] Plato, *Crito*, p. 49.   [2] Seneca, *De ira*, i. 5.
[3] *Ibid.* i. 16, ii. 6.
[4] *Ibid.* iii. 5. *Cf. ibid.* ii. 32, iii. 25 ; Seneca, *De clementia*, i. 5.
[5] *Idem*, *De ira*, iii. 26.   [6] *Ibid.* ii. 34.
[7] Epictetus, *Fragmenta*, 70.   [8] *Idem*, *Dissertationes*, iii. 22, 54.
[9] Pliny, *Epistolæ*, ix. 22 (viii. 22).
[10] Marcus Aurelius, *Commentarii*, vi. 6.
[11] *Ibid.* ii. 1.   [12] *Ibid.* xi. 18.   [13] *Ibid.* xi. 18.
[14] Seneca, *De ira*, ii. 32.   [15] *Romans* xii. 20.

A person who feels resentment may be a proper object of moral disapproval, not on account of the resentful impulse as such, but because it has been allowed to develop either into an intention or into a deliberate wish to make the other person suffer or, at any rate, into a wish that he shall have to suffer ; and the word resentment may be vaguely used in all these cases. Jesus' commandment, " Love your enemies," may imply something more than the next one, " Do good to them that hate you " : it may enjoin you to try to check your anger ; but it cannot reasonably make it an obligation for you to have a tender feeling towards your enemy. As Kant said,[1] " love, as an affection, cannot be commanded," and the reason for this is that it cannot be produced by any effort of will. But it is easy to see why thoughtful and sympathetic minds disapprove of resentment and retaliation springing from personal motives. Such resentment is apt to be partial. It is too often directed against persons whom impartial reflection finds to be no proper objects of indignation, and still more frequently it is unduly excessive. As Butler said, " We are in such a peculiar situation with respect to injuries done to ourselves, that we can scarce any more see them as they really are, than our eye can see itself." [2] " As bodies seem greater in a midst, so do little matters in a rage " ; hence the old rule that we ought not to punish whilst angry.[3] The restraining rule of like for like, which is frequently found among peoples whose customs permit or enjoin private revenge, has largely a social origin.[4] As resentment involves no accurate balancing of suffering against suffering, there may be a crying disproportion between the act of revenge and the injury evoking it ; a revengeful mind, said Sir Thomas Browne, " holds no rule in retaliations, requiring too often a head for a tooth, and the supreme revenge for trespasses, which a night's rest should obliterate." [5] But if the offender is a person with whose feelings men are ready to sympathise, their sympathy will keep the desire to see him suffer within certain limits ; and if, in ordinary circumstances, they tend to sympathise equally with both parties, the injurer

---

[1] Kant, *Grundlegung zur Metaphysik der Sitten*, sec. i (*Gesammelte Schriften*, iv [Berlin, 1911]), p. 399.

[2] J. Butler, ' Sermon IX.—Upon Forgiveness of Injuries,' in *The Analogy of Religion*, etc. (London, 1893), p. 469.

[3] Plutarch, *De cohibenda ira*, 11 ; Montaigne, *Essais*, ii. 31. " The sword of justice is ill-placed in the hands of an angry man " (Seneca, *De ira*, i. 19).

[4] See E. Westermarck, *The Origin and Development of the Moral Ideas*, i (London, 1912), p. 178 *sq.*

[5] T. Browne, *Christian Morals*, iii. 12 (Cambridge, 1716), p. 94.

and the person injured, and, in consequence, confer upon these equal rights, they will demand a retaliation which is only equal in degree to the offence. The more the moral consciousness is influenced by sympathy, the more severely it condemns any retributive infliction of pain which it regards as undeserved ; and it seems to be in the first place with a view to preventing such injustice that teachers of morality have enjoined upon men to love or be kind to their enemies.

Quite different from the resentment and retaliation springing from personal motives are moral resentment and the punishment in which it finds its expression. The moral indignation of Jesus was often intense. His attacks on the Pharisees, scribes, and lawyers were vehement in the extreme :

" Woe unto you, scribes and Pharisees, hypocrites ! for ye shut up the kingdom of heaven against men : for ye neither go in yourselves, neither suffer ye them that are entering to go in. Woe unto you, scribes and Pharisees, hypocrites ! for ye devour widows' houses, and for a pretence make long prayer : therefore ye shall receive the greater damnation. Woe unto you, scribes and Pharisees, hypocrites ! for ye compass sea and land to make one proselyte, and when he is made, ye make him twofold more the child of hell than yourselves. . . . Woe unto you, scribes and Pharisees, hypocrites ! for ye pay tithe of mint and anise and cummin, and have omitted the weightier matters of the law, judgment, mercy, and faith : these ought ye to have done, and not to leave the other undone. Ye blind guides, which strain at a gnat, and swallow a camel. Woe unto you scribes and Pharisees, hypocrites ! for ye make clean the outside of the cup and of the platter, but within they are full of extortion and excess. . . . Woe unto you, scribes and Pharisees, hypocrites ! for ye are like unto whited sepulchres, which indeed appear beautiful outward, but are within full of dead men's bones, and of all uncleanness. Even so ye also outwardly appear righteous unto men, but within ye are full of hypocrisy and iniquity. . . . Ye serpents, ye generation of vipers, how can ye escape the damnation of hell ? " (*Matthew* xxiii. 13–15, 23–25, 27, 28, 33).

" Beware of the scribes, which love to go in long clothing, and love salutations in the marketplaces, And the chief seats in the synagogues, and the uppermost rooms at feasts : Which devour widows' houses, and for a pretence make long prayers : these shall receive greater damnation " (*Mark* xii. 38–40).

In the Gospel of Luke there are similar attacks on the Pharisees and scribes, and on the lawyers as well (xi. 39 *sqq.*, xx. 46 *sq.*).

The moral indignation of Jesus even led him to violent activity. He " went into the temple of God, and cast out all them that sold and bought in the temple, and overthrew the tables of the moneychangers, and the seats of them that sold doves, And said unto them, It is written, My house shall be called the house of prayer ; but ye have made it a den of thieves." [1]

Resentment, moral and non-moral, varies indefinitely in intensity, and the same is the case with the act of retaliation to which it may lead. According to the teaching of Jesus, the future punishment of sinners is often enormous. As this is a fact which Christian apologists have ignored or smoothed over, I shall add other quotations from the gospels to those referring to the Pharisees, scribes, and lawyers :

" Whosoever shall say (to his brother), Thou fool, shall be in danger of hell fire " (*Matthew* v. 22).

" If thy right eye (or, ' thy right hand ') offend thee pluck it out (or, ' cut it off '), and cast it from thee : for it is profitable for thee that one of thy members should perish, and not that thy whole body should be cast into hell " (*ibid.* v. 29 *sq.*). See also *ibid.* xviii. 8 *sq.* ; *Mark* ix. 43–48.

" The children of the kingdom shall be cast out into outer darkness : there shall be weeping and gnashing of teeth " (*Matthew* viii. 12).

" Whosoever shall not receive you (the disciples), nor hear your words, when ye depart out of that house or city, shake off the dust of your feet. Verily I say unto you, It shall be more tolerable for the land of Sodom and Gomorrha in the day of judgment, than for that city " (*ibid.* x. 14 *sq.*).

" Fear him which is able to destroy both soul and body in hell " (*Matthew* x. 28).

" Woe unto thee, Chorazin ! woe unto thee, Bethsaida ! for if the mighty works, which were done in you, had been done in Tyre and Sidon, they would have repented long ago in sackcloth and ashes. But I say unto you, It shall be more tolerable for Tyre and Sidon at the day of judgment, than for you. And thou, Capernaum, which art exalted unto heaven, shalt be brought down to hell. . . . It shall be more tolerable for the land of Sodom in the day of judgment, than for thee " (*ibid.* xi. 21–24). See also *Luke* x. 12–15.

" The Son of man shall send forth his angels, and they shall gather out of his kingdom all things that offend, and them which do iniquity ; And shall cast them into a furnace of fire, there shall be wailing and gnashing of teeth. . . . So shall it

[1] *Matthew* xxi. 12 *sq.* See also *Mark* xi. 15–17 ; *Luke* xix. 45 *sq.*

be at the end of the world ; the angels shall come forth, and ever the wicked from among the just, And shall cast them into the furnace of fire : there shall be wailing and gnashing of teeth " (*Matthew*, xiii. 41, 42, 49 *sq.*).

" Whoso shall offend one of these little ones which believe in me, it were better for him that a millstone were hanged about his neck, and that he were drowned in the depth of the sea " (*ibid.* xviii. 6). See also *Mark* ix. 42.

When the Son of man shall come in his glory, and before him shall be gathered all nations, " he shall separate them one from another, as a shepherd divideth his sheep from the goats : And he shall set the sheep on his right hand, but the goats on the left. . . . Then shall he say unto them on the left hand, Depart from me, ye cursed, into everlasting fire, prepared for the devil and his angels. . . . And these shall go away into everlasting punishment " (*Matthew* xxv. 31–33, 41, 46).

" He that shall blaspheme against the Holy Ghost hath never forgiveness, but is in danger of eternal damnation " (*Mark* iii. 29). *Cf. Matthew* xii. 31 *sq.* ; *Luke* xii. 10.

" Except ye repent, ye shall all likewise perish " (*Luke* iii. 3, 5).

" Depart from me, all ye workers of iniquity. There shall be weeping and gnashing of teeth, when ye shall see Abraham, and Isaac, and Jacob, and all the prophets, in the kingdom of God, and you yourselves thrust out " (*ibid.* xiii. 27 *sq.*).

The rich man of the parable died and was buried, " and in hell he lift up his eyes, being in torments, and seeth Abraham far off, and Lazarus in his bosom. And he cried and said, . . . I am tormented in this flame " (*ibid.* xvi. 22–24).

When Jesus was asked, " Lord, are there few that be saved ? " he said : " Strive to enter in at the strait gate : for many, I say unto you, will seek to enter in, and shall not be able." [1] On another occasion, in his Sermon on the Mount, he said : " Wide is the gate, and broad is the way, that leadeth to destruction, and many there be which go in thereat : Because strait is the gate, and narrow is the way, which leadeth into life, and few there be that find it." [2] He also said : " There shall be weeping and gnashing of teeth. For many are called, but few are chosen." [3] Modern theology pretends to be better informed. In Hastings' *Encyclopædia of Religion and Ethics* we read that New Testament teaching, taken as a whole, suggests the salvation of the great bulk of mankind and repro-

[1] *Luke* xiii. 23 *sq.*   [2] *Matthew* vii. 13 *sq.*
[3] *Ibid.* xxii. 13 *sq.* See also *ibid.* xx. 16.

E

bation as the rare exception.[1] In support of this statement
the author quotes some inconclusive passages from John and
Timothy and only one from the synoptic gospels, namely the
saying that " the Son of man is come to save that which was
lost." [2] He is also very optimistic as to the condition of the
lost. He says that the general principle of the judgment will
be the loss of faculties which have been abused, and continues
" It is not necessary to regard the condition of the lost as
absolutely intolerable, though, in contrast with the bliss of the
redeemed, it will appear most sad. Its sadness will consist
mainly in regret for the loss of the Beatific Vision, and remorse
for the criminal folly which has led to their degradation from
the rank of responsible beings. On the other hand, their condition may admit of important alleviations. Thus they can
sin no more, and will perform the will of God unerringly, which
will surely be for their good. Moreover, their enjoyment of
natural goods, though impaired, will not be destroyed. In fact
it even seems possible to regard their condition as one of relative
happiness of a purely natural kind." [3] I should have thought
that there could not be much enjoyment of natural goods or
happiness in the furnace of hell.

It is, however, nowadays a widespread opinion that Jesus
did not believe in fiery torment in hell. The statements
referring to it in the gospels are said to be either non-authentic
—later glosses added in oral tradition or by the evangelists [4]—
or to be interpreted in a figurative sense. It is argued that they
are chiefly found in the first gospel, " the Jewish gospel," and
are absent from the parallel passages in the other gospels ; but
the fire of hell is nevertheless mentioned also by Mark and Luke
Another argument is that they are inconsistent with Jesus
true and original gospel of the love of God, which compels us
to regard them as metaphorical. But, as Dr. Cadoux remarks
" to have recourse to figurative interpretation whenever Jesus
words clash with modern knowledge or belief, in order to main
tain the complete conformity of our beliefs with his words, is
an unnatural and forced proceeding, which does violence to the
instinct of truth." [5] The explanation of the gospel passage
concerning hell seems simple enough. It is generally admitted
that Jesus shared with his Jewish contemporaries other belief

[1] C. Harris, ' State of the Dead (Christian),' in J. Hastings, Encyclopœdia of Religion and Ethics, xi (Edinburgh, 1920), p. 836 sq.
[2] Matthew xviii. 11.   [3] Harris, loc. cit. p. 837.
[4] Lily Dougall and C. W. Emmet, The Lord of Thought (London
1922), p. 249.
[5] C. J. Cadoux, Catholicism and Christianity (London, 1928), p. 21

which are now held untenable. The later pre-Christian Jewish writings contain a variety of detailed descriptions of future punishment in which torment and destruction by fire are constant features.[1] Of particular importance is the passage in which Isaiah speaks of the damnation of the wicked, when " the Lord will come with fire . . . to render his anger with fury, and his rebuke with flames," and of the carcasses of the men that have transgressed against him ; " for their worm shall not die, neither shall their fire be quenched." [2] This passage is evidently the source of Mark's reference to hell " where their worm dieth not, and the fire is not quenched." [3]

The immense bulk of Christians have naturally regarded hell and its agonies as material facts. Origen, who was a Platonist and a heretic in many respects, was severely censured for assuming that the souls of the unpurified ones pass into a cleansing fire which is only temporary and figurative, simply consisting in the torments of conscience ; [4] and in the ninth century Scotus Erigena showed unusual audacity in questioning the locality of hell and the material tortures of the condemned.[5] Some great Protestant divines, like Jeremy Taylor and Jonathan Edwards, were anxious to point out that the fire of hell is infinitely more painful than any fire on earth, being " fierce enough to melt the very rocks and elements." [6] This awful punishment also exceeds in dreadfulness anything which even the most vivid imagination can conceive, because it will last not for a passing moment, nor for a year or a hundred, thousand, million, or milliard years, but for ever and ever. In case any doubt should arise as regards the physical capacity of the damned to withstand the heat, we are assured by some reputed theologians that their bodies will be annealed like glass or asbestos-like or of the nature of salamanders,[7] which was already suggested by Augustine.[8] It would seem that even the felicity of the few who were saved must be seriously impaired by their contemplation of this endless and undescribable misery, but we are told that the case is just the reverse. They become

---

[1] *Ibid.* p. 523 ; F. Schwally, *Das Leben nach dem Tode nach den Vorstellungen des alten Israel und des Judentums einschliesslich des Volksglaubens im Zeitalter Christi* (Giessen, 1892), p. 174 *sqq.*

[2] *Isaiah* lxvi. 15, 24. [3] *Mark* ix. 43–48.

[4] Origen, περὶ ἀρχῶν, ii. 10. 4 ; *idem, Contra Celsum*, v. 15, vi. 26.

[5] H. H. Milman, *History of Latin Christianity*, ix (London, 1864), p. 88 n. k.

[6] W. R. Alger, *A Critical History of the Doctrine of a Future Life* (Philadelphia, 1864), p. 516 *sq.*

[7] *Ibid.* pp. 518, 520.

[8] Augustine, *De civitate Dei*, xxi. 4.

as merciless as their god.   Thomas Aquinas says that a perfect
sight of the punishment of the damned is granted them that
they " may enjoy their beatitude and the grace of God more
richly." [1]   And the Puritans, especially, have revelled in the
idea that " the sight of hell torments will exalt the happiness
of the saints for ever," as a sense of the opposite misery always
increases the relish of any pleasure.[2]

It was only in the nineteenth century that, at last, a more
considerable number of Christians began to feel shocked by the
ancient doctrine of eternal punishment.   Nowadays, according
to Dr. Major, the general belief in the English Church is " that
the soul at death passes into the spirit world, and never again
has anything to do with its fleshly integument, which has been
deposited in the grave " ;   and a conviction has grown up that
heaven and hell are thought of not as localities but as personal
states, and that there is every degree of purgatory between
them.[3]   Thus Mr. R. H. Charles has tried to show that the fire
spoken of by Jesus is not to be conceived sensuously, but as a
symbol of the divine wrath, and that the place of punishment
for the wicked is apparently a place of spiritual punishment
only.[4]   Modern theology constantly falls back upon symbolism
as an interpretation of unpalatable statements found in the
gospels.   This, it is said, safeguards the Saviour's infallibility.
But what about his honesty ?   In the recent Report of the
Commission on Christian Doctrine appointed by the Archbishops of Canterbury and York it is argued that eschatological
beliefs are inevitably expressed in symbolical language, being
matters in respect of which " eye hath not seen, nor ear heard,"
and the essence of hell is described as " exclusion from the
fellowship of God." [5]   This implies that Jesus said what he did
not mean, but terrified the simple and ignorant people to whom
he spoke, and countless succeeding generations, by words which
it has taken nearly two thousand years for learned theologians
to decipher.

XAs to the conception of the divine retribution for unrighteousness there are important differences between the teaching of the
gospels and that of the Old Testament.   According to the latter,

[1] Thomas Aquinas, *Summa theologica*, iii. Supplementum, xciv.
1. 2.
[2] J. Edwards, *Works*, vii (London, 1817), p. 480 ;   Alger, *op. cit.*
p. 541.
[3] H. D. A. Major, ' Towards Prayer Book Revision,' in *The Church
and the Twentieth Century*, ed. by G. L. H. Harvey, p. 99 *sq.*
[4] R. H. Charles, *A Critical History of the Doctrine of a Future Life
in Israel, in Judaism, and in Christianity* (London, 1913), pp. 399, 475.
[5] *Doctrine in the Church of England* (London, 1938), pp. 203, 219.

the judgment of God is carried out in this life, according to the former predominantly after death.[†] Among the Jews the belief in a future state began only in prophetic times, when it was clearly spoken of for the first time in the following passage in the book of Daniel : " Many of them that sleep in the dust of the earth shall awake, some to everlasting life, and some to shame and everlasting contempt. And they that be wise shall shine as the brightness of the firmament." [1] But belief in the resurrection of individuals and a final judgment had become elements of Jewish religion when Jesus was born.[2] The other difference between the ideas of retribution in the Old Testament and in the gospels was due to the Hebrew belief that sin affects the nation through the individual and entails guilt on succeeding generations. The anger of the Lord is kindled against the children of Israel on account of Achan's sin.[3] The sin of the sons of Eli is visited on his whole house from generation to generation.[4] Because Saul has slain the Gibeonites, the Lord sends in the days of David a three years' famine, which ceases only when seven of Saul's sons are hanged.[5] The notion of a jealous God who visits the iniquity of the fathers upon the children unto the third and fourth generation of them that hate him,[6] is also frequently met with in the Old Testament Apocrypha.[7]

The infliction of penal suffering on guiltless persons in consequence of the sins of others is contrary to the nature of moral indignation, which, as a retributive emotion, is a hostile attitude of mind towards a living being conceived as a cause of pain.[†] The retribution of a god is in many cases nothing but an outburst of sudden anger, or an act of private revenge, and is as such particularly liable to lack sufficient discrimination. It may also be extended beyond the limits of individual guilt, because sin is looked upon as a kind of material substance which may be transmitted from parents to offspring. To this day the Jews in Morocco sometimes go on their New Year's Day to the seashore or to a spring and remove their sins by throwing stones into the water. The words of the Psalmist, " Wash me thoroughly from mine iniquity, and cleanse me from my sin," [8]

[1] *Daniel* xii. 2 *sq.*
[2] A. Schweitzer, *Die Mystik des Apostels Paulus* (Tübingen, 1930), p. 89 *sq.*
[3] *Joshua* vii. 1.   [4] *1 Samuel* ii. 27 *sqq.*
[5] *2 Samuel* xxi. 1 *sqq.*
[6] *Exodus* xx. 5, 7 ; *Numbers* xiv. 18 ; *Deuteronomy* v. 9. *Cf. Leviticus* xxvi. 39.
[7] *Ecclesiasticus* xvi. 4, xli. 5 *sqq.* ; *Wisdom of Solomon* iii. 12, 16 *sqq.*
[8] *Psalms* li. 2.

were not altogether a figure of speech. That sin is contagious was expressly stated by Novatian, who said that " the one is defiled by the sin of the other, and the idolatry of the transgressor passes over to him who does not transgress." [1] In this materialistic conception of sin there is an obvious confusion between cause and effect, between the sin and its punishment. This carries with it the idea that the injurious energy inherent in sin will sooner or later discharge itself to the discomfort or destruction of anybody who is affected with it. The sick Chinese says of his sickness, " It is my sin," instead of saying, " It is the punishment of my sin " ; [2] and both in Hebrew and in the Vedic language the word for sin is used in a similar way. [3] " In the consciousness of the pious Israelite," says Schultz, " sin, guilt, and punishment, are ideas so directly connected that the words for them are interchangeable " ; the prophets frequently and emphatically declare that there is in sin itself a power which must destroy the sinner. [4] Finally it should be noticed that while the resentment of a man is a matter of experience, that of a god is a matter of inference. That some particular case of suffering is a divine punishment may therefore be assumed on the ground of the conviction that a certain heinous sin cannot be left unpunished. When the sinner himself escapes all punishment, leading a happy life till his death, the conclusion is thus near at hand that any grave misfortune which befalls his descendants is the delayed retribution of the offended god. [5] Such a conclusion may especially force itself upon a mind which has no idea of a hell with *post mortem* punishments for the wicked.

But a moral consciousness which is sufficiently guided by discrimination and sympathy cannot acquiesce in penal suffering being inflicted upon the guiltless. Protests against it are heard from different quarters both with reference to human justice and with reference to the retribution of gods. Plato lays down the rule that " the disgrace and punishment of the father is not to be visited on the children." [6] According to Roman law, " crimen vel poena paterna nullam maculam filio infligere

[1] Novatian, quoted by A. Harnack, *History of Dogma*, ii (London, 1896), p. 119.

[2] J. Edkins, *Religion in China* (London, 1878), p. 134.

[3] M. Holzman, ' Sünde und Sühne in den Rigvedahymnen und den Psalmen,' in *Zeitschrift für Völkerpsychologie und Sprachwissenschaft*, xv (Berlin, 1884), p. 9.

[4] H. Schultz, *Old Testament Theology*, ii (Edinburgh, 1892), pp. 306, 308 *sq.*

[5] *Cf.* Isocrates, *Oratio de pace*, 120 ; Cicero, *De natura deorum*, iii. 38.

[6] Plato, *Leges*, ix. 854.

potest." [1] The Deuteronomist enjoins : " The fathers shall not be put to death for the children, neither shall the children be put to death for the fathers : every man shall be put to death for his own sin." [2] And Jeremiah and Ezekiel broke with the old notion of divine vengeance by extending the law of individual responsibility to the sphere of religion. " Every one shall die for his own iniquity : every man that eateth the sour grape, his teeth shall be set on edge." [3] " The soul that sinneth, it shall die. The son shall not bear the iniquity of the father, neither shall the father bear the iniquity of the son : the righteousness of the righteous shall be upon him, and the wickedness of the wicked shall be upon him." [4]

While the belief in divine retribution after death favours the acceptance of the principle of individual responsibility, it lays itself open to criticism on the plea of being at variance with the moral justification of punishment. The punishment which society inflicts on a criminal is intrinsically an expression of its moral indignation. For ages it was looked upon as a matter of course that a person who has committed a crime should have to suffer for it because he deserves to be punished. This is still the notion of the multitude, as also of a host of theorisers, who by calling punishment an expiation, or a reparation, or a restoration of the disturbed equilibrium of justice, or some similar term, only endeavour to give philosophical sanction to a social institution which is rooted in an emotion. But the infliction of pain is not an act which the moral consciousness regards with indifference even in the case of a criminal ; and to many enlightened minds with keen sympathy for human suffering it has appeared both unreasonable and cruel that the State should wilfully torment him to no purpose. It may certainly be thought that men have no right to give vent to their moral resentment in a way which hurts their neighbours, unless some benefit may be expected from it. In the case of many other emotions we hold that the conative element in the emotion ought not to be allowed to develop into a distinct volition or act ; and it would seem that a similar view might be taken with reference to the aggressiveness of moral disapproval. It is a notion of this kind that is at the bottom of the condemnation of retributive punishment. But at the same time punishment itself is defended. It is only looked upon in

[1] *Digesta*, xlviii. 19. 26.   *Cf. ibid.* xlviii. 19. 20.
[2] *Deuteronomy* xxiv. 16.   *Cf. 2 Kings* xiv. 6.
[3] *Jeremiah* xxxi. 30.
[4] *Ezekiel* xviii. 20. For Talmudic views see E. Deutsch, *op. cit.* p. 52.

a different light, not as an end in itself but as the means of attaining an end. It is to be inflicted not because wrong has been done, but in order that wrong be not done. Its object is held to be either to deter from crime, or to reform the criminal, or by means of elimination or seclusion to make it physically impossible for him to commit fresh crimes.

A punishment inflicted after the death of the culprit cannot serve the aim of eliminating a dangerous individual, because he can no longer do any harm. Nor can it be of any use as a means of deterring him from committing fresh crimes, because he is incapable of doing it. Nor can it be supposed to have any reformatory effect of value to him or to anybody else, if the punishment is eternal. The only thing that may be gained by it is that the threat of it may intimidate the living. In an earlier chapter I have drawn attention to certain facts which seem to detract considerably from its usefulness in this respect ; but to inspire fear of damnation has certainly been a prominent object of Christian moralists from the very beginning till our own times, and not without some degree of success.[1]

On the other hand, as I have endeavoured to show in detail elsewhere,[2] those theorists who think it possible to make punishment independent of moral resentment are victims of an illusion. Whether they are advocates of the theory of determent or the theory of reformation, it has escaped them that they themselves are under the influence of the very principle they reject, because they have failed to grasp its true import. Rightly understood, resentment is preventive in its nature : it is not only aroused by pain, but is a hostile attitude towards its cause, and its tendency is to remove this cause. And it may aim at its removal by bringing about repentance in the offender, which is the reformationists' object of punishment. Thus resentment not only gives rise to punishment, but readily suggests as its proper end either determent or amendment or both. But first of all moral resentment raises a protest against wrong. And whatever theorists may say on the matter, the immediate aim of punishment has always been to give expression to the righteous indignation of the society which inflicts it.

The dependence of punishment upon moral resentment also shows itself in the fact that its degree is influenced by the degree of the resentment. Though a severe punishment may be the most effective deterrent, our feelings object to its application if the crime is slight ; and in any case they put a limit to the

---

[1] *Supra*, p. 28 *sq.*; *infra*, p. 406 *sq.*
[2] Westermarck, *op. cit.* i. 82 *sqq.* ; *idem, Ethical Relativity* (London 1932), p. 78 *sqq.*

intensity of suffering to be inflicted upon a criminal, whatever his crime may be. In former times burning was a penalty for certain offences which were considered particularly atrocious, but it is utterly revolting to the moral consciousness of modern men. Yet its agonies lasted only for a few minutes. What, then, shall we say of the everlasting torments in the furnace of hell as a punishment even for persons who " desire to walk in long robes, and love greetings in the markets, and the highest seats in the synagogues, and the chief rooms at feasts ; which devour widows' houses, and for a shew make long prayers " ? [1] The only thing which can be said in excuse of them is that their horror is never clearly perceived by any one who predicts them.

Side by side with the doctrine of retribution there is in the gospels the message of forgiveness. John the Baptist preached the baptism of repentance for the remission of sins, " and there went out unto him all the land of Judæa, and they of Jerusalem, and were all baptised of him in the river Jordan, confessing their sins." And he preached, saying : " There cometh one mightier than I after me, the latchet of whose shoes I am not worthy to stoop down and unloose. I indeed have baptised you with water : but he shall baptise you with the Holy Ghost." [2] " After that John was put in prison, Jesus came into Galilee, preaching the gospel of the kingdom of God, And saying, The time is fulfilled, and the kingdom of God is at hand : repent ye, and believe the gospel." [3] " I am not come to call the righteous, but sinners to repentance." [4] " Pray ye : Our Father which art in heaven, . . . forgive us our debts, as we forgive our debtors. . . . For if ye forgive men their trespasses, your heavenly Father will also forgive you ; But if ye forgive not men their trespasses, neither will your Father forgive your trespasses." [5] Yet there is a limit to forgiveness : " All manner of sin and blasphemy shall be forgiven unto men : but the blasphemy against the Holy Ghost shall not be forgiven unto men." [6]

That repentance is followed by forgiveness is found in other religions besides Christianity. According to Zoroastrianism, one element of atonement consists in repentance, as manifested by avowal of the guilt and by the recital of a formula, the *Patet*.[7]

---

[1] *Luke* xx. 46 *sq.*
[2] *Mark* i. 4, 5, 7 *sq.* Cf. *Matthew* iii. 1, 2, 5, 6, 11 ; *Luke* iii. 2, 3, 16.
[3] *Mark* i. 14 *sq.* Cf. *Matthew* iv. 17.
[4] *Luke* v. 32. See *infra*, p. 68.
[5] *Matthew* vi. 9, 12, 14 *sq.* Cf. *Luke* xi. 2, 4.
[6] *Matthew* xii. 31 *sq.* ; *Mark* iii. 29 ; *Luke* xii. 10.
[7] J. Darmesteter, ' Introduction to the Vendidâd,' in *The Sacred Books of the East*, iv (Oxford, 1880), p. lxxxvi.

It is said in the Laws of Manu : " In proportion as a man who has done wrong, himself confesses it, even so far he is freed from guilt, as a snake from its slough. . . . He who has committed a sin and has repented, is freed from that sin, but he is purified only by the resolution of ceasing to sin and thinking ' I will do so no more.' " [1] According to the Rig-Veda, the god Varuna inflicts terrible punishments on the hardened criminal, but is merciful to him who repents ; to Varuna the cry of anguish from remorse ascends, and before him the sinner comes to discharge himself of the burden of his guilt by confession.[2] So, also, Zeus pardons the repentant.[3] The main doctrine of Judaism on the subject of atonement is comprised in the single word Repentance. No teachers, says Montefiore, " exalted the place and power of repentance more than the Rabbis. There was no sin for which in their eyes a true repentance could not obtain forgiveness from God." [4] According to the Talmud, a space of only two fingers' breadth lies between hell and heaven : the sinner has only to repent sincerely, and the gates to everlasting bliss will spring open.[5]

But repentance not only blunts the edge of moral indignation and recommends the offender to the mercy of men and gods : it is the sole ground on which pardon can be given by a scrupulous judge. When sufficiently guided by deliberation and left to itself, without being unduly checked by other emotions, the feeling of moral resentment is apt to last as long as its cause remains unaltered, that is, until the will of the offender has ceased to be offensive ; and it ceases to be offensive only when he acknowledges his guilt and repents. It is true that the mere performance of certain ceremonies is frequently supposed to relieve the performer of his sin,[6] and the same end is thought to be attained by pleasing God in some way or other, by sacrifice, or almsgiving, or the like. But such ideas are objectionable to the moral consciousness of a higher type. They are based on the crude notion that sin is a material sub-

[1] *The Laws of Manu*, xi. 229, 231, *cf.* xi. 228, 230 ; in *The Sacred Books of the East*, xxv (1886).

[2] *Rig-Veda*, trans. into German by A. Ludwig (Prag, 1876, etc.), i. 25. 1 *sq.*, ii. 28. 5 *sqq.*, v. 85. 7 *sq.*, vii. 87. 7, 88. 6 *sq.*, 89. 1 *sqq.* ; A. Barth, *The Religions of India* (London, 1882), p. 17.

[3] *Ilias*, ix. 502 *sqq.*

[4] C. G. Montefiore, *Hibbert Lectures on the Religion of the Ancient Hebrews* (London, 1892), pp. 524, 335 n.

[5] Deutsch, *op. cit.* p. 53. *Cf. ibid.* p. 56 ; Katz, *op. cit.* p. 87 *sq.* ; G. F. Moore, ' Sacrifice,' in Cheyne and Black, *Encyclopœdia Biblica*, iv (London, 1903), p. 4224 *sq.*

[6] See E. Westermarck, *The Origin and Development of the Moral Ideas*, i. 53 *sqq.*

stance which may be removed by material means ; or on the belief that an offender may compound with the deity for sinning against him, in the same way as he pacifies his injured neighbour, by bribery or flattery. Hence the Reformation proscribed offerings for the redemption of sins, together with the trade in indulgences ; and we meet with an analogous movement in other comparatively advanced forms of religion. In reformed Brahmanism repentance is declared to be the only means of redeeming trespasses.[1] The idea expressed in the Psalms, that God delights not in burnt offerings, but that the sacrifices of God are a broken and a contrite heart,[2] became the prevailing opinion among the Rabbis, most of whom regarded repentance as the *conditio sine quâ non* of expiation and the forgiveness of sins.[3]

That moral indignation is appeased by repentance, and that repentance is the only proper ground for forgiveness, is due, not to the specifically moral character of such indignation, but to its being a form of resentment. This is confirmed by the fact that an angry and revengeful man is apt to be in a similar way influenced by the sincere apology of the offender. As Aristotle said, men are placable in regard to those who acknowledge and repent their guilt : " there is proof of this in the case of chastising servants ; for we chastise more violently those who contradict us, and deny their guilt ; but towards such as acknowledge themselves to be justly punished we cease from our wrath." [4] In the case of revenge external satisfaction or material compensation is often allowed to take the place of genuine repentance, and the humiliation of the adversary may be sufficient to quiet the angry passion. But the revenge felt by a reflecting mind is not so readily satisfied. It wants to remove the cause which aroused it. The object which resentment is chiefly intent upon, Adam Smith observes, " is not so much to make our enemy feel pain in his turn, as to make him conscious that he feels it upon account of his past conduct, to make him repent of that conduct, and to make him sensible, that the person whom he injured did not deserve to be treated in that manner." [5] The delight of revenge, says Bacon, " seemeth to be not so much in doing the hurt, as in making the party repent." [6]

[1] E. Goblet d'Alviella, *Hibbert Lectures on the Origin and Growth of the Conception of God* (London, 1892), p. 263.

[2] *Psalms* li. 16 *sq*.   [3] Moore, *loc. cit.* col. 4225.

[4] Aristotle, *Rhetorica*, ii. 3. 5.

[5] Adam Smith, *The Theory of Moral Sentiments* (London, 1887), p. 138 *sq*.

[6] Bacon, *Essays*, iv, ' Of Revenge.' *Cf*. Montaigne, *Essais*, ii. 27.

ᛣ While Jesus was capable of feeling intense moral indignation, his emotion of moral approval, of which moral praise or reward is the outward manifestation, plays an even more prominent part in his teaching, as is shown by the innumerable cases in which eternal reward is promised for righteousness. Modern theologians have been disconcerted by this fact and tried to minimise it. They have said that the hope of reward and consequently a eudemonistic motive " sometimes " is found in the teaching of Jesus ; [1] that " it cannot be denied that the idea of reward and punishment now and then peeps out from the context of Christian ethics " ; [2] that " no doubt Jesus did on occasion make an appeal to self-interest." [3] To disclose the inaccuracy of these statements, for which ignorance should be no excuse, the following quotations from the gospels may suffice :

" Blessed are the meek : for they shall inherit the earth. Blessed are they which do hunger and thirst after righteousness : for they shall be filled. Blessed are the merciful : for they shall obtain mercy. Blessed are the pure in heart : for they shall see God. Blessed are the peacemakers : for they shall be called the children of God. Blessed are they which are persecuted for righteousness' sake : for theirs is the kingdom of heaven. Blessed are ye, when men shall revile you, and persecute you, and shall say all manner of evil against you falsely, for my sake. Rejoice, and be exceeding glad : for great is your reward in heaven " (*Matthew* v. 5–12).

" When thou doest alms, let not thy left hand know what thy right hand doeth : That thine alms may be in secret : and thy Father which seeth in secret himself shall reward you openly. . . . When thou prayest, enter into thy closet, and when thou hast shut thy door, pray to thy Father which is in secret ; and thy Father which seeth in secret shall reward thee openly " (*ibid.* vi. 3, 4, 6).

" If ye forgive men their trespasses, your heavenly Father will also forgive you " (*ibid.* vi. 14). See *supra*, p. 57.

" When thou fasteth, anoint thine head, and wash thy face ; That thou appear not unto men to fast, but unto thy Father which is in secret : and thy Father, which seeth in secret, shall reward thee openly " (*ibid.* vi. 17 *sq.*).

" Not every one that saith unto me, Lord, Lord, shall enter

---

[1] T. Bohlin, *Das Grundproblem der Ethik* (Uppsala and Leipzig, 1923), p. 438.

[2] A. Nygren, *Filosofisk och kristen etik* (Lund and Leipzig, 1923), p. 312.

[3] E. W. Hirst, *Jesus and the Moralists* (London, 1935), p. 102.

into the kingdom of heaven ; but he that doeth the will of my Father which is in heaven " (*ibid.* vii. 21).

" Whosoever heareth these sayings of mine, and doeth them, I will liken him unto a wise man, which built his house upon a rock " (*ibid.* vii. 24). See also *Luke* vi. 47 *sq.*

" Ye shall be hated of all men for my name's sake : but he that endureth to the end shall be saved " (*Matthew* x. 22).

" He that receiveth a prophet in the name of a prophet shall receive a prophet's reward ; and he that receiveth a righteous man in the name of a righteous man shall receive a righteous man's reward. And whosoever shall give to drink unto one of these little ones a cup of cold water only in the name of a disciple, verily I say unto you, he shall in no wise lose his reward " (*Matthew* x. 41 *sq.*). See also *Mark* ix. 41.

" Then shall the righteous shine forth as the sun in the kingdom of their Father. Who has ears to hear, let him hear " (*Matthew* xiii. 43).

" Whosoever will save his life shall lose it ; and whosoever will lose his life for my sake shall find it. For what is a man profited, if he shall gain the whole world, and lose his own soul ? " (*ibid.* xvi. 25 *sq.*). See also *ibid.* x. 39 ; *Mark,* viii. 35 *sq.* ; *Luke,* ix. 24 *sq.*

" Every one that hath forsaken houses, or brethren, or sisters, or father, or mother, or wife, or children, or lands, for my name's sake, shall receive an hundredfold, and shall inherit everlasting life " (*Matthew* xix. 29). See also *Mark* x. 29 *sq.* ; *Luke* xviii. 29 *sq.*

" And before him shall be gathered all nations : and he shall separate them one from another, as a shepherd divideth his sheep from the goats : And he shall set the sheep on his right hand, but the goats on the left. Then shall the King say unto them on his right hand, Come, ye blessed of my Father, inherit the kingdom prepared for you from the foundation of the world : For I was an hungred, and ye gave me meat : I was thirsty, and ye gave me drink : I was a stranger, and ye took me in : Naked, and ye clothed me : I was sick, and ye visited me : I was in prison, and ye came unto me. . . . Verily I say unto you, Inasmuch as ye have done it unto one of the least of these my brethren, ye have done it unto me. . . . The righteous [shall go] into life eternal " (*Matthew* xxv. 32–36, 40, 46).

" Blessed are ye, when men shall hate you, and when they shall separate you from their company, and shall reproach you, and cast out your name as evil, for the Son of man's sake. Rejoice ye in that day, and leap for joy : for, behold, your reward is great in heaven " (*Luke* vi. 22 *sq.*).

" Love ye your enemies, and do good, and lend, hoping for nothing again ; and your reward shall be great, and ye shall be the children of the Highest : for he is kind unto the unthankful and to the evil. Be ye therefore merciful, as your Father also is merciful. Judge not, and ye shall not be judged ; condemn not, and ye shall not be condemned : forgive, and ye shall be forgiven : Give, and it shall be given unto you ; good measure, pressed down, and shaken together, and running over, shall men give into your bosom. For with the same measure that ye mete withal it shall be measured to you again " (ibid. vi. 35–38).

" Seek ye the kingdom of God ; and all these things (food and drink and clothing) shall be added unto you " (ibid. xii. 31).

" When thou makest a dinner or a supper, call not thy friends, nor thy brethren, neither thy kinsmen, nor thy rich neighbours ; lest they also bid thee again, and a recompense be made thee. But when thou makest a feast, call the poor, the maimed, the lame, the blind : And thou shalt be blessed ; for they cannot recompense thee : for thou shalt be recompensed at the resurrection of the just " (ibid. xiv. 12–14).

" Every one that exalteth himself shall be abased ; and he that humbleth himself shall be exalted " (ibid. xviii. 14).

When Jesus was asked by a certain ruler what he should do to inherit eternal life, and heard that he had kept all the commandments, " he said unto him, Yet lackest thou one thing ; sell all that thou hast, and distribute unto the poor, and thou shalt have treasure in heaven : and come, follow me " (ibid. xviii. 18, 20–22). See also Matthew, xix. 16, 18–21 ; Mark x. 17, 19–21.

As it, after all, cannot be denied that the gospels contain promises of reward, attempts have been made to extenuate their presence. It is said that they serve a " pedagogical " purpose being intended to influence people with a moral consciousness of an inferior type ;[1] that Jesus for this reason made use of an idea which was prevalent in Jewish thought, but in such a way as to abolish it " by transforming the reward into a gift of love, which transcends the claims that can be raised by the worker " ;[2] that the gospels speak of reward not to make people desirous of it, but to teach people that righteousness is pleasing to God, and must be followed by reward. When the world shows itself hostile to the good man, this belief serves

[1] C. Stange, Die christliche Ethik (Göttingen, 1892), p. 92 ; Bohlin, op. cit. p. 438 ; Nygren, op. cit. p. 312 ; Hirst, op. cit. p. 102.
[2] H. Jacoby, Neutestamentliche Ethik (Königsberg, 1899), p. 51.

to cheer and comfort him and make him persevere and progress in goodness.[1] This seems to be the general doctrine in Lutheran theology. But Luther admits that such an unselfish belief is hardly ever found in actual Christendom.[2]

It is easy to see why Christian theologians are perplexed by the promises of rewards in the gospels. Moral judgments are influenced by the motives of conduct. They are passed on intentions and deliberate wishes, and the motive of an act may itself be an intention or deliberate wish, but one referring to another act. When Brutus helped to kill Cæsar in order to save his country, his intention or deliberate wish, or hope, to save it was the reason, and therefore the motive, for his intention to kill Cæsar. But if we more carefully analyse our moral judgments, we find that they are not really passed on intentions or deliberate wishes in the abstract, but on the persons who have them : *they* are held blamable or worthy of praise on account of their intentions or wishes, because the moral emotions are reactionary attitudes towards living beings. Now we do not feel the emotion of moral approval or retributive kindliness towards a person if we recognise that he does a thing only in the selfish hope of being benefited by it, for example, if he saves another person from drowning merely because he expects a reward for it. The reason for this is not the specifically moral character of moral approval, but the fact of its being a retributive emotion. We do not feel grateful either to a person who bestows a benefit upon us, if we find that he does it only in his own interest.

As a matter of fact, however, moral judgments are commonly passed on acts without much regard being paid to their motives. Moral indignation and moral approval are in the first place aroused by conspicuous facts, and whilst intentions are expressed in the acts themselves, their motives are not. Men desire that certain acts shall be performed, and other acts refrained from. The motives, or conative causes of acts and forbearances are not equally interesting, and they are often mixed, uncertain, and hidden. As a mediæval writer puts it, " the devil himself knoweth not the thought of man." [3] Though we would not praise a person for some deed which we clearly recognise to reflect no merit on his will, the benefit which results from a good act easily induces us to exaggerate the goodness of the

---

[1] K. Thieme, *Die sittliche Triebkraft des Glaubens* (Leipzig, 1895), p. 179 *sq.*

[2] *Ibid.* p. 195.

[3] Quoted by F. Pollock and F. W. Maitland, *The History of the English Law before the Time of Edward I,* ii (Cambridge, 1898), p. 474.

agent. On the other hand, it is success alone that confers upon a man the full reward which he deserves; good intentions without corresponding deeds meet with little applause even when the failure is due to mere misfortune. But it is only from ignorance or want of due reflection that moral judgments are influenced by outward deeds. Owing to its very nature the moral consciousness, when sufficiently thoughtful, regards the will as the only proper object of moral disapproval or moral praise.

The teaching of Jesus certainly laid stress on the motives of conduct. It has been described as an ethic of inwardness: " he rebukes acquisitiveness rather than wealth, lust rather than adultery, hatred rather than war or violence." [1] He condemned the Pharisees, whose leaven was hypocrisy,[2] who for a pretence made long prayer, who made clean the outside of the cup and the platter, but whose inward part was full of wickedness.[3] He said: " That which cometh out of the man, that defileth the man. For from within, out of the heart of men, proceed evil thoughts, adulteries, fornications, murders, Thefts, covetousness, wickedness, deceit, lasciviousness, an evil eye, blasphemy, pride, foolishness: All these evil things come from within, and defile the man." [4] But in breaking with Pharisaism on the point of its mechanical conception of duty Jesus reverted, in fact, to the position taken up by the Prophets of Israel, whose teachings he must often have listened to in the synagogue at Nazareth.[5] " The Lord said, Forasmuch as this people draw near me with their mouth, and with their lips do honour me, but have removed their heart far from me, and their fear towards me is taught by the precept of men: Therefore, behold, I will proceed to do a marvellous work among this people, even a marvellous work and a wonder: for the wisdom of their wise men shall perish, and the understanding of their prudent men shall be hid." [6] " Thus saith the Lord to the men of Judah and Jerusalem, Break up your fallow ground, and sow not among thorns. Circumcise yourselves to the Lord, and take away the foreskins of your heart, ye men of Judah and inhabitants of Jerusalem: lest my fury come forth like fire, and burn that none can quench it, because of the evil of your doings. . . . O Jerusalem, wash thine heart from wickedness, that thou

---

[1] W. R. Inge, *Christian Ethics and Modern Problems* (London, 1932), p. 51.
[2] *Luke* xii. 1.   [3] *Supra*, p. 47.
[4] *Mark* vii. 20–3. See also *Matthew* xv. 18–20.
[5] *Cf.* H. H. Henson, *Christian Morality* (Oxford, 1936), p. 102.
[6] *Isaiah* xxix. 13 *sq.*

mayest be saved." [1] "Cast away from you all your transgressions, whereby ye have transgressed ; and make you a
new heart and a new spirit." [2] In the rabbinical literature
few sayings are quoted more frequently than the adage which
closes those tractates of the Mishna which deal with the sacrificial law : " He that brings few offerings is as he that brings
many ; let his heart be directed heavenward." [3] In the Talmud
it is said : " Before a man prays let him purify his heart " ; [4]
"Sin committed with a good motive is better than a precept
fulfilled from a bad motive " ; [5] " No charity is rewarded but
according to the degree of benevolence in it." [6]

That moral qualities are internal has indeed been recognised
by all great moralists. Confucius required an inward sincerity
in all outward practice, and poured scorn on the Pharisaism
which contented itself with cleaning the outside of the cup and
platter.[7] He said that " in the rites of mourning exceeding
grief with deficient rites is better than little demonstration of
grief with superabounding rites ; and that in those of sacrifice
exceeding reverence with deficient rites is better than an excess
of rites with but little reverence." [8] " Sacrifice is not a thing
coming to a man from without ; it issues from within him, and
has its birth in his heart. When the heart is deeply moved,
expression is given to it by ceremonies." [9] The virtuous man
offers his sacrifices " without seeking for anything to be gained
by them." [10] " The Master said : ' See what a man does, mark
his motives.' " [11] The popular Taoist work called ' The Book
of Secret Blessings ' inculcates the necessity of purifying the
heart as a preparation for all right-doing ; and in another
Taoist work it is written : " If you form in your heart a good
intention, although you may not have done any good, the good
spirits follow you. If you form in your heart a bad intention,
although you may not have done any harm, the evil spirits
follow you." [12] One of the Pahlavi texts puts the following

---

[1] *Jeremiah* iv. 3, 4, 14. *Cf. ibid.* xxiv. 7.
[2] *Ezekiel* xviii. 31. *Cf. ibid.* xi. 19, xxxvi. 26.
[3] Montefiore, *op. cit.* p. 484.   [4] *Ibid.* p. 174.
[5] *Nazir*, fol. 23*b*, quoted by P. I. Hershon, *Treasures of the Talmud*
London, 1882), p. 74.
[6] *Sukkah*, fol. 49*b*, quoted *ibid.* p. 11. See *infra*, p. 80.
[7] *Cf.* J. Legge, *The Religions of China* (London, 1880), p. 261 *sq.* ;
J. Girard de Rialle, *La mythologie comparée* (Paris, 1878), p. 214.
[8] *Lî Kî*, ii. 1. 2. 27 ; in *The Sacred Books of the East*, vol. xxvii.
Oxford, 1885). *Cf. Lun Yü*, iii. 4. 3 ; in J. Legge, *The Chinese Classics*,
(Oxford, 1893).
[9] *Lî Kî*, xxii. 1.   [10] *Ibid.* xxii. 2.   [11] *Lun Yü*, ii. 10. 1 *sq.*
[12] R. K. Douglas, *Confucianism and Taouism* (London, 1889), pp. 272,
270.

F

words into the mouth of the Spirit of Wisdom : " To be grateful in the world, and to wish happiness for every one ; this is greater and better than every good work." [1]   The religious legislator of Brahmanism, whilst assuming in accordance with the popular view that the fulfilment of religious duty will always be rewarded to some extent, whatever may be the motive, maintains that the man who fulfils his duties without regard to the rewards which follow the fulfilment, will enjoy the highest happiness in this life and eternal happiness here-after.[2]   " He who is pure in heart is the truest priest," said Buddha.[3]   According to ' Dhammapada,' " if a man speaks or acts with an evil thought, pain follows him, as the wheel follows the foot of the ox that draws the carriage. . . . If a man speaks or acts with a pure thought, happiness follows him, like a shadow that never leaves him." [4]   In his description of the Buddhists of Mongolia the Rev. James Gilmour observes : " Mongol priests recognise the power of motive in estimating actions. . . . The attitude of the mind decides the nature of the act. He that offers a cup of cold water only, in a proper spirit, has presented a gift quite as acceptable as the most magnificent of donations." [5]

Although Jesus insisted on inwardness and purity of heart, there is no indication that he regarded the hope of reward as an obstacle to gaining it. How could anybody make a promise and at the same time require that it should not influence the conduct of the promisee ? There is no inconsistency between benevolence being the immediate spring of action and the hope of reward being the ultimate motive for it : a person may aim at his own happiness as his ultimate end and at the same time aim sincerely at the happiness of his neighbour as a means to that end. Kant said that " morality is not properly the doctrine how we should *make* ourselves happy, but how we should become *worthy* of happiness." [6] But then he placed the virtuous man in a most precarious position. Even though he know that he is worthy of happiness, and even may hope to participate in it,[7] he must not allow any such hope to slip in

---

[1] *Dînâ-î-Maînôgî Khirad*, lxiii. 3 *sqq.* ; in *The Sacred Books of the East*, xxiv (Oxford, 1885).

[2] J. Talboys Wheeler, *The History of India*, ii (London, 1869), p. 478.

[3] E. W. Hopkins, *The Religions of India* (London, 1896), p. 319.

[4] *Dhammapada*, 1 *sq.* ; in *The Sacred Books of the East*, x (Oxford, 1898).

[5] J. Gilmour, *Among the Mongols* (London, [1892]), p. 239.

[6] Kant, *Kritik der praktischen Vernunft*, i. 2. 5 (*Gesammelte Schriften* v [Berlin, 1913], p. 129 *sq.*).

[7] *Idem, Kritik der reinen Vernunft*, Transcendentale Methodenlehre, ii. 2 (*Gesammelte Schriften*, iii [1911], p. 525 *sqq.*).

as a motive for his conduct ; for if he does so, he ceases to be virtuous and will not get the happiness he hopes for.

˟This was not the teaching of Jesus. To desire to gain divine favour, with everything implied in it, must certainly have been regarded by him as a right motive for our conduct. But then it cannot be said that there is in his message " no support for a hedonistic ethic." [1] He represents heaven as a place where his followers will receive ample compensation for all their present suffering. [2] They will enjoy the company of the great and good of former ages. Jesus will be there himself, in glory, to welcome them into everlasting habitations, and they will see God, the Father who is in heaven, face to face. They will have their old bodies, [3] and Jesus does not even scruple to throw into the picture a dash of material felicity, speaking of the drinking of wine in his Father's kingdom. [4] There is, however, this difference, mentioned in all the synoptic gospels, [5] that the children of resurrection will neither marry nor be given in marriage, but be as the angels of God in heaven. Neither can they die any more. [6] ┼

˟The ethics of Jesus are not only hedonism, but egoistic hedonism, as defined by Sidgwick, that is, " a system which prescribes actions as means to the end of the individual's happiness or pleasure." [7] ┼It cannot be said that the section of eighteenth-century hedonists who supported their theory by theological considerations [8] contradicted the teaching of Jesus, when they looked upon self-love as the ground for accepting the will of God as our rule ; nor that Waterland did so in his ' Sermon on Self-Love,' in which he said : " The wisest course for any man to take is to secure an interest in the life to come. . . . There can be no excess of fondness, or self-indulgence, in respect of eternal happiness. This is loving himself in the best manner, and to the best purposes. All virtue and piety are thus resolvable into a principle of self-love. . . . It is with reference to ourselves, and for our own sakes, that we love even God himself." [9] Paley defined virtue bluntly as " the doing good to mankind, in obedience to the will of God, and for the

---

[1] Hirst, *op. cit.* p. 101.
[2] *Cf.* J. Stalker, *The Ethic of Jesus* (London, 1909), p. 36 *sq.*
[3] *Matthew* v. 29 *sq.*, x. 28, xxvii. 52.
[4] *Ibid.* xxvi. 29.
[5] *Ibid.* xxii. 30 ; *Mark* xii. 25 ; *Luke* xx. 35.
[6] *Luke* xx. 36.
[7] H. Sidgwick, *The Methods of Ethics* (London, 1913), p. 89.
[8] See Westermarck, *Ethical Relativity*, p. 15 *sqq.*
[9] D. Waterland, ' Sermon on Self-Love,' in *The English Preacher*, i (London, 1773), p. 101 *sq.*

sake of everlasting happiness."[1] This motive is in agreement with Augustine's saying that in the heavenly city " there is only the piety that serves the true God and expects a reward."[2]

⋋ The most authoritative description of the ethics of Jesus as egoistic hedonism comes from a theologian of the highest repute, Nathan Söderblom, the late Archbishop of Sweden. He wrote in his book on the Sermon on the Mount : " If it is asked *why* everything which is commanded in the Sermon on the Mount is to be done, why we ought to love our enemies, not to put away our wife, and so forth, the ultimate answer, according to Jesus, is not, for the common good or progress of mankind, but the only uniform and satisfactory explanation of his whole ethics and injunction of piety runs : in order to save our soul. The infinite value of the individual human soul is the leading idea in the Sermon on the Mount and the whole message of Jesus. To this fact many of the moderns are perfectly blind." Jesus does not advocate " a careful weighing of one's own good against the good of others, but a ruthless egoism : build thou *thy* house upon a rock, so that it shall stand when the floods come and the winds blow."[3]

Another well-known Swedish theologian, professor Nygren, says on the contrary that " the evangelical ethics are the most anti-eudemonistic of all ethical theories,"[4] and even goes so far as to allege that according to the teaching of Jesus (as well as that of Paul) God's relations to the human beings are in no way influenced by their behaviour, but depend exclusively upon the nature of his love, which is " spontaneous " or " prompted by no motive."[5] In support of this allegation he quotes repeatedly the saying, " I came not to call the righteous, but sinners " ;[6] Luke adds : " to repentance."[7] This has been said to be clearly a gloss, since there is no notion at all that Jesus had brought with him into the world any new way of procuring forgiveness of sins but that of repentance.[8] It has been pointed out that the prodigal son in the parable is

[1] W. Paley, *The Principles of Moral and Political Philosophy*, i. 7 (Works [Edinburgh, 1834], p. 9).

[2] Augustine, *De civitate Dei*, xiv. 28.

[3] Söderblom, *op. cit.* p. 43.

[4] Nygren, *op. cit.* p. 313.

[5] *Ibid.* pp. 251, 252, 271 ; *idem, Urkristendom och reformation* (Lund, 1932), pp. 17, 71, 72, 74, 76, 78 *sqq.*

[6] *Matthew* ix. 13 (R.V.) ; *Mark* ii. 17 (R.V.) ; Nygren, *Urkristendom och reformation*, pp. 23, 27, 40, 78, 80, 153, 156.

[7] *Luke* v. 32.

[8] H. Rashdall, *The Idea of Atonement in Christian Theology* (London, 1919), p. 24 ; W. E. Barnes, *The Forgiveness of Jesus Christ* (London, 1936), p. 16.

nearer his father than the elder brother, and that there is more joy in heaven over one sinner that repenteth than over ninety-nine just men. But the prodigal son showed his repentance in thought and in word and in act ; and while we do not generally feel any positive pleasure because a person acts rightly, it is different when a sinner repents. Even Luther, whose authority is appealed to for the doctrine that God's love is prompted by no motive, demanded in the first of his ninety-nine theses that a Christian's whole life should be a continuous penitential act.

I am at a loss to understand how Professor Nygren can ignore sayings like these : " With what measure ye mete, it shall be measured to you again " ; [1] " Every idle word that men shall speak, they shall give account thereof in the day of judgment ; for by thy words thou shalt be justified, and by thy words thou shalt be condemned " ; [2] " The Son of man shall come in the glory of his Father with his angels ; and then he shall reward every man according to his works " ; [3]—and the number of others quoted above. The principle of reward and punishment permeates all the moral teaching of Jesus.

[1] *Matthew* vii. 2 ; *Luke* vi. 38.   [2] *Ibid.* xii. 36 *sq.*   [3] *Ibid.* xvi. 27.

CHAPTER IV

THE ETHICS OF JESUS : THEIR DISINTERESTEDNESS
AND ALTRUISM

WHILE Jesus' doctrine of punishment and reward is an outcome of the retributive character of the moral emotions, his teaching also emphasises that disinterestedness which distinguishes them from other, non-moral, retributive emotions. This he does in his enunciation of the " Golden Rule " : " All things whatsoever ye would that men should do to you, do ye even so to them " ; [1] or " As ye would that men should do to you, do ye also to them likewise." [2] The disinterestedness of the moral emotions also finds an echo in the rebuke : " Why beholdest thou the mote that is in thy brother's eye, but considerest not the beam that is in thine own eye ? . . . Thou hypocrite, first cast out the beam out of thine own eye ; and then shalt thou see clearly to cast out the mote out of thy brother's eye." [3]

The Golden Rule is much older than Christianity and, especially in its negative form, widespread. In the Sanskrit work ' Mahabharata ' it is said : " Let no man do to another that which would be repugnant to himself ; this is the sum of righteousness ; the rest is according to inclination. In refusing, in bestowing, in regard to pleasure and to pain, to what is agreeable and disagreeable, a man obtains the proper rule by regarding the case as like his own." [4] Similar words are ascribed to Confucius. When Tsze-kung asked if there is any one word which may serve as a rule of practice for all one's life, the Master answered : " Is not Reciprocity such a word ? What you do not want done to yourself, do not do to others." And in another utterance Confucius showed that the rule had for him not only a negative, but also a positive form. He said that, in the way of the superior man, there are four things to none of which he himself had as yet attained : to serve his

[1] *Matthew* vii. 12.   [2] *Luke* vi. 31.
[3] *Matthew* vii. 3, 5 ; *Luke* vi. 41 *sq.*
[4] *Mahabharata*, xiii. 5571 *sq.*, in J. Muir, *Religious and Moral Sentiments metrically rendered from the Sanskrit* (London, 1875), p. 107. *Cf. Pantschatantra*, iii. 104, trans. by Th. Benfey, ii (Leipzig, 1859), p. 235.

father as he would require his son to serve him, to serve his prince as he would require his minister to serve him, to serve his elder brother as he would require his younger brother to serve him, and to set the example in behaving to a friend as he would require the friend to behave to him.[1] In Greece Isocrates enunciated the maxim : " Do not do to others that which angers you when they do it to you." [2] Aristotle, when questioned how we should behave to our friends, is quoted by Diogenes Laertius as saying : " Exactly as we would they should behave to us." [3] Seneca wrote : " Let us put ourselves in the place of him with whom we are angry. . . . We are quite willing to do to others what we cannot endure should be done to ourselves " ; [4] and Epictetus : " That which thou wouldst not suffer thyself, seek not to lay upon others." [5] In its negative form the Golden Rule is also found in the earlier Judaism. Tobit said to his son : " Take heed to thyself, my child, in all thy works, and be discreet in thy behaviour ; what thou thyself hatest, do to no man." [6] When a heathen came to the famous rabbi Hillel and said to him that he would embrace Judaism on condition that he were taught the whole doctrine during the time that he stood on one leg, the rabbi replied : " What thou doest not like, do not do to thy neighbour ; that is the whole doctrine, all the rest is only explanation." [7] According to Augustine the precept that we must not do to others what we do not wish them to do to us, is a rule of behaviour which is by nature inherent in the human mind ; [8] and Hobbes speaks of the " laws of nature " expressed in " this one sentence, approved by all the world, Do not that to another, which thou thinkest unreasonable to be done by another to thy selfe." [9] They were perfectly right for the simple reason that disinterestedness is an essential characteristic of the moral emotions, without which there could be no moral precepts at all.

The Golden Rule also occurs in its prohibitive shape— ' that which ye will that other men do not unto you, do not that to other men "—in the earliest quotations of it which are

[1] *Lun Yü*, xv. 23, in J. Legge, *The Chinese Classics*, i (Oxford, 1893) ; *Chung Yung*, xiii. 4 (*ibid.*). *Cf. Lun Yü*, xii. 2 ; *Chung Yung*, xiii. 3.
[2] Isocrates, *Nicocles*, 61. *Cf. idem, Ad Demonicum*, 14.
[3] Diogenes Laertius, *De clarorum philosophicorum vitis*, v. 21.
[4] Seneca, *De ira*, iii. 12.
[5] Epictetus, *Fragmenta*, 42.   [6] *Tobit*, iv. 14 *sq.*
[7] *Shabboth*, 31a, quoted by A. Drews, *The Witnesses of the Historicity of Jesus* (London, 1912), p. 266 *sq.* For other parallels see C. Taylor, *Sayings of the Jewish Fathers* (Cambridge, 1897), p. 142 *sq.*
[8] Augustine, *De doctrina Christiana*, iii. 14 (Migne, *Patrologiæ cursus*, xxxiv. 74).
[9] T. Hobbes, *Leviathan*, ii. 26. 8 (Oxford, 1881), p. 210.

found in Christian literature outside the gospels. In this negative form it is already attached to the Apostolic Decree as early as the Western text to the Acts xv. 29, dating from the opening years of the second century if not from a still earlier period, and, in spite of its absence from the received text, it continued to hold a place in this passage of the Acts down to a comparatively late date.[1] The negative form is also observable in post-Biblical Christian writings.[2]

It is not difficult to explain why the negative Golden Rule is more widely spread than the positive one. Negative commandments spring from the disapproval of acts, whereas positive commandments spring from the disapproval of forbearances or omissions, and the indignation of men is much more easily aroused by action than by absence of action. A person who commits a harmful deed is a more obvious cause of pain than a person who causes harm by doing nothing, and this naturally affects the question of guilt in the eyes of most people. Moreover, the Golden Rule implies that it cannot be right for A to treat B in a manner in which it would be wrong for B to treat A, unless there is some difference between the natures or circumstances of the two individuals which can be regarded as a reasonable ground for difference of treatment; and such differences are generally more restricted in the case of acts that are forbidden than in the case of acts that are positively enjoined. The negative commandments are also more distinct: they condemn certain definite modes of behaviour, while the rules of benevolence often are more comprehensive. It seems that almost from the outset the rule of the gospels was in need of explanation and some limitation. In certain Latin versions the words " good things " were inserted after the word " whatsoever." Those who made the insertion recognised evidently that it is not everything which we may wish for ourselves that we are bound to do for others. We might wish for ourselves, for instance, some form of illicit or undesirable pleasure, and yet cannot be bound to provide for others such pleasure or assist them in obtaining it for themselves.[3]

The disinterestedness of the moral emotions partly underlies the rule, " Thou shalt love thy neighbour as thyself," which

[1] J. E. Carpenter and G. Harford, *The Composition of the Hexateuch* (London, 1902), p. 10 ; A. Harnack, ' Das Aposteldecret (Act 15, 29) und die Blass'sche Hypotese,' in *Sitzungsberichte der Königlich Preussischen Akademie der Wissenschaften zu Berlin*, Jahrgang 1899 (Berlin, 1899), p. 151 *sq.*

[2] W. A. Spooner, ' Golden Rule,' in J. Hastings, *Encyclopædia of Religion and Ethics*, vi (Edinburgh, 1913), p. 311.

[3] *Ibid.* p. 312.

occurs both in the Old Testament [1] and in the three synoptic gospels.[2] But this maxim contains much more than the disinterestedness of the conception of duty. When a person pronounces an act right or wrong, it implies that it is so *ceteris paribus*, whether he does it to another or another does it to him, but this has nothing to do with the particular nature of the act. When my own interests clash with those of my neighbour, I may have the right to prefer my own lesser good to the greater good of another, but only on condition that the other person also, in similar circumstances, is admitted to have the right to prefer his own lesser good to my greater good. No such right to prefer one's own lesser good to the greater good of another is recognised in the precept, " Thou shalt love thy neighbour as thyself " ; but this precept owes its origin to the strength of the altruistic sentiment in him who laid down the rule, and not merely to the disinterestedness of his moral emotions.

The precept inculcating love of one's neighbour is rooted in the altruistic sentiment, which, as I have pointed out above, has produced moral emotions, as distinguished from other retributive emotions not only by their disinterestedness, but also by their impartiality in other respects. Now the altruistic sentiment varies greatly both in strength and expanse, and so does consequently the love of neighbour which is prescribed as a duty by different moral codes. The groups of neighbours to which these rules refer may vary indefinitely, without interfering with the impartiality required by the moral emotions from which they sprang. If it is considered wrong of a person to cheat another belonging to his own group but not wrong to cheat a foreigner, the impartiality of the moral emotion of disapproval, which underlies the concept of wrongness, merely leads to a general rule that applies to all similar cases independently of the nationality of him who holds the view. If I maintain that a foreigner, or a member of another class in my own society, has a duty towards me but that I have not the same duty towards him, my opinion can be morally justified only on condition that there is some difference in the circumstances affecting the morality of the case. The impartiality of my moral emotions does not prevent me from promoting the welfare of my own family or country in preference to that of other families or countries. But they tell me that I must allow anybody else to show a similar preference for *his* family or country.

[1] *Leviticus* xix. 18.
[2] *Matthew* xix. 19, xxii. 39 ; *Mark* xii. 31 ; *Luke* x. 27.

The question is, then, who is my neighbour whom I ought to love as myself ?   This question was put to Jesus by a lawyer who asked him what he should do to inherit eternal life.   Jesus answered him by telling the parable of the traveller who fell among thieves and was left half dead, of the priest and the Levite who passed by on the other side, and of the good Samaritan who took care of the wounded man ; and he then asked the lawyer which of those three he thought was " neighbour unto him that fell among the thieves ?   And he said, He that shewed mercy on him.   Then said Jesus unto him, Go, and do thou likewise." [1]   This has been alleged to prove that in the thought of Jesus the idea of neighbour had lost all such limitations as in the earlier Jewish interpretation were imposed by national animosity, and embraced all men irrespective of race.   Much significance has also been attached to the word " men " in the passage, " All things whatsoever ye would that men should do to you, do ye even so to them " (*Matthew* vii. 12), [2] and to the word " whosoever " in the passage, " Whosoever shall do the will of my Father which is in heaven, the same is my brother, and sister, and mother " (*ibid*. xii. 50 ; *Mark* iii. 35). [3]   As to the alleged implications of these two passages, it must be said to be a poor case that is considered to need the support of such strained interpretations; indeed, the latter of them directly contains an important limitation.   And the parable of a Samaritan who takes pity on a wounded stranger is scarcely a clear answer to the question : Who is my neighbour whom I should love as myself ?

On the other hand, there is good evidence in the gospels that Jesus had not entirely discarded Jewish exclusiveness in these matters.   He seems to have felt himself as one who had come with a message to the people of Israel.   When he sent out his disciples as travelling apostles, he " commanded them, saying, Go not into the way of the Gentiles, and into any city of the Samaritans enter ye not : But go rather to the lost sheep of the house of Israel.   And as ye go, preach, saying, The kingdom of heaven is at hand." [4]   Again, a Syrophœnician woman came from the environs of Tyre, " and cried unto him, saying, Have mercy on me, O Lord, thou Son of David ; my daughter is grievously vexed with a devil.   But he answered her not a word.   And his disciples came and besought him,

---

[1] *Luke* x. 25–37.

[2] H. Bisseker, ' Brotherly Love (Christian),' in Hastings, *op. cit.* ii (1909), p. 873.

[3] E. W. Hirst, *Jesus and the Moralists* (London, 1935), p. 25.

[4] *Matthew* x. 5–7.

saying, Send her away ; for she crieth after us. But he answered
and said, I am not sent but unto the lost sheep of the house of
Israel. Then came she and worshipped him, saying, Lord,
help me. But he answered and said, It is not meet to take the
children's bread, and to cast it to dogs." When the woman,
admitting the truth of this, made the remark that the dogs eat
of the crumbs which fall from their masters' table, Jesus
"answered and said unto her, O woman, great is thy faith : be
it unto thee even as thou wilt." And her daughter was made
whole from that very hour.[1] By the children whose bread
should not be cast to the dogs, Jesus obviously meant the Jews.[2]
It was to Jewish sinners that Jesus addressed himself ; his
life was spent in wandering over the narrow strip of ground
between Capernaum and Jerusalem. He is sometimes represented as speaking of the gospel being preached " among all
nations," or " throughout the whole world," or " to every
creature " ; [3] but these utterances are scarcely congruous with
his belief in the imminence of the end of the world.[4] As Dean
Rashdall observes, " there is no critically unassailable evidence
that he ever spoke of actually converting the world to his gospel
or making gentiles into members of a world-wide Church." [5]
It has been argued that the belief in a common divine
fatherhood compels us to regard every man as a neighbour
whom we ought to love as ourselves. Among the Jews their
common descent from Abraham was always felt to bind them
together in mutual obligations. The novelty introduced by
Jesus, we are told, lies in the fact that he grounded such obligations on a common descent from God : " by substituting the
Father in Heaven for father Abraham, Christ made morality
universal. This phrase, which places not a certain number of
men, but all men, in the relation of brotherhood to each other,
destroys at once the partition-wall between Jew and Gentile,
Greek and barbarian." [6] Mr. Hirst writes : " Since the love
of God is a Father's love, man, being God's child, must love

[1] Ibid. xv. 21-8. Cf. Mark vii. 24-30.
[2] Cf. A. Aall, The Hellenistic Elements in Christianity (London, 1931),
p. 25.
[3] Matthew xxiv. 14 ; Mark xiii. 10, xiv. 9, xvi. 15 ; Luke xxiv. 47.
The commandment reported by Matthew xxviii. 19 could not have been
uttered by Jesus (see A. Harnack, History of Dogma, i [London, 1894],
p. 79, n. 1).
[4] Matthew iv. 17, xxiv. 34 sq. ; Mark i. 15, xiii. 30 sq. ; Luke xxi.
32 sq.
[5] H. Rashdall, The Idea of Atonement in Christian Theology (London,
1919), p. 17.
[6] J. R. Seeley, Ecce Homo (London, 1892), p. 122 sq.

him with filial devotion and other men as brothers." [1] And
Bishop Bohlin maintains not only that the principle of a human
brotherhood is derived from that of the fatherhood of God, but
even that without their belief in God as a Father the Christians
could never have formed the idea of a common human brotherhood. [2] As a matter of fact, however, we find in the gospels
neither the belief in a common divine fatherhood nor the idea
of a common human brotherhood.

By careful study of the passages in the New Testament in
which God is spoken of as a Father, Professor Mead has found
that he is called so with reference either to Christ in particular
or to Christ's believers. When Jesus is especially addressing the
Pharisees or others who are not in sympathy with him, he never
calls God their Father. He nowhere distinctly declares that
the fatherhood of God is universal, but he is recorded distinctly
to assert that it is not universal. When certain of the Jews,
in their dispute with Jesus, said to him : " We be not born of
fornication ; we have one Father, even God," he replied : " If
God were your Father, ye would love me. . . . Ye are of
your father the devil." [3] Again, when we examine the New
Testament passages which speak of men as the sons or children
of God, we find that the gospels, and particularly the words
of Jesus as recorded there, present not a single declaration to
the effect that all men are children of God. Wherever the
conception is found, it clearly and unmistakably is limited to
a portion of mankind. On one occasion Jesus said that those
who love their enemies become the children of the heavenly
Father. [4] Paul said : " As many as are led by the Spirit of
God, they are the sons of God." [5]

Nor do we find in the gospels the notion of a universal
brotherhood. In a passage quoted above Jesus says that his
brother is he who does the will of God. [6] John puts into his
mouth a saying in which he enjoins on his disciples brotherly
love of a very narrow compass : " A new commandment I give
unto you, That ye love one another ; as I have loved you,

----

[1] Hirst, *op. cit.* p. 49. He even says that " the Christian should
love himself, not of course for his own sake, but as being the child
of the Heavenly Father " (*ibid.* p. 21).

[2] T. Bohlin, *Das Grundproblem der Ethik* (Uppsala and Leipzig,
1923), p. 44.

[3] *John* viii. 41, 42, 44.　　　　　　[4] *Matthew* v. 44 *sq.*

[5] *Romans* viii. 14. See also *Galatians* iv. 5 ; *Philippians* ii. 14 *sq.* ;
Ephesians i. 5.—C. M. Mead, ' The Fatherhood of God,' in *The American
Journal of Theology*, i (Chicago, 1897), pp. 577–600. See also H. E.
Guillebaud, *Why the Cross ?* (London, 1937), pp. 49–59.

[6] *Supra*, p. 74.

that ye also love one another. By this all men know that ye are my disciples, if ye love one to another." [1] It has been pointed out that the prevalent sense of ἀδελφός in the New Testament is that of " fellow-Christian "—a restricted meaning which is sometimes markedly imposed by the immediate context [2]— and that the love required frequently refers to the brotherhood of believers only.[3] Even Paul, in spite of his cosmopolitan outlook, wrote to the Romans : " Be kindly affectioned one to another with brotherly love ; in honour preferring one another " ; [4] and to the Thessalonians : " As touching brotherly love ye need not that I write unto you : for ye yourselves are taught of God to love one another. And indeed ye do it toward all the brethren which are in all Macedonia." [5] In another epistle he wrote : " As we have . . . opportunity, let us do good unto all men, especially unto them who are of the household of faith." [6] Hospitality towards strangers is represented as a duty in the New Testament,[7] as it was by the Jews, but sometimes its exercise is expressly confined to the case of fellow-Christians.[8] Otherwise there is nothing specifically Christian about it. Hospitality seems to be a universal custom among the lower races whilst in their native state, as also among the early peoples of culture. But there is no doubt that it is in the main based on egoistic considerations, particularly connected with superstitious ideas about the unknown mysterious stranger, who is looked upon as a potential cause of evil if he is treated badly, and as a potential benefactor if he is received as a guest.[9] The latter idea is expressly mentioned as the reason for the injunction in the Epistle to the Hebrews : " Be not forgetful to entertain strangers : for thereby some have entertained angels unawares." [10]

As to the contention that without their belief in God as a father the Christians could never have formed the idea of a common human brotherhood, it should be noticed that tenets of universal love have been laid down both by the Stoics and by Eastern moralists, who had no notion of a divine fatherhood. The Chinese teachers of morality inculcated benevolence to all

---

[1] *John* xiii. 34 *sq.*   See also *ibid.* xv. 12, 17.
[2] See, for example, *1 Corinthians* v. 11, vi. 6.
[3] Bisseker, *loc. cit.* p. 873.   [4] *Romans* xii. 10.
[5] *1 Thessalonians* iv. 9 *sq.*   [6] *Galatians* vi. 10.
[7] *Matthew* xxv. 43, 45 ; *Romans* xii. 13 ; *1 Timothy* v. 10 ; *Hebrews* xiii. 2.
[8] *3 John* 5–8.
[9] E. Westermarck, *The Origin and Development of the Moral Ideas*, i (London, 1912), p. 572 *sqq.*
[10] *Hebrews* xiii. 2.

men, without making any reference to national distinctions.[1] Mih-tsze, who lived in the interval between Confucius and Mencius, even thought that we ought to love all men equally; but this called forth protests as abnegating the peculiar devotion due to relatives.[2] In 'Thâi-Shang' it is said that a good man will feel kindly towards every creature, and should not hurt even the insect tribes, grass, and trees.[3] Buddhism enjoins the duty of universal love : " As a mother, even at the risk of her own life, protects her son, her only son, so let a man cultivate goodwill without measure toward all beings, . . . unhindered love and friendliness toward the whole world, above, below, around." [4] According to the Hindu work ' Panchatantra ' it is the thought of little-minded persons to consider whether a man is one of ourselves or an alien, the whole earth being of kin to him who is generously disposed.[5]

Much importance has been attached to the fact that in the teaching of Jesus the two commandments enjoining the love of God and the love of neighbour, which in the Old Testament occur in different books,[6] have been put together in the saying : " Thou shalt love the Lord thy God with all thy heart, and with all thy soul, and with all thy mind. This is the first and great commandment. And the second is like unto it, Thou shalt love thy neighbour as thyself." [7] This combination has led to the conclusion that the love of neighbour follows from the love of God, and cannot exist without it.[8] I find no evidence for such a conclusion in the saying that the second commandment is " like unto " [9] the first. They are like each other in so far that both are commandments of love. But the word " love " cannot mean the same in both cases. The love of God implies reverence, gratitude,[10] devotion, and trust or faith ; the love of neighbour means practically benevolence. Love as a

[1] *Lun Yü*, xii. 22 ; Mencius, vii. 1. 45, in Legge, *op. cit.* ii (1895) ; R. K. Douglas, *Confucianism and Taouism* (London, 1889), pp. 108, 205.
[2] J. Edkins, *Religion in China* (London, 1878), p. 119 ; Legge, *op. cit.* ii. 476 n. 45 ; J. J. M. de Groot, *The Religious System of China*, vol. ii, book i (Leiden, 1894), p. 684.
[3] *Thâi-Shang*, 3 ; in *The Sacred Books of the East*, xl (Oxford, 1891).
[4] Quoted by T. W. Rhys Davids, *Hibbert Lectures on . . . the History of Indian Buddhism* (London, 1881), p. 111.
[5] Muir, *op. cit.* p. 109.
[6] *Deuteronomy* vi. 5 ; *Leviticus* xix. 18.
[7] *Matthew* xxii. 37–9 ; *Mark* xii. 30 *sq.*
[8] A. Nygren, *Filosofisk och kristen etik* (Lund and Leipzig, 1923), pp. 294, 298.
[9] In *Luke* (x. 27 *sq.*) these words are not found at all.
[10] " We love him, because he first loved us " (*1 John* iv. 19).

pure emotion cannot, of course, be commanded, but it readily develops into a volition, and becomes then a proper object of moral judgment. It is absurd, however, to suppose that benevolence towards a fellow-man could be merely derivative from the love of God. If it were, I am afraid that there would not be much of it even in the Christian world ; as Dean Inge says, " ' love of God ' is talked about more often than felt," [1] and while " god-fearing " is a common epithet for a devout Christian, " god-loving " is not found even in dictionaries. Paul speaks extremely rarely of the love of God. Instead of saying that the love of neighbour follows from the love of God, we may rather say, with John, that a man cannot love God, whom he has not seen, if he does not love his brother, whom he has seen.[2]

The altruistic sentiment, of which benevolence is a manifestation, is found in all mammalian species, at least as displayed in the mother's love of her young, and the duty of benevolence in every human society. There is no doubt that it was such a sentiment that led Jesus to enjoin men to love their neighbours as themselves, and to regard this duty as a command of God. His infinite kindness towards the sick, the needy, and the distressed is abundantly proved throughout the gospels, and finds its most touching expression in the words : " Come unto me, all ye that labour and are heavy laden, and I will give you rest. Take my yoke upon you and learn of me ; for I am meek and lowly in heart : and ye shall find rest unto your souls. For my yoke is easy, and my burden is light." [3]

Among the positive duties resulting from benevolence almsgiving holds a prominent position in the teaching of Jesus. He said : " Give to him that asketh thee, and from him that would borrow of thee turn not thou away." [4] When a young ruler who asked him what he should do that he might inherit eternal life, and told him that he had kept all the commandments from his youth, Jesus answered : " Yet lackest thou one thing : sell all that thou hast, and distribute unto the poor, and thou shalt have treasure in heaven." [5] Eternal life is promised to those who feed the hungry, give drink to the thirsty, take in the stranger, clothe the naked, visit the sick.[6]

[1] W. R. Inge, *Christian Ethics and Modern Problems* (London, 1932), p. 52.

[2] *1 John* iv. 20.

[3] *Matthew* xi. 28–30.

[4] *Ibid.* v. 42. See also *Luke* vi. 30.

[5] *Luke* xviii. 20–2. See also *Matthew* xix. 16, 18–21 ; *Mark* x. 17, 19–21.

[6] *Matthew* xxv. 34, 36, 40, 45 *sq.*

This insistence on the duty of charity, which for ages was destined to exercise a paramount influence on Christian morals, belonged to the Jewish heritage. " Thou shalt open thine hand wide unto thy brother, to thy poor, and to thy needy, in thy land " ; " for this thing the Lord thy God shall bless thee in all thy works, and in all that thou puttest thine hand unto." [1] Even " if thine enemy be hungry, give him bread to eat ; and if he be thirsty, give him water to drink : . . . the Lord shall reward thee." [2] Especially in the Old Testament apocrypha and in rabbinical literature almsgiving assumed an excessive importance—so much so that the word which in the older writings means " righteousness " in general came to be used for almsgiving in particular.[3] " Shut up alms in thy storehouses ; and it shall deliver thee from all affliction." [4] " As water will quench a flaming fire, so alms maketh an atonement for sins." [5] " For alms doth deliver from death, and shall purge away all sin. Those that exercise alms and righteousness shall be filled with life." [6] The charitable man is rewarded with the birth of male issue.[7] Almsgiving outweighs all other duties.[8] He who averts his eye from charity commits a sin equal to idolatry.[9] It must be extended equally to Jew and Gentile.[10] To such an extreme was almsgiving carried by the Jews that, while the giver must devote to charity at least a tenth of his income, some rabbis at length decreed that no man should give more than a fifth, lest he should come to seek charity himself.[11] But charity is not sufficient in itself : kind thoughts and words must go with it. To give liberally to the poor, but with sullen look, is to rob the deed of all virtue.[12] " Sow [a reward] for yourselves in giving alms as charity, you will reap according to the benevolence." [13] Like Jesus, the rabbis insisted that charity should be done in secret.[14] He that gives alms publicly is a sinner ; indeed, " better give no alms at all, than give them in public." [15]

[1] *Deuteronomy* xv. 11, 10. See also *ibid.* x. 18, xiv. 29, xv. 7–9, xvi. 11, 14, xxiv. 19–21 ; *Leviticus* xix. 9 *sq.*, xxv. 35 ; *Psalms* xli. 1 ; *Proverbs* xiv. 21.

[2] *Proverbs* xxv. 21 *sq.*

[3] W. E. Addis, ' Alms,' in T. K. Cheyne and J. S. Black, *Encyclopædia Biblica*, i (London, 1899), p. 118. *Cf.* C. G. Montefiore, *Hibbert Lectures on . . . the Religion of the Ancient Hebrews* (London, 1892) p. 484 *sq.*

[4] *Ecclesiasticus* xxix. 12.   [5] *Ibid.* iii. 30.

[6] *Tobit*, xii. 9. *Cf. ibid.* i. 3, 16 *sq.*, ii. 14, iv. 7–12, xii. 8 *sq.*

[7] *Baba Bathra*, fol. 10*b*.

[8] *Idem*, fol. 9*a* ; *Sukkah*, fol. 49*b*.

[9] *Kethuboth*, fol. 68*a*.   [10] *Gittin*, fol. 61*a*.

[11] *Kethuboth*, fol. 50*a*.   [12] *Baba Bathra*, fol. 9*b*.

[13] *Sukkah*, fol. 49*b*.   [14] *Baba Bathra*, fol. 9*b*.   [15] *Ḥagiga*, fol. 5*a*.

While the duty of almsgiving is in the first place based on
the altruistic sentiment and, therefore, is apt to assume a
religious character where the deity is looked upon as a being
who is kindly disposed towards mankind and a guardian of
morality, there are also some special reasons why it has been
so strenuously enjoined by religions of a higher type, including
others besides Hebrewism and Christianity.[1] There is an idea
that niggardliness exposes a person to supernatural danger,
whereas charity and liberality may entail supernatural reward,
on account of the curses or blessings of the poor. The ancient
Greeks believed that the beggar had his Erinys,[2] his avenging
demon, who was evidently a personification of his curse.[3] It is
said in the Proverbs : " He that giveth unto the poor shall
not lack : but he that hideth his eyes shall have many a curse " ;[4]
and in Deuteronomy : " Thou shalt not oppress an hired servant
that is poor and needy, . . . lest he cry against thee unto the
Lord, and it be sin unto thee." [5] The same idea is expressed in
Ecclesiasticus : " Turn not away thine eye from the needy,
and give him none occasion to curse thee : for if he curse thee
in the bitterness of his soul, his prayer shall be heard of him
that made him. . . . A prayer out of a poor man's mouth
reacheth to the ears of God, and his judgment cometh speedily." [6]
In a very early Christian work, the ' Shepherd ' of Hermas, it
is said : " Beware, ye that glory in your riches, lest perhaps
they groan who are in want, and their sighing come up to God,
and ye be shut out with your goods without the gate of the
tower." [7] And a poor man is able not only to punish the uncharitable by means of his curse, but also to reward the generous
giver by means of his blessing ; as it is said in Ecclesiasticus :
' Stretch thine hand unto the poor, that thy blessing may be
perfected. A gift hath grace in the sight of every man living." [8]
While he who withholdeth corn shall be cursed by the people,
" blessing shall be upon the head of him that selleth it." [9]
Hermas writes that as the vine is supported by the elm, so is
the rich man helped by the prayers of the poor. " The poor

[1] Westermarck, *op. cit.* i. 549 *sqq.*
[2] *Odyssey*, xvii. 575.
[3] Æschylus (*Eumenides*, 416 *sq.*) expressly designates the Erinyes
by the title of " curses " (ἀραί), and Pausanias (*Descriptio Græciæ*,
viii. 25. 6) derives the name Erinys from an Arcadian word signifying
fit of anger. *Cf.* Westermarck, *op. cit.* i. 60 n. 3.
[4] *Proverbs* xxviii. 27.
[5] *Deuteronomy* xxiv. 14 *sq. Cf. ibid.* xv. 9.
[6] *Ecclesiasticus*, iv. 5 *sq.*, xxi. 5.
[7] Hermas, *Pastor*, i. 3. 9.
[8] *Ecclesiasticus* vii. 32.   [9] *Proverbs* xi. 26.

praying unto the Lord for the rich are heard by him ; and their riches are increased, because they minister to the poor of their wealth." [1]

The curses and blessings, no doubt, partly account for the fact that almsgiving has come to be regarded as a religious duty. They have not necessarily the character of an appeal to a god, but may be believed to possess a purely magical power, independently of any superhuman will. This belief is rooted in the close association between the wish, more particularly the spoken wish, and the idea of its fulfilment. The wish is looked upon in the light of energy which may be transferred—by material contact, or by the eye, or by means of speech—to the person concerned, and then becomes a fact. This process, however, is not taken quite as a matter of course. There is always some mystery about it, and one—though not the only— method of giving the curse or the blessing that supernatural quality which alone can bring about the result desired is to invoke in it a god. His own feelings need not be considered at all : his holy name may simply be brought in to impart to it that mystic efficacy which the plain word lacks. In the Talmud there are traces of the idea that the name of the Lord might be used with advantage in any curse however undeserved.[2] But with the deepening of the religious sentiment this idea has to be given up. A righteous and mighty god can scarcely agree to be a mere tool in the hand of a wicked curser. Hence the curse comes to be looked upon as a prayer, which is not fulfilled if undeserved ; as it is said in the Proverbs, " the curse causeless shall not come." [3]   And the same is the case with a blessing. In ancient days Jacob could take away his brother's blessing by deceit ; [4] the blessing acted in the same way as a medicine, which cures the patient just as well if it is stolen as if it is bought. But later on its efficacy was limited by moral considerations. The Psalmist declares that only the offspring of the righteous can be blessed,[5] and according to the Apostolic Constitutions, " although a widow who eateth and is filled from the wicked, pray for them, she shall not be heard." [6]   On the other hand, curses and blessings, when well deserved, continued to draw down calamity or prosperity upon their objects, by inducing God to put them into effect. This notion prevails both in

[1] Hermas, *op. cit.* iii. 2.
[2] *Makkoth*, fol. 11a ; *Berakhoth*, foll. 19a, 56a.
[3] *Proverbs* xxvi. 2.
[4] *Genesis* xxvii. 23 *sqq.*
[5] *Psalms* xxxvii. 26.
[6] *Constitutiones Apostolicæ*, iv. 6. *Cf. Jeremiah*, vii. 16.

Judaism and Mohammedanism,[1] and underlies the Christian oath and benediction. As an uncharitable man deserves to be punished and a charitable man merits reward, the curses and blessings of the poor will be heard by a righteous God. " The Lord will plead their cause." [2]

Besides the belief in the efficacy of curses and blessings there is another, and more important, reason for the extraordinary stress which the higher religions lay on the duty of charity, namely the connection between almsgiving and sacrifice. When food is offered as a tribute to a god, he is supposed to enjoy its spiritual part only, while the substance of it is left behind and is in many cases eaten by the poor. And when the offering is continued in ceremonial survival in spite of the growing conviction that, after all, the deity does not need and cannot profit by it, the poor become the heirs of the god. The chief virtue of the act then lies in the self-abnegation of the donor, and its efficacy is measured by the " sacrifice " which it costs him.

Many instances may be quoted of sacrificed food being left for the poor or being distributed among them,[3] whilst in other cases almsgiving is itself regarded as a form of sacrifice, or takes the place of it.[4] When the destruction of the temple with its altar filled the Jews with alarm as they thought of their un-atoned sins, Johanan ben Zakkai comforted them saying : " You have another means of atonement as powerful as the altar, and that is the work of charity, for it is said, ' I desired mercy, and not sacrifice.' " [5] Several other passages show how closely the Jews associated almsgiving with sacrifice. " He that giveth alms sacrificeth praise." [6] " As sin-offering makes atonement for Israel, so alms for the Gentiles." [7] " Almsdeeds are more meritorious than all sacrifices." [8] An orphan is called an " altar to God." [9] Alms were systematically collected in the synagogues, and officers were appointed to make the collec-tion.[10] So also among the early Christians the collection of

[1] Cf. T. K. Cheyne, ' Blessings and Curses,' in Cheyne and Black, op. cit. i. 592 ; I. Goldziher, Abhandlungen zur arabischen Philologie, i (Leiden, 1896), i. 29 sqq.

[2] Proverbs xxii. 23.

[3] Westermarck, op. cit. i. 565 sq.   [4] Ibid. i. 566 sq.

[5] K. Kohler, in Jewish Encyclopedia, i (New York and London, 1901), p. 467 ; Hosea vi. 6.

[6] Ecclesiasticus xxxv. 2.

[7] Quoted by J. Levy, Neuhebräisches Wörterbuch über die Talmudim, iv (Leipzig, 1889), p. 173.

[8] Ibid. iv. 173.

[9] Constitutiones Apostolicæ, iv. 3.

[10] Addis, loc. cit. p. 119.

alms for the relief of the poor was an act of the Church life itself. Almsgiving took place in public worship, nay formed itself a part of worship. Gifts of natural produce, the so-called oblations, were connected with the celebration of the Lord's Supper. They were offered to God as the first-fruits of the creatures (*primitiæ creaturarum*), and a prayer was said : " O Lord, accept also the offerings of those who to-day bring an offering, as Thou didst accept the offerings of righteous Abel, the offering of our father Abraham, the incense of Zachariah, the alms of Cornelius, and the two mites of the widow." These oblations were not only used for the Lord's Supper, but also formed the chief means for the relief of the poor. They were regarded as sacrifice in the most special sense ; and as no unclean gift might be laid upon the Lord's altar, profit made from sinful occupations was not accepted as an oblation, neither were the oblations of impenitent sinners.[1]

The author of the Epistle to the Hebrews speaks of almsgiving as a sacrifice of thanksgiving which continues after the Jewish altar has been done away with.[2] Like sacrifice, almsgiving was connected with prayer, as a means of making the prayer efficacious and furnishing it with wings ; the angel said to Cornelius : " Thy prayers and thine alms are come up for a memorial before God." [3] When the Christians were reproached for having no sacrifice, Justin wrote : " We have been taught that the only honour that is worthy of Him is not to consume by fire what He has brought into being for our sustenance, but to use it for ourselves and those who need." [4] So also Irenæus observes that sacrifices are not abolished in the New Testament, though their form is indeed altered, because they are no longer offered by slaves, but by freemen, of which just the oblations are the proof.[5] And God has enjoined on Christians this sacrifice of oblations, not because He needs them, but " in order that themselves might be neither unfruitful nor ungrateful.[6] Augustine says : " The sacrifice of the Christians is the alms bestowed upon the poor." [7]

✕ By pointing out the magical and ritualistic elements in the formation of the religious duty of almsgiving I have, of course,

[1] G. Uhlhorn, *Die christliche Liebesthätigkeit*, i (Stuttgart, 1882), p. 135 *sqq.* ; A. Harnack, *History of Dogma*, i (London, 1894), p. 205.

[2] *Hebrews* xiii. 14 *sqq.*

[3] *Acts* x. 4 ; Cyprian, *De opere et eleemosynis*, 4 ; Chrysostom, *Homilia VII, de Pœnitentia* (Migne, *Patrologiæ cursus*, Ser. Gr., xlix sq. 332).

[4] Justin, *Apologia I. pro Christianis*, 13.

[5] Irenæus, *Adversus hæreses*, iv. 18. 82.   [6] *Ibid.* iv. 17. 5.

[7] Augustine, *Sermo XLII*. 1 (Migne, *op. cit.* xxxviii. 252).

by no means wanted to undermine its altruistic foundation, but only to explain why it has attained the same supreme importance as is otherwise attached only to devotional exercises. And this is certainly a problem by itself, for which the belief in a benevolent God interested in the worldly morality of his believers affords no adequate solution.

The altruism of the ethics of Jesus is also apparent in his insistence on those of the ten commandments which forbid men to do harm to their neighbours. Somewhat different was his attitude towards the commandment, " Honour thy father and thy mother : that thy days may be long upon the land which the Lord thy God giveth thee." It is unlike the others through its appeal to the worldly interests of those who follow it. Among the Hebrews, as among many other peoples,[1] the connection between filial submissiveness and religious beliefs was in a large measure due to the extreme significance attributed to parental blessings and curses. They thought that parents, and especially a father, could thereby determine the fate of their children ; [2] and we have every reason to assume that the reward which in the fifth commandment is held out to respectful children was originally the result of parental blessings. We meet with this idea in Ecclesiasticus, where it is said : " Honour thy father and mother in word and deed, that a blessing may come upon thee from them. For the blessing of the father establisheth the houses of children ; but the curse of the mother rooteth out foundations." [3] But a long life on earth was a poor reward compared with the eternal life in heaven. Jesus taught that every one that had forsaken father or mother for his name's sake would inherit everlasting life.[4] His church was a militant church. He had come not to send peace, but a sword, " to set a man at variance against his father, and the daughter against her mother." [5] Being chiefly addressed to the young, the new teaching naturally caused much disorder in families. Fathers disinherited their converted sons,[6] and children thought that they owed no duty to their parents when such a duty was opposed to the interests of their souls. According to Gregory the Great, we ought to ignore our parents, hating them, and flying from them when they are an obstacle to us in

---

[1] Westermarck, *op. cit.* i. 621 *sqq.*
[2] *Genesis* ix. 25 *sqq.*, xxvii. 4, 19, 23, 25, 27 *sqq.*, xlviii. 9, 14 *sqq.*, xlix. 4, 7 *sqq.* ; *Judges* xvii. 2.
[3] *Ecclesiasticus* iii. 8 *sq.* Cf. *ibid.* iii. 16.
[4] *Matthew* xix. 29 ; *Mark* x. 29 *sq.* ; *Luke* xviii. 29 *sq.*
[5] *Matthew* x. 34 *sq.* ; *Luke* xii. 51–3.
[6] Tertullian, *Apologeticus,* 3.

the way of the Lord; [1] and this became the accepted theory of the Church.[2] But it was not only in similar cases of conflict that Jesus spoke disparagingly of family ties that previously had been regarded with religious veneration. In all circumstances the relationship between child and parent was put in the shade by the relationship between man and God : " Call no man your father upon the earth : for one is your Father, which is in heaven." [3] And what would an orthodox Jew have thought if he heard the words : " If any man come to me, and hate not his father and mother, . . . he cannot be my disciple." [4] In his own conduct he did not always follow the law. When he, at the age of twelve, went to Jerusalem with his parents at the feast of the Passover, he tarried behind without their knowledge, and was found by them in the temple only after three days. The mother reproved him saying : " Son, why hast thou thus dealt with us ? behold, thy father and I have sought thee sorrowing " ; but afterwards he " was subject unto them." [5] Yet on one occasion his brusque treatment of his mother and brothers surprised the people around him : " There came then his brethren and his mother, and, standing without, sent unto him, calling him. And the multitude sat about him, and they said unto him, Behold, thy mother and thy brethren without seek for ·thee. And he answered them, saying, Who is my mother, or my brethren ? And he looked round about them which sat about him, and said, Behold my mother and my brethren ! For whosoever shall do the will of God, the same is my brother, and my sister, and mother." [6] According to John, the mother of Jesus was at a marriage in Cana, to which also he and his disciples were called. " When they wanted wine, the mother of Jesus saith unto him, They have no wine. Jesus saith unto her, Woman, what have I to do with thee ? mine hour is not yet come." Afterwards, however, he turned water into wine.[7] Yet in spite of utterances which must have jarred upon Jewish ears, the fifth commandment was left formally intact. It was mentioned by Jesus together with the other commandments which he enumerated in his answer to the man who asked him what he should do that he might inherit eternal life.[8]

---

[1] Gregory the Great, *Homiliæ in Evangelia*, xxxvii. 2 (Migne, *Patrologiæ cursus*, lxxvi. 1275).

[2] Thomas Aquinas, *Summa theologica*, ii.–ii. 101. 4.

[3] *Matthew* xxiii. 9.   [4] *Luke* xiv. 26.   [5] *Ibid.* ii. 42–8, 51.

[6] *Mark* iii. 31–5. See also *Matthew* xii. 46–50.

[7] *John* ii. 1–4, 6, 9.

[8] *Matthew* xix. 19 ; *Mark* x. 19 ; *Luke* xviii. 20. See also *Matthew* xv. 4 ; *Mark* vii. 10.

In an important point Jesus opposed the Jewish marriage law. In his teaching concerning divorce he stood up for the interests of the wife. The right of the husband to divorce his wife at his pleasure was the central thought in the system of Jewish divorce law, although the rabbis gradually tempered its severity by certain restrictive measures. Two restrictions are already found in the Deuteronomic code : the husband shall not put his wife away all his days if he has falsely accused her of ante-nuptial incontinence,[1] or if he has ravished her before marriage ;[2] but his loss of the right to divorce her in these cases was really a penalty inflicted upon him on account of his own offensive behaviour. To these restrictions the Mishna added a few others ;[3] but in the same period the very theory of the law was challenged by the school of Shammai, who held that according to Deuteronomy the husband cannot divorce his wife unless he has found her guilty of sexual immorality. The ancient doctrine was strongly supported by the school of Hillel, who went so far as to say that a man can divorce his wife even for the most trivial reason, for instance, for spoiling his food or if he sees another woman who pleases him better. Both schools based their opinions on the same passage in the Deuteronomic text : " When a man hath taken a wife, and married her, and it come to pass that she find no favour in his eyes, because he hath found some uncleanness in her : then let him write her a bill of divorcement, and give it in her hand, and send her out of his house." [4] But the school of Shammai maintained that the expression " some uncleanness " (lit. " the nakedness of a thing ") signified sexual immorality ; whereas the school of Hillel interpreted it to mean anything offensive to the husband and, besides, pressed the clause " if she find no favour in his eyes." [5] In legal respects the opinion of Hillel prevailed, although divorce without good cause is said to have been morally disapproved of by the rabbis in general.[6]

In the sayings of Jesus there are various passages bearing upon the question. A man who puts away his wife and marries

[1] *Deuteronomy* xxii. 13 *sqq.*
[2] *Ibid.* xxii. 28 *sq.*
[3] D. W. Amram, *The Jewish Law of Divorce according to Bible and Talmud* (London, 1897), p. 45 *sq.*
[4] *Deuteronomy* xxiv. 1.
[5] Amram, *op. cit.* p. 32 *sqq.* ; M. Mielziner, *The Jewish Law of Marriage and Divorce in Ancient and Modern Times* (Cincinnati, 1884), p. 118 *sq.* ; J. Bergel, *Die Eheverhältnisse der alten Juden* (Leipzig, 1881), p. 29 ; S. R. Driver, *A Critical and Exegetical Commentary on Deuteronomy* (Edinburgh, 1895), p. 270.
[6] Amram, *op. cit.* pp. 24, 52 *sq.*

another commits adultery,[1] he who marries a divorced wife is guilty of the same crime,[2] and so is a woman who puts away her husband and is married to another man.[3] A man shall cleave to his wife, " they twain shall be one flesh " ; and " what God hath joined together, let no man put asunder." [4] According to Matthew, however, Jesus, like Shammai and his school, taught that a man might put away his wife for fornication, but for no other reason. This exception is considered to be an interpolation.[5] But Dean Inge asks whether it was not Christ's method to make statements in an unguarded form, leaving it to the common sense of his hearers to make the necessary qualifications ; and he thinks it is a tenable view that the case of adultery was not in the speaker's mind at the time, and even that to a Jew the right of divorce for adultery might have been too obvious to need reaffirmation.[6] In any case, though the rule laid down by Jesus was, from the wife's point of view, a great improvement on the orthodox Jewish law, its stringency has certainly been a lasting cause of much matrimonial unhappiness in the Christian world.

[1] *Matthew* v. 32, xix. 9 ; *Mark* x. 11 ; *Luke* xvi. 18.
[2] *Matthew* v. 32, xix. 9 ; *Luke* xvi. 18.
[3] *Mark* x. 12.
[4] *Matthew* xix. 5 *sq.* ; *Mark* x. 7–9.
[5] Th. Keim, *The History of Jesus of Nazara,* v (London, 1881), p. 32 *sq.* ; N. Söderblom, *Jesu bärgspredikan* (Stockholm, 1899), p. 14 *sq.* ; K. Lake, *The Earlier Epistles of St. Paul* (London, 1911), p. 142 ; F. G. Peabody, *Jesus Christ and the Social Question* (New York, 1915), p. 152 *sqq.*
[6] Inge, *op. cit.* p. 370.

CHAPTER V

THE ETHICS OF JESUS (*concluded*)

THE ethical teaching of Jesus discussed in the two last chapters was found to be an expression of intense moral emotions in which both the retributive and the altruistic elements come out very prominently. Specific religious and eschatological beliefs were blended with the ideas springing from those emotions. Our duties to neighbours were founded upon our submission to the will of God,[1] and their sanctions were rewards or penalties for obedience or disobedience to his commandments.[†] But those beliefs have not essentially altered the contents of the commandments, as is testified by the innumerable parallels between the teaching of Jesus and that of other moralists. We even find that certain doctrines which had crept into the moral system of the Jews from their religion, but were alien to the emotional origin of morals, were opposed by him. This is particularly apparent in his attitude towards the sabbath.

It has been alleged that the abundant regulations of the rabbis had " tended to obscure in the general mind the original character and intention of the sabbath law." [2] These are evidently supposed to be explained by the words in the decalogue : " Remember the sabbath day, to keep it holy. Six days shalt thou labour, and do all thy work : But the seventh day is the sabbath of the Lord thy God : in it thou shalt not do any work. . . . For in six days the Lord made heaven and earth, the sea, and all that in them is, and rested the seventh day : wherefore the Lord blessed the sabbath day, and hallowed it." [3] It is evident, however, that the institution of the sabbath was not due to any idea of giving a weekly day of rest to men and animals, but to the belief that it was inauspicious or dangerous to work on the seventh day ; and there seems to be no doubt that the reason for this belief was the mystic connection which in the opinion of the ancient Hebrews existed between human activity and the changes of the moon. I have pointed out in another work that such a superstition is found among

---

[1] *Cf. Matthew* vii. 21, xii. 50 ; *Mark* iii. 35 ; *Luke* xi. 28.
[2] H. H. Henson, *Christian Morality* (Oxford, 1936), p. 106.
[3] *Exodus* xx. 8–11.

many peoples in different parts of the world.[1] It has been sufficiently demonstrated that the sabbath originally depended upon the new moon, and this carries with it the assumption that the Hebrews must at one time have observed a sabbath at intervals of seven days corresponding to the moon's phases.[2] In the Old Testament the new moon and the sabbath are repeatedly mentioned side by side ; [3] thus the oppressors of the poor are represented as saying : " When will the new moon be gone, that we may sell corn ? and the sabbath, that we may set forth wheat ? " [4] Among modern Jews, at the feast of the new moon, which is held every month on the first or on the first and second days of the month, the women are obliged to suspend all servile work, though the men are not required to interrupt their secular employment.[5]

Wellhausen suggested that the rest on the sabbath was originally the consequence of that day being the festal and sacrificial day of the week, and only gradually became its essential attribute on account of the regularity with which it every eighth day interrupted the round of everyday work. He argues that the sabbath as a day of rest cannot be very primitive, because such a day " presupposes agriculture and a tolerably hard-pressed working day-life." [6] But this argument appears quite untenable when we consider how frequently changes of the moon are believed to exercise an unfavourable influence upon work of any kind. That the superstitious fear of doing work on the seventh day developed into a religious prohibition, is only another instance of the tendency of magic forces to be transformed into divine volitions. Like the ancient Hebrews, the Assyrians and Babylonians looked upon the seventh day as an " evil day " ; and though they do not seem generally to have abstained from work on that day, there were royal taboos connected with it. The king was not to show himself in his chariot, not to hold court, not to bring sacrifices, not to change his clothes, not to eat a good dinner, nor even to curse his enemies.[7]

[1] E. Westermarck, *The Origin and Development of the Moral Ideas*, ii (London, 1917), p. 284 *sqq.*

[2] J. Wellhausen, *Prolegomena to the History of Israel* (London, 1885), p. 112 *sqq.* ; M. Jastrow, ' The Original Character of the Hebrew Sabbath,' in *The American Journal of Theology*, ii (Chicago, 1898), pp. 314, 327 ; H. Webster, *Rest Days* (New York, 1916), ch. viii.

[3] *2 Kings* iv. 23 ; *Isaiah* i. 13 ; *Hosea* ii. 11.   [4] *Amos* viii. 5.

[5] J. Allen, *Modern Judaism* (London, 1830), p. 390 *sq.*

[6] Wellhausen, *op. cit.* p. 114.

[7] E. Schrader, *Die Keilinschriften und das Alte Testament*, edited by H. Zimmern and H. Winckler (Berlin, 1903), p. 592 *sq.* ; H. Hirschfeld, ' Remarks on the Etymology of Sabbāth,' in *Journal of the Royal Asiatic Society*, 1896 (London), p. 358 ; Jastrow, *loc. cit.* pp. 320, 328.

Jesus exasperated the Pharisees by his treatment of the sabbath. He healed sick people on that day,[1] and defended it himself by saying that " it is lawful to do well on the sabbath days." [2] When the Pharisees blamed him for allowing his disciples to pluck the ears of corn as they went through corn-fields on the sabbath, he replied : " The sabbath was made for man, and not man for the sabbath. Therefore the Son of man is Lord also of the sabbath." [3] In defence of the Pharisees it has been pointed out that they authorised breaches of the sabbatic law in certain contingencies ; that they " permitted, nay required, the performance of all necessary works of mercy, but refused to extend the licence too indiscriminately, and never reconciled themselves to the theory that in general the perform-ance of a duty justified the infringement of a prohibition." [4] On such grounds even the accuracy of the reports concerning the indignant Pharisees has been called in question. Drews argues that since healing by merely stretching out one's hand over the patient, as Jesus is said to have done on the sabbath, was not forbidden by the rabbis, the Pharisees could not have been " filled with madness " on such an occasion.[5] But all Pharisees can scarcely be supposed to have been unanimous as to the emergencies in which the sabbath law might be dis-regarded ; and Jesus certainly traversed the Pharisaic position when he treated on the sabbath long-standing diseases, lingering maladies, and, generally, cases where the treatment could be postponed without fear of dangerous consequences.[6] We know that the early Christians considered the sabbath to have been abolished by Christ. Jewish converts no doubt continued to observe it, but this met with disapproval. In one of the epistles of Ignatius we find the exhortation not to " sabbatise," which was expanded by the subsequent paraphraser of these com-positions into a warning against keeping the sabbath, after the manner of the Jews, " as if delighting in idleness." [7] And in the fourth century a Council of the Church enacted that " the

---

[1] *Matthew* xii. 13, 15 ; *Mark* iii. 5 ; *Luke* vi. 10, xiii. 13, xiv. 4.

[2] *Matthew* xii. 12. See also *Luke* xiv. 3.

[3] *Mark* ii. 23, 24, 27 *sq.* See also *Matthew* xii. 1, 2, 8 ; *Luke* vi. 1, 2, 5.

[4] I. Abrahams, *Studies in Pharisaism and the Gospels*, 1st series (Cambridge, 1917), p. 135.

[5] A. Drews, *The Witnesses to the Historicity of Jesus* (London, 1912), p. 236.

[6] Abrahams, *op. cit.* p. 135.

[7] Ignatius, *Epistola ad Magnesios*, 9 ; E. V. Neale, *Feasts and Fasts* (London, 1845), p. 89.

Christians ought not to judaise and rest on the sabbath, but
ought to work on that day." [1]

Nor was the Christian Sunday originally in any way a
substitute for the Jewish sabbath. It was from early times a
recognised custom among the Christians to celebrate the first
day of the week in memory of Christ's resurrection by holding
a form of religious service; but there was no sabbatic regard
for it, and it was chiefly looked upon as a day of rejoicing.[2]
Tertullian is the first writer who speaks of abstinence from
secular care and labour on Sunday as a duty incumbent upon
Christians, lest they should " give place to the devil." [3] But
it is extremely doubtful whether the earliest Sunday law really
had a Christian origin. In 321 the Emperor Constantine issued
an edict to the effect that all judges and all city people and
tradesmen should rest on " the venerable Day of the Sun,"
whereas those living in the country should have full liberty
to attend to the culture of their fields, " since it frequently
happens that no other day is so fit for the sowing of grain or the
planting of vines." [4] In this rescript nothing is said of any
relation to Christianity, nor do we know that it in any way was
due to Christian influence.[5] It seems that Constantine, in his
capacity of Pontifex Maximus, only added the day of the sun—
whose worship was the characteristic of the new paganism—to
those inauspicious days, *religiosi dies*, which the Romans of old
regarded as unsuitable for worldly business and especially for
judicious proceedings.[6]

But although the obligatory Sunday rest in no case was a
continuance of the Jewish sabbath, it was gradually confounded
with it, owing to the recognition of the decalogue, with its

[1] *Concilium Laodicenum*, can. 29 (Labbe-Mansi, *Sacrorum Conciliorum collectio*, ii. 580).
[2] Justin Martyr, *Apologia I. pro Christia...,* *~idache*, 14; Barnabas, *Epistola catholica*, 15; Ph. Schaff, *History of the Christian Church: Anti-Nicene Christianity* (Edinburgh, 1884), p. 202 *sqq.*; J. A. Hessey, *Sunday* (London, 1889), p. 29 *sqq.*
[3] Tertullian, *De oratione*, 23.
[4] *Codex Justinianus*, iii. 12. 2 (3).
[5] *Cf.* A. H. Lewis, *A Critical History of Sunday Legislation* (New York, 1888), p. 18 *sqq.*; H. H. Milman, *History of Latin Christianity*, ii (London, 1867), p. 291 *sq.*
[6] Gellius, *Noctes Atticæ*, iv. 9. 5, vi. 9. 10; Varro, *De lingua Latina*, vi. 30; Neale, *op. cit.* pp. 5, 6, 86, 87, 206; W. W. Fowler, *The Roman Festivals of the Period of the Republic* (London, 1899), p. 8 *sq.* The Greeks, also, had " unblest and inauspicious " days, when no court or assembly was to be held, and work was to be abstained from (Plato, *Leges*, vii. 800; R. Karsten, *Studies in Primitive Greek Religion* [*Öfversigt af Finska Vetenskaps-Societetens Förhandlingar*, xlix, Helsingfors, 1906-1907, no. 1], p. 90).

injunction of a weekly day of rest, as the code of divine morality. From the sixth century upwards vexatious restrictions were made by civil rulers, councils, and ecclesiastical writers,[1] until in Puritanism the Christian Sunday became a perfect image of the Pharisaic sabbath, or even excelled it in the rigour with which abstinence from every kind of worldly activity was insisted upon. The theory that the keeping holy of one day out of seven is the essence of the fourth commandment reconciled people to the fact that the Jewish sabbath was the seventh day and Sunday the first. In England, in the seventeenth century, persons were punished for carrying coal on Sunday, for hanging out clothes to dry, for travelling on horseback, for rural strolls and walking about.[2] And there were Scotch clergymen who taught their congregations that on that day it was sinful even to save a vessel in distress.[3] Until quite recently the Scottish Sunday was observed with amazing rigour. Not only were ordinary recreations disallowed, but a ban was put even upon books and music, except such as were recognised as religious in the narrow sense. Indeed, no recreation remained but whisky-drinking; and a writer in Hastings' *Encyclopædia of Religion* attributes a great part of the drunkenness which is still common in Scotland to this strange sabbatarianism.

Jesus inaugurated his ministry by a fast of forty days;[4] the Jews associated fasting with divine revelations.[5] It also held a prominent position in Jewish ritual and in the Christian Church as well; but it is seldom mentioned by Jesus, though allusions to it have been interpolated in several places in later manuscripts of the New Testament.[6] To some extent he took it for granted. He said to his disciples : " When ye fast, be not, as the hypocrites, of a sad countenance : for they disfigure their faces, that they may appear unto men to fast. . . . But thou, when thou fastest, anoint thine head, and wash thy face ; That thou appear not unto men to fast, but unto thy Father which is in secret." [7] He speaks with scorn of the

[1] Hessey, *op. cit.* p. 87 *sqq.*

[2] G. Roberts, *The Social History of the People of the Southern Counties of England in Past Centuries* (London, 1856), p. 244 *sqq.*

[3] H. T. Buckle, *History of Civilization in England*, iii (London, 1894), p. 276.

[4] *Matthew* iv. 2 ; *Luke* iv. 2.

[5] *Exodus* xxxiv. 28 ; *Deuteronomy* ix. 9 ; *Daniel* ix. 3.

[6] *Matthew* xvii. 21 ; *Mark* ix. 29 ; *Acts* x. 30 ; *1 Corinthians* vii. 5. See W. R. Inge, *Christian Ethics and Modern Problems* (London, 1932), p. 98. The word "fasting" has been omitted in the Revised Edition.

[7] *Matthew* vi. 16–18.

Pharisee who " stood and prayed thus with himself, God, I thank thee, that I am not as other men are, extortioners, unjust, adulterers. . . . I fast twice in the week, I give tithes of all that I possess." [1] It was objected to Jesus that while the disciples of John and the Pharisees used to fast, his disciples did not fast. Jesus replied : " Can the children of the bridechamber fast, while the bridegroom is with them ? as long as they have the bridegroom with them, they cannot fast. But the days will come, when the bridegroom shall be taken away from them, and then shall they fast in those days." [2] Fasting after a death is a widespread practice,[3] and is also mentioned in the Old Testament. David and his people fasted for Saul and Jonathan until even on the day when the news of their death arrived.[4]

Jesus was not an ascetic like John the Baptist, who lived in the wilderness clothed with camel's hair and neither ate bread nor drank wine, but subsisted on locusts and wild honey.[5] He " came eating and drinking " and was even accused of being " a gluttonous man and a winebibber " who ate and drank with publicans and sinners.[6] He accepted invitations of Pharisees to dine in their houses, and according to John he was present at a wedding where he turned water into wine.[7] But he led a very simple wandering life, indifferent to all comfort. When a certain man came and said that he wished to follow him wherever he went, Jesus replied : " The foxes have holes, and the birds of the air have nests ; but the Son of man hath not where to lay his head." [8] And when he sent his disciples to preach the kingdom of God and to heal the sick, he said to them : " Provide neither gold, nor silver, nor brass in your purses, Nor scrip for your journey, neither two coats, neither shoes, nor yet staves " ; but admonished them to rely upon private hospitality.[9] On another occasion he said to his disciples : " Take no thought for your life, what ye shall eat, or what ye shall drink ; nor yet for your body, what ye shall put on. . . . For your heavenly Father knoweth that ye have need of all these things." [10]

[1] *Luke* xviii. 11 *sq.*
[2] *Mark* ii. 18–20. See also *Matthew* ix. 14 *sq.* ; *Luke* v. 33–5.
[3] Westermarck, *op. cit.* ii. 298 *sqq.*
[4] *2 Samuel* i. 12. *Cf. ibid.* iii. 35.
[5] *Matthew* iii. 1, 4 ; *Mark* i. 4, 6 ; *Luke* iii. 2, vii. 33.
[6] *Matthew* ix. 10 *sq.*, xi. 19 ; *Mark* ii. 15 *sq.* ; *Luke* v. 29 *sq.*, vii. 34.
[7] *John* ii. 1, 6–9.
[8] *Matthew* viii. 19 *sq.* ; *Luke* ix. 57 *sq.*
[9] *Matthew* x. 5, 9–11 ; *Mark* vi. 7–10 ; *Luke* ix. 2–4.
[10] *Matthew* vi. 25, 32 ; *Luke* xii. 22, 30.

In the opinion of Jesus wealth is of no value to a man but a peril : " Whosoever he be of you that forsaketh not all that he hath, he cannot be my disciple." [1] " Blessed be ye poor : for yours is the kingdom of God. Blessed are ye that hunger now : for ye shall be filled. . . . But woe unto you that are rich ! for ye have received your consolation. Woe unto you that are full ! for ye shall hunger." [2] " How hardly shall they that have riches enter into the kingdom of God ! . . . It is easier for a camel to go through the eye of a needle, than for a rich man to enter into the kingdom of God." [3] The beggar Lazarus died, " and was carried by the angels into Abraham's bosom : the rich man also died, and was buried. And in hell he lift up his eyes, being in torments, and seeth Abraham afar off, and Lazarus in his bosom. And he cried and said, Father Abraham, have mercy on me, and send Lazarus, that he may dip the tip of his finger in water, and cool my tongue ; for I am tormented in this flame. But Abraham said, Son, remember that thou in thy lifetime receivedst thy good things, and likewise Lazarus evil things : but now he is comforted, and thou art tormented." [4]

Jesus speaks of the folly of hoarding in the parable of the rich man who built greater barns : " God said unto him, Thou fool, this night thy soul shall be required of thee : then whose shall those things be, which thou hast provided ? " [5] Moreover, the end of the world was at hand : " Ye know neither the day nor the hour wherein the Son of man cometh." [6] The attitude of Jesus towards wealth was also connected with the idea that we ought to give in charity any superfluity of what we possess.[7] But the principal reason why Jesus was so severe upon the rich was the nothingness of all earthly possessions and their imperilling the soul. " He that layeth up treasure for himself . . . is not rich toward God." [8] " Lay not up for yourselves treasures upon earth, where moth and rust doth corrupt, and where thieves break through and steal : But lay up for yourselves treasures in heaven. . . . For where your treasure is, there will your heart be also. . . . No man can serve two masters : for either he will hate the one, and love the other ; or else he will hold to the one, and despise the

---

[1] *Luke* xiv. 33.
[2] *Ibid.* vi. 20, 21, 24 *sq.* Matthew (v. 3, 6) writes " the poor in spirit " and " they which do hunger and thirst after righteousness."
[3] *Mark* x. 23, 25 ; *Matthew* xix. 23 *sq.* ; *Luke* xviii. 24 *sq.*
[4] *Luke* xvi. 22–5.
[5] *Ibid.* xii. 20.   [6] *Matthew* xxv. 13.
[7] *Luke* xii. 33. See also *supra*, p. 79.
[8] *Luke* xii. 21.

other. Ye cannot serve God and mammon." [1] " What shall it profit a man, if he shall gain the whole world, and lose his own soul ? " [2]

This disdain for temporal anxieties and worldly goods has taken us to a new department in the ethics of Jesus, where the determining factor is no longer the natural constitution of the moral consciousness, but the influence of specific religious ideas. Such influence is also apparent in the importance which he attached to certain ritual practices, contrary to his disregard of certain others, such as the keeping of the sabbath, fasting, and sacrifice : " I will have mercy, and not sacrifice." [3] Prayer holds a very prominent position in his teaching : " Men ought always to pray, and not to faint." [4] " All things, whatsoever ye shall ask in prayer, believing, ye shall receive." [5] " Ask, and it shall be given you ; seek, and ye shall find ; knock, and it shall be opened unto you : For every one that asketh receiveth ; and he that seeketh findeth ; and to him that knocketh it shall be opened." [6] " But when ye pray, use not vain repetitions, as the heathen do : for they think that they shall be heard for their much speaking. Be not ye therefore like unto them : for your Father knoweth what things ye have need of, before ye ask him. After this manner therefore pray ye : Our Father which art in heaven, Hallowed be thy name " ; and so forth. [7] Isaiah also condemned those who did honour to the Lord with their lips, but had removed their heart far from him. [8]

Prayer is an act of humility, and the spirit of humility pervades the teaching of Jesus throughout : " Thy will be done in earth, as it is in heaven. . . . For thine is the kingdom, and the power, and the glory, for ever." [9] " Blessed are the meek : for they shall inherit the earth." [10] " Whosoever shall exalt himself shall be abased ; and he that shall humble himself shall be exalted." [11] It has been said that there is no more distinguishing mark of Christian ethics than humility. [12] But it was also insisted upon by the Prophets. Micah said : " What

---

[1] *Matthew* vi. 19–21, 24. See also *Luke* xvi. 13.
[2] *Mark* viii. 36. See also *Matthew* xvi. 26 ; *Luke* ix. 25.
[3] *Matthew* ix. 13, xii. 7.
[4] *Luke* xviii. 1. See also *ibid.* xxi. 36.
[5] *Matthew* xxi. 22.
[6] *Ibid.* vii. 7 *sq.* ; *Luke* xi. 9 *sq.*
[7] *Matthew* vi. 7–13.   [8] *Isaiah* xxix. 13 *sq.*
[9] *Matthew* vi. 10, 13 ; *Luke* xi. 2.   [10] *Matthew* v. 5.
[11] *Ibid.* xxiii. 12 ; *Luke* xiv. 11.
[12] J. Stalker, *The Ethic of Jesus* (London, 1909), p. 210.

doth the Lord require of thee, but to do justly, and to love mercy, and to walk humbly with thy God." [1]

Prayer and humility presuppose faith, which was stressed by the Prophets,[2] and assumed pre-eminence in the teaching of Jesus. "The apostles said unto the Lord, Increase our faith"; and he answered: "If ye had faith as a grain of mustard seed, ye might say unto this sycamine tree, Be thou plucked up by the root, and be thou planted in the sea; and it should obey you." [3] When Jesus caused a fig-tree which had leaves but no fruit suddenly to wither away, the disciples who saw it marvelled and said: "How soon is the fig-tree withered away." Jesus answered and said to them: "Verily I say unto you, If ye have faith, and doubt not, ye shall not only do this which is done to the fig-tree, but also if ye shall say unto this mountain, Be thou removed, and be thou cast into the sea; it shall be done. . . . And nothing shall be impossible unto you." [4]

Jesus particularly often speaks of faith in connection with his miracles. When he had entered into Capernaum, a centurion came and said to him: "Lord, my servant lieth at home sick of the palsy, grievously tormented." Jesus answered that he would come and heal him. The centurion said: "I am not worthy that thou shouldest come under my roof: but speak the word only, and my servant shall be healed. For I am a man under authority, having soldiers under me: and I say to this man, Go, and he goeth; and to another, Come, and he cometh; and to my servant, Do this, and he doeth it." When Jesus heard this, he marvelled and said to the people who followed him: "Verily I say unto you, I have not found so great faith, no, not in Israel." And he said to the centurion: "Go thy way; and as thou has believed, so be it done unto thee." And the servant was healed at once.[5]

A woman who was diseased with an issue of blood twelve years came behind Jesus and touched the hem of his garment, saying within herself: "If I may but touch his garment, I shall be whole." Jesus turned round, and when he saw her he said: "Daughter, be of good comfort; thy faith hath made

---

[1] *Micah* vi. 8.
[2] *Isaiah* vii. 9: "If ye will not believe, surely ye shall not be established"; *ibid.* xxviii. 16: "He that believeth shall not make haste"; *ibid.* xxx. 15: "Thus saith the Lord God, the Holy One of Israel; . . . in quietness and in confidence shall be your strength"; *Habakkuk* ii. 4: "The just shall live by his faith."
[3] *Luke* xvii. 5 *sq.*
[4] *Matthew* xxi. 19–22, xvii. 20. See also *Mark* xi. 22 *sq.*
[5] *Matthew* viii. 5–10, 13. See also *Luke* vii. 1–10.

thee whole." And the woman was made whole from that hour.[1]

Two blind men asked Jesus to have mercy on them. He asked them : " Believe ye that I am able to do this ? " They answered : " Yea, Lord." Then he touched their eyes, saying : " According to your faith be it unto you." And their eyes were opened.[2]

The woman of Canaan, mentioned above, whose daughter was vexed with a devil and who implored Jesus to heal her, but was rebuffed by him with the words, " It is not meet to take the children's bread and to cast it to dogs," replied : " Truth, Lord : yet the dogs eat of the crumbs which fall from their masters' table." Then Jesus said to her : " O woman, great is thy faith : be it unto thee even as thou wilt." And her daughter was made whole from that very hour.[3]

Once when Jesus was in a house preaching and there were many people gathered, four men came carrying a man sick of the palsy, but could not make their way through the crowd. They then uncovered the roof where he was, and when they had broken it up they let down the bed in which the sick man lay. " When Jesus saw their faith, he said unto the sick of the palsy, Son, thy sins be forgiven thee." Some of the scribes sitting there reasoned in their hearts : " Why doth this man thus speak blasphemies ? who can forgive sins but God only ? " Then Jesus, who read their thoughts, said : " That ye may know that the Son of man hath power on earth to forgive sins, (he saith to the sick of the palsy), I say unto thee, Arise, and take up thy bed, and go thy way into thine house." And immediately he arose, took up the bed, and went forth before them all.[4]

A man brought to Jesus his son who had been vexed with a dumb spirit since he was a child. He had spoken to the disciples that they should cast him out, but they could not, and now he implored Jesus, saying : " If thou canst do any thing, have compassion on us, and help us." Jesus answered : " If thou canst believe, all things are possible to him that believeth." Straightway the father of the child cried out, and said with tears : " Lord, I believe ; help thou mine unbelief." And Jesus cast the devil out. When the disciples asked him why they could not do it, Jesus answered, according to Mark :

[1] *Matthew* ix. 20-2. See also *Mark* v. 25-34 ; *Luke* viii. 43-8.
[2] *Matthew* ix. 27-30.
[3] *Supra*, p. 74 *sq.* ; *Matthew* xv. 22-8. See also *Mark* vii. 25-30, where Jesus is reported to have said, not " Great is thy faith," but, " For this saying go thy way."
[4] *Mark* ii. 1-12. See also *Matthew* ix. 2-7 ; *Luke* v. 17-25.

" This kind can come forth by nothing, but by prayer and fasting "; and according to Matthew : " Because of your unbelief. . . . Howbeit this kind goeth not out but by prayer and fasting." [1] But in these cases the word " fasting " is an interpolation.[2]

A blind man came to Jesus, who asked him : " What wilt thou that I should do unto thee ? " The blind man answered : " Lord, that I might receive my sight." Jesus said to him : " Go thy way ; thy faith hath made you whole." And immediately he received his sight.[3]

A man who was a ruler of the synagogue fell down at Jesus' feet, and besought him that he would come into his house, because he had a young daughter who was dying ; but the people thronged him. Then there came some one from his house and said to him : " Thy daughter is dead ; trouble not the Master." But when Jesus heard it he said : " Fear not : believe only, and she shall be made whole." When he came into the house he " took her by the hand, and called, saying, Maid, arise. And her spirit came again, and she arose straightway." [4]

When Jesus entered into a certain village ten lepers met him, and, standing afar off, cried out : " Jesus, Master, have mercy on us." When he saw them he said to them : " Go shew yourselves unto the priests." As they went they were cleansed. But one of them, who was a Samaritan, when he saw that he was healed, turned back and glorified God with a loud voice and fell down on his face at Jesus' feet, giving him thanks. Jesus said to him : " Were there not ten cleansed ? but where are the nine ? . . . Arise, go thy way : thy faith hath made thee whole." [5]

When Jesus was dining in a Pharisee's house, a woman who was a sinner brought an alabaster box of ointment, and, standing behind him weeping, began to wash his feet with tears, wiped them with the hair of her head, kissed his feet, and anointed them with the ointment. Now the Pharisee spoke within himself : " This man, if he were a prophet, would have known who and what manner of woman this is that toucheth him : for she is a sinner." Jesus turned to the woman, and said to the Pharisee : " Seest thou this woman ? I entered into thine house, thou gavest me no water for my feet : but she hath washed my feet with tears, and wiped them with the hairs of

---

[1] *Mark* ix. 17–29 ; *Matthew* xvii. 14–21.
[2] *Supra*, p. 93.
[3] *Mark* x. 46–52. See also *Luke* xviii. 35–43.
[4] *Luke* viii. 41, 42, 49–51, 54 *sq.* See also *Mark* v. 35, 36, 39, 41 *sq.*
[5] *Luke* xvii. 12–17, 19.

her head. Thou gavest me no kiss : but this woman since the time I came in hath not ceased to kiss my feet. My head with oil thou didst not anoint : but this woman hath anointed my feet with ointment. Wherefore I say unto thee, Her sins, which are many, are forgiven ; for she loved much : but to whom little is forgiven, the same loveth little." And he said to her : " Thy sins are forgiven. . . . Thy faith hath saved thee ; go in peace." [1]

Faith, then, is said to enable a person to work miracles, and to be a ground for the remission of sins and a cure for sickness. Faith in whom or in what ? It has been alleged that Jesus nearly always uses the word with the meaning of trust in the power and goodness of God.[2] In proof of this reference is made to the stories of the centurion whose servant was ill, of the four men who carried to Jesus the paralytic, and of the woman whose faith was shown by her answer that the dogs eat of the crumbs which fall from their masters' table. In these, and in the other cases of faith recorded in connection with his miracles, I can find nothing more than the belief that Jesus could cure sickness or forgive sins. This is particularly obvious from the question he put to the two blind men, " Believe ye that I am able to do this ? " and from their eyes being opened immediately after their answer, " Yea, Lord." On several occasions the faith was not even displayed by the person who was cured, but by the supplicant.

In any case faith, whether in God or in Jesus, is no moral quality, since the proper object of moral judgment is always the will ; and the reward for it is therefore no moral reward, but only a favour. At the same time there can be no objection to such a favour from the moral point of view ; whereas the case is quite different with the condemnation or punishment of the absence of faith. Of this little is heard in the sayings of Jesus reported in the synoptic gospels, but we nevertheless find there the germ of a doctrine which subsequently assumed enormous importance in Christian theology. He said : " Whosoever . . . shall confess me before men, him will I confess also before my Father which is in heaven. But whosoever shall deny me before men, him will I also deny before my Father which is in heaven." [3] Dean Rashdall suggests that here the representation of the evangelists may have been more or less coloured by the later belief of Christ's followers and by the teaching of Paul and the

---

[1] *Luke* vii. 36–9, 44–8, 50.

[2] W. Morgan, ' Faith (Christian),' in J. Hastings, *Encyclopædia of Religion and Ethics*, v (Edinburgh, 1912), p. 689.

[3] *Matthew* x. 32 *sq.* See also *Luke* xii. 8 *sq.*

whole early Church as to the importance of faith in Christ.[1]
Jesus is also reported to have said : " He that believeth and
is baptised shall be saved ; but he that believeth not shall be
damned." [2] Such reflection on the necessity of baptism betrays
the relatively late origin of the passage ; and it is known not
to have been an original part of Mark's gospel.[3] If Jesus had
regarded salvation as conditional on belief in his Messiahship
we might expect him to have emphasised it. This is what he
did according to John.[4] But, as said above, the fourth gospel
cannot be recognised as a reliable source of information about
the teaching of Jesus.

[1] H. Rashdall, *The Idea of Atonement in Christian Theology* (London,
1919), p. 21.
[2] *Mark* xvi. 16.
[3] J. V. Bartlet, ' Baptism (New Testament),' in Hastings, *op. cit.*
ii (1909), p. 376.
[4] *John* iii. 15, 16, 18, 36, vi. 40, 47, viii. 24, xx. 31, etc.

CHAPTER VI

THE ETHICS OF PAUL

THERE was once a great persecution against the church
at Jerusalem. A young man, whose name was Saul, then
entered into every house, and haling men and women committed them to prison. After that he went to the high priest
and desired of him letters to Damascus to the synagogues, that
if he found there any disciples of the Lord, whether they were
men or women, he might bring them bound to Jerusalem. As
he journeyed he came near Damascus ; and suddenly there
shone round about him a light from heaven. He fell to the
ground, and heard a voice saying to him : " Saul, Saul, why
persecutest thou me ? " He said : " Who art thou, Lord ? "
He heard the answer : " I am Jesus whom thou persecutest ;
it is hard for thee to kick against the pricks." He said,
astonished and trembling : " Lord, what wilt thou have me
to do ? " The answer was : " Arise, and go into the city, and
it shall be told thee what thou must do." The men who
journeyed with him stood speechless, hearing a voice but
seeing no man. When Saul rose from the ground he was blind,
and was led by them and brought into Damascus. There was
in the city a certain disciple, named Ananias, who also had a
vision in which Jesus commanded him to go and inquire for a man
called Saul, of Tarsus. "He is a chosen vessel unto me, to bear
my name before the Gentiles, and kings, and the children of
Israel." Ananias went to the house where Saul was staying,
put his hands on him, and told him that Jesus had sent him,
that Saul might receive his sight, and be filled with the Holy
Ghost. Immediately there fell from his eyes as it had been
scales. He arose and was baptised, and preached straightway
in the synagogues that Christ was the Son of God.[1]

There are in the Acts two other accounts of the vision and
conversion of Paul, represented as speeches delivered by himself.[2] In one of them, that addressed to King Agrippa, Ananias
is not mentioned at all, but Jesus is alleged to have said to
Paul : " I have appeared unto thee for this purpose, to make
thee a minister and a witness both of these things which thou

---

[1] *Acts* viii. 1, 3, ix. 1 *sqq.*   [2] *Ibid.* xxii. 6 *sqq.*, xxvi. 12 *sqq.*

hast seen, and of those things in the which I will appear unto thee ; Delivering thee from the people, and from the Gentiles, unto whom now I send thee, To open their eyes, and to turn them from darkness to light, and from the power of Satan unto God, that they may receive forgiveness of sins, and inheritance among them which are sanctified by faith that is in me." In his epistles Paul does not describe his vision, but insists that he has received the gospel by the revelation of Jesus Christ, "when it pleased God, who separated me from my mother's womb, and called me by his grace, To reveal his Son in me, that I might preach him among the heathen." [1] He also writes : " Am I not an apostle ? am I not free ? have I not seen Jesus Christ our Lord ? " [2] And after pointing out that Jesus was seen by all the apostles he adds : " And last of all he was seen of me also, as of one born out of due time." [3]

From all these accounts it is obvious that Paul's conversion was due to a vision in which he believed himself to have seen Christ risen in celestial glory ; he was evidently predisposed to visions and trances.[4] His vision of the risen Christ belonged to a type which is familiar to students of modern conversions, in which a complete division is established in the twinkling of an eye between the old life and the new. Those who have had such an experience carry away a feeling of its being a miracle. Voices are often heard, lights are seen, or visions are witnessed, and it always seems, after the surrender of the personal will, as if an extraneous higher power had flooded in and taken possession of the person, as if he were partaking directly of Christ's substance, as if the deity were present in him. Of this he has a joyous conviction, which has been called faith *par excellence*.[5] According to James, the most striking conversions of that kind have been permanent.[6] So also Starbuck has found that " the effect of conversion is to bring with it a changed attitude towards life, which is fairly constant and permanent, although the feelings fluctuate. . . . The persons who have passed through conversions, having once taken a stand for the religious life, tend to feel themselves identified with it, no matter how much their religious enthusiasm declines." [7]

[1] *Galatians* i. 11, 12, 15 *sq.*
[2] *1 Corinthians* ix. 1.   [3] *Ibid.* xv. 7 *sq.*
[4] *Acts* xvi. 9, xxii. 17 *sq.*, xxiii. 11, xxvii. 23 *sq.* ; *2 Corinthians* xii. 1 *sqq* ; *Galatians* ii. 2.
[5] W. James, *The Varieties of Religious Experience* (London, etc., 1903), ch. x *passim.*
[6] *Ibid.* pp. 257, 268.
[7] E. D. Starbuck, *The Psychology of Religion* (London, 1899), pp. 360, 357.

Of all these characteristics of conversion there is evidence in Paul's own sayings : " If any man be in Christ, he is a new creature." [1] " I am crucified with Christ : nevertheless I live ; yet not I, but Christ liveth in me : and the life which I now live in the flesh I live by the faith of the Son of God, who loved me, and gave himself for me." [2] " In him we live, and move, and have our being." [3] " If any man have not the Spirit of Christ, he is none of his. And if Christ be in you, the body is dead because of sin ; but the Spirit is life because of righteousness." [4] " We have the mind of Christ." [5] " Know ye not that ye are the temple of God, and that the Spirit of God dwelleth in you." [6] " To me to live is Christ." [7] According to Deissmann, the formula " in Christ " or " in the Lord " is found 164 times in the Pauline epistles.[8] The most conspicuous characteristic of all the elements of the conversion crisis is the ecstasy of happiness produced.[9] And Paul speaks again and again of the joy of faith, and exhorts his disciples to rejoice.[10] He says that " the fruit of the Spirit is love, joy, peace, long-suffering, gentleness, goodness, faith." [11] He speaks of " long-suffering with joyfulness " ; [12] and after recording his own torments and perils he writes : " I take pleasure in infirmities, in reproaches, in necessities, in persecutions, in distresses for Christ's sake : for when I am weak, then am I strong." [13]

Faith in Jesus Christ is the keystone of Paul's whole teaching. But this faith was not a belief in his miracles, nor even a belief in his Messiahship. In his estimation Christ was a divine being in whom " dwelleth all the fulness of the Godhead bodily," [14] " the image " of God,[15] and " the firstborn of every creature," [16] " the Son " of God [17] who " sitteth on the right hand of God." [18] And the Christ who had revealed himself

[1] *2 Corinthians* v. 17. See also *Galatians* vi. 15 ; *Colossians* iii. 10 ; *Ephesians* iv. 24.

[2] *Galatians* ii. 20.   [3] *Acts* xvii. 28.
[4] *Romans* viii. 9 *sq.*   [5] *1 Corinthians* ii. 16.
[6] *Ibid.* iii. 16.   [7] *Philippians* i. 21.

[8] G. A. Deissmann, *Paulus. Eine kultur- und religionsgeschichtliche Skizze* (Tübingen, 1925), p. 111.

[9] James, *op. cit.* p. 254 ; A. C. Underwood, *Conversion : Christian and Non-Christian* (London, 1925), p. 153 *sqq.*

[10] *Romans* xii. 12, xiv. 17, xv. 13 ; *2 Corinthians* i. 24, ii. 3, vi. 10, viii. 2 ; *Philippians,* i. 25, ii. 17 *sq.*, iii. 1, iv. 4 ; *1 Thessalonians* v. 16.

[11] *Galatians* v. 22.

[12] *Colossians* i. 11. See also *ibid.* i. 24.

[13] *2 Corinthians* xi. 23–33, xii. 10.   [14] *Colossians* ii. 9.

[15] *Ibid.* i. 15, iii. 10 ; *2 Corinthians* iv. 4.

[16] *Colossians* i. 15.

[17] *Ibid.* i. 18 ; *Galatians* ii. 20.

[18] *Colossians* iii. 1. *Cf. Ephesians* i. 20.

to Paul in his glory was the crucified and risen Christ, whom he now knew as a saviour, and whose message he felt called to preach to the world. † As Christ had risen from the grave, so also those who through their belief in it were possessed by him would rise and be justified. Jesus our Lord " was delivered for our offences, and was raised again for our justification. Therefore being justified by faith, we have peace with God through our Lord Jesus Christ. . . . Being now justified by his blood, we shall be saved from wrath through him . . . by whom we have now received the atonement." [1] " Since by man came death, by man came also the resurrection of the dead. For as in Adam all die, even so in Christ shall all be made alive." [2] " He which raised up the Lord Jesus shall raise up us also by Jesus." [3] " When Christ, who is our life, shall appear, then shall ye also appear with him in glory." [4] " Some man will say, How are the dead raised up ? and with what body do they come ? Thou fool, that which thou sowest is not quickened, except it die : And that which thou sowest, thou sowest not that body that shall be, but bare grain, it may chance of wheat, or of some other grain : But God giveth it a body as it hath pleased him, and to every seed his own body. . . . So also is the resurrection of the dead. It is sown in corruption ; it is raised in incorruption : It is sown in dishonour ; it is raised in glory : it is sown in weakness ; it is raised in power ; It is sown a natural body ; it is raised a spiritual body. . . . The trumpet shall sound, and the dead shall be raised incorruptible, and we shall be changed. For this corruptible must put on incorruption, and this mortal must put on immortality." [5]

By faith every one will be saved. The gospel of Christ " is the power of God unto salvation to every one that believeth ; to the Jew first, and also to the Greek. . . . For the same Lord over all is rich unto all that call upon him. For whosoever shall call upon the name of the Lord shall be saved." [6] God " hath made of one blood all nations of men for to dwell on all the face of the earth. . . . That they should seek the Lord, if haply they might feel after him, and find him." [7] " There is no respect of persons with God." [8] " There is neither Jew nor Greek, there is neither bond nor free, there is neither male nor female : for ye are all one in Christ Jesus " ; [9] " Christ

---

[1] *Romans* iv. 25, v. 1, 9, 11. [2] *1 Corinthians* xv. 21 *sq.*
[3] *2 Corinthians* iv. 14. [4] *Colossians* iii. 4.
[5] *1 Corinthians* xv. 35–8, 42–4, 52 *sq.*
[6] *Romans* i. 16, x. 12 *sq.*
[7] *Acts* xvii. 26 *sq.* [8] *Romans* ii. 11.
[9] *Galatians* iii. 28. See also *Colossians* iii. 11.

is all, and in all." [1]   And Paul had been commanded to " be
the minister of Jesus Christ to the Gentiles, ministering the
gospel of God." [2]

For this task he was pre-eminently suited. True, he was a
Jew of the tribe of Benjamin,[3] " a Pharisee, the son of a
Pharisee." [4] As Deissmann remarks, he " never departed from
the national and religious communion of his people ; he retained
with pride the name Hebrew, and the even more significant
names Israelite and Seed of Abraham, just as he also reckoned
himself one of the Israel of God." [5] He calls even the unconverted Jews " my brethren, my kinsmen according to the flesh " ; [6]
he could write that unto the Jews be became as a Jew that he
might gain the Jews, " to them that are under the law, as under
the law " ; [7] he constantly makes quotations from the Old
Testament. But he was a native of Tarsus in Cilicia,[8] a Græco-
Roman town, and spent most of his life before his conversion
there ; and he was a Roman citizen.[9]

At the beginning of our era Tarsus was a city of considerable
importance, which had reached a position of high standing on
account of its intellectual life and the general love of knowledge
displayed by his inhabitants. It had a university which was a
centre of Hellenistic philosophy, and even surpassed those of
Athens and Alexandria in respect of the eagerness of its students
and in filling its classroom with its own people, though it did
not surpass them in equipment or in standing and fame as a
seat of learning.[10] In Tarsus Paul came from his early boyhood
in close contact with the Græco-Roman world. He was a
man of education, who had received a Greek training. Greek
was the only language which he used in his epistles, and he read
his Old Testament first and chiefly in Greek translation. Even
though it cannot be proved that he possessed such accurate
knowledge of Greek literature and philosophy as some of the
Church Fathers have attributed to him,[11] he did not hesitate
to enter into discussion with persons trained in Greek
philosophy.[12] It is of particular interest to note that a famous
philosopher, Athenodorus (74 B.C.–A.D. 7), who had influenced

[1] *Colossians* iii. 11.
[2] *Romans* xv. 16. See also *Galatians* i. 16 ; *Ephesians* iii. 6.
[3] *Romans* xi. 1 ; *Philippians* iii. 5.
[4] *Acts* xxiii. 6 ; *Philippians* iii. 5.
[5] Deissmann, *op. cit.* p. 77.
[6] *Romans* ix. 3.   [7] *1 Corinthians* ix. 20.   [8] *Acts* xxii. 3.
[9] *Ibid.* xvi. 37, xxii. 25, 27, 29, xxiii. 27.
[10] Strabo, iv. 10. 13, p. 674 ; W. Ramsay, *The Cities of St. Paul*
(London, 1907), p. 232 *sq.*
[11] Socrates, *Historia ecclesiastica*, iii. 16.   [12] *Acts* xvii. 18 *sqq.*

considerably the thought of Seneca, had lived in Tarsus very near the time of which we are speaking, and whose teaching was undoubtedly influential in the university of Tarsus after his death.[1] There is reason to believe that Paul was brought up in a society which was permeated by Stoicism.[2] It is not improbable that his conversion, as has been found to be the case with other religious conversions,[3] was connected with a previous preparation for it in his own mind in the form of a subconscious incubation which, when ripe, burst into flower. If so, it is no wonder that he freed Christianity from its nationalistic fetters, and transformed it into a world-religion of salvation.

In Greece, philosophers had long before opposed national narrowness and prejudice. Democritus of Abdera said that every country is accessible to a wise man, and that a good soul's fatherland is the whole earth.[4] The same view was expressed by Theodorus, one of the later Cyrenaics, who denounced devotion to country as ridiculous.[5] The Cynics in particular, attached slight value to the citizenship of any special state, declaring themselves to be citizens of the world.[6] But, as Zeller observes, in the mouth of the Cynic this doctrine was meant to express not so much the essential oneness of all mankind, as the philosopher's independence of country and home.[7] It was the Stoic philosophy that first gave to the idea of a world-citizenship a definite positive meaning, and raised it to historical importance. The citizen of Alexander's huge empire had in a way become a citizen of the world ; and national dislikes were so much more readily overcome since the various nationalities comprised in it were united not only under a common government but also in a common culture.[8] Indeed, the founder of Stoicism was himself only half a Greek. But there is also an intrinsic connection between the cosmopolitan idea and the Stoic system in general. | According to the Stoics, human society has for its basis the identity of reason in individuals ; hence we have no ground for limiting this society to a single nation. We are all, says Seneca, members of one great body,

---

[1] Ramsay, *op. cit.* p. 217 *sqq.*
[2] See E. V. Arnold, *Roman Stoics* (Cambridge, 1911), p. 24.
[3] James, *op. cit.* p. 230.
[4] Stobæus, *Florilegium*, xl. 7, vol. ii. 80. *Cf.* P. Natorp, *Die Ethika des Demokritos* (Marburg, 1893), p. 117, n. 41.
[5] Diogenes Laertius, *Vitæ philosophorum*, ii. 98 *sq.*
[6] *Ibid.* vi. 12, 63, 72, 98 ; Epictetus, *Dissertationes*, iii. 24. 66 ; Stobæus, xlv. 28, vol. ii. 252.
[7] E. Zeller, *Socrates and the Socratic Schools* (London, 1885), p. 326 *sq.* ; *idem, The Stoics, Epicureans, and Sceptics* (London, 1892), p. 327.
[8] *Cf.* Plutarch, *De Alexandri Magni fortuna aut virtute*, i. 6, p. 329.

the universe; " we are all akin by Nature, who has formed us of the same elements, and placed us here together for the same end." [1] As Marcus Aurelius puts it, " the world is in a manner a state," including all rational beings, to which the individual states are related as the houses of a city are to the city collectively. [2] And the wise man will esteem it far above any particular community in which the accident of birth has placed him. [3]

Besides Stoic influence there may have been another cause that made for the universalising of Christianity, namely the Logos-doctrine, of which elements are clearly discernible in the Pauline epistles; it is difficult to doubt that this doctrine influenced his conception of Christ. It could look back to a long history, but assumed definite shape as a metaphysical theory particularly in the religious philosophy of Philo Judæus of Alexandria, who was a contemporary of Jesus. According to this theory nobody can approach God—the immaterial, unknowable, ineffable, self-existent Being. Nor was it possible that God should intervene directly in the process of creation; only indirectly could his function as cause of the universe be accomplished. God proceeded therefore according to a plan. He made use of an image of his own essence, an ideal image that remains intimately united with himself. The universe comes into existence through the instrumentality of this divine mediator. All that it possesses of spirit, soul, of forms and values, of patterns and ideas, issues from, or is rooted in, the supreme Reason, the Logos. The term *Logos* stood for many things, but in the teaching of Philo it was the equivalent of the world's wisdom or the world's image. [4] And in this sense it appears in Pauline literature. Jesus is spoken of as " the image of the invisible God, the firstborn of every creature : For by him were all things created, that are in heaven, and that are in earth, visible and invisible." [5]

Paul looked upon the process of redemption as a mystery. He declares that the wisdom he speaks of is " not the wisdom of this world," but " the wisdom of God in a mystery, even the hidden wisdom, which God ordained before the world unto our glory. . . . Let no man deceive himself. If any man among you seemeth to be wise in this world, let him become

[1] Seneca, *Epistulæ*, xcv. 52.
[2] Marcus Aurelius, *Commentarii*, iii. 11, iv. 4.
[3] Seneca, *De otio*, iv. 1 ; *idem*, *Epistulæ*, lxviii. 2 ; Epictetus, *Dissertationes* iii. 22. 83 *sqq*.
[4] A. Aall, *The Hellenistic Elements in Christianity* (London, 1931), pp. 57–9, 62 *sq*.
[5] *Colossians* i. 15 *sq*. See also *supra*, p. 104.

a fool, that he may be wise. For the wisdom of this world is foolishness with God. For it is written, He taketh the wise in their own craftiness. And again, The Lord knoweth the thoughts of the wise, that they are vain." [1] But the redemption is not only a mystery : there is also magic in it. This appears from the importance which Paul attaches to baptism and the Eucharist.

There is no evidence that Jesus instituted baptism, but every reason to believe that he did not do so. It never appears among the conditions of discipleship. The passage in Mark's gospel about him who believes and is baptised is not an original part of it.[2] John's report of Jesus' answer to Nicodemus, that " except a man be born of water and of the Spirit, he cannot enter into the kingdom of God," [3] cannot be relied upon. And the same is the case with the commandment attributed to Jesus by Matthew, " Go ye therefore, and teach all nations, baptising them in the name of the Father, and of the Son, and of the Holy Ghost," [4] which has been regarded as the central piece of evidence for the traditional view of the institution of baptism by Jesus.[5] Harnack points out that for two reasons Jesus could not have uttered it. First, it is only a later stage of the tradition that represents the risen Christ as delivering speeches and giving commandments — Paul knows nothing of it ; secondly, the Trinitarian formula is foreign to the mouth of Jesus and has not the authority in the Apostolic age which it must have had, if it descended from Jesus himself.[6] Further, if Paul had known of such a commission to baptise he could hardly have said, as he does : " Christ sent me not to baptise, but to preach the gospel." [7] At the same time he knows of no other way of receiving the Gentiles into the Christian community than by baptism. He writes : " By one Spirit are we all baptised into one body, whether we be Jews or Gentiles, whether we be bond or free." [8] We may perhaps assume that the practice of baptism was continued in consequence of Jesus' recognition of John the Baptist and his baptism, even after John himself was removed ; in the fourth gospel it is said that Jesus did not baptise, but that his disciples did.[9] John had preached " the baptism of repentance for the remission of

---

[1] *1 Corinthians* ii. 6 *sq.*, iii. 18–20. *Cf. Colossians* i. 26 *sq.*
[2] *Supra*, p. 101.   [3] *John* iii. 5.   [4] *Matthew* xxviii. 19.
[5] See K. Lake, ' Baptism (Early Christian),' in J. Hastings, *Encyclopædia of Religion and Ethics*, ii (Edinburgh, 1909), p. 380.
[6] Harnack, *op. cit.* i. 79 n. 1.   See also C. Clemen, *Primitive Christianity and its non-Jewish Sources* (Edinburgh, 1912), p. 214.
[7] *1 Corinthians* i. 17.
[8] *Ibid.* xii. 13.   [9] *John* iv. 2.

sins " ; [1] and Paul also regarded baptism as a cleansing from sin,[2] but predominantly as a reincarnation of Christ's death and rising to immortality : " Know ye not, that so many of us as were baptised into Jesus Christ were baptised into his death ? Therefore we are buried with him by baptism into death : that like as Christ was raised up from the dead by the glory of the Father, even so we also should walk in newness of life.   For if we have been planted together in the likeness of his death, we shall be also in the likeness of his resurrection : Knowing this, that our old man is crucified with him, that the body of sin might be destroyed, that henceforth we should not serve sin." [3]

Lietzmann observes that Paul's mystic sacramentalism in regard to baptism was in closest contact with the belief of the church of the " Hellenists " and must surely have appeared to many a Corinthian as an infallible means of purging away sin and as a guarantee of future salvation.[4]   In the Mysteries which at that time were spread throughout Asia Minor and Greece we find rites of ablution from which a new birth was expected ;   mention was made of " dying " in the figurative sense, as the high priest of Isis says in Apuleius ; [5] use was made of the magic power of a name or some other formula ; and the result was considered to be salvation due to the union of the initiate with the god.[6]   Tertullian noticed the resemblance, and argued that demons, whose chief employment was to prevent mankind from embracing the worship of the true God, endeavoured to preoccupy the minds of men by imitating rites having some similarity to those which were to be observed under the gospel, and that baptism was thus by their suggestion introduced into the Eleusinian mysteries as a mode of initiation, being an imitation of Christian baptism.[7]   The Eleusinian purificatory bath, from which the candidate emerged a new man with a new name, was also referred to by Greek Fathers, especially Clement of Alexandria, as a parallel to the Christian rite of baptism both in its nature and in its intended effects.[8]   In any case we must

---

[1] *Mark* i. 4.

[2] This is obviously implied in *1 Corinthians* vi. 11.

[3] *Romans* vi. 3–6.   See also *Colossians* ii. 12.

[4] H. Lietzmann, *The Beginnings of the Christian Church* (London, 1937), p. 184.

[5] Apuleius, *Metamorphoses*, xi. 21.

[6] Clemen, *op. cit.* p. 230 ; K. Lake, *The Earlier Epistles of St. Paul* (London, 1911), p. 389 *sq.*

[7] Tertullian, *De baptismo*, 5.   See also Justin, *Apologia I. pro Christianis*, 62.

[8] Clement of Alexandria, *Stromata*, v. 11 (Migne, *Patrologiœ cursus, Ser. Grœca*, ix. 107).

assume that the pagan sacrament influenced the latter and increased the importance attached to baptism in the Christian world.

Various writers regard Paul's sacramental conception of baptism as an alien body in his system as a whole, incongruous with his general doctrine of justification by faith ; [1] and, though he no doubt considered faith a necessary preliminary to it, it is fairly obvious that he attributed to baptism magical efficacy. Some statements to this effect have already been quoted, and others may be added, such as : " By one Spirit are we all baptised into one body " ; [2] " As many of you as have been baptised into Christ have put on Christ." [3] Paul's reference to the Corinthian custom of baptism for the dead—" What shall they do which are baptised for the dead, if the dead rise not at all ? why are they then baptised for the dead ? " [4]—also supports this view. It has been argued that he leaves us in the dark as to his own opinion about it. [5] But it seems more to the point that he does not reprove the Corinthians for practising it. [6]

Like baptism the Last Supper is mentioned in the synoptic gospels. They contain three passages dealing with it. When eating with his disciples Jesus " took bread, and blessed, and brake it, and gave to them, and said, Take, eat : this is my body. And he took the cup, and when he had given thanks, he gave it to them : and they all drank of it. And he said unto them, This is my blood of the new testament, which is shed for many. Verily I say unto you, I will drink no more of the fruit of the vine, until that day that I drink it new in the kingdom of God." [7] There is a similar account in Matthew, which is dependent on Mark. [8] The third account, found in Luke, contains the addition, " This do in remembrance of me." [9] This does not occur in some early Western authorities, and is therefore regarded by almost all critics as a later insertion influenced by the passage in Corinthians on the subject. [10] It

[1] W. Heitmüller, *Taufe und Abendmahl bei Paulus* (Göttingen, 1903), p. 22 *sq.* ; H. J. Holtzmann, *Lehrbuch der neutestamentlichen Theologie*, ii (Tübingen, 1911), p. 198 ; H. J. Weinel, *Biblische Theologie des neuen Testaments* (Tübingen, 1928), p. 251.
[2] *1 Corinthians* xii. 13.
[3] *Galatians* iii. 27.   [4] *1 Corinthians* xv. 29.
[5] E. Eidem, *Det kristna livet enligt Paulus* (Stockholm, 1927), p. 122 n. 2.
[6] *Cf.* A. Loisy, *Les mystères païens et le mystère chrétien* (Paris, 1914), p. 275.
[7] *Mark* xiv. 22-5.   [8] *Matthew* xxvi. 26-9.   [9] *Luke* xxii. 15-20.
[10] W. Sanday, ' Jesus Christ,' in J. Hastings, *A Dictionary of the Bible*, ii (Edinburgh, 1899), p. 636 ; P. Gardner, *The Religious Experience of Paul* (London and New York, 1911), p. 113 ; Holtzmann, *op. cit.* i. 377.

has also been contended by many scholars that the account of
Mark (on which Matthew depends) shows traces of Pauline
influence, especially in the language which describes the cup
as " my blood of the new testament, which is shed for many." [1]
Conybeare argues that the agreement is so close that either
Mark must have copied Paul or Paul Mark, and that the latter
hypothesis is ruled out by the fact that the Pauline epistle is
older than the Gospel of Mark.[2] Montefiore observes how difficult
it is to believe that a Palestinian or Galilæan Jew could have
suggested that, in drinking wine, his disciples were, even sym-
bolically, drinking blood, considering the horror with which
the drinking of blood was regarded by the Jews.[3]

In any case it is a widespread opinion that the only trace
of a mystic meaning given to the Eucharist in the gospels is a
later incorporation that could have no meaning save in the
mystery-salvation through Christ as conceived by Paul. For
him it was a sacrament and a mystical re-enactment of the
death and resurrection of Christ through which the believer
participates in his immortality, the bread and wine being an
incarnation of his body and blood : " The cup of blessing which
we bless, is it not the communion of the blood of Christ ? The
bread which we break, is it not the communion of the body of
Christ ? For we being many are one bread, and one body :
for we are all partakers of that one bread. Behold Israel after
the flesh : are not they which eat the sacrifices partakers of the
altar ? " [4] In reproving the Corinthians for profaning the
Lord's Supper Paul wrote to them : " As often as ye eat this
bread, and drink this cup, ye do show the Lord's death till he
come. Wherefore whosoever shall eat this bread, and drink
this cup of the Lord, unworthily, shall be guilty of the body
and blood of the Lord. But let a man examine himself, and
so let him eat of that bread, and drink of that cup. For he
that eateth and drinketh unworthily, eateth and drinketh
damnation to himself, not discerning the Lord's body." [5] As
Loisy observes, " in the ardent imagination of the Apostle, the
bread broken for the Lord's Supper assimilates itself to Christ
crucified for the elimination of sin, the wine of the cup identifies
itself with the blood spilt for the salvation of mankind." [6] The

---

[1] Loisy, op. cit. p. 284 ; Holtzmann, op. cit. i. 368 sq. ; M. Goguel,
The Life of Jesus (London, 1933), p. 448.

[2] F. C. Conybeare, Myth, Magic, and Morals (London, 1909), p. 270.

[3] C. G. Montefiore, The Synoptic Gospels, edited with an Introduction
and a Commentary, i (London, 1927), p. 332.

[4] 1 Corinthians x. 16–18.　　　　[5] Ibid. xi. 26–9.

[6] Loisy, op. cit. p. 286.

" worthy " participation in the Supper may have presupposed faith, but the essence of the rite was undoubtedly the magical effect ascribed to the bodily communion with Christ by partaking of his body and blood.

It is obvious that the sacramental form of the Eucharist exhibited by Paul cannot have been a creation of Jesus, nor can it have come from strict Judaism ; but there were striking parallels to it in the pagan world. There was a series of cults in the Roman Empire which offered a happy immortality to their initiates, and the method of obtaining it was by means of sacraments. In several of those mysteries blood played a very important part. It was an extremely common belief in the ancient world that by drinking the blood it was possible to absorb the qualities of the god whose blood was used.¹ All the mystery gods were intercessors and saviours, and the object of the initiates was to attain, through identification with the god, a share in his blessed immortality.² Paul was plainly aware of those pagan parallels. After speaking of the bread and the cup of communion, he refers to the things which the Gentiles " sacrifice to devils, and not to God," and warns the Corinthians that they " cannot be partakers of the Lord's table, and of the table of devils." ³ The Corinthians evidently regarded the Eucharist as food and drink by consuming which they enjoyed participation in the life of Jesus ; just as the participants in the Eleusinian mysteries believed that they became ἔνθεοι by means of a meal in which they partook, in some mysterious manner, of the body of Dionysus.⁴ The words of dislike and contempt with which Paul speaks of the pagan mysteries do not prove that he was uninfluenced by them. His own terminology rather suggests the reverse. He may have been, half-unconsciously, allured by them. Where ideas are in the air men may catch them by a sort of infection, and often without any notion whence they came.⁵

The centre of Paul's Christianity is the doctrine of redemption through the crucified and risen Christ. He never speaks of Jesus as a teacher or of his teaching, he extremely seldom appeals to any words of Jesus as a moral norm, he never refers to his example of life in any concrete situation.⁶ His pre-

¹ Cf. F. Cumont, Les religions orientales dans le paganisme romain Paris, 1929), p. 64.
² Ch. Guignebert, Jesus (London, 1935), p. 446 sq.
³ 1 Corinthians x. 20 sq.
⁴ K. Lake, The Earlier Epistles of St. Paul (London, 1911), p. 213 sq.
⁵ C. G. Montefiore, Judaism and St. Paul (London, 1914), p. 116 sq. ; Gardner, op. cit. p. 80.
⁶ Eidem, op. cit. pp. 236, 243, 250.

occupation with the death and resurrection of Jesus was no doubt immediately due to his vision, but to this vision he may have been predisposed by pagan cults known to him from his boyhood at Tarsus, which were much occupied with divine beings who had died and had risen again, who were, in fact, for ever dying and for ever rising again, to the joy of their worshippers. We have evidence that his native city was thronged with such mysteries, the myths and rites of Isis and Osiris, of Dionysus, Cybele, and Attis. The leading deities were Sandon-Herakles and Baal-Tarz. The former was popularly associated with the same ideas of death and resurrection as pervaded the worship of Adonis, Tammur, and Osiris. Baal-Tarz, again, pre-eminently " Lord of Tarsus," was the giver of vegetation and every good gift, and his picture, as seen on the coins of the fourth century before Christ, looks as noble as the Greek Zeus, whom he greatly resembled in character. Hans Böhlig has made it perfectly clear that Paul adopted his terminology, and perhaps his method of unfolding the redemptive scheme of a deified Christ, to the preconceptions of his Gentile fellow-citizens, who from childhood had been taught the mystic religion of Sandon.[1] But the resemblance between Paul's teaching and the mystery religions is not merely a formal one, apart from its sacramentalism, of which I have already spoken. In those religions, also, there was a divine saviour through which the believers hoped to reach a state of salvation not only in this life but in the world beyond the grave. While the synoptists emphasise a speedy coming of the Son of man to judge the nations and to found a reign of saints upon earth, Paul turned the eyes of Christians towards a spiritual heaven where he who dies with Christ will live for ever. This is a doctrine of the same class as the doctrines taught by pagan mystery religions.[2] From the moral point of view there is of course an enormous difference between Christ and the pagan gods. But those writers who maintain that Paul was in no way influenced by the mysteries—not even indirectly by the atmosphere which they diffused—fail to account for those points in which his teaching so closely resembles them.

At the same time Paul says himself that " Christ died for our

[1] C. M. Cobern, *The New Archæological Discoveries and their Bearing upon the New Testament and upon the Life and Times of the Primitive Church* (New York and London, 1928), p. 542 *sq.* ; H. Böhlig, *Die Geisteskultur von Tarsos im augustinischen Zeitalter* (Göttingen, 1913), pp. 67 *sqq.*, 89 *sqq.*

[2] *Cf.* Loisy, *op. cit.* pp. 248, 249, 333, 349, 357, etc. ; Gardner, *op. cit.* p. 87 *sqq.* ; Harnack, *op. cit.* ii. (1896), p. 10.

sins according to the scriptures." [1] Among the early Christians there was a belief that the Old Testament had prophesied the Passion of Christ.[2] There was, in particular, the famous prophecy in which Isaiah deals with the voluntary suffering and death of the servant of Yahveh, who " bore the sin of many." [3] This has obviously been the source of the words which Mark puts into the mouth of Jesus : " The Son of man came not to be ministered unto, but to minister, and to give his life a ransom for many " ; and, " This is my blood of the new testament, which is shed for many." [4] Johannes Weiss quotes with approval Jülicher's assertion that " Jesus himself never referred to his obligation to bear the form of a servant or to the mediatorial work of his death and sacrifice." [5]

It has been alleged that Paul's doctrine of justification by faith also is due to Hellenic influence,[6] while he himself refers to the Old Testament as his authority.[7] But it seems that the immense importance which he attaches to faith was in the first place the outcome of his ecstatic vision. This is suggested by knowledge which we have of other sudden conversions. " Beliefs," says William James, " are strengthened wherever automatisms corroborate them. Incursions from beyond the transmarginal region have a peculiar power to increase conviction." [8] There has been much discussion about the meaning of faith (*pistis*) in Paul's vocabulary.[9] He says himself that the word of faith which he teaches is " that if thou shalt confess with thy mouth the Lord Jesus, and shalt believe in thine heart that God hath raised him from the dead, thou shalt be saved." [10] Whatever else Paul's conception of faith may imply, such as trust, " enthusiastic adhesion," [11] and obedience,[12] it pre-

[1] *1 Corinthians* xv. 3.
[2] *Matthew* viii. 17 ; *Mark* ix. 12 ; *Acts* iii. 18, viii. 32 *sq.* ; *1 Peter* . 10 *sq.*, ii. 24 *sq.*
[3] *Isaiah* lii. 13–liii. 12.   [4] *Mark* x. 45, xiv. 24.
[5] J. Weiss, *Paul and Jesus* (London and New York, 1909), p. 11.
[6] Loisy, *op. cit.* p. 360.
[7] *Romans* x. 11.   [8] James, *op. cit.* p. 478.
[9] See, for example, J. Weiss, *Das Urchristentum* (Göttingen, 1917), . 322 *sqq.* ; R. Gyllenberg, *Pistis*, ii (Helsingfors, 1922), p. 2 *sqq.* ; V. H. P. Hatch, *The Idea of Faith in Christian Literature* (Strasbourg, 925), p. 9 *sq.* ; Eidem, *op. cit.* pp. 96 n., 115 *sqq.* ; E. Wissmann, *Das Verhältnis von* πίστις *und Christusfrömmigkeit bei Paulus* (Göttingen, 1926), pp. 38, 40, 66, 67, 81 *sqq.* ; C. A. A. Scott, *Christianity according to Paul* (Cambridge, 1927), p. 102 *sqq.*
[10] *Romans* x. 9.
[11] W. Sanday and A. C. Headlam, *Critical and Exegetical Commentary n the Epistle to the Romans* (Edinburgh, 1911), p. 33 *sq.*
[12] See W. Schlater, ' Glaube und Gehorsam,' in *Beiträge zur Förderung hristlicher Theologie*, v. (Gütersloh, 1901), fasc. 6.

supposes in the first place the acceptance of some fact as true ; and such a belief cannot be a proper object of moral judgment. But even if the sin of unbelief, as Thomas Aquinas argues, has its cause in the will because it consists in " contrary opposition to the faith, whereby one stands out against the hearing of the faith," [1] it could not be imputed to anybody who never heard of the faith. Paul considers this question in connection with his tenet that whosoever shall call upon the name of the Lord shall be saved : " How then shall they call on him in whom they have not believed ? and how shall they believe in him of whom they have not heard ? and how shall they hear without a preacher ? . . . I say, Have they not heard ? Yes verily, their sound went into all the earth, and their words unto the ends of the world." [2] Even now, after the lapse of nearly two thousand years this reassuring statement has not become true. In another passage, however, there is an indication that God might have mercy even upon unbelievers.[3]

In the most important cycle of Paul's teaching salvation is not, as it is generally depicted in the synoptic gospels, a reward for righteous conduct. " A man is justified by faith without the deeds of the law." [4] " Before faith came, we were kept under the law, shut up unto the faith which should afterwards be revealed. Wherefore the law was our schoolmaster to bring us unto Christ, that we might be justified by faith. But after that faith is come, we are no longer under a schoolmaster. For ye are all the children of God by faith in Christ Jesus." [5] " To him that worketh not, but believeth on him that justifieth the ungodly, his faith is counted for righteousness." [6] And the faith itself is a gift of God : " God hath dealt to every man the measure of faith." [7] Salvation depends upon an " election of grace." [8] " Whom he did foreknow, he also did predestinate to be conformed to the image of his Son, that he might be the firstborn among many brethren. Moreover, whom he did predestinate, them he also called : and whom he called, them he also justified : and whom he justified, them he also glorified." [9] " Is there unrighteousness with God ? God forbid. For he saith to Moses, I will have mercy on whom

---

[1] Thomas Aquinas, *Summa theologica*, ii.–ii. 10. 1.
[2] *Romans* x. 13, 14, 18.   [3] *Ibid*. xi. 32.
[4] *Romans* iii. 28. See also *ibid*. iii. 20, iv. 5, ix. 31 *sq*. ; *Galatians* ii. 16, iii. 11 ; *Ephesians* ii. 8 *sq*.
[5] *Galatians* iii. 23–6.   [6] *Romans* iv. 5.
[7] *Ibid*. xii. 3. See also *1 Corinthians* ii. 5 ; *Philippians* i. 29 ; *Ephesians* ii. 8. This point has been very strongly emphasised by A. Deissmann, *op. cit*. p. 132.
[8] *Romans* xi. 5.   [9] *Ibid*. viii. 29 *sq*.

I will have mercy, and I will have compassion on whom I will have compassion. So then it is not of him that willeth, nor of him that runneth, but of God that sheweth mercy. . . . Therefore hath he mercy on whom he will have mercy, and whom he will he hardeneth." [1]

Those who believe are justified by the grace of God " through the redemption that is in Christ Jesus. Whom God hath set forth to be a propitiation through faith in his blood, to declare his righteousness for the remission of sins that are past, through the forbearance of God." [2] Christ " died for all, that they which live should not henceforth live unto themselves, but unto him which died for them, and rose again. . . . God was in Christ, reconciling the world unto himself not imputing their trespasses unto them ; and hath committed unto us the word of reconciliation." [3] It is thus by the vicarious suffering of Jesus that the wrath of God, aroused by the sin of men, is appeased. How is that possible ? Paul writes : " As by one man sin entered into the world, and death by sin ; and so death passed upon all men, for that all have sinned. . . . If by one man's offence death reigned by one ; much more they which receive abundance of grace and of the gift of righteousness shall reign in life by one, Jesus Christ. Therefore as by the offence of one judgment came upon all men to condemnation ; even so by the righteousness of one the free gift came upon all men unto justification of life. . . . As sin hath reigned unto death, even so might grace reign through righteousness unto eternal life by Jesus Christ our Lord." [4]

The idea that all mankind are doomed to death on account of Adam's sin, which Paul no doubt had imbibed from his Jewish upbringing, is explicable by the conception of sin as a kind of material substance or infection which is transmitted by propagation.[5] As we have seen above, the Prophets already broke with the old notions of divine vengeance by declaring that " every one shall die for his own iniquity," that " the soul that sinneth, it shall die." [6] And Ezekiel added that as the wickedness of the wicked shall be upon him, so also " the righteousness of the righteous shall be upon him." [7] This is in agreement with the fact that the moral emotions of disapproval or approval, in their capacity of retributive emotions, are hostile

---

[1] *Romans* ix. 14–16, 18.   [2] *Ibid.* iii. 24 *sq.*
[3] *2 Corinthians* v. 15, 19.   See also *Romans* viii. 32 ; *1 Corinthians* xv. 3, 4, 14, 17 ; *Galatians* i. 4 ; *Colossians* i. 13, 14, 20 ; *Thessalonians* i. 10.
[4] *Romans* v. 12, 17, 18, 21.
[5] *Supra*, p. 53 *sq.*   [6] *Ibid.* p. 55.   [7] *Ezekiel* xviii. 20.

or friendly attitudes of mind towards living beings conceived as causes of pain or pleasure. They cannot admit that a person is punished or rewarded on account of another person's behaviour. There cannot be a merit by transfer.

But apart from this, Paul's doctrine of redemption raises the question how Christ's suffering and death could be a means of justification at all. Paul says that " Christ our passover is sacrificed for us." [1] The idea of Christ's death being a sacrifice is also found in the Epistle to the Ephesians,[2] the authorship of which is disputed, and is set forth in detail in the Epistle to the Hebrews,[3] which is related to Paulinism. The bloody sacrifices of the law have been succeeded by the redemption which Christ obtained for us " by the sacrifice of himself " being offered " to bear the sins of many." [4] " We are sanctified through the offering of the body of Jesus Christ once for all. . . . By one offering he hath perfected for ever them that are sanctified. . . . There is no more offering for sin." [5] This theory was subsequently elaborated by Cyprian. Christ's suffering and death constituted a sacrifice calculated to propitiate an angry God ; and this thought was never afterwards lost sight of in the West. I shall return to this subject in a following chapter.

Are we to conclude then that the teaching of Paul is devoid of all ethical significance. By no means. He asks : " What shall we say then ? Shall we continue in sin, that grace may abound ? God forbid. . . . Shall we sin, because we are not under the law, but under grace ? God forbid." [6] His epistles are full of moral injunctions. On the one hand he wrote that " Christ hath redeemed us from the curse of the law " ; [7] that he found " the commandment, which was ordained to life, . . . to be unto death " ; [8] that " the law worketh wrath " ; [9] that " the strength of sin is the law." [10] But on the other hand he also wrote that " the law is holy, and the commandment holy, and just, and good." [11] Different explanations have been given of these contradictory statements ; [12] but the most satisfactory one seems to be that when Paul speaks of the law he does not always mean the same thing.[13] He does not definitely distinguish

---

[1] *1 Corinthians* v. 7.
[2] *Ephesians* v. 2.
[3] *Hebrews* ch. ix *sq.*
[4] *Ibid.* ix. 26, 28.
[5] *Ibid.* x. 10, 14, 18.
[6] *Romans* vi. 1, 2, 15.
[7] *Galatians* iii. 13. See also *ibid.* iv. 4 *sq.* ; *Romans* vii. 6, x. 4.
[8] *Romans* vii. 10.
[9] *Ibid.* iv. 15.
[10] *1 Corinthians* xv. 56.
[11] *Romans* vii. 12.
[12] See, for example, A Juncker, *Die Ethik des Apostels Paulus,* i (Halle, 1904), p. 167 *sqq.* ; Weiss, *Das Urchristentum,* p. 427 *sq.* ; W. Wrede, *Paul* (London, 1907), p. 77 *sq.*
[13] *Cf.* Eidem, *op. cit.* p. 303 *sqq.*

between ritual and the strictly ethical parts of the Israelitish legislation. But he says that no man should be judged " in meat, or in drink, or in respect of an holyday, or of the new moon, or of the sabbath days : which are a shadow of things to come." [1] He contrasts " the circumcision, which is outward in the flesh," with the circumcision " of the heart." [2] And above all, he makes the parallel statements that all the law is fulfilled in one word, namely this : " Thou shalt love thy neighbour as thyself " ; [3] and that " he that loveth another hath fulfilled the law. For this, Thou shalt not commit adultery, Thou shalt not kill, Thou shalt not steal, Thou shalt not bear false witness, Thou shalt not covet ; and if there be any other commandment, it is briefly comprehended in this saying, namely, Thou shalt love thy neighbour as thyself. . . . Therefore love is the fulfilling of the law." [4] He also writes : " Bless them which persecute you : bless, and curse not. Rejoice with them that do rejoice, and weep with them that weep. . . . Recompense to no man evil for evil. Provide things honest in the sight of all men. If it be possible, as much as lieth in you, live peaceably with all men. . . . Avenge not yourselves, but rather give place unto wrath : for it is written, Vengeance is mine ; I will repay, saith the Lord. Therefore if thine enemy hunger, feed him ; if he thirst, give him drink : for in so doing thou shalt heap coals of fire on his head. Be not overcome of evil, but overcome evil with good." [5] " Put on therefore, as the elect of God, holy and beloved, bowels of mercies, kindness, humbleness of mind, meekness, long-suffering ; Forbearing one another, and forgiving one another, if any man have a quarrel against any. . . . And above all these things put on charity, which is the bond of perfectness." [6] " Though I speak with the tongues of men and of angels, and have not charity, I am become as sounding brass, or a tinkling cymbal. And though I have the gift of prophecy, and understand all mysteries, and all knowledge ; and though I have all faith, so that I could remove mountains, and have not charity, I am nothing. And though I bestow all my goods to feed the poor, and though I give my body to be burned, and have not charity, it profiteth me nothing. Charity suffereth long, and is kind ; charity envieth not ; charity vaunteth not itself, is not puffed up, Doth not behave itself unseemly, seeketh not her own, is not easily provoked, thinketh no evil ; Rejoiceth not in iniquity,

---

[1] *Colossians* ii. 16 *sq.*
[2] *Romans* ii. 28 *sq. Cf. Colossians* ii. 11.
[3] *Galatians* v. 14.   [4] *Romans* xiii. 8–10.
[5] *Ibid.* xii. 14, 15, 17–21.   [6] *Colossians* iii. 12–14.

but rejoiceth in the truth; Beareth all things, believeth all things, hopeth all things, endureth all things. Charity never faileth. . . . And now abideth faith, hope, charity, these three; but the greatest of these is charity." [1]

How can these sayings be reconciled with the doctrine of justification by faith only? An obvious answer would be that faith produces, or manifests itself in, obedience to the law and charity; that good works are not the condition of righteousness, but righteousness, received as a divine gift by faith, is the condition of good works. There are passages in the epistles which directly express this idea: "Do we then make void the law through faith? God forbid: yea, we establish the law." [2] "How shall we, that are dead to sin, live any longer therein?" [3] Faith "worketh by love"; [4] in another passage love is said to belong to "the fruit of the Spirit." [5] If Christ lives in the believer it must influence his whole conduct. The Christlikeness of the faithful is in some passages expressed in imperatives: "As ye have therefore received Christ Jesus the Lord, so walk ye in him"; [6] "Look not every man on his own things, but every man also on the things of others. Let this mind be in you, which was also in Christ Jesus"; [7] "Bear ye one another's burdens, and so fulfil the law of Christ." [8]

The great emphasis which Paul lays on charity is quite in agreement with what we find in modern narratives of conversion. "I had more tender feeling towards my family and friends";—"I spoke at once to a person with whom I had been angry";—"I felt for every one, and loved my friends better";—"I felt everybody to be my friend";—"I began to work for others";—these are so many expressions from the records collected by Starbuck. [9] Sainte-Beuve observes that in Christians of different epochs there is a fundamental and identical spirit of piety and charity, common to those who have received grace; an inner state which before all things is one of love and humility, of infinite confidence in God, and of severity for one's self, accompanied with tenderness for others. The fruits peculiar to this condition of the soul have the same savour in all, under distant suns and in different surroundings, in Saint Teresa of Avila just as in any Moravian brother of

---

[1] *1 Corinthians* xiii. 1–8, 13. The chapter in question has been regarded by some writers as a later interpolation, but this opinion has not been generally accepted (Eidem, *op. cit.* p. 187 n. 2).

[2] *Romans* iii. 31.   [3] *Ibid.* vi. 2.   [4] *Galatians* v. 6.

[5] *Ibid.* v. 22.   [6] *Colossians* ii. 6.

[7] *Philippians* ii. 4 *sq.*   [8] *Galatians* vi. 2.

[9] Starbuck, *op. cit.* p. 127. See also James, *op. cit.* pp. 274, 280 *sqq.*

Herrnhut.[1] Justin Martyr wrote about the wonderful change in manners of other converts : " We, who loved nothing like our possessions, now produce all we have in common and spread our whole stock before our indigent brethren ; we, who were pointed with mutual hatred and destruction, and would not so much as warm ourselves at the same fire with those of a different tribe on account of different institutions, now since the coming of Christ cohabit and diet together, and pray for our enemies ; and all our returns for evil are but the gentlest persuasives to convert those who unjustly hate us, that by living up to the same virtuous precepts of Christ they might be filled with the same comfortable hopes of obtaining the like happiness with ourselves, from that God who is Lord of all things. . . . I could give you a proof of the influence of such bright examples from many converts among us, who from men of violence and oppression were transformed into quite another nature." [2] Pagans bore witness to the correctness of the picture drawn by the apologetics.[3] Pliny wrote in a letter to Trojan that Christians said they had bound themselves by an oath not to commit any wicked deed, but to abstain from theft and robbery and adultery, and not withhold a deposit when reclaimed.[4] In recent times the Welsh revival of 1904-5 was accompanied by a real decrease in crime. Family life was restored by the abandonment of drinking habits, long-standing quarrels were made up, enemies were reconciled, ancient wrongs repaired, bad debts paid, stolen property restored.[5] Nowadays we also hear of moral reformation among converts to the Oxford Movement. A manifestation of the altruism of converted men and women is their missionary zeal—their burning desire to tell others of their experience that they may share their blessings. Throughout the history of Christianity those who have experienced the more sudden kind of conversion have generally been the most zealous missionaries.[6] Foremost among these was Paul.[7]

From the moral point of view, however, there is positive danger in a doctrine that relies upon love of fellow-men and good deeds as the fruits of faith. To an ecstatic convert like

[1] C.-A. Sainte-Beuve, *Port-Royal*, i (Paris, 1876), p. 106.
[2] Justin, *Apologia I. pro Christianis*, 17, 20.
[3] E. von Dobschütz, *Christian Life in the Primitive Church* (London, 1904), p. 371.
[4] Pliny, *Epistulæ*, x. 96 (97). 7.
[5] H. Bois, *Le Réveil au pays de Galles* (Toulouse, *s.d.*), pp. 582, 586 *sqq.*
[6] Underwood, *op. cit.* p. 234 *sqq.* ; W. Lawson Jones, *A Psychological Study of Religious Conversion* (London, 1937), p. 270.
[7] *Cf.* Eidem, *op. cit.* p. 171.

Paul faith may seem a sufficient source of such love and anything it carries with it, but in an established religion the faith
of the ordinary believer may fail entirely to produce similar
effects. Already in the Apostolic age his formula about
righteousness and salvation by faith alone was taken advantage
of as a cloak of laxity ; it was said that one might have the
true faith though in this case that faith remained dead or was
united with immorality.[1] James evidently saw this danger
when he wrote in his Epistle : " What doth it profit, my
brethren, though a man say he hath faith, and have not works ?
can faith save him ? . . . Faith without works is dead." [2]
Ordinary men are not mystics ; and ecstatic converts are
dangerous founders of religious creeds. The emphasis laid on
orthodox belief has not only, more than anything else, brought
the Christian religion into conflict with the nature of moral
emotions and ideas, but also, through the persecutions to which
it has led, been one of the most potent causes of misery in the
Christian world.

But we notice also another line of thought in the Pauline
epistles, which is more in harmony with the teaching of Jesus
as recorded in the synoptic gospels. He writes to the Romans
not only that a man is justified by faith without the deeds of
the law, but also that God will show himself as a righteous
judge " who will render to every man according to his deeds :
To them who by patient continuance in well doing seek for
glory and honour and immortality, eternal life : But unto them
that are contentious, and do not obey the truth, but obey
unrighteousness, indignation and wrath. . . . We shall all
stand before the judgment seat of Christ. . . . Every one of us
shall give account of himself to God." [3] In other epistles he
writes : " We must all appear before the judgment seat of
Christ ; that every one may receive the things done in his body,
according to that he hath done, whether it be good or bad." [4]
" Every man shall receive his own reward according to his own
labour. . . . Every man's work shall be made manifest : for
the day shall declare it, because it shall be revealed by fire ;
and the fire shall try every man's work of what sort it is. If
any man's work abide which he hath built thereupon, he shall
receive a reward. If any man's work shall be burned, he shall
suffer loss." [5] " Whatsoever a man soweth, that shall he also

[1] Harnack, *op. cit.* i (1894), p. 173.
[2] *The Epistle of James* ii. 14, 20.
[3] *Romans* ii. 5–8, xiv. 10, 12.
[4] *2 Corinthians* v. 10. See also *ibid.* ix. 6.
[5] *1 Corinthians* iii. 8, 13–15.

reap. For he that soweth to his flesh shall of the flesh reap corruption; but he that soweth to the Spirit shall of the Spirit reap life everlasting. And let us not be weary in well doing: for in due season we shall reap, if we faint not." [1]—" Whatsoever ye do, do it heartily, as to the Lord, and not unto men; Knowing that of the Lord ye shall receive the reward of the inheritance: for ye serve the Lord Christ. But he that doeth wrong shall receive for the wrong which he hath done: and there is no respect of persons." [2] When Paul mentions the deeds of men he does not overlook their cast of mind. He speaks of " the day when God shall judge the secrets of men by Jesus Christ," [3] when the Lord will come and " bring to light the hidden things of darkness, and will make manifest the counsels of the hearts." [4]

It may be argued that if a person is justified by his faith, which is a gift of God, and good deeds are manifestations of it, his " reward " for them is really due to the faith which God has given him, and that the damnation of a person who has done evil is due to the fact that he has not received the gift of faith from God; whereas if he receives such a gift, and is justified thereby, he will do no evil again. Such a conclusion might be drawn from the following passage: " Know ye not that the unrighteous shall not inherit the kingdom of God? Be not deceived: neither fornicators, nor idolators, nor adulterers, nor effeminate, nor abusers of themselves with mankind, Nor thieves, nor covetous, nor drunkards, nor revilers, nor extortioners, shall inherit the kingdom of God. And such were some of you: but ye are washed, but ye are sanctified, but ye are justified in the name of the Lord Jesus, and by the Spirit of our God." [5] But Paul was not a consistent thinker. On the one hand he teaches that justification depends upon faith alone, that faith is a gift of God, that man's work really is God's work, [6] nay that it even was God who gave Israel " the spirit of slumber, eyes that they should not see, and ears that they should not hear "; [7] but on the other hand he also looks upon the activity of the human will as a factor of importance. [8] His inconsistency is nowhere more glaring than in the passage in which he tells the Philippians to work out their own salvation

---

[1] *Galatians* vi. 7–9.   [2] *Colossians* iii. 23–5.   [3] *Romans* ii. 16.
[4] *1 Corinthians* iv. 5.   See also *ibid.* xiii. 3; *2 Corinthians* ix. 7.
[5] *1 Corinthians* vi. 9–11.
[6] *Philippians* i. 6; *1 Thessalonians* v. 24; *Ephesians* i. 11, ii. 10.
[7] *Romans* xi. 8.
[8] See, for example, *1 Corinthians* vii. 36 *sq.*, ix. 17, x. 27, xiv. 1, xvi. 12; *Philemon*, 14. *Cf.* Eidem, *op. cit.* p. 98 *sqq.*

" with fear and trembling," and then adds immediately : " For it is God which worketh in you both to will and to do of his good pleasure." [1] When he speaks of the retribution for good and evil deeds, he is obviously moved by his moral consciousness, which repeatedly finds expression without any reference to justification by faith. In his epistles to the Romans and to the Corinthians he frequently refers to " conscience," or *syneidēsis*, a term which he evidently had adopted from his Hellenistic surroundings,[2] and speaks of the " witness " it bears.[3] And he finds a conscience not only among the Christians, but in every man ; [4] and makes the following remarkable statement : " Not the hearers of the law are just before God, but the doers of the law shall be justified. For when the Gentiles, which have not the law, do by nature the things contained in the law, these, having not the law, are a law unto themselves : Which shew the work of the law written in their hearts, their conscience also bearing witness, and their thoughts the mean while accusing or else excusing one another." [5]

As Christ lives in the believer he must not soil his body : " Know ye not that ye are the temple of God, and that the Spirit of God dwelleth in you ? If any man defile the temple of God, him shall God destroy ; for the temple of God is holy, which temple ye are." [6] And as Christ was crucified, so the believer must crucify his flesh that he also may live eternally in the spirit, for the flesh is evil and contrary to the spirit. " If Christ be in you, the body is dead because of sin ; but the Spirit is life because of righteousness. But if the Spirit of him that raised up Jesus from the dead dwell in you, he that raised up Christ from the dead shall also quicken your mortal bodies by his Spirit that dwelleth in you. . . . If ye live after the flesh, ye shall die : but if ye through the Spirit do mortify the deeds of the body, ye shall live." [7] " Flesh and blood cannot inherit the kingdom of God ; neither doth corruption inherit incorruption." [8] " Walk in the Spirit, and ye shall not fulfil the lust of the flesh. For the flesh lusteth against the Spirit, and the Spirit against the flesh : and these are contrary the one to the other : so that ye cannot do the things that ye would. But if ye be led of the Spirit, ye are not under the law. Now the works of the flesh are manifest, which are these ; Adultery, fornication, uncleanness, lasciviousness, Idolatry, witchcraft,

---

[1] *Philippians* ii. 12 *sq.*
[2] *Cf.* Eidem, *op. cit.* p. 331.
[3] *Romans* ii. 15, ix. 1 ; *2 Corinthians* i. 12.
[4] *2 Corinthians* iv. 2.
[5] *Romans* ii. 13–15.
[6] *1 Corinthians* iii. 16 *sq.*
[7] *Romans* viii. 10, 11, 13.
[8] *1 Corinthians* xv. 50.

hatred, variance, emulations, wrath, strife, seditions, heresies, Envyings, murders, drunkenness, revellings, and such like: of the which I tell you before, as I have also told you in time past, that they which do such things shall not inherit the kingdom of God. But the fruit of the Spirit is love, joy, peace, long-suffering, gentleness, goodness, faith, Meekness, temperance: against such there is no law. And they that are Christ's have crucified the flesh with the affections and lusts. If we live in the Spirit, let us also walk in the Spirit. Let us not be desirous of vain glory, provoking one another, envying one another." [1] " To be carnally minded is death ; but to be spiritually minded is life and peace. Because the carnal mind is enmity against God : for it is not subject to the law of God, neither indeed can be. So then they that are in the flesh cannot please God. . . . They which are the children of the flesh, these are not the children of God." [2]

Though Paul connects his idea that the believer must die to the flesh, that he might live immortally in the spirit, with the death and resurrection of Christ, it may be asked where he had learnt to have such a moral contempt and horror of the flesh and to identify it with sin. This is not a Jewish conception. As Montefiore points out, Paul could not possibly have taken sin so sombrely as he did, had he been simply a Palestinian rabbi of his day. To the rabbinic Jew repentance and forgiveness were forces greater than sin, greater than the evil inclination. To Paul it was not so. He was no rabbinic Jew, and of the Law he knew little more than the fetters. He had always the horrid feeling of the unconquered evil inclination gnawing within his soul.[3] Nor did the rabbis oppose flesh and spirit in the same way as they are opposed in the writings of Paul. The spirit and flesh doctrine of the eighth chapter of the Epistle to the Romans could not have been devised by anyone who to his rabbinic antecedents merely added a conviction that the Messiah had appeared in the person of Jesus.[4] The man who devised that doctrine had been subjected to other influences. Paul, who was a Greek Jew, may have derived his idea of the sharp severance between flesh and spirit and his condemnation of the flesh from the Judaism of the Diaspora, which was greatly influenced by its Græco-Oriental environment. The antithesis of spirit and body was an old Platonic idea, and the doctrine that bodily enjoyments are low and degrading was taught by many pagan philosophers ; even a man like Cicero says that

---

[1] *Galatians* v. 16–26. [2] *Romans* viii. 6–8, ix. 8.
[3] Montefiore, *Judaism and St. Paul*, p. 114 *sq.*
[4] *Ibid.* p. 79 *sq.*

all corporeal pleasure is opposed to virtue and ought to be rejected.[1] And in the Neo-Platonic and Neo-Pythagorean schools of Alexandria an ascetic ideal of life was the natural outcome of their theory that God alone is pure and good, and matter impure and evil.

Paul's identification of flesh with evil led to various ascetic rules. " Every man that striveth for the mastery is temperate in all things." [2] " Mortify therefore your members which are upon the earth." [3] He submits himself to fastings, watchings, cold, and nakedness ; [4] he subdues his body after the manner of athletes ; [5] and he looks for similar action on the part of other seriously-minded followers of Christ. " I keep under my body, and bring it into subjection : lest that by any means, when I have preached to others, I myself should be a castaway." [6]

The worst of all sins of the flesh is sexual indulgence : " Flee fornication. Every sin that a man doeth is without the body ; but he that committeth fornication sinneth against his own body. What ? know ye not that your body is the temple of the Holy Ghost which is in you, which ye have of God, and ye are not your own." [7] Even marriage is permitted to man as a restraint, however imperfect, on the sinful licentiousness of the sexual impulse (Paul said nothing about propagation) : " It is good for a man not to touch a woman. Nevertheless, to avoid fornication, let every man have his own wife, and let every woman have her own husband. . . . I say therefore to the unmarried and widows, It is good for them if they abide even as I. But if they cannot contain, let them marry : for it is better to marry than to burn." He that giveth his virgin in marriage " doeth well ; but he that giveth her not in marriage doeth better." [8] For this inferiority of marriage to the un-married state he gives the following reason : " He that is unmarried careth for the things that belong to the Lord, how he may please the Lord : But he that is married careth for the things that are of the world, how he may please his wife. There is difference also between a wife and a virgin. The unmarried woman careth for the things of the Lord, that she may be holy both in body and in spirit : but she that is married careth for the things of the world, how she please her husband." [9]

This attitude towards marriage was utterly inconsistent with Jewish ideas : to marry and to have children were con-

---

[1] Cicero, *De officiis*, i. 30, iii. 33.
[2] *1 Corinthians* ix. 25.
[3] *Colossians* iii. 5.
[4] *2 Corinthians* xi. 27.
[5] *1 Corinthians* ix. 26.
[6] *Ibid.* ix. 27.
[7] *Ibid.* vi. 18 *sq.*
[8] *Ibid.* vii. 1, 2, 8, 9, 38.
[9] *Ibid.* vii. 32–4.

sidered matters of fundamental importance in Israel through all periods of its history. Nor does it receive much support from the synoptic gospels. Jesus was not himself married, and he is reported to have said that in the resurrection there will be neither marriage nor giving in marriage, but that those who rise will be as the angels in heaven.[1] When the disciples, after hearing Jesus' saying about divorce, wondered if it was good for a man to marry, he answered them that " all men cannot receive this saying, save they to whom it is given," and that there are " eunuchs, which have made themselves eunuchs for the kingdom of heaven's sake. He that is able to receive it, let him receive it." [2] Paul writes to the Corinthians : " Concerning virgins I have no commandment of the Lord : yet I give my judgment." [3] His view that celibacy is better than marriage was undoubtedly connected with his horror of sexuality as the worst sin of the flesh ; and for this there must have been some reason.

There was a small class of Hebrews, the Essenes, who renounced marriage, and esteemed " continence and the conquest over our passions to be virtue." [4] We have no evidence that Paul was influenced by them, but his sexual asceticism, like theirs,[5] may have been rooted in Greek ideas, Pythagorean and others. I wish particularly to draw attention to the notion that he who performs a sacred act or enters a holy place must be free from sexual pollution. In Greece priestesses were not infrequently required to be virgins, if not for their whole life, at any rate for the duration of their priesthood ; [6] and there were eunuch priests connected with the cults of the Ephesian Artemis,[7] the Phrygian Cybele,[8] and the Syrian Astarte.[9] Moreover, those who took part in certain religious festivals were obliged to be continent for some time previously.[10] Paul tells husbands and wives : " Defraud ye not one the other, except it be with consent for a time, that ye may give yourselves to

[1] *Supra*, p. 67.
[2] *Matthew* xix. 11 *sq.*   [3] *1 Corinthians* vii. 25.
[4] Josephus, *De bello Judaico*, ii. 8. 2. See also Solinus, *Collectanea rerum memorabilium*, xxxv. 9 *sq.*
[5] O. Zöckler, *Askese und Mönchtum*, i (Frankfurt a. M., 1897), p. 126.
[6] Strabo, xiv. 1. 23 ; Tertullian, *Ad uxorem*, i. 6 ; *idem*, *De exhortatione castitatis*, 13 ; W. Götte, *Das Delphische Orakel* (Leipzig, 1839), p. 78 *sq.* ; H. Blümner, *The Home Life of the Ancient Greeks* (London, 1893), p. 325.
[7] Strabo, xiv. 1. 23.
[8] Arnobius, *Adversus gentes*, v. 7.
[9] Lucian, *De dea Syria*, 15, 27, 50 *sqq.*
[10] W. Wachsmuth, *Hellenische Alterthumskunde*, ii (Halle, 1846), p. 560.

fasting and prayer." [1]   Again, Herodotus informs us that both the Greeks and the Egyptians " made it a point of religion to have no converse with women in the sacred places, and not to enter them without washing, after such converse " ; [2] and so far as the latter are concerned this statement is corroborated by a passage in the ' Book of the Dead.' [3]   Before entering the sanctuary of Mên Tyrannos, whose worship was extended over the whole of Asia Minor, the worshipper had to abstain from garlic, pork, and women, and had to wash his head. [4]   Among the Hebrews, also, it was a duty incumbent upon all to be free from sexual defilement before entering the temple. [5]   Now if, as Paul said, every believer is " the temple of God," he too must, consequently, be free from such defilement.

In order to explain in full the ascetic attitude towards sex, we have still to consider *why* sexual intercourse is looked upon as unclean and defiling. This implies that it is a presumed mysterious cause of danger. That the danger is supposed to be particularly alarming in the case of contact between the polluted individual and anything holy is merely an instance of the general belief ·that holiness is exceedingly sensitive to, and readily reacts against, external influences : indeed it is not only exceptionally susceptible to influences that are, or are supposed to be, injurious in other cases as well, but it is even affected or influenced by various acts or omissions which are otherwise considered perfectly harmless. [6]   It should be noticed that the mere discharge of sexual matter, even when quite involuntary and unaccompanied with any sexual desire, is held to be polluting both in Leviticus [7] and in the Christian Penitentials. [8]   It seems that the polluting effect ascribed to the discharge of such matter is largely due to its mysterious propensities and the veil of mystery which surrounds the whole sexual nature of man. There is the secrecy drawn over the sexual functions, and the feeling of sexual shame, [9] which give them the appearance of something illicit and sinful. But the

---

[1] *1 Corinthians* vii. 5.   [2] Herodotus, ii. 64.

[3] A. Wiedemann, *Herodots zweites Buch* (Leipzig, 1890), p. 269 *sq.*

[4] P. Foucart, *Des associations religieuses chez les Grecs* (Paris, 1873), pp. 119, 123 *sq.*

[5] *Leviticus* xii. 4, xv. 31.

[6] E. Westermarck, *Ritual and Belief in Morocco*, i (London, 1926), p. 250 *sqq.*

[7] *Leviticus* ch. xv.

[8] F. W. H. Wasserschleben, *Die Bussordnungen der abendländischen Kirche* (Halle, 1851), pp. 559, 560, 600.

[9] I have discussed the origin of sexual modesty in my book *The History of Human Marriage*, ii (London, 1921), ch. x.

defiling effects attributed to sexual intercourse are also, no
doubt, connected with the notion that woman is an unclean
being. Particularly during menstruation and childbirth she
is supposed to be charged with mysterious baleful energy, presumably on account of the marvellous nature of these processes
and especially the appearance of blood ; and such regular
temporary defilement of a specifically feminine character may
easily lead to the notion of the permanent uncleanness of the
female sex.

CHAPTER VII

THEOLOGICAL DOCTRINES BEFORE AUGUSTINE

THROUGHOUT the history of Christianity the principal subject of interest has been the question of salvation; but as to the means of procuring it there has been diversity of opinion. We have first and foremost to notice the antithesis between works and faith: between the moralistic view that eternal life is the wages and reward of a moral life, wrought out essentially by our own power, and the view that eternal life depends entirely on divine grace, connected with the faith in Christ as our redeemer through his death on the cross. In other words, there is, broadly speaking, the contrast between the moral teaching of Jesus as reported in the synoptic gospels and the Pauline formula of justification by faith alone.

In the sub-apostolic period both views are represented. The moralistic mode of thought is very prominent in the 'Shepherd' of Hermas, dating from the first half of the second century,[1] which is an important document for the Church Christianity of the age. "The true fast," he says, "is this: do nothing wickedly in thy life, but serve God with a pure mind, and keep his commandments, and walk according to his precepts, nor suffer any wicked desire to enter into thy mind. But trust in the Lord, that if thou dost these things, and fearest him, and abstainest from evil work, thou shalt live unto God."[2] "Fear God, and put thy trust in him, and love truth and righteousness, and do that which is good. If thou shalt do these things, thou shalt be an approved servant of God. . . . If thou shalt not observe these commands, but shalt neglect them, thou shalt not be saved, nor thy children, nor thy house."[3] "But if besides those things which the Lord hath commanded, thou shalt add some good thing, thou shalt purchase to thyself a greater dignity, and be in more favour with the Lord than thou shouldst otherwise have been."[4] Here we have the

[1] M. Dibelius, *A Fresh Approach to the New Testament and Early Christian Literature* (London, 1937), p. 132.

[2] Hermas, *Pastor*, iii. 5. 1.

[3] *Ibid.* ii. 12. 3. *Cf. ibid.* i. 1. 3, i. 2. 3, i. 3. 5, ii. 1. 8, iii. 6. 1, iii. 8. 7, iii. 10. 4.

[4] *Ibid.* iii. 5. 3. *Cf. ibid.* ii. 4. 4.

doctrine of merit in germ. Faith is repeatedly spoken of.[1]
By faith " the elect shall be saved . . . From faith proceeds
abstinence, from abstinence simplicity, from simplicity innocence, from innocence modesty, from modesty discipline and
charity." [2] " Put on faith, and trust in God, and thou shalt
receive all that thou shalt ask. . . . Faith promises all things,
and perfects all things." [3] But this faith is faith in God, not
in Christ. In the extensive writing of Hermas there is no
mention of the death and resurrection of Christ. But the Son
of God laboured very much, and suffered much, that he might
blot out the offences of those whom the Father delivered to
him. " For no vineyard can be digged without much labour
and pains. Wherefore having blotted out the sins of his people,
he showed to them the paths of life, giving them the law which
he had received of the Father." [4]

The same paramount importance attached to morality is
shown in the ' Teaching of the Twelve Apostles,' which is
usually cited by its Greek name as the ' Didache.' There also
nothing is said about the death and resurrection of Jesus and
the redemption of mankind. Thanks are given to God for the
knowledge of faith and immortality which he has made known
to us through Jesus, his servant,[5] who has shown us the way
of life in his teaching. The way of life " is this : first, thou
shalt love the God who made thee ; secondly, thy neighbour
as thyself ; and all things whatsoever thou wouldst not have
befall thee, thou too, do not to another." [6] Then there is a
series of sayings of Jesus, an enumeration of the commandments of the decalogue, and various other ethical injunctions.[7]
Particular emphasis is laid on almsgiving as a ransom for our
sins.[8] After this there is a description of the way of death,
which contains all sorts of wickedness and is full of curse.[9] At
the end we read the comforting words : " If thou art able to
bear the whole yoke of the Lord, thou shalt be perfect ; but
if thou art not able, what thou art able, that do." [10] The
warning is given : " Watch for your life's sake ; let your lamp
not go out, and your loins not be relaxed, but be ready ; for
ye know not the hour in which our Lord cometh. . . . In the
last days the false prophets and the corrupters shall be multiplied,
and the sheep shall be turned into wolves, and love shall be
turned into hate. . . . Then all created men shall come into
the fire of trial, and many shall be made to stumble and shall

[1] *Ibid.* i. 3. 5, 6, 8, i. 4. 1, ii. 1, ii. 6. 1 *sq.*, ii. 8, ii. 12. 5.
[2] *Ibid.* i. 3. 8. [3] *Ibid.* ii. 9. [4] *Ibid.* iii. 5. 6.
[5] *Didache*, 10. [6] *Ibid.* 1. [7] *Ibid.* 1–4.
[8] *Ibid.* 4. [9] *Ibid.* 5. [10] *Ibid.* 6.

perish. But they that endure in their faith shall be saved from this curse." [1]

To the moralistic group of writings belongs also the so-called ' Second Epistle of Clement of Rome,' which was in fact a sermon delivered by a presbyter to the Church. He quotes the saying of Jesus : " Whosoever therefore shall confess me before men, him will I confess also before my Father which is in heaven," [2] and asks : " Wherein must we confess him ? " His answer is : " In doing those things which he saith, and not disobeying his commandments—by worshipping him not with our lips only, but with all our heart, and with all our mind." [3] " If we do the will of Christ we shall find rest ; but if not, nothing shall deliver us from eternal punishment if we shall disobey his commands." [4] " Beautiful, therefore, is almsgiving, even as repentance from sin. Better is fasting than prayer, but almsgiving is better than both. Love covereth a multitude of sins. But prayer out of a good conscience delivereth from death." [5] " Let us repent. Let us recover ourselves unto that which is good, for we are full of much madness and evil. Let us wipe away from us our former sins, and repent with all our hearts, and be saved." [6] " Blessed are they who obey these ordinances. Though for a short season they suffer affliction in the world, they shall gather in the immortal fruit of the resurrection." [7]

In the genuine epistle of Clement, which is of an earlier date, there is an echo of Paul's teaching. We " are not justified by ourselves, neither by our own wisdom, or knowledge, or piety, or the works which we have done in the holiness of our hearts," but by faith. This, however, is " that faith by which God almighty has justified all men from the beginning," [8] not faith in the Pauline sense of the word. " We must fix our minds by faith towards God, and seek those things that are pleasing and acceptable unto him." [9] " We see how all righteous men have been adorned with good works ; wherefore even the Lord himself, having adorned himself with his works, rejoiced. Having therefore such an example, let us without delay fulfil his will, and with all our strength work the work of righteousness. The good workman with confidence receives the bread of his labour ; but the sluggish and lazy cannot look him in the face that sets him on work. We must therefore be ready and forward in well-doing ; for from him are all things.

---

[1] *Didache*, 16.   [2] *Matthew* x. 32.
[3] Clement of Rome, *Epistola II. ad Corinthios*, 3.
[4] *Ibid.* 6.   [5] *Ibid.* 16.   [6] *Ibid.* 13.   [7] *Ibid.* 19.
[8] Clement of Rome, *Epistola I. ad Corinthios*, 32.   [9] *Ibid.* 35.

And thus he foretells us, ' Behold, the Lord cometh, and his reward is with him, even before his face, to render to every one according to his work ' " (*Isaiah* xl. 10, lxii. 11).[1] " Let the wise man shew forth his wisdom, not in words but in good works," [2] we are " justified by our actions, and not our words." [3] " Happy then shall we be, beloved, if we shall have fulfilled the commandments of God, in the unity of love : that so, through love, our sins may be forgiven us.   For so it is written, ' Blessed are they whose iniquities are forgiven, and whose sins are covered ' " (*Psalms* xxxii. 1).[4] Clement also speaks of keeping the commandments of Christ.[5] He calls him " our high priest and protector," [6] whose blood, being shed for our salvation, has obtained the grace of repentance for all the world.[7] There shall be a future resurrection of which God has made our Lord Jesus Christ the first-fruits, raising him from the dead ; and some other guarantees of our own resurrection are also mentioned, among others that of the wonderful bird phœnix, seen in Arabia.[8] Though Clement occasionally directly refers to Paul there is no genuine Paulinism in his epistle. " The Roman Christians," says Lietzmann, " had not felt the least breath of the Pauline spirit.   It is not an eviscerated Paulinism but a Hellenistic proselyte Christianity that we meet with here in a pure form, an independent growth from a root in the early Church, of importance for the future." [9]

The letter bearing the name of James, which was known in Rome at the end of the first century or shortly after, and was accepted into the canon of the Western Church in the fourth century,[10] looks like a definite polemic against Paul's teaching of justification by faith only, although his name is not mentioned.[11] " What doth it profit, my brethren, though a man say he hath faith, and have not works ? can faith save him ? . . . Faith without works is dead.   Was not Abraham our father justified by works, when he had offered Isaac his son upon the altar ?   Seest thou how faith wrought with his works, and by works was faith made perfect ? . . .   By works a man is justified, and not by faith only.   Likewise also was not Rahab the harlot justified by works, when she had received

---

[1] *Ibid.* 33 *sq.*
[2] *Ibid.* 38.   [3] *Ibid.* 30.   [4] *Ibid.* 50.   [5] *Ibid.* 49.
[6] *Ibid.* 64.   [7] *Ibid.* 7. *Cf. ibid.* 21.   [8] *Ibid.* 24 *sq.*
[9] H. Lietzmann, *The Beginnings of the Christian Church* (London, 1937), p. 267.
[10] F. B. Clogg, *An Introduction to the New Testament* (London, 1937), p. 146 *sq.*
[11] See Dibelius, *op. cit.* p. 227 *sq.*

the messengers, and had sent them out another way ? '' [1]   But unlike Paul, the author of this epistle means by faith merely belief, or the acceptance of something as true : '' Thou believest that there is one God ; thou doest well : the devils also believe, and tremble.'' [2]   There is no reference to the resurrection of Jesus, whose name is mentioned only twice, and then quite incidentally. [3]

An addendum to the series of the Pauline epistles is the Epistle to the Hebrews, which was quoted already by Clement of Rome [4] and was accepted as canonical by the Eastern Church from early times, but in the West only since the fourth century. [5] The author's conception of Jesus and his work is similar to Paul's, although he expresses it in his own way.   Jesus is the Son of God, by whom he has made the worlds. [6]   He became man and equal to us in every respect : '' In all things it behoved him to be made like unto his brethren, that he might be a merciful and faithful high priest in things pertaining to God, to make reconciliation for the sins of the people.   For in that he himself hath suffered being tempted, he is able to succour them that are tempted.'' [7]   Being thus the perfect representative of humanity in the sight of God, he sanctified us once for all by offering his body, [8] and '' became the author of eternal salvation unto all them that obey him.'' [9]   '' But this man, after he had offered one sacrifice for sins for ever, sat down on the right hand of God.'' [10]   '' If we sin wilfully after that we have received the knowledge of the truth, there remaineth no more sacrifice for sins.'' [11]   Sore punishment awaits him '' who hath trodden under foot the Son of God, and hath counted the blood of the covenant, wherewith he was sanctified, an unholy thing.'' [12] The writer cites the saying about the righteous man who lives by faith. [13]   But faith does not mean for him personal trust in Christ, as it meant for Paul : '' Faith is the substance of things hoped for, the evidence of things not seen. . . .   Through faith we understand that the worlds were framed by the word of God, so that things which are seen were not made of things which do appear. . . .   Without faith it is impossible to please him : for he that cometh to God must believe that he is, and that he is a rewarder of them that diligently seek him.'' [14]   We

---

[1] *The Epistle of James* ii. 14, 20-2, 24 *sq.*
[2] *Ibid.* ii. 19.   [3] *Ibid.* i. 1, ii. 1.
[4] Clement, *Epistola I.*, 36.   [5] Clogg, *op. cit.* pp. 134, 142.
[6] *The Epistle to the Hebrews* i. 2.
[7] *Ibid.* ii. 16–18.   [8] *Ibid.* x. 10.   [9] *Ibid.* v. 9.
[10] *Ibid.* x. 12.   [11] *Ibid.* x. 26.   [12] *Ibid.* x. 29.
[13] *Ibid.* x. 38.   [14] *Ibid.* xi. 1, 3, 6.

have Jesus as " the author and finisher of our faith " ; [1] but the writer also speaks of the faith of Abel, Enoch, Noah, Abraham, Isaac, Jacob, Moses, and other saints of the past, " of whom the world was not worthy." [2]   There is some Judaising moralism in the comforting saying addressed to the readers, that God would not be so unjust as to forget their work and their loving deeds which they had done to his honour at an earlier date and were now doing in the service of the saints. [3]

Tertullian attributed this epistle to Barnabas, [4] who is interpreted in Acts as one able to give consolation, [5] but this seems to be a mere guess.   There is, however, another writer current under the name of Barnabas, whom Origen even describes as " Catholic," that is canonical. [6]   The Paulinism of his epistle is well marked.   Faith, love, and hope of that life which is to come are the characteristics of a Christian ; [7] and the assistants of our faith are fear and patience. [8]   Our Lord vouchsafes to give up his body to destruction, that through the forgiveness of our sins we might be sanctified, that is, by the sprinkling of his blood " ; [9] and he " shall come to judge both the quick and the dead." [10]   As his kingdom was founded upon the cross, " they that put their trust in him shall live for ever " ; [11] whereas " a man will justly perish, if having the knowledge of the way of truth, he shall nevertheless not refrain himself from the way of darkness." [12]   The whole of Christianity was already foretold in the Old Testament ; it is as if it had been said there : " Put your trust in Jesus, who shall be manifested to you in the flesh." [13]   But the Jews were not worthy to receive the covenant which God had promised to give them, because they had transgressed his commandments, being deceived by the evil one. [14]   There is also a moral strain in this epistle : " Learning the just commands of the Lord, . . . we should walk in them.   For he who does such things shall be glorified in the kingdom of God. But he that chooses the other part shall be destroyed together with his works.   For this cause there shall be both a resurrection and a retribution." [15]

The chief representative of Paulinism among the Apostolic Fathers is Ignatius, who was bishop of Antioch in the beginning

---

[1] *The Epistle to the Hebrews* xii. 2.
[2] *Ibid.* xi. 4 *sqq.*
[4] Tertullian, *De pudicitia*, 20.
[6] Clogg, *op. cit.* p. 145.
[7] Barnabas, *Epistola catholica*, 1.
[8] *Ibid.* 2.
[11] *Ibid.* 8.
[14] *Ibid.* 9, 14.

[3] *Ibid.* vi. 10.
[5] *Acts* iv. 36.

[9] *Ibid.* 5.
[12] *Ibid.* 5 ; *cf.* 20.

[10] *Ibid.* 7.
[13] *Ibid.* 6.
[15] *Ibid.* 21.

of the second century.[1] We have seven letters from his hand, all written in imitation of the epistles of Paul. Like him he speaks of believers both " being found in Christ," [2] and of " having Christ within themselves," [3] and exhort them to keep their bodies " as the temples of God." [4] " Faith and charity in Christ Jesus . . . are the beginning and end of life ; for the beginning is faith, the end charity. And these two, joined together, are of God." [5] Nothing is to be preferred to them.[6] Jesus Christ died for us, that we, by believing in his death, might escape death ; [7] and " he was also truly raised from the dead by his Father, after the manner as he will also raise up us who believe in him, by Jesus Christ, without whom we have no true life." [8] On the other hand, if people " believe not in the blood of Christ, it shall be them to condemnation." [9] He calls faith " the flesh of the Lord " and charity " the blood of Jesus Christ " : " Renew yourselves in faith, that is, the flesh of the Lord ; and in charity, that is, the blood of Jesus Christ." [10] All other things which concern a holy life are the consequences of faith and charity.[11] " Let your works be your charge, that so you may receive a suitable reward." [12] We must not judaise : " If we still continue to live according to the Jewish law, we do confess ourselves not to have received grace." [13]

The antitheses of Paul between law and gospel and between wrath and grace were carried to an extreme by Marcion. He was a native of Sinope in Pontus, where his father was bishop, but as a grown man he came to Rome in the reign of Antoninus Pius, and gained influence in the Church there until sharp oppositions arose. He separated himself from the Church Catholic and founded his own Church, which spread with such rapidity that wherever Christians were numerous about the year 160 there were probably Marcionite communities. The work in which he brought his teaching together has not been preserved, and its contents can therefore only be deduced from the notices which are found in the writings of opponents, particularly in Tertullian's five volumes against Marcion.

[1] Lietzmann, op. cit. p. 315.
[2] Ignatius, Epistola ad Trallianos, 2.
[3] Idem, Epistola ad Romanos, 6.
[4] Idem, Epistola ad Philodelphenses, 7.
[5] Idem, Epistola ad Ephesios, 14.
[6] Idem, Epistola ad Magnesios, 1 ; idem, Epistola ad Smyrnœos, 6
[7] Idem, Trallianos, 2 ; idem, Smyrnœos, 6.
[8] Idem, Trallianos, 9.   [9] Idem, Smyrnœos, 6
[10] Idem, Trallianos, 8. Cf. idem, Romanos, 7.
[11] Idem, Ephesios, 14.
[12] Idem, Epistola ad Polycarpum, 6.   [13] Magnesios, 8.

They have been assembled by Harnack,[1] and I shall avail myself of his collection.

Contrary to some other writers of the age, Marcion explained the Old Testament in its literal sense and rejected every allegorical interpretation. He recognised it as the revelation of the creator of the world and the god of the Jews, but placed it, just on that account, in sharpest contrast to the gospel. This god created the world out of material substance ; and he also created Adam weak in body and soul and then, tolerating the wiles of the devil through the Law, he brought sin and death upon mankind. His character was stern justice, and therefore anger, contentiousness, and unmercifulness. He wished to enforce the carrying out of his commandments by a system of punishments which rested upon the idea of retaliation : an eye for an eye, a tooth for a tooth, blood for blood was its principle, and this made him an unmerciful judge who punished the sins of the fathers on the children down to the fourth generation. His ideal was " righteousness," and therefore he might be called the " righteous God."

But there is also another god, the good God of love, who was absolutely unknown before Christ, but was revealed by him. Men were also in every respect strange to him ; but out of pure goodness and mercy he espoused their cause, as he could not bear to have them any longer tormented by their just and yet malevolent god. Rejecting Old Testament righteousness, Christ preached the gospel of the unknown God, taught gentleness and patience instead of cruelty and wrath, love of enemies and forgiveness instead of hate and retribution, compassionate kindness instead of calculating righteousness. He taught these things as the will of God and showed them forth in both word and deed. Then he died on the cross the death accursed by the creator god (*Galatians* iii. 13), and thereby paid him the ransom money and thus redeemed us, " the strangers," from our previous owners and gained us for the good God ; and not only those of us who were then living or who should live, but also the dead. For he descended into hell and liberated all the sinners, the whole multitude of heathen who suffered in the fiery wrath of the revenging god. The difference between the two gods had been clearly expounded by Paul, whom Christ had inspired by a special revelation, lest the gospel of the grace of God should be lost by falsifications. None of the twelve apostles whom Christ chose had understood him ; they had regarded him erroneously as the Messiah of the Jewish god.

[1] A. Harnack, *Marcion : das Evangelium vom fremden Gott* (Leipzig, 1921).

Therefore Christ had revealed the truth once again and had called Paul as its herald, who alone had maintained it in its purity. Marcion set himself boldly to the task of restoring the genuine and true gospel which had been known to Paul, by removing the Judaising interpolations and altering the text. But his gospel had also been misunderstood, nay his epistles had been falsified in many passages, in order to make them teach the identity of the god of creation and the God of redemption.   And Marcion attempted to purify them too from interpolations and restore the genuine Paulinism, which was just the gospel itself.

Nearly all ecclesiastical writers from Justin to Origen opposed Marcion.   He was said to be the most wicked and shameless of all heretics, worse than a heathen, a blasphemous emissary of demons, the first-born of Satan.[1] Yet he was too important to be ignored. Harnack maintains that the duty of accommodating herself to the Pauline epistles was actually forced upon the Church by Marcion and some other heretics, and that, but for this constraint, she would hardly have incorporated them with the canon.[2] Whatever else may be said about Marcion we must give him credit for having perceived clearly the vital difference between the teaching of Jesus as reported in the synoptic gospels and the teaching of Paul, as we know it, which modern theologians have been so apt to slur.

The early Christian Apologists—Aristides, Justin, Athenagoras, Tatian, Theophilus, and Minucius Felix—are earnest moralists. Man was created free to choose ; there is no virtue where there is no choice, and evil may therefore be necessary for the production of virtue.[3] Justin introduces Jesus with the formula " the teacher Christ," [4] represents him as the Socrates of the barbarians, and propounds the theory that this teacher is the incarnate reason of God.[5] The prophets of the Jews, however, were also inspired by the divine wisdom or Logos ; [6] hence the Mosaic law comprehended the unchangeable and fundamental principles of morality, and those who had lived up to it before the coming of Christ would be saved by him.[7] Man is naturally endowed with a " sperm of Logos." [8] But a revelation of the rational was necessary because he had

[1] A. Harnack, *History of Dogma*, i (London, 1894), p. 284 *sq.*
[2] *Ibid.* ii (1896), p. 51.
[3] E. Hatch, *Hibbert Lectures on the Influence of Greek Ideas and Usages upon the Christian Church* (London, 1890), p. 232.
[4] Justin, *Apologia I. pro Christianis*, 4.
[5] *Ibid.* 5.   [6] *Ibid.* 33, 36.
[7] Justin, *Dialogus cum Tryphone Judæo*, 45.
[8] *Idem, Apologia II. pro Christianis*, 8.

fallen under the sway of demons, and by the appearance of
Christ the very Logos, or Reason itself, took upon himself a
human form and nature to assist man and rescue him from the
power of the demons, and thus enable him to follow his reason
and freedom to do what is good.[1] God is " the Father of
righteousness," [2] who rewards goodness and punishes wickedness. " Every one is stepping forward into everlasting misery
or happiness according to his works." [3] They who walk
according to the will of God, " and demonstrate their worthiness
by their works, we are sure will be admitted into the Divine
presence, there to reign with him, where corruption and suffering
never come " ; [4] whereas every one according to his demerits
shall suffer in eternal fire.[5] But no one can be accountable for
any action of his unless mankind has the power to choose the
good and refuse the evil. " For if it be not so, but all things
are determined by fate, then farewell freedom of will ; and if
this man is destined to be good, and that evil, then neither the
one nor the other can be justly approved or condemned." [6]
" By maintaining, therefore, that future events have been
foretold by the prophets, we do not maintain that the things
foretold came to pass by any fatal necessity, but from that
divine prescience which foresees all the actions of men, without
necessitating them to act." [7] Only this is destiny, inevitable
destiny, that those who choose to walk in the paths of virtue
shall meet with proportionate returns of honour, and those
who prefer the contrary course shall be punished accordingly,
for God has not made man like trees or beasts, without the
power of election.[8]

But although Christ is considered to have accomplished
salvation as a divine teacher and to be a redeemer by helping
men to withstand the power of evil demons, Justin also refers
to the cross, saying that the sinless Christ submitted to his
ignominious death in obedience to the will of his Father, in
order that he might rescue them from the penalty due to their
sins,[9] and that in order to secure the benefits from Christ's
death repentance and a renunciation of our past evil habits
are necessary.[10] He also says that men are purified by faith
through the blood and death of Christ,[11] and that we are sure to
have a life incorruptible if we ask for it in faith.[12] But it has

---

[1] Justin, *Apologia I.*, 5.
[2] *Ibid.* 6.   [3] *Ibid.* 12.   [4] *Ibid.* 10.
[5] *Ibid.* 12, 21.   [6] *Ibid.* 43.   [7] *Ibid.* 44.
[8] *Ibid.* 43.   [9] Justin, *Dialogus cum Tryphone Judæo*, 41.
[10] *Ibid.* 44, 95.   [11] *Ibid.* 13.
[12] Justin, *Apologia I.*, 16.

been pointed out that these are mere words which have nothing at all corresponding to them in Justin's general system of thought. To him Christianity is essentially the belief, founded on the words of Christ, that God rewards righteousness with eternal life, and punishes wickedness with eternal punishment.[1]

The other Apologists mentioned above did not enter closely into the significance of Christ. They, also, maintained that true wisdom can be learnt only by divine revelation, from the prophets and Christ, whose teaching was identical with or a continuation of theirs.[2] But while Minucius Felix, like the Greek Apologists, perceives the teachings of the prophets and Christ to be divine truth,[3] he also says that Christian truth chiefly presents itself as the wisdom implanted by nature in every man,[4] and finds Christian ethics to be the expression of the Stoic.[5] That the moral interest is dominant in all the Apologists is the more natural on account of the calumnious accusations circulated against the Christians. Aristides, a philosopher of Athens, portrays Christianity by portraying Christian morality. The Christians " know and believe in God, the creator of heaven and earth, by whom all things consist, . . . and from whom they have received the commandments which they have written in their hearts, commandments which they keep in the hope and expectation of the world to come." [6]

Tertullian was the first Apologist after Justin who considered it necessary to give a detailed account of Christ as the incarnation of the Logos.[7] He repeatedly urges that the whole work of Christ is comprised in the death on the cross, and indeed that this death was the aim of his mission ; [8] we are redeemed by the blood of the Lord and the Lamb,[9] and such is the efficacy of this blood, that it not only cleanses men from sin and brings them out of darkness into light, but preserves them also in a state of purity if they continue to walk in the light.[10] He also speaks of a repentance which is justified by faith, *pœnitentiam ex fide justificatam*,[11] and of justification by faith without the ordi-

---

[1] M. von Engelhardt, *Das Christenthum Justins des Märtyrers* (Erlangen, 1878), p. 199 *sqq.*
[2] Athenagoras, *Legatio pro christianis*, 7 ; Tatian, *Oratio adversus Græcos*, 29 ; Theophilus, *Ad Autolycum*, i. 14.
[3] Minucius Felix, *Octavius*, 34.
[4] *Ibid.* 16.   [5] *Ibid.* 31 *sqq.*   [6] Aristides, *Apologia*, 15.
[7] Tertullian, *Apologeticus*, 21.
[8] *Idem*, *De baptismo*, 11 ; *idem*, *Adversus Marcionem*, iii. 8.
[9] *Idem*, *De pudicitia*, 6.   Cf. *idem*, *Ad uxorem*, ii. 3.
[10] *Idem*, *De pudicitia*, 19.
[11] *Idem*, *Adversus Marcionem*, iv. 18.

nances of the law.[1] But in Tertullian the mystic doctrine of
salvation is rudimentary, and there are many inconsistencies
in his treatment both of dogmatic and moral questions. In
the first place he was a moralist and a legalist, who looked upon
the whole life of the Christian after baptism as strictly a life
under the law, its motives being hope of reward and fear of
punishment and the result determined purely according to legal
standards. He tells us that God keeps a register of our works,[2]
that we shall be restored to life to answer for them, whether
they be good or evil.[3] All good works are in general meritorious,
but merit in a peculiar sense attaches to such as go beyond the
strict demands of God. Tertullian distinguishes between precepts and counsels, between *jussa* and *suasa*, in consequence
of expressions found in Paul's first epistle to the Corinthians,[4]
a distinction which had previously been made by Hermas.[5]
The retribution is strictly according to merit.[6] " The worshippers of God shall be clothed upon with a substance proper
for everlasting duration, and fixed in a perpetual union with
God ; but the profane and the hypocrite shall be doomed to
a lake of everflowing fire, and fuelled with incorruptibility from
the divine indefectible nature of that flame which torments
them."[7] But Tertullian also speaks of a kind of purgatory,
where, in the interval between death and the general resurrection, the souls of those who are destined to eternal happiness
undergo a purification from the stains which even the best
men contract during their lives.[8]

Of predestination we find no trace in Tertullian's writings.
When men sin the guilt is strictly and properly their own,[9] for
they possess by nature freedom of will.[10] " Some argue," he
says, " that whatever happens, happens by the will of God ;
for if God had not willed, it would not have happened. But
this is to strike at the root of all virtue, and to offer an apology
for every sin. The sophistry, moreover, of the argument is
not less glaring than its pernicious tendency. For if nothing
happens but what God wills, God wills the commission of crime ;
in other words, he wills what he forbids. . . . Man has also a
will, which ought always to coincide with the will of God, but
is often at variance with it."[11] But at the same time he says that

[1] *Ibid.* iv. 35.
[2] Tertullian, *Apologeticus*, 36.   [3] *Ibid.* 48.
[4] Tertullian, *Ad uxorem*, ii. 1 ; *1 Corinthians*, vii.
[5] *Supra*, p. 130.
[6] Tertullian, *Adversus gnosticos scorpiace*, 6 ; idem, *De patientia*, 10.
[7] *Idem, Apologeticus*, 48.   [8] *Idem, De anima*, 57 *sq.*
[9] *Idem, De monogamia*, 14.   [10] *Idem, De anima*, 21.
[11] *Idem, De exhortatione castitatis*, 2.

man's freedom of will is subject to the influence of divine grace.[1] Tertullian has often given a Stoic colouring to Christian ethics and rules of life.

The influence of Paul shows itself clearly in Irenæus, although it was by no means so great as the frequency of his citations from him might suggest.[2] He adopted from Paul the thought that Christ's real work of salvation consists in his death on the cross,[3] but his moralistic teaching differed from Paul's. He applied the benefits of Christ's work to those who listen to the Saviour's words and adorn them with works of righteousness.[4] Christ is the teacher who reforms mankind by his preaching, calling upon them to direct their freedom of will to obedience to the divine commandment and thereby strengthening this freedom.[5] The fundamental knowledge of God and the moral law of nature were already revealed to man and placed in his heart by the creator.[6] He who preserves these, as the patriarchs did, is justified.[7] But the great majority of men wandered away from God ; hence he gave his people the written law, the decalogue, though it contains nothing else than the moral law of nature, which had fallen in oblivion.[8] Christ did not abolish it, but extended and fulfilled it.[9] It is the same truth which we can learn from the prophets and again from Christ and the apostles. It is Christ that prohesied and appeared in the Old Testament ; he is the householder who produced both Old and New Testaments.[10]

In the Alexandrian school of catechists, which was modelled to some extent after the manner of the Academy of Plato, Greek philosophy was made to serve the purpose of Christian apologetics. The goodness of God and the responsibility of man are the central ideas. According to Clement of Alexandria, it is the will of God that he who obeys the commandments and repents his sins should be saved.[11] The law and the gospel are only parts of the same economy, in which the same God is revealed to mankind : " There is in truth one covenant of salvation, extending from the foundation of the world to our time, which, according to the difference of generations and

---

[1] Tertullian, De anima, 21.
[2] See J. Werner, Der Paulinism des Irenæus (Leipzig, 1889), p. 213 sq.
[3] Irenæus, Contra hæreses, ii. 20. 3.
[4] Ibid. iv. 36. 6.
[5] Ibid. v. 1. 1, iii. 23. 2, iii. 5. 3, iv. 24. 1.
[6] Ibid. iv. 13. 1, iv. 15. 1.　　　　[7] Ibid. iv. 16. 3.
[8] Ibid. iv. 16. 3.　　　　　　　　　[9] Ibid. iv. 13. 1.
[10] Ibid. iv. 2. 3, iv. 9. 1.
[11] Clement of Alexandria, Stromata, ii. 16 (Migne, Patrologiæ cursus, Ser. Græca, viii. 1012).

seasons, is supposed to be given in different forms." [1] Before
the coming of the Lord philosophy was necessary to the Greeks
for justification,[2] but it was much later than the philosophy of
the Hebrews, from which it was in fact borrowed.[3] Yet the
Greek philosophy, though it possessed the Logos—the source of
all the true knowledge to which man attains—is not sufficient
for salvation, which must be obtained through faith in Christ ;
for that which was hidden from former generations is now
revealed to mankind.[4] " The law was given to the Jews,
philosophy to the Greeks, until the advent of Christ, who was
to collect all men, Greeks and barbarians into one peculiar
righteous people through the teaching of faith." [5] The Son
of God is the saviour of all men ; " but especially, as the Apostle
says, of those who believe." [6]

Clement speaks of the redemption of man as effected by the
death of Christ,[7] but he really regards Christ as of no importance
to " gnostics "—who are wise men and not merely simple
believers—except as a teacher, who " taught the good life, in
order that afterwards as God he might grant everlasting life." [8]
God confers eternal salvation on those who work together with
him in knowledge and good actions ; the performance of his
commandments being in our power.[9] This freedom of will,
however, does not exclude the operation of divine grace : " by
grace we are saved," but not without good works.[10] Clement
also speaks of justification by faith, referring to the Epistle to
the Hebrews, which he ascribes to Paul.[11] He quotes almost
all the epistles of Paul, and yet there is not much of Paul in
his teaching. He defines faith as the rational assent of a soul
free to choose,[12] and, in another place, as obedience to the word.[13]
But knowledge is superior to faith,[14] through knowledge faith is
perfected ; [15] or the first saving change is from heathenism to
faith, the second is from faith to knowledge, which is perfected
in love.[16] If the choice were proposed to the gnostic either to

[1] *Ibid.* vi. 13 (Migne, ix. 328). [2] *Ibid.* i. 5 (Migne, viii. 717).
[3] *Ibid.* i. 14 (Migne, viii. 757). [4] *Ibid.* v. 13 (Migne, ix. 128).
[5] *Ibid.* vi. 17 (Migne, ix. 392). [6] *Ibid.* vi. 17 (Migne, ix. 393).
[7] Clement of Alexandria, *Pædagogus*, i. 5 (Migne, viii. 277), i. 6
(Migne, viii. 301), i. 11 (Migne, viii. 365), ii. 8 (Migne, viii. 488).
[8] *Idem, Cohortatio ad gentes*, 1 (Migne, viii. 61).
[9] *Idem, Stromata*, vii. 7 (Migne, ix. 469).
[10] *Ibid.* v. 1 (Migne, ix. 16).
[11] *Ibid.* ii. 4 (Migne, viii. 944).
[12] *Ibid.* v. 1 (Migne, ix. 12), v. 13 (Migne, ix. 128).
[13] Clement of Alexandria, *Pædagogus*, i. 13 (Migne, viii. 372).
[14] *Idem, Stromata*, vi. 14 (Migne, ix. 332).
[15] *Ibid.* vii. 10 (Migne, ix. 477).
[16] *Ibid.* vii. 10 (Migne, ix. 481).

know God or to obtain eternal salvation, he would choose the former. And he does not strive to attain to the knowledge of God for any consequences which will flow from the attainment : he does not do good for fame nor for reward.[1] Clement's strict moralism is also apparent in his sayings that different degrees of reward will be assigned to different degrees of virtue,[2] and that in inflicting punishment God does not wish to avenge himself but " has three things in view : to amend the transgressor, to admonish those who can be saved by example, and to prevent the injured party from becoming an object of contempt, and being thereby exposed to future injustice." [3] Sins committed after baptism are to be purged by public confession and profession of repentance ; and if the purifying discipline does not take place in this life, it must do so after death, being effected by fire, " not by a destructive, but a discriminating fire, pervading the soul which passes through it." [4]

Like Clement his great disciple Origen modified the gospel doctrine of the state of sinners after death, with its everlasting torments in the fire of hell. He assumed that the souls of the unpurified ones pass into a cleansing fire which is only temporary and figurative, simply consisting in the torments of conscience ; [5] and that in the end all the spirits in heaven and earth, nay even the demons, are purged and brought back to the Logos-Christ.[6] But he treated this doctrine as an esoteric one : " for the common man it is sufficient to know that the sinner is punished." [7] Origen regarded the two Testaments as the absolute reliable divine revelation, while he also recognised revelations of God in Greek philosophy ; [8] but he maintained that the Christianity which is fitted for the comprehension of the multitude is the best doctrine only in a relative sense, that the " common man " must be reformed by the prospect of rewards and punishments, and that the truth can be communicated to him only in veiled forms and images.[9] When faith is elevated to knowledge and clear vision, it is found that God rewards in justice and punishes in kindness.[10] No spirit can be saved without entering into fellowship with the Logos, who, as also the Apologists maintained, has been revealing himself from the

[1] Clement of Alexandria, Stromata, iv. 22 (Migne, viii. 1348).
[2] Ibid. iv. 6 (Migne, viii. 1248).
[3] Ibid. iv. 24 (Migne, viii. 1364).
[4] Ibid. vii. 6 (Migne, ix. 449).
[5] Origen, περὶ ἀρχῶν, ii. 10. 4 ; idem, Contra Celsum, v. 15, vi. 26.
[6] Idem, περὶ ἀρχῶν, i. 6. 1 sqq., iii. 6. 1 sqq.
[7] Idem, Contra Celsum, vi. 26.
[8] Ibid. ii. 335.
[9] Ibid. iii. 78 sq.
[10] Origen, περὶ ἀρχῶν, ii. 5. 3 sq.

beginning. In the lower stages this is effected through faith and sure conviction of the reality of a historical fact, the redeeming death of Christ, but in the higher stage it is accomplished through knowledge and love, which grasp the eternal essence of the Logos.[1] For this purpose the wise man requires a perfect, in other words, a divine teacher ; while " to know Christ crucified is the knowledge of babes." [2]

Porphyry says of Origen : " His outward life was that of a Christian and opposed to the law, but in regard to his views of things and of the Deity he thought like the Greeks, inasmuch as he introduced their ideas into the myths of other peoples " ; [3] and we can everywhere verify this observation from his works and particularly from the books written against Celsus. In the East the history of the Church during the succeeding centuries is the history of Origen's philosophy ; and among the theologians of ecclesiastical antiquity he was the most important and influential alongside of Augustine.

---

[1] C. Bigg, *The Christian Platonists of Alexandria* (Oxford, 1913), p. 211 *sq.*

[2] Origen, *Contra Celsum*, iii. 28, 61 ; *idem, Commentaria in Evangelium Joannis*, i. 20 *sqq.*

[3] Eusebius, *Historia ecclesiastica*, vi. 19.

CHAPTER VIII

LATER THEOLOGICAL DOCTRINES

IN the West Augustine dominated more or less the history of piety and dogma from the beginning of the fifth century to the eve of Reformation, and continued to exert his influence afterwards as well. His own reformation was essentially a Pauline reaction against the prevailing piety, though a Paulinism modified by popular Catholic elements.[1] Like Paul, Augustine experienced a sudden conversion, a momentary ecstacy in which he became absorbed in the love of God, and his mind underwent a complete change; he had been a slave of lust, as he describes himself, but was now set free from all propensity to sensual indulgence. The conversion took place when he was in his thirty-second year. He tells us in his ' Confessions ' that in Milan, where he was staying, he retired into a garden and, greatly agitated, cast himself down under a fig-tree, and, weeping in most bitter contrition of his heart, prayed to God to put an end to his uncleanness. Then he heard from a neighbouring house a voice, " as of a boy or girl," singing and repeating the words, " *Tolle lege* " (" take up and read "). " Instantly," he writes, " with a changed countenance, I began to think most intently, whether boys in any kind of game used to sing such a phrase ; nor could I remember ever to have heard the like. So checking the torrent of my tears, I arose, interpreting it to no other than a divine command, to open the book and read the first chapter I should find. . . . I seized, opened, and in silence read the passage upon which my eyes first fell : ' Let us walk honestly, as in the day ; not in rioting and drunkenness, not in chambering and wantonness, not in strife and envying ; but put ye on the Lord Jesus Christ, and make not provision for the flesh, to fulfil the lusts thereof ' " (*Romans* xiii. 13 *sq.*). Then his friend Alypius, who was with him, disclosed to him the following passage, " Him that is weak in the faith receive " (*ibid.* xiv. 1).[2]

Next to the conversion of Paul, there has been no other conversion fraught with so far-reaching consequences in the

[1] *Cf.* H. Reuter, *Augustinische Studien* (Gotha, 1887), p. 494 *sqq.*
[2] Augustine, *Confessiones*, viii. 12.

history of Christianity as that of Augustine. In innumerable passages Augustine, like Paul, extols faith as the element in which the soul lives, as the beginning, middle, and end of piety. But to him the object of the faith which is necessary for salvation was the truth guaranteed by the Catholic Church, which he regarded as infallible in consequence of its authority as based on apostolicity.[1] Augustine had forced his way through scepticism to the truth of the Church and looked upon the latter as the rock on which his faith was founded. It constitutes a real unity with Christ, so that all Catholics are " the true members of his body " ; whereas heretics and schismatics " are cut off from this body," [2] and consequently cannot be saved. At the same time, faith is only a preliminary condition of salvation. We must not fancy that faith by itself protects from future judgment : it is only the faith that works in love, faith and work, that does so.[3] Faith and hope without love are useless; it is love that decides the measure of goodness possessed by a man.[4] According to Augustine, faith, love, and merit are successive steps in the way to final salvation ; and this became the view of the Catholic Church.

But while the conception of merits, which had been current in the Church from the days of Tertullian [5] and Cyprian [6] was accepted by Augustine, he reconciled this principle—as also Ambrose had done [7]—with the doctrine of grace, by teaching that God crowned his own gifts in crowning our merits.[8] A man is justified not by the merits of his own deeds, but by free grace. Faith and love and merits are all God's gifts ; [9] and ' no one is saved except by undeserved mercy, and no one condemned except by a deserved judgment." [10] As Paul taught in his epistle to the Romans, the elect are saved because God, in virtue of his eternal decree of salvation, has predestinated, chosen, called, justified, sanctified, and preserved them.[11] He would not have been blamed if he had redeemed no one after Adam's fall ; so neither is he to be blamed if in his mercy he redeems only a few, that none may boast of his own merits. God's will is expressed in the case of the lost as much as in that of the saved : " in the very deed by which they opposed his

---

[1] *Idem, Contra epistolam Manichæ*, i. 5.
[2] *Idem, De civitate Dei*, xxi. 25.   [3] *Idem, Enchiridion*, 67 *sq.*
[4] *Ibid.* 117.   [5] *Supra*, p. 141.
[6] Cyprian, *De habitu virginum*, 23.
[7] Ambrose, *De viduis*, 12.
[8] Augustine, *De gratia et libero arbitrio*, 15 ; idem, *De gestis Pelagii*, 5 ; idem, *Epistola CXCIV*.
[9] *Idem, Enchiridion*, 30-2, 107.   [10] *Ibid.* 94.
[11] Augustine, *De prædestinatione sanctorum*, 17 (34).

will, his will regarding them was done." [1]   When Adam, in the
hope of becoming like God, transgressed his command not to
eat the fruit, all conceivable sins were compressed into his sin ;
and children are infected not only by Adam's sin, but also by
the sins of their parents, nay even unbaptised infants will
receive damnation.[2]   Indeed, their very birth is corrupt,
because their parents have produced them in sinful lust.[3]
Adam's fall was all the more dreadful as it was easy for him
to observe God's command and refrain from sin.   He might
have forborne one fruit when there were so many besides it,
and no lust then opposed his will.[4]   But the Fall of man was
the suicide of his free will, and since then he is subject to the
dreary necessity of being unable to refrain from sin.[5]   And
even inherited sin is enough for damnation.

Since all men are by nature children of wrath, and are
burdened both by original sin and their own sins, a mediator
was necessary, who should appease that wrath by presenting a
unique sacrifice.   That this was done constitutes the grace of
God through Jesus Christ, who was conceived not by the
libido matris, but by faith and therefore sinlessly.[6]   Christ, the
man who was deemed worthy to be assumed by God to form
one person with him, is the most splendid example of grace
given *gratis* and not according to merits.[7]   He submitted to
death, not from compulsion, but in order to let the devil receive
his rights.[8]   He became a sacrifice for sin, representing our sin
in the flesh in which he was crucified, " that in some way he
might die to sin, in dying to the flesh," and from the resurrection might seal our new life.[9]

In the future state there will be different degrees both of
felicity [10] and damnation.   Those of the latter will depend in
each case on the measure of sin ; those will have the mildest
punishment who have only original but not actual sin.[11]   It
is credible that a purifying fire exists for *believers* even after
death.[12]   In the intermediate state departed souls may obtain
mitigation through the mass and the alms of survivors in the
Church ; for there are many souls not good enough to be able
to dispense with this provision, and not bad enough not to be

[1] Agustine, *Enchiridion*, 98–100.
[2] Ibid. 45 ; Augustine, *De peccato originali*, 31.
[3] Idem, *Enchiridion*, 34, 46 ; idem, *De nuptiis et concupiscentia*, ii. 15.
[4] Idem, *De civitate Dei*, xiv. 12.   On the primitive state see *idem*,
De correptione et gratia, 28–33.
[5] Idem, *Enchiridion*, 30.
[6] Ibid. 34, 41.　　　[7] Ibid. 36.　　　[8] Ibid. 49.　　　[9] Ibid. 41.
[10] Augustine, *De civitate Dei*, xxii. 30.
[11] Idem, *Enchiridion*, 93.　　　　　　　　　[12] Ibid. 69.

benefited by it. What the Church does for the dead is not inconsistent with the sayings of Paul in his epistle to the Romans (xiv. 10) and in his second epistle to the Corinthians (v. 10). For those who are wholly good it is a thanksgiving, for those not altogether bad an atonement, for those entirely wicked it is resultless, but gives comfort to the survivors; nay, while it makes remission complete, it renders damnation more tolerable.[1] After the judgment there are only two states, though there are different grades in them. We must believe in the eternal duration of the pains of hell, although we may perhaps suppose that from time to time God lightens the punishment of the lost, or permits some sort of mitigation. " Death will continue without end, just as the collective eternal life of all saints will continue." [2]

From the moral point of view the relation between the grace of God and the faith, love, and merit of man in Augustine's doctrine of salvation is an absurdity. If the latter are gifts of God, he rewards man with eternal felicity for what he himself has given him ; and if man's freedom of will is restricted in such a way as to make him unable to refrain from sin, he might possibly reject the offer of the gift, but he certainly deserves no reward for refraining from doing so.

Augustine's idea that God has predestinated some persons to salvation and others to damnation takes us to the problem of free will and moral responsibility. We have seen that a moral emotion is a reactionary attitude of mind towards a person conceived as the cause of a certain mode of conduct, and that a moral judgment is consequently passed on him as the cause of it. But we impute a person's conduct to *him* only in so far as we consider it to be due, directly or indirectly, to his will. This is not the case if he acts under compulsion. In such circumstances even ordinary anger tends to cease ; as Seneca said, " Who but an unjust person can be angry with what is done under compulsion ? " [3] When a man's whole conduct is determined by an external power ruling over human affairs, a god or an all-powerful fate, he can obviously not be held responsible for what he does under the influence of such constraint ; the logical outcome of radical fatalism is a denial of all moral imputability and a rejection of all moral judgment. The same has been said to apply to determinism. Determinism has been confounded with fatalism, causation confounded with compulsion, the cause which determines the will being looked upon in the light of a constraining power outside the will. This

---

[1] *Ibid.* 110.   [2] *Ibid.* 111–13.   [3] Seneca, *De ira*, ii. 30.

is an obvious mistake.   While fatalism presupposes the existence of a person who is constrained by an outward power, determinism regards the person himself as in every respect a product of causes. It does not assume any part of his will to have existed previous to his formation by these causes ; his will cannot possibly be constrained by them because there is nothing to constrain, it is made by them.   When we say of a person that he is influenced by external circumstances or subdued by fate, we regard *him* as existing independently of that which influences or subdues him, we attribute to him a will, or character, which is acted upon from the outside.   He would have been different if he had lived under different conditions of life, or if fate had left him alone.   But how could we say that he would have been different if he had been the offspring of different parents ?   *He* would not have existed at all.   This is the pivot of the whole question. A moral emotion and a moral judgment presuppose the existence of a certain individual with an innate character, it is towards him that the emotion is felt, on him that the judgment is passed ; beyond that they cannot go.   In the very strictest sense of the term, the proper subject of moral judgment is the innate character,[1] and any succeeding change a person's character undergoes is imputable to *him* only in so far as it is caused by the character with which he was born.   The moral consciousness should, so far as possible, consider the influences to which his innate character has been subjected from the outside world, but it cannot consider the causes from which it sprang.   To do so would be foreign to its very nature.   The moral emotions are no more concerned with the origin of the innate character than the æsthetic emotions are concerned with the origin of the beautiful object: when we enjoy the music of a violin, we do not consider that it is produced by the rubbing of hairs from a horse-tail against the dried intestines of sheep.   In their capacity of retributive emotions, they are essentially directed towards sensitive and volitional entities conceived, not as uncaused themselves, but only as causes of pleasure or pain.

Nor can Augustine's conception of original sin satisfy even the most elementary moral claims.   His opinion of the enormity of Adam's sin shocked even a schoolman like Duns Scotus, who argued that the act to which he allowed himself to be led was not in its nature an immoral act, but only transgression of a command imposed for the purpose of testing, and that Adam accordingly sinned only indirectly against the command to love God, while at the same time he transgressed the law of neigh

---

[1] See my book *Ethical Relativity* (London, 1932), p. 177 *sqq.*

bourly love by overpassing, through his pliancy, the proper limit. His sin did not arise from uncontrolled self-love, but had its root in uncontrolled love for the partner associated with him, which, however, was not libidinous, since in the primitive state there was no *libido*.[1] The punishment for his offence was also enormous, and unjust beyond all bounds; it consisted not only in his own death but in the death of all other men, his descendants, who were supposed to be infected with his sin. And at the same time they had also, for no fault of theirs, to pay for the sin contracted by their parents producing them in sinful lust.

It would seem that from the Augustinian point of view the salvation of man might have been accomplished simply by the grace of God, without the assistance of the death of Christ; but Paul had written that " Christ died for all," and this had to be explained. Augustine, however, had no new explanation to offer. Origen, though considering that the crucified Christ was of no account for the gnostic, was the first to set up the theory that the devil had acquired a legal claim on men, and therefore to regard the death of Christ (or his soul) as a ransom paid to the devil. He associated this view with the notion of a deception practised on the devil. By his successful temptation the devil acquired such a right, and this right could not be destroyed, but only bought off. God offered the devil Christ's soul in exchange for the souls of men. But this proposal of exchange was insincere, as God knew that the devil could not keep hold of Christ's soul, because a sinless soul could not but cause him torture. The devil agreed to the bargain and was duped; hence Christ did not fall into the power of death and the devil, but overcame both.[2] This theory was widely accepted, by Augustine and Gregory the Great amongst others. The latter gives it in a very drastic form: the humanity of Christ was the bait, the fish—that is the devil—snapped at it, and was left hanging on the invisible hook, Christ's divinity.[3] But in Augustine we also find echoes of another thought, namely that God must be propitiated. This view, too, had been expressed by Origen, who was the first to introduce into the Church a theology of sacrifice or propitiation based on the death of Christ.[4]

While Augustine insisted on the eternal duration of the pains of hell, he moralised somewhat this doctrine by admitting

---

[1] K. Werner, *Johannes Duns Scotus* (Wien, 1881), p. 412.
[2] Harnack, *History of Dogma*, ii (London, 1896), p. 367 n. 1.
[3] Gregory the Great, *Moralia*, xxxiii. 7.
[4] Harnack, *op. cit.* ii. 307 n. 1, iii. (1897), p. 308.

different degrees of damnation. The notion of different degrees
of damnation and blessedness did not originate in him, but
seems to have been very common even before his days.[1] Nor
was his suggestion of a purifying fire after death a novel one.
The idea of a kind of purgatory is found in Tertullian,[2] and
Clement and Origen had assumed a purgatory in the shape of a
cleansing fire.[3] From the East this conception passed to
Ambrose, who established it in the West, after the way for it
had been prepared by Tertullian.[4] The scriptural proof was
Paul's first epistle to the Corinthians (iii. 13–15).

Augustinianism was accepted by the Western Church, though
" with the secret reservation that it was to be moulded by its
own mode of thought," when it did not harmonise with the
tendencies of the Church. Its greatest and most influential
champion was Thomas Aquinas, particularly with regard to
its doctrines of God, predestination, sin, and grace. The
turning from Realism to Nominalism was an anti-Augustinian
movement, but in the fourteenth century Bradwardine, on
whom Wyclif was dependent as a theologian, gave the impulse
to Augustinian reactions which accompanied the history of the
Church till the time of Staupnitz and Luther, and prepared the
way for the Reformation. It has been said that the work of
Augustine was finally brought to completion by Luther, since
Augustine, by going back to Paulinism, began the work of
breaking down and re-casting the ruling dogmatic tradition
and of restoring theology to faith. In Roman Catholicism the
Augustinian reaction of the fifteenth and sixteenth centuries
partly embodied itself in the decrees of Trent, but was fully
checked again, after a struggle for three hundred years, in the
nineteenth century.[5]

Augustine's doctrine that faith in the truth guaranteed by
the Catholic Church is necessary for salvation, was universally
accepted by the Church. It was admitted that a certain belief
or " unbelief " never is by itself a sufficient ground for damnation ; but Thomas Aquinas points out that there is yet a sin
of unbelief consisting in " contrary opposition to the faith
whereby one stands out against the hearing of the faith, or
even despises faith," and that, though such unbelief is in the
intellect, the cause of it is in the will. He adds that in those
who have heard nothing of the faith, unbelief has not the character of a sin, " but rather of a penalty, inasmuch as such

[1] Harnack, *op. cit.* iii. 188 n. 1.
[2] *Supra*, p. 141.   [3] *Supra*, p. 144.
[4] Harnack, *op. cit.* iii. 189 n. 1.
[5] *Ibid.* vi (1899), pp. 169, 170, 275.

ignorance of divine things is a consequence of the sin of our first parent." [1]   The sin of unbelief is greater than all sins of moral perversity.[2]

In spite of Thomas' adherence to Augustinianism we find in him a timid revision of it in a moralistic direction.   He makes an earnest endeavour to assert the sole efficacy of divine grace, but his line of statement takes ultimately a different direction. Although " without grace man cannot merit eternal life," [3] there must for justification co-operate a movement of free will, a movement of faith, and a hatred of sin [4]—in other words there is an intermingling of grace and self-action ;   and only then justification takes place.[5]   Man cannot acquire merit before God in the absolute sense of strict righteousness, but certainly in virtue of a benevolent arrangement of God.   " Meritorious work of man can be looked at in two ways : on the one hand in so far as it proceeds from free will, on the other hand in so far as it proceeds from the grace of the Holy Spirit." [6]   Thus, according to Thomas, the process of grace realises itself with the consent of free will, but this consent is at the same time an effect of grace.   Other theologians, such as Halesius, Bonaventura, and Scotus, yielded to a much more decided tendency to render the doctrine of grace less effectual by means of the doctrine of merit ;   and from the middle of the fourteenth century their views gained the ascendancy in the Church through the victorious conflicts of the Scotists against the Thomists.[7]   According to Scotus, merit always precedes grace.[8] The Council of Trent declared that " while God touches the heart of man by the illumination of the Holy Ghost, neither is man himself utterly without doing anything while he receives that inspiration, forasmuch as he is also able to reject it, yet is he not able, by his own free will, without the grace of God, to move himself unto justice in His sight." [9]

As to the election of grace, Thomas took over Augustine's doctrine of predestination in all its strictness : in virtue of his decree God determines some to be elected and others to be reprobated.[10]   Bonaventura, on the other hand, makes predestination dependent on prescience and limits the causation of God by teaching that another contingent cause is the free

---

[1] Thomas Aquinas, *Summa theologica*, ii.–ii. 10. 1 *sq.*
[2] *Ibid.* ii.–ii. 10. 3.   [3] *Ibid.* ii.–i. 109. 5.
[4] *Ibid.* ii.–i. 113. 3–5.   [5] *Ibid.* ii. 8. 113. 6.
[6] *Ibid.* ii.–i. 114. 3.   [7] Harnack, *op. cit.* vi. 300 *sq.*
[8] R. Seeberg, *Die Theologie des Johannes Duns Scotus* (Leipzig, 1900), p. 301 *sq.* ; Werner, *op. cit.* p. 418 *sqq.*
[9] *Canones et decreta Concilii Tridentini*, sess. vi. ch. 5.
[10] Thomas, *op. cit.* i. 23. 3.

will of man.[1] In the ninth century Rabanus had already declared that when God foresees evil, he predestines punishment for those who should not deserve to be redeemed by grace ; [2] and John of Damascus, whose doctrines became final in the Greek Church, taught that God, in virtue of his omniscience, knows everything from all eternity, and therefore assists by his grace those who will avail themselves of it.[3]

It was not easy for Thomas to construe the doctrine of free will, since in the doctrine of God he had applied throughout the thought of sole divine causality, even the consent of man's will being conceived as an effect of divine grace. But he wants free will in order to strengthen the Augustinian concept of merit. His doctrine of grace culminates in the " evangelical counsels." He points out, as others had done before him, that there are both precepts and counsels. A precept is compulsory, whereas a counsel is dependent on the option of him to whom it is given. Precepts are necessary to, and also sufficient for, eternal life, " but there ought to be counsels regarding those things by which man can attain the appointed end better and more readily." They consist in relinquishing entirely, so far as it is possible, the benefits of this world, such as the possession of outward goods, sexual pleasures, and the possession of honours ; and the adoption of even one of these counsels has a corresponding worth, e.g. when one gives alms to a poor man beyond what is obligatory, abstains from marriage for a long time for the sake of prayer, or does good to his enemies in excess of what is due, and so forth. The following of these counsels is a ground of merit in a still higher degree than the following of the commands, so that here in a pre-eminent way it holds good, that God gives eternal life to man, not merely in grace, but also by virtue of divine righteousness.[4] All merit, so far as it proceeds from the free will is de congruo, and so far as it proceeds from grace de condigno.[5] The doctrine that eternal salvation must be merited by good works is common to all the mediæval schoolmen, and the Council of Trent stamped it with its approval. It decreed that " to those who perform good works on to the end, and who hope in God, there is to be offered eternal life, both as grace mercifully promised to the sons of God through Christ Jesus, and as a reward to be faith-

---

[1] Bonaventura, Sententiæ, i. 40. 2. 1.
[2] Harnack, op. cit. v. (1898), p. 298.
[3] John of Damascus, De fide orthodoxa, ii. 29 sq., iv. 22.
[4] Thomas Aquinas, op. cit. ii.-i. 108. 4, ii.-ii. 184 sqq.
[5] F. Loofs, Leitfaden zum Studium der Dogmengeschichte (Halle a. S., 1906), p. 551 sq.

fully rendered, in terms of the promise of God himself, to their good works and merits." [1] Bellarmine briefly sums up the Roman Catholic point of view when he says : " The common opinion of all Catholics is that good works are truly and properly meritorious, and that not merely of some particular reward, but of eternal life itself." [2]

The distinction between command and counsel, between a higher and a lower Christian life, is in agreement with Paul's saying that the virgin state is superior to the married, but that he who marries has not sinned. [3] A similar distinction meets us in many later writers, such as Hermas, [4] Tertullian, [5] Cyprian, [6] Origen, [7] Ambrose, [8] Augustine. [9] It has certainly a solid foundation in our moral consciousness, in so far that a command implies the concept of duty, which is based on the emotion of moral disapproval, and a counsel implies the concept of goodness, which derives its origin from the emotion of moral approval. [10] But at the same time goodness and meritoriousness, the latter of which lays claim to praiseworthiness, are not identical with the superobligatory. Although the concept of duty has nothing to do with praise, we may nevertheless praise a person for doing his duty and even consider him worthy of praise. Practically, no doubt, there is a general antagonism between duty and merit. We praise, and especially we regard as deserving praise, only what is above the average, and we censure what is below it. But although thus most acts that are deemed meritorious fall outside the ordinary limits of duty as roughly drawn by the popular mind, we are, on the other hand, often disposed to attribute merit to a man on account of an act which from a strict point of view is his duty, but a duty that most people in the same circumstances would have left undischarged. This shows that the antagonism between duty and merit is not absolute. And in the concept of merit *per se* no such antagonism is involved.

But while " meritorious " is not identical with " superobligatory," it is obvious that if a course of conduct which is not regarded as a duty is held to be meritorious, it is *eo ipso*

[1] *Canones et decreta Concilii Tridentini*, sess. vi. ch. 16.
[2] R. Bellarmine, *De justificatione*, v. 1.
[3] *1 Corinthians* vii. 25 *sqq.*
[4] Hermas, *Pastor*, ii. 4. 4, iii. 5. 3.
[5] Tertullian, *Ad uxorem*, i. 3, ii. 1 ; *Adversus Marcionem*, i. 29 ; *De monogamia*, 1 ; *De pudicitia*, 16.
[6] Cyprian, *De habitu virginum*, 23.
[7] Origen, *Commentarii in Epistolam B. Pauli ad Romanos*, iii. 3.
[8] Ambrose, *De officiis ministrorum*, i. 11 ; *idem, De viduis*, 12.
[9] Augustine, *Enchiridion*, 121, etc.   [10] See *supra*, pp. 16, 17, 19.

admitted that a man can do more than his duty. This is denied both by those who derive goodness from duty and consider that what is good is what ought to be done, and by those who derive duty from goodness and consider that everybody ought to do the best he is able to do. Duty, which is the minimum of morality, in so far that it implies that the opposite mode of conduct is wrong, is identified with the supreme moral ideal, which requires the best possible conduct for its realisation. This rigorism is not supported by our practical moral judgments, but is a mere theory, which may be traced either to the direct or indirect influence of Protestant theology with its denial of all works of supererogation, or to the endeavour of normative moralists to preach the most elevated kind of morality they can conceive. For my own part I do not see how such a doctrine could serve any useful purpose at all. The recognition of a " superobligatory " does not lower the moral ideal, but on the contrary tends to raise it ; and at the same time it makes it more possible to vindicate the moral law and administer it more strictly. It is nowadays a recognised principle in legislation that a law loses much of its weight if it cannot be enforced. If the realisation of the highest moral ideal is commanded by a moral law, such a law will always remain a dead letter, and morality will gain nothing. It seems to me that far above the anxious effort to fulfil the commandments of duty stands the free and lofty aspiration to live up to an ideal, which, unattainable as it may be, threatens neither with blame nor remorse him who fails to reach its summits. Does not experience show that those whose minds are constantly prepossessed with thoughts of duty are apt to become inhuman, intolerant, indeed intolerable ?

At the same time there are in the Roman Catholic doctrine of merit certain very objectionable features. It implies that a good deed stands in the same relation to a bad deed as a claim to a debt ; that the claim is made on the same person to whom the debt is due, that is God, even though it only be by his mercy ; and that the debt consequently may be compensated for in the same way as the infliction of a loss or damage may be compensated for by the payment of an indemnity. This doctrine of reparation comes inevitably to attach badness and goodness to external acts rather than to mental facts. No reparation can be given for badness. It can only be forgiven, and moral forgiveness can be granted only on condition that the agent's mind has undergone a radical alteration for the better, that the badness of the will has given way to repentance. This point was certainly not overlooked by the Catholic moralists, but even the most ardent apology cannot explain away the idea of reparation in the Catholic doctrine of the justification of man.[1] Penance consists of contrition, confession, and satisfaction, and contrition itself is chiefly " a willingness to compensate." [2] Moreover, vicarious efficacy is attributed to good deeds. It is said that Chri t has done more by his suffering than was required for redemption, and that even many saints have acquired for themselves merit which God's grace rewards. This surplus merit, or " treasury of supererogatory works," must necessarily fall to the benefit of the Church, since neither Christ nor the saints can derive further advantage from it. The theory of a treasury of merits which the Church administers and from which indemnifications can be derived for the sins of others was first adopted by Halesius,[3] but owes its recognition within the Catholic Church chiefly to Thomas Aquinas.[4] It has been argued that, since we are all regenerated unto Christ by being washed in the same baptism, made partakers of the same sacraments, and especially of the same meat and drink, the body and blood of Christ, we are all members of the same body. " As, then, the foot does not perform its functions solely for itself, but also for the benefit of the eyes ; and as the eyes exercise their sight, not for their own, but for the common benefit of all the members ; so should works of satisfaction be deemed common to all the members of the Church." [5]

Augustine's doctrine of original sin was modified to some extent by Thomas. The sin which originated with Adam was loss of natural goodness, and accordingly led to rebellion of the lower parts of man against the higher, but the natural capacity to know and to will the good was only weakened, not eradicated ; that sin could remove it is unthinkable.[6] He thus emphasised the negative side of sin more strongly than Augustine. Yet he taught a stricter doctrine than Anselm, who really only accentuated the negative side, and began to waver even in regard to the character of guilt ; he rejected the damnation of infants.[7] To him Duns Scotus attached himself. He separated the question about concupiscence, which is natural, from the question about original sin; and there remains for it merely the being deprived of the supernatural good, which

[1] A. Manzoni, *Osservazioni sulla morale cattolica* (Firenze, 1887), p. 100.
[2] *The Catechism of the Council of Trent*, ii. 5. 22.
[3] Harnack, *op. cit.* vi. 263 n. 1.
[4] Thomas Aquinas, *op. cit.* iii. Supplementum, xxv. 1.
[5] *The Catechism of the Council of Trent*, ii. 5. 72.
[6] Thomas Aquinas, *op. cit.* ii.–i. 82 *sqq.*
[7] Anselm, *De conceptu virginali et originali peccato*, 27 *sq.*

certainly has a disturbing effect upon the nature of man, while however nothing is really lost of the natural goodness. The guilt of inherited sin, which is considerably reduced even in Thomas, appears in Duns quite insignificant. Even the consequences of sin are presented by him in another light : it has not attacked the very nature of man.[1] Scholasticism ultimately lost sight entirely of the Augustinian starting-point.[2] In its decree on original sin the Council of Trent rejects in strong terms Pelagianism, which denies that sin can be inherited, but the positive propositions are so shrewdly constructed that it is always *possible* still to connect with them a meaning that widely diverges from that of Augustine.[3]

Augustine's answer to the question how Christ's suffering and death can be a means of justification, namely, that it is a ransom paid to the devil, who has acquired a legal claim on men—a theory which had previously been set forth by Origen— was accepted by the most important of the Western Fathers. This, however, did not exclude the other thought that Christ's suffering and death constituted a sacrifice presented by him to God in order to propitiate him. But rival explanations were also suggested. Among these Anselm's theory in his *Cur Deus homo* deserves special consideration because it has given the impulse to permanent treatment of the subject and is still regarded in our own day and by evangelical theologians, too, as essentially a model ; both Luther and Calvin took over many of its presuppositions, and quite recently Principal Denney described *Cur Deus homo* as " the truest and greatest book on the Atonement that has ever been written." [4] It is an attempt to prove both the necessity of the appearing of the God-man and the necessity of his death. Anselm denies that the devil had obtained any claim upon us, since over against God he has absolutely no right.[5] Every rational creature owes to God entire subjection to his will. This is the only honour that God demands, and he who does not pay it dishonours God by withholding from him his own. This robbery he cannot tolerate, he must defend his honour ; hence every sinner must furnish a satisfaction.[6] But what can man give God which he was not already required to give him in any case ? He has nothing that he can render back for his sin,[7] and how much he would

[1] Seeberg, *op. cit.* p. 218.   [2] Harnack, *op. cit.* vi. 305.
[3] *Canones et decreta Concilii Tridentini*, sess. v. ' Decree concerning original sin.' *Cf.* Harnack, *op. cit.* vii. 58.
[4] J. Denney, *The Death of Christ* (London, etc., 1911), p. 295.
[5] Anselm, *Cur Deus homo*, i. 6 *sq.*
[6] *Ibid.* i. 11.   [7] *Ibid.* i. 20.

have to do ! Even the smallest disobedience entails an infinite
guilt,[1] and man has therefore to furnish an infinitely great
satisfaction.[2] The incapacity of human nature to furnish such
satisfaction can make no change on this law, which follows
from the honour of God.[3] So there remains only one solution :
there must be some one who shall pay to God for the sin of man
something greater than all that is apart from God, but since
there is nothing above all that is not God save God, no one is
able to make this satisfaction save God. Again, it cannot be
made by anybody save man ; consequently, it is necessary that
the God-man shall make it.[4] If the God-man surrenders his
life voluntarily to God, the satisfaction sought for is obtained ;
it must be his life, because only this he is not under obligation
to offer to God.[5] The worth of such a life as a satisfaction is
infinite ; the acceptance of the death of such a God-man is an
infinite good for God which far surpasses the loss by sin.[6] The
God-man acts for himself, by no means as the representative of
mankind ; and the Father must recompense him for that.[7]
Though nothing can be given to the Son, since he has all, it
would be outrageous to assume that the whole action of the
Son should remain without effect. Hence it is necessary that
it should be for the advantage of another, and if this is willed
by the son the Father cannot object, otherwise he would be
unjust. " But to whom more fittingly shall he impart the
fruit and recompense of his death than to those for whose
salvation, as true reason has taught us, he made himself man,
and to whom, as we have said, he gave in dying the example of
dying for righteousness' sake ? In vain surely shall they be
imitators of him, if they are not to be partakers of his merit.
Or whom shall he more justly make heirs of that which is due
to him, but which he does not need, . . . than his own parents
and brethren, whom he looks on, burdened in their poverty
with so many and so great debts, and languishing in the depths
of misery, that what they owe for their sin may be remitted to
them, and what, by reason of their sin, they lack, may be given
to them ? " [8] Anselm's theory does not guarantee to the
individual that he really becomes saved ; it aims rather at only
showing for all the possibility of their being saved. Whether
they shall be so depends " on the measure in which men come
to partake of so great grace, and on the degree in which they
live under it," that is, on how they fulfil the commandments of

---

[1] *Ibid.* i. 21.

[2] *Ibid.* i. 23.

[3] *Ibid.* i. 24.

[4] *Ibid.* ii. 6.

[5] *Ibid.* ii. 11.

[6] *Ibid.* ii. 14.

[7] *Ibid.* ii. 20 (19).

[8] *Ibid.* ii. 20 (19).

holy scripture.[1] This statement introduces a moral element into the theory, which it otherwise lacks. It is true that the suffering of Christ is not regarded as a vicarious punishment : Anselm did not say, like Athanasius, that justice was satisfied by his taking upon himself the punishment to be inflicted for our sins.[2] But at the same time the benefit he provided was to make us " partakers of his merit."

The meritoriousness of the work of Christ rapidly came to the front. It was strongly emphasised by the Lombard and Thomas Aquinas, both of whom combined various points of view which had been furnished by earlier theologians. By his passion, says Thomas, Christ merited *exaltatio*,[3] but as the exaltation could not be conferred upon him it passed over to the Church of which he is the head, " the head and the members are, as it were, one mystical person, and thus the satisfaction of Christ belongs to all believers just as to his own members."[4] Both Thomas and the Lombard are in agreement with Abelard's view that the death of Christ is a proof of love, which awakens counter-love.[5] The Lombard writes : " So great a pledge of love having been given to us, we are both moved and kindled to love God who did such great things for us ; and by this we are justified, that is, being loosed from our sins we are made just. The death of Christ therefore justifies us, inasmuch as through it charity is stirred up in our hearts."[6] Duns Scotus, again, and his school abandoned the principle of strict equivalence, which was fundamental to Anselm, in favour of a theory which makes the efficacy of the atonement depend upon the gracious acceptance of God rather than upon its own inherent merit constituting it an exact equivalent for the punishment deserved by man.[7] Neither Catholics nor Protestants, however, have maintained that the self-sacrifice of Christ acts automatically as a means of salvation. To the Catholic theologian the atonement only forms the basis of the whole system of ecclesiastical machinery upon which man's salvation is supposed to depend. To the Protestant it is his warrant for rejecting this machinery as superfluous. Through the atonement of Christ the price of man's redemption has been paid once for all, but he can appropriate its benefits only through faith.[8]

[1] Anselm, *Cur Deus homo*, ii. 20 (19).
[2] Athanasius, *Adversus Arianos*, i. 60.
[3] Thomas Aquinas, *op. cit.* iii. 49. 6.
[4] *Ibid.* iii. 48. 2.   [5] Harnack, *op. cit.* vi. 78, 79, 81.
[6] Peter the Lombard, *Sententiæ*, iii. 19. 1.
[7] Seeberg, *op. cit.* p. 284 *sqq.*
[8] *Cf.* W. A. Brown, ' Expiation and Atonement (Christian),' in Hastings, *Encyclopædia of Religion and Ethics*, v (1912), p. 645.

That the suffering and death of Christ was a propitiatory substitutionary sacrifice, or a penalty of guilt in the interests of God, has undoubtedly remained the most popular view. In Anglican Article II. it is said that the Son of God " suffered, was crucified, dead and buried, to reconcile his Father to us, and to be a sacrifice, not only for original guilt, but also for all actual sins of men." A recent writer asserts that the teaching of the New Testament is faithfully expressed in the popular hymn :

> Bearing shame and scoffing rude,
> In my place condemned He stood ;
> Sealed my pardon with His blood :
> Hallelujah ! what a Saviour.[1]

Yet there is an increasing number of disbelievers even within the Church. An English theologian asks if the theory that Jesus, by his propitiatory sacrifice and by his resurrection, has restored to mankind what had been lost by the Fall can be held to-day by people of education ; and he adds, " It is doubtful even if those who profess to believe in propitiatory sacrifice really do believe in it ; and how rapidly they are diminishing in numbers." [2] The bishop of Birmingham writes that " in some way or another the fact of the atonement must be preserved," but that " we can no longer maintain the Evangelical tradition which uses for the atonement a substitutionary theory of the death of Christ " ; [3] yet he does not tell us what other explanation should take its place. In the last century a Swedish bishop, the famous poet Esaias Tegnér, called the doctrine of a blood-atonement " a butcher's idea, blasphemous against both God and reason." [4] While the older Evangelicals hold a particularly crude doctrine of the atonement, the liberal modern ones, though they have retained a full recognition of Christ's work of redemption, have deliberately discouraged attempts to inquire too closely into the manner in which it was accomplished.[5] The authorities of the Church of England even declared in their Report (in spite of Article II.) that " the Church as a whole has never formally accepted any particular explanation of the fact." [6] It has been argued that there never

---

[1] H. E. Guillebaud, *Why the Cross ?* (London, 1937), p. 181.
[2] H. D. A. Major, ' Towards Prayer Book Revision,' in *The Church and the Twentieth Century*, edited by G. L. Harvey (London, 1930), p. 74.
[3] The bishop of Birmingham (Dr. E. W. Barnes), ' Foreword,' in *The Church and the Twentieth Century*, p. x.
[4] E. Tegnér, *Samlade skrifter*, iii (Stockholm, 1920), p. 447.
[5] L. Elliott Binns, ' Evangelicalism in the Twentieth Century,' in *The Church and the Twentieth Century*, p. 369.
[6] *Doctrine in the Church of England* (London, 1938), p. 90.

can be a single theory of the atonement, since " God's plan of
salvation is too vast to be embraced in any one single explanation." [1]   But though none of the many theories of the atonement is held finally satisfactory, there is said to be neither
doubt nor difficulty about the fact itself, the saving power of
the cross of Christ being a matter of common Christian experience.[2]   It is alleged that we " perceive " the effect of the
cross,[3] and that what took place at Calvary " can be appre-
hended only by faith." [4]   But faith is no testimony.   Dr.
Murray maintains that " Our Lord's own words . . . leave no
doubt that with clear consciousness and deliberate intent in
accordance with the prophetic anticipation (Isaiah liii. 10–12),[5]
He accepted the position as victim on behalf of His people with
the institution of the sin-offering prefigured." [6]   But modern
scholars have denied that Jesus ever spoke such words ; [7] and
even Mr. Thornton, who attaches much importance to Old
Testament Servant-prophecies as a basis for the theology of
the atonement, does not seem quite convinced that they are
mistaken.   He writes, however, that " even if our Lord never
spoke such words as those in Mark x. 45, there still remains the
possibility that His life and teaching as a whole, crowned by the
death and resurrection, are most fitly interpreted in the light
of the Servant passages." [8]   But according to the Hebrew text
Israel was smitten for its own iniquities, not for the iniquities
of other peoples ; and, as Dujardin remarks, the idea of Israel
atoning for the sins of the world was impossible before the
Christian era.[9]   Dean Rashdall maintains that " the only
doctrine of the atonement which can with any certainty, or
even with any probability, be traced back to our Lord himself
is the simple doctrine that his death, like his life, was one of
self-sacrifice for his followers." [10]

From the moral point of view the doctrines of salvation

[1] P. Green, *Our Lord and Saviour* (London, 1928), p. 78.   See also
J. G. Riddell, *Why did Jesus die ?* (London, 1938), p. 60 *sq.*
[2] Riddell, *op. cit.* p. 63 ; J. Dickie, *The Organism of Christian Truth*
(London, *s.d.*), p. 43 ; H. R. Mackintosh, *The Christian Experience of
Forgiveness* (London, 1927), p. 194.
[3] Mackintosh, *op. cit.* p. 195.
[4] Riddell, *op. cit.* p. 31.   [5] See *supra*, p. 115.
[6] J. O. F. Murray, *The Obedience of the Cross* (London, 1938), p. 36.
[7] *Supra*, p. 115.
[8] L. S. Thornton, *The Doctrine of the Atonement* (London, 1937),
p. 55.
[9] É. Dujardin, *The Source of the Christian Tradition* (London, 1911),
p. 189.
[10] H. Rashdall, *The Idea of Atonement in Christian Theology* (London,
1919), p. 45.

through the suffering and death of Jesus and the various explanations given of it make a distressing chapter in the history of Christian dogma. All of them imply the idea of vicarious merit or of vicarious punishment or of both. Yet moral justification is claimed for them. In the Report of the Archbishops' Commission we are told that " the Cross is a satisfaction for sin so far as the moral order of the universe makes it impossible that human souls should be redeemed from sin except at a cost. . . . The redeeming love of God, through the life of Jesus Christ sacrificially offered in death upon the Cross, acted with cleansing power upon a sin-stained world, and so enables us to be cleansed." [1] So also Harnack refers to the demand that sin must be expiated by suffering, and to the conviction that the expiation may be effected by the suffering of a righteous person. " No reflection of the ' reason,' no deliberation of the ' intelligence,' " he says, " will ever be able to expunge from the moral ideas of mankind the conviction that injustice and sin deserve to be punished, and that everywhere that the just man suffers, an atonement is made which puts us to shame and purifies us. It is a conviction which is impenetrable." [2] An idea of this kind is found among children. M. Piaget has shown that they accept the equity of collective punishment if the guilty one is unknown, not in the least because the group is responsible as a whole for the fault of one of its members, but simply because there must be punishment at all costs. [3]

To me it seems that even the slightest degree of reflection should show how incompatible the infliction of punishment on an innocent person in place of the culprit is with the very nature of our moral consciousness, moral indignation being a hostile attitude of mind towards a living being conceived as a cause of pain. Dean Inge says that " it may be worth while to distinguish between vicarious punishment, which is immoral, and vicarious suffering, which love is willing to endure." [4] Other writers [5] refer to John's saying, " Greater love hath no man than this, that a man lay down his life for his friends." [6] This is quite true, but does not explain why the self-sacrifice of

[1] *Doctrine in the Church of England*, p. 92 *sq.*
[2] A. Harnack, *What is Christianity?* (London, 1904), p. 162.
[3] J. Piaget, *Le jugement moral chez l'enfant* (Paris, 1932), p. 279.
[4] W. R. Inge, *Christian Ethics and Moral Problems* (London, 1932), p. 54 *sq.*
[5] *E.g.* the bishop of London (Dr. Winnington Ingram), ' Are we forgetting the Message of the Cross ? ' in the *Daily Mail*, April 14, 1938 ; R. Fangen, *Paulus* (Stockholm, 1937), p. 64.
[6] *John* xv. 13.

Christ makes amends for the sins of mankind. Our moral consciousness does not admit that the execution of an innocent person can cancel the guilt of a criminal, and, in addition, finds it outrageous that, as in the present case, the sinner, in order to benefit by the death of the innocent person, must have faith in such an order of things established by a righteous God. It sounds like mockery to be told that " the righteousness of God may be discerned in the death of Christ." [1] The Socinians argued that the doctrine of vicarious suffering blunts the conscience and leads easily to moral laxity ; [2] and the doctrine of vicarious merit may certainly have a similar effect.

The modifications of Augustinianism which took place in Scholasticism had generally a moralistic tendency. The ethical interest is particularly predominant in Abelard, who was sure that what answers to the moral law also is holy and good before God, and consequently endeavoured to show that in the doctrinal system of the Church the principles of morality shall have as much justice done to them as the fundamental theological speculations on nature. [3] That his success in carrying conviction was small is not to be wondered at ; his contemporaries felt repelled by many of his propositions. They certainly suffered from contradictions ; but above all, the conflict between morality and the religion of the Church was too great to allow any considerable modifications of her dogmas or their interpretations.

The Reformation implied an Augustinian reaction and a restoration of Paulinism. It substituted the Bible for the authority of the Church, and the kernel and marrow of the Bible was in particular the epistles of Paul. Luther passed through a crisis of the same kind as that which Paul had experienced in his day. It implied the conviction that in faith in Jesus he had a gracious God, who had revealed himself in the gospel, that is, in the incarnated, crucified, and risen Christ. We are justified by faith alone, this justification is the forgiveness of sins, [4] and the faith through which it takes place should make the believer feel an absolute confidence in his own personal and complete salvation. [5] Sometimes he pushes his insistence upon faith, and faith only, to the point of disparaging repentance.

---

[1] Riddell, *op. cit.* p. 99.

[2] *The Racovian Catechism* (London, 1818), v. 8, p. 306.

[3] Harnack, *History of Dogma*, vi. 40 n.

[4] K. Holl, *Gesammelte Aufsätze zur Kirchengeschichte*, i (Tübingen, 1927), pp. 69, 71, 75, 117.

[5] Luther, ' Operationis in Psalmos, 1519-1521,' in *Werke*, v (Weimar, 1892), p. 395.

" Priests," he declares, " err and are mad, not to absolve people unless they are contrite, and they ask, ' Son, do you grieve for your sins ? ' " They should only say, " Dost thou believe ? Believe and have confidence." " Thus Christ said to the sinful woman, ' Thy sins are forgiven thee. I absolve thee, go in peace, because thou believest.' " [1]   The Schoolmen had developed the hint contained in Paul's expression " faith working by love," and distinguished between an " unformed " faith—a mere intellectual belief—and a " formed " faith, which includes love, and which alone justifies and saves. But to Luther the doctrine that we are saved by faith formed by charity is an abominable blasphemy.[2] " We can be saved without charity, . . . but not without pure doctrine and faith." [3] " No good work can profit an unbeliever to justification and salvation ; and, on the other hand, no evil work makes him an evil and condemned person, but that unbelief, which makes the person and the tree bad, makes his works evil and condemned. Wherefore, when any man is made good or bad, this does not arise from his works, but from his faith or unbelief." [4] But Luther even denied that we can do any good work at all. Among the famous ninety-five theses which he nailed on the church door of Wittenberg there were the assertions that " the just man sins in every good work," and that " our best work is a venial sin." But in his explanation the last thesis is withdrawn in favour of the assertion that every good work of the just man is a mortal sin if it were judged by the judgment of God.[5] Both Augustine and the Schoolmen had taught that after justification, with the assistance of divine grace and of the divine spirit, the Christian really did become capable of good works, well-pleasing to God, and this was just what Luther in his more dogmatic moments categorically denied.[6] Yet in his more moderate statements he can declare that the sanctifying grace given after the man has been justified by faith enables him to do good works. He writes : " If thou believest, good works will neces-

[1] *Idem*, ' De sacerdotum dignitate Sermo,' *ibid.* iv (Weimar, 1886), p. 658. See also ' Assertio omnium articulorum M. Lutheri per bullam Leonis novissimam damnatorum, 1520,' *ibid.* vii (Weimar, 1897), p. 119.
[2] *Idem*, ' In epistolam S. Pauli ad Galatas Commentarius [1531], 1535,' *ibid.* xl. i (Weimar, 1911), p. 254.
[3] *Ibid.* xl. ii (Weimar, 1914), p. 51.
[4] *Idem*, ' Von der Freiheit eines Christenmenschen. 1520,' *ibid.* vii. Weimar, 1897), p. 32 *sq.*
[5] *Idem*, ' Assertio omnium articulorum M. Lutheri per bullam Leonis X. novissimam damnatorum,' *ibid.* vii (Weimar, 1897), pp. 136, 38 *sq.*
[6] *Cf.* H. Rashdall, *The Idea of Atonement in Christian Theology* (London, 1919), p. 402.

sarily follow thy faith," [1] and even : " He believeth not truly if works of charity follow not his faith." [2] At the same time the good works which are done when the man has been justified are not really done by him but by God. " To sleep and to do nothing is the work of Christians," he exclaims in a sermon on Jacob's dream.[3] As Luther grew older, his conception of faith became more and more intellectual, till at last it comprised little beyond the assent of mind to certain articles of an orthodox creed.[4] " One little point of doctrine," he says, " is of more value than heaven and earth ; therefore we do not suffer it (*i.e.* doctrine) to be injured in the smallest particular. But at errors of life we may very well connive." [5]

Luther took over the Augustinian doctrine of the entire incapacity of fallen man and of the bondage of the will. True, he describes Paul's teaching of the derivation of human sin from Adam as " a laughable doctrine," and asks what can be more ridiculous than the fact that Adam, by taking a bite of an apple, put all men, to the very end of the world, into the power of death.[6] But he knows how to answer charges of this kind. " It is," he says, " a quality of faith that it wrings the neck of reason and strangles the beast, which else the whole world, with all creatures, could not strangle. But how ? It holds to God's Word : lets it be right and true, no matter how foolish and impossible it sounds." [7] The Fall itself and the penalties which it brought with it were predestined. Luther accepted Augustine's doctrine of predestination.

Although Luther would not hear of any human merit, he believed in the merit of Christ, who, as the Confession of Augsburg put it, " suffered and died that he might reconcile the Father to us, and be a sacrifice, not only for original guilt, but also for all actual sins of men." [8] Christ's righteousness is

[1] Luther, ' Predigten des Jahres 1523,' in *Werke*, xii (Weimar, 1891), p. 559.

[2] *Idem*, ' In epistolam S. Pauli ad Galatas Commentarius,' *ibid.* xl. ii (Weimar, 1914), p. 37.

[3] *Idem*, ' Predigten Luthers gesammelt von Joh. Poliander 1519–1521,' *ibid.* ix (Weimar, 1893), p. 407.

[4] See C. Beard, *The Reformation of the Sixteenth Century* (London, 1885), p. 132, and the references.

[5] Luther, ' In epistolam S. Pauli ad Galatas Commentarius,' in *Werke*, xl. ii (Weimar, 1914), p. 52.

[6] *Idem*, ' Auslegung des 15. Capitels der I. Epistel St. Pauli an die Corinther, von der Auferstehung der Todten (anno 1534),' in *Sämtliche Schriften*, viii (Halle, 1742), col. 1240 *sq.*

[7] *Idem*, ' Ausführliche Erklärung der Epistel an die Galater,' *ibid.* viii. 2042.

[8] *Augustana Confessio*, art. 3.

imputed to us.[1] " Christ, that rich and pious husband, takes
as a wife a needy and impious harlot, redeeming her from all
her evils and supplying her with all his good things. It is
impossible now that her sins should destroy her, since they
have been laid upon Christ and swallowed up in him." [2] Our
faith in Christ makes his piety ours, and makes our sins his.
He was the greatest of all sinners, " because he assumed in his
body the sins we had committed, to make satisfaction for them
by his own blood." [3] " He was crucified and died for us, and
offered up our sins in his own body." [4] And Christ is represented as not merely dying instead of us, but also as keeping the
law instead of us. " This is the gospel . . . that the law has
been fulfilled, that is, by Christ, so that it is not necessary for
us to fulfil it, but only to adhere and be conformed to him who
fulfils it." [5] We meet with this idea also in the Reformed
Church. Jonathan Edwards says that " Christ's perfect
obedience shall be reckoned to our account, so that we shall
have the benefit of it, as though we had performed it ourselves." [6]
But Dean Rashdall is probably right in saying that Luther's
' insistence on correctness of doctrine and his contempt for
' mere morality ' would be difficult to parallel from any previous
writer." [7]

The other Reformers were, generally, in substantial agreement with Luther.[8] Zwingli likewise substituted the authority
of the Bible for the authority of the Church, and preached the
justification by faith alone. He denied, however, that he was
dependent on Luther (who was exactly of his own age), and
though he spoke in admiring language of him, he would not be
called a Lutheran. He says he took his doctrine from Scripture
and preached it before even he heard the name of Luther.[9] A dis-

---

[1] Luther, ' Sermo de triplici iusticia, 1518,' in *Werke*, ii (Weimar,
884), p. 44 *sq.*
[2] *Idem*, ' Von der Freiheit eines Christenmenschen. 1520,' *ibid.*
vii (Weimar, 1897), p. 26.
[3] *Idem*, ' In epistolam S. Pauli ad Galatas Commentarius,' *ibid.*
xl. i (Weimar, 1911), p. 433.
[4] *Ibid.* xl. i (Weimar, 1911), p. 224.
[5] *Idem*, ' Sermo Dominica II. Adventus ' (1516), in *Werke*, i (Weimar,
883), p. 105.
[6] J. Edwards, ' Justification by Faith Alone,' in *Works*, vi (London,
817), p. 257.
[7] Rashdall, *op. cit.* p. 414.
[8] Melanchthon, who may be taken in general as the systematiser
of Luther's thought, however, did not accept his doctrine of predestination (R. Bring, *Förhållandet mellan tro och gärning inom luthersk teologi
Acta Academiæ Aboensis*, ix. Åbo, 1934]), p. 94 *sqq.*
[9] Zwingli, *Werke*, i (Zürich, 1828), p. 253 *sqq.*

tinction has been drawn between their attitudes towards Scripture : Luther, it is said, was willing to abide by any existing doctrine or usage which he did not find expressly forbidden by it, whereas Zwingli demanded distinct warrant of it for whatever he was willing to allow. But the latter took a wider view of what Scripture was. He was more biblical than Pauline : he did not so exclusively as Luther take his gospel from Paul's epistles and then read it into the whole Bible. It is significant that the Epistle to the Romans finds no place in his scheme of scriptural instruction.[1] He was much more than Luther a humanist, and more a moralist as well. He writes, for instance, that the Christian life is " an innocent life after Christ's pattern "; [2] that " we are not born that we may live to ourselves, but that we may be all things to all men "; [3] that " it is the part of a Christian man not to talk magnificently of doctrines, but always with God to do great and hard things." [4] And his more reasonable view of the sacraments [5] caused an irreparable breach between him and Luther, which became a rock on which Reformation was wrecked.

Calvin was a full generation younger than Luther and Zwingli. He is the only one of the great Reformers who can justly be called international. In Switzerland the influence of Zwingli paled before that of his countryman, the Genevese Reformer. Calvinism soon found a footing even in Germany especially in the Palatinate. In France it was the religion of the Huguenots. In its strength the Dutch Republic was sustained, and the American Republic was founded. It partly turned the current of the English Reformation in the direction of Puritanism. It made Scotland what it is. Its leading ideas are generally ideas which Zwingli had already put forward in a less precise and systematic form ; but in his great work, the ' Institution of the Christian Religion,' he gathered up all the diverse threads of the new thought and wove them into a homogeneous system. In his appeal from the authority of the Church to Scripture he took the Bible much more as a whole than Luther did. He was full of a Hebrew spirit, and used references to the Old Testament to modify the too great humanity of the gospel. This accounts for the fact that among the English Puritans of the seventeenth century the Mosaic

---

[1] Beard, *op. cit.* p. 239 *sq.*

[2] Zwingli, ' De vera et falsa religione commentarius,' in *Opera*, ii (Turici, 1832), p. 201.

[3] *Idem*, ' Quo pacto adolescentes formandi,' in *Opera*, iv (Turici 1841), p. 155.

[4] *Ibid.* in *Opera*, iv. 158.   [5] *Infra*, pp. 196, 197, 200

legislation and the Jewish kingdom and church took a place to which the earlier history of Christianity offers no parallel. Like Luther, Calvin was an Augustinian in assuming the absolute foreknowledge and determining power of God, the servitude of the human will, the corruption and incapacity of man's nature. To him, however, the main thing was not the sinner's personal relation to Christ and his appropriation of the Saviour's work, but the awful omnipotence of the Divine decree fixing the unalterable succession of events, shutting out all co-operation of the human will. God chose certain individuals as his elect, predestining them to salvation from eternity by " his gratuitous mercy, totally irrespective of human merit," and consigned the remainder to eternal damnation, by " a just and irreprehensible, but incomprehensible judgment." [1] To apply earthly standards of justice to God's sovereign decrees is meaningless and an insult to his majesty, since he and he alone is free, subject to no law. To assume that human merit and guilt play a part in determining the destiny of man would be to think of God's absolutely free decrees, which have been settled from eternity, as subject to change by human influence, an impossible contradiction. And since his decrees cannot change, it is as impossible for those to whom his grace has been granted to lose it, as it is impossible to attain it for those to whom he has denied it. [2]

It might seem that such ideas must be fatal to morals and produce slackness of will. Yet we find that Calvinists have been among the most strenuous of men : Calvin himself, John Knox, William of Nassau, Oliver Cromwell, and many others. This is congruous with the fact that " no true Calvinist, save one perhaps here and there, ever believes that he is finally reprobate ; . . . on the contrary, he feels himself to be an instrument of the Omnipotent Will, and bends to whatever toil he undertakes in the unshakable conviction that he is on the side of God." [3] Indeed, it is held to be an absolute duty to consider oneself chosen, and to combat all doubts as temptations of the devil, since lack of self-confidence is the result of insufficient faith, hence of imperfect grace. [4] In order to attain such self-confidence, intense worldly activity, which serves to increase the glory of God, is recommended as the most suitable means. However useless good works might be as a means of attaining salvation, nevertheless they are indispensable as a sign of election. They are the technical means, not of pur-

---

[1] Calvin, *Institutio Christianæ religionis*, iii. 21. 7.
[2] See Max Weber, *Gesammelte Aufsätze zur Religionssoziologie*, i (Tübingen, 1922), p. 92 *sq*.
[3] Beard, *op. cit.* p. 257.   [4] Weber, *op. cit.* i. 105.

chasing salvation, but of getting rid of the fear of damnation.[1] Lutherans have again and again accused this line of thought of reversion to the Catholic doctrine of salvation by works. But the God of Calvinism did not demand of his believers an accumulation of individual good works to one's credit. The Calvinist's conviction of salvation depends rather on a systematic self-control, on a life of good works combined into a unified system. Max Weber observes that it is no accident that the name of Methodists stuck to the participants in the last great revival of Puritan ideas in the eighteenth century.[2]

Calvin's conception of God's law shows itself in the reign of terror which he established at Geneva. He laid down in the ' Institution ' that the Church has not the right of the sword to punish or restrain and knows of no punishment save exclusion from the Lord's Supper,[3] but he used the State as its instrument in punishing, for the honour of God, such acts as he assumed to be opposed to the Divine mind and purpose. They were many and varied, and the punishments inflicted were worse than Draconian. Adultery was repeatedly punished with death. Banishment, imprisonment, in some cases drowning, were penalties inflicted on unchastity. It was a punishable offence to wear clothes of forbidden stuff or make ; to give a feast to too many guests or of too many dishes ; to dance at a wedding. A child was beheaded for having struck father and mother.[4] Calvinism accounts for the strict home discipline among the English Puritans, with its liberal use of the rod. Its doctrine of original sin led to an utter distrust of child nature. Even Bunyan bids parents remember that children are cursed creatures, whose wills, being evil, are to be broken.[5]

The English Reformation has no name to show beside those of Luther, Zwingli, and Calvin. But during the reign of Edward VI. communications were opened with the Reformed Churches of the Continent, which resulted in a strong foreign influence of Protestant theologians, whose theology was more Calvinistic than Lutheran. It was when this influence was at its height that the English Prayer-book was shaped and the foundation laid of the Thirty-nine Articles. At the same time the English Reformation is characterised by the continuity of the Anglican Church which makes it impossible to fix the point where the old Church ends and the new begins ; she is the heir of the Catholic tradition as well as of the Reformation. The materials of the Prayer-book were quarried in the mines of English mediæval

---

[1] Weber, *op. cit.* i. 105, 106, 110.　　[2] *Ibid.* i. 111 *sqq.*
[3] Calvin, *op. cit.* iv. 11. 3.　　[4] Beard, *op. cit.* pp. 249, 250, 255.
[5] H. G. Wood, ' Puritanism,' in Hastings, *op. cit.* x (1918), p. 513.

piety, while the theology of the Thirty-nine Articles is that of the Confession of Augsburg. During the reign of Elizabeth there was a growing prevalence of Calvinistic theology. Puritanism, which was chiefly Calvinistic, spread in every diocese, and in the Nine Lambeth Articles of 1595 the main points of Calvinism were laid down with uncompromising rigidity.[1] They were never imposed upon the English Church, but in the following century Puritanism was still in the ascendant. It did not, however, establish itself as the controlling power in English religion. While Scotland was strongly Calvinistic and Presbyterian, the Puritans in England did not capture the Church, and were compelled to struggle hard for the right to follow their own consciences.[2]

Reformation was a protest not only against doctrines taught by the Catholic Church, but also against moral abuses practised in its name, such as benefactions being accepted in atonement for flagrant sin, and escape from purgatory being bought of wandering indulgence-mongers in any market-place. But at the same time the Reformers rejected the sound moral principles which were defiled by such corrupt practices. They denied altogether the value of good deeds, however sincere, and the different degrees of sinfulness of which the doctrine of purgatory was an expression ; and while they condemned to eternal damnation the most virtuous man who lacks the orthodox belief, which has nothing to do with morality, Luther, as we have seen, even went so far as to promise salvation to the greatest sinner who has such a belief. No wonder that such an attractive doctrine was taken advantage of. Von Döllinger has accumulated a vast mass of evidence to show that the immediate result of the Reformation was a dissolution of morals ; that the restraint of religion was relaxed, and that the characters of the Protestant preachers themselves were by no means without stain. Part of this evidence is drawn from the works of Catholic theologians, who were altogether out of harmony with the Reformation ; part from those of humanists who grew dissatisfied with it before they died ; part from the utterances of men who retreated from the Protestant into the Catholic ranks. All of them lay the blame of the neglect of morals upon the doctrine of justification by faith alone.[3] Evidence from such sources is certainly

[1] Beard, *op. cit.* p. 320.

[2] H. Balmforth ' Disrupta membra : Developments in England,' in *History of Christian Thought*, ed. by E. G. Selwyn (London, 1937), p. 154.

[3] J. J. I. von Döllinger, *Die Reformation, ihre Entwicklung und ihre Wirkungen im Umfange des Lutherischen Bekenntnisses* (Regensburg, 1846–8).

not above suspicion; but there remain a series of painful confessions of disappointment with the moral results of their work on the part of the Reformers themselves, and especially of Luther. " In passage after passage Luther declares that the last state of things was worse than the first; that vice of every kind had increased since the Reformation; that the nobles were greedy, the peasants brutal; that the corruption of morals in Wittenberg itself was so great that he contemplated shaking off the dust of his feet against it; that Christian liberality had altogether ceased to flow; and that the preachers were neither held in respect nor supported by the people. Towards the close of his life, these complaints became more bitter and more frequent. Sometimes the Devil is called in to account for so painful and perplexing a state of things. . . . But it is significant that Luther himself does not altogether acquit the doctrine of justification—though in his view misapprehended—of blame in this matter." [1] Harnack writes: " The holding to the ' faith alone ' (' fides sola ') necessarily resulted in dangerous laxity. What would really have been required here would have been to lead Christians to see that only the ' fides caritate formata ' has a real value before God. . . . If one has persuaded himself that everything that suggests ' good works ' must be dropped out of the religious sequence, there ultimately remains over only the readiness to subject one's self to faith, *i.e.* to the pure doctrine. . . . The Lutheran Church had to pay dearly for turning away from ' legal righteousness,' ' sacrifice,' and ' satisfactions.' Through having the resolute wish to go back to *religion* and to it alone, it neglected far too much the moral problem, the ' Be ye holy, for I am holy.' " [2] Thus the demoralising effect of Paul's teaching of justification by faith alone, which already was noticed in Apostolic times, was again testified at the Reformation.

In the history of moral protests against Christian dogmas Pelagianism, which played an important part in the beginning of the fifth century, has to be mentioned; indeed, it has been justly said that in the study of no other controversy can we learn so much about the connection and the distinction between morality and religion. The two earnest monks Pelagius and Cælestius and their associate, the wordly bishop Julian of Eclanum, taught that as God's highest attributes are his goodness and righteousness, everything created by him must be good, and that human nature must remain so indestructively, though it may be modified accidentally. To its constitution belongs the will as free choice, and this free choice, with which reason is

---

[1] Beard, *op. cit.* p. 145 *sq.* *Cf.* Rashdall, *op. cit.* p. 417.
[2] Harnack, *op. cit.* vii. 256, 267.

implied, is the highest good in man's constitution. We are free to abstain from sin, as Adam was before the fall : his sin—which Julian esteemed of slight account—was not transmitted. The doctrine of inherited or original sin is blasphemous and absurd : it annuls God's righteousness, it contradicts the fact that there can be no sin where there is no free will, it leads to the condemnation of marriage when original sin is assumed to be propagated by sexual intercourse. In the discussion of divine grace the statements of the Pelagians are often contradictory or ambiguous. Sometimes it is said to be necessary to every good work, sometimes to facilitate goodness, and sometimes to be superfluous. The two latter positions, which to a certain extent can be combined, seem to give their real opinion ; " for it was assuredly the chief intention of Pelagius to deprive Christians of their indolent reliance on grace, and Julian's main object was to show that the human constitution bore merit and salvation in its own lap." There are three states of grace. In the first place, there is the grace of creation, which is so glorious that even heathens and Jews may be perfect men ; Julian sneers at the saying that the virtuous of the heathen are only splendid vices. In the second place, grace denotes the law of God ; indeed all grace, in so far as it is not nature, can have no other character than that of illumination and instruction (*doctrina*), which facilitates the doing of good. Thirdly, grace means the grace of God through Christ, which also is at bottom " illumination and instruction " : Christ works by his example. Pelagius and Julian admit that the habit of sinning was so great that Christ's appearance was necessary. This grace through Christ is quite compatible with the righteousness of God, because the latter does not preclude an increase of benefit, but that grace is given according to our merits ; in any other case God would have been unjust.[1]

The Pelagians never came to form a sect or schismatical party. They were suppressed, chiefly by the influence of Augustine, in the years after A.D. 418, without it being necessary to apply any special force, and in the West Pelagianism brought upon itself a kind of universal anathema. Although the subsequent development of Christian thought has tended to confirm certain individual propositions of the Pelagian system, it was rejected both by Catholics and Protestants. From a moral point of view it was superior to the doctrines of both.

[1] For the Pelagian doctrine see Harnack, *op. cit.* v. 188–203 ; F. Wörter, *Der Pelagianismus* (Freiburg, i. B., 1874) ; F. Klasen, *Die innere Entwicklung des Pelagianismus* (Freiburg, i. B., 1882) ; A., Bruckner, *Julian von Eclanum* (Leipzig, 1897) ; *idem, Die vier Bücher Julians von Æclanum an Turbantius* (Berlin, 1910).

CHAPTER IX

ASCETICISM

THE ethical value of the doctrine that good works are essential to salvation is much reduced by the fact that merit is particularly ascribed to works which our moral consciousness is apt to regard as indifferent or even to disapprove of, namely, ascetic practices, not in the sense of strict self-discipline but of deliberate maltreatment of the body.

Such practices were not prescribed in the original body of Christian doctrine as necessary to salvation, but the ascetic principle soon made way for itself in the development of the Christian Church. The beginnings of early Christian asceticism were due to the influence of Greek and Judæo-Hellenic philosophy. According to the conception of Eastern theologians religion and morality were closely bound together : " God does not accept doctrine without good works, nor works separated from the dogmas of religion." [1] But there was one kind of good works which did not appear to be merely subordinate to religious faith and hope, but seemed to anticipate the future blessings or to put man into the condition of being able to receive them immediately. This was asceticism, which was regarded as the adequate and principal disposition for the reception of salvation. The achievement of more positive morality appeared as a minimum, to which the shadow of imperfection always clung. Clement of Alexandria deemed the performance of any act by which the senses are gratified, for the purpose of obtaining that gratification, derogatory from Christian perfection, nay even sinful : [2] " a sensual life is unseemly, opprobrious, hateful, and contemptible." [3] Origen remained an enthusiastic panegyrist of world-renunciation and mortification of the flesh, even after he had repented the hyper-ascetic excesses of his youth, especially his self-emasculation. [4] John of Damascus characterised asceticism as a salutary means of correcting the deterioration

---

[1] Cyril of Jerusalem, *Cathesis*, iv. 2.

[2] Clement of Alexandria, *Pædagogus*, ii. 10 (Migne, *Patrologiæ cursus, Ser. Græca*, viii. 508).

[3] *Ibid.* iii. 7 (Migne, *Ser. Gr.*, viii. 608).

[4] Eusebius, *Historia ecclesiastica*, vi. 8.

of the human state : " Asceticism and its toils were not invented to procure the virtue that comes from without, but to remove superinduced and unnatural vileness, just as we restore the natural brightness of iron by carefully removing the rust, which is not natural, but has come to it through negligence." [1]

Western Christianity kept real life more distinctly in view. In spite of the asceticism which Ambrose also preached, he constantly discussed all the concrete affairs of the time and the moral wants of the community. He thus represents the intimate union of the ascetic ideal with energetic insistence on positive morality,[2] and this union the Western mediæval Church never lost, however much practical life was subordinated to the contemplative. Augustine looked upon the ascetic life as the ideal for the individual, but at the same time broke through the barren system which made blessedness consist in contemplation alone by urging the monastic ascetics to engage in active work ; and although the *merita* which he said would be crowned at the Judgment were works thoroughly ascetic, he did not consider it necessary for everybody to practise asceticism.[3] Before his time Clement had distinguished between ordinary and extraordinary rules of life, the latter of which are laid down for Christians perfected in knowledge, but are too pure and spiritual to be comprehended by the great mass of believers.[4] Tertullian had also, like Augustine, made a difference between precepts and counsels, and the same was subsequently done by Thomas Aquinas, who considered the following of the counsels, by relinquishing the benefits of this world, to be more meritorious than the following of the precepts.[5]

In Christian asceticism fasting came gradually to hold a prominent position. In the primitive Church there were two weekly fast-days, which undoubtedly were a Pharisaic inheritance, although the days were different. It is said in the ' Didache ' that the " hypocrites " fast on Monday and Thursday, but that the Christians should fast on Wednesday and Friday ; [6] and fasting is also prescribed as preparatory to baptism, both for the baptiser and the baptised.[7] Fasting was an accompaniment of prayer. In the ' Shepherd ' of Hermas we read : " All prayer needeth humiliation ; fast therefore, and thou shalt

---

[1] John of Damascus, *De fide orthodoxa*, iii. 14.
[2] Th. Förster, *Ambrosius Bischof von Mailand* (Halle a. S., 1884), p. 186 *sqq.*
[3] A. Harnack, *History of Dogma*, v (London, 1898), pp. 138, 209 n. 3, 235.
[4] Clement of Alexandria, *Stromata*, i. 1 etc.
[5] *Supra*, pp. 141, 155.   [6] *Didache*, 8.   [7] *Ibid.* 7.

learn from the Lord that which thou dost ask." [1] Clement of Alexandria also speaks of fasting on Wednesday and Friday,[2] and from his day these fasts became more and more general both in the East and the West.[3] In Tertullian's time a half-fast terminating at three in the afternoon was kept in the Catholic Church, though he contended that the fast ought to be prolonged till the evening.[4] These were voluntary fasts, and observed on the authority of tradition, Wednesday being selected because on that day the Jews took counsel to destroy Christ, and Friday because that was the day of his crucifixion. But there was also a fast that was considered obligatory upon all Christians, namely, the Lent fast, consisting in a total abstinence from food during the interval between Christ's passion and resurrection.[5] The Montanists were anxious to introduce a more rigorous discipline in the observance of fasts, and their two weeks' " xerophagy," which implied abstinence from flesh and wine, induced the Church to prolong her Lent fast.[6] Indeed, she gradually extended the fast which lasted for forty hours, the time when Christ lay in the grave, to forty days, in imitation of the forty days' fasts of Moses, Elijah, and Christ.[7] A custom which is known to have existed at the beginning of the fifth century and subsequently, slowly, became general in the Western Church is that of observing every Saturday as a fast-day.[8]

Many other fasts of a longer or shorter duration were also introduced, before religious festivals or in connection with them ; so that in the Roman Catholic Church, since the ninth century, fasting is more or less obligatory on about 120 days of the year.[9] But a conscientious member of the Greek Church abstains from flesh at least 180 days and from fish as well about 140 days. Most of these fasts are known to have existed there from the fourth or sixth century onwards.[10] There are, in addition, compulsory individual fasts connected with baptism, confirmation, communion, ordination, and nuptials, as also penitential

[1] Hermas, *Pastor*, i. 3. 10.

[2] Clement of Alexandria, *Stromata*, vii. 12 (Migne, *Patrologiæ cursus, Ser. Græca*, ix. 504).

[3] O. Zöckler, *Askese und Mönchtum* (Frankfurt a. M., 1897), p. 154.

[4] Tertullian, *De jejuniis*, 2, 10.

[5] *Ibid.* 2 ; Irenæus, quoted by Eusebius, *op. cit.* v. 24.

[6] Zöckler, *op. cit.* p. 155.

[7] Leo I., *Sermo XLIV.* (*alias* XLIII.) ; Jerome, *Commentarii in Jonam*, 3 (Migne, *Patrologiæ cursus*, xxv. 1140) ; Augustine, *Epistola LV.* (*alias* CXIX.), ' Ad inquisitiones Januarii,' 15 (Migne, xxxiii. 217 *sq.*) ; Funk, ' Die Entwicklung des Osterfastens,' in *Theologische Quartalschrift*, lxxv (Tübingen, 1893), p. 209.

[8] Zöckler, *op. cit.* p. 434 *sq.*

[9] *Ibid.* p. 435 *sqq.*

[10] *Ibid.* pp. 302, 305.

fasts.[1] Besides these there are voluntary fasts. Of some of
these incredible stories have been told as the highest proof of
excellence.   Jerome declares that he had seen a monk who for
thirty years had lived exclusively on barley bread and muddy
water, while another, who lived in an old cistern, kept himself
alive on five dried figs a day.[2] Of a famous saint it is asserted
that for three years his only nourishment was the sacrament,
which was brought him on Sundays.[3] In Mesopotamia and
part of Syria there existed a whole sect known by the name of
" Grazers," who never lived under a roof, but spent their time
for ever on the mountain-side and ate grass like cattle.[4]

There were other ascetic practices equally appalling. We
read of hermits who lived in deserted dens of wild beasts, or in
dried-up wells, or in tombs ; who disdained all clothes, and
crawled abroad like animals covered only by their matted hair ;
who spent forty days and nights in the middle of thornbushes,
and for forty years never lay down.[5] In the early days of
Christian monasticism " the cleanliness of the body was regarded
as the pollution of the soul." The saints who were most
admired were those who had become one hideous mass of clotted
filth. Athanasius relates with enthusiasm how St. Antony, the
patriarch of monasticism, never washed his feet, " nor even
endured so much as to put them into water, unless compelled
by necessity." [6] St. Simeon Stylites, who was generally pronounced to be the highest model of a Christian saint, bound a
rope round himself so that it became imbedded in his flesh and
caused putrefaction ; and it is said that " a horrible stench,
intolerable to the bystanders, exhaled from his body, and
worms dropped from him whenever he moved, and they filled
his bed." [7] Even a philosopher like Clement of Alexandria
asserts that while women may bathe for cleanliness and health,
men may only bathe for health.[8]

The most important form of asceticism has been abstinence
from sexual relationships. From the earliest period there were
circles of ascetics in the Christian communities who required
of all, as an inviolable law under the name of Christian perfection,

---

[1] *Ibid.* p. 439 *sq.*   [2] Jerome, *Vita Pauli*, 6.

[3] Rufinus, *Historia monachorum*, 15.

[4] Sozomen, *Historia ecclesiastica*, vi. 33.

[5] Evagrius, *Historia ecclesiastica*, i. 21 (Migne, *Patrologiæ cursus, Ser.
Græca*, lxxxvi. 2475 *sqq.*); W. E. H. Lecky, *History of European Morals*,
ii (London, 1890), p. 108 *sq.*

[6] Athanasius, *Vita S. Antoni*, 47.

[7] Lecky, *op. cit.* ii. 111 *sq.*

[8] Clement of Alexandria, *Pædagogus*, iii. 9 (Migne, *Ser. Græca*,
viii. 617).

N

complete abstinence from marriage. As Jesus had been unmarried and his mother was a virgin, did not this represent the
divine ideal for men and women who sought to be like him ?
The Marcionites permitted no union of the sexes, and those who
were married had to separate ere they could be received by
baptism into the community.[1] Hierarcas, a disciple of Origen
who lived at the close of the third and in the first half of the
fourth century, insisted on the suppression of the sexual impulse
as a demand of the Logos-Christ, and consequently required
celibacy as a Christian law.[2] The Eustathians also condemned
marriage. They were opposed by the Synod of Gangra ;[3] but
the numerous tractates *De virginitate* show how near the great
Fathers of the Church came to the Eustathian view. Clement
of Alexandria combats the notions of the heretics who, like
Marcion, enjoined abstinence from marriage in order that the
world created by the Demiurge might not be peopled ; or, like
Tatian, dared to ascribe the institution of marriage to the devil,
contending that the binding of the woman to the man, mentioned by Paul (1 *Corinthians* vii. 39), meant the union of the
flesh to corruption.[4] But he limits the lawful use of marriage
to the procreation of children.[5] According to Methodius, in
whom we have the final stage of Greek theology, marriage is
not forbidden,[6] but unstained virginity is ranked high above
the married state. It is the condition of Christlikeness,[7] and
all Christians must strive towards it. It is like a spring flower
always softly exhaling immortality from its white petals.[8] It
is " the flower and first fruits of incorruption, and therefore the
Lord promises to admit those who have preserved their virginity
into the kingdom of heaven."[9]

The apologist Justin asserts that the Christians either
abstained from marriage altogether or married with the sole
view of having children, and that such as refuse to marry contain
perpetually within the bounds of chastity.[10] According t
Athenagoras, procreation is the measure of a Christian's indul
gence in appetite, just as the husbandman throwing the seed
into the ground awaits the harvest, not sowing more upon it
" Many among us," he adds, " both men and women, have
grown old in a state of celibacy, through the hope that the

---

[1] Harnack, *op. cit.* i. 277.   [2] *Ibid.* iii. 98.

[3] C. J. von Hefele, *Conciliengeschichte*, i. (Freiburg i. B., 1873
p. 779 *sq.*

[4] Clement of Alexandria, *Stromata*, iii. 3, 12.

[5] *Ibid.* ii. 23.

[6] Methodius, *Convivium decem virginum*, ii. 1 *sq.*

[7] *Ibid.* i. 5.   [8] *Ibid.* vii. 1.   [9] *Ibid.* i. 1.

[10] Justin, *Apologia I. pro Christianis*, 29.

shall thereby be more closely united to God. But if the condition of virgins and eunuchs is more acceptable to God and even thoughts and desires exclude us from his presence, surely we shall renounce the act when we shun the very wish." [1] Tertullian, on the authority of the new prophecy of Montanus, if not actually condemning marriage, yet on all occasions gives a decided preference to a life of celibacy. Commenting on the words of the Apostle that " it is better to marry than to burn," he points out that what is better is not necessarily good. It is better to lose one eye than two, but neither is good; so also, though it is better to marry than to burn, it is far better neither to marry nor to burn.[2] Marriage unfits the soul for devotional exercises.[3] It " consists of that which is the essence of fornication," [4] and is only allowed under the gospel in condescension to human infirmity. " The union of the sexes was, it is true, in the beginning blessed by God, being devised for the purpose of peopling the earth, and on that account permitted." [5] On the other hand, continence " is a means whereby a man will traffic in a mighty substance of sanctity " ; [6] the Lord himself opens the kingdoms of the heavens to eunuchs.[7] Yet when Tertullian is opposing Marcion and other heretics who condemned marriage altogether, he speaks of it as a pure and honourable state; [8] and he even breaks out into a glowing description of the blessedness of that marriage in the celebration of which none of the forms required by the Church has been omitted.[9] He was himself married; but the Romish commentators attempt to get rid of this perplexing fact by saying that when he became a priest, he ceased to cohabit with his wife. If Jerome consented to praise marriage, it was merely because it produced virgins.[10]

Ambrose celebrated virginity as the real novelty in Christian morality : this virtue is our exclusive possession, the heathen had it not.[11] It works miracles : Mary, the sister of Moses, leading the female band, passed on foot over the straits of the sea, and by the same grace Thecla was reverenced even by lions, so that the unfed beasts, lying at the feet of their prey, underwent a holy fast, neither with wanton look nor sharp

[1] Athenagoras, *Legatio pro Christianis*, 33.
[2] Tertullian, *Ad uxorem*, i. 3 ; *idem*, *De monogamia*, 3.
[3] *Idem*, *De exhortatione castitatis*, 9 *sq*.   [4] *Ibid*. 9.
[5] *Idem*, *Ad uxorem*, i. 2. See also *idem*, *De exhortatione castitatis*, 5.
[6] *Idem*, *De exhortatione castitatis*, 10.
[7] *Idem*, *De monogamia*, 3.
[8] *Idem*, *De anima*, 27 ; *idem*, *Adversus Marcionem*, v. 15.
[9] *Idem*, *Ad uxorem*, ii. 9.   [10] Jerome, *Epistola XXII*. 20.
[11] Ambrose, *De virginibus*, i. 4.

claw venturing to harm the virgin.[1]   But Ambrose admitted
that though virginity is the shortest way to the camp of the
faithful, the way of matrimony also arrives there, by a longer
circuit.[2]   According to Augustine, pride in relation to God and
concupiscence show that man is sinful in soul and body ; but
the emphasis falls on concupiscence, the lust of the flesh.   The
motus genitalium, independent even of will, teaches us that
nature is corrupt.   But although the involuntariness of the
impulse should exclude the possibility of its being sinful,
Augustine concludes that there is a sin which belongs to nature
and not to the sphere of the will.   Children possess original sin
because their parents have procreated them in lust,[3] whereas
Christ was sinless because he was not born of marriage.[4]   Augustine imagined paradisiacal marriages in which children were
begotten without lust, or, as Julian says jerkingly, were to be
shaken from trees.   Similar views had been expressed before
by Marcion and others.   Gregory of Nyssa,[5] and in a later time
John of Damascus, held the opinion that virginity belonged
to the nature of man and that if Adam had preserved his
obedience to the Creator some harmless method of vegetation
would have peopled paradise with a race of innocent and
immortal beings—an opinion which was opposed by Thomas
Aquinas, who maintained that the human race from the beginning was propagated by means of sexual intercourse, but that
such intercourse originally was free from all carnal desire.
One would think that Augustine's conception of the sinfulness
mingled with all procreation should have led him to reject
marriage.   But he argues that many things are permitted by
the Apostles, although they are sinful, matrimonial intercourse
being one of these, and that many things which custom has
brought us to look on lightly, for example unchastity, are
dreadful, even though Church discipline itself has become lax
in dealing with them.[7]   So far as marriage is concerned, this
argument is extraordinary considering that Augustine ranked
concupiscence practically above alienation from God, and
treated original sin, resulting from it, as if it were more serious
than actual sin, in so far that while the former can only be
washed out by baptism, the latter can be atoned for by penance

---

[1] Ambrose, *Epistola LXIII.* 34 (Migne, *Ser. Latina*, xvi. 1198 *sq.*)
[2] *Ibid.* 40 (Migne, xvi. 1200).
[3] Augustine, *De nuptiis et concupiscentia*, ii. 15.
[4] *Idem, Enchiridion*, 34, 41.
[5] Gregory of Nyssa, *De hominis opificio*, 17.
[6] H. von Eicken, *Geschichte und System der mittelalterlichen Weltanschauung* (Stuttgart, 1887), p. 437 *sq.*
[7] Augustine, *Enchiridion*, 78, 80.   [8] Harnack, *op. cit.* v. 220

It is interesting to notice that Pelagius almost rivalled his great antagonist Augustine in his praise of virginity. He deduced not inherited sin, which he denied, but the actual existence of sin from the snares of the devil and sensual lusts, and condemned concupiscence accordingly. Pelagius' associate, Bishop Julian, however, argued that if the substance of the flesh was good, its desires, which frequently do not spring from the will, must have been permitted by the Creator; and he attacked inexorably Augustine's view that marriage is allowed although concupiscence is sinful. The case of marriage, which is unthinkable without sexual desire, convinced Julian that the latter is in itself indifferent and innocent, while excess follows from a fault of the will. Christ himself possessed concupiscence [1]

In Scholasticism a clear distinction is drawn between sinful and innocent concupiscence: the latter is involved in man's earthly nature and is kept within appointed limits, as it may be as a result of his baptism. Duns Scotus, who found no reason to regard the sperm as more infectious than blood and saliva, also separated the question about concupiscence, which he regarded as natural, from the question about original sin. [2] Following Augustine, the Catholic Church declared sexual desire to be sinful, but at the same time accepted marriage. Before his time, in the earlier part of the fourth century, the Council of Gangra expressly condemned any one who maintained that marriage prevented a Christian from entering the kingdom of God; [3] but at the end of the same century a Council also excommunicated the monk Jovinian because he denied that virginity is more meritorious than marriage. [4] The Church declared marriage a sacrament. Virginity is ordained to the good of the soul in the contemplative life, which is to " think of the things of the Lord "; marriage, on the other hand, is ordained to the good of the body, the bodily multiplication of the human race, and belongs to the active life, because husband and wife, living in the married state, are under necessity to think of " the things of the world." [5] The Council of Trent condemned any one who does not regard the unmarried state as better than the married. [6]

[1] F. Klasen, *Die innere Entwicklung des Pelagianismus* (Freiburg B., 1882), p. 195 *sq.*

[2] R. Seeberg, *Die Theologie des Johannes Duns Scotus* (Leipzig, 1900), p. 218.

[3] *Concilium Gangrense*, can. 1 (Labbe-Mansi, *Sacrorum Conciliorum Collectio*, ii. 1106).

[4] *Concilium Mediolanense*, A.D. 390 (*ibid.* iii. 689 *sq.*).

[5] Thomas Aquinas, *Summa theologica*, ii.–ii. 152. 4.

[6] *Canones et decreta Concilii Tridentini*, sess. xxiv, can. 10.

Yet the Church by no means encouraged the adoption of virginity as a general practice among her members, but on the contrary resolutely declared war on all attempts to make it a law for everybody.   While she distinguished between a higher and a lower, though sufficient, morality, she repudiated any claim that the higher morality should be the only authoritative one.   A religion that commanded all alike to renounce the world would have closed the world against it.   She graded her members as priests, monks, and laity, and assigned to them different standards of duty.

The earliest form of compulsory celibacy was imposed on persons who had been married before.   The command in the First Epistle to Timothy (iii. 2, 12) that a bishop and a deacon should be the husband of one wife was believed, rightly or wrongly, to be prohibitory of second marriages.   But such marriages were in early times looked upon as more or less discreditable or inadmissible even if contracted by the laity. Hermas says that if a husband or a wife dies the party which survives does not sin in marrying again; " howbeit, if he shall remain single, he shall thereby gain to himself great honour before the Lord." [1]   But if a man puts away an unfaithful wife and marries another woman, he too commits adultery.[2]   According to Justin, divorced persons who contract new marriages are guilty of the same crime.[3]   Athenagoras calls a second marriage a " decorous adultery," for Christ says that " whosoever puts away his wife and marries another commits adultery "; and he who cuts himself off from his first wife, even though she be dead, is a concealed adulterer.[4]   Clement of Alexandria does not pronounce second marriages positively unlawful, but asserts that a man who marries again after the decease of his wife falls short of human perfection.[5]   Tertullian, referring to the injunction of the Apostle, argues that what is forbidden to the clergy is not allowed to the laity : all Christians are really priests, who in case of need must exercise the functions of the priesthood, and consequently must also live up to its standard of morality. And he also adduces another argument : you have lost your wife, it was therefore the will of God that you should become a widower ; by marrying again you cease to be a widower, and thereby strive against the will of God.[7]   This doctrine was

<hr>

[1] Hermas, *op. cit.* ii. 4. 4.   [2] *Ibid.* ii. 4. 1.
[3] Justin, *Apologia I. pro Christianis*, 15.
[4] Athenagoras, *op. cit.* 33.
[5] Clement of Alexandria, *Stromata*, iii. 1 (Migne, *Ser. Græca*, viii 1104).
[6] Tertullian, *De exhortatione castitatis*, 7.   [7] *Ibid.* 2.

branded by the Church as heretical when it was elevated into
an article of belief by the Montanists; but those who married
a second time were subject to penance. In 484 we find the
Pope Gelasius obliged to remind the faithful that marriages of
this kind are not to be refused to laymen. On the other hand,
it became firmly and irrevocably established that no husband
of a second wife was admissible to holy orders.[1] The Council
of Elvira, in 365, which admitted that in cases of extreme
necessity a layman might administer baptism, was careful to
specify that he must not be a " digamus," or husband of a
second wife.[2] The restriction on the priesthood, however, was
not easily enforced. Jerome asserts that the world is full of
prelates who evade it, not only in the lower orders but in the
episcopate.[3]

The rule in question drew for the first time a distinct line
of separation between the great body of the faithful and those
who officiated as ministers of Christ. Shortly afterwards there
was a revival of the Levitical law that required the priesthood
to marry none but virgins.[4] The Council of Elvira declared
in the most positive manner that all concerned in the ministry
of the altar should maintain entire abstinence from their wives
under pain of forfeiting their positions; [5] but this was simply
the legislation of a local synod in Spain, and its canons were
not entitled to respect or obedience beyond the limits of the
churches directly represented. At the end of the fourth century
we find, for the first time, a papal command imposing perpetual
celibacy as an absolute rule of discipline on the ministers of the
altar.[6] Energetic protests were not wanting, nor the more
perplexing stubbornness of passive resistance. The most
energetic endeavours to enforce the celibacy of the clergy were
made, in the latter part of the eleventh century, by Gregory VII.,
who ordered that no one in future should be admitted to orders
without a vow of celibacy, and authorised the laity to with-
draw their obedience from all prelates and priests who dis-
regarded this rule. He was resolved that his decree should
not remain, like the decretals of innumerable Councils, a mere
protest, and took immediate measures to have it enforced
wherever the authority of Rome extended.[7] Yet the reform
for which he laboured was not carried through in the various

[1] H. C. Lea, *History of Sacerdotal Celibacy in the Christian Church*, i
(London, 1907), p. 24 *sq.*
[2] *Concilium Eliberitanum*, A.D. 305, ch. 38 (Labbe-Mansi, ii. 12).
[3] Jerome, *Epistola LXIX.* 2.   [4] Lea, *op. cit.* i. 27.
[5] *Concilium Eliberitanum*, ch. 33 (Labbe-Mansi, ii. 11).
[6] Lea, *op. cit.* i. 62.   [7] *Ibid.* i. 185 *sqq.*

Roman Catholic countries till the end of the twelfth or even late in the thirteenth century.[1]

In the Eastern Church, where sexual asceticism continued to flourish as in its birthplace, there is no trace of any official attempt to render it universally imperative. The East only preserved the traditions of earlier times, as recorded in the Apostolic Constitutions and Canons, prohibiting marriage in orders and the ordination of digami, but imposing no compulsory separation on those who had been married previous to ordination.[2] In these respects the early traditions of the Greek Church have remained unaltered to the present day. The lower grades of the clergy are free to marry, and they are not separated from their wives when promoted to the sacred functions of the diaconate or priesthood. The bishops, again, are selected from the regular clergy or monks, and, being bound by the vow of chastity, are of course unmarried and unable to marry.[3]

The Reformation of the sixteenth century rejected the demands for the celibacy of the clergy. This was due not only to its denial of merits of any kind, but also to its rejection of the double standard of moral excellence which was accepted by Catholicism, and of its different attitude towards asceticism in general and towards sexual abstinence in particular. Luther appreciated all the lawful enjoyments of life. " If our Lord God," he said, " may make excellent large pike and good Rhenish wine, I may very well venture to eat and to drink. Thou mayest enjoy every pleasure in the world that is not sinful : that thy God forbids thee not, but much rather wills it. And it is pleasing to the dear God whenever thou rejoicest or laughest from the bottom of your heart." [4]   The German Pietism of the seventeenth century, however, returned to the principles and practices of strict asceticism in the matters both of fasting and of abstinence from worldly pleasures and enjoyments ; even strolls, games, and laughter were condemned by the more rigorous section of Pietists. Calvin attached much importance to a strict ecclesiastical discipline as a means of holiness.[5]   This gave birth to the austere holiness of Scottish Presbyterianism and English Puritanism with their occasional excesses of harsh casuistry and sabbatarian gloom. Among the Evangelicals there was a real distrust of pleasure as pleasure. Sport was

---

[1] Zöckler, *op. cit.* p. 446.
[2] Lea, *op. cit.* i. 91.   [3] *Ibid.* i. 97.
[4] K. Hagen, *Deutschland's literarische und religiöse Verhältnisse im Reformationszeitalter*, ii (Erlangen, 1843), p. 232.
[5] Calvin, *Institutio Christianæ religionis*, iv. 12.

accepted if it served a rational purpose, that of recreation necessary for physical efficacy, but in so far as it became purely a means of enjoyment, it was strictly condemned. Sexual intercourse was permitted, even within marriage, only as the means willed by God for the increase of his glory according to the commandment, " Be fruitful and multiply." A moderate vegetable diet and cold baths were remedies against sexual temptations.[1] Children were kept away from the fire in cold weather ; and if flagellation had gone out of fashion in the monasteries, it was religiously practised in schools and in the home. We read of a typical Evangelical of the eighteenth century, John Fletcher of Madeley, who sat up every week for reading, meditation and prayer, and lived wholly upon vegetarian food.[2] The early Methodist and Baptist sects even favoured the principle of celibacy. These tendencies to withdrawal from the world led for the most part to no permanent results. But a more enduring character belongs to the ascetic efforts of various branches of British and American Methodism, particularly in the sphere of the crusade against alcohol.[3]

A common characteristic of all forms of asceticism is that it involves suffering or privation, and in religious asceticism this is supposed to be pleasing or gratifying to the deity, or lead to something having such an effect. From the days of Tertullian and Cyprian the Latins were familiar with the notion that the Christian has to propitiate God, that cries of pain, sufferings and deprivations are means of appeasing his anger, that God takes strict account of the quantity of the atonement, and that where there is no guilt to be blotted out those very means are regarded as merits.[4] According to the doctrine of the Church, penitential asceticism should in all grave cases be preceded by sorrow for the sin and also by confession, either public or private; but only too often the notion was adopted that the outward practice itself was a compensation for sin, that a man was at liberty to do whatever he pleased provided he was prepared to do penance afterwards, and that a person who, conscious of his frailty, had laid in a large stock of vicarious penance in anticipation of future necessity, had a right " to work it out,"

[1] Max Weber, *Gesammelte Aufsätze zur Religionssoziologie*, i (Tübingen, 1922), pp. 170, 171, 184, 187.

[2] W. R. Inge, *Christian Ethics and Modern Problems* (London, 1932), p. 132 *sq.*

[3] Zöckler, *op. cit.* p. 572 *sqq.* ; *idem*, ' Asceticism (Christian),' in J. Hastings, *Encyclopædia of Religion and Ethics*, ii (Edinburgh, 1909), p. 79.

[4] Tertullian, *De jejuniis*, 7 ; *idem*, *De resurrectione carnis*, 8 ; *idem*, *De patientia*, 13 ; Harnack, *op. cit.* ii. 110, 132 *sqq.*, iii. 311.

and spend it in sins. How largely ascetic practices are due to
the idea of expiation is indicated by the fact that they scarcely
occur among nations which have no vivid sense of sin, like the
Chinese before the introduction of Taoism and Buddhism,[1]
and the ancient Greeks, Romans, and Scandinavians. In
Greece, however, people sometimes voluntarily sacrificed a part
of their happiness in order to avoid the envy of the gods, who
would not allow to man more than a moderate share of good
fortune. Yet, though fear is a tremendous incentive to self-
mortification, the impulse to expiate and do penance may also
be an immediate and spontaneous expression of self-despair
and devotion. " There are saints," says William James, " who
have literally fed on the negative principle, on humiliation and
privation, and the thought of suffering and death, their souls
growing in happiness just in proportion as their outward state
grew more intolerable." [2]

The most extreme instance of the infliction of suffering as
a means of salvation was the practice of flagellation. In this
practice there was a considerable difference between Eastern
and Western Christians. The former aimed at weeping in their
devotional acts, tears being a sign of contrition, and as self-
scourging was thought by them to be an excellent expedient
for obtaining tears, they had frequent recourse to it for the
purpose of bringing them into this saving state. Western
Christians, on the other hand, resorted to flagellation as a direct
and immediate method of compensation for past sins.[3] It
came into prominence in Europe in the eleventh century through
the practices of the monk Dominicus Loricatus and Cardinal
Peter Damian. It was advocated as a substitute for the reading
of penitential psalms, a thousand strokes of the lash being equal
to ten psalms ; but the most complete course went up to three
million strokes.[4] The first serious outbreak of public flagellation began in Italy. just after the middle of the thirteenth
century ; and a still more famous gregarious outbreak came
about a hundred years later, and led to the formation of the
Brotherhood of the Flagellants, whose members, stripping to
the waist, lashed themselves with scourges, sometimes knotted
and sometimes supplied with iron points which embedded
themselves in the flesh. They believed that their blood would

[1] A. Réville, La religion Chinoise (Paris, 1889), p. 221.
[2] W. James, The Varieties of Religious Experience (London, etc.,
1903), p. 50. See also ibid. p. 302.
[3] W. M. Cooper, Flagellations and the Flagellants (London, s.d.),
p. 115.
[4] Zöckler, op. cit. p. 529 n. 1.

mingle with the shed blood of Christ, and that this penitential flagellation, continued for thirty-three days and a half, would wash the soul free of all taint of sin. Being voluntary, it was thought to be more meritorious than martyrdom, and to supply the want of all other good works.[1] When the Flagellants thus felt that the means of salvation were in their own hands, and that the mediation of the Church and its priesthood could be dispensed with, the Church launched her anathemas against them, and on several occasions they were forced to seal their testimonies at the stake. The mania then took the form of private whipping, and in cells and rooms they belaboured the sinful flesh with infinite satisfaction. This was especially the case in Bavaria, which may be termed the classic land of the scourge.[2]

Suffering is not only sought as a means of wiping off sins committed, but is also endured with a view to preventing the commission of sin. This is another important idea upon which Christian asceticism rests. The gratification of every worldly desire is sinful, the flesh should be the abject slave of the spirit intent upon unearthly things. Man was created for a life in spiritual communion with God, but yielded to the seduction of evil demons, who availed themselves of the sensuous side of his nature to draw him away from the contemplation of the divine and lead him to the earthly. Goodness, therefore, consists in renouncing all sensuous pleasures, in separating from the world, in living solely after the spirit, in imitating the perfection and purity of God. The contrast between good and evil is the contrast between God and the world, and the conception of the world includes not only the objects of bodily appetites but all human institutions. This antithesis of spirit and body, which we have met with already in Paul, was an old Platonic conception, which the Fathers of the Church regarded as the contrast between what was precious and what was to be mortified. In the Neo-Platonic and Neo-Pythagorean schools of Alexandria, an ascetic ideal of life was the natural outcome of their theory that God alone is pure and good, and matter impure and evil. The idea that man ought to liberate himself from the bondage of earthly desires is the conclusion of a contemplative mind reflecting upon the short duration and emptiness of all bodily pleasures and the allurements by which they lead men into misery and sin. And separation from the material world is the ideal of the religious enthusiast whose highest aspiration

[1] R. M. Jones, ' Flagellants,' in J. Hastings, *Encyclopædia of Religion and Ethics*, vi (Edinburgh, 1913), p. 49 *sq.* ; Cooper, *op. cit.* p. 117.
[2] Cooper, *op. cit.* p. 118.

is union with God conceived as an immaterial being, as pure spirit.

There are yet other ideas at the bottom of particular ascetic practices. Fasting is frequently adopted as a means of having supernatural converse, or of acquiring supernatural powers.[1] Chrysostom says that fasting " makes the soul brighter, and gives it wings to mount up and soar on high." [2] An idea of this kind partly underlies the common practice of abstaining from food before or in connection with the performance of a magical or religious ceremony ; [3] but there is also another ground for this practice. The effect attributed to fasting is not merely psychical, but it also prevents pollution.[4] In Christianity we meet with it as a rite of purification, when practised before a religious festival or a religious rite, like prayer or a sacramental act. In the early Church catechumens were accustomed to fast before baptism.[5] At least as early as the time of Tertullian it was usual for communicants to prepare themselves by fasting for the reception of the Eucharist ; [6] and to this day Roman Catholicism regards it as unlawful to consecrate or partake of it after food or drink.[7] The Lent fast itself was partly interpreted as a purifying preparation for the holy table ; [8] but its archetype, the fast which lasted for forty hours only, the time when Christ lay in the grave, belonged to the very common type of fasting after a death. The mourning fast may be ascribed to different causes,[9] but in this case it was undoubtedly an expression of sorrow.

Moreover, there is a close connection between fasting and almsgiving. This was the case among the Jews,[10] and from

---

[1] E. Westermarck, *The Origin and Development of the Moral Ideas*, ii (London, 1917), p. 292 *sq.*

[2] Chrysostom, *In Cap. I. Genes. Homil. X.* 2 (Migne, *Ser. Græca*, liii. 83). *Cf.* Tertullian, *De jejuniis*, 6 *sqq.* ; B. Haug, *Die Alterthümmer der Christen* (Stuttgart, 1785), pp. 476, 482.

[3] Westermarck, *op. cit.* ii. 293 *sqq.* Among the Jews fasting was a means of giving special efficacy to prayer (L. Löw, *Gesammelte Schriften*, i [Szegedin, 1889], p. 108 ; W. Nowack, *Lehrbuch der hebräischen Archäologie*, ii [Freiburg i. B. and Leipzig, 1894], p. 271 ; I. T. Benzinger, ' Fasting, Fasts,' in *Encyclopædia Biblica*, ii [London, 1901], p. 1507), and fasting and praying became in fact a constant combination of words (*Judith*, iv. 9, 11 ; *Tobit*, xii. 8 ; *Ecclesiasticus*, xxxiv. 26).

[4] Westermarck, *op. cit.* ii. 294 *sq.*

[5] Justin Martyr, *Apologia I. pro Christianis*, 61 ; Augustine, *De fide et operibus*, vi. 8.

[6] Tertullian, *De oratione*, 19.

[7] *The Catechism of the Council of Trent*, ii. 4, 6.

[8] Jerome, *In Jonam*, 3 (Migne, *Patrologiæ cursus*, xxv. 1140).

[9] Westermarck, *op. cit.* ii. 302 *sqq.*

[10] *Ibid*, ii. 317.

Judaism the combination of fasting and almsgiving passed over into Christianity. We read in the ' Shepherd ' of Hermas : " That day on which thou fastest thou shalt taste nothing at all but bread and water ; and computing the quantity of food which thou art wont to eat upon other days, thou shalt lay aside the expense which thou shouldst have made that day, and give it unto the widow, the fatherless, and the poor. And thus thou shalt perfect the humiliation of thy soul, that he who receives of it may satisfy his soul, and his prayer come up to the Lord God for thee. If, therefore, thou shalt thus accomplish thy fast, as I command thee, thy sacrifice shall be acceptable unto the Lord, and thy fast shall be written in his book." [1] Aristides writes that if there is among Christians " a man who is poor or needy, and they have not an abundance of necessaries, they fast two or three days that they may supply the needy with their necessary food." [2] According to Augustine, alms and fasting are the two wings which enable a man's prayer to fly upward to God.[3] But fasting without almsgiving " is not so much as counted for fasting " ; [4] that which is gained by the fast at dinner ought not to be turned into a feast at supper, but should be expended on the bellies of the poor.[5] And if a person is too weak to fast without injuring his health he should give more plentiful alms.[6] Tertullian calls fastings " sacrifices that are acceptable to God." [7] But fasting, as well as temperance, has also from early times been advocated by Christian writers on the ground that it is " the beginning of chastity," [8] whereas " through love of eating love of impurity finds passage." [9] Thomas Aquinas says that fasting serves principally three ends : " First, to repress the concupiscences of the flesh ; hence the Apostle says, ' In fastings, in chastity,' because by fasting chastity is preserved. Secondly, it is taken up that the mind

---

[1] Hermas, *op. cit.* iii. 5. 3.   [2] Aristides, *Apologia*, 15.

[3] Augustine, *Enarratio in Psalmum XLXII.* 8 (Migne, *Patrologiæ cursus*, xxxvi. 482).

[4] *Idem, Sermones supposititü,* cxlii. 2, 6 (Migne, xxxix. 2023 *sq.*) ; Chrysostom, *In Matthæum Homilia, LXXVII. (al. LXXVIII.)* 6 (Migne, *Ser. Græca*, lviii. 710).

[5] Augustine, *Sermones supposititü,* cxli. 4 (Migne, xxxix. 2021). *Cf. Canons enacted under King Edgar*, ' Of Powerful Men,' 3 (*Ancient Laws and Institutes of England* [London, 1840], p. 415) ; *Ecclesiastical Institutes*, 38 (*ibid.* p. 486).

[6] Augustine, *Sermones supposititü,* cxlii. 1 (Migne, xxxix. 2022 *sq.*) ; Chrysostom, *In Cap. I. Genes. Homil. X.* 2 (Migne, *Ser. Græca*, liii. 83).

[7] Tertullian, *De resurrectione carnis*, 8.

[8] Chrysostom, *In Epist. II. ad Thessal. Cap. I. Homil. I.* 2 (Migne, *Ser. Græca*, lxii. 470).

[9] Tertullian, *De jejuniis*, 1.

may be more freely raised to the contemplation of high things ;
hence Daniel, after a three weeks' fast, received a revelation
from God. Thirdly, to satisfy for sin." [1] That fasting serves
the general purpose of religious asceticism as a means of pro-
pitiating God by self-inflicted suffering is also kept in view by
Tertullian when he explains its necessity as the result of Adam's
fall. He fell by yielding to his appetite, and from this fact it
follows that the sure way for man to regain the favour of God
is to mortify his appetite : Adam offended by eating, his
descendants must remedy the evil consequences of the offence
by fasting.[2]

So also religious celibacy and abstinence from sexual intercourse are enjoined or commended as means of self-mortification
supposed to appease an angry god. We find them side by side
with other ascetic observances practised for similar purposes.
Among the early Christians those young women who took a vow
of chastity " did not look upon virginity as any thing if it were
not attended with great mortification, with silence, retirement,
poverty, labour, fastings, watchings, and continual praying.
They were not esteemed as virgins who would not deny themselves the common diversions of the world, even the most
innocent." [3] Tertullian enumerates virginity, widowhood, and
the modest restraint in secret on the marriage-bed among those
fragrant offerings acceptable to God which the flesh performs
to its own especial suffering.[4] But sexual asceticism may be
traced to other sources as well.

In various religions a priestess is regarded as married to the
god whom she is serving, and is therefore forbidden to have
sexual intercourse with any man. In the Egyptian texts there
are frequent references to " the divine " consort, a position
which was generally held by the ruling queen, and the king was
believed to be the offspring of such a union.[5] As Plutarch
states, the Egyptians thought it quite possible for a woman
to be impregnated by the approach of some divine spirit, though
they denied that a man could have corporeal intercourse with
a goddess.[6] Nor was the idea of a nuptial relation between a
woman and the deity foreign to the early Christians. Cyprian

[1] Thomas Aquinas, op. cit. ii.–ii. 147. 1.
[2] Tertullian, De jejuniis, 3.
[3] C. Fleury, An Historical Account of the Manners and Behaviour of
the Christians (London, 1698), p. 128 sq.
[4] Tertullian, De resurrectione carnis, 8.
[5] A. Wiedemann, Herodots zeites Buch mit sachlichen Erläuterungen
(Leipzig, 1890), p. 268. Cf. A. Erman, Life in Ancient Egypt (London,
1894), p. 295 sq.
[6] Plutarch, Numa, iv. 5 ; idem, Symposiaca problemata, viii. 1. 6 sq.

speaks of women who had no husband and lord but Christ, with whom they lived in a spiritual matrimony—who had " dedicated themselves to Christ, and, retiring from carnal lust, vowed themselves to God in flesh and spirit." [1] In the following words he condemns the cohabitation of such virgins with unmarried ecclesiastics, under the pretence of a purely spiritual connection : " If a husband come and see his wife lying with another man, is he not indignant and maddened, and does he not in the violence of his jealousy perhaps even seize the sword ? What ? How indignant and angered then must Christ our Lord and Judge be, when he sees a virgin, dedicated to himself, and consecrated to his holiness, lying with a man ! and what punishments does he threaten against such impure connections. . . . She who has been guilty of this crime is an adulteress, not against a husband, but Christ." [2] According to the gospel of Pseudo-Matthew, the Virgin Mary had in a similar manner dedicated herself as a virgin to God.[3]

An extremely important cause of sexual asceticism is the view that sexual intercourse is defiling, and that sexual pollution is particularly injurious to holiness, as also to anybody who comes into contact with anything holy—a view the origin of which I have discussed in an earlier chapter.[4] The Christians prescribed strict continence as a preparation for baptism [5] and the partaking of the Eucharist.[6] They enjoined that no married persons should participate in any of the great festivals of the Church if the night before they had lain together ; [7] and in the ' Vision ' of Alberic, dating from the twelfth century, a special place of torture, consisting of a lake of mingled lead, pitch, and resin, is represented as existing in hell for the punishment of married people who have had intercourse on Sundays, church

[1] Cyprian, *De habitu virginum*, 4, 22. *Cf.* Methodius, *Convivium decem virginum*, vii. 1.

[2] Cyprian, *Epistola LXII., ad Pomponium de virginibus*, 3 sq. (Migne, *Patrologiæ cursus*, iv. 368 sqq.). See also J. Neander, *General History of the Christian Religion and Church*, i (Edinburgh, 1847), p. 378. The Council of Elvira decreed that such fallen virgins, if they refused to return back to their former condition, should be denied communion even at the moment of death (*Concilium Eliberitanum*, A.D. 305, ch. 13 [Labbe-Mansi, ii. 8]).

[3] *The Gospel of Pseudo-Matthew*, 8 (*Anti-Nicene Christian Library*, xvi [Edinburgh, 1870], p. 25). See also *The Gospel of the Nativity of Mary*, 7 (*ibid.* xvi. 57 sq.).

[4] *Supra*, p. 128 sq.

[5] Augustine, *De fide et operibus*, vi. 8.

[6] Jerome, *Epistola XLVIII.* 15 (Migne, xxii. 505 sq.).

[7] Gregory the Great, *Dialogi*, i. 10 (Migne, lxxvii. 200 sq.) ; Lecky, *op. cit.* ii. 324.

festivals, or fast-days.[1] They abstained from the marriage-bed
at other times also, when they were disposed more freely to
give themselves to prayer.[2] Newly married couples were
admonished to practice continence during the wedding-day and
the night following, out of reverence for the sacrament ; and
in some instances their abstinence lasted even for two or three
days.[3] The Penitential of Theodore commands those who
contract a first marriage to abstain from entering a church for
thirty days, after which they are to perform penance for forty
more.[4] The Syrian philosopher Jamblichus speaks of the belief
that " the gods do not hear him who invokes them, if he is
impure from venereal connections." [5] A similar notion prevailed among the early Christians ; with reference to a passage
in the First Epistle to the Corinthians (vii. 5), Tertullian remarks
that the Apostle added the recommendation of a temporary
abstinence for the sake of adding efficacy to prayers.[6] Carried
further, the idea underlying all these rules and practices led to
the notions, that celibacy is more pleasing to God than marriage
and a religious duty for those members of the community whose
special office is to attend to the sacred cult.   For a nation like
the Jews, whose ambition was to live and to multiply, celibacy
could never become an ideal ; whereas the Christians, who
professed the utmost indifference to all earthly matters, found
no difficulty in glorifying a state which, however opposed it
was to the interests of the race and the nation, made men pre-
eminently fit to approach their god.   Indeed, far from being
a benefit to the kingdom of God by propagating the species,
sexual intercourse was on the contrary detrimental to it by
being the great transmitter of the sin of our first parents.

Finally, it was argued that marriage prevents a person from
serving God perfectly, because it induces him to occupy himself
too much with worldly things.[7] Though not contrary to the
act of charity or the love of God, says Thomas Aquinas, it is

---

[1] Albericus, *Visio* (Ariano, 1899), ch. 5, p. 17 ; J. O. Delepierre,
L'enfer décrit par ceux qui l'ont vu (London, 1864-5), p. 57 *sq.* On this
subject see also J. Müller, *Das sexuelle Leben der christlichen Kulturvölker*
(Leipzig, 1904), pp. 52, 53, 120 *sq.*

[2] Jerome, *Epistola XLVIII*. 15 (Migne, xxii. 505) ; Fleury, *op. cit.*
p. 75.

[3] L. A. Muratori, *Dissertazioni sopra le antichità Italiane*, 20, vol. i
(Milano, 1836), p. 347.

[4] G. May, *Social Control of Sex Expression* (London, 1930), p. 63.

[5] Jamblichus, *De mysteriis*, iv. 11.

[6] Tertullian, *De exhortatione castitatis*, 10.

[7] Vincentius Bellovacensis, *Speculum naturale* (Venetijs, 1494),
xxx. 43.

nevertheless an obstacle to it.[1] This was one, but certainly not the only, cause of the obligatory celibacy which the Roman Church imposed upon her clergy. Even in the East, where there was no such compulsory celibacy, we find Eusebius stating that it is becoming in those who are engaged in the ministry of God to abstain from their wives in order to be relieved from family cares and anxieties.[2]

[1] Thomas Aquinas, *op. cit.* ii.–ii. 184, 3.
[2] Eusebius, *Demonstratio evangelica*, i. 9.

CHAPTER X

THE SACRAMENTS

IN previous chapters we have considered two different trends
of thought as regards the means of procuring salvation.
On the one hand there is the moralistic view that salvation is
the reward of a moral life wrought out essentially by our own
power, and on the other hand there is the belief that it depends
upon divine grace, connected with the faith in Christ as our
redeemer through his death on the cross. In the Catholic
Church the two views were combined by the idea that merits
are the gifts of God, while in Protestantism justification was
declared to be due to faith alone and good works to be merely
the fruits of faith. But as a matter of fact, whatever importance
was attached either to merits or to faith, the doctrine of salvation
was at the same time influenced by the belief in a mystical
efficacy of sacraments.

What is a sacrament ? It was found easier to describe the
particular rites called by that name than to give a general
definition of it. Augustine made various statements on the
notion of the sacrament, but evolved no harmonious theory on
the subject. He says that when " the Word is added to the
element . . . a sacrament is constituted, itself being, as it were,
a visible Word "; [1] and in many passages the sign is described
as a figure, although at the same time it is not an empty sgin.
" It is not that which is seen that feeds, but that which is
believed." [2] The gift conveyed in the Eucharist is a spiritual
gift, and the eating and drinking are a spiritual process.[3] That
of which we partake is not the sensual flesh, but of this flesh we
receive its essence, the spirit which quickens it.[4] The Schoolmen's doctrine of the sacraments has its root in that of Augustine,
but goes beyond it both formally and materially. The " word "
disappears behind the sacramental sign, and the conception
becomes still more magical. The definition of the Lombard,
which lies at the foundation of the later definitions, runs thus :

[1] Augustine, *In Joannis evangelium*, lxxx. 3.
[2] *Idem, Sermo CXII.* 5.
[3] *Idem, Sermo CXXXI.* 1.
[4] *Idem, In Joannis evangelium*, xxvii. 5.

194

" That is properly called a sacrament which is a sign of the grace of God, and a form of invisible grace in such a way that it bears the image thereof and exists as a cause. Sacraments, therefore, are instituted for the purpose, not merely of signifying, but also of sanctifying." [1]

Thomas Aquinas, however, does not accept without guarding clauses the statement that the sacrament " exists as a cause." He says that it only " in some way " causes grace ; that the principal cause of grace is God, who works as the fire does by its warmth, communicating in grace his own nature, and that the sacrament is merely an " instrumental cause," which acts through the impulse it receives from the principal agent. Anyhow, " the sacraments of the new law are at the same time causes and signs, and hence it is commonly said of them that they effect what they symbolise." [2] But while the principal cause of grace is God, the humanity of Christ is, so to speak, a conjoined instrument. Yielding himself up as an offering and sacrifice to God, he initiated by his passion the ritual of the Christian religion, " whence it is manifest that the sacraments of the Church have their efficacy principally from the passion of Christ, of which the virtue is in some way united to us through receiving the sacraments, as a sign of which there flowed from Christ as he hung upon the cross water and blood, of which the one relates to baptism, the other to the Eucharist, which are the most potent sacraments." [3] The ultimate end of the sacrament is life eternal ; and a sacrament may thus be defined as " a sign commemorative of what went before, namely, the passion of Christ, and representative of what is effected in us by the passion of Christ, namely, grace, and anticipatory, that is, predictive of future glory." [4] It must always be a sensible thing, because it corresponds with the nature of man that he should attain to the knowledge of intelligible, through sensible things.[5] Though the inner effect of the sacrament, which is justification, can be produced only by God, a man (the priest), by way of administering it, becomes an instrumental cause of that effect.[6] Whether he is good or bad does not come into account here, since " the instrument does not work by its own form of virtue, but by the virtue of him by whom it is moved." [7] Bad servants commit a mortal sin when they celebrate the sacraments, but the sin does not extend to the receiver, " who

[1] Petrus Lombard, *Sententiæ*, iv. 2.
[2] Thomas Aquinas, *Summa theologica*, iii. 62. 1.
[3] *Ibid.* iii. 62. 5.　　　　　[4] *Ibid.* iii. 60. 3.
[5] *Ibid.* iii. 60. 4.　　　　　[6] *Ibid.* iii. 64. 1.
[7] *Ibid.* iii. 64. 5.

does not communicate with the sin of the bad minister, but with the Church." [1]

The doctrine of Thomas underwent afterwards considerable modification from the time of Duns Scotus onwards—although Scotus himself, in spite of his criticism, does not stand very far from him in his doctrine of the sacraments,[2]—but became finally dominant. This is noticeable in what the Council of Trent has to say on the subject. In the prologue to the decree of Session vii, it declares that " by means of the sacraments all true righteousness either begins or, having been begun, is increased or, having been lost, is restored." As in the doctrine of Aquinas, a regard to faith is lacking, and this silence is the more significant since it shows that just the sacrament itself as externally applied is held to be the means of salvation. In the canons, anathema is pronounced on those who assert that man can be justified before God without the sacraments by faith alone ; [3] on those who teach that the sacraments are instituted for the sake of only nourishing faith ; [4] on those who say that " grace is not conveyed *ex opere operato* by the sacraments of the new law, but that faith alone in the divine promise is sufficient for obtaining grace." [5] If the negative definitions which the Council adopted in these and other statements are translated into a positive form, they come close to Thomism. They are really protests against Protestantism.

Luther insisted that the sacraments do not become efficacious in their being celebrated, but in their being believed in. He maintained that both baptism and the Eucharist, which were the only sacraments recognised by him, work forgiveness of sin and thereby procure life and blessedness, but not without faith. He says that in baptism " this is not done certainly by the water, but by the Word of God, which is with and beside the water, and by the faith which trusts in such Word of God in the water " ; [6] and so also the eating of the bread and the drinking of the wine in the Eucharist must be combined with faith in the Word in order to produce forgiveness of sins, for only then it can be said with truth, " This bread is my body, this wine is my blood." [7] According to Zwingli, on the other hand, " all sacraments are so far from conferring grace that

---

[1] Thomas Aquinas, *Summa theologica*, iii. 64. 6.
[2] See Harnack, *op. cit.* vi (London, 1899), p. 219 *sqq.* ; R. Seeberg, *Die Theologie des Johannes Duns Scotus* (Leipzig, 1900), p. 346 *sqq.*
[3] *Canones et decreta Concilii Tridentini*, sess. vii, can. 4.
[4] *Ibid.* vii. 5.   [5] *Ibid.* vii. 8.
[6] Luther, ' Der kleine Catechismus,' in *Sämmtliche Werke*, xx (Erlangen, 1832), p. 17.
[7] *Ibid.* xxi. 20.

they do not even bring or dispense it. . . . Sacraments are given for a public testimony of that grace which is previously present to each individual. . . . A sacrament is a sign of a sacred thing, that is, of grace which has been given." [1] Calvin, again, tried to steer a middle course between the theories of Luther and Zwingli. He defined a sacrament as " an external sign, by which the Lord seals to our consciences his promises of goodwill towards us, in order to sustain the weakness of our faith, and we in our turn testify our piety towards him, both before himself and before angels as well as men." [2] But was not the sacrament then a superfluity, since the true will of God was sufficiently known through the Word, and the sacrament could make us no wiser ? Calvin makes the reply : " Sacraments bring with them the clearest promises, and, when compared with the Word, have this peculiarity that they represent promises to the life, as if painted in a picture." They are like seals which are affixed to diplomas and other public deeds, which " are nothing considered in themselves, and would be affixed to no purpose if nothing were written on the parchment, and yet this does not prevent them from sealing and confirming when they are appended to writing." [3]

The doctrine of the sacraments was developed under the disadvantage of not knowing for certain to what sacred acts the general conceptions were to be applied. As to their number the greatest vacillation prevailed for centuries. Still, theology had already wrought for long with the number seven, before this number was officially recognised by the Church,[4] which happened in 1439.[5] The only sacred acts in a pre-eminent sense, which had been handed down from ecclesiastical antiquity were baptism and the Eucharist.

Baptism was regarded as the bath of regeneration, by which the sins of the past were blotted out. Speaking of " the repentance of baptism," Hermas says that when we go down into the water we receive the forgiveness of our sins ; we " go down under the obligation unto death, but come up appointed unto life." [6] According to the ' Didache,' the pronouncing of the name of Father and Son and the Holy Spirit is essential, but if immersion is not practicable water may be poured upon the

---

[1] Zwingli, ' Fidei ratio,' in *Eine Auswahl aus seinen Schriften* (Zürich, 1918), p. 748 *sq.*

[2] Calvin, *Institutio Christianæ religionis*, iv. 12. 1.

[3] *Ibid.* iv. 14. 5.   [4] Harnack, *op. cit.* vi. 201 *sqq.*

[5] Eugene IV., ' Decretum,' in Labbe-Mansi, *Sacrorum Conciliorum collectio*, xxxi (Venetiis, 1798), col. 1054 *sqq.*

[6] Hermas, *Pastor*, ii. 4. 3, iii. 9. 16.

head thrice.[1] Personal faith was looked upon as a necessary condition.[2] Tertullian argues that baptism, in order to be effectual to the pardon of sin, presupposes a renunciation of all sinful habits on the part of him who is to receive it; men are admitted to baptism because they have repented and reformed their lives, not in order that they may afterwards repent and reform.[3] The converts from heathenism went through a course of instruction in the principles and doctrines of the gospel, and were subjected to a strict probation before they were admitted to the rite of baptism. Tertullian says that this rite must not be hastily conferred; and recommends delay in the case not only of infants but also of unmarried persons and widows, whom he considers particularly exposed to temptation.[4] He and the Christians of his day were impressed by the belief that the external rite was absolutely necessary to salvation, and thought it better that it should be performed by a layman than that it should not be performed at all. But although he maintains that the laity possess the right to administer baptism in case of necessity, he does not extend this right to women, and stigmatises the attempt on their part to baptise as a most flagrant act of presumption.[5]

Augustine considers likewise baptism indispensable for salvation. Its necessity rests on the " stamp," and it cannot be rendered invalid by sin or heresy;[6] it may even cause a momentary forgiveness of sin in the case of heretics.[7] But the importance of the Catholic Church is strictly guarded. Baptism is set in the foreground as the grand mystery in the cross of Christ, for according to Paul it is nothing but the similitude of Christ's death; but the death of Christ crucified is nothing but the remission of sin, that as in him a true death took place, so in us a true remission of sins.[8] Thomas Aquinas asserts that while generally the sacraments as a whole are necessary to salvation, this applies specifically, in the strictest sense, to baptism.[9] It is the medicine for the consequences of the Fall, and lays the basis of the new life. It has thus both a negative and a positive effect. It abolishes the guilt both of original

---

[1] *Didache*, 7.
[2] Justin Martyr, *Apologia I. pro Christianis*, 61; Tertullian, *De baptismo*, 14; *idem, De pœnitentia*, 6.
[3] Tertullian, *De pœnitentia*, 6.
[4] *Idem, De baptismo*, 18.
[5] *Ibid.* 17; Tertullian, *De præscriptione hæreticorum*, 41.
[6] Augustine, *De peccato originali*, i. 34.
[7] *Idem, De baptismo*, i. 19.
[8] *Idem, Enchiridion*, 52.
[9] Thomas Aquinas, *op. cit.* iii. 66. 2, iii. 68. 1 *sq.*

sin and of the previously committed sinful deeds without exception.[1] The penalty is thereby remitted, and the disorder of the passions is rectified, so that man is now capable of resisting or keeping within appointed limits the concupiscence which is involved in his earthly nature.[2] The positive effect of baptism is summed up in the term " regeneration." [3] Baptism cannot be repeated.[4] It is valid when it is performed with water and with the words of institution, and is regularly dispensed by the priest. Yet in an emergency a deacon,[5] and even a layman, nay a woman, can baptise.[6] The Council of Trent only systematised the earlier doctrine and practice of baptism,[7] which, in fact, had not essentially altered in the Church since the middle of the second century. In the ' Confession of Augsburg ' the Lutherans asserted the absolute necessity of baptism quite as emphatically as the Tridentine theologians.[8] The Anglican Article XXVII. speaks of baptism as a sign of regeneration " whereby, as by an instrument, they that receive Baptism rightly are grafted into the Church," the promises of the forgiveness of sin being visibly signed and sealed. The Archbishops' Commission on Doctrine in the Church of England admits that the baptism of infants cannot clean from actual sin, since no such sin has been committed, but maintains that it " is a means of deliverance from the domination of influences which predispose to sin." [9]

Infant baptism is a subject of great, though melancholy, interest. We have no testimony regarding it from an earlier time than that of Irenæus [10] and Tertullian, but then it had already become quite general. Tertullian alludes to the custom of having sponsors, who made, in the name of the children brought to the font, those promises which they were unable to make for themselves. He thinks, however, that it is more advantageous to delay baptism till the children are growing up and are able to know Christ ; " for why is it necessary for the sponsors also to be thrust into danger ? " [11] Augustine, on the other hand, regarded infant baptism as indispensable : even the youngest children who have done nothing sinful pass justly into damnation if they die unbaptised, because they possess

---

[1] *Ibid.* iii. 69. 1 *sq.*   [2] *Ibid.* iii. 69. 4.
[3] *Ibid.* iii. 66. 9, iii. 69. 10.
[4] *Ibid.* iii. 66. 9.   [5] *Ibid.* iii. 67. 1.
[6] *Ibid.* iii. 67. 3 *sq.*
[7] *Canones et decreta Concilii Tridentini*, sess. vii.
[8] *Augustana Confessio*, art. 9.
[9] *Doctrine in the Church of England* (London, 1938), p. 137.
[10] Irenæus, *Contra hæreses*, ii. 22. 4.
[11] Tertullian, *De baptismo*, 18.

original sin and are burdened with concupiscence. He admitted, however, that the punishment of such children was of the mildest sort.[1]   Other writers were more severe ; Fulgentius condemned to " everlasting punishment in eternal fire " even infants who died in their mother's womb.[2]   But the notion that unbaptised children will be tormented gave gradually way to a more humane opinion.   In the middle of the twelfth century Peter Lombard determined that the proper punishment of original sin, when no actual sin is added to it, is loss of heaven and the sight of God, but not positive torment.[3]   This doctrine was confirmed by Innocentius III. and shared by the whole troop of the School-men, who assumed the existence of a place called *limbus*, or *infernus puerorum*, where unbaptised infants will dwell without being subject to torture.[4]   But the older view was again set up by the Protestants, who generally maintained that the due punishment of original sin is, in strictness, damnation in hell, although many of them were inclined to think that if a child dies by misfortune before it is baptised, the parents' sincere intention of baptising it, together with their prayers, will be accepted with God for the deed.[5]   Luther, who declared that baptism is useless in the absence of faith,[6] nevertheless retained infant baptism not only as a symbol, but as an efficacious act.[7] The Confession of Augsburg emphatically condemns the doctrine of the Anabaptists that God would not damn a little child for a drop of water.[8]   Zwingli regarded the salvation of the un-baptised children of Christians as certain, and hoped apparently for the salvation of all other infants as well.[9]   But the damna-tion of infants who died unbaptised was an acknowledged belief of Calvinism,[10] although an exception was made for the children of pious parents, provided " there is neither sloth, nor contempt,

[1] Augustine, *De peccatorum meritis et remissione*, i. 16 ; *idem*, *Enchiridion*, 93.
[2] Fulgentius, *De fide*, 27.
[3] Petrus Lombard, *op. cit.* ii. 33. 5.
[4] W. Wall, *The History of Infant-Baptism*, i (Oxford, 1862), p. 460 *sq.*
[5] *Ibid.* i. 462, 468.
[6] Luther, ' Der grosse Catechismus,' in *Sämmtliche Werke*, xxi (Erlangen, 1832), p. 133.
[7] *Ibid.* xxi. 136 *sqq.*
[8] *Augustana Confessio*, i. 9.
[9] Zwingli, ' De providentia Dei,' in *Opera*, iv (Turici, 1841), p. 125 *sqq.*
[10] Calvin, *op. cit.* iv. 15. 10 : " Even infants bring their condemnation with them from their mother's womb ; for although they have not yet brought forth the fruits of their unrighteousness, they have its seed included in them.   Nay, their whole nature is, as it were, a seed of sin, and, therefore, cannot but be odious and abominable to God " ; A. Norton, *Tracts concerning Christianity* (Cambridge, 1852), p. 179 *sqq.*

nor negligence." [1] Yet in the latter part of the eighteenth century Toplady, who was a violent Calvinist, avowed his belief in the universal salvation of all departed infants, whether baptised or unbaptised ; [2] and a hundred years later Dr. Hodge thought he was justified in stating that the common belief of evangelical Protestants was that all who die in infancy are saved. [3] The accuracy of this statement, however, seems somewhat doubtful. In 1883 Mr. Prentiss wrote of the doctrine of infant salvation independently of baptism : "My own impression is that, had it been taught as unequivocally in the Presbyterian Church even a third of a century ago by a theologian less eminent than Dr. Hodge for orthodoxy, piety, and weight of character, it would have called forth an immediate protest from some of the more conservative, old-fashioned Calvinists." [4]

Like the sacrament of baptism, the Eucharist also evidently owes its sacramental character to Paul. He looked upon it as a mystical re-enactment of the death and resurrection of Christ through which the believer participates in his immortality, the bread and wine being an incarnation of his body and blood. A similar conception is found in the Gospel of John, where the following words are put into the mouth of Jesus : " Whoso eateth my flesh, and drinketh my blood, hath eternal life ; and I will raise him up at the last day. For my flesh is meat indeed, and my blood is drink indeed. He that eateth my flesh, and drinketh my blood, dwelleth in me, and I in him." [5] In this respect there was a great resemblance between the teaching of Paul and John and certain mystic saviour cults in the Græco-Roman world, in which the believer shares in and is assimilated to a divine being who dies and is reborn to immortal life. [6] In the case of Pauline Christianity the breaking of bread and the drinking of wine, as well as baptism, were efficacious sacraments, as the instruments of an intimate union with Christ through faith, but they were not sufficient for salvation.

The Lord's Supper soon became the central point both for the worship of the Church and for its very life as a Church, the common meal being a fitting expression of the brotherly unity

---

[1] Calvin, op. cit. iv. 15. 22 ; W. Anderson, ' Introductory Essay ' to W. Logan, Words of Comfort for Parents Bereaved of Little Children (London, 1851), p. xxi.

[2] A. M. Toplady, Works (London, 1852), p. 645 sq.

[3] C. Hodge, Systematic Theology, i (London and Edinburgh, 1871), p. 26 sq.

[4] G. L. Prentiss, ' Infant Salvation and its Theological Bearings,' in The Presbyterian Review, iv (New York, 1883), p. 559. See also Anderson, loc. cit. p. xxiii.

[5] John vi. 54-6.   [6] Supra, p. 113.

of the community.[1] It is said in the ' Didache ' : " On the
Lord's day do ye assemble and break bread, and give thanks,
after confessing your transgressions, in order that your sacrifice
may be pure. But every one that hath controversy with his
friend, let him not come together with you, until they be reconciled, that your sacrifice may not be profaned." [2] Agapes, or
love-feasts, were held in connection with the Supper, and the
bread and wine for the holy celebration were taken out of the
payments in kind that were necessary for them. The presenta-
tion of the elements for the holy ordinance was also extended
to the offering of gifts for the poor brethren.[3] The wealthy
and the willing, for every one is at liberty, contribute as they
think fitting ; and this collection is deposited with the bishop,
who out of this relieves the orphan and the widow, and such
as are in bonds, and strangers that come from afar.[4]

But in the first place the Lord's Supper was a blessing to
the individual who partook of it. Ignatius calls the breaking
of bread " the medicine of immortality, our antidote that we
should not die, but live for ever in Christ Jesus." [5] As to the
connection between the elements and the body and blood of
Christ, he seems to have expressed himself in a strictly realistic
way in several passages,[6] but in others he gives evidence of a
very different conception, as when he equates the flesh of the
Lord partaken of at the Supper with faith and the blood with
love,[7] or when he calls the blood " incorruptible love " [8] and
the gospel " the flesh of Christ." [9] Justin, on the other hand,
presupposed the identity, miraculously produced by the Logos,
of the consecrated bread and the body he had assumed ; in
this we have undoubtedly to recognise an influence of pagan
mysteries where " bread and a cup of water, with a certain form
of words " were made use of as an initiation ceremony, according
to Justin at the instigation of evil spirits.[10] Tertullian says that
owing to the devil the consecration of the bread in the Eucharist
was imitated in the mysteries of Mithra.[11] Harnack observes
that " there was plainly a remodelling of the ritual in imitation
of the ancient mysteries and of the heathen sacrificial system,"
and that this fact is admitted by Protestant scholars of all

[1] Cf. 1 Corinthians x. 17, xii. 13.   [2] Didache, 14.
[3] Supra, p. 84.   [4] Justin, op. cit. 67.
[5] Ignatius, Epistola ad Ephesios, 20.
[6] See, for example, idem, Epistola ad Smyrnœos, 7.
[7] Idem, Epistola ad Trallianos, 8.
[8] Idem, Epistola ad Romanos, 7.
[9] Idem, Epistola ad Philodelphenses, 5.
[10] Justin, op. cit. 66.
[11] Tertullian, De præscriptione hæreticorum, 40.

parties.[1] But the doctrine in question is essentially that of Paul, and there is no reason to suppose that the pagan influence was only of a later date.

Clement and Origen, like Ignatius, assign a spiritual significance to the flesh and blood of Christ. According to the former, " there is a twofold blood of the Lord : the one carnal, by which we are redeemed from corruption, the other spiritual, by which we are anointed." [2] " His notion," says Bishop Kaye, " seems to have been that by partaking of the bread and wine in the Eucharist, the soul of the believer is united to the Spirit, and that by this union the principle of immortality is imparted to the flesh." [3] In Origen's view the eucharistic body is only the word of God or of Logos as being a substitute for his appearance in the flesh ; whenever he speaks of the Supper, or in a more general sense of eating of the flesh or of the drinking of the blood of Christ, he does this without any reference to the body which he had as a man or to the blood which flowed in the veins of this body.[4] But Origen's disciple Gregory of Nyssa maintained that the actual body of Christ as immortal is the only remedy against death, and that it therefore must be partaken of bodily in the Supper ; through the act of consecration the bread and wine are changed into the flesh and blood of the Lord in order that by partaking of them our body may be transformed into the body of Christ.[5] Chrysostom agreed with Gregory in the assumption of an essentially corporeal effect of the participation, and speaks like him of a refashioning and transforming of the elements which Christ effects through the priest by means of the invocation. He says that Christ, in proof of his love, has given us his body pierced with nails, " that we might hold it in our hands and eat it ; for we often bite those whom we love much." [6] The classical doctrine of the Lord's Supper in the Greek Church up to the present day is that of John of Damascus, who perfected the conception of the identity of the eucharistic and the real body of Christ. By

[1] Harnack, op. cit. ii. 138.
[2] Clement of Alexandria, Pædagogus, ii. 2 (Migne, Ser. Græca, viii. 409).
[3] J. Kaye, Some Account of the Writings and Opinions of Clement of Alexandria (London, s.d.), p. 265.
[4] G. E. Steitz, ' Die Abendmahlslehre der griechischen Kirche in ihrer geschichtlichen Entwickelung,' in Jahrbücher für deutsche Theologie, x (Gotha, 1865), p. 99.
[5] Gregory of Nyssa, Oratio catechetica magna, 37. Cf. Steitz, loc. cit. p. 446 sqq.
[6] Chrysostom, In Epistolam primam ad Corinthios Homilia XXIV. 4 ; Steitz, loc. cit. x. 446 sqq.

the Holy Ghost bread and wine are received into the body of Christ. The eucharistic body is that which was born of the virgin, not, however, by a transubstantiation, as if the body of Christ descended suddenly from heaven and took the place of the elements, but by a transformation and assumption, just as in the incarnation. The bread-body is received into the real body and is thus identical with it.[1]

Roman Catholic writers are desirous to allege Tertullian's authority in support of the doctrine of transubstantiation. He speaks indeed of " the feeding on the fatness of the Lord's body, that is, on the Eucharist," [2] and of " our flesh being fed on the body and blood of Christ, in order that our soul may be sated with God." [3] But when compared with other passages in his writings these appear to have been used in a figurative sense.[4] And in other places he expressly calls the bread only the representation of the body of Christ.[5] So also Augustine resists the realistic interpretation of the Supper.[6] But towards the end of the period of Louis the Pious, Paschasius Radbertus asserted as doctrine what had been felt by the majority, that the real historical body of Christ is sacrificed in the Mass and partaken of in the Lord's Supper.[7] At the beginning of the thirteenth century the doctrine of transubstantiation was practically settled by the Lateran Council of 1215. The words run : " There is one universal Church of the faithful, outside of which no one whatever can be saved, in which Jesus Christ is at once priest and sacrifice, whose body and blood are truly contained in the sacrifice of the altar under the appearances of bread and wine, the bread being transubstantiated into the body, and the wine into the blood by divine power, so that for the effecting of the mystery of unity we receive of his what he received of ours. And this sacrament especially no one can administer but the priest who has been duly ordained according to the Church authority which Jesus Christ himself gave to the Apostles and their successors." [8] The conception of the

---

[1] John of Damascus, De fide orthodoxa, iv. 13. Cf. Steitz, loc. cit. xii (1867), pp. 216, 275 sqq.

[2] Tertullian, De pudicitia, 9.

[3] Idem, De resurrectione carnis, 8.

[4] See John, bishop of Bristol, The Ecclesiastical History of the Second and Third Centuries illustrated from the Writings of Tertullian (London, s.d.), p. 224 sq.

[5] Tertullian, Adversus Marcionem, i. 14, iii. 19, iv. 40 ; idem, Ad uxorem, ii. 5 ; idem, De anima, 17 ; idem, Adversus Judæos, 10.

[6] Augustine, Enarratio in Psalmum xcviii. 9 ; supra, p. 194.

[7] Harnack, op. cit. v. 311 sqq.

[8] Mansi, Sacrorum Conciliorum collectio, xxii. 982.

Eucharist as a sacrifice is already found in the early Church ; [1] and Cyprian's statement that every celebration of the Lord's Supper is a repetition or imitation of Christ's sacrifice of himself, and therefore has an expiatory value, still continues to be repeated by the Romish Church to the present day. [2] While Greek Catholicism interpreted the Eucharist as the mystery whereby life eternal was mediated to the faithful, the Eucharist of Latin Catholicism centred more upon the sacrifice, forgiveness rather than immortality being mediated by it. [3]

Thomas Aquinas, who gives a systematic exposition of the notion of transubstantiation, [4] says of the effects of the Eucharist that it conveys grace, gives aid for eternal life, blots out venial sins but not mortal sins, guards against future transgressions, and as a sacrifice profits the spectators also, although it as a sacrament profits only the receiver. [5] Although in strict theory comparatively slight results were attributed to the Eucharist as a sacrifice, the people looked upon it as much more important than the sacrament, which formed the central part of divine service. And the dignity of the priest came most distinctly to view when he in the Mass appeared as priest of the body of Christ and in a very real sense as the mediator between God and men. But the doctrine of transubstantiation increased the dignity of the priest also in his capacity of administering the sacrament because, in order that the wine might not be spilt and the sacrament thereby profaned, it was considered safer that the layman should receive it only in the form of the bread, while the priest drank the cup in the name of all. [6] In defiance of history, the Council of Trent alleged that the doctrine of transubstantiation had always prevailed in the Church. [7]

Luther rejected the Scholastic doctrine of transubstantiation on the grounds that it lacks support in revelation and is not the most reasonable way of asserting the presence of the real flesh and blood of Christ ; but he does not claim that all others also should reject it. His own opinion is that in the consecrated sacrament the substances of the bread and wine remain, although the real flesh and blood of Christ are there also. Why should not Christ be able to include his body within the substance of the bread as well as within the accidents ? " In the sacra-

---

[1] See *supra*, p. 202 ; Harnack, *op. cit.* i. 209 n. 1.
[2] Harnack, *op. cit.* ii. 137 *sq.*
[3] *Cf.* J. Moffatt, *The First Five Centuries of the Church* (London, 1938), p. 145.
[4] Thomas Aquinas, *op. cit.* iii. 73 *sqq.*
[5] *Ibid.* iii. 79. 1–4, 6 *sq.*   [6] *Ibid.* iii. 80. 12.
[7] *Canones et decreta Concilii Tridentini*, sess. xiii, ch. 3 *sq.*

ment it is not necessary to the presence of the real body and
real blood that the bread and wine should be transubstantiated,
so that Christ may be contained beneath the accidents; but
while both bread and wine continue there, it can be said with
truth, ' This bread is my body, this wine is my blood,' and
conversely." [1] When Melanchthon went to hold conferences
with Butzer, Luther could give him the instruction, that " in
and with the bread the body of Christ is truly partaken of, that
accordingly all that takes place actively and passively in the
bread takes place actively and passively in the body of Christ,
that the latter is distributed, eaten and masticated with the
teeth." [2] Brenz, who after Luther's death was among the
most active opponents of union with the Reformed theologians,
asks what would be the consequence if, by any accident, the
consecrated bread were eaten by a mouse. He decides that
the mouse would have eaten the true body of Christ.[3]

Zwingli allowed only a symbolical explanation of the body
and blood of Christ in the sacrament. Calvin, again, stood
between Zwingli and Luther : the body of Christ is not now
present on earth anywhere as substance, but it is present as
power, and in the Eucharist it is so to our benefit.[4] The
Socinians expressly rejected the Catholic, Lutheran, and
Calvinistic doctrines of the Supper, and attempted to restore
to the Eucharist its original meaning. The Racovian Catechism of 1609, in which their doctrines are set forth in detail,
says that " it is an institution of the Lord Christ, that believers
in him should break and eat bread and drink of a cup together,
with the view of commemorating him, or showing forth his
death." He is said to have instituted that rite because he
wished the remembrance of this to be above all other things
celebrated in the Church; for of all the actions which he
undertook with a view to our salvation, his death was the most
difficult and exhibited the strongest proof of his love towards
us.[5]

The sacraments of baptism and the Eucharist are rooted
in magical ideas, and the efficacy ascribed to them has always
retained a more or less magical character. In the Report of
the Archbishops' Commission on Doctrine in the Church of

[1] Luther, ' De captivitate Babylonica ecclesiæ præludium. 1520,'
in *Werke*, vi (Weimar, 1888), p. 508 *sqq.*
[2] Harnack, *op. cit.* vii. 264.
[3] D. Schenkel, *Das Wesen des Protestantismus*, i (Schaffhausen,
1845), p. 563 *sq.*
[4] Calvin, *op. cit.* iv. 17. 18.
[5] *The Racovian Catechism* (London, 1818), p. 263 *sq.*

England it is said that there is " at once a sharp distinction of Sacraments from magic. In magic the use of the formula is held to enable the wizard to control powers other than human. Belief in the efficacy of Sacraments is rooted in faith in the revealed will of God to bestow gifts of grace through certain appointed signs." [1] But then, how is it that the appointed signs are so similar to certain pagan rites with which Christianity had come into contact, and which certainly contained a lot of magic ? Wizards are not necessary for the performance of magical acts. In magic man simply makes use of supernatural means which act mechanically. Eusebius tells the story of a sick old man who was longing to die, and whose wish was fulfilled by a few drops from a moistened piece of Eucharistic bread being dropped into his mouth.[2] But in the case of the Eucharist there really is a wizard who administers it, or what else shall I call the priest who, according to the main tradition of the Church, has to celebrate the rite in order to make it valid ? [3] Is he not supposed to possess some quality capable of bringing about a supernatural effect which other persons lack ? The bishop of Birmingham, who was not a member of the Commission, writes that the modern world rejects as an absurdity such priestly pretensions as this that any priest could associate the spiritual presence of Christ with the consecrated elements of bread and wine.[4]

For the saving effect attributed to baptism and the Eucharist there is no moral justification. A righteous God does not forgive a sinner unless he repents, and if he repents he is forgiven without any external rite. Repentance is not much spoken of in connection with those sacraments. In the case of baptism it was formerly expected of converts. In Tertullian's time the teachers who undertook to prepare the catechumens for reception at the baptismal font insisted on the necessity of repentance and amendment of life.[5] But he tells us that when the proselyte heard that baptism conferred upon him who received it the remission of all his former sins, he persuaded himself that he might with safety defer the work of repentance, and passed the time allotted for his probation in a more unrestrained enjoyment of those worldly and sensual pleasures

[1] *Doctrine in the Church of England*, p. 128.
[2] Eusebius, *Historia ecclesiastica*, vi. 44.
[3] *Doctrine in the Church of England*, p. 132.
[4] The bishop of Birmingham (E. W. Barnes), 'Foreword,' in *The Church and the Twentieth Century*, edited by G. L. H. Harvey (London, 1936), p. xv.
[5] Tertullian, *De pœnitentia*, 1–5.

in which he knew that after baptism he could not indulge without forfeiting his hopes of eternal happiness. So general had this practice become that Tertullian devotes a considerable portion of the tract *De pœnitentia* to the exposure of its wickedness.[1] When infant baptism was introduced repentance ceased of course even nominally to be required of him who was going to be baptised.

While baptism blots out the sins of the past, the Roman Catholic Church has another sacrament for the remission of sins committed afterwards, that of penance, which became practically the most important means of grace. Certain statements of Jesus [2] left no doubt as to the general power vested in the Church to forgive all manner of sins ; such is the belief reasserted in the decree *Lamentabili* of 3rd July 1907. In the earliest times it was held by the Christian Church that after baptism, while lighter sins needed only to be confessed to the gracious God,[3] serious sins excluded the offender altogether from the community.[4] But this rigorous practice was soon broken through, and by a public confession of sins even gross sinners were allowed restoration, though at first not more than once. Hermas gives assurances of forgiveness for all sins except blasphemy against the Lord and betrayal of the brethren ; but " to the servants of God there is but one repentance " [5]—a restriction which later writers apply to public penance only.[6] Tertullian treats as a fixed regulation a custom established in the course of the latter half of the second century, according to which a baptised person in the case of a first relapse might be restored to the favour of God and of the Church by making a public confession of his guilt. It was not sufficient that the offender felt the deepest remorse : he was required to express his contrition by some public acts which consisted in various external marks of humility. The penitent was clothed in the meanest apparel ; he lay in sack-cloth and ashes ; he either fasted entirely or lived upon bread and water; he passed whole days and nights in tears and lamentations, he embraced the knees of the presbyters as they entered the church, and entreated the brethren to intercede by their prayers in his behalf. In this state of degradation and exclusion from the communion of the

[1] See particularly *ibid.* 6.
[2] *Matthew* xvi. 19, xviii. 18 ; *John* xx. 21–3.
[3] *1 John* i. 9.
[4] F. Loofs, *Leitfaden zum Studium der Dogmengeschichte* (Halle, 1906), p. 205.
[5] Hermas, *Pastor*, iii. 9. 19, ii. 4. 1.
[6] Tertullian, *De pœnitentia*, 7, 9 ; Origen, *Homilia in Leviticum* xv. 2 ; Ambrose, *De pœnitentia*, ii. 95.

faithful he remained a longer or a shorter period, according to the magnitude of his offence ; and when that period was expired the bishop publicly pronounced his absolution, by which he was restored to the favour of God and to the communion of the Church.[1] The benefits of this penance could be obtained only once.[2] But although a penitent who relapsed could not be reconciled to the Church in this world, Tertullian does not exclude him from all hope of pardon in the next. He expressly distinguishes between remission of sins by the Church and by God ; and affirms that the sincere penitent, though he may not by his tears and lamentations obtain readmission into the Church, may yet secure his reception into the kingdom of heaven.[3] In the tract *De pœnitentia* he spoke as if all crimes committed after baptism might once, though only once, be pardoned upon repentance.[4] But in the tract *De pudicitia*, which was written after he became a Montanist, we find him drawing a distinction between greater and less offences, between those which could not and those which could be pardoned by the Church.[5] Among the venial sins he classes such as being angry without a cause and allowing the sun to go down upon our wrath, acts of violence, evil-speaking, rash swearing, non-performance of contracts, and white lies ; and among the heinous sins, homicide, idolatry, fraud, denial of Christ, blasphemy, adultery, fornication,[6] and even second marriages.[7] Of these he says that there is no remission, and that even Christ will not intercede for those who commit them. *De pudicitia* was directed against an edict, issued by Pope Calixtus, which allowed adulterers and fornicators to be readmitted to the communion of the Church if they had done penance. In another tract Tertullian maintained that the stain of mortal sin after baptism could only be washed away by martyrdom, by the baptism of the sinner in his own blood.[8] The milder practice with regard to the sins of the flesh prevailed, and in the latter part of the third century certain concessions were allowed in the case of relapse into idolatry. Moreover, the assumption that there can be only one repentance after baptism became untenable.[9]

An important change was that private confession in the presence of the priest became the rule. This state of matters

[1] Tertullian, *De pudicitia*, 5, 13, 18.
[2] *Idem, De pœnitentia*, 7, 9.
[3] *Idem, De pudicitia*, 3, 11, 18.　　[4] *Idem, De pœnitentia*, 8.
[5] *Idem, De pudicitia*, 1, 2, 18.
[6] *Ibid.* 19.　　[7] *Ibid.* 1.
[8] Tertullian, *Scorpiace*, 6.　　[9] Harnack, *op. cit.* ii. 111 *sq.*

P

began in the Iro-Scottish Church, where penitential regulations were drawn up for the laity, who were directed to confess their sins to the priest, as the monks had long been enjoined to do in their cloisters. From Ireland books dealing with penance came to the Anglo-Saxons and Franks and to Rome.[1] The Fourth Lateran Council definitely laid down the rule that " every believer of either sex, after arriving at the years of discretion, must by himself faithfully confess all his sins at least once a year to his own priest, and must study to carry out to the best of his ability the repentance enjoined upon him." [2]

This doctrine appears in perfected form in Thomas Aquinas. He shows that penance is a sacrament, and that the words " I absolve thee " are the form of it; for this sacrament receives its full effect from those things which are spoken by the priest. These words have been appointed by Christ (*Matthew* xvi); and the general rule that God alone forgives sin is not violated by the priest's absolution, since the priests are " authorised ministers." [3] The salvation of the sinner—that is, that his sin be removed from him—is not possible without the sacrament of penance, in which there operates the virtue of Christ's passion through the absolution of the priest together with the work of the penitent, who co-operates with grace for the destruction of sin. " When once anyone has fallen into sin, love, faith, and mercy do not deliver the man from sin without penitence; for love requires that a man grieve for the offence committed against his friend, and that a man be anxious to satisfy his friend; faith also requires that he seek to be justified from his sins through the virtue of the passion of Christ, which operates in the sacraments of the Church; rightly directed mercy also requires that a man find a remedy in his repenting for the misery into which his sin has plunged him." [4] " Penitence is twofold, namely, internal and external. That is internal penitence in which one grieves over sin committed, and such penitence ought to last till the close of life. . . . That is external penitence in which one shows external signs of grief, and verbally confesses his sins to the priest who absolves him, and makes satisfaction according to the priest's judgment; and such penitence does not need to continue till the end of life, but only for a time determined by the measure of the sin." [5] Thomas—as others had done before him—distinguishes between attrition and contrition : the former is a certain displeasure over sins committed. but only an approach to perfect contrition,

---

[1] Harnack, *op. cit.* v. 325.　　　　[2] Mansi, xxii. 1007 *sqq.*
[3] Thomas Aquinas, *op. cit.* iii. 84. 1, 3.
[4] *Ibid.* iii. 84. 5.　　　　[5] *Ibid.* iii. 84. 8.

which is a perfect penitent disposition.[1] As to the necessity of
confession, he points out that though according to divine law
only those guilty of mortal sin after baptism are obliged to
confess, yet according to positive law (that is, the decree of the
Council of 1215) all Christians must confess at least once a
year,[2] and that a dispensation exempting from confession can
on no account whatever be given.[3] As to the administrator of
confession it is said that as " he only is the minister of the
sacraments in which grace is given who has a ministry in connection with the true body of Christ," confession must be made
to him only.[4] But it is conceded that " in case of necessity a
layman supplies the place of the priest, so that it is possible to
make confession to him." [5] Thomas very strongly accentuates
the reticence of the minister : " it is of the essence of the sacrament that one conceal confession, and he sins as a violator of
the sacraments who reveals confession." [6] The confession made
before the priest is followed by absolution. Thomas has
developed the doctrine of " the power of the keys," and pointed
out that the priest's absolution is " the instrumental cause " of
the forgiveness of sin.[7] He explains that even the bad priest
retains the keys.[8] But absolution is preceded by the appoint-
ment of satisfaction, if such has not already been made ; here
the priest acts as a skilled physician and impartial judge.[9]
This performance is the necessary manifestation of sorrow
through works that are fitted to furnish a certain satisfaction
to the injured God, especially prayer, fasting, and alms.[10] It
is shown that one can render satisfaction for another ; yet this
thesis has its guarding clauses.[11]

Thomas' doctrine of the sacrament of penitence underwent
modifications made by the Scotists,[12] but it became permanent in
substance. The Council of Trent declared that " the universal
Church has always understood that the entire confession of
sins is of divine right necessary for all who have fallen after
baptism, because Christ has left behind him priests, repre-
sentatives of himself, as overseers and judges to whom all mortal
offences are to be made known " ; [13] and it pronounced anathema
on any one who shall deny that, " for the entire and perfect

[1] *Ibid*. iii. Suppl. 1. 2.　　　　　[2] *Ibid*. iii. Suppl. 6. 3.
[3] *Ibid*. iii. Suppl. 6. 6.　　　　　[4] *Ibid*. iii. Suppl. 8. 1.
[5] *Ibid*. iii. Suppl. 8. 2.　　　　　[6] *Ibid*. iii. Suppl. 11.
[7] *Ibid*. iii. Suppl. 17 *sqq*.
[8] *Ibid*. iii. Suppl. 19. 5.　　　　　[9] *Ibid*. iii. Suppl. 12 *sqq*.
[10] *Ibid*. iii. Suppl. 15. 3.　　　　[11] *Ibid*. iii. Suppl. 13. 2.
[12] D. A. W. Dieckhoff, *Der Ablassstreit* (Gotha, 1886), p. 19 *sq*.
[13] *Canones et decreta Concilii Tridentini*, sess. xiv, ch. 4.

remission of sins, three acts are required in the penitent, forming
as it were, the material of the sacrament of penance, namely
contrition, confession, and satisfaction, which are called th
three parts of penance." [1] Thus the party which declare
attrition to be enough for saving reception of the sacramen
did not succeed in asserting itself. At the same time attritio
is called " imperfect contrition " and is described as " a gif
of God and an impulse of the Holy Spirit " ; and it is said tha
although attrition cannot of itself conduct the sinner to justif
cation, " it disposes him to obtain the grace of God in th
sacrament of penance." [2]

For the inner penitent temper, the confession of sin, and th
satisfaction, Luther substituted repentance alone, which h
conceived of as the crushed feeling about sin awakened b
faith, and he also abolished the necessity for priestly co-opera
tion by substituting for the Catholic sacrament of penance th
thought of justification by faith. This became the gener.
Protestant doctrine. In England the Wesleyans have Churc
discipline, and so had the Calvinistic and Presbyterian bodie
but no confession, while the Salvation Army practises an
recommends public confession. The Anglicans do not prescrib
auricular confession, but merely advise it, when necessary,
satisfy one's conscience, and to the sick if they feel their co
science troubled. The Oxford Movement revived it to
considerable extent. [3] It should be noticed that confessio
even when unconnected with any formal absolution, serves
a means of purgation. We find this also among savages. " Tl
Akikuyu of British East Africa hold that sin is essential
remissible, and one needs only to confess it. The confession
made, usually, to a sorcerer or to a medicine-man who expe
the sin by a ceremony in which one subjects himself to tl
effects of a pretended emetic, *kotahikio*, a word derived fro
tahikia, ' to vomit.' " Such a view is found among son
American Indians as well, the words " to vomit " and " to co
fess " being synonymous, or nearly so. [4]

The sacrament of penance differs from the other sacramen
by having a distinctly ethical foundation. The starting-poi
is the contrition, or at any rate attrition, of the penitent, wh
the real sacrament is the external acts of him and the pries

---

[1] *Canones et decreta Concillii Tridentini*, sess. xiv, can. 4.

[2] *Ibid*. sess. xiv, ch. 4.

[3] E. L. van Becelaere, ' Penance (Roman Catholic),' in J. Hastin
Encyclopædia of Religion and Ethics, ix (Edinburgh, 1917), p. 715.

[4] H. S. Darlington, ' The Confession of Sins,' in *The Psychoanaly
Review*, xxiv (1937), p. 150 *sq*.

[5] See Thomas Aquinas, *op. cit.* iii. 84. 1.

But as the contrition did not constitute the actual sacrament, the opinion could easily creep in that in the case of sacramental penitence the addition of the sacrament completes the imperfect contrition; and as a matter of fact this opinion became dominant.[1] The priest became the most important person. As Joh. von Paltz says, very few men are really contrite, though every one can bring himself in the end to an imperfect contrition, and then the priest, through the sacrament of penance, transfers the imperfect contrition into a perfect one and saves the soul of the penitent.[2] The satisfaction preceding absolution, again, became a sheer travesty through the practice of indulgences, which implied the exchange of more arduous penitential acts for very small performances, such as the payment of penance money—with such excellent result that the Church dispensed from the temporal pains of purgatory all, whether living or departed, who either themselves or vicariously performed those ecclesiastical exercises.

The practice and theory of indulgences were strenuously attacked by Wyclif and Huss, by Wesel and Wessel, and, as everybody knows, by Luther. But his own doctrine that only such repentance has value before God as springs from faith, is also open to severe criticism, though of a very different kind. It alienates repentance widely from the sphere of morality, and is fraught with serious consequences. It makes it as constant as faith. The first of Luther's ninety-five theses runs : " Our Lord and Master Jesus Christ in saying : ' Repent ye,' etc., intended that the whole life of believers should be penitence." A Lutheran theologian remarks that if men are told that they must constantly repent, and that particular acts of repentance are of no use, there are few who will ever repent.[3]

[1] Dieckhoff, *op. cit.* p. 12.
[2] J. von Paltz, *Cœlifodina*, published 1510, quoted by Dieckhoff, *op. cit.*
[3] Harnack, *op. cit.* vii. 252 *sq.*

CHAPTER XI

CHRISTIANITY AND THE REGARD FOR HUMAN LIFE

IN the preceding chapters we have studied Christian ethics as expressed in theories of salvation, and examined how far these theories are in agreement with the nature of our moral emotions. The remaining portion of the book will be devoted to a discussion of the influence which Christianity has exercised in concrete cases upon ideas and behaviour within different branches of morality.

It inspired a greater regard for human life than was felt anywhere in pagan society. The extraordinary importance it attached to this earthly life as a preparation for the life to come naturally increased the guilt of any one who, by cutting it short, not only killed the body, but probably to all eternity injured the soul ; and in a still higher degree than most other crimes, homicide was regarded as an offence against God, because man had been made in his image.[1] Gratian says that even the slayer of a Jew or a heathen has to undergo a severe penance, " quia imaginem Dei et spem futuræ conversionis exterminat." [2] The early Christians, in fact, condemned homicide of any kind as a heinous sin ; and in this, as in all other questions of moral concern, the distinction of nationality or race was ignored by them.

The sanctity which they attached to the life of every human being led to a total condemnation of warfare, sharply contrasting with the prevailing sentiment in the Roman Empire. In accordance with the general spirit of their religion, as also with special passages in the Bible,[3] they considered war unlawful in all circumstances. Justin Martyr quotes the prophecy of Isaiah, that " nation shall not lift up sword against nation, neither shall they learn war any more," [4] and proceeds to say that the instruction in the Word of God which was given by the

[1] L. Thomassin, *Dictionnaire de discipline ecclésiastique*, ii (Paris 1856), pp. 1069, 1074.
[2] Gratian, *Decretum*, i. 50, 40.
[3] *Matthew* v. 9, 39, 44, xxvi. 52 ; *Romans* xii. 17 ; *Ephesians* vi. 12
[4] *Isaiah* ii. 4.

twelve Apostles " had so good effect that we, who heretofore
were continually devouring each other, will not now so much
as lift up our hand against our enemies." [1] Lactantius asserts
that " to engage in war cannot be lawful for the righteous man,
whose warfare is that of righteousness itself." [2] Tertullian
asks : " Can it be lawful to handle the sword, when the Lord
himself has declared that he who uses the sword shall perish by
it ? " [3] And in another passage he states that " the Lord by
his disarming of Peter disarmed every soldier from that time
forward." [4] Origen calls the Christians the children of peace,
who, for the sake of Jesus, never take up the sword against any
nation ; who fight for their monarch by praying for him, but
who take no part in his wars, even though he urge them.[5] It
is true that even in early times Christian soldiers were not
unknown ; Tertullian alludes to such as were engaged in military
pursuits together with their heathen countrymen.[6] But the
number of Christians enrolled in the army seems not to have
been very considerable before the era of Constantine,[7] and
though they were not cut off from the Church, their profession
was looked upon as hardly compatible with their religion.
Basil says that soldiers, after their term of military service has
expired, are to be excluded from the sacrament of the communion for three whole years.[8] And according to one of the
canons of the Council of Nice, those Christians who, having
abandoned the profession of arms, afterwards returned to it,
" as dogs to their vomit," were for some years to occupy in the
Church the place of penitents.[9]

A divine law which prohibited all resistance to enemies
could certainly not be accepted by the State, especially at a
time when the Empire was seriously threatened by foreign
invaders. Christianity could therefore never become a State
religion unless it gave up its attitude towards war. And it
gave it up. In 314 a Council condemned soldiers who, from
religious motives, deserted their colours.[10] Athanasius, " the

[1] Justin, *Apologia I. pro Christianis*, 39.
[2] Lactantius, *Divinæ institutiones*, vi (' De vero cultu '), 20.
[3] Tertullian, *De corona*, 11.   [4] *Idem, De idolatria*, 19.
[5] Origen, *Contra Celsum*, v. 33, viii. 73.
[6] Tertullian, *Apologeticus*, 42.
[7] E. Le Blant, *Inscriptions chrétiennes de la Gaule antérieures au VIII.
siècle*, i (Paris, 1856), p. 84 sqq.
[8] Basil, *Epistola CLXXXVIII., ad Amphilochium*, can. 13 (Migne,
Patrologiæ cursus, Ser. Græca, xxxii. 681 sq.).
[9] *Concilium Nicænum*, A.D. 325, can. 12 (Labbe-Mansi, *Sacrorum
Conciliorum collectio*, ii. 674).
[10] *Concilium Arelatense I.*, A.D. 314, can. 3 (Labbe-Mansi, *op. cit.
i. 471). Cf.* Le Blant, *op. cit.* i. lxxxii.

father of orthodoxy," ventured to say that it was not only permissible, but praiseworthy, to kill enemies in war.[1] Ambrose eulogised the warlike courage which prefers death to bondage and disgrace, and claimed the Old Testament warriors as spiritual ancestors; nay, he adopted the classical maxim that one who does not defend a friend from injury is as much at fault as he who commits the injury.[2] Augustine, who was forced to face the question by the havoc of the Teutonic migrations and the peril of the Empire, explored the subject very fully. He tried to prove that the practice of war was quite compatible with the teaching of the New Testament. The soldiers who were seeking for a knowledge of salvation were not directed to throw aside their arms and renounce their profession, but were advised to be content with their wages.[3] St. Peter baptised Cornelius, the centurion, in the name of Christ, without exhorting him to give up the military life.[4] St. Paul himself took care to have a strong guard of soldiers for his defence.[5] And was not the history of David, the " man after God's own heart," an evidence of those being wrong who say that " no one who wages war can please God." [6] When Christ declared that " all they that take the sword shall perish with the sword," he referred to such persons only as arm themselves to shed the blood of others without either command or permission of any lawful authority.[7] A great deal depends on the causes for which men undertake war, and on the authority they have for doing so. Those wars are just which are waged with a view to obtaining redress for wrongs, or to chastising the undue arrogance of another State. The monarch has the power of making war when he thinks it advisable, and, even if he be a sacrilegious king, a Christian may fight under him, provided that what he enjoined upon the soldier personally is not contrary to the precept of God.[8] In short, though peace is our final good, though in the City of God there is peace in eternity,[9] war may sometimes be a necessity in this sinful world.

By the writings of Augustine the theoretical attitude of the Church towards war was definitely settled, and later theologians

[1] Athanasius, ' Epistola ad Amunem monachum,' in Migne, Patrologiæ cursus, Ser. Græca, xxiii. 1173.
[2] Ambrose, De officiis ministrorum, i. 35, 36, 40.
[3] Augustine, Epistola CXXXVIII. ad Marcellinum, 15 (Migne, Patrologiæ cursus, xxxiii. 531 sq.).
[4] Idem, Epistola CLXXXIX. ad Bonifacium, 4 (Migne, xxxiii. 855).
[5] Idem, Epistola XLVII. ad Publicolam, 5 (Migne, xxxiii. 187).
[6] Idem, Epistola CLXXXIX. ad Bonifacium, 4 (Migne, xxxiii. 855).
[7] Idem, Contra Faustum Manichæum, xxii. 70.
[8] Ibid. xxii. 75.   [9] Idem, De civitate Dei, xix. 11.

only reproduced or further elaborated his view. Thomas
Aquinas says that there are three requisites for a war to be just.
The first thing is the authority of the prince by whose command
the war is to be waged. It does not belong to a private person
to start a war, for he can prosecute his claim in the court of
his superior. But since the care of the commonwealth is
entrusted to princes, it belongs to them not only to defend it
with the sword against inward disturbances by punishing malefactors, but also to protect it from enemies without by the
sword of war. The second requisite is a just cause, so that they
who are assailed should deserve to be assailed for some fault
that they have committed; as Augustine says: " Just wars
are usually defined as those which avenge injuries, in cases
where a nation or city has to be chastised for having either
neglected to punish the wicked doings of its people, or neglected
to restore what has been wrongfully taken away." The third
requisite is a right intention of promoting good or avoiding
evil; as Augustine says: " Eagerness to hurt, bloodthirsty
desire to revenge, an untamed and unforgiving temper, ferocity
in renewing the struggle, lust of empire,—these and the like
excesses are justly blamed in war." [1]

Yet it was not with a perfectly safe conscience that the
Church thus sanctioned the practice of war. There was a
feeling that a soldier scarcely could make a good Christian. In
the middle of the fifth century, Leo the Pope declared it to be
contrary to the rules of the Church that persons after the action
of penance—that is, persons then considered to be pre-eminently
bound to obey the law of Christ—should revert to the profession
of arms. [2] Various Councils forbade the clergy to engage in
warfare, [3] and certain canons excluded from ordination all who

[1] Thomas Aquinas, *Summa theologica*, ii.-ii. 40. 1.
[2] Leo Magnus, *Epistola XC. ad Rusticum*, 12 (Migne, liv. 1206 *sq.*).
[3] One of the Apostolic Canons requires that any bishop, priest, or
deacon who devotes himself to military service shall be degraded from
his ecclesiastical rank (*Canones ecclesiastici qui dicuntur Apostolorum*,
83 [74] [C. C. J. Bunsen, *Analecta Ante-Nicœna*, ii, London, 1854, p. 31]).
The Councils of Toulouse, in 633 (ch. 45, in Labbe-Mansi, x. 630), and of
Meaux, in 845 (can. 37, *ibid.* xiv. 827), condemned to a similar punishment those of the clergy who ventured to take up arms. Gratian says
(*Decretum*, ii. 23. 8. 4) that the Church refuses to pray for the soul of a
priest who died on the battle-field. But notwithstanding the canons of
Councils and the decrees of popes, ecclesiastics frequently participated
in battles (Nicolaus I., *Epistolœ et Decreta*, 83 [Migne, cxix. 922]; W.
Robertson, *The History of the Reign of the Emperor Charles V.*, i [London,
1806], pp. 330, 385; R. Ward, *An Enquiry into the Foundation and History
of the Law of Nations in Europe, from the Time of the Greeks and Romans,
to the Age of Grotius*, i [London, 1795], p. 365 *sq.*; H. T. Buckle, *History of*

had served in an army after baptism.[1] Penance was prescribed for those who had shed blood on the battle-field.[2]   Thus
the ecclesiastical canons made in William the Conqueror's reign
by the Norman prelates, and confirmed by the Pope, directed
that he who was aware that he had killed a man in a battle
should do penance for one year, and that he who had killed
several should do a year's penance for each.[3]   Occasionally
the Church seemed to wake up to the evils of war in a more
effective way : there are several notorious instances of wars
being forbidden by popes.   But in such cases the prohibition
was only too often due to the fact that some particular war was
disadvantageous to the interests of the Church.   And while
doing comparatively little to discourage wars which did not
interfere with her own interests, the Church did all the more
to excite war against those who were objects of her hatred.

It has been suggested that the transition from the peaceful
principles of the primitive Church to the essentially military
Christianity of the crusades was chiefly due to the terrors and
the example of Islam.   " The spirit of Mohammedanism,"
says Lecky, " slowly passed into Christianity, and transformed
it into its image."   Until then, " war was rather condoned
than consecrated, and, whatever might be the case with a few
isolated prelates, the Church did nothing to increase or encourage
it." [4]   But this view is hardly consistent with facts.   Christianity had entered on the war-path already before it came into
contact with Mohammedanism.   Wars against Arian peoples
had been represented as holy wars, for which the combatants
would be rewarded by Heaven.[5]   The war which Chlodwig made
upon the Visigoths was not only undertaken with the approval

Civilization in England [London, 1894], i. 204, ii. 464 ; J. F. Bethune-
Baker, The Influence of Christianity on War [Cambridge, 1888], p. 52 ;
E. Dümmler, Geschichte des Ostfränkischen Reichs [Berlin and Leipzig,
1862–88], ii. 637).

[1] H. Grotius, De jure belli et pacis, i. 2. 10. 10 ; J. Bingham, Antiquities of the Christian Church, iv. 4. 1 (Works, ii. [Oxford, 1855], p. 55).

[2] Pœnitentiale Bigotianum, iv. 1. 4 (F. W. H. Wasserschleben, Die
Bussordnungen der abendländischen Kirche [Halle, 1851], p. 453) ;
Pœnit. Vigilanum, 27 (ibid. p. 529) ; Pœnit. Pseudo-Theodori, xxi. 15 (ibid.
p. 587 sq.).   Cf. La mort de Garin le Loherin (Paris, 1846), p. 213 : " Ainz
se repent et se claime cheti ; Ses pechiés plore au soir et au matin, De ce
qu'il a tans homes mors et pris."

[3] D. Wilkins, Concilia Magnæ Britanniæ et Hiberniæ, i (London,
1737), p. 366.

[4] W. E. H. Lecky, History of European Morals from Augustus to
Charlemagne, ii (London, 1890), p. 251 sq.

[5] J. Gibb, ' The Christian Church and War,' in The British Quarterly
Review, lxxiii (London, 1881), p. 86.

of the clergy, but it was " properly their war, and Chlodwig undertook it in the capacity of a religious champion in all things but the disinterestedness which ought to distinguish that character." Remigius of Reims assisted him by his countenance and advice, and the Catholic priesthood set every engine of their craft in motion to second and encourage him.[1] In the Church itself there were germs out of which a military spirit would naturally develop itself. The famous dictum, " Nulla salus extra ecclesiam," was promulgated as early as the days of Cyprian. The general view of mediæval orthodoxy was that those beyond the pale of the Church, heathen and heretics alike, were unalterably doomed to hell, whereas those who would acknowledge her authority, confess their sins, receive the sacrament of baptism, partake of the Eucharist, and obey the priest, would be infallibly saved. If war was allowed by God, could there be a more proper object for it than the salvation of souls otherwise lost ? And for those who refused to accept the gift of grace offered them, could there be a juster punishment than death ? Moreover, had not the Israelites fought great battles " for the laws and the sanctuary ? "[2] Had not the Lord Himself commissioned them to attack, subdue, and destroy his enemies ? Had he not commanded them to root out the natives of Canaan, who, because of their abominations, had fallen under God's judgment, and to kill man and beast in the Israelitish cities which had given themselves to idolatry, and to burn all the spoil, with the city itself, as a whole offering to Jehovah ?[3] There was no need, then, for the Christians to go to the Mohammedans in order to learn the art of religious war. The Old Testament, the revelation of God, gave better lessons in it than the Koran, and was constantly cited in justification of any cruelty committed in the name of religion.[4]

It was thus in perfect consistency with the general teachings of the Church that she regarded an exploit achieved against the infidels as a merit which might obliterate the guilt of the most atrocious crimes. Such a deed was the instrument of pardon to Henry II. for the murder of Becket,[5] and was supposed to be the means of cure to St. Louis in a dangerous illness.

[1] T. Greenwood, *The First Book of the History of the Germans* (London, 1836), p. 518.

[2] *1 Maccabees* xiii. 3. Thomas Aquinas (*op. cit.* ii.–ii. 188. 3) quotes this passage in support of the doctrine that fighting may be directed to the preservation of divine worship.

[3] *Deuteronomy* xiii. 15 *sq.*

[4] *Cf.* B. Constant, *De la religion*, ii (Paris, 1825), p. 229 *sq.*

[5] G. Lyttelton, *The History of the Life of King Henry the Second*, iii (London, 1771), p. 96.

Fighting against infidels took rank with fastings, penitential discipline, visits to shrines, and almsgivings, as meriting the divine mercy.[1] He who fell in the battle could be confident that his soul was admitted directly into the joys of paradise.[2] And this held good not only of wars against Mohammedans. The massacres of Jews and heretics seemed no less meritorious than the slaughter of the more remote enemies of the gospel. Nay, even a slight shade of difference from the liturgy of Rome became at last a legitimate cause of war.

It is true that these views were not shared by all. At the Council of Lyons, in 1274, the opinion was pronounced, and of course eagerly attacked, that it was contrary to the examples of Christ and the apostles to uphold religion with the sword and to shed the blood of unbelievers.[3] In the following century Bonet maintained that, according to the Scriptures, a Saracen or any other disbeliever could not be compelled by force to accept the Christian faith.[4] Franciscus a Victoria declared that " diversity of religion is not a cause of just war ";[5] and a similar opinion was expressed by Soto,[6] Covarruvias a Leyva,[7] and Suarez.[8]   According to Balthazar Ayala, the most illustrious Spanish lawyer of the sixteenth century, it does not belong to the Church to punish infidels who have never received the Christian faith, whereas those who, having once received it, afterwards endeavour to prevent the propagation of the gospel, may, like other heretics, be justly persecuted with the sword.[9] But the majority of jurisconsults, as well as of canonists, were in favour of the orthodox view that unbelief is a legitimate reason for going to war.[10]   And this principle was, professedly, acted upon to an extent which made the history of Christianity

[1] Cf. H. H. Milman, History of Latin Christianity, iv (London, 1867), p. 209.

[2] Cf. F. Laurent, Études sur l'histoire de l'Humanité, vii (Paris, 1865), p. 257.

[3] Bethune-Baker, op. cit. p. 73.

[4] H. Bonet, L'arbre des batailles (Bruxelles and Leipzig, 1883), iv. 2, p. 86.

[5] Franciscus a Victoria, Relectiones Theologicæ (Lugduni, 1587), vi. 10, p. 231.   Yet infidels may be compelled to allow the gospel to be preached (ibid. v. 3. 12, p. 214 sq.).

[6] D. Soto, De justitia et jure (Lugduni, 1582), v. 3. 5, fol. 154.

[7] D. de Covarruvias a Leyva, Regulæ, Peccatum, ii. 10. 2 (Opera omnia, i [Antverpiae, 1638], p. 496).

[8] Suarez, quoted by E. Nys, Le droit de la guerre et les précurseurs de Grotius (Bruxelles and Leipzig, 1882), p. 98.

[9] B. Ayala, De iure et officiis bellicis et disciplina militari (Duaci, 1582), i. 2. 29 sq.

[10] Nys, op. cit. p. 89 ; idem, in his Introduction to Bonet's L'arbre des batailles, p. xxiv.

for many centuries a perpetual crusade, and transformed the Christian Church into a military power even more formidable than Rome under Cæsar and Augustus. Very often religious zeal was a mere pretext for wars which in reality were caused by avarice or desire for power. The aim of the Church was to be the master of the earth, rather than the servant of heaven. She preached crusades not only against infidels and heretics, but against any disobedient prince who opposed her boundless pretensions. And she encouraged war when rich spoils were to be expected from the victor, as a thankoffering to God for the victory He had granted, or as an atonement for the excesses which had been committed.

Out of this union between war and Christianity there was born that curious bastard, Chivalry. The secular germ of it existed already in the German forests. According to Tacitus, the young German who aspired to be a warrior was brought into the midst of the assembly of the chiefs, where his father, or some other relative, solemnly equipped him for his future vocation with shield and javelin.[1] Assuming arms was thus made a social distinction, which subsequently derived its name from one of its most essential characteristics, riding a war-horse. But Chivalry became something quite different from what the word indicates. The Church knew how to lay hold of knighthood for her own purposes. The investiture, which was originally of a purely civil nature, became, even before the time of the crusades, as it were, a sacrament.[2] The priest delivered the sword into the hand of the person who was to be made a knight, with the following words : " Serve Christi, sis miles in nomine Patris, Filii, et Spiritus Sancti, Amen." [3] The sword was said to be made in semblance of the cross so as to signify " how our Lord God vanquished in the cross the death of human lying " ; [4] and the word " Jesus " was sometimes

---

[1] Tacitus, *Germania*, 13. According to Honoré de Sainte Marie (*Dissertations historiques et critiques sur la chevalerie* [Paris, 1718], p. 30 *sqq.*), Chivalry is of Roman, according to some other writers, of Arabic origin. L. Gautier (*La Chevalerie* [Paris, 1884], pp. 14, 16) repudiates these theories, and regards Chivalry as " un usage germain idéalisé par l'Église." See also A. Rambaud, *Histoire de la civilisation française*, i (Paris, 1893), p. 178 *sq.*

[2] W. Scott, ' An Essay on Chivalry,' in *Miscellaneous Prose Works*, vi (Edinburgh, 1827), p. 16 ; C. Mills, *The History of Chivalry*, i (London, 1826), p. 10 *sq.* For a description of the various religious ceremonies accompanying the investiture, see *The Book of the Ordre of Chyualry or Knyghthode* (Westminster, 1484 ?), fol. 27b *sqq. Cf.* also A. Favyn, *The Theater of Honour and Knight-Hood*, i (London, 1623), p. 52.

[3] Favyn, *op. cit.* i. 52.

[4] *Ordre of Chyualry*, fol. 31a *sq.*

engraven on its hilt.[1]   God Himself had chosen the knight to
defeat with arms the miscreants who wished to destroy his
Holy Church, in the same way as he had chosen the clergy to
maintain the Catholic faith with Scripture and reasons.[2]   The
knight was to the body politic what the arms are to the human
body : the Church was the head, Chivalry the arms, the citizens,
merchants, and labourers the inferior members ; and the arms
were placed in the middle to render them equally capable of
defending the inferior members and the head.[3]   " The greatest
amity that should be in this world," says the author of ' The
Book of the Ordre of Chyualry,' " ought to be between the
knights and clerks." [4]   The several gradations of knighthood
were regarded as parallel to those of the Church.[5]   And after
the conquest of the Holy Land the union between the profession
of arms and the religion of Christ became still more intimate by
the institution of the two military orders of monks, the Knights
Templars and Knights of St. John of Jerusalem.

The duties which a knight took on himself by oath were
very extensive, but not very well defined. He should defend
the holy Catholic faith, he should defend justice, he should
defend women, widows, and orphans, and all those of either
sex that were powerless, ill at ease, and groaning under oppression and injustice.[6]   In the name of religion and justice he could
thus practically wage war almost at will. Though much real
oppression was undoubtedly avenged by these soldiers of the
Church, the knight seems as a rule to have cared little for the
cause or necessity of his doing battle. " La guerre est ma patrie,
Mon harnois ma maison : Et en toute saison Combatre c'est
ma vie," was a saying much in use in the sixteenth century.[7]
The general impression which Froissart gives us in his history
is, that the age in which he lived was completely given over to
fighting, and cared about nothing else whatever.[8]   The French
knights never spoke of war but as a feast, a game, a pastime.
" Let them play their game," they said of the cross-bow men
who were showering down arrows on them ; and " to play a
great game," *jouer gros jeu*, was their description of a battle.[9]
Previous to the institution of Chivalry there certainly existed

[1] Mills, *op. cit.* i. 71.   [2] *Ordre of Chyualry*, fol. 11*b*.
[3] *Le Jouuencel* (Paris, 1493), fol. 94 *sqq.*
[4] *Ordre of Chyualry*, fol. 12*a*.   [5] Scott, *loc. cit.* p. 15.
[6] *Ordre of Chyualry*, fols. 11*b*, 17*a* ;   De la Curne de Sainte-Palaye,
Mémoires sur l'ancienne chevalerie, i (Paris, 1781), pp. 75, 129.
[7] F. de la Nouë, *Discours politiques et militaires* (Basle, 1587), p. 215.
[8] See Sir James Stephen's essay on ' Froissart's Chronicles,' in his
Horæ Sabbaticæ, i (London, 1891), p. 22 *sqq.*
[9] Sainte-Palaye, *op. cit.* ii. 61.

much fighting in Christian countries, but knighthood rendered war " a fashionable accomplishment." [1] And so all-absorbing became the passion for it that, as real injuries were not likely to occur every day, artificial grievances were created, and tilts and tournaments were invented in order to keep in action the sons of war when they had no other employments for their courage. Even in these images of war—which were by no means so harmless as they have sometimes been represented to be [2]—the intimate connection between Chivalry and religion displays itself in various ways. Before the tournament began, the coats of arms, helmets, and other objects were carried into a monastery, and after the victory was gained the arms and the horses which had been used in the fight were offered up at the church. [3] The proclamations at the tournaments were generally in the name of God and the Virgin Mary. Before battle the knights confessed and heard mass ; and when they entered the lists, they held a sort of image with which they made the sign of the cross. [4] Moreover, " as the feasts of the tournaments were accompanied by these acts of devotion, so the feasts of the Church were sometimes adorned with the images of the tournaments." [5] It is true that the Church now and then made attempts to stop these performances. [6] But then she did so avowedly because they prevented many knights from joining the holy wars, or because they swallowed up treasures which might otherwise with advantage have been poured into the Holy Land. [7]

Closely connected with the feudal system was the practice of private war. Though tribunals had been instituted, and even long after the kings' courts had become well-organised and powerful institutions, a nobleman had a right to wage war upon another nobleman from whom he had suffered some gross injury. [8] On such occasions not only the relatives, but also the

---

[1] J. G. Millingen, *The History of Duelling*, i (London, 1841), p. 70.

[2] Sainte-Palaye, *op. cit.* i. 179, ii. 75 ; C. D. Du Cange, ' Dissertations ou Réflexions sur l'histoire de S. Louys,' in Petitot, *Collection complète des Mémoires relatifs à l'histoire de France* (Paris, 1819–29), iii. 122 *sq.* ; Honoré de Sainte Marie, *op. cit.* p. 186.

[3] Sainte-Palaye, *op. cit.* i. 151.   [4] *Ibid.* ii. 57.   [5] *Ibid.* ii. 57 *sq.*

[6] Du Cange, *loc. cit.* p. 124 *sqq.* ; Honoré de Sainte Marie, *op. cit.* p. 186 ; Sainte-Palaye, *op. cit.* ii. 75.

[7] Du Cange, *loc. cit.* p. 125 *sq.*

[8] The right of private war generally supposed nobility of birth and equality of rank in both the contending parties (Ph. de Beaumanoir, *Les coutumes du Beauvoisis* [Paris, 1842], lix. 5 *sq.*, vol. ii. 355 *sq* ; W. Robertson, *The History of the Reign of the Emperor Charles V.*, i [London, 1806], p. 329). But it was also granted to the French *communes* and to the free towns in Germany, Italy, and Spain (A. Du Boys, *Histoire du droit criminel des peuples modernes*, ii [Paris, 1858], p. 348).

vassals, of the injured man were bound to help him in his quarrel, and the same obligation existed in the case of the aggressor.[1] Only greater crimes were regarded as legitimate causes of private war,[2] but this rule was not at all strictly observed. We read of a nobleman who declared war against Frankfort, because a lady residing there had promised to dance with his cousin, but danced with another ; and the city was obliged to satisfy the wounded honour of the gentleman.[3] The barons fled to arms upon every quarrel ; he who could raise a small force at once made war upon him who had anything to lose. The nations of Europe were subdivided into innumerable states of inferior rank, which were almost independent, and declared war and made treaties with all the vigour and all the ceremonies of powerful monarchs. Contemporary historians describe the excesses committed in prosecution of these intestine quarrels in such terms as excite astonishment and horror ; and great parts of Europe were in consequence reduced to the condition of a desert, which it ceased to be worth while to cultivate.

The Church made some feeble attempts to put an end to this state of things. Thus, about the year 990, ordinances were directed against the practice of private war by several bishops in the south of France, who agreed to exclude him who violated their ordinances from all Christian privileges during his life, and to deny him Christian burial after his death.[4] A little later, men engaged in warfare were exhorted, by sacred relics and by the bodies of saints, to lay down their arms and to swear that they would never again disturb the public peace by their private hostilities.[5] But it is hardly likely that such directions had much effect as long as the bishops and abbots themselves were allowed to wage private war by means of their vidames, and exercised this right scarcely less frequently than the barons.[6]

---

[1] Du Cange, *loc. cit.* pp. 450, 458.

[2] *Ibid.* p. 445 *sq.* ; W. Arnold, *Deutsche Urzeit* (Gotha, 1879), p. 341 ; C. G. von Wächter, *Beiträge zur deutschen Geschichte* (Tübingen, 1845), p. 46.

[3] Von Wächter, *op. cit.* p. 57.

[4] ' Charta de Treuga et Pace per Aniciensem Praesulem Widonem in Congregatione quamplurium Episcoporum, Principium, et Nobilium hujus Terrae sancita,' in J. Dumont, *Corps universel diplomatique du droit des gens,* i (Amsterdam, 1726), p. 41.

[5] R. Glaber, *Historiæ sui temporis,* iv. 5 (M. Bouquet, *Recueil des Historiens des Gaules et de la France,* x [Paris, 1760], p. 49) ; Robertson, *op. cit.* i. 335.

[6] N. Brussel, *Nouvel examen de l'usage général des fiefs en France,* i (Paris, 1750), p. 144. How much the prelates were infected by the general spirit of the age, appears from a characteristic story of an arch-

Nor does it seem that the Church brought about any considerable change for the better by establishing the Truce of God, involving obligatory respite from hostilities during the great festivals of the Church, as also from the evening of Wednesday in each week to the morning of Monday in the week ensuing.[1] We are assured by good authorities that the Truce was generally disregarded, though the violator was threatened with the penalty of excommunication.[2] Most barons could probably say with Bertram de Born : " La paix ne me convient pas ; la guerre seule me plaît. Je n'ai égard ni aux lundis, ni aux mardis. Les semaines, les mois, les années, tout m'est égal. En tout temps, je veux perdre quiconque me nuit." [3] The ordinance enjoining the *treuga Dei* was transgressed even by the popes.[4] It was too unpractical a direction to be obeyed, and was soon given up even in theory by the authorities of the Church. Thomas Aquinas says that, as physicians may lawfully apply remedies to men on feast-days, so just wars may be lawfully prosecuted on such days for the defence of the commonwealth of the faithful, if necessity so requires ; " for it would be tempting God for a man to want to keep his hands from war under stress of such necessity." [5] And in support of this opinion he quotes the First Book of the Maccabees, where it is said : " Whosoever shall come to make battle with us on the sabbath day, we will fight against him." [6]

It seems that the main cause of the abolition of private war was not any measure taken by the Church, but the increase of the authority of emperors or kings. In France the right of waging private war was moderated by Louis IX., checked by Philip IV., suppressed by Charles VI.[7] In England, after the Norman Conquest, private wars seem to have occurred more

bishop of Cologne who gave to one of his vassals a castle situated on a sterile rock. When the vassal objected that he could not subsist on such a soil, the archbishop answered : " Why do you complain ? Four roads unite under the walls of your castle " (A. Du Boys, *Histoire du droit criminel de l'Espagne* [Paris, 1870], p. 504).

[1] Glaber, *op. cit.* v. i (Bouquet, *op. cit.* x. 59) ; C. D. Du Cange *Glossarium ad scriptores mediæ et infimæ Latinitatis*, vi (Parisiis, 1736), p. 1267 *sq.* ; C. J. F. Henault, *Nouvel abrégé chronologique de l'histoire de France* (Paris, 1752), p. 106.

[2] Du Cange, *Glossarium*, vi. 1272 ; E. Nys, *op. cit.* p. 114.

[3] A. F. Villemain, *Cours de littérature française, Littérature du moyen âge*, i (Paris, 1830), p. 122 *sq.*

[4] Belli, *De re militari*, quoted by Nys, *op. cit.* p. 115.

[5] Thomas Aquinas, *op. cit.* ii.–ii. 40. 4.   [6] *1 Maccabees* ii. 41.

[7] Robertson, *op. cit.* i. 55, 56, 338 *sqq.* ; H. Hallam, *View of the State of Europe during the Middle Ages*, i (London, 1860), p. 207 ; Brussel, *op. cit.* i. 142.

Q

rarely than on the Continent, probably owing to the strength
of the royal authority, which made the execution of justice more
vigorous and the jurisdiction of the King's court more extensive
than was the case in most other countries.[1] Freeman mentions
as the last instance of private war in England one from the time
of Edward IV.[2] In Scotland the practice of private war
received its final blow only late in the eighteenth century, when
the clans were reduced to order after the rebellion of 1745.[3]
While, then, it is impossible to ascribe to the Church any
considerable part in the movement which ultimately led to the
entire abolition of private war, we have, on the other hand,
to take into account the encouragement which the Church gave
to the warlike spirit of the time by the establishment of
Chivalry,[4] and by sanctioning war as a divine institution. Before
a battle, the service of mass was usually performed by both
armies in the presence of each other, and no warrior would
fight without secretly breathing a prayer.[5] Pope Adrian IV.
says that a war commenced under the auspices of religion
cannot but be fortunate ; [6] and it was commonly believed that
God took no less interest in the battle than did the fighting
warriors. Bonet, who wrote in the fourteenth century, puts
to himself the question, why there are so many wars in the
world, and gives the answer, " que toutes sont pour le pechié
du siecle dont nostre seigneur Dieu pour le pugnir permet les
guerres, car ainsi le maintient l'escripture." [7] The Catechism
of the Council of Trent brings home that there are on record
instances of slaughter executed by the special command of God
Himself, as when the sons of Levi, who put to death so many
thousands in one day, after the slaughter were thus addressed
by Moses : " Ye have consecrated your hands this day to the
Lord." [8] Even quite modern Catholic writers refer to the
canonists who held that a State might lawfully make war upon
a heretic people which is spreading heresy, and upon a pagan
people which prevents the preaching of the gospel.[9]

[1] Brussel, op. cit. i. 343 sq.
[2] E. A. Freeman, Comparative Politics (London, 1896), p. 328 sq.
[3] T. J. Lawrence, Essays on some disputed Questions in Modern International Law (Cambridge, 1885), p. 254 sq.
[4] I do not understand how Gautier can say (op. cit. p. 6) that
Chivalry was the most beautiful of those means by which the Church
endeavoured to check war.
[5] Mills, op. cit. i. 147.   [6] Laurent, op. cit. vii. 245.
[7] Bonet, op. cit. iv. 54, p. 150.
[8] The Catechism of the Council of Trent, iii. 6. 5.
[9] W. E. Addis and T. Arnold, A Catholic Dictionary (London, 1903),
p. 944.

In its attitude towards war Protestantism was in general agreement with Catholicism. Luther defended vigorously the Christian soldier.[1] Calvin argued that war is a branch of the work of retributive justice which has been entrusted by God to the civil magistrate, and that it has the same moral justification as the police measures which protect the citizens against criminals. If it be objected that the New Testament does not expressly permit Christians to fight, it is to be observed that the gospel does not undertake to legislate about civil polity, and that it presupposes the Old Testament, " in which the greatest men of God, like Moses and David, were mighty men of valour in the service of God." [2] The subject received prominence in the Protestant Confessions, which found it desirable to allay any misgivings that might be felt by princes as to the political implications of evangelical religion. They explicitly claimed for the State the right of waging war, and the Anabaptists were condemned because they considered war unlawful for a Christian.[3] Even the necessity of a just cause as a reason for taking part in warfare, which was reasserted at the time of the Reformation, was subsequently allowed to drop out of sight. It is noticeable that in the Anglican Article XXXVII., which is to the effect that a Christian at the command of the magistrate may wear weapons and serve in the wars, the word *justa* in the Latin form preceding the word *bella* has been omitted altogether. The Lutheran clergy, however, have followed the tradition of the Catholic Church that military service is inconsistent with the clerical office ; [4] and the Anglican Church reaffirmed its adherence to it during the recent war by forbidding the clergy to offer themselves for such service. The Reformed Churches have occasionally left it to ministers to judge for themselves as to whether the necessity was such as to require them to offer their services as fighting men to the State. This was lately done by the Church of Scotland.[5]

Nor did the old opinion that war is a providential institution and a judgment of God die with the Middle Ages. Bacon looks upon wars as " the highest trials of right ; when princes and states that acknowledge no superior upon earth shall put themselves upon the justice of God, for the deciding of their controversies by such success as it shall please Him to give on

---

[1] Luther, *Ob Kriegsleute auch im seligen Stande sein können*, 1526.
[2] Calvin, *Institutio Christianæ religionis*, 1559, iv. 20. 10–12.
[3] *Augsburg Confession*, i. 16 ; *Second Helvetic Confession*, xxx. 4.
[4] H. Martensen, *Christian Ethics. Special Part. Second Division* (Edinburgh, 1882), p. 236.
[5] W. P. Paterson, ' War,' in J. Hastings, *Encyclopædia of Religion and Ethics*, xii (Edinburgh, 1921), p. 680.

either side." [1] Réal de Curban says that a war is seldom successful unless it be just, hence the victor may presume that God is on his side.[2] According to Jeremy Taylor, " kings are in the place of God, who strikes whole nations, and towns, and villages ; and war is the rod of God in the hands of princes." [3] And it is not only looked upon as an instrument of divine justice, but it is also said, generally, " to work out the noble purposes of God." [4] Its tendency, as a theological writer assures us, is " to rectify and exalt the popular conception of God," there being nothing among men " like the smell of gunpowder for making a nation perceive the fragrance of divinity in truth." [5] By war the different countries " have been opened up to the advance of true religion." [6] " No people ever did, or ever could, feel the power of Christian principle growing up like an inspiration through the national manhood, until the worth of it had been thundered on the battle-field." [7] War is, " when God sends it, a means of grace and of national renovation " ; it is " a solemn duty in which usually only the best Christians and most trustworthy men should be commissioned to hold the sword." [8] According to Proudhon, it is the most sublime phenomenon of our moral life,[9] a divine revelation more authoritative than the gospel itself.[10] The warlike people is the religious people ; [11] war is the sign of human grandeur, peace a thing for beavers and sheep. " Philanthrope, vous parlez d'abolir la guerre ; prenez garde de dégrader le genre humain." [12]

In order to prove the consistency of war with Christianity appeals are still, as in former days, made to the Bible : to the divinely-sanctioned example of the ancient Israelites, to the fact that Jesus never prohibited those around him from bearing arms, to the instances of the centurions mentioned in the gospel, to Paul's predilection for taking his spiritual metaphors from the profession of the soldier, and so on.[13] According to

[1] Bacon, *Letters and Life*, i (*Works*, viii [London, 1862]), p. 146.
[2] G. de Réal de Curban, *La science du gouvernement*, v (Paris, 1764), p. 394 *sq.*
[3] J. Taylor, *The Whole Works of*, xii (London, 1822), p. 164.
[4] ' The Sword and Christianity,' in *The Boston Review. Devoted to Theology and Literature*, iii (Boston, 1863), p. 261.
[5] *Ibid.* iii. 259, 257.
[6] T. A. Holland, *A Time of War* (Brighton, 1885), p. 14.
[7] *Boston Review*, iii. 257.
[8] ' Christianity and War,' in *The Christian Review*, xxvi (Rochester, 1861), p. 604.
[9] P.-J. Proudhon, *La guerre et la paix*, ii (Bruxelles, [1861]), p. 420.
[10] *Ibid.* i. 62, ii. 435.   [11] *Ibid.* i. 45.   [12] *Ibid.* i. 43.
[13] See, for example, E. H. Browne, *An Exposition of the Thirty-Nine Articles* (London, 1887), p. 827 *sq.* ; *Christian Review*, xxvi. 603 *sq.*

Canon Mozley, the Christian recognition of the right of war was contained in Christianity's original recognition of nations.[1] " By a fortunate necessity," a universal empire is impossible.[2] Each nation is a centre by itself, and when questions of right and justice arise between these independent centres, they cannot be decided except by mutual agreement or force. The aim of the nation going to war is exactly the same as that of the individual in entering a court, and the Church, which has no right to decide which is the right side, cannot but stand neutral and contemplate war forensically, as a mode of settling national questions, which is justified by the want of any other mode.[3] A natural justice, Canon Mozley adds, is inherent not only in wars of self-defence ; there is an instinctive reaching in nations and masses of people after alteration and readjustment, which has justice in it. And there are wars of progress which, so far as they are really necessary for the due advantage of mankind, are approved of by Christianity.[4] As a matter of fact, it would be impossible to mention a single instance of a war waged by a Protestant country, from any motive whatsoever, to which the bulk of its clergy, being in the service of the State, have not given their sanction and support. As Mr. Gibb observes, the Protestant minister has been as ready with his Thanksgiving Sermon for the victories of a profligate war as the Catholic priest has been with his *Te Deum* ; " indeed, the latter was probably the more independent of the two, because of his allegiance to Rome." [5] The opposition against war has generally come from other quarters.

There have been, and still are, Christian sects which, on religious grounds, condemn war of any kind. In the fourteenth century the Lollards taught that homicide in war is expressly contrary to the New Testament ; they were persecuted partly on this account.[6] Of the same opinion were the Anabaptists of the sixteenth century, who suffered imprisonment and death rather than bear arms ; their insistence upon peace was the main cause of the constant war made upon them. They could claim on their side the words of men like Colet and Erasmus. From the pulpit of St. Paul's Colet thundered that " an unjust

[1] J. B. Mozley, *Sermons preached before the University of Oxford* (London, 1883), p. 119.
[2] *Ibid.* p. 112.   [3] *Ibid.* p. 100 *sqq.*
[4] *Ibid.* p. 104 *sq.* So also Rothe, in his *Theologische Ethik*, iii (Wittenberg, 1848), p. 960, defends the war of conquest as legitimate in order to the replacement of a lower by a higher civilisation.
[5] Gibb, *loc. cit.* p. 90.
[6] G. G. Perry, *A History of the English Church. First Period* (London, 1881), pp. 455, 467.

peace is better than the justest war," and that, "when men out of hatred and ambition fight with and destroy one another, they fight under the banner, not of Christ, but of the Devil." [1] According to Erasmus, "nothing is more impious, more calamitous, more widely pernicious, more inveterate, more base, or in sum more unworthy of a man, not to say of a Christian," than war. It is worse than brutal ; to man no wild beast is more destructive than his fellow-man. When brutes fight, they fight with weapons which nature has given them, whereas we arm ourselves for mutual slaughter with weapons which nature never thought of. Neither do beasts break out in hostile rage for trifling causes, but either when hunger drives them to madness, or when they find themselves attacked, or when they are alarmed for the safety of their young. But we, on frivolous pretences, what tragedies do we act on the theatre of war ! Under colour of some obsolete and disputable claim to territory ; in a childish passion for a mistress ; for causes even more ridiculous than these, we kindle the flame of war. Transactions truly hellish are called holy wars. Bishops and grave divines, decrepit as they are in person, fight from the pulpit the battles of the princes, promising remission of sins to all who will take part in the war of the prince, and exclaiming to the latter that God will fight for him, if he only keeps his mind favourable to the cause of religion. And yet, how could it ever enter into our hearts, that a Christian should imbrue his hands in the blood of a Christian ! What is war but murder and theft committed by great numbers on great numbers ! Does not the gospel declare in decisive words that we must not revile again those who revile us, that we should do good to those who use us ill, that we should give up the whole of our possessions to those who take a part, that we should pray for those who design to take away our lives ? "The man who engages in war by choice, that man, whoever he is, is a wicked man ; he sins against nature, against God, against man, and is guilty of the most aggravated and complicated impiety." [2]

In Protestantism the chief opponents of war have been sectarians. Among these the Quakers are the most important. By virtue of various passages in the Old and the New Testament,[3] they contend that all warfare, whatever be its peculiar features, circumstances, or pretexts, is wholly at variance with the Christian religion. It is always the duty of

---

[1] J. R. Green, *History of the English People*, ii (London, 1878), p. 93.
[2] Erasmus, *Adagia* (Coloniæ Allobrogum, 1612), iv. 1, col. 893 *sqq.*
[3] *Isaiah* ii. *sqq.* ; *Micah* iv. 1 *sqq.* ; *Matthew* v. 38 *sqq.*, xxvi. 52; *Luke* vi. 27 *sqq.* ; *John* xviii. 36 ; *Romans* xii. 19 *sqq.* ; *1 Peter* iii. 9.

Christians to obey their Master's high and holy law—to suffer wrong, to return good for evil, to love their enemies. War is also inconsistent with the Christian principle that human life is sacred, and that death is followed by infinite consequences. Since man is destined for eternity, the future welfare of a single individual is of greater importance than the merely temporal prosperity of a whole nation. When cutting short the days of their neighbour and transmitting him, prepared or unprepared, to the awful realities of an everlasting state, Christians take upon themselves a most unwarrantable responsibility, unless such an action is expressly sanctioned by their divine Master, as was the case among the Israelites. In the New Testament there is no such sanction, hence it must be concluded that, under the Christian dispensation, it is utterly unlawful for one man to kill another, under whatever circumstances of expediency or provocation the deed may be committed. And a Christian who fights by the command of his prince, and in behalf of his country, not only commits sin in his own person, but aids and abets the national transgression.[1]

Similar views, however, are also found independently of any particular form of sectarianism. According to Dr. Wayland, all wars, defensive as well as offensive, are contrary to the revealed will of God, aggression from a foreign nation calling not for retaliation and injury, but rather for special kindness and goodwill.[2] Theodor Parker, the Congregational minister, looks upon war as a sin, a corrupter of public morals, a practical denial of Christianity, a violation of God's eternal love.[3] W. Stokes, the Baptist, observes that Christianity cannot sanction war, whether offensive or defensive, because war is an " immeasurable evil, by hurling unnumbered myriads of our fellow-men to a premature judgment and endless despair." [4] Even before the outbreak of the Great War it was said that those who compared the state of opinion during later years with that of former periods, could not fail to observe a marked progress of a sentiment antagonistic to war in the various sections of the Christian Church.[5] Yet the duties which compulsory military service imposes upon the male population of most Christian countries presuppose that a Christian should have no scruples

[1] J. J. Gurney, *Observations on the Distinguishing Views and Practices of the Society of Friends* (London, 1834), p. 375 *sqq.*

[2] F. Wayland, *The Elements of Moral Science* (London, 1863), pp. 375, 379.

[3] T. Parker, *A Sermon of War* (Boston, 1846), p. 23.

[4] W. Stokes, *All War inconsistent with the Christian Religion* (London, 1855), p. 41.

[5] *Cf.* Gibb, *loc. cit.* p. 81.

about taking part in any war waged by the State ; and they are recognised as binding by the clergy of those countries. What, then, about " conscientious objectors " ? In France, during the Great War, the authorities considered that it was not the business of the State to decide whether a man's dislike of fighting was due to conscience, want of patriotism, or personal cowardice ; and in consequence the few who refused to serve were shot. In England, even after compulsory service was instituted, men were allowed to plead conscientious scruples ; but things were not made pleasant for them, and they were on the whole condemned by public opinion.[1]

It is significant that the protest against war which has, presumably, exercised the widest influence on public opinion, came from a school of moralists whose tendencies were not only anti-orthodox, but distinctly hostile to the most essential dogmas of Christian theology. Bayle, in his ' Dictionary,' calls Erasmus' essay against war one of the most beautiful dissertations ever written.[2] He observes that the more we consider the inevitable consequences of war, the more we feel disposed to detest those who are the causes of it.[3] Its usual fruits may, indeed, " make those tremble who undertake or advise it, to prevent evils which, perhaps, may never happen and which, at the worst, would often be much less than those which necessarily follow a rupture."[4] To Voltaire war is an " infernal enterprise," the strangest feature of which is that " every chief of the ruffians has his colours consecrated, and solemnly prays to God before he goes to destroy his neighbour."[5] He asks what the Church has done to suppress this crime. Bourdaloue preached against impurity, but what sermon did he ever direct against the murder, rapine, brigandage, and universal rage, which desolate the world ? " Miserable physicians of souls, you declaim for five quarters of an hour against the mere pricks of a pin, and say no word on the curse which tears us into a thousand pieces."[6] Voltaire admits that in certain circumstances war is an inevitable curse, but rebukes Montesquieu for saying that natural defence sometimes involves the necessity of attack, when a nation perceives that a longer peace would

---

[1] W. R. Inge, *Christian Ethics and Modern Problems* (London, 1932), p. 310.

[2] P. Bayle, *Dictionnaire historique et critique*, vi (Paris, 1820), p. 239, art. Erasme.

[3] *Ibid.* ii. 463, art. Artaxata.

[4] *Ibid.* i. 472, art. Alting (Henri).

[5] Voltaire, *Dictionnaire philosophique*, art. Guerre (*Œuvres complètes*, xl [*s.l.*, 1785], p. 562).

[6] *Ibid.* xl. 564.

place another nation in a position to destroy it.[1] Such a war,
he argues, is as illegitimate as possible. " It is to go and kill
your neighbour for fear that your neighbour, who does not
attack you, should be in a condition to attack you ; that is
to say, you must run the risk of ruining your country, in the
hope of ruining without reason some other country ; this is,
to be sure, neither fair nor useful." [2] The chief causes which
induce men to massacre in all loyalty thousands of their
brothers and to expose their own people to the most terrible
misery, are the ambitions and jealousies of princes and their
ministers.[3] Similar views are expressed in the great ' Encyclopédie.' " La guerre est le plus terrible des fléaux qui détruisent
l'espèce humaine : elle n'épargne pas même les vainqueurs ;
la plus heureuse est funeste. . . . Ce ne sont plus aujourd'-
hui les peuples qui déclarent la guerre, c'est la cupidité des
rois qui leur fait prendre les armes ; c'est l'indigence qui les
met aux mains de leurs sujets." [4]

However vehemently Voltaire and the Encyclopædists condemned war, they did not dream of a time when all wars would
cease. Other writers were more optimistic. In the early part
of the eighteenth century Abbé Saint-Pierre—whose abbotship
involved only a nominal connection with the Church—published
a project of perpetual peace, which was based on the idea of a
general confederation of European nations.[5] This project was
much laughed at ; Voltaire himself calls its author " un homme
moitié philosophe, moitié fou." But once called into being,
the idea of a perpetual peace and of a European confederation
did not die. It was successively conceived by Rousseau,[6]
Bentham,[7] and Kant.[8] But on the other hand it met with a
formidable enemy in the awakening spirit of nationalism.

The Napoleonic oppression called forth resistance. Philosophers and poets sounded the war-trumpet. The dream of a
universal monarchy was looked upon as absurd and hateful,
and the individuality of a nation as the only possible security

---

[1] Montesquieu, *De l'esprit des lois*, x. 2 (*Œuvres* [Paris, 1837], p.
256).

[2] Voltaire, *op. cit.* xl. 565.

[3] *Ibid.* pp. 466, 564.

[4] *Encyclopédie méthodique*, Art militaire, ii. 618 *sq.*

[5] Saint-Pierre, *Projet de Traité pour rendre la paix perpétuelle entre les
souverains Chrétiens.*

[6] Rousseau, *Extrait du Projet de paix perpétuelle, de M. l'Abbé de
Saint-Pierre* (*Œuvres complètes*, i [Paris, 1837], p. 606 *sqq.*).

[7] J. Bentham, *A Plan for an universal and perpetual Peace* (*Works*, ii
[Edinburgh, 1843], p. 546 *sqq.*).

[8] Kant, *Zum ewigen Frieden.*

for its virtue.[1] War was no longer attributed to the pretended interests of princes or to the caprices of their advisers. It was praised as a vehicle of the highest right,[2] as a source of national renovation.[3] By war, says Hegel, " finite pursuits are rendered unstable, and the ethical health of peoples is preserved. Just as the movement of the ocean prevents the corruption which would be the result of perpetual calm, so by war people escape the corruption which would be occasioned by a continuous or eternal peace." [4] Similar views have been expressed by later writers. War is glorified as a stimulus to the elevated virtues of courage, disinterestedness, and patriotism.[5] It has done more great things in the world than the love of man, says Nietzsche.[6] It is the mother of art and of all civil virtues, says Ruskin.[7] Others defend war, not as a positive good, but as a necessary means of deciding the most serious international controversies, denying that arbitration can be a substitute for all kinds of war. Questions which are intimately connected with national passions and national aspirations, and questions which are vital to a nation's safety, will never, they say, be left to arbitration. Each State must be the guardian of its own security, and cannot allow its independence to be calmly discussed and adjudicated upon by an external tribunal.[8] Moreover, arbitration would prove effective only where the contradictory pretensions could be juridically formulated, and these instances are by far the less numerous and the less important.[9] And would it not, in many cases, be impossible to find impartial arbiters ? Would not arbitration often be influenced by a calculation of the forces which every power interested could bring into the field, and would not war be resorted to where arbitration failed to reconcile conflicting

[1] Fichte, *Reden an die deutsche Nation* (Leipzig, 1824). *Cf. idem, Ueber den Begriff des wahrhaften Krieges* (Tübingen, 1815).
[2] Arndt, quoted by M. Jähns, *Ueber Krieg, Frieden und Kultur* (Berlin, 1893), p. 302.
[3] P. J. A. von Feuerbach, *Ueber die Unterdrückung und Wiederbefreiung Europens* (München and Leipzig, 1813).
[4] Hegel, *Grundlinien der Philosophie des Rechts*, § 324, p. 317 (English translation [London, 1896], p. 331).
[5] See, for example, P. Mabille, *La guerre* (Paris, 1884), p. 139.
[6] Nietzsche, *Also sprach Zarathustra*, i (Chemnitz and Leipzig, 1883), p. 63.
[7] Ruskin, ' Crown of Wild Olive, Lecture on War,' in *Works*, vi (Keston, Orpington, 1873), pp. 99, 105.
[8] T. J. Lawrence, *op. cit.* p. 275 *sq.* ; H. Sidgwick, ' The Morality of Strife,' in *International Journal of Ethics*, i (London and Philadelphia, 1891), p. 13.
[9] Geffken, quoted by Jähns, *op. cit.* p. 352 n. 2.

interests, or where a decision was opposed to a high-spirited people's sense of justice ? The prediction of such difficulties hampering the work of a League of Nations has, indeed, been amply confirmed by recent events.

✗ It is said that, although Christianity has not abolished war, it has nevertheless, even in war, asserted the principle that human life is sacred by prohibiting all needless destruction. ┼ The Canon ' De treuga et pace ' laid down the rule that non-resisting persons should be spared ; [1] and Franciscus a Victoria maintained not only that between Christian enemies those who made no resistance could not lawfully be slain, [2] but that even in war against the Turks it was wrong to kill children and women. [3] This doctrine of mercy, however, was far in advance of the habits and general opinion of the time. [4] If the simple peasant often was spared, that was largely from motives of prudence, [5] or because the valiant knight considered him unworthy of the lance. [6] As late as the seventeenth century, Grotius was certainly not supported by the spirit of the age when he argued that, " if justice do not require, at least mercy does, that we should not, except for weighty causes tending to the safety of many, undertake anything which may involve innocent persons in destruction " ; [7] or when he recommended enemies willing to surrender on fair conditions, or unconditionally, to be spared. [8] Pufendorf, in echoing the doctrine of Grotius, [9] spoke to a world which was already convinced ; and in the eighteenth century Bynkershoek stands alone in giving to a belligerent unlimited rights of violence. [10] In reference to the assumption that this change of opinion is due to the influence of the Christian religion, it is instructive to note that Grotius, in support of his doctrine, appealed chiefly to pagan authorities ; and that even savage peoples, without the aid of Christianity,

---

[1] Gregory IX., ' Decretales,' i. 34. 2 (in *Corpus juris canonici*, ed. by A. Friedberg, ii [Lipsiae, 1881]).

[2] Franciscus a Victoria, *op. cit.* vi. 13, 35, 48, pp. 232, 241, 246 *sq.*

[3] *Ibid.* vi. 36, p. 241.

[4] *Cf.* W. E. Hall, *A Treatise on International Law* (Oxford, 1890), p. 395 n. 1.

[5] B. d'Argentré, *L'histoire de Bretaigne* (Paris, 1618), p. 391.

[6] Mills, *op. cit.* p. 132.

[7] Grotius, *op. cit.* iii. 11. 8.

[8] *Ibid.* iii. 11. 14 *sqq.*

[9] S. Pufendorf, *De jure naturæ et gentium* (Amstelodami, 1688), viii. 6. 8, p. 885.

[10] C. van Bynkershoek, *Questiones juris publici* (Lugduni Batavorum, 1737), i. 1, p. 3 : " Omnes enim vis in bello justa est " ; Hall, *op. cit.* p. 395 n. 1.

have arrived at the rule which in war forbids the destruction of helpless persons and captives.[1]

It is also remarkable that Augustine was under an obligation to Cicero for his attitude towards war, which was adopted by the Church. According to Cicero, a war, to be just, ought to be necessary, the sole object of war being to enable us to live undisturbed in peace. There are two modes of settling controversies, one by discussion, the other by a resort to force. The first is proper to man, the second is proper to brutes, and ought never to be adopted except where the first is not available. And when we obtain the victory we are bound to exercise consideration towards those whom we have conquered by force, and to receive into our protection those who throw themselves upon the honour of our general and lay down their arms.[2] Seneca anticipates Erasmus in his condemnation of war, which he regards as a " glorious crime," comparable to murder. " What is forbidden in private life is commanded by public ordinance. Actions which, committed by stealth, would meet with capital punishment, we praise because committed by soldiers. Men, by nature the mildest species of the animal race, are not ashamed to find delight in mutual slaughter, to wage wars, and to transmit them to be waged by their children, when even dumb animals and wild beasts live at peace with one another." [3] History attests that the Romans, in their intercourse with other nations, did not act upon Cicero's and Seneca's lofty theories of international morality; as Plutarch observes, the two names " peace " and " war " are mostly used only as coins, to procure, not what is just, but what is expedient.[4] This remark has never ceased to be true. War is a rock on which Christian principles have suffered the most miserable shipwreck.

---

[1] E. Westermarck, *The Origin and Development of the Moral Ideas*, i (London, 1912), p. 335 *sq.*
[2] Cicero, *De officiis*, i. 11.   [3] Seneca, *Epistulæ*, 95.
[4] Plutarch, *Vita Pyrrhi*, xii. 3, p. 389.

CHAPTER XII

CHRISTIANITY AND THE REGARD FOR HUMAN LIFE
(concluded)

WHILE the early Fathers utterly failed to put a stop to war, they succeeded in their endeavour to bring about a change of ideas with regard to another practice involving the destruction of human life, to wit, the practice of exposing new-born infants, which was very common in the Pagan Empire.

The exposure of deformed or sickly infants was an ancient custom in Greece; in Sparta, at least, it was enjoined by law. It was also approved of by the most enlightened among the Greek philosophers. Plato condemns all those children who are imperfect in limbs, as also those who are born from depraved citizens, to be buried in some obscure and unknown place; he maintains, moreover, that when both sexes have passed the age assigned for presenting children to the State, no child is to be brought to light, and that any infant who is by accident born alive shall be done away with.[1] Aristotle not only lays down the law with respect to the exposing or bringing up of children, that " nothing imperfect or maimed shall be brought up," but proposes that the number of children allowed to each marriage shall be regulated by the State, and that, if any woman be pregnant after she has produced the prescribed number, an abortion shall be procured before the fetus has life.[2] These views were in perfect harmony with the general tendency of the Greeks to subordinate the feelings of the individual to the interest of the State. Confined as they were to a very limited territory, they were naturally afraid of being burdened with the maintenance of persons whose life could be of no use. It is necessary, says Aristotle, to take care that the increase of the people shall not exceed a certain number, in order to avoid poverty and its concomitants, sedition and other evils.[3] It has been said that the exposure of healthy infants, which was frequently practised in Greece, was hardly approved of by

---

[1] Plato, *Respublica*, v. 460 *sq.*
[2] Aristotle, *Politica*, vii. 16, p. 1335.
[3] *Ibid.* ii. 6, p. 1265.

public opinion, although tolerated,[1] except at Thebes, where it was, according to Ælian, a crime punishable by death.[2] But recent researches have revealed the extraordinary prevalence of infanticide in ancient Greece. According to Mr. Zimmern, it remained a universal custom, so far as we know at least down to the fourth century, that it was within the discretion of the father whether a new-born child should be allowed to live. On the fifth day after birth, at the earliest, the infant was solemnly presented to the household and admitted to its membership. Up to the time of this ceremony the father had a complete power of selection, and it appears that this was quite frequently exercised, particularly in the case of female infants. The provision of a dowry for his daughters weighed heavily on a Greek father's mind, and what was easier than to evade it by pleading inability at the outset ? When it was decided that the infant was not to be " nourished," it would be packed in a cradle or a pot, and exposed in a public place. The Athenian " had a traditional abhorrence of violence, and interfered when he could on behalf of the helpless. If he consented to exercise his immemorial right over his own offspring, he did so with regret, for the sake of the city and his other children, because it was more merciful in the long run."[3] Dr. Inge has found from the speeches of Isæus, who lived in the fourth century before Christ, that in the pedigrees of eleven typical Athenian families, belonging to the middle class, the names of 97 males are mentioned, and of only 37 females.[4] Mr. Tarn writes that the prevalence of infanticide in Greece has been strenuously asserted from the literary texts, and as strenuously denied, but that for the late third and the second centuries the inscriptions are conclusive. " Of some thousand families from Greece who received Milesian citizenship c. 228–220, details of 79, with their children, remain ; these brought 118 sons and 28 daughters, many being minors ; no natural causes can account for those proportions. . . . More than one daughter was practically never reared, bearing out Poseidippus' statement that ' even a rich man always exposes a daughter.' Of 600 families from Delphic inscriptions, second century, just one per cent. reared two daughters."[5] Polybius says that the Greeks in the middle

[1] L. Schmidt, *Die Ethik der alten Griechen*, ii (Berlin, 1882), pp. 138, 463 ; C. F. Hermann-H. Blümner, *Lehrbuch der Griechischen Privat-alterthümer* (Freiburg i. B. and Tübingen, 1882), p. 77.

[2] Ælian, *Variæ historiæ*, ii. 7.

[3] A. Zimmern, *The Greek Commonwealth* (Oxford, 1931), p. 330 *sq.*

[4] W. R. Inge, *Christian Ethics and Modern Problems* (London, 1932), p. 263.

[5] W. W. Tarn, *Hellenistic Civilisation* (London, 1930), p. 92 *sq.*

of the second century refused to rear more than one or, at most, two children ;[1] and, according to Tarn, there is plenty of evidence to bear him out.[2]

In Rome custom or law enjoined the destruction of deformed infants. According to a law of the Twelve Tables, referred to by Cicero, monstrous abortions were not suffered to live.[3] With reference to a much later period Seneca writes : " We destroy monstrous births, and we also drown our children if they are born weakly and unnaturally formed " ; he adds that it is an act of reason thus to separate what is useless from what is sound.[4] But there was no tendency in Rome to encourage infanticide beyond these limits. While the Greek policy was to restrain, the Roman policy was to encourage population. Being engaged in incessant wars of conquest, Rome was never afraid of being over-populated, but, on the contrary, tried to increase the number of its citizens by according special privileges to the fathers of many children, and exempting poor parents from most of the burden of taxation.[5] The power of life and death which the Roman father possessed over his children undoubtedly involved the legal right of destroying or exposing newborn infants ; but it is equally certain that the act was in ordinary circumstances disapproved of.[6] An ancient " law," ascribed to Romulus—which according to Mommsen could have been merely a priestly direction [7]—enjoined the father to bring up all his sons and at least his eldest daughter, and forbade him to destroy any well-formed child till it had completed its third year, when the affection of the parent might be supposed to be developed.[8] In later times we find exposure of children condemned by poets, historians, philosophers, jurists. Among nefarious acts committed in sign of grief on the day when Germanicus died Suetonius mentions the exposure of new-born babes.[9] Epictetus indignantly opposes the saying of Epicurus that men should not rear children : " Even a sheep will not desert its young, nor a wolf ; and shall a man ? " [10]

---

[1] Polybius, *Historiarum reliquiæ*, xxxvi. 17. 7.
[2] Tarn, *op. cit.* p. 92.   [3] Cicero, *De legibus*, iii. 8.
[4] Seneca, *De ira*, i. 15.
[5] Montesquieu, *De l'esprit des lois*, xxiii. 20 *sq.* (*Œuvres* [Paris, 1837], p. 398 *sqq.*) ; W. E. H. Lecky, *History of European Morals*, ii (London, 1890), p. 27.
[6] J. Denis, *Histoire des théories et des idées morales dans l'antiquité*, ii (Paris, 1856), p. 110.
[7] T. Mommsen, *Römisches Strafrecht* (Leipzig, 1899), p. 619.
[8] Dionysius of Halicarnassus, *Antiquitates Romanæ*, ii. 15.
[9] Suetonius, *Caligula*, 5.
[10] Epictetus, *Dissertationes*, i. 23.

Julius Paulus, the jurist, pronounced him who refused nourishment to his child, or exposed it in a public place, to be guilty of murder [1]—a statement which is to be understood, not as a legal prohibition of exposure, but only as the expression of a moral opinion. [2]　On the other hand, though the exposure of healthy infants was disapproved of in Pagan Rome, it was not generally regarded as an offence of very great magnitude, especially if the parents were destitute. [3]　During the Empire it was practised on an extensive scale, and in the literature of the time it is spoken of with frigid indifference.　Since the life of the victim was frequently saved by some benevolent person or with a view to profit, [4] it was not looked upon in the light of downright infanticide, which in the case of a healthy infant seems to have been strictly prohibited by custom. [5]

The practice of exposing new-born infants was vehemently denounced by the early Christian Fathers. [6]　They tried to convince men that if the abandoned infant died, the unnatural parent was guilty of nothing less than murder, while the fact that such foundlings, girls and boys, were trained up for the service of lust formed another argument against exposure. [7] The enormity of the crime of causing an infant's death was enhanced by the notion that children who had died unbaptised were doomed to eternal perdition. [8]　According to a decree of the Council of Mentz in 852, the penance imposed on the mother was heavier if she killed an unbaptised than if she killed a baptised child. [9]　In the year 1556 Henry II. of France made a law which punished as a child-murderess any woman who had concealed her pregnancy and delivery, and whose child was found dead, " privé, tant du saint sacrement de baptesme, que

---

[1] *Digesta*, xxv. 3. 4.

[2] G. Noodt, ' Julius Paulus, sive de partus expositione et nece apud veteres,' in *Opera omnia*, i (Lugduni Batavorum, 1767), p. 465 *sqq.* ; F. Walter, *Geschichte des Römischen Rechts bis auf Justinian*, § 538, vol. ii (Bonn, 1861), p. 148 *sq.* ; Spangenberg, ' Ueber das Verbrechen des Kindermords und der Aussetzung der Kinder,' in *Neues Archiv des Criminalrechts*, iii (Halle, 1819–20), p. 10 *sqq.* ; Mommsen, *op. cit.* p. 620 n. 1.

[3] Quintilian, *Declamationes*, 306 ; Plutarch, *De amore prolis*, 5.

[4] L. Lallemand, *Histoire des enfants abandonnés et délaissés* (Paris, 1885), p. 59 ; Lecky, *op. cit.* ii. 28.

[5] Mommsen, *op. cit.* p. 619.

[6] See J.-F. Terme and J.-B. Montfalcon, *Histoire des enfans trouvés* (Paris, 1840), p. 67 *sqq.*

[7] Justin Martyr, *Apologia I. pro Christianis*, 27, 29.

[8] *Cf.* Spangenberg, *loc. cit.* p. 20.

[9] *Canon Hludowici regis*, 9 (G. H. Pertz, *Monumenta Germaniæ historica*, *Leges*, iii [Hannoveræ], p. 413).

sépulture publique et accoustumée." [1] This statute—to which
there is a counterpart in England in the statute 21 Jac. 1, c. 27,[2]
and in the Scotch law of 1690, c. 21 [3]—thus went so far as to
constitute a presumptive murder, avowedly under the influence
of that Christian dogma to which Lecky generously attributes,
in the first instance, " the healthy sense of the value and sanctity
of infant life which so broadly distinguishes Christian from
Pagan societies." [4]

If the Pagans had been comparatively indifferent to the
sufferings of the exposed infant, the Christians became all the
more cruel to the unfortunate mother, who, perhaps in a fit of
despair, had put to death her new-born child. The Christian
emperor Valentinian I. made infanticide a capital offence.[5]
According to the ' Coutume de Loudunois,' a mother who killed
her child was burned.[6] In Germany and Switzerland she was
buried alive with a pale thrust through her body ; [7] this punishment was prescribed by the criminal code of Charles V., side
by side with drowning.[8] Until the end of the eighteenth or the
beginning of the nineteenth century infanticide was a capital
crime everywhere in Europe, except in Russia.[9] Then, under
the humanising influence of that rationalistic movement which
compelled men to rectify so many preconceived opinions,[10] it
became manifest that an unmarried woman who destroys her
illegitimate child is not in the same category as an ordinary
murderess.[11] It was pointed out that shame and fear, the excite-

---

[1] Isambert, Decrusy, and Armet, *Recueil général des Anciennes Lois
Françaises*, xiii (Paris, 1828), p. 472 *sq.*

[2] W. Blackstone, *The Commentaries on the Laws of England*, iv
(London, 1876), p. 198.

[3] J. Erskine of Carnock, *Principles of the Law of Scotland* (Edinburgh,
1890), p. 560.

[4] Lecky, *op. cit.* ii. 23.

[5] *Codex Theodosianus*, ix. 14. 1 ; *Institutiones*, ix. 16. 7.

[6] J. Tissot, *Le droit pénal*, ii (Paris, 1860), p. 40.

[7] E. Osenbrüggen, *Das Alamannische Strafrecht* (Schaffhausen, 1860),
p. 229 *sq.* ; *idem*, *Studien zur deutschen und schweizerischen Rechtsgeschichte* (Schaffhausen, 1868), p. 358.

[8] Charles V., *Die Peinliche Gerichtsordnung*, art. 131 (Heidelberg, 1842).

[9] D. de Feyfer, *Verhandeling over den Kindermoord* (Utrecht, 1866),
p. 225 ; H. von Fabrice, *Die Lehre von der Kindsabtreibung und vom
Kindsmord* (Erlangen, 1868), p. 251.

[10] A. F. Berner, *Lehrbuch des Deutschen Strafrechtes* (Leipzig, 1881),
p. 497.

[11] Bentham maintained (*Theory of Legislation* [London, 1882],
p. 264 *sq.*) that infanticide ought not to be punished as a principal
offence. " The offence," he says, " is what is improperly called the death
of an infant, who has ceased to be, before knowing what existence is—
a result of a nature not to give the slightest inquietude to the most timid

ment of mind, and the difficulty in rearing a poor bastard, could induce the unfortunate mother to commit a crime which she herself abhorred. That no notice had been taken of all this is explicable from the extreme severity with which female unchastity was looked upon by the Church. At present most European law-books do not punish infanticide committed by an unmarried woman even nominally with death.[1] In France the law which regards infanticide as an aggravated form of *meurtre* [2] has become a dead letter; [3] and Stephen wrote in 1883 that in England no woman seems for a long time to have been executed for killing her new-born child under the distress of mind and fear of shame caused by childbirth.[4] Yet the law takes its grim course. The judge dons his black cap, the death sentence is pronounced, and although reprieve is certain, the unfortunate prisoner is condemned to cruel and unnecessary mental torture. In order to put an end to this gruesome formality, Lord Dawson's Infanticide Bill, which was given a second reading in the House of Lords shortly before this was written, provided that a woman proved guilty of causing the death of her baby, under the age of twelve months, should be convicted of manslaughter and not of murder.

Hand in hand with the custom of infanticide goes feticide, or the destruction of the embryo before it has left the mother's womb. In ancient Greece, as we have seen, it was in certain circumstances recommended by Plato and Aristotle, in preference to infanticide. In Rome it was prohibited by Septimius Severus and Antoninus, but the prohibition seems to have referred only to those married women who, by procuring abortion, defrauded their husbands of children.[5] During the Pagan Empire abortion was extensively practised, either from poverty, or licentiousness, or vanity; and although severely disapproved of by some,[6] it was probably regarded by the average Romans

imagination; and which can cause no regrets but to the very person who, through a sentiment of shame and pity, has refused to prolong a life begun under the auspices of misery."

[1] de Feyfer, *op. cit.* p. 228. For modern legislation on infanticide, see also Spangenberg, in *Neues Archiv des Criminalrechts*, iii. 360 *sqq.*; von Fabrice, *op. cit.* p. 254 *sqq.*

[2] *Code Pénal*, arts. 300, 302.

[3] R. Garraud, *Traité théorique et pratique du droit pénal Français*, iv (Paris, 1891), 251.

[4] J. F. Stephen, *A History of the Criminal Law of England*, iii (London, 1883), p. 86.

[5] *Digesta*, xlvii. 11. 4. *Cf.* W. Rein, *Das Criminalrecht der Römer* (Leipzig, 1844), p. 447.

[6] Paulus, quoted in *Digesta*, xxv. 3. 4.

of the later days of Paganism as so venial as scarcely to deserve
censure.[1] Seneca thinks Helvia worthy of special praise because
she had never destroyed her expected child within her womb,
" after the fashion of many other women, whose attractions are
to be found in their beauty alone." [2] The Romans drew a
broad line between feticide and infanticide. An unborn child
was not looked upon as a human being, it was a *spes animantis*,
not an *infans*.[3] It was said to be merely a part of the mother,
as the fruit is a part of the tree till it becomes ripe and falls
down.[4]

Very different opinions were held by the Christians. A
sanctity, previously unheard of, was attached to human life
from the very beginning. Feticide was regarded as a form of
murder. " Prevention of birth," says Tertullian, " is a precipitation of murder ; nor does it matter whether one take
away a life when formed, or drive it away while forming. He
also is a man who is about to be one. Even every fruit already
exists in its seed." [5] Augustine, again, makes a distinction
between an embryo which has already been formed and an
embryo as yet unformed. From the creation of Adam, he
says, it appears that the body is made before the soul. Before
the embryo has been endowed with a soul it is an *embryo inform-
atus*, and its artificial abortion is to be punished with a fine only ;
but the *embryo formatus* is an animate being, and to destroy it
is nothing less than murder, a crime punishable with death.[6]
This distinction between an animate and inanimate fetus was
embodied both in Canon [7] and Justinian law,[8] and passed sub-

---

[1] Lecky, *op. cit.* ii. 21 *sq.*
[2] Seneca, *Ad Helviam*, 16.
[3] Spangenberg, ' Ueber das Verbrechen der Abtreibung der Leibes-
frucht,' in *Neues Archiv des Criminalrechts*, ii (Halle, 1818), p. 23.
[4] *Ibid.* ii. 22.
[5] Tertullian, *Apologeticus*, 9.
[6] Augustine, *Questiones in Exodum*, 80 ; *idem*, *Questiones Veteris et
Novi Testamenti*, 23 (Migne, *Patrologiæ cursus*, xxxiv.–xxxv. 626,
2229).
[7] Gratian, *Decretum*, ii. 32. 2. 8 *sq.*
[8] As regards the time from which the fetus was considered to be
animate a curious distinction was drawn between the male and the female
fetus. The former was regarded as *animatus* forty days after its conception, the latter eighty days. This theory, however—which was
derived, as it seems, either from an absurd misinterpretation of *Leviticus*
xii. 2–5, or from the views of Aristotle (*De animalibus historiæ*, vii. 3 ;
cf. Pliny, *Historia naturalis*, vii. 6)—was not accepted by the glossarist
of the Justinian Code, who fixed the animation of the female, as well as
of the male, fetus at forty days after its conception ; and this view was
adopted by later jurists (Spangenberg, in *Neues Archiv des Criminalrechts*, ii. 37 *sqq.*).

sequently into various law-books.[1]   And a woman who destroyed her animate embryo was punished with death.[2]

The criminality of artificial abortion was increased by the belief that an *embryo formatus*, being endowed with an immortal soul, was in need of baptism for its salvation.   In his highly esteemed treatise ' De Fide,' written in the sixth century, Fulgentius says : " It is to be believed beyond doubt that not only men who are come to the use of reason, but infants, whether they die in their mother's womb, or after they are born, without baptism, in the name of the Father, Son, and Holy Ghost, are punished with everlasting punishment in eternal fire, because, though they have no actual sin of their own, yet they carry along with them the condemnation of original sin from their first conception and birth." [3]   And in the ' Lex Bajuwariorum ' this doctrine is expressly referred to in a paragraph which prescribes a daily compensation for children killed in the womb on account of the daily suffering of those children in hell.[4] Subsequently, however, Fulgentius' dictum was called in question, and no less a person than Thomas Aquinas suggested the possibility of salvation for an infant who died before its birth.[5]   Apart from this, the doctrine that the life of an embryo is equally sacred with the life of an infant was so much opposed to popular feelings, that the law concerning feticide had to be altered.   Modern legislation, though treating the fetus as a distinct being from the moment of its conception,[6] punishes criminal abortion less severely than infanticide.[7]   The very frequent occurrence of it is an evidence of the comparative indifference with which it is practically looked upon by large numbers of people in Christian countries ; and there is to-day in more than one of these countries a growing demand for legal facilities of abortion.   A moral ground for this demand is that legalised abortion, allowed only by skilled operators, will kill off the demand for quack abortion with its direful results.[8]   In

[1] von Fabrice, *op. cit.* p. 202 *sq.* ; Berner, *op. cit.* p. 501 ; W. E. Wilda, *Das Strafrecht der Germanen* (Halle, 1842), p. 720 *sqq.*

[2] Fleta, *seu Commentarius Juris Anglicani* (London, 1735), i. 23. 12 (England) ; Charles V.'s *Peinliche Gerichts Ordnung*, art. 133 ; Spangenberg, in *Neues Archiv des Criminalrechts*, ii. 16.

[3] Fulgentius, *De fide*, 27.

[4] *Lex Bajuwariorum*, viii. 21 (vii. 20).

[5] W. E. H. Lecky, *History of the Rise and Influence of the Spirit of Rationalism in Europe*, i (London, 1893), p. 360 n. 2.

[6] A. Henke, *Lehrbuch der gerichtlichen Medicin* (Berlin, 1859), § 99, p. 75 ; Berner, *op. cit.* p. 502.

[7] von Fabrice, *op. cit.* p. 199.

[8] *Cf.* D. White, ' Religion and Sex,' in *The Church and the Twentieth Century*, ed. by G. L. H. Harvey (London, 1936), p. 294.

Great Britain it is only allowed where there is danger to the woman's life or health.

The best preventive against abortion is the use of contraceptives ; it is particularly for this reason that in Soviet Russia instruction in contraception may be obtained freely by any one seeking it.[1] But any such interference with the course of nature is contrary to the old Catholic rule that the only legitimate object of sexual intercourse even between husband and wife is the continuance of the human species. This rule was confirmed by the Pope's encyclical of December 31, 1930, forbidding the use of contraceptives on the ground that " the connubial act is naturally designed to evoke new life." [2] Among orthodox Christians of other confessions we also find, to some extent, the theory that sexual intercourse is justifiable only as a means of generation ; but it is certainly on the wane. Some interesting information on this point comes from America. Dr. Katharine B. Davis, who carried out a study on a thousand educated married women and about a thousand unmarried college women, put to them the question, " Are married people justified having intercourse except for the purpose of having children ? " Only a small minority (15·3 per cent.) of those answering definitely this question replied negatively.[3] The enormous frequency of the use of contraceptives also bears testimony to people's feelings concerning it. The leader in the movement has been France, a largely Catholic country, where it started in the middle of the last century in the great cities and in the fertile districts of the south ; [4] and the proportion of Catholic women who apply for advice at Margaret Sanger's clinic in New York is only one percentage lower than the proportion of Protestant women.[5] In England the change in public opinion since the time when Bradlaugh, who was regarded as the protagonist of the movement, was called " the unsavoury member for Northampton," has been enormous.[6] Dr. A. W.

---

[1] Fannie W. Halle, *Die Frau in Sowjetrussland* (Berlin, etc., 1932), p. 202 ; Margaret Sanger, ' Birth Control in Soviet Russia,' in *Birth Control Review*, June 1935 (New York), p. 3.

[2] F. E. Traumann, ' Das Rundschreiben des Papstes Pius XI über die christliche Ehe und die Sexualreform,' in *Zeitschrift für Sexualwissenschaft und Sexualpolitik*, xviii (Berlin and Köln, 1931), p. 124.

[3] Katharine B. Davis, *Factors in the Sex Life of Twenty-two Hundred Women* (New York and London, 1929), p. 355 *sqq.* See also G. V. Hamilton, *A Research in Marriage* (New York, 1929), p. 382.

[4] H. Harmsen, *Bevölkerungspolitik Frankreichs* (Berlin, 1927), reviewed in *Zeitschrift für Sexualwissenschaft und Sexualpolitik*, xv (Berlin and Köln, 1929), p. 588.

[5] Havelock Ellis, *More Essays of Love and Virtue* (London, 1931), p. 36 n. 1. [6] Inge, *op. cit.* p. 273.

Thomas wrote in 1906 : " From my experience as a general practitioner, I have no hesitation in saying that 90 per cent. of young married couples of the comfortably-off classes use preventives " ; [1] and this rough estimate does not seem to be over the mark.[2] In Germany birth control was very prevalent before the War,[3] and greatly increased afterwards.[4] In the United States 74·11 per cent. of the 985 married women who answered Dr. Davis's question referring to the use of contraceptives admitted it.[5] At the same time contraception has still many opponents also in Protestant countries, and not only on political grounds as lowering the birth-rate. In Denmark there seems to be quite a widespread feeling against it.[6] But it is obvious that those who condemn it are defending a lost cause. Even among Anglican clericals there has in this respect been a decisive breach with ecclesiastical tradition. Though the 15th Resolution of the Lambeth Conference of 1930 concerning the use of contraceptives by Christians was so carefully conditioned that it might well appear practically valueless, the large Committee of Bishops who considered the subject of marriage and sex frankly stated in their ' Report ' that the prohibition of the use of preventive methods is not founded on any directions given in the New Testament, nor has behind it the authority of any Œcumenical Council of the Church, and that "the Communion which most strongly condemns in principle all preventive methods, nevertheless in practice recognises that there are occasions when a rigid insistence on the principle is impossible." [7]

The early Christians' regard for human life also displays itself in their condemnation of capital punishment.[8] But when

[1] A. W. Thomas, ' The Decline in the Birth Rate,' in *British Medical Journal*, 1906, vol. ii (London), p. 1066.

[2] See Havelock Ellis, *Studies in the Psychology of Sex*, vi (Philadelphia, 1923), p. 589.

[3] L. D. Pesl, ' Fruchtabtreibung und Findelhaus,' in *Zeitschrift für Sexualwissenschaft und Sexualpolitik*, xv (Berlin and Köln, 1928), p. 260.

[4] A. Moll, ' Der " reaktionäre " Kongress für Sexualforschung,' *ibid.* xiii (Bonn, 1927), p. 330 ; F. Burgdörfer, *Der Geburtenrückgang und die Zukunft des deutschen Volkes* (Berlin, 1928), quoted *ibid.* xvi (Berlin and Köln, 1929), p. 67. See also A. V. Knack, ' Die Wegbereitung einer vernunftgemässen Bevölkerungspolitik,' in A. Weil, *Sexualreform und Sexualwissenschaft* (Stuttgart, 1922), p. 203.

[5] Davis, *op. cit.* p. 14. See also Hamilton, *op. cit.* p. 134.

[6] S. Ranulf, ' Die moralische Reaktion gegen neomalthusianische Propaganda in Dänemark,' in *Zeitschrift für Sexualwissenschaft und Sexualpolitik*, xvi (Berlin and Köln, 1929), p. 47 *sqq.*

[7] H. H. Henson, *Christian Morality* (Oxford, 1936), p. 216 *sq.*

[8] H. Hetzel, *Die Todesstrafe in ihrer kulturgeschichtlichen Entwicklung* (Berlin, 1870), p. 71 *sqq.* ; L. Günther, *Die Idee der Wiedervergeltung*, i

the Church obtained an ascendency, the condemnation was modified into the doctrine that a priest must not take part in a capital charge. If he passed a sentence of death, he was punished with degradation and imprisonment for life ; [1] nor was he allowed to write or dictate anything with a view to bringing about such a sentence.[2] From the twelfth century, at least, he might assist at judicial proceedings resulting in a sentence of death, if only he withdrew for the moment when the sentence was passed.[3] These rules were due to that horror of blood-pollution which is so generally felt in the case of anybody or anything connected with the religious cult.

The shedding of blood is commonly prohibited in sacred places.[4] At Athens the prosecution for homicide began with debarring the criminal from all sanctuaries and assemblies consecrated by religious observances.[5] According to Greek notions purification was an essential preliminary to an acceptable sacrifice.[6] Hector said : " I shrink from offering a libation of gleaming wine to Zeus with hands unwashed ; nor can it be in any way wise that one should pray to the son of Kronos, god of the storm-cloud, all defiled with blood and filth." [7] In Morocco it is a common, though not universal, rule that a man who has slain another person is never afterwards allowed to kill with his own hands the sacrificial sheep at the " Great Feast." [8] When David had in his heart to build a temple, God said to him : " Thou shalt not build an house for my name, because thou hast been a man of war, and hast shed blood." [9] A decree of the penitential discipline of the Christian Church, which was enforced even against emperors and generals, forbade

(Erlangen, 1889), p. 271 ; Lactantius, *Divinæ institutiones*, vi. 20 : " . . . occidere hominem sit semper nefas, quem Deus sanctum animal esse voluit."

[1] Gratian, *Decretum*, ii. 23. 8. 30.

[2] *Concilium Lateranense IV.*, A.D. 1215, ch. 18 (Mansi, *Sacrorum Conciliorum collectio*, xxii. 1007).

[3] Gerhohus, ' De ædificio Dei,' 35 (Migne, *Patrologiæ cursus*, cxciv. 1282).

[4] E. Westermarck, *The Origin and Development of the Moral Ideas*, i (London, 1912), p. 380.

[5] Aristotle, *De republica Atheniensium*, 57 ; C. O. Müller, *Dissertations on the Eumenides of Æschylus* (London and Cambridge, 1853), p. 103.

[6] J. Donaldson, ' On the Expiatory and Substitutionary Sacrifices of the Greeks,' in *Transactions of the Royal Society of Edinburgh*, xxvii (Edinburgh, 1876), p. 433 ; L. R. Farnell, *The Cults of the Greek States*, i (Oxford, 1896), p. 72.

[7] *Iliad*, vi. 266 *sqq.* Cf. Vergil, *Æneid*, ii. 717 *sqq.*

[8] E. Westermarck, *Ritual and Belief in Morocco* (London, 1926), i. 237, ii. 12.　　　　　[9] *1 Chronicles* xxviii. 2 *sq.*

any one whose hands had been imbrued in blood to approach the altar without a preparatory period of penance.[1]

While, from fear of contaminating anything holy, casual restrictions have thus been imposed on all kinds of manslayers, whether murderers or those who have killed an enemy in righteous warfare, more stringent rules have been laid down for persons permanently connected with the religious cult. Adair states that the " holy men " of the North American Indians, like the Jewish priests, were by their function absolutely forbidden to shed human blood, "notwithstanding their propensity thereto, even for small injuries." [2] The Druids of Gaul never went to war ; it is true, they sacrificed human victims to their gods, but those they burnt.[3] The Christian Church, whilst ostentatiously sticking to her principle that " the Church does not shed blood," [4] had frequent recourse to the convenient method of punishing heretics by relegating the execution of the sentence of death to the civil power, with a prayer that the culprit should be punished " as mildly as possible and without the effusion of blood," that is, by the death of fire.[5] To the same class of facts belong those decrees of the Church which forbade clergymen taking part in a battle, for which Thomas Aquinas gives the reason that fighting " tends to the spilling of blood." [6] It is said that this was taken so literally that martial prelates in the Middle Ages went into battle with heavy maces, with which they could pound their enemies into pulp without breaking the skin.[7] If a priest killed a robber in order to save his life, he had to do penance till his death ; the hands which had to distribute the blood of the Lamb of God were not to be polluted with the blood of those for whose salvation it was shed.[8] He must not even perform a surgical operation by help of fire or iron.[9]

In spite of the early Christians' condemnation of the punishment of death, the number of capital offences became considerably greater than before under the Christian emperors and, in

[1] Lecky, *History of European Morals*, ii. 39.

[2] J. Adair, *The History of the American Indians* (London, 1775), p. 152.

[3] Cæsar, *De bello Gallico*, vi. 14, 16. *Cf.* H. d'Arbois de Jubainville, *La civilisation des Celtes* (Paris, 1899), p. 254.

[4] E. Katz, *Ein Grundriss des kanonischen Strafrechts* (Berlin and Leipzig, 1881), p. 54.

[5] Lecky, *op. cit.* ii. 41.

[6] Thomas Aquinas, *Summa theologica*, ii.–ii. 40. 2.

[7] Inge, *op. cit.* p. 309.

[8] L. Thomassin, *Dictionnaire de discipline ecclésiastique*, ii (Paris, 1856), pp. 1069, 1074.

[9] *Concilium Lateranense IV.*, A.D. 1215, ch. 18 (Mansi, xxii. 1007).

Teutonic countries, under the Christian kings.[1] During the Middle Ages and later the severity of the penal codes, in general, increased very greatly ; and the chief explanation of this lies in their connection with despotism or religion or both.[2] Every crime came to be regarded as a crime against the king. Indeed, breach of the King's peace became the foundation of the whole criminal law of England ; the right of pardon, for instance, as a prerogative of the Crown, took its origin in the fact that the king was supposed to be injured by the crime, and could therefore waive his remedy.[3] But the king was not only regarded as the fountain of social justice : he was also regarded as the earthly representative of the heavenly lawgiver and judge.[4] The Christian Church and Christian governments adopted the Hebrew notions [5] that it is man's duty to avenge offences against God, that every crime involves a breach of God's law and is punishable as such, and that hardly any punishment is too severe to be inflicted on the ungodly.[6] The principle stated in the Laws of Cnut, that " it belongs very rightly to a Christian king to avenge God's anger very deeply, according as the deed may be," [7] was acted upon till quite modern times, and largely contributed to the increasing severity of the penal codes. It was therefore one of the most important steps towards a more humane legislation when, in the eighteenth century, this principle was superseded by the contrary doctrine, " Il faut faire honorer la Divinité, et ne la venger jamais." [8]

In modern times the views of the early Christians regarding capital punishment have been revived by the Anabaptists [9]

[1] Lecky, *op. cit.* ii. 42, 43 n. 1.

[2] See Westermarck, *The Origin and Development of the Moral Ideas,* i. 193 *sqq.*

[3] R. R. Cherry, *Lectures on the Growth of Criminal Law in Ancient Communities* (London, 1890), pp. 68, 105.

[4] E. Henke, *Grundriss einer Geschichte des deutschen peinlichen Rechts und der peinlichen Rechtswissenschaft,* ii (Sulzbach, 1809), p. 310 ; J. F. H. Abegg, *Die verschiedenen Strafrechtstheorieen* (Neustadt a.d. O., 1835), p. 117 ; A. Du Boys, *Histoire du droit criminel de l'Espagne* (Paris, 1870), p. 323.

[5] *Cf.* W. Robertson Smith, *Lectures on the Religion of the Semites* (London, 1894), p. 162 *sq.*

[6] H. von Eicken, *Geschichte und System der mittelalterlichen Weltanschauung* (Stuttgart, 1887), p. 563 *sqq.* ; Abegg, *op. cit.* p. 111 *sq.* ; W. E. Wilda, *op. cit.* p. 530 *sq.* ; Günther, *op. cit.* ii. 12 *sqq.* ; Henke, *op. cit.* ii. 310 *sq.* ; H. Brunner, *Deutsche Rechtsgeschichte,* ii (Leipzig, 1892), p. 587.

[7] *Laws of Cnut,* ii. 40.

[8] Montesquieu, *op. cit.* xii. 4 (*Œuvres,* p. 282).

[9] W. J. McGlothlin, ' Anabaptism,' in J. Hastings, *Encyclopædia of Religion and Ethics,* i (Edinburgh, 1908), p. 411.

and the Quakers ; [1] but the powerful movement in favour of its abolition chiefly derives its origin from the writings of Beccaria and the French Encyclopædists. The great motive force of this movement has been sympathy with human suffering and horror of the destruction of human life—feelings which have been able to operate the more freely, the less they have been checked either by the belief in the social expediency of capital punishment, or by the notion of a vindictive god who can be conciliated only by the death of the offender. During the last century Western legislation has undergone a radical change with reference to the punishment of death. In several European and American States it has been formally abolished, or is nowadays never inflicted,[2] whilst in the rest it is practically restricted to cases of wilful murder. But it still has as strenuous advocates as ever. It is said that the abolition of it would remove one of the best safeguards of society ; [3] and, as usual, religion is also called in to give strength to the argument. Several writers have argued that the statements in the Bible which command capital punishment have an obligatory power on all Christian legislators ; [4] and we meet with the assertion that its object is not the protection of civil society, but to carry out the justice of God, in whose name " the judge should sentence and the executioner strike." [5] But I venture to believe that the chief motive for retaining the punishment of death in modern legislation is the strong hold which the principle of talion has on the minds of legislators as well as on the public mind. This supposition derives much support from the fact that capital punishment is popular only in the case of murder. " Blood, it is said, will have blood, and the imagination is flattered with the notion of the similarity of the suffering, produced by the punishment, with that inflicted by the criminal." [6]

In no question of morality was there a greater difference between classical [7] and Christian doctrines than in regard to

[1] J. J. Gurney, *Observations on the Distinguishing Views and Practices of the Society of Friends* (London, 1834), pp. 377 n. 1, 389.

[2] Günther, *op. cit.* iii. 347 *sqq.* ; F. von Liszt, *Lehrbuch des deutschen Strafrechts* (Berlin, 1912), p. 258 *sq.*

[3] For arguments against and for its abolition, see Westermarck, *The Origin and Development of the Moral Ideas*, i. 494 *sqq.*

[4] C. J. A. von Mittermaier, *Die Todesstrafe* (Heidelberg, 1862), p. 128 *sqq.*

[5] W. L. Clay, *The Prison Chaplain* (Cambridge, 1861), p. 357.

[6] J. Bentham, *The Rationale of Punishment* (London, 1830), p. 191.

[7] See Westermarck, *The Origin and Development of the Moral Ideas*, ii (1917), p. 247 *sqq.*

suicide. The Greek tragedians frequently give expression to the notion that suicide in certain circumstances is becoming to a noble mind.[1] According to the Platonic Socrates, however, " there may be reason in saying that a man should wait, and not take his own life until God summons him " ; [2] and Aristotle maintains that he who kills himself from rage commits a wrong against the State.[3] But the opinions of the philosophers were anything but unanimous.[4] Plato himself, in his ' Laws,' has no word of censure for him who deprives himself by violence of his appointed share of life under the compulsion of some painful and inevitable misfortune, or out of irremediable and intolerable shame.[5] According to Epicurus, we ought to consider " whether it be better that death should come to us, or we go to him." [6] The Stoics, especially, advocated suicide as a relief from all kinds of misery.[7] Seneca remarks that it is a man's own fault if he suffers, as, by putting an end to himself, he can put an end to his misery. " As I would choose a ship to sail in, or a house to live in, so would I choose the most tolerable death when about to die. . . . Human affairs are in such a happy situation, that no one need be wretched but by choice. Do you like to be wretched ? Live. Do you like it not ? It is in your power to return from whence you came." [8] Epictetus opposes indiscriminate suicide on religious grounds : " Friends, wait for God ; when he shall give the signal and release you from this service, then go to him ; but for the present endure to dwell in the place where he has put you." [9] But such a signal is given often enough : it may consist in incurable disease, intolerable pain, or misery of any kind. " Remember this : the door is open ; be not more timid than little children, but as they say, when the thing does not please them, ' I will play no longer,' so do you, when things seem to you of such a kind, say I will no longer play, and be gone : but if you stay, do not complain." [10] Pliny says that the power of dying when you please is the best

---

[1] See L. Schmidt, *Die Ethik der alten Griechen*, ii (Berlin, 1882), p. 442 *sqq.*

[2] Plato, *Phœdo*, p. 62.

[3] Aristotle, *Ethica Nicomachea*, v. 11. 3.

[4] See K. A. Geiger, *Der Selbstmord im klassischen Altertum* (Augsburg, 1888), p. 5 *sqq.*

[5] Plato, *Leges*, ix. 873.

[6] Epicurus, quoted by Seneca, *Epistulæ*, 26.

[7] See Geiger, *op. cit.* p. 15 *sqq.*

[8] Seneca, *Epistulæ*, 70. See also *idem, De ira*, iii. 15 ; *idem, Consolatio ad Marciam*, 20.

[9] Epictetus, *Dissertationes*, i. 9. 16.

[10] *Ibid.* i. 24. 20, i. 25. 20 *sq.*, ii. 16. 37 *sqq.*, iii. 13. 14, iii. 24. 95 *sqq.*

thing that God has given to man amidst all the sufferings of life.[1]

It seems that the Roman people, before the influence of Christianity made itself felt, regarded suicide with considerable moral indifference. Vergil enumerates self-murderers not among the guilty, but among the unfortunate, confounding them with infants who have died prematurely and persons who have been condemned to die on a false charge.[2] Throughout the whole history of pagan Rome there was no statute declaring it to be a crime for an ordinary citizen to take his own life, though it was prohibited in the case of soldiers.[3] The self-murderer's rights were in no way affected by his deed, his memory was no less honoured than if he had died a natural death, his will was recognised by law, and the regular order of succession was not interfered with.[4] On the other hand, it seems to have been the general opinion in Rome that suicide in certain circumstances is an heroic and praiseworthy act.[5] Even Cicero, who professed the doctrine of Pythagoras that we should not abandon our station in life without the orders of God,[6] approved of the death of Cato.[7]

The earlier Christian Fathers still allowed, or even approved of, suicide in certain cases, namely, when committed in order to procure martyrdom,[8] or to avoid apostasy, or to retain the crown of virginity. To bring death upon ourselves voluntarily, says Lactantius, is a wicked and impious death ; " but when urged to the alternative, either of forsaking God and relinquishing faith, or of expecting all torture and death, then it is that undaunted in spirit we defy that death with all its previous threats and terrors which others fear." [9] Eusebius and other ecclesiastical writers mention several instances of Christian women putting an end to their lives when their chastity was in danger, and their acts are spoken of with tenderness or even

---

[1] Pliny, *Historia naturalis*, ii. 5 (7).

[2] Vergil, *Æneid*, vi. 426 *sqq.*   [3] *Digesta*, xlix. 16. 6. 7.

[4] F. Bourquelot, ' Recherches sur les opinions et la législation en matière de mort volontaire pendant le moyen âge,' in *Bibliothèque de l'École des Chartes*, iii (Paris, 1841), p. 544 ; Geiger, *op. cit.* p. 64 *sqq.* ; C. van Bynkershoek, *Observationes Juris Romani* (Lugduni Batavorum, 1710), iv. 4, p. 350.

[5] C. F. Stäudlin, *Geschichte der Vorstellungen und Lehren vom Selbstmorde* (Göttingen, 1824), p. 62 *sq.*

[6] Cicero, *Cato Major*, 20 (72 *sq.*).

[7] *Idem*, *De officiis*, i. 31 (112).

[8] See J. Barbeyrac, *Traité de la morale des Pères de l'Église* (Amsterdam, 1728), pp. 18, 122 *sq.* ; A. Buonafede, *Istoria critica e filosofica del suicidio* (Venezia, 1788), p. 135 *sqq.* ; Lecky, *op. cit.* ii. 45 *sq.*

[9] Lactantius, *Divinæ institutiones*, vi. 17.

admiration, nay some of them were admitted into the calendar
of saints.[1] This admission was due to the extreme honour in
which virginity was held ; Jerome, who denied that it was lawful
in times of persecution to die by one's own hands, made an
exception for cases in which a person's chastity was at stake.[2]
But even this exception was abolished by Augustine. He
allows that the virgins who laid violent hands upon themselves
are worthy of compassion, but declares that there was no
necessity for their doing so, since chastity is a virtue of the
mind which is not lost by the body being in captivity to the
will and superior force of another. He argues that there is no
passage in the canonical Scriptures which permits us to destroy
ourselves either with a view to obtaining immortality or to
avoiding calamity. On the contrary, suicide is prohibited in
the commandment, " Thou shalt not kill," namely, " neither
thyself nor another " ; for he who kills himself kills no other
but a man.[3] This doctrine, which assimilates suicide with
murder, was evidently not the Hebrew view on the subject,
since in the few cases of suicide which are mentioned in the
Old Testament no censure is passed on the perpetrator of the
deed,[4] and of Ahithophel it is said that he was buried in the
sepulchre of his father ; [5] but it became the doctrine of the
Church.[6] Nay, self-murder was declared to be the worst form
of murder, " the most grievous thing of all " ; [7] Chrysostom
had already insisted that " if it is base to destroy others, much
more is it to destroy one's self." [8] It was even said that Judas
committed a greater sin in killing himself than in betraying his
master Christ to a certain death.[9] The self-murderer was
deprived of rights which were granted to all other criminals.
In the sixth century a Council of Orleans enjoined that " the

---

[1] Eusebius, *Historia ecclesiastica*, viii. 12, 14 ; Ambrose, *De virgini-bus*, xiii. 7 ; Chrysostom, *Homilia encomiastica in S. Martyrem Pelagiam*
(Migne, *Patrologiæ cursus, Ser. Græca*, 1. 579 *sqq.*).
[2] Jerome, *Commentarii in Jonam*, i. 12 (Migne, *Patrologiæ cursus*,
xxv. 1129).
[3] Augustine, *De civitate Dei*, i. 16 *sqq.*
[4] *1 Samuel* xxxi. 4 *sq.* ;   *1 Kings* xvi. 18 ;   *2 Maccabees* xiv. 4 *sqq.*
[5] *2 Samuel* xvii. 23.   [6] Gratian, *Decretum*, ii. 23. 5. 9. 3.
[7] Thomas Aquinas, *op. cit.* ii.-ii. 64. 5. 3.
[8] Chrysostom, *In Epistolam ad Galatas commentarius*, i. 4 (Migne, *Ser. Græca*, lxi. 618 *sq.*).
[9] J. de Damhouder, *Praxis rerum criminalium* (Antverpiæ, 1570),
lviii. 2 *sq.*, p. 258. See Gratian, ii. 33. 3. 3. 38. At the trial of the
Marquise de Brinvilliers in 1676, the presiding judge said to the prisoner
that " the greatest of all her crimes, horrible as they were, was, not the
poisoning of her father and brothers, but her attempt to poison herself "
(G. Ives, *The Classification of Crimes* [London, 1904], p. 36).

oblations of those who were killed in the commission of any crime may be received, except of such as laid violent hands on themselves " ; [1] and a subsequent Council denied self-murderers the usual rites of Christian burial. [2]

According to the Christian doctrine, as formulated by Thomas Aquinas, suicide is utterly unlawful for three reasons. First, everything naturally loves itself and preserves itself in being ; suicide is against a natural inclination and contrary to the charity which a man ought to bear towards himself, and consequently a mortal sin. Secondly, by killing himself a person does an injury to the community of which he is a part. Thirdly, " life is a gift divinely bestowed on man, and subject to His power who ' killeth and maketh alive ' ; and therefore he who takes his own life sins against God, as he who kills another man's slave sins against the master to whom the slave belongs, and as he who usurps the office of judge on a point not referred to him ; for to God alone belongs judgment of life and death." [3] The second of the three arguments is borrowed from Aristotle, and is entirely foreign to the spirit of early Christianity. The notion of patriotism being a moral duty was habitually discouraged by it, and, as has been truly observed, " it was impossible to urge the civic argument against suicide without at the same time condemning the hermit life, which in the third century became the ideal of the Church." [4] But certain other arguments were deeply rooted in some of the fundamental doctrines of Christianity—in the sacredness of human life, in the duty of absolute submission to God's will, and in the extreme importance attached to the moment of death. The earthly life is a preparation for eternity ; sufferings which are sent by God are not to be evaded, but to be endured. [5] The man who deliberately takes away the life which was given him by the Creator displays the utmost disregard for the will and authority of his Master ; and, worst of all, he does so in the very last minute of his life, when his doom is sealed for ever. His deed, as Aquinas says, is " the most dangerous thing of all, because no time is left to expiate it by repentance." [6] He who kills a fellow-creature does not in the same degree renounce the protection of God ; he kills only the body, whereas the self-murderer

[1] *Concilium Aurelianense II.*, A.D. 533, can. 15 (Labbe-Mansi, viii. 837). See also *Concilium Autisiodorense*, A.D. 578, can. 17 (*ibid.* ix. 913).
[2] *Concilium Bracarense II.*, A.D. 563, cap. 16 (Labbe-Mansi, ix. 779).
[3] Thomas Aquinas, *op. cit.* ii.-ii. 64. 5.
[4] Lecky, *op. cit.* ii. 44.
[5] *Cf.* Augustine, *De civitate Dei*, i. 23.
[6] Thomas Aquinas, *op. cit.* ii.-ii. 64. 5. 3. *Cf.* Augustine, *De civitate Dei*, i. 25.

kills both the body and soul.[1] By denying the latter the right
of Christian burial the Church recognises that he has placed
himself outside her pale.

The condemnation of the Church influenced the secular
legislation. The provisions of the Councils were introduced
into the law-books. In France Louis IX. enforced the penalty
of confiscating the self-murderer's property,[2] and laws to the
same effect were passed in other European countries.[3] Louis
XIV. assimilated the crime of suicide to that of lèse-majesté.[4]
According to the law of Scotland, " self-murder is as highly
criminal as the killing of our neighbour." [5] So also in England
suicide is regarded by the law as murder committed by a man
on himself ; [6] and, unless declared insane, the self-murderer
forfeited his property as late as the year 1870, when forfeitures
for felony were abolished.[7]

The horror of suicide also found a vent in outrages committed on the dead body. Of a woman who drowned herself
in Edinburgh in 1598 we are told that her body was " harled
through the town backwards, and thereafter hanged on the
gallows." [8] In France, as late as the middle of the eighteenth
century, self-murderers were dragged upon a hurdle through
the streets with the face turned to the ground ; they were then
hanged up with the head downwards, and finally thrown into
the common sewer.[9] In most cases, however, the treatment to
which suicides' bodies were subjected was not meant as a
punishment, but was intended to prevent their spirits from
causing mischief. All over Europe wandering tendencies have
been ascribed to their ghosts. In some countries the corpse of
a suicide is supposed to make barren the earth with which it
comes in contact, or to produce hailstorms or tempests or
drought. The practice of burying suicides apart from other

[1] Damhouder, op. cit. lxxxviii. 1 sq., p. 258.
[2] Les Établissements de Saint Louis, i. 92 (ed. by P. Viollet [Paris,
1881–6], vol. ii. 150).
[3] Bourquelot, op. cit. iv. 263 ; E. Morselli, Il suicidio (Milano, 1879),
p. 196 sq.
[4] Louis XIV., ' Ordonnance criminelle,' A.D. 1670, xxii. 1, in Isambert, Decrusy, and Taillandier, op. cit. xviii. 414.
[5] Erskine of Carnock, op. cit. p. 559.
[6] Stephen, op. cit. iii. 104. For earlier times see H. de Bracton, De
Legibus et Consuetudinibus Angliæ, fol. 150 (ed. by T. Twiss, London,
1878–9, vol. ii. 504 sq.).
[7] Stephen, op. cit. iii. 105.
[8] A. Ross, ' Superstitions as to burying suicides in the Highlands,' in
Celtic Magazine, xii (Inverness, 1887), p. 354.
[9] F. Serpillon, Code Criminel, ou Commentaire sur l'Ordonnance de
1670, ii (Lyon, 1784), p. 223.

dead has been very widespread in Europe, and in many cases there are obvious indications that it arose from fear.[1] In England persons against whom a coroner's jury had found a verdict of *felo de se* were buried at cross-roads, with a stake driven through the body in order to prevent their ghosts from walking—a custom which was formally abolished only in 1823 by 4 Geo. IV., c. 52.[2] For the same purpose the bodies of suicides were in many cases burned. And when removed from the house where the act had been committed, they were commonly carried out, not by the door, but by a window, or through a perforation specially made for the occasion in the door, or through a hole under the threshold, in order that the ghost should not find its way back into the house, or perhaps with a view to keeping the entrance of the house free from dangerous infection.[3]

Side by side with the extreme severity with which suicide is viewed by the Christian Church, however, we find even in the Middle Ages instances of more humane feelings towards its perpetrator. In mediæval tales and ballads true lovers die together and are buried in the same grave ; two roses spring through the turf and twine lovingly together.[4] In the later Middle Ages, says Bourquelot, " on voit qu'à mesure qu'on avance, l'antagonisme devient plus prononcé entre l'esprit religieux et les idées mondaines relativement à la mort volontaire. Le clergé continue à suivre la route qui a été tracée par Saint Augustin et à déclarer le suicide criminel et impie ; mais la tristesse et le désespoir n'entendent pas sa voix, ne se souviennent pas de ses prescriptions." [5] The revival of classical learning, accompanied as it was by admiration for antiquity and a desire to imitate its great men, not only increased the number of suicides, but influenced popular sentiments on the subject.[6] Even the Catholic casuists, and later on philosophers of the school of Grotius and others, began to distinguish certain cases of legitimate suicide, such as that committed to avoid dishonour

[1] Westermarck, *The Origin and Development of the Moral Ideas*, ii. 254 *sqq.*

[2] Stephen, *op. cit.* iii. 105. I have elsewhere suggested that suicides may have been buried at cross-roads because the cross was supposed to disperse the evil energy ascribed to their bodies. Both in Europe and India the cross-road has since ancient times been a favourite place to divest oneself of diseases or other evil influences (*op. cit.* ii. 256 *sq.* n. 1).

[3] Westermarck, *op. cit.* ii. 256 *sq.*

[4] See Bourquelot, *loc. cit.* iv. 248 ; F. B. Gummere, *Germanic Origins* (London, 1892), p. 322.

[5] Bourquelot, *loc. cit.* iv. 253.

[6] *Ibid.* iv. 464 ; Morselli, *op. cit.* p. 35.

or probable sin, or that of a condemned person saving himself from torture by anticipating an inevitable death, or that of a man offering himself to death for the sake of his friend.[1] Sir Thomas More, in his *Utopia*, permits a person who is suffering from an incurable and painful disease to take his own life, provided that he does so with the agreement of the priests and magistrates ; nay, he even maintains that these should exhort such a man to put an end to a life which is only a burden to himself and others.[2] Donne, the well-known Dean of St. Paul's, wrote in his younger days a book in defence of suicide, " a Declaration," as he called it, " of that paradoxe, or thesis, that Self-homicide is not so naturally sin, that it may never be other-wise." He there pointed out the fact—which ought never to be overlooked by those who derive their arguments from " nature " —that some things may be natural to the species, and yet not natural to every individual member of it.[3] In one of his essays Montaigne pictures classical cases of suicide with colours of unmistakable sympathy. " La plus volontaire mort," he says, " c'est la plus belle. La vie despend de la volonté d'aultruy ; la mort, de la nostre." [4]

The rationalism of the eighteenth century led to numerous attacks both upon the views of the Church and upon the laws of the State concerning suicide. Montesquieu advocated its legitimacy :—" La société est fondée sur un avantage mutuel ; mais lorsqu'elle me devient onéreuse, qui m'empêche d'y renoncer ? La vie m'a été donnée comme une faveur ; je puis donc la rendre lorsqu' elle ne l'est plus : la cause cesse, l'effet doit donc cesser aussi." [5] Voltaire strongly opposed the cruel laws which subjected a suicide's body to outrage and deprived his children of their heritage.[6] If his act is a wrong against society, what is to be said of the voluntary homicides committed in war, which are permitted by the laws of all countries ? Are they not much more harmful to the human race than self-murder, which nature prevents from ever being practised by any large number of men ? [7] Beccaria pointed out

---

[1] Buonafede, *op. cit.* p. 148 *sqq.* ; Lecky, *op. cit.* ii. 55.

[2] T. More, *Utopia* (London, 1869), p. 122.

[3] J. Donne, *Biathanatos* (London, 1648), p. 45. Donne's book was first committed to the press in 1644, by his son.

[4] Montaigne, *Essais*, ii. 3 (*Œuvres*, Paris, 1837), p. 187.

[5] Montesquieu, *Lettres Persanes*, 76 (*Œuvres* [Paris, 1837], p. 53).

[6] Voltaire, *Commentaire sur le livre Des délits et des peines*, 19 (*Œuvres complètes*, v [Paris, 1837], p. 416) ; *idem, Prix de la justice et de l'humanité*, 5 (*ibid.* v. 424).

[7] *Idem, Note to Olympie acte v. scène 7 (Œuvres complètes*, i [Paris, 1836], p. 826 n. *b*) ; *idem, Dictionnaire philosophique*, art. Suicide (*ibid.* viii. 1836, p. 236).

that the State is more wronged by the emigrant than by the suicide, since the former takes his property with him, whereas the latter leaves his behind.[1] According to Holbach, he who kills himself is guilty of no outrage on nature or its author ; on the contrary, he follows an indication given by nature when he parts from his sufferings through the only door which has been left open. Nor has his country or his family any right to complain of a member whom it has no means of rendering happy, and from whom it consequently has nothing more to hope.[2] Others eulogised suicide when committed for a noble end,[3] or recommended it on certain occasions. " Suppose," says Hume, " that it is no longer in my power to promote the interest of society ; suppose that I am a burthen to it ; suppose that my life hinders some person from being much more useful to society. In such cases my resignation of life must not only be innocent but laudable."[4] Hume also attacks the doctrine that suicide is a transgression of our duty to God. " If it would be no crime in me to divert the Nile from its course, were I able to do so, how could it be a crime to turn a few ounces of blood from their natural channel ? Were the disposal of human life so much reserved as the peculiar province of the Almighty that it were an encroachment on his right for men to dispose of their own lives, would it not be equally wrong of them to lengthen out their lives beyond the period which by the general laws of nature he had assigned to it ? My death, however voluntary, does not happen without the consent of Providence ; when I fall upon my own sword, I receive my death equally from the hands of the Deity as if it had proceeded from a lion, a precipice, or a fever."[5]

Thus the main arguments against suicide which had been set forth by Christian theologians were scrutinised and found unsatisfactory or at least insufficient to justify that severe and wholesale censure which was passed on it by the Church and the State. But a doctrine which has for ages been inculcated by the leading authorities on morals is not easily overthrown ; and when the old arguments are found fault with new ones are invented. Kant maintained that a person who disposes of his own life degrades the humanity subsisting in his person and

[1] C. Beccaria Bonesana, *Dei delitti e delle pene*, § 35 (*Opere*, i [Milano, 1821], p. 101).
[2] P. H. D. d'Holbach, *Système de la nature*, i (Paris, 1821), p. 369.
[3] In the early part of the nineteenth century this was done by J. F. Fries, *Neue oder anthropologische Kritik der Vernunft*, iii (Heidelberg, 1831), p. 197.
[4] Hume, ' Suicide,' in *Philosophical Works*, iv (London, 1875), p. 413.
[5] *Ibid.* iv. 407 *sqq.*

entrusted to him to the end that he might uphold it.[1] Fichte
argued that it is our duty to preserve our life and to will to live,
not for the sake of life, but because our life is the exclusive
condition of the realisation of the moral law through us.[2]
According to Hegel it is a contradiction to speak of a person's
right over his life, since this would imply a right of a person
over himself, and no one can stand above and execute himself.[3]
Paley, again, feared that if religion and morality allowed us to
kill ourselves in any case, mankind would have to live in continual alarm for the fate of their friends and dearest relations [4]—
just as if there were a strong temptation for men to shorten
their lives which could be overcome only by religious and moral
prescriptions. But common sense is neither a metaphysician
nor a sophist. When not restrained by the yoke of a narrow
theology, it is inclined in most cases to regard the self-murderer
as a proper object of compassion rather than of condemnation,
and in some instances as a hero. The legislation on the subject
therefore changed as soon as the religious influence was weakened. The laws against suicide were abolished in France by
the Revolution,[5] and afterwards in various other continental
countries ; [6] whilst in England it became the custom of jurymen
to presume absence of mind in the self-murderer—perjury, as
Bentham said, being the penance which prevented an outrage
on humanity.[7] These measures undoubtedly indicate not only
a greater regard for the innocent relatives of the self-murderer,
but also a change in the moral ideas concerning the act itself.
Durkheim thought that the more lenient judgment passed on
it by the public conscience of the present time is merely
accidental and transient.[8] But then he failed to notice that
the chief cause of the extreme severity with which it was treated
in Christian countries was an antiquated theology, which stands
no chance of being revived.

[1] Kant, *Metaphysische Anfangungsgründe der Tugendlehre* (Königsberg, 1803), p. 73.
[2] Fichte, *Das System der Sittenlehre* (Jena and Leipzig, 1798), p. 339
sqq. See also *ibid.* pp. 360, 391.
[3] Hegel, *Grundlinien der Philosophie des Rechts*, § 70, Zusatz, p. 72.
[4] W. Paley, *Principles of Moral and Political Philosophy*, iv. 3 (*Complete Works*, ii [London, 1825], p. 230).
[5] A. Legoyt, *Le suicide ancien et moderne* (Paris, 1881), p. 109.
[6] Bourquelot, *loc. cit.* iv. 475.
[7] J. Bentham, *Principles of Penal Law*, ii. 4. 4 (*Works*, i [Edinburgh,
1838], p. 479 *sq.*).
[8] É. Durkheim, *Le Suicide* (Paris, 1897), p. 377.

CHAPTER XIII

CHRISTIANITY AND ECONOMICS

JESUS' attitude towards the question of possessions was that we should seek first the kingdom of God and not to be anxious for the morrow. He allowed everybody to earn his living by work ; many of his parables dealt with the use of money, without any reproof on account of its possession ; he did not denounce ownership in goods or land, except among the small missionary group of his immediate disciples. But he condemned wealth, which he regarded as a peril to the soul.

The story of the rich young ruler who was told by Jesus that he would have treasure in heaven if he sold all that he had and distributed to the poor, was regarded by the early Christians as a counsel of perfection. It was apparently followed by many of the adherents to the little community of believers at Jerusalem which is mentioned in Acts.[1] The essence of its primitive communism was the formation of a common fund, which was applied in the first instance to the relief of the necessities of the poorer members ; but another outstanding feature of the community was fellowship expressed in common meals. The communistic organisation of the little Church in Jerusalem may have been an isolated experiment—Paul knows nothing of such communism [2]—but the common fund maintained by weekly subscription from rich and poor of which he speaks, the relief of the necessities of the poorer members, and the expression of the spirit of brotherhood in the Agape or Love-feast, became normal features of Church-life.[3] On the other hand, the surrender of private property was fundamental in monastic communism. " The principle is that the monk may *possess* nothing—nothing whatsoever—may look on nothing as his own, but must always recognise that whatever he may have for his personal use is all the common property of the community and that he must not have anything at all except what the abbot has given him or permitted him to have." [4]

[1] *Acts* ii. 44–7, iv. 32–5.

[2] *1 Corinthians* xvi. 2 ; *2 Corinthians* ix. 7, xii. 14.

[3] H. G. Wood, *Communism, Christian and Marxist* (London, 1935), p. 23 *sqq.*

[4] Cuthbert Butler, *Benedictine Monachism* (London, 1924), p. 147.

The patristic view was that this principle was the most perfect way of life, but that for mankind in general some organisation of ownership became necessary, human nature being what it is. Clement of Alexandria argues that if the gospel required men to renounce their worldly possessions, it would be impossible for them to fulfil our Saviour's injunctions to feed the hungry, clothe the naked, and so forth ; and the precepts of the Gospel would be found at variance with each other.[1] But wealth is like a viper, which is harmless if man knows how to take hold of it, though if he does not, it will twine round his hand and bite him.[2] Wealth ill-directed is the citadel of wickedness, and they who are earnest about their salvation must understand that all possession is for use.[3] Property is limited to the necessary minimum of existence ; all that is superfluous must be given away. But for different positions in life the existence minimum which is permitted is different.[4] According to Ambrose, it was the will of God that the earth should be the common possession of men, and should furnish its fruits to all; hence it is just that the man who claims for his private ownership that which was given to the human race in common should at least distribute some of this to the poor.[5] So also Augustine maintains that the right of possession is limited by the use to which it is put, and that a man who does not use his property rightly has no valid claim to it.[6] He very contemptuously sets aside the claim of the Donatists to hold as their property that which they had accumulated by their labour.[7]

Similar doctrines are laid down by Gratian, the compiler of the Canon Law in the twelfth century. He says that by the law of nature all things are common to all men, and that private property is lawful only as an accommodation to the imperfect and vicious character of human nature.[8] He cites a passage from Ambrose denouncing as unjust and avaricious the man who consumes in luxury what might have supplied the needs of those who are in want, and refers to a saying which he attributes to Jerome, to the effect that a man who keeps for himself more than he needs is guilty of taking that which belongs to another.[9] At the same time, however, he appeals to the

---

[1] Clement of Alexandria, *Quis dives salvatur ? passim.*
[2] *Idem, Pædagogus,* iii. 6. [3] *Ibid.* ii. 3. [4] *Ibid.* ii. 1.
[5] Ambrose, *In Psalmum David CXVIII. Expositio,* viii. 22 (Migne, *Patrologiæ cursus,* xv. 1303 *sq.*).
[6] Augustine, *Sermo L.* 4. [7] *Idem, Epistola XCIII.* 11.
[8] Gratian, *Decretum,* dist. viii. 1.
[9] *Ibid.* dist. xlvii. 8. 3, dist. xlii. 1.

authority of Augustine when he urges that the needs of different people vary, and that the rich are therefore not required to use the same food as the poor, but may have such food as their infirmity has made necessary for them, though they ought to lament the fact that they require this indulgence.[1] These principles are somewhat modified by Thomas Aquinas. According to him private property, while not an institution of the natural law is not contrary to it, but a thing added to it by human reason.[2] And it is not only lawful for a man to have property of his own, but also necessary to human life for various reasons : because every one is more careful to look after a thing that is his own private concern than after what is common to all or to many ; because there would be confusion if every one indiscriminately took the management of anything he pleased ; and because a peaceful state of society is thus better ensured, every one being contented with his own lot, whereas disputes arise not uncommonly among those who have any possession in joint stock. But a man ought not to hold exterior goods so exclusively as his own, that he does not readily share them with others in their need.[3] Aquinas even maintains that if " a need be so plain and pressing that clearly the urgent necessity has to be relieved from whatever comes to hand, as when danger is threatening a person and there is no other means of succouring him, then the man may lawfully relieve his distress out of the property of another, taking it either openly or secretly ; nor does this proceeding properly bear the stamp of either theft or robbery." [4] But it is only his superfluity that a person is obliged to distribute in alms : every one must first provide for himself and for those the care of whom is incumbent on him, and not deprive himself of so much of his own goods that he becomes unable to pass his life suitably to his state and to the calls of business. Yet it is praiseworthy to do so in the case of extreme need in some private person or in the commonwealth.[5]

In conformity with the doctrine that if a man possesses more than he needs, he has no personal right to it by natural law, but is only a steward of God, as well as with the direct teaching of Christ, almsgiving became one of the chief instruments of salvation. Very soon the charitable activity merged itself in ascetic achievements whose principal aim was not to help the poor but to secure eternal life for the donor In the ' Didache '

[1] Gratian, *Decretum*, dist. xli. 3.
[2] Thomas Aquinas, *Summa theologica*, ii.–ii. 66. 2. 1.
[3] *Ibid.* ii.–ii. 66. 2.   [4] *Ibid.* ii.–ii. 66. 7.
[5] *Ibid.* ii.–ii. 32. 5 *sq.*

it is said : " If thou hast anything, by thy hands thou shalt give a ransom for thy sins." [1] Countless times is the thought expressed that almsgiving is a safe investment of money at good interest with God in heaven. [2] Cyprian establishes an arithmetical relation between the number of alms-offerings and the blotting out of sins. [3] According to Augustine, " God is to be propitiated for past sins by alms " ; and at the Last Judgment the decision turns on almsgiving. [4] He also speaks of the mitigation obtained by departed souls through the alms of survivors, as well as through the Mass, saying that there are many souls not good enough to be able to dispense with this provision, and not bad enough not to be benefited by it. [5] " The food of the needy," says Leo the Great, " is the purchase-money of the kingdom of heaven." [6] " As long as the market lasts," says Chrysostom, " let us buy alms, or rather let us purchase salvation through alms." [7] The habit was gradually introduced to redeem with alms, after the fashion of the Teutonic *wergeld*, the various penitential penalties. The rich man is only a debtor ; all that he possesses beyond what is necessary, belongs to the poor, and ought to be given to them. [8] The poor, nc longer looked down upon, became tools of salvation. To them was given the first place in the church and in the Christian community. Chrysostom says of them : " As fountains flow near the place of prayer that the hands that are about to be raised to heaven may be washed, so were the poor placed by our fathers near to the door of the church, that our hands might be consecrated by benevolence before they are raised to God." [9] Gregory the Great announces, and the Middle Ages re-echo : " The poor are not to be lightly esteemed and despised, but to be honoured as patrons." [10]

It has been claimed that the virtue of charity " is beyond dispute one of the greatest gifts which Christianity has bestowed on the world." [11] As to this it may be pointed out that it has also, since ancient times, been very prominent among the civilised nations of the East and often strenuously enjoined

[1] *Didache*, 4.
[2] See G. Uhlhorn, *Die christliche Liebesthätigkeit*, i (Stuttgart, 1882), p. 270.
[3] Cyprian, *De opere et eleemosynis*, 24.
[4] Augustine, *Enchiridion*, 70, 72, 73, 75, 77.   [5] *Ibid.* 109.
[6] Leo the Great, *Sermo X., de Collectis*, 5.
[7] Chrysostom, *Homilia VII., de Pœnitentia*, 7
[8] Uhlhorn, *op. cit.* i. 294 *sq.*
[9] Chrysostom, *De verbis Apostoli, Habentes eumdem spiritum*, iii. 11.
[10] Gregory the Great, quoted by Uhlhorn, *op. cit.* i. 315.
[11] P. Gardner, *Evolution in Christian Ethics* (London, 1918), p. 124.

by their religions; [1] and that the Christian insistence on it belonged to its Jewish inheritance.[2] " The Hebrew race, throughout its entire history, has been endowed with a peculiar sense of responsibility for its weaker brethren, and in modern life is excelled by no element in any community in thoroughness and magnificence of organised charity." [3] Nor can we blame the ancient Greeks and Romans for neglecting their poor. Among them slavery in a great measure replaced pauperism; and what slavery did for the very poor, the Roman system of clientage did for those of a somewhat higher rank.[4] Moreover, the relief of the indigent was an important function of the State.[5] The Areopagus provided public works for the poor.[6] At Rome gratuitous distribution of corn was the rule for many centuries; [7] agrarian laws furnished free homesteads to the landless on conquered or public territory.[8] Nerva enjoined the support of poor children in all the cities of Italy.[9] The tablet Veleia records the charitable measures adopted by Trajan, which were continued by Hadrian.[10] All the emperors from Vespasian to Marcus Aurelius made liberal provision for the higher studies.[11] But while the emperors were responding to the call of charity by using the resources of the State, private benevolence is said to have been even more active. Friedländer writes that the rich and great were always expected to employ their excess both to support the poor and to allow them to participate largely in their own pleasures and to afford them advantages and amusements in which the modern world gives them no share. In public buildings, institutions, and feeding the poor private generosity went hand in hand with communal

---

[1] E. Westermarck, *The Origin and Development of the Moral Ideas*, i (London, 1912), p. 549 *sqq.*

[2] *Supra*, p. 80.

[3] F. G. Peabody, *Jesus Christ and the Social Question* (New York, 1915), p. 228.

[4] W. E. H. Lecky, *History of European Morals*, ii (London, 1890), p. 73.

[5] G. Boissier, *La religion romaine d'Auguste aux Antonins*, ii (Paris, 1874), p. 206.

[6] J. A. Farrer, *Paganism and Christianity* (London and Edinburgh, 1891), p. 183.

[7] Naudet, ' Des secours publics chez les Romains,' in *Mémoires de l'Institut Royal de France, Académie des Inscriptions et Belles-Lettres*, xiii (Paris, 1838), p. 43 *sq.*

[8] *Ibid.* p. 71 *sq.*

[9] Aurelius Victor, *Epitome*, xii. 8.

[10] S. Dill, *Roman Society from Nero to Marcus Aurelius* (London, 1904), p. 192.

[11] *Ibid.* p. 192.

activity. " Endowments, gifts, and legacies for purchase of oil and meal for free distribution or cheap sale were frequent, and endowments to put poor parents in the position to educate their children up to wage-earning age not unusual." [1] Nor were the aged and the sick forgotten. The countless gifts and legacies to the colleges, which were the refuge of the poor in that age, in every region of the Roman world, are an irresistible proof of an overflowing charity. Dill says that Pliny had a conception of the uses and responsibilities of wealth which, in spite of the teaching of Galilee, is not yet very common; " although he was not a very wealthy man, he acted up to his principles on a scale and proportion which only a few of our millionaires have yet reached." And Pliny, whose lavish generosity is a commonplace of social history, is only a shining example of a numerous class of more obscure benefactors, as the stone records abundantly tell those who care to read them. [2] Stoicism inculcated the duty of charity. " The wise man will help those who weep, but not imitate them. He will give his hand to the shipwrecked, hospitality to the exile, and aid to the poor; not proudly, like many who wish to seem compassionate, . . . but like a man who helps his fellow-men on account of the universal brotherhood." [3] Beneficence and liberality are " virtues that are the most agreeable to the nature of man." [4] Peabody observes : " It was in this soil of the surviving traditions of Rome and the still flourishing traditions of Israel that the philanthropy of the Christian religion took root. Without such a soil Christian charity would have been a seed sown by the wayside." [5]

There was, however, an essential difference between the charity of the Christians and that taught by the Stoics. Among the former indiscriminate almsgiving was looked upon as a duty, in accordance with the precept given by Jesus : " Give to him that asketh thee, and from him that would borrow of thee turn not thou away." Hermas said that they who receive without a real need shall give an account for it to God, whereas " he that gives shall be innocent; for he has fulfilled his duty as he received it from God; not making any choice to whom he should give, and to whom not." [6] In a much later age Thomas Aquinas denied that it is our duty to give alms to a

---

[1] L. Friedländer, *Roman Life and Manners under the Early Empire*, ii (London, 1909), p. 228.
[2] Dill, *op. cit.* p. 193 *sqq.*
[3] Seneca, *De clementia*, ii. 6. 2.
[4] Cicero, *De officiis*, i. 14.
[5] Peabody, *op. cit.* p. 230. [6] Hermas, *Pastor*, ii. 2.

person who is not in need,[1] but nevertheless raised the question whether we are bound to do the work of mercy to a distressed client if there is an appearance of possible relief for him by his own exertions or otherwise, and answered it by saying that " you are not absolutely bound under pain of sin to relieve his distress ; though if you do relieve him without such absolute obligation, your generosity is to be commended "[2]—though he might do it himself by his own exertions. A different spirit meets us in the sayings of Seneca. The wise man " will choose out the worthiest with the utmost care, and never give without sufficient reason ; for unwise gifts must be reckoned among foolish extravagances ; his purse will open easily, but never leak."[3] " He errs who thinks it easy to give alms ; it is very difficult, if they are to be distributed with any purpose, and not merely thrown away by chance. . . . Never do I take more pains in any investments than in these."[4] " Giving to a base man is neither noble nor generous."[5] Cicero likewise points out that the virtues of beneficence and liberality involve many precautionary considerations. Thus " we are to take care lest our kindness should hurt both those whom it is meant to assist and others," and " it ought to be rendered to each in proportion to his worth " ; " they who do kindnesses which prove of disservice to the person they pretend to oblige, should not be esteemed beneficent nor generous, but injurious sycophants."[6] Again, whilst among the Christians attention was concentrated on the supposed profit which almsgiving brought to the bestower, Seneca laid down the rule, " Give the kindness for its own sake, thinking only of the receiver's interests."[7]

In one respect, however, Christian charity was not always unlimited. In the Epistles of the New Testament the love spoken of frequently refers to the brotherhood of believers only.[8] Clement of Rome insists that charity shall be " without respect of persons, alike towards all such as religiously fear God."[9] The principle of the Church was, " Omnem hominem *fidelem* tuum esse fratrem." As an instance of this may be mentioned the attempts made in the latter part of the Middle Ages by Councils and sovereigns to abolish the ancient custom of seizing the goods of persons who had been shipwrecked : they concerned Christian sailors only, whereas the robbing of

[1] Thomas Aquinas, *op. cit.* ii.–ii. 32. 5.
[2] *Ibid.* ii.–ii. 71. 1.   [3] Seneca, *De vita beata*, xxiii. 5.
[4] *Ibid.* xxiv. 1.   [5] Seneca, *De beneficiis*, iv. 9. 3.
[6] Cicero, *op. cit.* i. 14.   [7] Seneca, *De beneficiis*, iv. 9. 1.
[8] *Supra*, p. 76 *sq.*
[9] Clement of Rome, *Epistola I.*, 21.

shipwrecked infidels was not prohibited.[1] Nor was that principle followed by the Catholics alone : in the seventeenth century the Scotch clergy taught that food and shelter must on no occasion be given to a starving man unless his opinions were orthodox.[2] How different was the Stoic maxim that the wise man will give his hand to the shipwrecked and aid to the poor on account of the universal brotherhood. Among the Jews also we meet with a rule of similar loftiness : it is said in the Talmud, with reference to the treatment of the poor, that no distinction should be made between such as are Jews and such as are not.[3]

Thus it cannot be denied that the kind of charity which was established by Christianity and continued during the longest period of its existence suffered from grave defects, in theory and practice, which had been avoided outside its pale and are utterly condemned by enlightened moral opinion. The ideal of poverty, which was supported both by the belief in the redeeming effect of almsgiving and the teaching of Jesus, and the desire to imitate his own poor life and that of his apostles, led to the breeding of parasites and beggars, hordes of whom were turned out by the mendicant orders in particular. It also led to the depreciation of work. It is true that the contempt in which manual labour was held by the ancient pagans [4] could not be shared by the early Christians. Jesus had been born in a carpenter's family, his apostles belonged to the working class, and so did originally most of his followers. Origen accepts with pride the reproach of Celsus, when he accuses Christians of worshipping the son of a poor workwoman, who had earned her bread by spinning,[5] and contrasts with the wisdom of Plato, that of Paul the tent-maker, of Peter, the fisherman, of John, who had abandoned his father's nets.[6] In the Epistles to the Thessalonians the duty of personal industry is pressed on them ; " if any would not work, neither should he eat." [7] But the teaching of Jesus makes it quite plain that he considered work of value only in so far as it is necessary to life ; all that men have to do is to live by the day, trusting their heavenly Father

---

[1] F. Laurent, *Études sur l'histoire de l'Humanité*, vii (Paris, 1865), pp. 323, 413 n. 3 ; H. von Eicken, *Geschichte und System der mittelalter-lichen Weltanschauung* (Stuttgart, 1887), p. 570.

[2] H. T. Buckle, *History of Civilization in England*, iii (London, 1894), p. 277.

[3] Giṭṭin, fol. 61a, quoted by A. Katz, *Der wahre Talmudjude* (Berlin, 1893), p. 38. *Cf.* A. Chaikin, *Apologie des Juifs* (Paris, 1887), p. 10.

[4] See Westermarck, *op. cit.* ii. 278 *sqq.*

[5] Origen, *Contra Celsum*, i. 28 *sq.*　　　　[6] *Ibid.* vi. 7.

[7] *1 Thessalonians* iv. 11 ; *2 Thessalonians* iii. 10.

to provide for the morrow. The ancient Fathers also say remarkably little about work ; the significance of labour in a calling for the exercise of the Christian life and the furtherance of the kingdom of God is never expressed by any of them.[1]   In the original sinless state of mankind labour was unknown. It was to punish man for his disobedience that God caused him to eat daily bread in the sweat of his face.[2]   Since then work is a necessity ; but the contemplative life is better than the active life.[3]   Bonaventura points out that Jesus preferred the meditating Mary to the busy Martha,[4] and that he himself seems to have done no work till his thirtieth year.[5]   Work is of no value by itself ; its highest object is to further contemplation, to macerate the body, to curb concupiscence.[6]   For this purpose, indeed, it was strongly insisted upon by several founders of religious orders.   According to St. Benedict, " idleness is an enemy to the soul ; and therefore at certain seasons the brethren ought to occupy themselves in the labour of their hands, and at others in holy reading."[7]   St. Bernard writes : " The handmaid of Christ ought always to pray, to read, to work, lest haply the spirit of uncleanness should lead astray the slothful mind. The delight of the flesh is overcome by labour. . . .   The body tired by work is less delighted with vice."[8]   But the active life must not be pursued to such an extent as to hinder what it is intended to promote ; for it is impossible for any man to be at once occupied with exterior actions and at the same time apply himself to divine contemplation.[9]   Thomas Aquinas says that while he who has nothing else to live upon is bound to work, it is a sin to try to acquire riches beyond the limit of those which are necessary to his life according to his rank and station.[10]

However restricted was the amount of work which might

---

[1] *Cf.* E. Troeltsch, *The Social Teaching of the Christian Churches* (London and New York, 1931), p. 184 *sq.*

[2] *Genesis* iii. 19.

[3] Thomas Aquinas, *op. cit.* ii.–ii. 182. 1 *sq.* ; von Eicken, *op. cit.* p. 488 *sqq.*

[4] Bonaventura, *Meditationes vitæ Christi*, 45 (*Opera*, xii [Venetiis, 1756], p. 452).

[5] *Ibid.* 15 (*Opera*, xii. 405).

[6] Guigo, *Epistola ad Fratres de Monte-Dei*, i. 8 (in St. Bernard, *Opera omnia*, ii [Parisiis, 1719], p. 214) : " Non spiritualia exercitia sunt propter corporalia, sed corporalia propter spiritualia " ; von Eicken, *op. cit.* p. 491 *sqq.*

[7] St. Benedict, *Regula monachorum* (Lipsiae, 1895), 48.

[8] St. Bernard, *De modo bene vivendi*, 51 (*op. cit.* ii. 883 *sq.*).

[9] *Speculum monachorum*, in St. Bernard, *op. cit.* ii. 818 ; von Eicken, *op. cit.* p. 494 *sq.* Cf. Thomas Aquinas, *op. cit.* ii.–ii. 182. 3.

[10] Thomas Aquinas, *op. cit.* ii.–ii. 187. 3, 118. 1.

erve as a source of income, the acquisition of money without
work was prohibited in the ecclesiastical legislation on the
subject of " usury." This word did not signify, as nowadays,
an excessive rate of interest on a loan, but the taking of any
payment for a loan of money. At first the prohibition of lending
money for gain was a disciplinary regulation binding only on
the clergy, but it was subsequently extended to the laity in
Western Europe by the capitularies of Charles the Great and
various Councils. It was ordained that manifest usurers should
not be admitted to communion, nor, if they died in their sin,
receive Christian burial, and that no priest should accept their
alms. The wills of unrepentant usurers—of usurers who did
not make restitution—should be without validity ; and any
person who denied that usury was a sin should be treated as a
heretic.[1] The prohibition of usury was in the first place an
attempt to enforce the precept, " Lend, hoping for nothing
again," [2] but it was also supported by references to the Jewish
law (*Exodus* xxii. 25), which only permitted interest to be taken
from aliens,[3] while the evils of usury were abundantly illustrated
by the grievous results exercised by that practised by the Jews.[4]
There was further the feeling that usury was an exploitation of
distress, and, as Leo X. ruled in the fifth Lateran Council, an
" attempt to draw profit and increment, without labour, without cost, and without risk, out of the use of a thing that does
not fructify." In those days there was but a very small field
for the investment of capital ; [5] and as ample security was
usually given for the return of the money lent, and the alternative to lending was that the money remained idle in the hands
of its possessor, he was just in the same position when his money
came back to him as if he had never parted with it. In the
sixteenth century the theory arose that not all taking of reward
was usurious, but only the taking more than a certain percentage.[6]

A particularly difficult question was that of trade. It was
suspect from the ascetic point of view because it assumed
pleasure in possession and in gain, and it was suspect from the
point of view of the principle of love because it meant taking
away from one to give to another and enriching oneself at the
expense of others ; as the trader does not himself add to the

[1] W. J. Ashley, *An Introduction to English Economic History and
Theory*, i (London, 1894), p. 148 *sqq.*
[2] *Luke* vi. 35.
[3] Thomas Aquinas, *op. cit.* ii.–ii. 78. 1. 2.
[4] Ashley, *op. cit.* i. 156.
[5] *Cf.* W. Roscher, *Political Economy*, ii (New York, 1878), p. 128.
[6] Ashley, *op. cit.* p. 154.

value of his wares, and yet gains more for them than he has paid, his gain—it was argued—must be another's loss.[1] Even Augustine wrote that business is itself an evil, because " it turns men from seeking true rest, which is God." [2] More sober churchmen, such as Leo the Great, however, replied that it is the way in which a man carries on his trade that determines whether it is good or bad : " The nature of their gains either excuses or condemns the trafficker, because there is an honourable and a base kind of profit." [3] So also Aquinas admits that gain " does not essentially involve any element of vice," since there is nothing to hinder it from being referred to an end which is necessary or even honourable. Thus it is lawful when the trader refers the moderate gain which he seeks to the sustenance of his family or to the relief of the distressed, or when he " applies to trade on behalf of the public interest, that the necessaries of life may not be wanting to his country, and seeks gain, not as an end, but as the wages of his labour." [4] In any case, " to sell a thing dearer or buy it cheaper than it is worth, is a proceeding in itself unjust and unlawful." [5] But what is the just price, representing the value of a thing ? Aquinas maintained that prices should correspond with the labour and costs of the producer, though they may vary with " the diversity of place or time." [6] To him value was something objective, something outside the will of the individual purchaser or seller, something attached to the thing itself, existing whether he liked it or not and that he ought to recognise.[7] The principle of the Roman law, on the other hand, had been that the price of a thing was entirely a matter to be determined by free contract ; [8] and so also several Schoolmen of the fourteenth century, emphasising the subjective element in value, insisted that the essence of value was utility, and drew the conclusion that a fair price was most likely to be reached under freedom of contract, since the mere fact that a bargain had been struck showed that both parties were satisfied.[9]

[1] Troeltsch, *op. cit.* p. 116 ; J. Kautz, *Theorie und Geschichte der National-Oekonomik*, ii (Wien, 1860), p. 209.

[2] Augustine, quoted by Gratian, *op. cit.* dist. lxxxviii. 12.

[3] Leo the Great, *Epistola CLXVII.* 11 (Migne, *Patrologiæ cursus* liv. 1206).

[4] Thomas Aquinas, *op. cit.* ii.–ii. 77. 4.

[5] *Ibid.* ii.–ii. 77. 1.   [6] *Ibid.* ii.–ii. 77. 4. 2.

[7] *Cf.* W. Endemann, *Studien in der romanisch-kanonistischen Wirthschafts- und Rechtslehre*, ii (Berlin, 1883), p. 37.

[8] Justinian, *Digesta*, iv. 4. 16.

[9] R. H. Tawney, *Religion and the Rise of Capitalism* (London, 1933) p. 40.

While trade, when conducted properly, was admitted to laymen, Aquinas rules that it must not be practised by clerics, who "ought to abstain, not only from things in themselves evil, but also from things that have the appearance of evil." This observation applies to trade "both because it refers to earthly gain, of which the clergy ought to be despisers ; as also because of the vices frequently found in persons engaged in trade," a merchant being "hardly free from sins of the lips " (*Ecclesiasticus* xxvi. 28) ; and because trade too much entangles the soul in secular cares and withdraws from spirituality ; hence the Apostle says : "No man being a soldier to God, entangleth himself with secular business " (*2 Timothy* ii. 4).[1] As a matter of fact, however, this rule was constantly transgressed. From time to time complaints are made that priests engage in trade, as also that they take usury ; and from the middle of the thirteenth century a continuous wail arises against the avarice of the Church.[2] While she did little at any time to curb the greed of the strong, Mammon's victory within the bosom of the Church herself was still more signal, "inspiring it to the discovery and cultivation of doctrines and rites which became ever finer instruments for the acquisition of wealth."[3] She capitalised the fear of purgatory by selling exemptions from torment, and went further still by selling the right to sin, under the name of " indulgence."

This state of things was from the outset denounced by the Reformers. But in other respects their attitude in economic matters was far from revolutionary. "In the sixteenth century," says Mr. Tawney, "religious teachers of all shades of opinion still searched the Bible, the Fathers, and the *Corpus Juris Canonici* for light on practical questions of social morality, and, as far as the first generation of reformers was concerned, there was no intention, among either Lutherans, or Calvinists, or Anglicans, of relaxing the rules of good conscience, which were supposed to control economic transactions and social relations. If anything, indeed, their tendency was to interpret them with a more rigorous severity, as a protest against the moral laxity of the Renaissance, and, in particular, against the avarice which was thought to be peculiarly the sin of Rome.[4] Most characteristic features of the mediæval economic ethics reappear in Lutheranism ; but a novelty was the insistence on

---

[1] Thomas Aquinas, *op. cit.* ii.–ii. 77. 4. 3.
[2] Tawney, *op. cit.* p. 28 *sq.*
[3] J. A. Hobson, *God and Mammon* (London, 1931), p. 20 *sq.*
[4] Tawney, *op. cit.* p. 65.

labour within one's calling as a divinely ordained duty.[1] A person's endeavour ought not to exceed the requirements of his rank, and it is against all law, both natural and divine, to wish to rise in the world ; we ought to be satisfied with a very moderate standard of living, and not try day and night to reach something higher.[2] The mediæval prohibition of usury was taken for granted, nay demanded with increased urgency by Luther, though the later Lutherans did not perpetuate his severe attitude towards it ; [3] he even denounced the payment of interest as compensation for loss and the practice of investing in rent-charges, both of which the canon law in his day allowed.[4] But in its attitude towards almsgiving and mendicancy Lutheranism differed radically from that of the mediæval Church. Its doctrine of justification by faith alone deprived almsgiving of all merit and, consequently, of all attraction as a means of salvation. No beggars should be tolerated in Christian countries, and each town should organise charity for the support of the honest poor.[5]

Like Luther, Calvin advocated labour as a universal duty and condemned mendicancy and indiscriminate almsgiving ; the ecclesiastical authorities should regularly visit every family to ascertain whether the members were idle, or drunken, or otherwise undesirable. He, too, regarded work as the practical exercise of a calling appointed by God, as well as a method of self-discipline and of diverting evil desires. The Calvinistic economic ethic, moreover, agreed with the Lutheran one in its urgent desire for modesty and moderation, its observance of distinctions in rank, and its campaign against luxury, which was prosecuted with unexampled severity by laws against it, and which was checked ecclesiastically by the moral tribune.[6] But at the same time Calvin influenced the Reformed economic ethic in a manner which was utterly alien to the spirit of Lutheranism and led to the religious sanction of capitalism.

While Luther considered that the most admirable form of life was the self-contained family life of the peasant, based as far as possible on primitive methods of production, Calvin set the profits of trade and finance on the same level of respecta-

---

[1] Max Weber, *Gesammelte Aufsätze zur Religionssoziologie*, i (Tübingen 1922), p. 69 *sqq.*
[2] Luther, ' Kirchenpostille,' in *Sämmtliche Werke*, x (Erlangen, 1827) p. 233 *sq.* ; Weber, *op. cit.* i. 76 ; Troeltsch, *op. cit.* p. 870.
[3] Troeltsch, *op. cit.* p. 870.
[4] Luther, ' An den christlichen Adel deutscher Nation von des christlichen Standes Besserung. 1520,' in *Werke*, vi (Weimar, 1888), p. 466
[5] *Ibid.* vi (Weimar, 1888), p. 450.   [6] Troeltsch, *op. cit.* 641.

bility as the earnings of the labourer and the rents of the land-lord. He quite approved of the fact that greater profits were made in trade than in agriculture, since they were simply the reward of carefulness and industry.[1] He rejected the canonical veto on usury and the scholastic theory of money. He argued that the payment of interest for capital is as reasonable as the payment of rent for land, and only urged that it should not exceed the amount dictated by natural justice and the Golden Rule.[2] In his opinion the supposed scriptural prohibition of usury rests on an error of translation, referring not to interest as such but to the abuse of it.[3]

The direction which the ethics of Calvinism evolved was evidently connected with the conditions which governed the practical situation in Geneva. Calvin, who himself had a great deal to do with questions of industrial production, found capitalism acceptable as a calling which suited the existing conditions of the city, and which was capable of being com-bined with loyalty, seriousness, honesty, thrift, and considera-tion for one's neighbour.[4] Mr. Tawney feels that " there have been few systems in which the practical conclusions flow by so inevitable a logic from the theological premises." [5] To me it seems much more likely that Calvin's theological deductions were mainly influenced by economic circumstances. The dogma of predestination is the core of his theology. God has chosen certain individuals as his elect, predestined to salvation from eternity, while the remainder have been consigned to eternal damnation. The aim of man's existence is not salvation, to which human effort is quite irrelevant, but the glorification of God ; good works are not a way of attaining salvation, but are indispensable as a proof that salvation has been attained.[6] But why are the good works of Calvinism not such as were conceived of by Jesus and the mediæval Church, but such as suited urban industry and commercial enterprise ? Why is profit looked upon as the sign of the blessing of God on the faithful exercise of one's calling, and success as the hall-mark of godliness ? It may be that the Puritans' excessive deference to the Old Testament had something to do with that association of divine favour and mundane prosperity, which also marked

[1] *Ibid.* p. 642.
[2] *Ibid.* p. 643 ; Tawney, *op. cit.* p. 107.
[3] Margaret James, ' The effect of the religious changes of the sixteenth and seventeenth centuries on economic theory and development,' in *European Civilization Its Origin and Development,* by various contri-butors under the direction of E. Eyre, v (Oxford, 1937), p. 45.
[4] Troeltsch, *op. cit.* p. 642 *sq.*
[5] Tawney, *op. cit.* p. 108.   [6] *Supra,* p. 169 *sq.*

the religion of ancient Israel.[1]   But I maintain that the chief
solution of the problem lies in the influence of the capitalist
spirit over theological dogma.   Mr. Tawney himself points out
that there was plenty of this spirit in fifteenth-century Venice
and Florence, in South Germany and Flanders, for the simple
reason that these areas were the greatest commercial and
financial centres of the age, though all were, at least nominally,
Catholic, and that the development of capitalism in Holland
and England in the sixteenth and seventeenth centuries was
due, not to the fact that they were Protestant powers, but to
" large economic movements, in particular the Discoveries and
the results which flowed from them." [2]

The " ethic of the calling " was most consistently set forth
in Puritanism, which was an offshoot of Calvinism and is rightly
regarded as the most representative interpretation of Protestant
morality among English-speaking peoples.   It was most elabor-
ately and authoritatively expounded by Baxter in his *Christian
Directory*.   The first duty of a Christian is to make the most
of his powers and possessions in whatever might be his calling.
" It is for action that God maintaineth us." . . .   It is action
that God is most served and honoured by." [3]   " Keep up a
high esteem of time and be every day more careful that you
lose none of your time, than you are that you lose none of your
gold and silver.   And if vain recreations, dressings, feastings,
idle talk, unprofitable company, or sleep, be any of them
temptations to rob you of any of your time, accordingly heighten
your watchfulness." [4]   " You may cast off all such excess of
worldly cares or business as unnecessarily hinder you in spiritual
things.   But you may not cast off all bodily employment and
mental labour in which you serve the common good.   Every
one that is a member of Church or Commonwealth must employ
their parts to the utmost for the good of the Church and the
Commonwealth." [5]   " He is most beholden to God, that is most
exercised in good works : the more we *do*, the more we receive
from him." [6]   Unwillingness to work is a symptom of the lack
of grace.   Wealth does not except any one from this uncon-
ditional command.[7]   Wealth and poverty come of God's gifts,
and either is to be accepted as from him.   The seventeenth-
century moralists do not ignore the spiritual and moral dangers

[1] *Cf.* H. H. Henson, *Christian Morality* (Oxford, 1936), p. 278.
[2] Tawney, *op. cit.* p. 319 *sq.*
[3] R. Baxter, *A Christian Directory : a Summ of Practical Theologie
and Cases of Conscience*, i (London, 1678), p. 376.
[4] *Ibid.* ii (1677), p. 70.   [5] *Ibid.* i. 111 ; *cf. ibid.* i. 336.
[6] *Ibid.* i. 107.   [7] *Ibid.* i. 108 *sqq.*, 376.

of wealth, indeed they are most anxious to direct the man of means in the employment of his money. But as they regard the possession of wealth as something ordained of God, they take up a conservative attitude towards class distinctions and class standards of living.[1] Differences in wealth are incidental to God's education of mankind. "We may this day be rich, to-morrow we may be beggars ; for the riches be chanceable unto us, but not unto God : for God knoweth when, and to whom, he will give them or take them away again." [2] In the midst of many wise cautions against prodigality Baxter reserves the expenditure necessary for the maintenance of class distinctions. When he asks, "What may be accounted prodigality in the costliness of apparel ? " the answer begins with the sentence : "Not that which is only for a distinction of superiors from inferiors, or which is needful to keep up the vulgar's reverence to magistrates." [3] And when he discusses how far the rich may spend on themselves while the poor suffer want, he writes : "It must be confessed, that some few persons may be of so much worth and use to the commonwealth (as kings and magis-trates) and some of so little ; that the maintaining of the honour and succours of the former, may be more necessary than the saving of the lives of the latter. But take heed lest pride or cruelty teach you, to misunderstand this, or abuse it for your-selves." [4] Professor Barker observes that "Puritanism helped to dig the gulf—which is apparent in the history of English thought, and not least of English education, from the end of the seventeenth century onwards—between a possessional class, regarded as justified in its possessions by its moral and spiritual merits, and a class of labouring poor conceived as condemned to poverty by its moral and spiritual defects." [5] Although the Puritans regarded riches as God's gift and no man as absolute owner, but all men as God's stewards who must render an account of their stewardship, they seldom attached much weight to the claim which the poor can make on the rich in virtue of the social character of all wealth.[6]

The Puritan divines followed Calvin in rejecting the Canon

[1] H. G. Wood, ' The influence of the Reformation on ideas concerning wealth and property,' in *Property Its Duties and Rights*. Essays by various writers (London, 1913), p. 148.

[2] H. Latimer, *Works*, i (Cambridge, 1844), p. 478.

[3] Baxter, *op. cit.* iv (1677), p. 223.   [4] *Ibid.* iv. 225.

[5] E. Barker, *National Character and the Factors in its Formation* (London, 1927), p. 209. See also W. Cunningham, *The Moral Witness of the Church on the Investment of Money and the Use of Wealth* (Cambridge, 1909), p. 26.

[6] Wood, *loc. cit.* pp. 156, 162.

Law against usury. In his book *De conscientia*, which was the most influential work on social ethics written in the first half of the seventeenth century, Ames argues that there is no difference between a man who buys a farm and takes a rent for it—which is considered just—and a man who lends the money to another to buy the farm and gets that other to pay interest instead of rent.[1] But although the Puritan moralists generally admitted the right to take interest, they were never tired of insisting on moderation in terms on which money is lent. Baxter's counsels are somewhat vague, and he does not refer to any statutory limitation of interest, but he is clear that all usury is sinful when it is against justice and charity. The attitude of Puritanism towards monopolies, both in theory and practice, is also in line with Baxter's repudiation of getting all you can for your goods.[2] The Christian must not desire " to get another's goods or labour for less than it is worth." He must not secure a good price for his own wares " by extortion working upon men's ignorance, error or necessity." Rivalry in trade is inevitable, but the Christian must not snatch a good bargain " out of greedy covetousness, nor to the injury of the poor." And so forth.[3]

Of the rules of morality elaborated by Baxter, Mr. Tawney remarks that " they were like seeds carried by birds from a distant and fertile plain, and dropped upon a glacier," where they were at once embalmed and sterilised in a river of ice. He finds the roots of their failure, not merely in the obstacles offered by the ever more recalcitrant opposition of a commercial environment, but in certain tendencies in Puritanism itself, which were to make it later a potent ally of the movement against the control of economic relations when political and economic changes had prepared a congenial surrounding for their growth. This rejection of all traditional restrictions on economic enterprise was not only the temper of the English business world after the Civil War, but it took place in all other Calvinist countries as well.[4] In any case it was another instance of capitalism triumphing over religious doctrine, when the wave of commercial and financial expansion came, in the form of companies, colonies, capitalism in textiles, in mining, in finance, and so forth. As Miss James observes, " Puritanism was

[1] W. Ames, *De conscientia et eius iure* (Amstelodami, 1631), p. 384.
[2] Wood, *loc. cit.* pp. 141-3, 145.
[3] Selections from those parts of the *Christian Directory* which bear on social ethics are published by Jeannette Tawney, *Chapters from Richard Baxter's Christian Directory* (London, 1925).
[4] Tawney, *op. cit.* p. 226 *sq.*

strongest among those classes who were best able to take care of themselves and had nothing to gain and all to lose by the interference of Church and State in economic affairs." [1]

We notice a similar development within Methodism. While the early Wesleyans buoyed up enthusiasm, kept their virtue amid the temptations of the world, and were distinguished by devotion to public and private charities, their restrictive austerity weakened when the early enthusiasm waned. The theory of the divine ownership, which ordered the disposition of all money above the bare needs of the individual for the good of the community, was taken seriously only in the early vital period of the revival. Hand in hand with the altering economic social status of society members, the sense of class consciousness began to assert itself. And at the end of the century, after Wesley's death, philanthropy was in danger of being defined again in the old traditional terms of dutiful alms. Wesley and the early Methodists were felt to be too radical, and a rising group of prosperous Methodists repudiated the inconvenient part of the teaching by the apparently innocuous judgment that in this respect Wesley was simply impracticable.[2] Of the Established Church of England it has been said that its ordinary attitude, as expressed in Congresses or other authoritative utterances " is one of platitudinarianism, loose, suave, non-committal, on all important proposals of economic reform. This is due partly to a genuine disbelief in its competency to handle economic issues, partly to its feeling of personal sympathy with the wealthy business classes whose assistance is more than ever needed to enable it to carry on the recognised work of a modern parish." [3]

The teaching of Jesus can certainly not be recognised as applicable to economics. This is due not merely to the enormous difference between the social conditions of Judæa in the time of Jesus and those of the modern world, but also to certain general precepts which lack the support of the moral consciousness in any circumstances. One is that we should respond to every call of need, even though this should involve indiscriminate charity. Backed up by the hope of heavenly reward this rule was followed in a large measure by early and mediæval Christianity, but with unfortunate results. The Reformation brought about a change, and even led to a religious doctrine

---

[1] Margaret James, *Social Problems and Policy during the Puritan Revolution* (London, 1930), p. 16.

[2] W. J. Warner, *The Wesleyan Movement in the Industrial Revolution* (London, 1930), p. 247.

[3] Hobson, *op. cit.* p. 46.

which was utterly inconsistent with Jesus' recommendation of poverty as a state of blessedness and his warning against anxiety for the morrow. The poor were no longer looked upon as God's friends, but as objects of his hatred. Prosperity was the reward for moral superiority and the sign of salvation, poverty the punishment for moral failings and the sign of damnation. In connection with Puritanism a school of opinion arose that regarded with repugnance the whole body of social theory of which both private charity and public relief had been the expression. " The generall rule of all England," wrote a pamphleteer in 1646, " is to whip and punish the wandring beggars." The poor are the victims, not of circumstances, but of their own " idle, irregular, and wicked courses," and the truest charity is not to enervate them by relief, but so to reform their characters that relief may be unnecessary. The rigours of economic exploitation were preached as a public duty. Some thought that salvation might be found by reducing the number of days kept as holidays. Bishop Berkeley, with the conditions of Ireland before his eyes, suggested that all sturdy beggars should be seized and made slaves to the public for a certain term of years.[1] Innumerable writers advanced schemes for reformed workhouses which should be places at once of punishment and of training.[2] When we thus find within Christianity itself such absolutely conflicting religious opinions about the proper treatment of the poor, we have certainly good reason for accepting the modern view that this department of economics should be governed by social considerations in a humanitarian spirit without the interference of any religious doctrine at all.

Besides the duty of indiscriminate almsgiving there is another rule which should be observed in economic relations if these are to be regulated by the teaching of Jesus, namely, the maxim that you ought to love your neighbour as yourself. This rule would of course, as Mr. Hobson points out, be completely impracticable in the intricacies of a highly organised national or world market, where " no man knows whom he serves or who consumes the goods to the making of which he contributes some fractional share." [3] But this is not the only objection that may be raised to its application. Contrary to the Golden Rule, it is not merely an expression of the disinterestedness of the concept of duty, which implies that when an act is pronounced to be my duty it is so independently of any reference it might have to me personally. This has nothing to do with

[1] G. Berkeley, *Works*, iii (Oxford, 1871), p. 387.
[2] Tawney, *op. cit.* pp. 264-7, 270.
[3] Hobson, *op. cit.* p. 50 *sq.*

the particular nature of the act. When my own interests clash with those of my neighbour, I may have the right to prefer my own lesser good to the greater good of another, though only on condition that the other person also, in similar circumstances, is admitted to have the right to prefer his own lesser good to my greater good. No such right to prefer one's own lesser good to the greater good of another is recognised in the precept, " Thou shalt love thy neighbour as thyself." As I have pointed out above,[1] this precept owes its origin to the strength of the altruistic sentiment in him who laid down the rule, and not merely to the disinterestedness of his moral emotions.

The altruistic sentiment varies in range and strength, and in so far as it is stronger in some persons than in others, it is more apt to influence their consciences with regard to their own conduct and their judgments on other people's conduct. The utilitarian proposition, " I ought not to prefer my own lesser good to the greater good of another," which, as Stuart Mill pointed out, is identical with the precept of Jesus,[2] presented itself to Sidgwick as no less evident than the mathematical axiom that " if equals be added to equals the wholes are equal " ; he called it the axiom or principle of " rational benevolence." He admitted that the duty of benevolence as recognised by common sense seems to fall somewhat short of this principle ; but he thought " that a ' plain man ' in a modern civilised society, if his conscience were fairly brought to consider the hypothetical question, whether it would be morally right for him to seek his own happiness on any occasion if it involved a certain sacrifice of the greater happiness of some other human being—without any counterbalancing gain to any one else,— would answer unhesitatingly in the negative."[3] Well, in many cases he undoubtedly would, but in other cases he most decidedly would not. Suppose that if I by sacrificing my own life could save another person's life, which is a greater good to him or to others than my life is to me or others, would it be my duty to make such a sacrifice ? Or suppose that I endeavour to obtain a good which another person also tries to obtain, and that I do so in spite of my belief that it will be a lesser good to me than it would be to him if he succeeded in achieving it ; would common sense condemn my action, even though I could claim no counterbalancing gain to any one else as an excuse for my behaviour ? For example, would it require that I, being a merchant, should abstain from some business if it is likely that

---

[1] *Supra*, pp. 38, 73.
[2] J. S. Mill, *Utilitarianism* (London, 1895), p. 24 *sq.*
[3] H. Sidgwick, *The Methods of Ethics* (London, 1913), p. 382 *sq.*

another competing merchant would make a larger profit than I could by engaging in the business ? [1] Can anybody doubt that common sense, without hesitation, would answer these questions in the negative ? It seems fairly obvious that Sidgwick has considerably exaggerated even that limited support his principle of rational benevolence could receive from the " plain man." Everybody will undoubtedly agree that some amount of self-sacrifice is a duty in certain circumstances, but the amount and the circumstances cannot be fixed in general rules, and on the whole, in cases of conflicting interests the judgment must to a large extent remain a matter of private opinion. Hutcheson, in whose system benevolence is the very essence of virtue and who was apparently the author of the utilitarian formula that " that action is best which procures the greatest happiness for the greatest numbers," [2] goes so far as to say that " we do not positively condemn those as evil, who will not sacrifice their private interest to the advancement of the positive good of others, unless the private interest is very small, and the public good very great." [3]

What has been said of our right to prefer our own lesser good to the greater good of another also applies to preferring our own good when it may involve a lessening of somebody else's good, as is generally the case in competition. There is nothing in the intrinsic nature of the moral emotions that prevents us from doing so, provided that we allow the other person in similar circumstances to increase his own good. The indictment made against our economic system that it is necessarily wrong because it is competitive is therefore unjustified, although it is certainly incompatible with the teaching of Jesus. This, of course, does not imply that it will be regarded as right in all circumstances. There are certain generally accepted moral principles which cannot be transgressed without disapproval, and these principles are very often ignored in our business life. " Look at the results of our present capitalistic system," says Dr. Lofthouse, " which places those who have only their labour to sell, where the market is overstocked, in the position of slaves ; at the operations of money and finance in the modern world, whereby those who possess the power of dispensing or withholding credit can control the whole of industry, capital

---

[1] Cf. G. Cohn, Etik og sociologi (Kjöbenhavn and Kristiania, 1913), p. 62 sqq.

[2] F. Hutcheson, An Inquiry into the Original of our Ideas of Beauty and Virtue (London, 1753), p. 185.

[3] Idem, An Essay on the Nature and Conduct of the Passions and Affections. With Illustrations on the Moral Sense (London, 1756), p. 318.

and labour alike. The result is what every one can recognise and no one can overcome ; poverty and distress in a world where science and skill can supply its wants as quickly as they can arise ; and a universal shortage, experienced and dreaded, which makes every man look on his neighbour as his foe ; which binds men into groups whose mutual rivalries leave the rivalries of individuals far behind ; and a heartless or despairing acquiescence in the misery that flows from defeat or from the terrors that still hang over the world." [1] Professor Knight remarks that if there is anything on which divergent interpretations of Christianity would have to agree, it would be the admission that the Christian conception of goodness is the antithesis of the competitive system.[2] " Compromise," writes Mr. Tawney, " is as impossible between the Church of Christ and the idolatry of wealth, which is the practical religion of capitalist societies, as it was between the Church and the State idolatry of the Roman Empire." [3]

It is not my task, however, to examine in detail the moral implications of the present economic system, which operates partly by competition and partly by monopoly. I am concerned with the influence of the Christian religion on economics ; and this influence has decidedly collapsed. " The established Episcopal Church of this country," says Mr. Hobson, " has inclined, in its ordinary preaching and teaching, to renounce all claims to regulate business life in conformity with Christian principles, as distinct from inculcating the ethics of personal integrity and justice." Among the nonconformists there are Christian Socialists, who have made " a pathetic attempt to rally some remnant of belief and moral authority for the churches." [4] But on the Continent the break of Socialism with the religion of the churches, Catholic or Protestant, is almost complete, largely accepting Marx's asseveration that the idea of God must be destroyed, being the keystone of a perverted civilisation. In his conflict with God, Mammon has carried the day.

[1] W. F. Lofthouse, *Christianity in the Social State* (London, 1936), p. 99 *sq.*
[2] F. H. Knight, *The Ethics of Competition and other Essays* (London, 1935), p. 72.
[3] Tawney, *op. cit.* p. 286.   [4] Hobson, *op. cit.* p. 46 *sq.*

CHAPTER XIV

CHRISTIANITY AND SLAVERY

THERE still remains a branch of economics where we might expect to find conspicuous traces of Christian influence, especially as the very objects that it is concerned with are human beings—I mean the institution of slavery.

Slavery is essentially an industrial institution, which implies compulsory labour beyond the limits of family relations. The master has a right to avail himself of the working power of his slave, without previous agreement on the part of the latter. This I take to be the essence of slavery ; but connected with such a right there are others which hardly admit of a strict definition, or which belong to the master in some cases though not in all. He is entitled to claim obedience and to enforce this claim with more or less severity, but his authority is not necessarily absolute, and the restrictions imposed on it are not everywhere the same. Voluntary slavery is spoken of, as when a person sells himself as a slave, but this is only an imitation of slavery true and proper : the person who gives up his liberty confers upon another, by contract, either for a limited period or for ever the same rights over himself as a master possesses over his slave. If slavery proper could be based upon a contract between the parties concerned, I fail to see how to distinguish between a servant and a slave.

Christianity recognised slavery from the beginning. Paul wrote : " By one Spirit are we all baptised into one body, whether we be Jews or Gentiles, whether we be bond or free." [1] But he also wrote : " Let every man abide in the same calling wherein he was called. Art thou called being a servant ? care not for it : but if thou mayest be made free, use it rather. For he that is called in the Lord, being a servant, is the Lord's freeman : likewise also he that is called, being free, is Christ's servant. Ye are bought with a price ; be not ye the servants of men. Brethren, let every man, wherein he is called, therein abide with God." [2] Masters are told to give to their servants

[1] *1 Corinthians* xii. 13. See also *Galatians* iii. 27 *sq.* ; *Colossians* iii. 11.
[2] *1 Corinthians* vii. 20–4.

282

that which is just and equal; [1] but in the first place servants
are commanded to obey in all things their masters " according
to the flesh; not with eyeservice, as men-pleasers; but in
singleness of heart, fearing God." [2] Peter says that they shall
be subject to their masters with all fear; " not only to the good
and gentle but also to the froward." [3] There are a few references to slavery in the Apostolic Fathers. Ignatius writes:
" Overlook not the men and maid-servants: neither let them
be puffed up; but rather let them be the more subject, to the
glory of God, that they may obtain from him a better liberty.
Let them not desire to be set free at the public cost, that they
be not slaves to their own lusts." [4] Barnabas tells masters not
to be bitter in their commands towards any of their servants
that trust in God.[5] The same injunction is found in the
' Didache,' together with the order that slaves shall be subject
to their lords, " as to God's image." [6]

ᕽChristianity's acceptance of slavery belonged to its Jewish
heritage.⁺ Among the Hebrews the slave class consisted of
captives taken in war; [7] of persons bought with money from
neighbouring nations or from foreign residents in the land; [8]
of children of slaves born in the house; [9] of native Hebrews
who had been sold by their fathers,[10] or who either alone or with
their wives and children had fallen into slavery in consequence
of poverty,[11] or who had been sold by the authorities as slaves
on account of theft when unable to pay compensation for the
stolen property.[12] Slaves of foreign extraction were not to be
emancipated, but should remain slaves for ever.[13] But in no case
had the master absolute power over his slave. Whether the
latter was an Israelite or a foreigner, his life, and to some extent
his body, were protected by law. If a man by blows destroyed
an eye or a tooth, or any other member belonging to his man-
servant or maid-servant, he was bound to let the injured person
go free.[14] And a master who smites his slave so that he dies
under his hand, " shall be surely punished "; but if the slave

---

[1] *Colossians* iv. 1. See also *Ephesians* vi. 9.
[2] *Colossians* iii. 22. See also *Ephesians* vi. 5–8 ; *1 Timothy* vi. 1 *sq.* ;
Titus ii. 9 *sq.*
[3] *1 Peter* ii. 18.
[4] Ignatius, *Epistola ad Polycarpum*, 4.
[5] Barnabas, *Epistola catholica*, 19.
[6] *Didache*, 4.   [7] *Deuteronomy* xx. 14.
[8] *Leviticus* xxv. 44 *sqq.*   [9] *Genesis* xiv. 14.
[10] *Exodus* xxi. 7.
[11] *Ibid.* xxi. 2 *sq.* ; *Leviticus* xxv. 39, 47.
[12] *Exodus* xxii. 3.   [13] *Leviticus* xxv. 46.
[14] *Exodus* xxi. 26 *sq.*

continues to live for a day or two after the assault, the master goes free on the score that the slave is " his money." [1]   In the Talmud masters are repeatedly admonished to treat their slaves with kindness; [2] and emancipation of slaves is practically encouraged in various ways,[3] in spite of the dictum of certain rabbis that he who emancipates his slave transgresses the positive precept of Leviticus xxv. 46, " They shall be your bondmen for ever." [4]

Paul also knew the slavery of the Græco-Roman world. The power, originally unlimited, which the Roman master had over his slave was during the Pagan Empire limited in various ways.   Claudius [5] and Antoninus Pius [6] put check on his legal right to kill his slave.   The Lex Petronia, A.D. 61, forbade masters to compel their slaves to fight with wild beasts.[7]   In the time of Nero an official was appointed to hear complaints of the wrongs done by masters to their slaves.[8]   But in those days when Roman slavery had lost its original patriarchal and, to speak with Mommsen,[9] " in some measure innocent " character, when the victories of Rome and the increasing slave-trade had introduced into the city innumerable slaves, when those simpler habits of life which in early times somewhat mitigated the rigour of the law had changed—the lot of the Roman slave was often extremely hard, and numerous acts of shocking cruelty were committed.[10]   At the same time we also hear, from the early days of the Empire, that masters who had been cruel to their slaves were pointed at with disgust in all parts of the city, and were hated and loathed.[11]   And with a fervour which can scarcely be surpassed Seneca and other Stoics argued that the slave is a being with human dignity and human rights, born of the same race as ourselves, living the same life, and dying the

---

[1] *Exodus* xxi. 20 *sq.*

[2] *Ecclesiasticus* xxxiii. 31 ; A. Katz, *Der wahre Talmudjude* (Berlin, 1893), p. 59 *sqq.*

[3] J. Winter, *Die Stellung der Sklaven bei den Juden in rechtlicher und gesellschaftlicher Beziehung nach talmudischen Quellen* (Breslau, 1886), p. 41.

[4] *Berakhoth*, fol. 47b, quoted by P. I. Hershon, *Treasures of the Talmud* (London, 1882), p. 81 ; R. Samuel, quoted by T. André, *L'esclavage chez les anciens Hébreux* (Paris, 1892), p. 180 *sq.*

[5] Suetonius, *Claudius*, 25.

[6] Gaius, *Institutionum juris civilis commentarii*, i. 53 ; *Institutiones*, i. 8. 2.

[7] *Digesta*, xlviii. 8. 11. 2.   [8] Seneca, *De beneficiis*, iii. 22. 3.

[9] T. Mommsen, *History of Rome*, iii (London, 1894), p. 305.

[10] W. E. H. Lecky, *History of European Morals from Augustus to Charlemagne*, i (London, 1890), p. 302 *sq.*

[11] Seneca, *De clementia*, i. 18. 3.

same death—in short, that our slaves " are also men, and friends, and our fellow-servants." [1] Epictetus even went so far as to condemn altogether the keeping of slaves. " What you avoid suffering yourself," he says, " seek not to impose on others. You avoid slavery, for instance ; take care not to enslave. For if you can bear to exact slavery from others, you appear to have been yourself a slave." [2] These teachings could not fail to influence both legislation and public sentiment. Imbued with the Stoic philosophy, the jurists of the classical period declared that all men are originally free by the Law of Nature, and that slavery is only " an institution of the Law of Nations, by which one man is made the property of another, in opposition to natural right." [3]

Considering that Christianity has commonly been represented as almost the sole cause of the mitigation and final abolishment of slavery in Europe, it deserves special notice that the chief improvement in the condition of slaves at Rome took place at so early a period that Christianity could have absolutely no share in it. Nay, for about two hundred years after it was made the official religion of the Empire there was an almost complete pause in the legislation on the subject.[4] Beyond a law of Constantine, to the effect that a master who put his slave to death in a non-judicial way was to be punished as a murderer,[5] the Christian emperors seem to have done little to guard the life of the slave. Whilst it was provided that any master who applied to his slave certain atrocious tortures with the object of killing him should be deemed a manslayer, it was emphatically said that no charge whatever should be brought against him if the slave died under moderate punishment, or under any punishment not inflicted with the intention of killing him.[6] Arcadius and Honorius even passed a law refusing protection to a slave who should fly to a church for refuge from his master ; [7] but this law was, in the West, followed by regulations of an opposite character.[8] Under Justinian certain reforms were introduced :—enfranchisement was facilitated in various ways ; [9]

---

[1] *Idem, Epistolæ*, 47 ; *idem, De beneficiis*, iii. 28 ; Epictetus, *Dissertationes*, i. 13. See also the collection of statements referring to slavery made by F. M. Holland, *The Reign of the Stoics* (New York, *s.d.*), p. 186 *sqq.*

[2] Epictetus, *Fragmenta*, 42.   [3] *Institutiones*, i. 3. 2.

[4] *Cf.* Lecky, *op. cit.* ii. 64.   [5] *Codex Theodosianus*, ix. 12. 1.

[6] *Ibid.* ix. 12 ; Lecky, *op. cit.* ii. 62 *sq.*

[7] *Codex Theodosianus*, ix. 45. 3.

[8] C. Babington, *The Influence of Christianity in promoting the Abolition of Slavery in Europe* (Cambridge, 1846), p. 37 ; É. Biot, *De l'abolition de l'esclavage ancien en Occident* (Paris, 1840), p. 239.

[9] *Institutiones*, i. 5 *sqq.*

the rights of Roman citizens were granted to emancipated slaves, who had previously occupied an intermediate position between slavery and perfect freedom ; [1] and though the law still refused to recognise the marriages of slaves, Justinian gave them a legal value after emancipation in establishing rights of succession. [2] But the inferior position of the slave was asserted as sternly as ever. He belonged to the " corporeal " property of his master, he was reckoned among things which are tangible by their nature, like land, raiment, gold, and silver. [3] The constitution of Antoninus Pius restraining severity on the part of masters was enforced, but the motive for this was not evangelic humanity. [4] It is said in the ' Institutes ' of Justinian : " This decision is a just one ; for it greatly concerns the public weal, that no one be permitted to misuse even his own property." [5]

It is strange that the inconsistency of slavery with the tenet, " Do to others as you would be done by," though emphasised by a pagan philosopher, never seems to have occurred to any of the early Christian writers. The principle that all men are spiritually equal in Christ does not imply that they should be socially equal in the world. Slavery does not prevent anybody from performing the duties incumbent on a Christian, it does not bar the way to heaven, it is an external affair only, nothing but a name. He only is really a slave who commits sin. [6] Augustine says that slavery is a burden which has justly been laid upon the back of transgression. Man when created by God was free, and nobody was the slave of another until that just man Noah cursed Ham, his offending son ; slavery, then, is a punishment sent by Him who best knows how to proportionate punishment to offence, [7] and the slave himself ought not to desire to become free. [8] Not one of the Fathers of the Church hints that slavery is unlawful or improper. In the early age martyrs possessed slaves, and so did abbots, bishops, popes, monasteries, and

[1] *Institutiones*, i. 5. 3, iii. 7. 4.
[2] *Ibid*. iii. 7 pr.
[3] *Ibid*. ii. 2. 1.
[4] *Cf.* H. H. Milman, *History of Latin Christianity*, ii (London, 1867), p. 14.
[5] *Institutiones*, i. 8. 2.
[6] Gregory Nazianzen, *Orationes*, xiv. 25 (Migne, *Patrologiæ cursus, Ser. Græca*, xxxv. 891 *sq.*) ; *idem, Carmina*, i. 2. 26. 29 (*ibid.* xxxvii. 853), i. 2. 33. 133 *sqq.* (*ibid.* xxxvii. 937 *sq.*) ; Chrysostom, *In cap. IX. Genes. Homilia XXIX.* 7 (*ibid.* liii. 270) ; *idem, In Epist. I. ad Cor. Homilia XIX.* 5 (*ibid.* lxi. 158) ; Ambrose, *In Epistolam ad Colossenses*, 3 (Migne, *Patrologiæ cursus*, xvii. 439).
[7] Augustine, *De civitate Dei*, xix. 15.
[8] *Idem, Ennaratio in Psalmum CXXIV.* 7 (Migne, *Patrologiæ cursus*, xxxvii. 1653).

churches ; [1] Jews and pagans only were prohibited from acquiring Christian slaves.[2] So little was the abolition of slavery thought of that a Council at Orleans, in the middle of the sixth century, expressly decreed the perpetuity of servitude among the descendants of slaves.[3] On the other hand, the Church showed a zeal to prevent accessions to slavery from capture, but her exertions were restricted to Christian prisoners of war.[4] As late as the nineteenth century the right of enslaving captives was defended by Bishop Bouvier.[5]

Like the Apostles, Councils and popes reminded slaves of their duties towards their masters, and masters of their duties towards their slaves. The Council of Gangra, about the year 324, pronounced its anathema on any one who should teach a slave to despise his master on pretence of religion ; [6] and so much importance was attached to this decree that it was inserted in the epitome of canons which Hadrian I. in 773 presented to Charlemagne in Rome.[7] But there are also many instances in which masters are recommended to show humanity to their slaves.[8] According to Gregory IX. " the slaves who were washed in the fountain of holy baptism should be more liberally treated in consideration of their having received so great a benefit." [9] Slaves who had taken refuge from their masters in churches or monasteries were not to be given up until the master had sworn not to punish the fugitive ; [10] or they were

[1] C. Babington, *The Influence of Christianity in promoting the Abolition of Slavery in Europe* (Cambridge, 1846), p. 22 ; J. Potgiesser, *Commentarii juris Germanici de'statu servorum* (Lemgoviæ, 1736), i. 4. 8, p. 176 ; L. A. Muratori, *Dissertazioni sopra le antichità Italiane,* i (Milano, 1836), p. 244.

[2] *Concilium Toletanum IV.*, A.D. 633, can. 66 (Labbe-Mansi, *Conciliorum collectio*, x. 635) ; R. Blakey, *The Temporal Benefits of Christianity* (London, 1849), p. 397 ; K. H. Digby, *Mores Catholici*, ii (London, 1846), p. 341 ; L. Cibrario, *Della schiavitù e del servaggio*, i (Milano, 1868), p. 272 ; A. Rivière, *L'Église et l'esclavage* (Paris, 1864), p. 350.

[3] *Concilium Aurelianense IV.*, about A.D. 545, can. 32 (Labbe-Mansi, ix. 118 *sq.*).

[4] *Concilium Rhemense*, about A.D. 630, can. 22 (Labbe-Mansi, x. 597) ; Gratian, *Decretum*, ii. 12. 2. 13 *sqq.* ; C. Baronius, *Annales Ecclesiastici*, A.D. 1263, ch. 74, xxii. 124 ; E. Le Blant, *Inscriptions chrétiennes de la Gaule antérieures au VIII. siècle*, ii (Paris, 1865), p. 284 *sqq.* ; Babington, *op. cit.* pp. 51 *sqq.*, 94 *sq.* ; E. Nys, *Le droit de la guerre et les précurseurs de Grotius* (Bruxelles and Leipzig, 1882), p. 114.

[5] J.-B. Bouvier, *Institutiones philosophicæ* (Paris, 1844), p. 566.

[6] *Concilium Gangrense*, can. 3 (Labbe-Mansi, ii. 1102, 1106, 1110).

[7] ' Epitome canonum, quam Hadrianus I. Carolo magno obtulit, A.D. DCCLXXIII.,' in Labbe-Mansi, xii. 863.

[8] Babington, *op. cit.* p. 58 *sqq.*

[9] Baronius, *Annales Ecclesiastici*, A.D. 1238, ch. 62, vol. xxi. 204.

[10] Milman, *op. cit.* ii. 51 ; Rivière, *op. cit.* p. 306 ; A. Du Bois, *Histoire du droit criminel des peuples modernes*, ii (Paris, 1858), p. 246 n. 1.

never given up, but became slaves to the sanctuary.¹ Faithful
to her principle that human life is sacred, the Church made
efforts to secure the life of the slave against the violence of the
master ; but neither the ecclesiastical nor the secular legislation
gave him the same protection as was bestowed upon the free
member of the Church and State. Various Councils punished
the murder of a slave with two years' excommunication only,
if the slave had been killed " sine conscientia judicis " ; ² and
the same punishment was adopted by some Penitentials.³
Edgar made the penance last three years, whereas if a freeman
was killed, the penance was of seven years' duration.⁴ Facts
do not justify Lecky's statement that, " in the penal system of
the Church, the distinction between wrongs done to a freeman,
and wrongs done to a slave, which lay at the very root of the
whole civil legislation, was repudiated." ⁵ The Church prohibited the sale of Christian slaves to Jews and heathen nations.⁶
The Council of Chalons, in the middle of the seventh century,
ordered that no Christian should be sold outside the kingdom of
Clovis, so that they might not get into captivity or become the
slaves of Jewish masters ; ⁷ and some Anglo-Saxon laws
similarly forbade the sale of Christians out of the country, and
especially into bondage to heathen, " that those souls perish not
that Christ bought with his own life." ⁸ The clergy sometimes

¹ ' Concilium Kingesburiense sub Bertulpho,' in D. Wilkins, *Concilia
Magnæ Britanniæ et Hiberniæ*, i (London, 1737), p. 181.
² *Concilium Agathense*, A.D. 506, can. 62 (Labbe-Mansi, viii. 335) ;
Concilium Epaonense, A.D. 517, can. 34 (*ibid.* viii. 563) ; *Concilium
Wormatiense*, A.D. 868, can. 38 (*ibid.* xv. 876).
³ *Pœnitentiale Cummeani*, vi. 29 (F. W. H. Wasserschleben, *Die
Bussordnungen der abendländischen Kirche* [Halle, 1851], p. 480) ;
Pœnitentiale Pseudo-Theodori, xxi. 12 (*ibid.* p. 587).
⁴ *Canons enacted under Edgar, Modus imponendi pœnitentiam*, 4, 11
(*Ancient Laws and Institutes of England* [London, 1840], p. 405 *sq.*).
⁵ Lecky, *op. cit.* ii. 66.   Lecky states (*ibid.* ii. 66 *sq.*) that the Council
of Illiberis excluded for ever from the communion a master who killed his
slave.   I have only been able to find the following enactment made by a
Council held at Illiberis in the beginning of the fourth century : " Si qua
domina furore zeli accensa flagris verberaverit ancillam suam, ita ut in
tertium diem animam cum cruciatu effundat ; eo quod incertum sit,
voluntate, an casu occiderit ; si voluntate, post septem annos ; si casu,
post quinquennii tempora, acta legitima pœnitentia, ad communionem
placuit admitti " (*Concilium Eliberitanum*, ch. 5 [Labbe-Mansi, ii. 6]).
⁶ *Concilium Rhemense*, about A.D. 630, can. 11 (Labbe-Mansi, x. 596) ;
Concilium Liptinense, A.D. 743, can. 3 (*ibid.* xii. 371) ; C. J. Hefele,
Beiträge zur Kirchengeschichte, Archäologie und Liturgie, i (Tübingen,
1864), p. 218 ; idem, *A History of the Councils of the Church*, v (Edinburgh, 1896), p. 211.
⁷ *Concilium Cabilonense*, about A.D. 650, can. 9 (Labbe-Mansi, x. 1191).
⁸ *Laws of Ethelred*, v. 2, vi. 9 ; *Laws of Cnut*, ii. 3.

remonstrated against slave-markets; but their indignation
never reached the trade in heathen slaves,[1] nor was the master's
right of selling any of his slaves whenever he pleased called in
question at all.

✗ The assertion made by many writers that the Church exercised an extremely favourable influence upon slavery surely
involves a great exaggeration. As late as the thirteenth century
the master had practically the power of life and death over his
slave.[2] Throughout Christendom the purchase and the sale of
men, as property transferred from vendor to buyer, was recognised as a legal transaction of the same validity with the sale of
other merchandise, land or cattle.[3] Slaves had a title to nothing
but subsistence and clothes from their masters, all the profits of
their labour accruing to the latter; and if a master from indulgence gave his slaves any *peculium*, or fixed allowance for their
subsistence, they had no right of property in what they saved
out of that, but all that they accumulated belonged to the
master.[4] A slave or a freedman was not allowed to bring a
criminal charge against a free person, except in the case of a
crimen læsæ majestatis,[5] and slaves were incapable of being
received as witnesses against freemen.[6] The old distinction
between the marriage of the freeman and the concubinage of the
slave was long recognised by the Church: slaves could not
marry, but had only a right of *contubernium*, and their unions
did not receive the nuptial benediction of a priest.[7] Subsequently, when conjunction between slaves came to be considered a lawful marriage, they were not permitted to marry
without the consent of their master, and such as transgressed
this rule were punished very severely, sometimes even with
death.[8]

The gradual disappearance of slavery in Europe during the

---

[1] K. D. Hüllmann, *Stædtewesen des Mittelalters*, i (Bonn, 1826),
p. 80 *sq.*; C. Loring Brace, *Gesta Christi* (London, 1890), p. 229;
Rivière, *op. cit.* p. 325.

[2] E. Westermarck, *The Origin and Development of the Moral Ideas*, i
(London, 1912), p. 427 *sq.*

[3] Potgiesser, *op. cit.* ii. 4. 5, p. 429; Milman, *op. cit.* ii. 16.

[4] Potgiesser, *op. cit.* ii. 10, p. 528 *sqq.*; C. D. Du Cange, *Glossarium
ad scriptores mediæ et infimæ Latinitatis*, vi (Parisiis, 1736), p. 451;
W. Robertson, *The History of the Reign of the Emperor Charles V.*, i
(London, 1806), p. 274.

[5] Potgiesser, *op. cit.* iii. 3. 2, p. 612.

[6] Ph. de Beaumanoir, *Les coutumes du Beauvoisis* (Paris, 1842),
xxxix. 32, vol. ii. 103; Du Cange, *op. cit.* vi. 452; Potgiesser, *op. cit.*
iii. 3. 1, p. 611.

[7] Potgiesser, *op. cit.* ii. 2. 10 *sq.*, p. 354 *sq.*

[8] *Ibid.* ii. 2. 12, p. 355 *sq.*

latter period of the Middle Ages has also commonly been in the main attributed to the influence of the Church.[1] But this opinion is scarcely supported by facts. It is true that the Church in some degree encouraged the manumission of slaves. Though slavery was considered a perfectly lawful institution, the enfranchisement of a fellow-Christian was deemed a meritorious act, and was sometimes recommended on Christian principles. At the close of the sixth century it was affirmed that, as Christ had come to break the chain of our servitude and restore our primitive liberty, so it was well for us to imitate him by making free those whom the law of nations had reduced to slavery ; [2] and the same doctrine was again proclaimed at various times down to the sixteenth century.[3] In the Carlovingian period the abbot Smaragdus expressed the opinion that among other good and salutary works each one ought to let slaves go free, considering that not nature but sin had subjected them to their masters.[4] In the latter part of the twelfth century the prelates of France, and in particular the archbishop of Sens, pretended that it was an obligation of conscience to accord liberty to all Christians, relying on a decree of a Council held at Rome by Pope Alexander III.[5] And in one of the later compilations of German mediæval law it was said that the Lord Jesus, by his injunction to render unto Cæsar the things which are Cæsar's and unto God the things that are God's, indicated that no man is the property

---

[1] T. Clarkson, *An Essay on the Slavery and Commerce of the Human Species* (London, 1788), p. 19 *sq.* ; Biot, *op. cit.* p. xi. ; Abbé Thérou, *Le Christianisme et l'esclavage* (Paris, 1841), p. 147 ; H. Martin, *Histoire de France jusqu'en 1789*, iii (Paris, 1878), p. 11 n. 2 ; J. Balmes, *El Protestantismo comparado con el Catolicismo en sus relaciones con la civilizacion Europea*, i (Barcelona, 1844), p. 285 ; Blakey, *op. cit.* p. 170 ; J. Yanoski, *De l'abolition de l'esclavage ancien au moyen âge* (Paris, 1860), p. 75 ; A. Cochin, *L'abolition de l'esclavage*, ii (Paris, 1861), pp. 349, 458 ; É. Littré, *Études sur les Barbares et le Moyen Age* (Paris, 1867), p. 230 *sq.* ; P. Allard, *Les esclaves chrétiens depuis les premiers temps de l'Église* (Paris, 1876), p. 490 ; P. Tedeschi, *La schiavitù* (Piacenza, 1882), p. 68 ; W. E. H. Lecky, *History of the Rise and Influence of the Spirit of Rationalism in Europe*, ii (London, 1893), pp. 216, 236 *sqq.* ; H. S. Maine, *International Law* (London, 1888), p. 160 ; B. Kidd, *Social Evolution* (London, 1894), p. 168 ; W. F. Lofthouse, *Christianity in the Social State* (London, 1936), p. 96.
[2] Gregory the Great, *Epistolæ*, vi. 12 (Migne, *Patrologiæ cursus*, lxxvii. 803 *sq.*) ; Gratian, *op. cit.* ii. 12. 2. 68 ; Potgiesser, *op. cit.* iv. 1. 3, p. 666 *sq.*
[3] Babington, *op. cit.* p. 180.
[4] Smaragdus, *Via Regia*, 30 (L. d'Achery, *Spicilegium*, i [Parisiis, 1723], p. 253).
[5] De Boulainvilliers, *Histoire de l'ancien gouvernement de la France*, i (La Haye and Amsterdam, 1727), p. 312.

of another, but that every man belongs to God.[1]   Slaves were
liberated " for God's love," or " for the remedy " or " ransom of
the soul." [2]   In the formularies of manumission given by the
monk Marculfus in the seventh century we read, for instance:
" He that releases his slave who is bound to him, may trust that
God will recompense him in the next world " ; [3]   " For the remission of my sins, I absolve thee " ; [4]   " For the glory of God's
name and for my eternal retribution," etc.[5]   Too much importance, however, has often been attached to these phrases.   For
the most trivial occurrences, such as giving a book to a
monastery, are commonly accompanied by similar expressions ; [6] and it appears from certain formulas that slaves were not
only liberated, but also bought and sold, " in the name of God." [7]

Nor can we suppose that it was from religious motives only
that manumissions were encouraged by the clergy.   It has been
pointed out that " as dying persons were frequently inclined to
make considerable donations for pious uses, it was more immediately for the interest of churchmen, that people of inferior
condition should be rendered capable of acquiring property, and
should have the free disposal of what they had acquired."   It
also seems that those who obtained their liberty by the influence
of the clergy had to reward their benefactors, and that the
manumission should for this reason be confirmed by the Church.[8]
And while the Church favoured liberation of the slaves of laymen,
she took care to prevent liberation of her own slaves ; like a
physician she did not herself swallow the medicine which she
prescribed to others.   She allowed alienation of such slaves only
as showed a disposition to run away.[9]   The Council of Agatho,
in 506, considered it unfair to enfranchise the slaves of monasteries, seeing that the monks themselves were daily compelled
to labour ; [10] and, as a matter of fact, the slaves of monasteries

---

[1] *Speculum Saxonum*, iii. 42 (M. Goldast, *Collectio consuetudinum et
legum imperialium* [Francofordiæ ad Mœnum, 1613], p. 158).
[2] Du Cange, *op. cit.* iv. 460 *sqq.* ;   Potgiesser, *op. cit.* iv. 12. 5,
p. 751 *sqq.* ; Muratori, *op. cit.* i. 249 ; Robertson, *op. cit.* i. 323 ; Milman,
op. cit. ii. 51 *sq.*
[3] Marculfus, *Formulæ*, ii. 32 (Migne, *Patrologiæ cursus*, lxxxvii. 747).
[4] *Ibid.* ii. 33 (Migne, lxxxvii. 748).
[5] *Ibid.* ii. 34 (Migne, lxxxvii. 748).
[6] Babington, *op. cit.* p. 61 n. 6.
[7] *Formulæ Bignonianæ*, 2, ' Venditio de servo ' (S. Baluze, *Capitu-
laria regum Francorum*, ii [Parisiis, 1677], p. 497 :   " Domino magnifico
fratri illi emptori, ego in Dei nomine ille venditor."
[8] J. Millar, *The Origin of the Distribution of Ranks* (Edinburgh, 1806),
p. 274 *sq.*
[9] Gratian, *op. cit.* ii. 12. 2. 54.
[10] *Concilium Agathense*, can. 56 (Labbe-Mansi, viii. 334).

were everywhere among the last who were manumitted.[1] In the seventh century a Council at Toledo threatened with damnation any bishop who should liberate a slave belonging to the Church, without giving due compensation from his property, as it was thought impious to inflict a loss on the Church of Christ ; [2] and according to several ecclesiastical regulations no bishop or priest was allowed to manumit a slave in the patrimony of the Church unless he put in his place two slaves of equal value.[3] Nay, the Church was anxious not only to prevent a reduction of her slaves, but to increase their number. She zealously encouraged people to give up themselves and their posterity to be the slaves of churches and monasteries, to enslave their bodies— as some of the charters put it—in order to procure the liberty of their souls.[4] And in the middle of the seventh century a Council decreed that the children of incontinent priests should become the slaves of the churches where their fathers officiated.[5]

The disappearance of mediæval slavery has further, to some extent, been attributed to the efforts of kings to weaken the power of the nobles.[6] Thus Louis X. and Philip the Long of France issued ordinances declaring that, as all men were by nature free, and as their kingdom was called the kingdom of the Franks, they would have the fact to correspond with the name, and emancipated all persons in the royal domains upon paying a just compensation, as an example for other lords to follow.[7] Muratori believes that in Italy the wars during the twelfth and following centuries contributed more than anything else to the decline of slavery, as there was a need of soldiers and soldiers must be freemen.[8] According to others, the disappearance of slavery was largely effected by the great famines and epidemics with which Europe was visited during the tenth, eleventh, and twelfth centuries.[9] The number of slaves was also considerably reduced by the ancient usage of enslaving prisoners of war being replaced by the more humane practice of accepting ransom for

[1] H. Hallam, *View of the State of Europe during the Middle Ages*, i (London, 1837), p. 221.

[2] *Concilium Toletanum IV.*, A.D. 633, can. 67 (Labbe-Mansi, x. 635).

[3] Gratian, *op. cit.* ii. 12. 2. 58 ; Potgiesser, *op. cit.* iv. 2. 4, p. 673.

[4] Du Cange, *op. cit.* iv. 1286 ; Potgiesser, *op. cit.* i. 1. 6 *sq.*, p. 5 *sqq.* ; Robertson, *op. cit.* i. 326.

[5] *Concilium Toletanum IX.*, A.D. 655, can. 10 (Labbe-Mansi, xi. 29).

[6] Robertson, *op. cit.* i. 47 *sq.* ; Millar, *op. cit.* p. 276 *sqq.*

[7] Decrusy, Isambert, and Jourdan, *Recueil général des anciennes lois Françaises*, iii. 102 *sqq.*

[8] Muratori, *op. cit.* i. 234 *sq.* ; *idem, Rerum Italicarum scriptores,* xviii (Mediolani, 1731), pp. 268, 292.

[9] Biot, *op. cit.* p. 318 *sqq.* ; J. A. Saco, *Historia de la esclavitud*, iii (Paris and Barcelona, 1878), p. 241 *sqq.*

them, which became the general rule in the latter part of the Middle Ages, at least in the case of Christian captives.[1] But it seems that the chief cause of the extinction of slavery in Europe was its transformation into serfdom.

This transformation has been traced to the diminished supply of slaves, which made it the interest of each family to preserve indefinitely its own hereditary slaves, and to keep up their number by the method of propagation. The existence and physical well-being of the slave became consequently an object of greater value to his master, and the latter found it more profitable to attach his slaves to certain pieces of land.[2] Moreover, the cultivation of the ground required that the slaves should have a fixed residence in different parts of the master's estate, and when a slave had thus been for a long time engaged in a particular farm, he was so much the better qualified to continue in the management of it for the future. By degrees he therefore came to be regarded as belonging to the stock upon the ground, and was disposed of as a part of the estate which he had been accustomed to cultivate.[3]

But serfdom itself was merely a transitory condition destined to lead up to a state of entire liberty. I have elsewhere discussed the causes of this process.[4] As a quite subordinate one may be mentioned instances of lords liberating their villeins at the intercession of their spiritual confessors, the clergy availing themselves of every opportunity to lessen the formidable power of their great rivals, the temporal nobility.[5] The influence which the Church exercised in favour of the enfranchisement of serfs was even less than her share in the abolition of slavery proper.[6] She represented serfdom as a divine institution,[7] as a school of

[1] R. Ward, *An Enquiry into the Foundation and History of the Law of Nations in Europe*, i (London, 1795), p. 298 *sq.* ; Babington, *op. cit.* p. 147 ; B. Ayala, *De jure et officiis bellicis et disciplina militari* (Angers, 1591), i. 5. 19. In the sixteenth century the statutes of some Italian towns make mention of the sale of slaves, who probably were Turkish captives (Nys, *op. cit.* p. 140).

[2] H. Storch, *Cours d'économie politique*, iv (St. Pétersbourg, 1815), p. 260 ; J. K. Ingram, *A History of Slavery and Serfdom* (London, 1895), p. 72.

[3] Millar, *op. cit.* p. 263 *sqq.*

[4] Westermarck, *op. cit.* i. 701 *sqq.*

[5] Thomas Smith, *The Common-wealth of England* (London, 1635), p. 250 ; F. M. Eden, *The State of the Poor*, i (London, 1797), p. 10 ; S. Sugenheim, *Geschichte der Aufhebung der Leibeigenschaft und Hörigkeit in Europa* (St. Petersburg, 1861), p. 109.

[6] *Cf.* Rivière, *op. cit.* p. 511 ; Babington, *op. cit.* p. 148 *sqq.*

[7] Bonaventura, quoted by F. Laurent, *Études sur l'histoire de l'Humanité*, vii (Paris, 1865), p. 522 : " Non solum secundum humanam institutionem, sed etiam secundum divinam dispensationem, inter

humility, as a road to future glory.[1]   Luther was horrified when
the German peasants demanded that villeinage should end,
because " Christ has delivered and redeemed us all, the lowly as
well as the great, without exception, by the shedding of his
precious blood." [2]   According to him, the spiritual kingdom of
Christ must not be changed into an external worldly one : " An
earthly kingdom cannot exist without inequality of persons.
Some must be free, others serfs, some rulers, others subjects.
As St. Paul says, ' Before Christ both master and slave are
one.' " [3]   The Catholic Church, again, was herself the greatest
serf-holder ; and so strenuously did she persist in retaining her
villeins, that after Voltaire had raised his powerful outcry in
favour of liberty, and Louis XVI. himself had been induced to
abolish " the right of servitude " in consideration of " the love
of humanity," the Church still refused to emancipate her serfs.[4]

Not long after serfdom had begun to disappear in the most
advanced communities of Christendom a new kind of slavery was
established in the colonies of European states.   It grew up in
circumstances particularly favourable to the employment of
slaves.   Whether slave or free labour is more profitable to the
employer depends on the wages of the free labourer, and these
again depend on the numbers of the labouring population compared with the capital and land.   In the rich and underpeopled
soil of the West Indies and in the Southern States of America
the balance of the profits between free and slave labour was on
the side of slavery.   Hence slavery was introduced there, and
flourished, and could be abolished only with the greatest
difficulty.[5]

From the moral point of view negro slavery is interesting
chiefly because it existed in the midst of a highly developed
Christian civilisation, and nevertheless, at least in the British
colonies and the United States, was the most brutal form of
slavery ever known.   First there was the capture of the negroes
in Africa, then the " middle passage " with its indescribable

Christianos sunt domini et servi." See also Adalbero, *Carmen ad
Rotbertum regem Francorum*, 291, 292, 297 sqq. (in M. Bouquet, *Recueil
des Historiens des Gaules et de la France*, x [Paris, 1865], p. 70).

[1] Laurent, *op. cit.* vii. 523.

[2] J. S. Schapiro, *Social Reform and the Reformation* (New York, 1909),
p. 139.

[3] Luther, ' Ermahnung zum Frieden auf die zwölf Artikel der Bauer-
schaft in Schwaben. 1525,' in *Werke*, xviii (Weimar, 1908), p. 327.

[4] H. Hettner, *Geschichte der französchen Literatur im achtzehnten
Jahrhundert* (Braunschweig, 1894), p. 169 ; Babington, *op. cit.* p. 108 ;
Sugenheim, *op. cit.* p. 156 sqq ; Laurent, *op. cit.* vii. 537 sq.

[5] J. S. Mill, *Principles of Political Economy*, i (London, 1865), p. 311.

horrors, and lastly the miserable existence in the new country. It may be worth while to consider more closely some points of the legislation relating to this particular outgrowth of Christian civilisation.

In America, as elsewhere, the state of slavery was hereditary. The child of a female slave was itself a slave and belonged to the owner of its mother, even if its father was a freeman, whereas the child of a free woman was free even if its father was a slave.[1] When the slave-trade was prohibited, heredity remained the only legitimate source of slavery ; but even then a freeborn negro was far from safe. In the British colonies and in all the Slave States except one, every negro was presumed to be a slave until he could prove the reverse.[2] A man who, within the limits of a slave-holding State, could exhibit a person of African extraction in his custody was exempted from all necessity of making proof how he had obtained him or by what authority he claimed him as a slave. Nay more, through direct action of Congress it became law that persons known to be free should be sold as slaves in order to cover the costs of imprisonment which they had suffered on account of the false suspicion that they were runaway slaves. This law was repeatedly put into effect. " How many crowned despots," says Professor von Holst, " can be mentioned in the history of the Old World, who have done things which compare in accursedness with this law to which the democratic republic gave birth ? "[3]

Slaves were defined as " chattels personal in the hands of their respective owners or possessors, and their executors, administrators, and assigns, to all intents and purposes whatsoever."[4] In the British colonies and the American Slave States

[1] G. M. Stroud, *A Sketch of the Laws relating to Slavery in the several States of the United States of America* (Philadelphia, 1856), p. 16 *sqq.* ; T. R. R. Cobb, *An Inquiry into the Law of Negro Slavery in the United States of America* (Philadelphia and Savannah, 1858), p. 68 ; J. Stephen, *The Slavery of the British West India Colonies delineated*, i (London, 1824), p. 122 ; *Le Code Noir* (Paris, 1767), Édit du mois de Mars 1685, art. 13, p. 35 *sq.*, and Édit donné au mois de Mars 1724, art. 10, p. 288 *sq.* In Maryland, according to an early enactment, which obtained till the year 1699 or 1700, all the children born of a slave were slaves " as their fathers were " (Stroud, *op. cit.* p. 14 *sqq.*). In Cuba the nobler parent determined the rank of the offspring (F. W. Newman, *Anglo-Saxon Abolition of Negro Slavery* [London, 1889], p. 17).

[2] Stephen, *op. cit.* i. 369 *sq.* ; Stroud, *op. cit.* pp. 125, 126, 130 ; Cobb, *op. cit.* p. 67 ; J. D. Wheeler, *A Practical Treatise on the Law of Slavery* (New York and New Orleans, 1837), p. 5.

[3] H. von Holst, *The Constitutional and Political History of the United States*, i (Chicago, 1876), p. 305.

[4] J. Brevard, *An Alphabetical Digest of the Public Statute Law of South Carolina*, ii (Charleston, S.C., 1814), p. 229 ; O. H. Prince, *A Digest of the*

they were at all times liable to be sold or otherwise alienated at the will of their masters, as absolutely as cattle or any other personal effects. They were also liable to be sold by process of law for satisfaction of the debts of a living, or the debts or bequests of a deceased master, at the suit of creditors or legatees. They were transmitted by inheritance or by will to heirs at law or to legatees, and in the distribution of estates they were distributed like other property.[1] No regard was paid to family ties. Except in Louisiana, where children under ten years of age could not be sold separately from their mothers,[2] no law existed to prevent the violent separation of parents from their children or from each other.[3] And what the law did not prevent, the slave-owners did not omit doing; thus Virginia was known as a breeding-place out of which the members of one household were sold into every part of the country.[4] All this, however, holds true of the British colonies and the Slave States only. In the Spanish, Portuguese, and French colonies plantation slaves were real estate, attached to the soil they cultivated. They partook therewith of all the restraints upon voluntary alienation to which the possessor of the land was there liable, and they could not be seized or sold by creditors, for satisfaction of the debts of the owner.[5] As regards the sale of members of the same family the ' Code Noir ' expressly says : " Ne pourront être saisis et vendus séparément, le mari et la femme, et leurs enfans impubéres, s'ils sont tous sous la puissance du même Maître." [6]

A slave could make no contract ; he could not even contract marriage, in the juridical sense of the word. The association which took place among slaves and was called marriage was virtually the same as the Roman *contubernium*, a relation which had no sanctity and to which no civil rights were attached.[7]

Laws of the State of Georgia (Athens, U.S., 1837), p. 777. In the French *Code Noir* (Édit du mois de Mars 1685, art. 44, p. 49 ; Édit donné au mois de Mars 1724, art. 40, p. 305 [Paris, 1767]), slaves are declared to be " meubles."

[1] Stephen, *op. cit.* i. 62 ; Stroud, *op. cit.* p. 84 ; W. Goodell, *The American Slave Code in Theory and Practice* (New York, 1853), p. 63 *sqq.*

[2] L. Peirce, M. Taylor, and W. W. King, *The Consolidation and Revision of the Statutes of the State* [*Louisiana*] (New Orleans, 1852), pp. 523, 550 *sq.*

[3] Stephen, *op. cit.* i. 62 *sq.* ; Stroud, *op. cit.* p. 82.

[4] C. H. Pearson, *National Life and Character* (London, 1893), p. 210.

[5] Stephen, *op. cit.* i. 69.

[6] *Code Noir*, Édit du mois de Mars 1685, art. 47, p. 51 ; Édit donné au mois de Mars 1724, art. 43, p. 306.

[7] Cobb, *op. cit.* p. 240 *sqq.* ; Stroud, *op. cit.* p. 99 ; Goodell, *op. cit.* p. 105 *sqq.* ; Wheeler, *op. cit.* p. 199.

The master could whenever he liked separate the " husband " and " wife," he could, if he pleased, commit " adultery " with the " wife," and was the absolute owner of all the children born by her. A slave had " no more legal authority over his child than a cow has over her calf." On the other hand, the common rules of sexual morality were not enforced on the slaves. They were not admonished for incontinence, nor punished for " adultery," nor prosecuted for " bigamy." Incontinence was rather thought a matter of course in the slave. We are told that even in Puritan New England female slaves in ministers' and magistrates' families bore children, black or yellow, without marriage, that no one inquired who their fathers were, and that nothing more was thought of it than of the breeding of sheep or swine. And concerning the " slave-quarters " connected with the plantations the universal testimony was that the sexes were there " herded together promiscuously, like beasts." [1] In the answer given to a query which, in 1835, was presented to a Baptist Association of ministers, the fact leaks out that slave cohabitation was enforced by the authority of the masters for the increase of their human chattels.[2]

Yet though slaves were regarded as chattels, the master could not do with his slave exactly what he pleased. The life of the slave was in some degree protected by law. In most of the British colonies it was only by force of comparatively recent acts, made for the most part subsequent to the year 1797, that the same punishment was prescribed for the murder of a slave as for the murder of a free person. Prior to this period the former crime was subject only to a small pecuniary penalty, in Barbadoes not exceeding £15.[3] In the French colonies, according to the ' Code Noir,' a master who killed his slave should be punished " selon l'atrocité des circonstances." [4] In all the North American Slave States there was a time when the murder of a slave, whether by his master or a third person, was atoned for by a fine. In South Carolina this was the case as late as 1821, and only since then the wilful, malicious, and premeditated killing of a slave, by whomsoever perpetrated, was a capital offence in all the slave-holding States.[5] But this does not mean that no distinction was made between the killing of a slave and the killing of a freeman. In South Carolina, according to an enactment of 1821, he who killed a slave on a sudden heat or

---

[1] Goodell, *op. cit.* p. 111.
[2] *Idem, Slavery and Anti-Slavery* (New York, 1852), p. 185.
[3] Stephen, *op. cit.* i. 36, 38.
[4] *Code Noir*, Édit donné au mois de Mars 1724, art. 39, p. 304.
[5] Brevard, *op. cit.* ii. 240 *sq.* ; Stroud, *op. cit.* p. 55 *sq.*

passion was punished simply with a fine of five hundred dollars and imprisonment not exceeding six months.[1] In the Statutes of Tennessee the law referring to the wilful murder of a slave contained the provision that it should not be extended to " any person killing any slave in the act of resistance to his lawful owner or master, or any slave dying under moderate correction " ;[2] and a very similar provision was made by the laws of Georgia.[3] In other words, a correction causing the death of the victim was not necessarily immoderate in the eye of the law. In a still higher degree the life of the slave was endangered by another law, which prevailed universally both in the Slave States and in the British colonies. Neither a slave, nor a free negro, nor any descendant of a native of Africa whatever might be the shade of his complexion, could be a witness against a white person, either in a civil or a criminal case.[4] This law placed the slave, who was seldom within the view of more than one white man at a time, entirely at the mercy of this individual, and its consequences were obvious. Speaking of slavery in the United States in 1853, Goodell remarks : " Upon the most diligent inquiry and public challenge, for fifteen or twenty years past, not one single case has yet been ascertained in which, either during that time or previously, a master killing his slave, or indeed any other white man, has suffered the penalty of death for the murder of a slave." Nevertheless, murders of slaves by white men had been notoriously frequent.[5]

In the North American Slave States and in the colonies of all European Powers the master could inflict any number of blows upon his slave, but if he mutilated him he was fined or subjected to a very moderate term of imprisonment.[6] Again, the maltreatment of another person's slave was regarded as an injury done to the master. In the Negro Act of 1740 for South Carolina it was prescribed that if a slave was beaten by any person who had not sufficient cause or lawful authority for so

---

[1] Stroud, *op. cit.* p. 64.

[2] R. L. Caruthers and A. O. P. Nicholson, *A Compilation of the Statutes of Tennessee* (Nashville, Tenn., 1836), p. 677.

[3] Prince, *op. cit.* p. 787.

[4] Brevard, *op. cit.* ii. 242 ; Stroud, *op. cit.* p. 106 *sq.* ; Stephen, *op. cit.* i. 166, 174. In the French colonies, also, slaves could not be legal witnesses, but their testimony might be heard by the judge, merely to serve as a suggestion, or unauthenticated information, which might throw light on the evidence of other witnesses (*Code Noir*, Édit du mois de Mars 1685, art. 30, p. 44).

[5] Goodell, *The American Slave Code*, p. 209 *sq.*

[6] ' Negro Act ' of 1740, § 37, in Brevard, *op. cit.* ii. 241 ; Stephen, *op. cit.* i. 36 *sq.* ; B. Edwards, *The History of the British West Indies*, ii (London, 1819), p. 192.

doing, and if he was maimed or disabled by such beating from performing his or her work, the offender should pay to the owner of the slave " the sum of 15 shillings current money per diem, for every day of his lost time, and also the charge of the cure of such slave." [1]   But if the beating of the slave caused no loss of service to his master, the offender was not, as a rule, punished by law. [2]   A decision of the Supreme Court of Maryland established expressly the law to be, in that State, that trespass would not lie by a master for an assault and battery on his slave, unless it were attended with a loss of service. [3]   If, on the other hand, the offender was a slave and his victim a white man the injury was regarded in a very different light.   We read in an act of Georgia passed in 1770 : " If any slave shall presume to strike any white person, such slave . . . shall . . . for the second offence suffer death : But in case any such slave shall grievously wound, maim, or bruise any white person, though it shall be only the first offence, such slave shall suffer death." [4]   And to offer violence, to strike, attempt to strike, struggle with, or resist any white person, was, even by the latest meliorating laws issued in the British colonies, declared to be a crime in a slave which, if the white person had been wounded or hurt, and in some islands even without that condition, should subject the offender to death, dismemberment, or other severe penalties. [5]

The law also took care to prohibit the master from doing things which were considered injurious to the community or the State.   There was a great fear of teaching negroes to read and write.   William Knox, in a tract addressed to " the venerable Society for propagation of the Gospel in foreign parts " in the year 1768, remarks that " instruction renders them less fit or less willing to labour," and that, if they were universally taught to read, there would undoubtedly be a general insurrection of the negroes leading to the massacre of their owners. [6]   A similar fear underlies the laws on the subject which we meet with in the

[1] Brevard, *op. cit.* ii. 231 *sq.*

[2] Of all the Slave States, so far as I know, Kentucky was the only one where the owner of a slave might bring an action of trespass against any one who whipped, stroke, or otherwise abused the slave without the owner's consent, notwithstanding the slave was not so injured that the master lost his services thereby (C. S. Morehead and M. Brown, *A Digest of the Statute Laws of Kentucky*, ii [Frankfort, Ky., 1834], p. 1481).

[3] T. Harris and R. Johnson, *Reports of Cases argued and determined in the General Court of Appeals of the State of Maryland from 1800 to 1805, inclusive*, i (Annapolis, 1821), p. 4.

[4] Prince, *op. cit.* p. 781.

[5] Stephen, *op. cit.* i. 188 ; Edwards, *op. cit.* ii. 202 *sq.*

[6] W. Knox, *Three Tracts respecting the Conversion and Instruction of the Free Indians and Negro Slaves in the Colonies* (London, 1789), p. 15 *sq.*

codes of some of the Slave States. According to the Negro Act
of 1740 for South Carolina, any person who instructed a slave
in writing was subject to a fine of one hundred pounds ; [1] but
this enactment was later on considered too liberal. A law of
1834 placed under the ban all efforts to teach the coloured race
either reading or writing, and the punishment was no longer a
pecuniary fine only, but, besides, imprisonment for six months
or a shorter time or, if the offender was a free person of colour,
whipping not exceeding fifty lashes.[2]   In Georgia a law of 1770,
which prohibited the instruction of slaves in reading and writing,
was in 1833 followed by an act which extended the prohibition
to free persons of colour.[3]   In Louisiana the teaching of slaves
was punished with imprisonment for not less than a month nor
more than twelve months.[4]   North Carolina allowed slaves to
be acquainted with arithmetical calculations, but sternly interdicted instruction in reading and writing ; [5]   whilst Alabama
warred with the rudiments of reading, forbidding any coloured
persons, bond or free, to be taught not only reading and writing,
but spelling.[6]   In all these States the prohibition referred to the
master of the slave as well as to other persons. In Virginia, on
the other hand, the master might teach his slaves whatever he
liked, but others might not.[7]

There is yet another point in which the master's power was
restricted in a most unusual manner : in many cases he was not
allowed to liberate his slave, or great obstacles were put in the
way of manumission, both in many of the Slave States [8] and
throughout the British West Indies prior to the Emancipation
Act.[9]   In Saint Christopher, in the year 1802, a tax of £1,000
was imposed on the manumission of any slave who was not a

[1] Brevard, op. cit. ii. 243.
[2] D. J. McCord, The Statutes at large of South Carolina (Columbia,
S.C., 1836–41), vii. 468.
[3] Prince, op. cit. pp. 658, 785.
[4] Peirce, Taylor, and King, op. cit. p. 552.
[5] The Revised Statutes of North Carolina passed by the General Assembly
at the Session of 1836–7, xxxiv. 74, cxi. 27, vol. i. (Raleigh, 1837), pp. 209,
578.
[6] C. C. Clay, A Digest of the Laws of the State of Alabama (Tuskaloosa,
1843), p. 543.
[7] The Code of Virginia, cxcviii. 31 sq., vol. ii (Richmond, 1849),
p. 747 sq. ; Stroud, op. cit. p. 142.
[8] Morgan, Civil Code of Louisiana, p. 29 sqq. ; Revised Statutes of
North Carolina, cxi. 58, vol. i. 585 ; Brevard, op. cit. ii. 255 sq. (South
Carolina) ; Prince, op. cit. p. 787 (Georgia) ; Stroud, op. cit. p. 231
(Alabama) ; T. J. F. Alden and J. A. van Hoesen, Digest of the Laws of
Mississippi (New York, 1839), p. 761 ; J. Haywood and R. L. Cobbs,
The Statute Laws of the State of Tennessee, i (Knoxville, 1831), p. 327 sq.
[9] Cobb, op. cit. p. 282.

native of, or had not resided for two years within, the island,
while natives or residents might be enfranchised at half that
price. But the authors of this enactment went further still.
They considered that a master, though unwilling to pay £1,000
or £500 for the legal enfranchisement of his slave, might, during
his own life, make him or her practically free by not exercising
his own rights as master. Hence they enacted " that if any
proprietor of a slave should, by any contract in writing or otherwise, dispense with the slave's service, or should be proved
before a justice of peace not to have exercised any right of
ownership over such slave, and maintained him or her at his
own expense, within a month, the slave should be publicly sold
at vendue by the provost-marshal ; and should become the
property of the purchaser, and the purchase-money should be
paid into the colonial treasury." [1] In St. Vincents £100 should
be paid into the treasury for each slave sought to be manumitted,[2] whilst in Barbadoes a person minded to manumit a
slave should pay £50 to the churchwarden of the parish in which
he resided.[3] Very different were the Spanish laws on the subject
of manumission. According to a law of 1528, a negro slave who
had served a certain length of time was entitled to his liberty
upon the payment of a certain sum, not less than twenty marks
of gold, the exact amount to be settled by the royal authorities.[4]
In 1540 a law was issued to the effect that " if any negro, or
negress, or any other persons reputed slaves, should publicly
demand their liberty, they should be heard, and justice be done
to them, and care be taken that they should not on that account
be maltreated by their masters." [5] Nay, a slave who wished to
change his master and could prevail on any other person to buy
him by appraisement, could demand and compel such a transfer,[6]
and a master who treated his slaves inhumanly could be by the
judge deprived of them.[7] In the French islands a negro who
had been cruelly treated, contrary to royal ordinances, was
forfeited to the crown, and acquired, if not freedom, at least
deliverance from a tyrannical master ; [8] but the Court which

---

[1] Stephen, *op. cit.* i. 401 *sq.* [2] Cobb, *op. cit.* p. 282 *sq.*
[3] S. Moore, *The Public Acts in force; passed by the Legislature of
Barbados* 1762–1800 (London, 1801), p. 224 *sq.*
[4] A. Helps, *The Spanish Conquest in America*, iv (London, 1861),
p. 373.
[5] *Recopilacion de leyes de los reinos de las Indias*, vii. 5. 8, vol. ii
Madrid, 1841), p. 321.
[6] Barre Saint Venant, quoted by Stephen, *op. cit.* i. 119 *sq.*
[7] Edwards, *op. cit.* iv. 451.
[8] *Code Noir*, Édit du mois de Mars 1685, art. 42, p. 48 *sq.* ; Édit donné
au mois de Mars 1724, art. 38, p. 303 *sq.*

adjudged the offence might also decree the sufferer to be manu-
mitted.[1] In most of the British colonies and American Slave
States, on the other hand, the slave had no legal right to obtain
a change of master when cruel treatment made it necessary for
his relief or preservation.[2] The exceptions to this rule [3] were
few and of little practical value.

This extraordinary system of slavery was not only recognised
by Christian governments, but was supported by the large bulk
of the clergy, Catholic [4] and Protestant alike. In the beginning
of the abolitionist movement the Churches acknowledged slavery
to be a great evil, but with the making of this acknowledgment
they believed that they had done their share, and denied that
there was any obligation on them, or even that they had any
right, to proceed against the slave-holders. But things did not
stop here. The lamentations of resignation were gradually
changed into excuses, and the excuses into justifications.[5] The
Bible, it was said, contains no prohibition of slavery; on the
contrary, slavery is recognised both in the Old and New Testaments. Abraham, the father of the faithful and the friend of
God, had slaves; the Hebrews were directed to make slaves of
the surrounding nations; St. Paul and St. Peter approved of the
relation of master and slave when they gave admonitions to
both as to their reciprocal behaviour; the Saviour himself said
nothing in condemnation of slavery, although it existed in great
aggravation while he was upon earth. If slavery were sinful,

---

[1] Stephen, *op. cit.* i. 119.
[2] *Ibid.* i. 106; Stroud, *op. cit.* p. 93.
[3] Morgan, *Civil Code of Louisiana*, art. 192, p. 33; Morehead and
Brown, *op. cit.* ii. 1481 (Kentucky); Edwards, *op. cit.* ii. 192 (Jamaica);
Stephen, *op. cit.* i. 106 (some other British colonies).
[4] The attempts to represent the Roman Catholic clergy as ardent
abolitionists (A. Cochin, *L'abolition de l'esclavage*, ii [Paris, 1861], p. 443;
S. de Locqueneuille, *L'esclavage, ses promoteurs et ses adversaires* [Liège,
1890], p. 193) are certainly not justified by facts. Among the Catholics
of the United States there were some advocates of emancipation, but
their number was not large (Goodell, *Slavery and Anti-Slavery*, p. 195 *sq.*;
T. Parker, *Collected Works*, vi [London, 1864], p. 127 *sq.*). Dr. England,
the Catholic bishop of Charleston, South Carolina, undertook in public to
prove that the Catholic Church had always been the uncompromising
friend of slave-holding (Parker, *op. cit.* v [1863], p. 57). In Brazil it was
common for clergymen not only to possess slaves, but to buy and sell
them with as little scruple as other merchandises (L. A. da Fonseca, *A
escravidão, o clero e o abolicionismo* [Bahia, 1887], pp. 28, 33). Bishop
Bouvier wrote (*op. cit.* p. 568): " Servi autem dominis suis obedire
sortem suam patienter tolerare et officia sibi imposita fideliter exsequi
debent, quoadusque libertas ipsis concedatur. Meminerint præsentem
vitam esse momentaneam, futuram vero æternam."
[5] Von Holst, *op. cit.* ii. 231 *sqq.*

would it have been too much to expect that the Almighty had directed at least one little word against it in the last revelation of His will ? [1]   Nay, God not only permitted slavery, but absolutely provided for its perpetuity ; [2] it is the very legislation of Heaven itself ; [3] it is an institution which it is a religious duty to maintain,[4] and which cannot be abolished, because " God is pledged to sustain it." [5]   According to some, slavery was founded on the judgment of God on a damned race, the descendants of Ham (as Augustine said) ; according to others it was only in this way that the African could be raised to a participation of Christianity and civilisation.[6] With the name of " abolitionist " was thus associated the idea of infidelity, and the emancipation movement was branded as an attempt to spread the evils of scepticism through the land.[7] According to Governor Macduffie, of South Carolina, no human institution is more manifestly consistent with the will of God than slavery, and every community ought to punish the interference of abolitionists with death, without the benefit of clergy, " regarding the authors of it as enemies of the human race." [8]   It is true that religious arguments were also adduced in favour of abolition.   To hold men in bondage was said to be utterly inconsistent with the inalienable rights which the Creator had granted mankind, and still more obviously at variance with the dictates of Christian love.[9] Many clergymen also joined the abolitionists. But it seems that in the middle of the nineteenth century the Quakers and the United Brethren were the only religious bodies that regarded slave-holding and slave-dealing as ecclesiastical offences.[10] The American Churches were said to be " the bulwarks of American slavery." [11]

[1] A. Barnes, *The Church and Slavery* (Philadelphia, 1857), p. 15 ; J. G. Birney, *Letter to the Churches* (on the subject of slavery) (*s.l.*, 1834), p. 3 *sq.* ; A. T. Bledsoe, *An Essay on Liberty and Slavery* (Philadelphia, 1857), p. 138 *sqq.* ; Gerrit Smith, *Letter to Rev. James Smylie* (New York, 1837), p. 3 ; Cobb, *op. cit.* p. 54 *sqq.* ; Goodell, *Slavery and Anti-Slavery*, pp. 154–6, 167, 176, 181, 184, 186, etc. ; T. Parker, *op. cit.* v. 157.
[2] Thornton, quoted by Goodell, *Slavery and Anti-Slavery*, p. 147 ; Fisk, quoted *ibid.* p. 147.
[3] Bledsoe, *op. cit.* p. 138.
[4] Smylie, quoted by Gerrit Smith, *op. cit.* p. 3.
[5] Quoted by Goodell, *Slavery and Anti-Slavery*, p. 347.
[6] Barnes, *op. cit.* p. 16.
[7] *Ibid.* p. 18 ; Newman, *op. cit.* p. 56 ; Bledsoe, *op. cit.* p. 223.
[8] Newman, *op. cit.* p. 53 ; von Holst, *op. cit.* ii. 118 n. 1.
[9] J. J. Gurney, *Observations on the Distinguishing Views and Practices of the Society of Friends* (London, 1834), p. 390 ; ' Anti-Slavery Declaration of 1833,' quoted by Goodell, *Slavery and Anti-Slavery*, p. 398 ; J. G. Birney, *Second Letter on the subject of Slavery* (*s.l.* [1834 ?]), p. 1.
[10] Parker, *op. cit.* v. 56.   [11] Von Holst, *op. cit.* ii. 230.

Nobody would suppose that this attitude towards slavery was due to religious zeal. It was one of those cases, only too frequent in the history of morals, in which religion is called in to lend its sanction to a social institution agreeable to the leaders of religious opinion. Many clergymen and missionaries were themselves slave-holders,[1] the chapel funds largely rested on slave property,[2] and the ministers naturally desired to be on friendly terms with the more important members of their respective congregations, who were commonly owners of slaves. It is interesting to notice how slow the anti-slavery movement among the Quakers was towards practical achievement. It was in 1675 that a companion of George Fox, after visiting Barbadoes, delivered a remonstrance to Friends in Maryland and Virginia against slave-holding; but although from that time on sporadic protests against it were made in Pennsylvania, " the Society gave these memorials a cold reception. The love of gain and power was too strong on the part of the wealthy and influential planters and merchants, who had become slave-holders, to allow the scruples of the Chester meeting to take the shape of discipline." Not until John Woolman had devoted the latter part of his life (from 1742 to 1762) to a crusade against slave-dealing and slave-holding was the Society solidly converted to the cause of abolition.[3] But Adam Smith makes the remark that the resolution of the Quakers in Pennsylvania to set at liberty all their slaves, was due to the fact that the principal produce there was corn, the raising of which cannot afford the expense of slave cultivation; had the slaves " made any considerable part of their property, such a resolution could never have been agreed to."[4] As regards the Parliamentary act against the slave trade in 1807 and the emancipation of all slaves in British dominions in 1833, it has been pointed out that " the success of the abolitionists lay, among other things, in the economic aspects of the question. While the long battle for the abolition of the slave trade was being waged, it became evident that it would be far cheaper to increase the number of slaves by propagation than to continue importing fresh supplies from Africa; and later, when the abolitionists turned their attention to the extinction of slavery itself, the change in the economic condition of the West Indies gave added impetus to the anti-slavery cause."[5]

[1] Barnes, *op. cit.* p. 13; Goodell, *Slavery and Anti-Slavery*, pp. 151, 186 *sqq.*

[2] Newman, *op. cit.* p. 53.

[3] J. A. Hobson, *God and Mammon* (London, 1931), p. 39 *sq.*

[4] Adam Smith, *An Inquiry into the Nature and Causes of the Wealth of Nations* (Edinburgh, 1863), p. 172.

[5] E. L. Griggs, *Thomas Clarkson* (London, 1936), p. 20.

To explain the establishment of colonial slavery, the laws relating to it, and the difficulties in the way of its abolition, it is necessary to consider not only economic conditions and the motive of self-interest, but also the want of sympathy for, or positive antipathy to, the coloured race. The negro was looked upon almost as an animal, according to some he was a being without a soul.[1] Even the free negro was a pariah, subject to special laws and regulations. In the Code of Louisiana it is said : " Free people of colour ought never to insult or strike white people, nor presume to conceive themselves equal to the whites ; but, on the contrary, they ought to yield to them on every occasion, and never speak or answer them but with respect, under the penalty of imprisonment, according to the nature of the offence." [2] The ' Code Noir ' prohibited white men and women from marrying negroes, " à peine de punition et d'amende arbitraire " ; [3] and in the Revised Statutes of North Carolina we read : " If any white man or woman, being free, shall marry with an Indian, negro, mustee or mulatto man or woman, or any person of mixed blood to the third generation, bond or free, he shall, by judgment of the county court, forfeit and pay the sum of one hundred dollars to the use of the county." [4] In Mississippi a free negro or mulatto was legally punished with thirty-nine lashes if he exercised the functions of a minister of the gospel.[5] Coloured men in the North were excluded from colleges and high schools, from theological seminaries and from respectable churches, as also from the town hall, the ballot, and the cemetery where white people were interred.[6] The Anglo-Saxon aversion to the black race is thus expressed by an English writer : " We hate slavery, but we hate the negroes still more." [7] Among the Spaniards and Portuguese racial antipathies were not so strong, and their slaves were consequently better treated.[8]

As the slavery existing in Mohammedan countries has partly served as an excuse for their annexation by Christian powers, it is interesting to compare Islam's attitude towards slavery with that which not long before had prevailed in the Christian world. The slave should be treated with kindness ; the Prophet said :

---

[1] Von Holst, op. cit. i. 279 ; M. M. Malloch, ' How the Church dealt with Slavery,' in The Month, xxvii (London, 1876), p. 454.
[2] Quoted by Stroud, op. cit. p. 157.
[3] Code Noir, Édit donné au mois de Mars 1724, art. 6, p. 286.
[4] Revised Statutes of North Carolina, lxxi. 5, vol. i. 386 sq.
[5] Alden and Van Hoesen, op. cit. p. 771.
[6] Parker, op. cit. v. 58 ; Goodell, Slavery and Anti-Slavery, p. 200.
[7] Seward, quoted by Newman, op. cit. p. 54.
[8] L. Couty, L'esclavage au Brésil (Paris, 1881), p. 8 sqq.

" A man who behaves ill to his slave will not enter into paradise."
The master should give to his slaves of the food which he eats
himself, and of the clothes with which he clothes himself. He
should not order them to do anything beyond their power, and
in the hot season, during the hottest hours of the day, he should
let them rest. He may marry them to whom he will, but he may
not separate them when married ; nor must he separate a mother
from her child. The Prophet said : " Whoever is the cause of
separation between mother and child, by selling or giving, God
will separate him from his friends on the day of resurrection."
To liberate a slave is regarded as an act highly acceptable to
God, and as an expiation for certain sins. These rules, it should
be added, are not only recognised in theory, but derive additional
support from general usage. In the Mohammedan world the
slave generally lives on easy terms with his master. He is often
treated as a member of the family, and occasionally exercises
much influence upon its affairs.[1] This could of course not be
expected in the case of colonial slavery ; and some of its laws
were no doubt inspired by fear on account of the multitude of
slaves in a wealthy nation.

[1] Westermarck, *op. cit.* i. 686 *sq.*

CHAPTER XV

THE REGARD FOR TRUTH

IN the New Testament there are several passages condemning lying. According to the Apocalypse, " whosoever loveth and maketh a lie " may not enter the heavenly city,[1] but " all liars shall have their part in the lake which burneth with fire and brimstone." [2] In the Epistle to the Ephesians it is said : " Putting away lying, speak every man truth with his neighbour : for we are members one of another." [3] Paul wrote to the Colossians : " Lie not one to another, seeing that ye have put off the old man with his deeds." [4] In his first letter to the Corinthians, however, he describes himself as something of a hypocrite : [5] " Unto the Jews I became as a Jew, That I might gain the Jews ; to them that are under the law, as under the law, that I might gain them that are under the law ; To them that are without law, as without law (being not without law to God, but under the law to Christ), that I might gain them that are without law. To the weak became I as weak, that I might gain the weak : I am made all things to all men, that I might by all means save some. And this I do for the gospel's sake, that I might be partaker thereof with you." [6]

According to Augustine, a lie is always and necessarily sinful ; it is not permissible even when told with a view to saving the life of a neighbour, " since by lying eternal life is lost, never for any man's temporal life must a lie be told." [7] Yet all lies are not equally sinful : the degree of sinfulness depends on the mind of the liar and on the nature of the subject on which the lie is told.[8] Jokes which " bear with them in the tone of voice, and in the very mood of the joker a most evident indication that he means

[1] *Revelation* xxii. 15.
[2] *Ibid.* xxi. 8.
[3] *Ephesians* iv. 25.
[4] *Colossians* iii. 9.
[5] *Cf.* A. Nygren, *Urkristendom och reformation* (Lund, 1932), p. 149.
[6] *1 Corinthians* ix. 20–3.
[7] Augustine, *De mendacio*, 6.
[8] *Idem, Enchiridion*, 18 ; *idem, De mendacio*, 21. For Augustine's views on lying see also his treatise *Contra mendacium*, addressed to Consentius (Migne, *Patrologiæ cursus*, xl. 517 *sqq.*).

no deceit, are not accounted lies, though the thing he utters be
not true." [1]   This statement is also incorporated in Gratian's
Decretum.[2]   Thomas Aquinas discusses with his usual thoroughness the questions whether a lie is always a sin, and whether
every lie is a mortal sin.   " A lie has the character of sinfulness,
not only from the damage done to a neighbour, but also from its
own inordinateness.   Now it is not lawful to employ any unlawful inordinateness for the hindering of hurts and losses to
others ;   as it is not lawful to steal in order to give alms.   And
therefore it is not lawful to tell a lie to deliver another from any
danger whatever.   It is lawful, however, to hide the truth
prudently under some dissimulation, as Augustine says."   A lie
is a mortal sin, if it is opposed to charity by being uttered either
to the injury of God or to the hurt of our neighbour in his person,
wealth, or good name.   " But if the end intended be not contrary to charity, neither will the lie be a mortal sin in this respect ;   as appears in a jocose lie, that is intended to create some
slight amusement, and in an officious lie, in which is intended
even the advantage of our neighbour." [3]

From early times, however, we meet within the Christian
Church a much less rigorous doctrine, which soon came to exercise a more powerful influence on the practice and feelings of
men.   It was argued that an untruth is not a lie when there is a
" just cause " for it ;   and as a just cause was regarded not only
self-defence, but also zeal for God's honour.   This zeal, together
with an indiscriminate devotion to the Church, led to those
" pious frauds," those innumerable falsifications of documents,
inventions of legends, and forgeries of every description, which
made the Church a veritable seat of lying, and most seriously
impaired the sense of truth in the minds of Christians.[4]   Thus
by a fiction Papacy, as a divine institution, was traced back to
the age of the Apostles ;   and in virtue of another fiction Constantine was alleged to have abdicated his imperial authority in

[1] Augustine, *De mendacio*, 2 ; *idem*, *Quæstiones in Genesim*, 145, *ad*
Gen. xliv. 15 (Migne, xxxiv. 587).

[2] Gratian, *Decretum*, ii. 22. 2. 12, 17 *sq*.

[3] Thomas Aquinas, *Summa theologica*, ii.-ii. 110. 3 *sq*.

[4] W. Gass, *Geschichte der christlichen Ethik*, i (Berlin, 1881), pp. 91, 92,
236 *sqq*. ;   J. H. Newman, *Apologia pro vita sua* (London, 1873), p. 349 *sq*. ;
J. L. von Mosheim, *Institutes of Ecclesiastical History*, i (London, 1863),
p. 275 ;   C. Middleton, *A Free Inquiry into the Miraculous Powers, Which*
are supposed to have subsisted in the Christian Church (London, 1749),
passim ;   W. E. H. Lecky, *History of the Rise and Influence of the Spirit of*
Rationalism in Europe, i (London, 1893), p. 396 *sqq*. ;   H. von Eicken,
Geschichte und System der mittelalterlichen Weltanschauung (Stuttgart,
1887), pp. 654–6, 663 ;   A. Harnack, *History of Dogma*, iii (London, 1897),
pp. 184, 185, 219 *sq*.

Italy in favour of the successor of St. Peter.[1] The Bishop of
Rome assumed the privilege of disengaging men from their oaths
and promises. An oath which was contrary to the good of the
Church was declared not to be binding.[2] The theory was laid
down that as faith was not to be kept with a tyrant, pirate, or
robber, who kills the body, it was still less to be kept with an
heretic, who kills the soul.[3] Origen, Gregory of Nyssa, and
most of the later Fathers even charged God with falsehood in
dealing with his enemy, the devil, by offering him Christ's soul
in exchange for the souls of men, although he knew that the
devil could not keep hold of Christ's sinless soul, which would
only cause him torture.[4] It would not have been the first time
that God had recourse to deceit for the purpose of carrying out
his plans. In order to ruin Ahab he commissioned a lying spirit
to deceive his prophets ; [5] and once he threatened to use deception as a means of taking revenge upon idolaters.[6]

Private protestations were thought sufficient to relieve men
in conscience from being bound by a solemn treaty or from the
duty of speaking the truth ; and an equivocation, or play upon
words in which one sense is taken by the speaker and another
sense intended by him for the hearer, was in some cases also held
permissible. According to Alfonso de' Liguori—who lived in
the eighteenth century and was beatified in the nineteenth, and
whose writings were declared by high authority not to contain
a word that could be justly found fault with [7]—there are three
sorts of equivocation which may be employed for a good reason,
even with the addition of a solemn oath. We are allowed to use
ambiguously words having two senses, as the word *volo*, which
means both to " wish " and to " fly " ; sentences bearing two
main meanings, as " This book is Peter's," which may mean
either that the book belongs to Peter or that Peter is the author
of it ; words having two senses, one more common than the
other or one literal and the other metaphorical—for instance, if
a man is asked about something which it is in his interest to
conceal, he may answer, " No, I say," that is, " I say the word

---

[1] Von Eicken, *op. cit.* p. 656 ; R. Lane Poole, *Illustrations of the
History of Mediæval Thought in the Departments of Theology and Ecclesi-
stical Politics* (London, 1884), p. 249.

[2] Gregory IX., *Decretales*, ii. 24. 27.

[3] J. Simancas, *De catholicis institutionibus liber* (Romæ, 1575),
lvi. 52 *sq.*, p. 365 *sq.*

[4] See *supra*, pp. 151, 158.   [5] *1 Kings* xxii. 20 *sqq.*

[6] *Ezekiel* xiv. 7 *sqq.*

[7] F. Meyrick, *Moral and Devotional Theory of the Church of Rome.*
Vo. I. S. *Alfonso de' Liguori's Theory of Truthfulness* (London, 1855),
p. 3.

' no '." [1] As for mental reservations, again, such as are
" purely mental," and on that account cannot in any manner
be discovered by other persons, are not permissible ; but we
may, for a good reason, make use of a " non-pure " mental
reservation, which in the nature of things is discoverable,
although it is not discovered by the person with whom we are
dealing. [2] Thus it would be wrong secretly to insert the word
" no " in an affirmative oath without any external sign ; but it
would not be wrong to insert it in a whispering voice or under the
cover of a cough.   The " good reason " for which equivocations
and non-pure mental reservations may be employed is defined as
" any honest object, such as keeping our goods spiritual or
temporal." [3]   In support of this casuistry it is uniformly said
by Catholic apologists that each man has a right to act upon the
defensive, that he has a right to keep guard over the knowledge
which he possesses in the same way as he may defend his goods;
and as for there being any deceit in the matter—why, soldiers
use stratagems in war, and opponents use feints in fencing. [4]

Protestant moralists reject the doctrine of mental reservation, and adopt a less formal view as to falsehood than is taken
by the Roman Catholic theologians.   They teach that the
malice of lying consists in its being an offence against justice,
truth being a debt which we owe our fellow-men, and that when
that debt ceases falsehood is legitimate. [5]   But there have also
been the Puritan insistence on literal truthfulness and distrust
of works of imagination, alike poetry and romance, and the early
Quakers' battle against insincerity in their theeing and thouing
and refusal of giving titles of respect.   Thomas Ellwood wrote
in his autobiography : " I durst not say, Sir, Master, My Lord,
Madam (or My dame) ; or say Your Servant to any one to whom
I did not stand in the real relation of a servant, which I had never
done to any. . . .   Again, the corrupt and unsound form of
speaking in the plural number to a single person, *you* to one,
instead of *thou*, contrary to the pure, plain, and single language
of truth, *thou* to one, and *you* to more than one, which had always
been used by God and men, and men to God, as well as one to
another . . . hath greatly debased the spirits and depraved the
manners of men." [6]

[1] Alfonso de' Liguori, *Theologia moralis* (Bassani, 1822), iii. 151,
vol. i. 249.
[2] *Ibid.* iii. 152, vol. i. 249.
[3] *Ibid.* iii. 151, vol. i. 249.   [4] Meyrick, *op. cit.* i. 25.
[5] G. H. Joyce, ' Mental Reservation,' in J. Hastings, *Encyclopædia of
Religion and Ethics*, viii (Edinburgh, 1915), p. 555.
[6] *The History of the Life of Thomas Ellwood, written by his own hand*
(London, 1900), p. 19.

According to the Catholic doctrine, formulated by Aquinas, the most grievous and mortal of all lies is that which is contrary to the charity of God, whose truth is obscured or misrepresented by it ; and " a lie of this nature is not only opposed to the virtue of charity, but also to the virtue of faith and religion." [1] As Augustine said, " it is far more tolerable to lie in those things that are unconnected with religion than to be deceived in those without belief in, or knowledge of, which God cannot be worshipped." [2] In agreement with Augustine, who defined faith as " cum assensione cogitare," Aquinas also asserts that it is " an act of the intellect, assenting to divine truth by command of the will, moved by God's grace ; and thus is under the control of freewill in reference to God. Hence the act of faith may be meritorious." [3] So also unbelief is in the intellect, but the cause of it is in the will, and therefore it is a sin, and indeed a sin greater than all sins of moral perversity.[4] By insisting that unbelief is " in the will as its prime mover " Aquinas thinks that he has proved its sinful character.

The faith which the Christian Churches have regarded as an indispensable condition of salvation implies belief in the power and dignity of Christ as Messiah and Lord and in the reality of his redemption. In the Catholic conception of faith it is faith in the Church, who is the guarantor of the truth of her doctrines.[5] What then about those who have never heard of Christ and his Church, and whose unbelief therefore cannot possibly be due to their will ? Some early Fathers admitted the possible salvation of pagans—Justin Martyr expressly said that Socrates and Heraclitus in the sight of God were Christians [6]—but the vast majority of the Fathers and the Church held a different opinion.[7] " Hold most firmly," said Fulgentius, " and doubt not that not only all pagans but also all Jews, heretics, and schismatics who depart from this present life outside the Catholic Church are about to go into eternal fire, prepared for the devil and his angels." [8] This doctrine was deemed so prominent and unquestionable that the Council of Carthage, in the fourth century, made it one of the test-questions put to every bishop before

---

[1] Thomas Aquinas, *op. cit.* ii.-ii. 110. 4.
[2] Augustine, *Enchiridion*, 18.
[3] Thomas Aquinas, *op. cit.* ii.-ii. 2. 9.
[4] *Ibid.* ii.-ii. 10. 2 *sq.*   [5] *Ibid.* ii.-ii. 10. 12.
[6] Justin, ' Apologia II. pro Christianis,' in *Opera omnia*, ed. by F. Sylburg (1593), p. 65.
[7] J. Barbeyrac, *Traité de la morale des Pères de l'Église* (Amsterdam, 1728), p. 159 ; W. Palmer, *A Treatise on the Church of Christ*, i (London, 1842), 12.
[8] Fulgentius, *De fide*, 81.

ordination.[1] Aquinas, again, argues that in those who have heard nothing of the faith, unbelief has not the character of a sin, but rather of a penalty, inasmuch as such ignorance of divine things is a consequence of the sin of our first parent, and that, consequently, " unbelievers of this class are damned for other sins that cannot be forgiven without faith, but they are not damned for the sin of unbelief." [2]

All the Lutherans and Reformed and the sects which separated from them held that faith in the Church, their own Church, or at any rate faith in Christ, was necessary for salvation.[3] Luther is clear that outside Christendom there is no forgiveness and can be no holiness.[4] Calvin says : " Beyond the bosom of the Church, no remission of sins is to be hoped for, nor any salvation." [5] The Anglican Article XIII. denies that " works done before the grace of Christ " are pleasant to God ; " yea rather, for that they are not done as God hath willed and commanded them to be done, we doubt not but they have the nature of sin." In the Westminster Confession of Faith the divines declared the opinion that men not professing Christianity may be saved to be " very pernicious, and to be detested " ; [6] and in their Larger Catechism they expressly said that " they who, having never heard the gospel, know not Jesus Christ, and believe not in him, cannot be saved, be they never so diligent to frame their lives according to the light of nature, or the laws of that religion which they profess." [7] Among the leading Reformers Zwingli was the only one who openly and unequivocally repudiated the doctrine of exclusive salvation. In a Confession of Faith which he wrote just before his death he described that future " assembly of all the saintly, the heroic, the faithful, and the virtuous," when Abel and Enoch, Noah and Abraham, Isaac and Jacob, will mingle with " Socrates, Aristides, and Antigonus, with Numa and Camillus, Hercules and Theseus, the Scipios and the Catos," and when every upright and holy man who has ever lived will be present with God. On reading this Luther said he despaired of the salvation of Zwingli.[8] Even in the case of Christians errors in belief on such

---

[1] Palmer, *op. cit.* i. 13.

[2] Thomas Aquinas, *op. cit.* ii.–ii. 10. 1.

[3] Palmer, *op. cit.* i. 13.

[4] Luther, ' Der grosse Katechismus 1529,' pt. ii. art. 1, in *Sämmtliche Werke*, xxi (Erlangen, 1832), p. 98 *sqq.*

[5] Calvin, *Institutio Christianæ religionis*, iv. 1. 4.

[6] *The Confession of Faith*, x. 4.

[7] *The Larger Catechism*, Answer to Question 60.

[8] Zwingli, ' Fidei Christianæ expositio,' in *Opera*, iv (Turici, 1841), p. 65 ; J. B. Bossuet, *Histoire des variations des Eglises Protestantes*, i (Paris, 1688), p. 72 *sqq.*

subjects as church government, the Trinity, transubstantiation, original sin, and predestination, have been declared to expose the guilty to eternal damnation.[1] In the seventeenth century it was a common theme of certain Roman Catholic writers that " Protestancy unrepented destroys salvation," [2] while the Protestants on their part taxed Du Moulin with culpable laxity for admitting that some Roman Catholics might escape the torments of hell.[3]

Unfortunately it was not left to the Almighty alone to avenge the injury done to him by the sin of unbelief, but in this case also the principle that it belongs to the worldly authorities to appease his anger was acted upon. And a lie about divine things is not only an offence against God, but also a corruption of the faith, whereby the life of the soul is sustained ; and this is much worse than to temper with the coinage, which is only an aid to temporal life. " Hence," says Aquinas, " if coiners or other malefactors are at once handed over by secular princes to a just death, much more may heretics, immediately they are convicted of heresy, be not only excommunicated, but also justly done to die." [4]

The opinions of the early Fathers on persecution were divided. Those who wrote when a pagan or heretical power was supreme were the champions of toleration, but those who wrote when the Church was in the ascendency usually inclined to persecution. Foremost among the latter was Augustine. As long as the Donatists had the upper hand in Africa he stood for the rights of conscience, but when the balance of material force was with Catholicism he changed his mind. It was merciful, he contended, to punish heretics even by death, if this could save them or others from the eternal suffering that awaited the unconverted ; and he adduced as applicable precedents all the worst persecutions mentioned in the Old Testament.[5] From the moment the Church obtained civil power under Constantine the general principle of coercion was admitted and acted on both against Jews, heretics, and pagans.[6] The first law that has come

[1] E. Abbot, ' Literature of the Doctrine of a Future Life,' in W. R. Alger, *A Critical History of the Doctrine of a Future Life* (Philadelphia, 1864), p. 863.

[2] M. Wilson, *Charity Mistaken, with the Want whereof Catholickes are unjustly charged, for affirming . . . that Protestancy unrepented destroys Salvation* (St. Omer, 1630).

[3] Abbot, *loc. cit.* p. 860.   [4] Thomas Aquinas, *op. cit.* ii.–ii. 11. 3.

[5] Augustine, *Contra Gaudentium*, i. 19 ; *idem*, *Contra epistolam Parmeniani*, i. 8 ; *idem*, *Epistola XCIII.* 17.

[6] H. H. Milman, *History of Latin Christianity*, ii (London, 1864), p. 33 *sq.* ; Lecky, *op. cit.* ii. 13 *sqq.*

down to us in which the penalty of death is annexed to the simple profession of a heresy, is law 9 ' De Hereticis ' in the Theodosian Code, which was made by Theodosius the Great, but it was applicable only to some sects of Manichæans.[1] For a long time, however, the clergy were reluctant to sanction the death of heretics, though very desirous to suppress their worship by force, and to banish their teachers from the empire. Spain was the first country to shed a Christian's blood for the sake of Christian orthodoxy. The emperor and the bishops responsible for murdering Priscillian were Spaniards ; and it was in a letter to a Spanish bishop (in 447) that Bishop Leo of Rome frankly rejoiced to think how the civil power aids the Church's " law of gentleness " by inflicting capital punishment on heretics like the Priscillians.[2]

After the suppression of paganism in the Roman Empire, however, religious persecution was very rare for centuries, because heresies scarcely appeared, and the few that arose were quite insignificant. But as soon as the revival of learning commenced there was a change. This happened in the eleventh and twelfth centuries. In 1199 Innocentius III. issued a decree which led to the foundation of the Inquisition.[3] Shortly afterwards began the massacre of the Albigenses in the south of France. The papal legate wrote jubilantly that at the capture of Béziers nearly 20,000 persons were killed—men, women, and children together. When some of the soldiers asked how they should distinguish orthodox from heretics, the legate gave the order, " Kill them all, for God knows his own." [4] In 1215 the Fourth Council of the Lateran enjoined all rulers as they desired to be esteemed faithful, to swear a public oath that they would labour earnestly, and to the full extent of their power, to exterminate from their dominions all those who were branded as heretics by the Church.[5] She excommunicated princes who refused to execute the heretics whom the Inquisition handed over to them.[6]

In 1231 burning alive was made the regular mode of execution ; and it took place after the constancy of the victim had been tried by the most excruciating torture. Not infrequently he was burnt alive by a slow fire, which was said to give him

---

[1] *Codex Theodosianum,* xvi. 8.
[2] J. Moffatt, *The First Five Centuries of the Church* (London, 1938), p. 100 *sq.*
[3] G. G. Coulton, *The Inquisition* (London, 1929), p. 20 *sqq.*
[4] H. C. Lea, *A History of the Inquisition,* i (New York, 1906), p. 154.
[5] N. Eymericus, *Directorium Inquisitorum* (Romæ, 1578), p. 60.
[6] Coulton, *op. cit.* p. 49.

more time for repentance.[1] It was the invariable rule to confiscate the entire property of the impenitent heretic [2]—a rule which the Sicilian inquisitor Paramo justified on the ground that the crime of the heretic is so great that something of his impurity falls upon all who are related to him, and that the Almighty—whom he terms the First Inquisitor—deprived both Adam and his descendants of the Garden of Eden.[3] Nay, all the possessions of a person ceased to be his from the mere fact that he had been accused of heresy.[4]

The number of persons who suffered death at the stake cannot be given with any confidence. Llorente, who had free access to the archives of the Spanish Inquisition, assures us that by that tribunal alone more than 31,000 persons were burnt, and more than 290,000 condemned to punishments less severe than death.[5] On August 24 (St. Bartholomew's Day) 1572 began the famous massacres in France in which about 70,000 Huguenots were slain. After the beginning of the eighteenth century, persecution became less sanguinary, though in Spain over a thousand persons are said to have been burnt in the first half of the century.[6] But there was no relaxation in Catholic theory. In 1808 Napoleon abolished the Spanish Inquisition ; but when his power fell, it was restored there and in the Papal States.[7] In 1885, in the encyclical ' Immortale Dei,' Leo XIII. blamed all States that granted equal rights to every creed ; and in 1888 he issued another encyclical, in which he laid down that the State ought to profess only Catholicism, and that " although in the extraordinary condition of these times the Church usually acquiesces in certain modern liberties . . . because she judges it expedient to permit them, she would in happier times exercise her own liberty." [8] In *The Catholic Encyclopedia*, published in New York between 1907 and 1914, it is said that the rigours of the Inquisition offend the feelings of later ages in which there is less regard for the purity of faith, but that they did not antagonise the feelings of their own time, when heresy was looked upon as more malignant than treason. " Toleration came in only when faith went out ; lenient measures were

---

[1] Lecky, *op. cit.* ii. 34.

[2] Eymericus, *op. cit.* iii. 110 *sqq.*, p. 390.

[3] L. Paramo, *De origine et progressu Sanctæ Inquisitionis* (Matriti, 1598), i. 2. 7, p. 45.

[4] Lea, *op. cit.* i. 517.

[5] J. A. Llorente, *Histoire de l'Inquisition d'Espagne*, iv (Paris, 1818), p. 271.

[6] C. J. Cadoux, *Catholicism and Christianity* (London, 1928), pp. 570, 573.

[7] *Ibid.* p. 574.   [8] *Ibid.* p. 578 *sq.*

resorted to only where the power to apply more severe measures was wanting." [1]

Religious persecution was not peculiar to the Catholics but was also practised by the Protestants, though on a smaller scale. The early documents of the Reformation contain brilliant declarations of the rights of conscience ; [2] it was, of course, only by an appeal to those rights that the Reformers could justify their own attitude towards Roman Catholicism. But it is one thing to claim liberty for oneself, and another to accord it to others. All round about Luther and Melanchthon sprang up a crop of heresies with which they had no sympathy.[3] Luther writes to the Elector John, begging him to silence a certain Hans Mohr, who was spreading Zwinglian opinions in Coburg ; [4] and in another place he lays down as a rule for the treatment of unbelievers in an evangelical State that if after instruction they still persist, they are to be made to hold their tongues.[5] But his intolerance chiefly spends itself in violent words, and he objects to inflicting capital punishment in cases of heresy. In 1526 he writes in reference to Anabaptists : " It is not right, and I think it great pity, that such wretched people should be so miserably slain, burned, cruelly put to death ; every one should be allowed to believe what he will. If he believes wrongly, he will have punishment enough in the eternal fire of hell." [6] In another letter he writes : " I am slow to adopt the judgment of blood, even where it is abundantly deserved. . . . I can in no way admit that false teachers should be put to death ; it is enough that they should be banished." [7] Melanchthon was less merciful. He writes that sedition ought to be suppressed by the sword, and that blasphemers, even if not seditious, should be put to death by the civil magistrate ; there were precedents for this course in the law of Moses.[8] And he did not hesitate to express his entire approval of the burning of the " blasphemer " Servetus, whom Calvin had arrested and condemned to the

[1] J. Wilhelm, ' Heresy,' in The Catholic Encyclopedia, vii (New York, 1910), p. 262.

[2] Luther, ' Von weltlicher Oberkeit, wie weit man ihr Gehorsam schuldig sei. 1523,' in Sämmtliche Werke, xxii (Erlangen, 1833), p. 59 sqq. ; ' Sermon vom Bann. 1519,' ibid. xxvii (Erlangen, 1833), p. 50 sqq.

[3] See C. Beard, The Reformation of the Sixteenth Century (London, 1885), p. 170 sqq.

[4] Luther, Briefe, Sendschreiben und Bedenken, iii (Berlin, 1827), p. 256 sq.

[5] Ibid. iii. 498.

[6] Luther, Sämmtliche Werke, xxvi (Erlangen, 1830), p. 256.

[7] Idem, Briefe, Sendschreiben und Bedenken, iii. 347 sq.

[8] Ph. Melanchthon, ' Epistolæ, v.,' in Opera, ii (Halis Saxonum, 1835), p. 17 sq.

flames,[1] although he was only a wayfarer in Geneva, over whom neither Calvin nor the magistrates of the city had a shadow of jurisdiction. Calvin lays down with great distinctness the duty of repressing heresy by force.[2] Even Zwingli, who speaks of a heaven in which Christians may expect to meet the wise and good of heathen antiquity, approved of putting false teachers to death,[3] which actually happened when Anabaptist leaders were judicially drowned in the Lake of Zürich.[4]

In England, on the accession of Elizabeth, a law was made prohibiting any religious service other than the Prayer-book, the penalty for the third offence being imprisonment for life. Both before the Reformation, and during the Reformation, and after the Reformation—down to 1678—it was a rule of the common law that an Englishman could be burned as a heretic by virtue of a State writ.[5] Presbyterians, through a long succession of reigns, were imprisoned, branded, mutilated, scourged, and exposed in pillory ; many Catholics under false pretences were tortured and hung ; Anabaptists and Arians were burnt alive. In Ireland the religion of the immense majority of the people was banned and prescribed, and when in 1626 the Government manifested some slight wish to grant it partial relief, nearly all the Protestant bishops assembled to protest in a solemn resolution against the indulgence.[6] When the Reformation triumphed in Scotland, one of its first fruits was a law which declared that whoever either said mass, or was present while it was said, should for the first offence lose his goods, for the second offence be exiled, and for the third offence be put to death.[7] According to Lecky, it was in Scotland, in 1697, that the last execution for heresy on British soil took place, and in Scotland again, in 1727, that the sin of witchcraft was last punished with death by any British authority. He believes that in no part of Protestant Europe prosecutions for witchcraft were so frequent, persistent, and ferocious as there. It was to the ministers that the persecution was mainly due ; and in 1736 the associated Presbytery

---

[1] *Idem*, ' Epistolæ, xii.,' in *Opera*, viii (1841), p. 362.

[2] P. Henry, *The Life and Times of John Calvin*, ii (London, 1849), p. 241.

[3] Zwingli, ' Fidei Christianæ expositio,' in *Opera*, iv (Turici, 1841), p. 65.

[4] H. Bullinger, *Reformationsgeschichte* (Frauenfeld, 1838), i. 382, ii. 14.

[5] E. Barker, in the review of a book in *The Sociological Review*, xxix (London, 1937), p. 210.

[6] Lecky, *op. cit.* ii. 39 *sqq.*

[7] H. T. Buckle, *History of Civilization in England*, iii (London, 1894), p. 82.

left a solemn protest against the repeal of the laws against witchcraft as an infraction of the express word of God.[1] The Puritans, who, when a minority, demanded freedom as passionately as minorities always will, were no lovers of toleration for its own sake : " where they controlled the State, as they showed in New England, they were ready to enforce conformity to their own views, and to exert a discipline no less drastic than that of their enemies." Even Cromwell, who called God to witness that " no man in England doth suffer for the testimony of Jesus," was unable in his hour of triumph to grant freedom to Anglicans and Catholics.[2]

After discussing the persecutions of the Christian Churches, Dean Inge [3] expresses the opinion that almost everything which offends the antagonists of Christianity comes from ecclesiasticism, not from Christianity. True, in its early days there were no other persecutions than those of which the Christians themselves were the victims. But it cannot be denied that early Christianity contained seeds productive of the persecuting spirit. It accepted the divine authority of the Old Testament. Like other monotheistic religions that attribute human emotions and passions to their godhead—Zoroastrianism and Mohammedanism —that of the Hebrews was an intolerant religion. Yahveh said : " Thou shalt have no other gods before me. . . . I the Lord thy God is a jealous God." In the pre-prophetic period the existence of other gods was recognised, but they were not to be worshipped by Yahveh's people. Nor was any mercy to be shown to their followers, for Yahveh was " a man of war." [4] The god of Christianity inherited his jealousy ; and Augustine and other advocates of religious persecutions expressly appealed in justification of them to those mentioned in the Old Testament. Polytheism, on the other hand, is by nature tolerant : a god who is always used to share with other gods the worship of his believers cannot be a very jealous god. Among the early Greeks and Romans it was a principle that the religion of the State should be the religion of the people, as its welfare was supposed to depend upon a strict observance of the established cult ; but the gods mainly cared for external worship, and took little notice even of expressed opinions. Philosophers openly

[1] W. E. H. Lecky, *A History of England in the Eighteenth Century*, ii (London, 1878), pp. 80, 83.
[2] E. Barker, *National Character and the Factors in its Formation* (London, 1827), p. 203.
[3] W. R. Inge, *Christian Ethics and Moral Problems* (London, 1932), p. 196.
[4] *Exodus* xv. 3.

despised the very rites which they both defended and practised ; and religion was more a pretext than a real motive for the persecutions of men like Anaxagoras, Protagoras, Socrates, and Aristotle.[1] In the collection of Roman laws before Constantine we search in vain for any enactment aimed at free thought, and in the history of the Emperors there was no prosecution of abstract doctrine. The measures by which the Romans in earlier times repressed the introduction of new religions were largely suggested by worldly considerations ; and it has been sufficiently proved that the persecutions of the Christians during the pagan Empire sprang from motives quite different to religious intolerance. Liberty of worship was a general principle of the Imperial rule. That it was denied the Christians was due to their own aggressiveness, as also to political suspicion. They grossly insulted the pagan cult, denouncing it as the worship of demons ; they refused to offer sacrifice on behalf of the Emperor ; and calamities that fell upon the Empire were in consequence regarded by the populace as the righteous vengeance of the offended gods. Their proselytism disturbed the peace of families and towns. Their secret meetings aroused suspicion of political danger ; and this suspicion was increased by the doctrines they professed. They considered the Roman Empire a manifestation of Antichrist, they looked forward with longing to its destruction, and many of them refused to take part in its defence. The greatest and best among the pagans spoke of the Christians as " enemies," or " haters of the human race." [2]

An ecclesiastical reason for the Christian persecutions was undoubtedly that the cohesion and power of the Church, which regarded itself as the sole possessor of divine truth, depended upon a strict adherence to its doctrines. There were also worldly grounds for them. One was greed. The inquisitor Eymeric complained in 1375 : " In our days there are no more rich heretics, so that princes, not seeing much money in prospect, will not put themselves to any expense ; it is a pity that so salutary an institution as ours should be so uncertain of its future." [3] Another ground which induced Christian princes to persecute heretics was fear of their political influence. Certain heresies, as Manichæism and Donatism, were expressly declared to affect the common welfare ; and the Frankish kings treated heretics not only as rebels against the Church, but as traitors to the State, as confederates of hostile Visigoths or Burgundians or

[1] L. Schmidt, *Die Ethik der alten Griechen*, ii (Berlin, 1882), p. 24 *sqq.*
[2] E. Westermarck, *The Origin and Development of the Moral Ideas*, ii (London, 1917), p. 649.
[3] Coulton, *op. cit.* p. 47.

Lombards.[1] But whatever other grounds there may have been for the persecutions committed by the Christians, the principal one was unquestionably the doctrine of exclusive justification by faith ; and this was not an ecclesiastical invention, but the leading idea in the Pauline epistles. Thus Paul, who before his conversion had been persecuting the Christians, became afterwards an indirect cause of religious persecution on an infinitely greater scale, to which there has been no parallel outside Christendom. It is significant that the reviver of Paulinism, Augustine, also was the spiritual father of persecution.

The persecutions were by no means ineffective. Before operating in any district the inquisitors used to make a proclamation offering pardon under certain conditions to those who confessed and retracted their heresies within thirty or forty days ; and Mariana says that when such a proclamation was made on the first establishment of the Inquisition in Andalusia, 17,000 recantations followed.[2] This was presumably regarded as a triumph of truth ; but it was scarcely a triumph of truthfulness. Augustine himself writes that we must avoid the lie and, even when we err in our thought, must always say what we think.[3] But it is not only by persecutions that the Christian Churches have impaired the spirit of truth : they have also done it by softer means—by inducing the State to make the profession of a certain creed, or at any rate the performance of certain religious rites, a condition of the enjoyment of full civic rights. And this is what even Protestant countries have been doing up to our own time. In the case of the clergy, too, there is considerable inducement to insincerity. Mr. Harvey writes in a book on *The Church and the Twentieth Century* : " It is to be feared that even now the Church is not universally regarded as pre-eminently the home of truthfulness. The more intelligent layman suspects his clergyman of practising a good deal of mental reservation." [4] " While a man's livelihood and the happiness of his wife and children," says the Rev. R. Roberts, " are dependant on his defence of orthodoxy he is most certainly forced into conformity. . . . It is orthodoxy holding the pistol of starvation at the heretic's head in the name of religion." [5]

---

[1] H. H. Milman, *History of Latin Christianity*, ii (London, 1867), pp. 33, 61.

[2] I. Mariana, *Historiæ de rebus Hispaniæ*, ii (Moguntiæ, 1605), bk. xxiv, ch. 17.

[3] Augustine, *Enchiridion*, 22.

[4] G. L. H. Harvey, ' Nova et vetera,' in *The Church and the Twentieth Century*, ed. by himself (London, 1936), p. 420.

[5] R. Roberts, ' The Tyranny of Intolerance,' in *R.P.A. Annual 1913* (London), p. 46 *sq.*

According to Dean Rashdall the most deadly result of the doctrine of justification by faith is that it has fostered the belief that honest thinking is sinful and blind credulity meritorious. " It deters the clergy from study, from thought, and from openly teaching what they themselves really believe." [1]

The highest regard for truth is not to profess it, but to seek for it. In this respect the Christian Churches have been most lamentably deficient. While the knowledge of religious truth has been held to be a necessary requirement of salvation, all other knowledge was for a long time regarded not only as valueless but even as sinful. " The wisdom of this world," says Paul, " is foolishness with God." [2] Tertullian expresses the ecclesiastical contempt of scientific knowledge in the famous formula, *Credo quia impossibile*, " I believe because it is impossible." Lactantius in particular expatiated on the nothingness of all worldly wisdom.[3] According to Aquinas, eagerness to learn the truth may be a vice ; as " when one seeks to learn the truth about creatures without reference to the due end, which is the knowledge of God. Hence Augustine says : ' We must not gratify a curiosity, idle and sure to be thrown away over the study of creatures ; but we must make of that study a ladder to ascend to immortal and everlasting goods.' " [4] Throughout the Middle Ages there is a conflict between the learning of the Church and the study of the classics. The latter might be useful only as a dialectic training calculated to promote a scientific exposition and defence of the ecclesiastical doctrines.[5] Aquinas points out that " though the study of philosophy in itself is lawful and praiseworthy, still because some philosophers abuse it to assail the faith, the Apostle says : [6] ' Beware lest any man spoil you through philosophy and vain deceit, after the tradition of men, after the rudiments of the world, and not after Christ.' " [7]

For centuries afterwards, as Lecky remarks, " every mental disposition which philosophy pronounces to be essential to a legitimate research was almost uniformly branded as a sin, and a large proportion of the most deadly intellectual vices were deliberately inculcated as virtues. It was a sin to doubt the opinions that had been instilled in childhood before they had

---

[1] H. Rashdall, *The Idea of Atonement in Christian Theology* (London, 1919), p. 429.
[2] *1 Corinthians* iii. 19.
[3] Lactantius, *Divinæ institutiones*, iii. 3, etc.
[4] Thomas Aquinas, *op. cit.* ii.–ii. 167. 1.
[5] H. von Eicken, *op. cit.* p. 591 *sqq.*   [6] *Colossians* ii. 8.
[7] Thomas Aquinas, *op. cit.* ii.–ii. 187. 1. 3.

been examined. It was a virtue to hold them with unwavering, unreasoning credulity. It was a sin to notice and develop to its full consequences every objection to those opinions, it was a virtue to stifle every objection as a suggestion of the devil. It was sinful to study with equal attention and with an indifferent mind the writings on both sides, sinful to resolve to follow the light of evidence wherever it might lead, sinful to remain poised in doubt between conflicting opinions, sinful to give only a qualified assent to indecisive arguments, sinful even to recognise the moral or intellectual excellence of opponents. In a word, there is scarcely a disposition that marks the love of abstract truth, and scarcely a rule which reason teaches as essential for its attainment, that theologians did not for centuries stigmatise as offensive to the Almighty." [1]

Lecky adds that from this frightful condition was Europe at last rescued by the intellectual influences that produced the Reformation. This may be true in a manner, but it was not the Reformation itself that marked the change. It held out no hand of welcome to awakening science; and it has been justly observed that even at a later time the divines who looked most askance at it and claimed for their statements an entire independence of modern knowledge were those who most loudly declared their allegiance to the theology of the Reformation.[2] With Luther himself reason and faith were mortal enemies : what Scripture imposes upon us was precisely what reason would bid us reject. " All the articles of our Christian faith," he writes, " which God has revealed to us in His Word are in presence of reason sheerly impossible " ; [3] and when his natural reason rebelled against the violence which orthodox faith offered to it, the revolt was ascribed to the direct agency of the devil.[4] In the middle of the seventeenth century a powerful party was rising in England who said that all learning was unfavourable to religion, and that it was sufficient for everybody to be acquainted with his mother-tongue alone.[5] Mr. Harvey asserts that the Church of the nine-teenth century lost the reputation of putting truth in the first place ; though the position is not so bad as it was when Hort could speak of " a favourable specimen of the conventional English ecclesiastical scholar, who does not willingly violate

[1] Lecky, *op. cit.* ii. 87 *sq.*   [2] Beard, *op. cit.* p. 298.
[3] Luther, 'Ausführliche Erklärung der Epistel an die Galater. 1523,' in *Sämtliche Schriften*, viii (Halle, 1742), col. 2042.
[4] *Idem*, ' Auslegung des vierzehenten funfzehenten und sechzehenten Capitels St. Johannis. 1538,' *ibid.* viii. 571.
[5] L. Twells and others, *The Lives of Dr. E. Pocock*, etc. (London, 1816), p. 176.

truth, but has never discovered that there is such a thing as truth." [1]

Nevertheless we are told, even by highly respectable writers, that the modern world owes its scientific spirit to the extreme importance which Christianity assigned to the possession of truth, of *the* truth.[2] According to Réville, " it was the orthodox intolerance of the Church in the Middle Ages which impressed on Christian society this disposition to seek truth at any price, of which the modern scientific spirit is only the application. The more importance the Church attached to the profession of the truth—to the extent even of considering involuntary error as in the highest degree a damnable crime—so much the more the sentiment of the immense value of this truth arose in the general persuasion, along with a resolve to conquer it wherever it was felt not to be possessed. How otherwise can we explain that science was not developed and has not been pursued with constancy, except in the midst of Christian societies ? " [3] This statement is a curious instance of the common tendency to attribute to the influence of the Christian religion almost anything good which may be found among Christian peoples. But surely, the patient and impartial search after hidden truth, for the sake of truth, which constitutes the essence of scientific research, is not congenial to, but the very opposite of, that ready acceptance of a revealed truth for the sake of eternal salvation, which was insisted on by the Churches. And what about that singular love of abstract knowledge which flourished in ancient Athens, where Aristotle declared it a sacred duty to prefer truth to everything else,[4] and Socrates sacrificed his life on its altar ? The modern scientific spirit is only a revival and development of a mental disposition which for ages was suppressed by the persecuting tendencies of the Church, as also—it must be added —by the extreme contempt of learning displayed by the barbarian invaders and their descendants. Even when they had settled in the countries which they had conquered, the Teutons

---

[1] Harvey, *loc. cit.* p. 403 ; *Life and Letters of F. J. A. Hort*, ii (London, 1896), p. 102.

[2] D. G. Ritchie, *Natural Rights* (London, 1895), p. 172. *Cf.* A. Kuenen, *Hibbert Lectures on National Religions and Universal Religions* (London, 1882), p. 290.

[3] A. Réville, *Prolegomena of the History of Religions* (London, 1884), p. 226.

[4] Aristotle, *Ethica Nicomachea*, i. 6. 1. Ritchie argues (*op. cit.* p. 172) that a devotion to truth as such was in the ancient world known only to a few philosophers. T. Fowler is probably more correct in saying (*Progressive Morality* [London, 1895], p. 114 ; J. M. Wilson and Fowler, *The Principles of Morals*, ii [Oxford, 1887], pp. 45, 220 *sq.*) that it was more common amongst the Greeks than amongst ourselves.

would not permit their children to be instructed in any science, for fear lest they should become effeminate and averse from war ; [1] and long afterwards it was held that a nobleman ought not to know letters, and that to write and read was a shame to gentry.[2]

Religious toleration certainly does not mean passive indifference with regard to dissenting religious ideas. The tolerant man may be a great propagandist. He may do his utmost to suppress by arguments what he considers to be a false belief. He may even favour stronger measures against those who do mischief in the name of religion. But he does not persecute anybody for the sake of his faith. Nor does he believe in an intolerant and persecuting god.

[1] Procopius, *De bello Gothorum*, i. 2 ; W. Robertson, *The History of the Reign of the Emperor Charles V.*, i (London, 1806), p. 234 ; J. G. Millingen, *The History of Duelling*, i (London, 1841), p. 22 *sq.* n. †.

[2] Alain Chartier, quoted by De la Curne de Sainte-Palaye, *Mémoires sur l'ancienne chevalerie*, ii (Paris, 1781), p. 104. See also F. De la Noüe, *Discours politiques et militaires* (Basle, 1587), p. 238 ; G. Lyttelton, *The History of the Life of King Henry the Second*, ii (London, 1767), p. 246 *sq.*

CHAPTER XVI

CHRISTIANITY AND MARRIAGE

THE founder of Christianity did not prescribe any particular ceremony in connection with marriage, but it has been assumed that the celebration of it among Christians was from the very first accompanied with suitable acts of religious worship. The testimony of the Fathers, from the middle of the third century onwards, shows that marriages contracted without any formal benediction did occur, but they were discountenanced by the Church.[1] Yet, though the dogma that marriage is a sacrament gradually developed from the words in the Epistle to the Ephesians τὸ μυστήριον τοῦτο μέγα ἐστίν,[2] in the Vulgate translated " Sacramentum hoc magnum est," and was fully recognised in the twelfth century,[3] marriage without benediction was nevertheless regarded as valid in the Church till the year 1563, when the Council of Trent decreed that thenceforth no marriage should be considered valid unless celebrated by a presence of two or three witnesses.[4]

Marriage was already instituted by God in Paradise for the propagation of the human race ; but according to Thomas Aquinas it was only raised to the position of a sacrament by Christ, inasmuch as he made it the picture of his union with the Church, thereby establishing anew its indissoluble character, and also united with marriage a saving gift.[5] It may seem strange that marriage was made a sacrament, in view of the extraordinary reverence in which virginity was held ; but as a matter of fact there was an intrinsic connection between the sanctification of marriage and the worship of virginity. By declaring marriage a sacrament the Church got some control over the *copula carnalis*, which even in marriage was not supposed to differ materially from fornication, and brought that union of the sexes under ecclesiastical jurisdiction. Moreover, it was in some measure

[1] Tertullian, *Ad uxorem*, ii. 9 ; *idem, De pudicitia*, 4.
[2] *Ephesians* v. 32.
[3] A. von Scheurl, *Das gemeine deutsche Eherecht* (Erlangen, 1882), p. 15.
[4] E. Roguin, *Traité de droit civil comparé. Le mariage* (Paris, 1904), pp. 103, 104, 128 *sqq.*
[5] Thomas Aquinas, *Summa theologica*, iii. Suppl. 41. 1, 42. 2 *sq.*

purified by the priest's " sacramental " blessing.¹ But the office of the priest was not restricted to the performance of the nuptial ceremony : according to Catholic rituals he had also to bless the bridal bed, and this was considered one of the most important of marriage rites. Thus in England, in the papal times, no marriage could be consummated until the bed had been blessed. On the evening of the wedding-day, when the married couple sat in state in the bridal bed, before the exclusion of the guests, one or more priests, attended by acolytes swinging to and fro lighted censers, appeared in the crowded chamber to bless the couch, its occupants, and the truckle-bed, and fumigate the room with hallowing incense ; ² and the parties were also sprinkled with holy water.³ The object of the ceremony was partly to bestow upon the couple a long life and progeny and other good things, but partly also to protect them against evil influences ; as appears from the formula given in the manual for the use of Salisbury, where it is said : " Benedic, Domine, thalamum istum et omnes habitantes in eo ; ut in tua pace consistant, et in tua voluntate permaneant ; et in amore tuo vivant et senescant et multiplicentur in longitudine dierum. . . . Qui custodis Israel, custodi famulos tuos in hoc lecto quiescentes *ab omnibus fantasmaticis demonum illusionibus.*" ⁴ The idea that sexual intercourse is defiling, even when practised by husband and wife, shows itself in various prescriptions relating to it which have been mentioned in an earlier chapter.⁵

The Reformers maintained that matrimonial affairs belong not to the Church, but to the jurists ; Luther called marriage a " worldly thing," and Calvin put it on the same level as house-building, farming, or shoe-making.⁶ This opinion, however, was not accepted by the legislators of the Protestant countries. Marriage certainly ceased to be thought of as a sacrament, but continued to be regarded as a divine institution ; and sacerdotal nuptials became no less obligatory on Protestants than on

¹ Thomas Aquinas, *op. cit.* iii. Suppl. 42. 1.
² J. C. Jeaffreson, *Brides and Bridals*, i (London, 1872), p. 98.
³ F. Douce, *Illustrations of Shakespeare* (London, 1839), p. 123.
⁴ *Ibid.* p. 123. In Norway the custom of the clergy blessing the bridal bed still persisted in the beginning of the seventeenth century, although formally abolished by the Reformation (T. F. Troels-Lund, *Dagligt Liv i Norden i det 16 Aarhundrede*, xi [Köbenhavn, 1904], p. 66 *sq.*). Among German Catholics it is found to this day (E. H. Meyer, *Badisches Volksleben im neunzehnten Jahrhundert* [Strassburg, 1900], p. 306 ; K. Reiser, *Sagen, Gebräuche und Sprichwörter des Allgäus*, ii [Kempten, 1894], p. 250 *sq.*).
⁵ *Supra*, p. 191 *sq.*
⁶ Havelock Ellis, *Sex in Relation to Society* (London, 1937), p. 350.

Catholics. It was the French Revolution that first gave rise to an alteration in this respect. The Constitution of September 3, 1791, declares in its seventh article, title ii : " La loi ne considère le mariage que comme contrat civil. Le pouvoir législatif établira pour tous les habitants, sans distinction, le mode par lequel les naissances, mariages et décès seront constatés et il désignera les officiers publics qui en recevront les actes." [1] To this obligatory civil act a sacerdotal benediction may be added, if the parties wish it. Since then civil marriage has gradually become widespread in the Christian world, also among Roman Catholics, although, by a papal decree of 1907, it has been declared to be not only sinful and unlawful, which it was before, but actually null and void. [2] In some countries, as in England, the parties may choose the religious or the civil rite, just as they like, both making marriage equally valid by law. [3]

The decisive external sign of the sacrament of marriage is the expressed " consensus " of the partners to the marriage. [4] Under the jurisprudence of Justinian a father could not force his son or daughter in marriage. [5] But at the same time the right of a voice in his children's marriages was stoutly maintained : the consent of the head of the family remained essential to the validity of the marriage of any one under his power, irrespective of age. [6] Canon Law also adopted the principle that no marriage can be concluded without the consent of the persons who marry ; but, unlike Justinian law, as a consequence of its doctrine that marriage is a sacrament, it ruled that, however young the bride-groom and bride may be, the consent of their parents or guardians is not necessary to make the marriage valid. [7] The Church disapproved of marriages contracted without such consent : the lack of it was a " prohibitory impediment " (impedimentum impediens) rendering the marriage illicit, but not a " diriment impediment " (impedimentum dirimens) rendering it null and void. [8] The stipulations of Canon Law influenced secular

[1] E. Glasson, Le mariage civil et le divorce (Paris, 1880), p. 253 ; Roguin, op. cit. p. 140 sq.

[2] Ellis, op. cit. p. 345 n. 1.

[3] See Roguin, op. cit. p. 141 sqq. ; Glasson, op. cit. p. 282.

[4] Thomas Aquinas, op. cit. iii. 42. 1.

[5] Codex Justinianus, v. 4. 14 ; Digesta, xxiii. 2. 21. Cf. W. A. Hunter, A Systematical and Historical Exposition of Roman Law (London, 1903), p. 680.

[6] O. Karlowa, Römische Rechtsgeschichte, ii (Leipzig, 1901), p. 174 ; Hunter, op. cit. p. 680.

[7] Gratian, Decretum, ii. 27. 2. 2.

[8] E. Friedberg, Lehrbuch des katholischen und evangelischen Kirchenrechts (Leipzig, 1909), p. 422 ; A. Winroth, Offentlig rätt. Familjerätt : Äktenskapshindren (Lund, 1890), p. 52.

legislation. An edict of Clothaire I. in 560 prohibited the forcing of women to marry against their will.[1] According to the Laws of Cnut, no woman or girl could be compelled to marry a man whom she disliked.[2] In an Anglo-Saxon betrothal formula from the tenth century the girl's consent is unconditionally required.[3] And various early Teutonic law-books in continental countries likewise prohibited the forcing of a woman into marriage against her will.[4]

As to the canonical prescription that a marriage is valid without the consent of parents or guardians, it seems that the English temporal law more or less acquiesced in it, although it regarded " wardship and marriage " as a valuable piece of property.[5] In England, by the common law, the marriages of minors who had attained the age of consent—fixed at fourteen years for males and twelve years for females—were valid without the consent of parents until the year 1753, when Lord Hardwicke's Marriage Act (26 Geo. 2, c. 33, 11) declared such marriages void.[6] According to the present law of England, " where a person, not being a widower nor widow, is under the age of twenty-one years, the father, if living, or, if he is dead, the guardian or guardians, or one of them, or if there is no guardian lawfully appointed, then the mother, if she has not remarried, has authority to consent to his or her marriage ; and such consent is required except where there is no person having authority to give it." [7] Yet the marriage of a minor without the requisite consent is not invalid, whether it is by banns or licence or superintendent registrar's certificate ; but there may be forfeiture of all the rights and interest in any property accruing to the offending party by force of the marriage.[8] In Scotland, on the other hand, no consent of parents or guardian

---

[1] J. M. Pardessus, *Loi Salique* (Paris, 1843), p. 666.

[2] *Laws of Cnut*, ii. 75.

[3] F. Roeder, *Die Familie bei den Angelsachsen* (Halle a. S., 1899), p. 24 *sq.*

[4] J. J. Nordström, *Bidrag till den svenska samhälls-författningens historia*, ii (Helsingfors, 1840), p. 15 *sq.* ; W. E. Wilda, *Das Strafrecht der Germanen* (Halle, 1842), p. 803 ; K. Weinhold, *Die deutschen Frauen in dem Mittelalter*, i (Wien, 1882), p. 304 ; Winroth, *op. cit.* p. 55 *sq.* ; J. M. Ludlow, ' Consent to Marriage,' in W. Smith and S. Cheetham, *A Dictionary of Christian Antiquities*, i (London, 1875), p. 434 *sq.*

[5] F. Pollock and F. W. Maitland, *The History of the English Law before the Time of Edward I.*, ii (Cambridge, 1898), p. 389. *Cf.*, however, Roeder, *op. cit.* p. 25.

[6] W. Blackstone, *The Commentaries on the Laws of England*, i (London, 1876), p. 408 *sq.*

[7] Earl of Halsbury, *The Laws of England*, xvi (London, 1911), p. 296.

[8] *Ibid.* xvi. 297 *sq.*

is required even for minors who have attained the age of puberty ; [1] and by the common law of the United States, which was not affected by Lord Hardwicke's Marriage Act, the marriage of minors without the parental consent is likewise good. There are " statutes which forbid the celebration of the nuptials of minors without permission from the parent or guardian ; but, in the absence of a clause of nullity, which most of them do not contain, a marriage in disobedience is valid, while yet the participators in it may be subject to a penalty or punishment." [2]

In the later Middle Ages German women were able to marry without parental consent, though at the risk of being disinherited.[3] The ' Schwabenspiegel,' which is a faithful echo of canonical ideas, says that when a young man has completed his fourteenth year he can take a wife without the consent of his father, that a maiden is marriageable at twelve years, and that her marriage subsists even if contracted in spite of her father or other relatives.[4] But the feelings of the people seemed to have been opposed to such a marriage and required the consent of parents. Ulrich von Lichtenstein says in his ' Frauenbuch ' : " A girl who has no parents should follow the advice of her kinsfolk ; if she gives herself to a man of her own accord, she may live with shame." [5] Attempts were made to induce the Church to change its law on the subject, but in vain ; the matter was definitely settled at the Council of Trent, after a lively discussion.[6] Luther and other Reformers were of a different opinion : they maintained that a marriage contracted without the consent of parents should be regarded as invalid, unless the consent was given afterwards.[7] This principle was gradually accepted by most legislators in Protestant countries, but with the modification that parental consent could be refused for good

---

[1] J. Erskine of Carnock, *Principles of the Law of Scotland*, ed. by J. Rankine (Edinburgh, 1890), p. 61.

[2] J. P. Bishop, *New Commentaries on Marriage, Divorce, and Separation*, i (Chicago, 1891), p. 239 *sq.*

[3] W. T. Kraut, *Die Vormundschaft nach den Grundsätzen des deutschen Rechts*, i (Göttingen, 1835), p. 326 ; R. Schroeder, *Lehrbuch der deutschen Rechtsgeschichte* (Leipzig, 1902), p. 733 ; R. Sohm, *Das Recht der Eheschliessung aus dem deutschen und canonischen Recht geschichtlich entwickelt* (Weimar, 1875), p. 51 *sq.* ; E. Friedberg, *Das Recht der Eheschliessung in seiner geschichtlichen Entwicklung* (Leipzig, 1865), p. 104 *sq.*

[4] *Der Schwabenspiegel*, Landrecht (Tübingen, 1840), § 55.

[5] Weinhold, *op. cit.* i. 305.

[6] Friedberg, *Das Recht der Eheschliessung*, p. 122 *sq.* ; Winroth, *op. cit.* p. 52 *sq.*

[7] H. Colberg, *Ueber das Ehehinderniss der Entführung* (Halle, 1869), p. 114 *sqq.* ; Friedberg, *Das Recht der Eheschliessung*, p. 105 *sq.* ; *idem*, *Lehrbuch des katholischen und evangelischen Kirchenrechts*, p. 422 *sq.*

reasons only and, in case of need, the consent of the authorities could take its place.[1]

In Catholic countries, also, the canonical doctrine met with opposition ; legislators declared parental consent to be necessary for the validity of a marriage, and no appeal could be made in the case of refusal.[2]   In France and other Latin countries the Roman notions of parental rights and filial duties left behind traces which lasted throughout the Middle Ages and long after. Bodin wrote, in the latter part of the sixteenth century, that although the monarch commands his subjects, the master his disciples, the captain his soldiers, there is none to whom nature has given any command except the father, "who is the true image of the great sovereign God, universal father of all things." [3] Henry II. of France decreed, in 1556, that a marriage contracted by a minor without the consent of ascendants was null and void ; and the later legislation went further in the same direction.   If a marriage was contracted without such consent by a person who was below the age of twenty-five, it was annulled ; if contracted by a person between twenty-five and thirty, it was valid, but disinheritance might be the consequence ; and if contracted by a person above the age of thirty, it had still to be notified to the ascendant by " three respectful acts." [4]   Indeed, according to the French ' Code Civil,' a son under twenty-five and a daughter under twenty-one could not, until 1907, marry without parental consent.[5]   According to the present law of France, a son and daughter under the age of twenty-one cannot marry without the consent of the father and mother, or of the father only if they disagree, or of the survivor if one be dead.   If both father and mother are dead, or in a condition which renders them unable to consent, the grandparents take their place.   Between the ages of twenty-one and thirty the parties must still obtain parental consent, but if this be refused it can be regulated by means of an act before a notary, and if the consent is not given within thirty days the marriage can take place without it.[6]   In Italy the consent of parents, or of the father, or of the survivor if one of the parents is dead, is required for a son who has not completed his twenty-fifth year and for a daughter who has not completed

---

[1] Colberg, *op. cit.* p. 121 ; Friedberg, *Das Recht der Eheschliessung*, p. 106 ; Sohm, *op. cit.* p. 206 *sq.* n. 16.

[2] *Cf.* Winroth, *op. cit.* p. 53.

[3] J. Bodin, *De Republica* (Ursellis, 1601), i. 4, p. 31.

[4] J.-E. Guétat, *Histoire élémentaire du droit français* (Paris, 1884), p. 364 *sq.*

[5] *Code civil*, art. 148.

[6] *Ibid.* arts. 148–51, 154.

her twenty-first; but in case of refusal of consent provision is made for an appeal to court.[1]

The Justinian principle that a father cannot force his child in marriage has been universally adopted in Christian countries, but, as we have just seen, not the canonical rule that the consent of the persons who contract a marriage is always sufficient to make it valid. The value of this concession was much reduced by the fact that the Church adopted the stipulation of the Roman law concerning the lowest age at which a person was allowed to marry—fourteen years for a man and twelve for a woman. This regulation is still in force in Great Britain, in some of the United States, and in several Roman Catholic countries; but the general tendency of the later legislation has been to raise the age-limit, which may even be as high as twenty-one for men and eighteen for women. In many countries, however, where the canonic age-limit has not been preserved, the obstacle to marrying at an earlier age than that which the law admits may be removed by dispensation.[2]

Under the influence of the ascetic ideas prevalent in the Church the degrees of relationship within which no marriage was allowed were greatly extended. In the Eastern Church marriage was prohibited within the seventh degree according to the Roman method of computing degrees of relationship, which was to count from one of the parties up to a common ancestor and then down to the other party, so that, for example, first cousins were held to be related in the fourth degree and uncle and niece in the third. This rule is still in force in the Eastern Church.[3] The Western Church went still farther in her prohibitions. The forbidden degrees became gradually as many as seven according to the new Western reckoning, or "canonical computation," by which seven degrees were practically equivalent to seven generations; brother and sister were related in the first degree, first cousins in the second degree, second cousins in the third degree, and similarly beyond.[4] The seventh degree seems to have been chosen by rigorous theorists who would have forbidden a marriage between kinsfolk however remote; for it seems to have been a common rule among the Teutonic peoples that for the

---

[1] *Codice civile del regno d'Italia,* §§ 63, 67.

[2] E. Westermarck, *The History of Human Marriage,* i (London, 1921), p. 387 *sq.*

[3] J. Zhishman, *Das Eherecht der Orientalischen Kirche* (Wien, 1863), p. 241 *sqq.* For the reckoning of degrees see *ibid.* p. 217 *sqq.*

[4] J. Freisen, *Geschichte des Canonischen Eherechts bis zum Verfall der Glossenlitteratur* (Tübingen, 1888), p. 393 *sqq.*; O. D. Watkins, *Holy Matrimony* (London, 1895), p. 702 *sq.* For the canonical computation see Freisen, p. 423 *sqq.*

purposes of inheritance kinship could not be traced beyond the seventh generation, and so to prohibit marriage within seven degrees was to prohibit it among all persons who for any legal purpose could claim blood-relationship with each other.[1] The fourth Lateran Council, held A.D. 1215 under Innocent III., reduced the prohibited degrees from seven to four, that is, marriage was permitted beyond the degree of third cousins ; [2] and since then there has been no change.[3] The forbidden degrees of the Western Church thus almost coincide with those of the Eastern Church, the fourth degree of canonical computation corresponding to the seventh and eighth degrees of the Roman reckoning.[4] But there is this important difference between the legislation of the two Churches, that in the Eastern Church no dispensation is held possible from any of the prohibited degrees,[5] whereas in the West dispensation is not only allowed but has since early times been practised on a very large scale. It does not seem, however, that the field of the Levitical prohibitions was entered upon by the papal dispensing claims till the fifteenth century.[6]

The Reformers went in principle back to the prohibited degrees of the Mosaic law.[7] Henry VIII. declared in 1540 that nothing, " God's law except, shall trouble or impeach any marriage without the Levitical degrees " ; as the farthest of which was considered that between uncle and niece.[8] In Catholic countries also the ecclesiastical law of prohibited degrees has ceased to be recognised by the legislators. The prohibition of marriage between cousins is a late survival of it in a few law-books, unless it has been removed quite recently.[9] The Catholic Church forbids marriage with a deceased wife's sister, though the prohibition may be dispensed with.[10] In England such marriages were condemned by the canon law of the English Church, and their illegality was confirmed in 1835 ; [11] and, as is well known, it was only after many futile attempts and in the face of very strong opposition that an Act legalising marriage with a

---

[1] Pollock and Maitland, op. cit. ii. 387 sq. ; Winroth, op. cit. p. 181.
[2] Concilium Lateranense IV., ch. 50 (Labbe-Mansi, Sacrorum Conciliorum collectio, xxii. 1037 sq.).
[3] Freisen, op. cit. p. 405.   [4] Cf. Zhishman, op. cit. p. 253.
[5] Ibid. p. 713.   [6] Watkins, op. cit. p. 704.
[7] A. von Scheurl and E. Sehling, ' Eherecht,' in J. J. Herzog, Realencyklopädie für protestantische Theologie und Kirche, ed. by A. Hauck, v (Leipzig, 1898), p. 210 ; Winroth, op. cit. p. 186.
[8] H. J. Stephen, New Commentaries on the Laws of England, ii (London, 1914), p. 386.
[9] Westermarck, op. cit. ii. 101.
[10] Roguin, op. cit. p. 87 sq.   [11] Ibid. p. 88.

deceased wife's sister in the United Kingdom was passed in 1907.[1] Marriage with a deceased brother's widow was also prohibited by Canon Law,[2] and is prohibited by the laws of many, especially Latin, countries although dispensation is easily obtained.[3]

The Church not only encumbered marriage with all those prohibitions on the ground of kinship, but introduced a new obstacle to it by establishing the so-called *cognatio spiritualis*, or " spiritual relationship." The Emperor Justinian passed a law forbidding a man to marry a woman for whom he had stood godfather in baptism, the tie of the godfather and godchild being so analogous to that of father and child as to make such a marriage appear improper.[4] To this law the Church added various other prohibitions on account of spiritual relationship, for instance, against marriage between the minister of the sacrament and the person baptised and that person's parents as well, between a godfather and a sister of the godchild, between two sponsors, and between a sponsor and the child of another sponsor born after the act of baptism. Similar impediments arose from relationships created by confirmation.[5]

In addition to these prohibitions difference of religion was made a bar to intermarriage. As according to the law of the Talmud and the Rabbinical code a Jew could not marry a Christian,[6] so also were marriages between Jews and Christians forbidden by the latter—by Constantine and later emperors and by various Councils ; and during the Middle Ages they were universally avoided.[7] Indeed, owing to the intense Jewish hatred for the sacred name of Christ, the early Church was more opposed to wedlock with Jews than with pagans. Although Paul indicates that a Christian must not marry a heathen,[8] and

---

[1] Earl of Halsbury, *op. cit.* xvi. 284.

[2] Roguin, *op. cit.* p. 87 *sq.*

[3] *Ibid.* p. 88 ; Winroth, *op. cit.* p. 206.

[4] *Codex Justinianus*, v. 4. 26.

[5] For prohibitions on account of spiritual relationship see Freisen, *op. cit.* p. 508 *sqq.* ; Zhishman, *op. cit.* p. 265 *sqq.* ; Watkins, *op. cit.* p. 700 *sqq.* ; A. Boudinhon, ' Impediments, Canonical,' in *The Catholic Encyclopedia*, vii (New York, 1910), p. 697 ; Winroth, *op. cit.* p. 183.

[6] M. Mielziner, *The Jewish Law of Marriage and Divorce in Ancient and Modern Times* (Cincinnati, 1884), p. 45 *sq.*

[7] *Ibid.* p. 46 n. 6 ; K. Kohler, ' Intermarriage,' in *Jewish Encyclopedia*, vi (New York and London, *s.d.*), p. 611 ; L. Löw, *Gesammelte Schriften*, iii (Szegedin, 1893), p. 175 ; R. Andree, *Zur Volkskunde der Juden* (Bielefeld and Leipzig, 1881), p. 48 ; A. Neubauer, ' Notes on the Race-Types of the Jews,' in *The Journal of the Anthropological Institute*, xv (London, 1886), p. 19.

[8] 1 *Corinthians* vii. 39.

Tertullian calls such an alliance fornication,[1] the Church, in early times, often even encouraged marriages of this sort as a means of propagating Christianity ; and it was only when its success was certain that it actually prohibited them.[2]   When the 'Decretum' of Gratian was published, in the twelfth century, the impediment *disparitas cultus* became part of the Canon Law of the Church,[3] and from that time forward all marriages contracted between Catholics and infidels were held to be invalid unless a dispensation had been obtained from the ecclesiastical authority.   Marriages between Catholics and heretics, on the other hand, were considered valid, though illicit if a dispensation *mixtæ religionis* had not been obtained ; but there had been much opposition to such unions from early times, and various Councils had legislated against them.   The Council of Trent declared all matrimonial unions between Catholics and non-Catholics null and void, unless entered into before the ecclesiastical authority ; but by degrees the Popes felt constrained to make various concessions for mixed marriages.   " The Church," says Taunton, " has always abhorred these marriages both on account of the danger of perversion and the difficulty of educating the offspring, as well as on account of the *communicatio in sacris*." [4]   The Protestants also originally forbade them.[5]   But mixed marriages are not now contrary to the civil law either in Roman Catholic or Protestant countries.   The case is, or has been, different in countries belonging to the Greek Church, where the ecclesiastical restrictions were adopted by the State. The Eastern Church declared marriages between Catholics and heretics null and void, and has also shown herself opposed to marriages with members of the Roman Church ; and in Russia various laws were passed ordering that such marriages be not permitted unless the children of the union were to be brought up in the Orthodox faith.[6]

It has been asserted that Jesus " definitely condemned polygamy," [7] and was unusually explicit " in his insistence that marriage should be monogamous." [8]   Such conclusions have been drawn from the saying that a man who puts away his wife and marries another commits adultery.   But in 1 Timothy it is

---

[1] Tertullian, *Ad uxorem*, ii. 3.   [2] Winroth, *op. cit.* p. 212.
[3] Gratian, *Decretum*, ii. 28. 1. 1.
[4] E. Taunton, *The Law of the Church* (London, 1906), p. 439.
[5] Von Scheurl and Sehling, *loc. cit.* p. 211.
[6] Zhishman, *op. cit.* p. 519 *sqq.* ; W. Fanning, ' Marriage, Mixed,' in *The Catholic Encyclopedia*, ix (New York, 1910), p. 698 *sq.* ; Winroth, *op. cit.* p. 213 *sqq.*
[7] H. H. Henson, *Christian Morality* (Oxford, 1936), p. 203.
[8] E. W. Hirst, *Jesus and the Moralists* (London, 1935), p. 14.

said that a bishop and a deacon must be " the husband of one wife," [1] which seems to suggest that polygamy was not actually held unlawful for other Christians and occasionally occurred among them, though no doubt monogamy was assumed as the normal and ideal form of marriage. That injunction, however, has been interpreted as a prohibition of contracting a second marriage by persons who had been married before ; and, as we have seen, such marriages were actually held objectionable even if contracted by the laity.[2] Augustine points out that among the ancient fathers it was lawful for the husband of a barren wife to take another woman that from her might be born sons common to both, and adds that he would not hastily pronounce whether it still was lawful for him to do so, with the good will of the wife.[3] It has been argued that it was not necessary for the first Christian teachers to condemn polygamy because monogamy was the universal rule among the peoples in whose midst they were preaching ; but this is certainly not true of the Jews, who still both permitted and practised polygamy in the beginning of the Christian era. Some of the Fathers accused the Jewish rabbis of sensuality ; [4] but no Council of the Church in the earliest centuries opposed polygamy, and no obstacle was put in the way of its practice by kings in countries where it had occurred in the times of paganism. In the middle of the sixth century Diarmait, king of Ireland, had two queens and two concubines.[5] Polygamy was frequently practised by the Merovingian kings. Charlemagne had two wives and many concubines ; and one of his laws seems to imply that polygamy was not unknown even among priests.[6] This, of course, does not mean that such a practice was recognised by the Church ; nor must the permissions granted to kings be taken as evidence of her rules, for, as the Council of Constantinople decided in 809, " Divine law can do nothing against Kings." [7] Yet in the earlier part of the Middle Ages the strenuous general rule of monogamy was relaxed in certain exceptional circumstances, as

[1] *1 Timothy* iii. 2, 12.
[2] *Supra*, p. 182.
[3] Augustine, *De bono conjugali*, 15.
[4] S. Krauss, *Talmudische Archäologie*, ii (Leipzig, 1911), p. 28.
[5] H. d'Arbois de Jubainville, *Cours de littérature celtique*, vi (Paris, 1899), p. 292.
[6] A. Thierry, *Narratives of the Merovingian Era* (London, 1845), p. 17 *sqq.* ; F. von Hellwald, *Die menschliche Familie* (Leipzig, 1889), p. 558 n. 1 ; H. Hallam, *View of the State of Europe during the Middle Ages*, i (Paris, 1840), p. 420 n. 2.
[7] W. Smith and S. Cheetham, *A Dictionary of Christian Antiquities*, i (London, 1875), p. 207.

in cases of sexual impotency and of enforced or voluntary desertion.[1]

In later times Philip of Hesse and Frederick William II. of Prussia contracted bigamous marriages with the sanction of the Lutheran clergy.[2] Luther himself approved of the bigamy of the former, and so did Melanchthon.[3] On various occasions Luther speaks of polygamy with considerable toleration. It had not been forbidden by God ; even Abraham, who was a " perfect Christian," had two wives. God had allowed such marriages to certain men of the Old Testament in particular circumstances, and if a Christian wanted to follow their example he had to show that the circumstances were similar in his case ; [4] but polygamy was undoubtedly preferable to divorce.[5] In 1650, soon after the Peace of Westphalia, when the population had been greatly reduced by the Thirty Years War, the Frankish *Kreistag* at Nuremberg passed the resolution that thenceforth every man should be allowed to marry two women.[6] Certain Christian sects have even advocated polygamy with much fervour. In 1531 the Anabaptists openly preached at Munster that he who wants to be a true Christian must have several wives.[7] Among the Mormons the duty of polygamy, when economic resources permitted, was urged upon men, both as a means of securing eternal salvation and as a step in harmony with their earthly interest. Group-marriage or, as it was called, " complex marriage " was practised by the Oneida Community in Madison county, New York, which was established in 1848 by John Humphrey Noyes and consisted mostly of New England Puritans. All the men within the community were the actual or potential husbands of all the women ; and this community of wives was based on Noyes' interpretation of certain passages of the New Testament, though he also appealed to the law of nature in support of it.[8]

In no case was it Christianity that first introduced obligatory monogamy into Europe. There can be little doubt that monogamy was the only recognised form of marriage in Greece. Concubinage existed at Athens at all times, and was hardly censured by public opinion, but it was well distinguished from

---

[1] H. Ellis, *Studies in the Psychology of Sex*, vi (Philadelphia, 1923), p. 499.

[2] Friedberg, *Lehrbuch des katholischen und evangelischen Kirchenrechts*, p. 436, note to § 143.

[3] J. Köstlin, *Martin Luther*, ii (Berlin, 1903), p. 475 *sqq.*

[4] *Ibid.* i. 693 *sq.*   [5] *Ibid.* i. 347, ii. 257.

[6] Von Hellwald, *op. cit.* p. 559 n.   [7] *Ibid.* p. 558 n. 1.

[8] J. H. Noyes, *History of American Socialism* (Philadelphia and London, 1870), p. 624 *sqq.*

marriage : it conferred no rights on the concubine, and the children were bastards.[1] Roman marriage was strictly monogamous. A second marriage concluded by a married person was invalid, although it was not subject to punishment during the Republic and the early Empire ; Diocletian was the first who punished bigamy.[2] Liaisons between married men and mistresses were not uncommon by the close of the Republic ; [3] but such a relation was not considered lawful in after times. According to the jurist Paulus, a man who had an *uxor* could not have a *concubina* at the same time.[4]

In ancient times the power which the Roman father possessed over his daughter was generally, if not always,[5] by marriage transferred to the husband.[6] When marrying a woman passed in *manum viri*, as a wife she was *filiæ loco*, that is, in law she was her husband's daughter.[7] And as the Roman house-father originally had the *jus vitæ necisque* over his children, the husband naturally had the same power over his wife. But from her being destitute of all legal rights we must not conclude that she was treated with indignity. On the contrary, she generally had a respected and influential position in the family ; [8] and though the husband could repudiate her at will, it was said that for five hundred and twenty years *a condita urbe* there was no such thing as a divorce in Rome.[9] As Lord Bryce points out, we cannot doubt that the wide power which the law gave to the husband " was in point of fact restrained within narrow limits, not only by affection, but also by the vigilant public opinion of a comparatively small community." [10] Gradually, however, marriage with *manus* fell into disuse, and was, under the Empire, generally superseded by marriage without *manus*, a form of wedlock which conferred on the husband scarcely any authority at all over his wife. Instead of passing into his power, she remained in the power of her father ; and since the tendency of the later law was to reduce the old *patria potestas* to a nullity, she became prac-

---

[1] Westermarck, *op. cit.* iii. 48 *sq.*

[2] T. Mommsen, *Römisches Strafrecht* (Leipzig, 1899), p. 701.

[3] Cicero, *De oratore*, i. 40, § 183.

[4] *Digesta*, i. 16. 144.

[5] A. Rossbach, *Untersuchungen über die römische Ehe* (Stuttgart, 1853), p. 64 ; H. S. Maine, *Ancient Law* (London, 1885), p. 155.

[6] Or, properly speaking, to the husband's father, if he was alive.

[7] B. W. Leist, *Alt-arisches Jus Civile*, i (Jena, 1892), p. 175.

[8] Rossbach, *op. cit.* pp. 36, 117.

[9] Valerius Maximus, ii. 1 (*De matrimoniorum ritu*), 4 ; Aulus Gellius, *Noctes Atticæ*, iv. 3. 1.

[10] Lord Bryce, *Studies in History and Jurisprudence*, ii (Oxford, 1901), p. 389.

tically independent.[1] She could bring an action against others and, with some limitations, against her husband also. She could hold property and dispose of it freely—a very considerable portion of Roman wealth thus passed into the uncontrolled possession of women ; and the tyranny exercised by rich wives over their husbands—to whom it is said they sometimes lent money at high interest—was a continual theme of satirists.[2]

This remarkable liberty granted to married women was not agreeable to the opinion which the new religion held about the female sex. The Hebrews represented woman as the source of evil and death on earth—" Of the woman came the beginning of sin, and through her we all die " ; [3] and this notion passed into Christianity—" Adam was not deceived, but the woman being deceived was in the transgression." [4] Tertullian maintains that a woman should go about in humble garb, mourning and repentant, in order to expiate that which she derives from Eve, the ignominy of the first sin, and the odium attaching to her as the cause of human perdition. " Do you not know," he exclaims, " that you are each an Eve ? The sentence of God on this sex of yours lives in this age ; the guilt must of necessity live too. You are the devil's gateway ; you are the unsealer of that [forbidden] tree ; you are the first deserter of the divine law ; you are she who persuaded him whom the devil was not valiant enough to attack. You destroyed so easily God's image, man. On account of your desert—that is, death—even the Son of God had to die." [5] In the ' Testament ' of Reuben, one of the " twelve Patriarchs," it is said : " Evil are women. . . . Women are overcome by the spirit of fornication more than men, and in their heat they plot against men ; and by means of their adornment they deceive first their minds, and by the glance of the eye instil the poison, and then through the accomplished act they take them captive. . . . If you wish to be pure in mind, guard your senses from every woman." [6] According to Gregory Thaumaturgus, " a person may find one man chaste among a thousand, but a woman never." [7] At the Council of Mâcon, in 585, a bishop expressed the opinion that woman had no soul ;

---

[1] Rossbach, *op. cit.* pp. 30, 42 ; Maine, *op. cit.* p. 155 *sq.* ; L. Friedländer, *Darstellungen aus der Sittengeschichte Roms*, i (Leipzig, 1881), p. 418 *sqq.*

[2] F. Girard, *Manuel élémentaire du droit romain* (Paris, 1898), p. 160 *sq.*

[3] *Ecclesiasticus* xxv. 24.   [4] *1 Timothy* ii. 14.

[5] Tertullian, *De cultu feminarum*, i. 1.

[6] ' The Testament of Reuben,' 5 *sq.*, in R. H. Charles, *The Testaments of the Twelve Patriarchs* (London, 1917), p. 28 *sq.*

[7] Gregory Thaumaturgus, *Metaphrasis in Ecclesiasten*, vii. 28 (Migne, *Patrologiæ cursus, Ser. Græca*, x. 1007 *sq.*).

but he was corrected by his colleagues.[1] Some Fathers of the Church, however, were careful to emphasise that womanhood only belongs to this earthly existence, and that on the day of resurrection all women will appear in the shape of sexless beings.[2]

On account of their uncleanness women were excluded from sacred functions, in striking contrast with both heathen and heretical practice. In the early Church, it is true, there were " deaconesses " and clerical " widows," but their offices were merely to perform some inferior services of the church,[3] and even these very modest posts were open only to virgins or widows of a considerable age.[4] Whilst a layman could in case of necessity administer baptism, a woman could never, as it seems, perform such an act.[5] Nor was a woman allowed to preach publicly in the church, either by the Apostle's rules or those of succeeding ages,[6] and it was a serious complaint against certain heretics that they allowed such a practice. " The heretic women," Tertullian exclaims, " how wanton are they ! they who dare to teach, to dispute, to practise exorcisms, to promise cures, perchance, also, to baptise " ![7] A Council held at Auxerre at the end of the sixth century forbade women to receive the Eucharist into their naked hands ;[8] and in various canons women were enjoined not to come near to the altar while mass was celebrating.[9] To such an extent was this opposition against women carried that the Church of the Middle Ages did not hesitate to provide herself with eunuchs in order to supply cathedral choirs with the soprano tones inhering by nature in women alone.

The low opinion held about women affected also their social

---

[1] Gregory of Tours, *Historia Francorum*, viii. 20.

[2] Hilary, *Commentarius in Matthæum*, xxiii. 4 (Migne, *Patrologiæ Cursus*, ix. 1045 *sq.*) ; Basil, *Homilia in Psalmum CXIV*. 5 (*ibid. Ser. Græca*, xxix. 492).

[3] L. Zscharnack, *Der Dienst der Frau in den ersten Jahrhunderten der christlichen Kirche* (Göttingen, 1902), p. 99 *sqq.* ; C. Robinson, *The Ministry of Deaconesses* (London, 1898), *passim*.

[4] Robinson, *op. cit.* pp. 113, 114, 125.

[5] J. Bingham, *Works*, iv (Oxford, 1855), p. 45 ; Zscharnack, *op. cit.* p. 93.

[6] Bingham, *op. cit.* v. 107 *sqq.* ; Zscharnack, *op. cit.* p. 73 *sqq.*

[7] Tertullian, *De præscriptionibus adversus hæreticos*, 41. Cf. *idem*, *De baptismo*, 17.

[8] *Concilium Autisiodorense*, A.D. 578, can. 36 (Labbe-Mansi, *Sacrorum Conciliorum collectio*, ix. 915).

[9] *Canones Concilii Laodiceni*, 44 (Labbe-Mansi, ii. 581, 589) ; *Epitome canonum, quam Hadrianus I. Carolo Magno obtulit*, A.D. DCCLXXIII., in Labbe-Mansi, xii. 868 ; *Canons enacted under King Edgar*, 44, in *Ancient Laws and Institutes of England* (London, 1840), p. 399.

status. Paul's saying that among those who have been baptised into Christ and put on Christ there is neither male nor female, all being the children of God by faith,[1] did not imply that they were equal in this world. As the head of every man is Christ and the head of Christ is God, so is the man the head of the woman ; and as the man is the image and glory of God, so is the woman the glory of the man. " For the man is not of the woman ; but the woman of the man. Neither was the man created for the woman ; but the woman for the man. For this cause ought the woman to have power on her head." [2] While husbands should love their wives and not be bitter against them, wives should submit themselves to their husbands, " as it is fit in the Lord." [3] In support of the former rule the Epistle to the Ephesians appeals to the husband's love of himself : men ought to love their wives " as their own bodies. He that loveth his wife loveth himself. For no man ever yet hated his own flesh ; but nourisheth and cherisheth it." [4] Augustine says that a good *mater familias* must not be ashamed to call herself her husband's servant (*ancilla*).[5] Principal Donaldson observes that, although the woman has been continually said to owe her present high position to Christianity, as well as to the influence of the Teutonic mind, an examination of the facts has led him to the opinion that there was no sign of this revolution in the first three centuries of the Christian era, and that the position of women among Christians was lower, and the notions in regard to them were more degraded, than they were in the first.[6]

The latest Roman law, so far as it is touched by the Constitutions of the Christian emperors, already bears some marks of a reaction against the liberal doctrines of the great Antonine jurisconsults, who assumed the equality of the sexes as a principle of their code of equity.[7] This tendency was supported by Teutonic custom and law. Among the Teutons a husband's authority over his wife was the same as a father's over his unmarried daughter,[8] and gave him in certain circumstances a right to kill or sell his wife.[9] It certainly contained more than

---

[1] *Galatians*, iii. 27 *sq.*　　[2] *1 Corinthians* xi. 3, 7-10.
[3] *Colossians* iii. 18 *sq.*　　[4] *Ephesians* v. 28 *sq.*
[5] Augustine, *Sermo XXXVII.* 6.
[6] J. Donaldson, *Woman* (London, 1907), p. 148.
[7] Maine, *op. cit.* pp. 154, 156.
[8] H. Brunner, *Deutsche Rechtsgeschichte*, i (Leipzig, 1887), p. 75 ; C. L. E. Stemann, *Den danske retshistorie indtil Christian V.'s Lov* (Kjöbenhavn, 1871), p. 323.
[9] J. Grimm, *Deutsche Rechtsalterthümer* (Leipzig, 1899), p. 450 *sq.* ; Brunner, *op. cit.* i. 75 ; R. Schröder, *Lehrbuch der deutschen Rechtsgeschichte* (Leipzig, 1898), p. 303.

the Church could approve of; but she is all the same largely responsible for those heavy disabilities with regard to personal liberty, as well as with regard to property, from which married women have suffered up to quite recent times. The systems, says Sir Henry Maine, "which are least indulgent to married women are invariably those which have followed the Canon Law exclusively, or those which, from the lateness of their contact with European civilisation, have never had their archaisms weeded out." [1]

Nor did the Reformers improve the position of married women. In agreement with the dictum of Paul, an extensive masculine domination of a patriarchal kind belongs to the very essence of Lutheranism, which looks upon the physical superiority of man as the expression of a superior relationship willed by God. The house-father represents the law; he is the bread-winner, the pastor, and the priest of his household. By submission to her husband the wife atones for Eve's transgression, although she ought to be considered on a level with him so far as religion is concerned.[2] In England, where from the Norman Conquest onwards the unmarried woman, on attaining her majority, became fully equipped with legal and civil rights,[3] the wife remained in every respect subject to her husband. Blackstone wrote: "The very being or legal existence of the woman is suspended during the marriage, or at least is incorporated and consolidated into that of the husband: under whose wing, protection and cover, she performs every thing. . . . For this reason, a man cannot grant any thing to his wife, or enter into covenant with her: for the grant would be to suppose her separate existence, and to covenant with her would be only to covenant with himself." He is bound to provide her with necessaries, but for anything besides necessaries he is not chargeable. If she be injured in her person or property, she can bring no action for redress without his concurrence, neither can she be sued without making him a defendant. In criminal persecutions she may be indicted and punished separately, but she is considered as acting under his orders, and in some felonies (though not treason or murder) she is excused, if acting under his constraint. "The husband also (by the old law) might give his wife moderate correction. For, as he is to answer for her misbehaviour, the law thought it reasonable to intrust him with the power of restraining her, by domestic chastisement, in the same modera-

---

[1] Maine, *op. cit.* p. 159.
[2] E. Troeltsch, *The Social Teaching of the Christian Church* (London and New York, 1931), p. 546.
[3] Pollock and Maitland, *op. cit.* ii. 435.

tion that a man is allowed to correct his servants or children. . . .
But, with us, in the politer reign of Charles II., this power of
correction began to be doubted : and a wife may now have
security of the peace against her husband ; or, in return, a
husband against his wife. Yet the lower rank of people, who
were always fond of the old common law, still claim and exert
their ancient privilege : and the courts of law will still permit a
husband to restrain a wife of her liberty in case of any gross
misbehaviour." [1] Blackstone wrote two centuries after the
Reformation ; but, as I said, the reformers did not improve the
status of the wife. The influence of the Old Testament rather
tended to harden their views of the prerogatives of the husband.
This is particularly noticeable in Puritanism. Baxter published
in 1650 a book, called *The Husband's Authority Unvail'd*, in
which " it is moderately discussed whether it be fit or lawfull for
a *good man* to beat his *bad Wife*." He maintains that if wives
" cannot or will not cary, in some degree, conformable to the
Prescript and Patern of that *Weaker Vessell* set down as moulded
and framed by the holy Ghost ; they must permit their Husband,
in some proportion, to exercise that knowledge and coactive
power which God hath imparted to him " ; and " they must not
disdain a little scratch on their Body, or to be deplum'd of a
little Pride by their discreet and conscientious *Husband* for their
good." [2]

After English women had acquired personal protection from
the wife-beating husband, their property, except when protected
by settlement, still remained at the absolute disposal of their
lord and master. That protection was a privilege of the daughters of the propertied classes ; but there was literally no protection for the wife of a drunkard struggling to support her
children by the labour of her hands from the husband who should
choose to sponge upon what she earned. It was only by the
Married Women's Property Act of 1870 that such earnings were
emancipated from the husband's control. In 1882 the same
principles were applied to all property ; and the English law,
which was the most backward in Europe, became the most
forward. [3] But there have been movements in the same direction
in other countries, though the process is not yet complete.

It has thus taken nearly 2,000 years for the married woman
to get back that personal independence which she enjoyed under

[1] W. Blackstone, *Commentaries on the Laws of England*, i (Oxford,
1765), p. 430 *sqq.*
[2] Quoted by Sir Josiah Stamp, *Motive and Method in a Christian Order*
(London, 1936), p. 123 *sqq.*
[3] L. T. Hobhouse, *Morals in Evolution* (London, 1915), p. 223.

the later Roman law, but lost through the influence which Christianity exercised on European legislation.   And it may be truly said that she has regained it, not by the aid of the Churches, but despite their opposition.[1]

[1] See J. McCabe, *The Religion of Woman* (London, 1905), ch. vi, ' The Churches and the Modern Woman Movement.'

CHAPTER XVII

CHRISTIANITY AND DIVORCE

CHRISTIANITY revolutionised European legislation with regard to divorce. In pagan times Roman law was as liberal as possible so far as the husband's right to divorce his wife was concerned, and in the case of a " free " marriage, which implied that the wife did not fall under the *manus*, or power, of her husband, equally liberal with regard to the wife's right to dissolve the marriage. The dissolution of such a marriage could be brought about either by mutual agreement between both parties or by the will of one party only, and in this respect the legal position of the wife was the same as that of the husband.[1] The rules of divorce which were recognised in the case of a free marriage were afterwards extended to marriages with *manus* ; and in the end marriage with *manus* fell into disuse altogether.[2]

In the New Testament there are various passages bearing upon the question of divorce.[3] A man who puts away his wife and marries another commits adultery against her, and a woman who puts away her husband and is married to another is guilty of the same crime : " What God hath joined together, let no man put asunder." There are, however, two exceptions to this rule. Like Shammai and his school, Jesus taught, according to St. Matthew, that a man might put away his wife for fornication, which, however, has been considered to be an emendation made by the editor of the first gospel, but for no other reason ;[4] and Paul lays down the rule that if a Christian is married to an unbeliever and the latter departs, the Christian " is not under bondage." [5] But, largely under the influence of Augustine, the Western Church gradually made up her mind to deny the dissolubility of a valid Christian marriage, at least if it had been

---

[1] R. Sohm, *The Institutes* (Oxford, 1907), p. 475 *sq.* ; W. A. Hunter, *A Systematical and Historical Exposition of Roman Law* (London, 1903), p. 691.

[2] Sohm, *op. cit.* p. 476 ; Karlowa, *Römische Rechtsgeschichte*, ii (Leipzig, 1901), p. 189.

[3] *Matthew* v. 32, xix. 3 *sqq.* ; *Mark* x. 2 *sqq* ; *Luke* xvi. 18 ; *Romans* vii. 2 ; *1 Corinthians* vii. 10–15, 39.

[4] See *supra*, p. 88.

[5] *1 Corinthians* vii. 15.

consummated.[1] Her doctrine on the subject was in the twelfth century definitely fixed by Gratian and Peter Lombard ; [2] it was dogmatically asserted by the Council of Trent,[3] and was in the nineteenth century reaffirmed by Pius IX. and Leo XIII.[4] A consummated Christian marriage is a sacrament and must as such remain valid for ever. It represents the union between Christ and the Church, and is consequently as indissoluble as that union.[5] It is also permanent according to the law of nature, because only as permanent can marriage fulfil its object. And God made it so at the very beginning of our race, when He decreed [6] that a man shall leave his father and his mother and shall cleave unto his wife, and they shall be one flesh.[7]

On the other hand, a Christian marriage which has not been consummated is not indissoluble ; it is only by consummation that such a marriage becomes a sacrament and a symbol of the union between Christ and the Church.[8] The Council of Trent decreed that " matrimony contracted but not consummated " might be dissolved by " the solemn profession of religion by one of the married parties " ; [9] and it may also be dissolved for other reasons by an act of Papal authority.[10] Non-Christian marriage is not a sacrament, even though consummated ; [11] hence it is in

---

[1] E. Loening, *Geschichte des deutschen Kirchenrechts*, ii (Strassburg, 1878), p. 607 *sqq.* ; E. von Moy, *Das Eherecht der Christen in der morgen-ländischen und abendländischen Kirche bis zur Zeit Karls des Grossen* (Regensburg, 1833), p. 11 *sqq.* ; J. Freisen, *Geschichte des Canonischen Eherechts bis zum Verfall der Glossenlitteratur* (Tübingen, 1885), p. 770 *sqq.* ; A. Esmein, *Le mariage en droit canonique*, ii (Paris, 1891), p. 49 *sqq.*

[2] Esmein, *op. cit.* ii. 73 *sqq.* ; Gratian, *Decretum*, ii. 32. 7. 2 : " Nulla ratione dissolvitur conjugium, quod semel initum probatur."

[3] While the indissolubility of marriage on the ground of adultery was expressed in somewhat guarded terms (*Canones et decreta Concilii Tridentini*, sess. xxiv, can. 7) out of consideration for the Eastern Church (see Esmein, *op. cit.* ii. 305), the other causes for divorce were expressly condemned in the fifth canon, where it is said : " Si quis dixerit, propter hæresim, aut molestam cohabitationem, aut affectatam absentiam a coniuge dissolvi posse matrimonii vinculum : anathema sit." This con-demnation was particularly directed against the Protestants.

[4] Esmein, *op. cit.* ii. 307.

[5] Freisen, *op. cit.* p. 802 *sq.* ; Loening, *op. cit.* ii. 610 *sq.*

[6] *Genesis* ii. 24. [7] Esmein, *op. cit.* i. 64 *sqq.*

[8] Gratian, ii. 27. 2. 39 ; Freisen, *op. cit.* p. 802 *sq.*

[9] *Canones et decreta Concilii Tridentini*, xxiv. 6.

[10] A. Ballerini, *Opus theologicum morale*, ed. by D. Palmieri, vi (Prati, 1892), p. 367 *sq.* ; Freisen, *op. cit.* pp. 212, 213, 826 *sq.* ; F. Walter, *Lehrbuch des Kirchenrechts aller christlichen Confessionen*, ed. by H. Gerlach (Bonn, 1871), p. 714 *sq.* ; E. Friedberg, *Lehrbuch des katholischen und evangelischen Kirchenrechts* (Leipzig, 1909), p. 503.

[11] Friedberg, *op. cit.* p. 503 ; Esmein, *op. cit.* i. 222.

certain circumstances dissoluble, in accordance with Paul's dictum that a Christian married to an infidel is not under bondage if the latter depart. Innocent III. declared authoritatively that if, in the case of a marriage between two infidels, one of them became a Christian, the convert was justified in entering into another marriage, provided that either the non-Christian was unwilling to live with the other or such cohabitation would cause the blasphemy of the Divine name or be an incentive to mortal sin.[1] It was argued that this so-called *privilegium Paulinum* is no exception to the rule that Christian marriage is indissoluble, because in the case in question the marriage is dissolved not by the Christian but by the infidel, and the Church has nothing to do with the marriages of infidels.[2]

While asserting the indissolubility of a Christian marriage the Church admitted a *divortium imperfectum* or *separatio quoad thorum et mensam*, a " separation from bed and board," which discharged the parties from the duty of living together but at the same time left them husband and wife and consequently unable to marry any other person. According to the Council of Trent, such separation may take place " for many causes," either for a determinate or for an indeterminate period.[3] The chief cause is adultery or other carnal sin, equivalent to it; but Augustine had already spoken of a *fornicatio spirituale* as a ground for separation,[4] and this view was accepted by Gratian, who regarded as such apostasy,[5] heresy,[6] and incitement to evil deeds.[7] Subsequently a distinction was made between permanent and temporary separation.[8] According to some writers, perpetual separation may be granted only for *fornicatio carnalis*, unless it has been condoned or unless both parties have been guilty of it.[9] According to others, it may also be granted for defection of the faith whether by the rejection of Christianity or by heresy, and on account of entrance into religious life on the part of the wife or of the husband or by the reception of Holy Orders on the part of the husband. The cases justifying temporary separation may be summed up under the general notion of " danger to body or soul."[10]

Yet in spite of the theory of the indissolubility of Christian

[1] Ballerini, *op. cit.* vi. 325. See also Friedberg, *op. cit.* p. 503.
[2] Freisen, *op. cit.* p. 806 *sqq.*
[3] *Canones et decreta Concilii Tridentini*, xxiv. 8.
[4] Freisen, *op. cit.* p. 836. [5] Gratian, ii. 28. 1. 6.
[6] *Idem*, ii. 28. 2. 2. [7] *Idem*, ii. 28. 1. 5.
[8] Freisen, *op. cit.* p. 837.
[9] *Ibid.* p. 830 *sqq.*; Friedberg, *op. cit.* p. 508; Walter, *op. cit.* p. 716.
[10] Ballerini, *op. cit.* vi. 381 *sqq.*; A. Lehmkuhl, ' Divorce,' in *The Catholic Encyclopedia*, v (New York, 1909), p. 63 *sq.*

marriage, the Roman Catholic doctrine gives ecclesiastics a large practical power of dissolving marriages which may have appeared perfectly valid. The Church recognised a legal process which was popularly, though incorrectly, called a divorce a *vinculo matrimonii*, " from the bond of matrimony," in case the union had been unlawful from the beginning on the ground of some canonical impediment, such as relationship or earlier engagement of marriage. This only implied that a marriage which never had been valid would remain invalid ; but practically it led to the possibility of dissolving marriages which in theory were indissoluble. For, as Lord Bryce observes, " the rules regarding impediments were so numerous and so intricate that it was easy, given a sufficient motive, whether political or pecuniary, to discover some ground for declaring almost any marriage invalid." [1]

The doctrine of the Western Church influenced profoundly the secular legislation of the countries in which she was established. For a long time, however, it was not accepted in full by the legislators. The Christian emperors laid down certain grounds on which a husband could divorce his wife and a wife her husband without blame. According to Constantine, a man was allowed to dissolve the marriage if the wife was an adulteress, a preparer of poisons, or a procuress ; and the wife could do so if her husband was guilty of murder, prepared poisons, or violated tombs. [2] After some further legislation on the subject by later emperors, [3] Justinian repealed the earlier constitutions and resettled the grounds of divorce. A marriage could be dissolved for a variety of specified reasons. Thus, a man might repudiate his wife if she committed adultery, and a wife might repudiate her husband if he took a woman to live in the same house with her, or if he persisted in frequenting any other house in the same town with any woman after being warned more than once by his wife or her parents or other persons of respectability. [4] At the same time the old right of either party to dissolve the marriage at will by simple notice to the other party was not formally abolished even by the legislation of the Christian Empire ; but it was provided that when a marriage was dissolved without any statutory ground of divorce, the offending

[1] Lord Bryce, *Studies in History and Jurisprudence*, ii (Oxford, 1901), p. 434 ; W. E. H. Lecky, *Democracy and Liberty*, ii (London, 1899), p. 193 *sq.* ; F. Pollock and F. W. Maitland, *The History of the English Law before the Time of Edward I.*, ii (Cambridge, 1898), p. 393.

[2] *Codex Theodosianus*, iii. 16. 1.

[3] *Ibid.* iii. 16. 2 (Honorius and Theodosius) ; *Codex Justinianus*, v. 17. 8. 2 (Theodosius and Valentinian).

[4] *Novellæ*, cxvii. 8 *sq.*

party should suffer certain penalties. When a wife repudiated the marriage without sufficient cause she forfeited her dowry, and when the husband was the offender he was deprived of his *donatio propter nuptias,* in other words, he was required actually to pay over the *donatio* he had covenanted to pay.[1] Justinian also prohibited divorce by mutual consent—which until then seems to have taken place without any legal check whatever—except when the husband was impotent, when either he or the wife desired to enter a monastery, and when either of them was in captivity for a certain length of time.[2] Subsequently Justinian even enacted that persons dissolving a marriage by mutual consent should forfeit all their property and be confined for life in a monastery.[3] But his nephew and successor, Justin the Second, repealed his uncle's prohibitions relating to this kind of divorce.[4]

The facility of divorce by mutual consent also remained in the Roman codes of the German kings, and, as under the older Roman legislation, a man might besides divorce his wife for certain offences.[5] Those subjects of the Western rulers who elected to live under the old Teutonic systems of law seem to have had an equal facility.[6] Thus the dooms of Æthelbirht, Christian though they be, suggest that the marriage might be dissolved at the will of both parties or even at the will of one of them.[7] Even the Anglo-Saxon and Frankish penitentials allow a divorce in various cases.[8] According to Theodore's Penitential the husband may divorce an adulterous wife and marry another, and she, too, may marry again, though only after five years of penance ;[9] but a wife cannot dissolve the marriage on account of the adultery of her husband.[10] The husband may also marry another woman if the wife is carried into captivity [11] or if she deserts him, but in the latter case only after five years have elapsed and with the bishop's consent.[12] Since the days of Charlemagne, however, the canonical doctrine of the indis-

---

[1] Sohm, *Institutes,* p. 476 ; Hunter, *op. cit.* p. 692 *sq.*

[2] *Novellœ,* cxvii. 12.   [3] *Ibid.* cxxxiv. 11.   [4] *Ibid.* cxl. 1.

[5] Freisen, *op. cit.* p. 776 *sqq.* ; O. D. Watkins, *Holy Matrimony* (London, 1895), p. 380 *sq.*

[6] *Ibid.* p. 778 *sqq.*

[7] *Laws of Æthelbirht,* 79 *sqq.*   *Cf.* Pollock and Maitland, *op. cit.* ii. 393.

[8] Freisen, *op. cit.* p. 785 *sqq.*

[9] *Pœnitentiale Theodori,* ii. 5 (in A. W. Haddan and W. Stubbs, *Councils and Ecclesiastical Documents relating to Great Britain and Ireland,* iii [Oxford, 1878], p. 199).

[10] *Ibid.* ii. 12. 6 (vol. iii. 199).

[11] *Ibid.* ii. 12. 23 (vol. iii. 200 *sq.*).

[12] *Ibid.* ii. 12. 19 (vol. iii. 200).

solubility of marriage entered the secular legislation of German peoples, and in the tenth century the ecclesiastical rules and courts gained there exclusive control of this branch of law.[1] At a somewhat earlier date the provisions of the Roman law had been superseded by new rules enforced by the Church in the regions where the imperial law had been observed.[2]

While the Western Church in the matter of divorce at last completely triumphed in the countries under her sway, the Eastern Church, instead of shaping the secular law, was on the contrary greatly influenced by it. It is true that the Council of Trullo in 692 expressly condemned divorce by mutual consent, and that largely in consequence of this condemnation the emperor Leo III. (the Isaurian) in 740 put a stop to the legality of it ; and at the end of the ninth century the prohibition against it was reinforced, never again to be relaxed.[3] But of the long list of specified grounds of divorce which were admitted by the secular law none, except that of absence without tidings, appears even to have been questioned by the Eastern Church. " The enactments of the emperors and princes as to the grounds of divorce," says Zhishman, " never met with an ecclesiastical contradiction. No Council, no patriarch, no bishop of the East has ever in that matter called the emperors to account, assigned penalties to them, or forced them to the repeal of their enactments." [4] The grounds of divorce with the right of remarriage are those admitted by the laws of Justinian with certain modifications introduced in later times. In the Eastern Churches divorce is permitted on the following grounds, with penalty attached : high treason, designs of either of the partners on the life of the other, adultery, circumstances affording presumption of adultery or equivalent to adultery, the procuring of abortion, difference of religion arising from the conversion to Christianity of one of the partners, and the acting as sponsor for one's own child in baptism. There are further grounds for divorce, without penalty attached, namely : impotence, absence without tidings received, captivity and slavery, insanity and imbecility, the undertaking of monastic obligations, and episcopal consecration.[5]

The canonical doctrines that marriage is a sacrament and that it is indissoluble save by death were rejected by the Reformers. They all agreed that divorce, with liberty for the

---

[1] H. Brunner, *Grundzüge der deutschen Rechtsgeschichte* (München and Leipzig, 1913), p. 224.

[2] Lord Bryce, *op. cit.* ii. 433.

[3] Zhishman, *op. cit.* p. 104 *sqq.*   [4] *Ibid.* p. 115.

[5] *Ibid.* pp. 107 *sqq.*, 729 *sqq.* A summary of Zhishman's account is given by Watkins, *op. cit.* p. 353 *sqq.*

innocent party to remarry, should be granted for adultery, and most of them regarded malicious desertion as a second legitimate cause for the dissolution of marriage.[1] The latter opinion was based on Paul's dictum that a Christian married to an unbeliever " is not under bondage " if the unbeliever depart, which was broadened by Luther so as to include malicious desertion even without a religious motive.[2] The same reformer admits that the worldly authorities may allow divorce also on other strong grounds,[3] and mentions himself obstinate refusal of conjugal intercourse as sufficient cause for it.[4] Several reformers went farther than Luther.[5] Lambert of Avignon argued that if a wife leaves her husband because she is constantly ill-treated by him without cause, this should be counted as repudiation by the man and not as desertion by the woman ; [6] and Melanchthon likewise justified divorce in the case of ill-treatment.[7] The views of the Reformers exercised a lasting influence upon the Protestant legislators both in Germany and in other continental countries. Thus the Danish law-book issued by Christian V. in 1684 mentions as sufficient grounds for divorce desertion for at least three years, impotence which has lasted for the same period, and leprosy which has been concealed and communicated to the other party.[8] The Swedish code of 1734 allows divorce for malicious desertion, for long absence without tidings, and for bodily incapacity or incurable contagious disease deliberately concealed.[9]

The Fathers of English Protestantism as a body were more conservative than the brethren on the Continent. But they were unanimous in allowing the husband to put away an unfaithful wife and contract another marriage ; and prevailing opinion appears also to have accorded a similar privilege to the wife on like provocation, although there were undoubtedly some in the Protestant ranks who were not so liberal in her behalf.[10] A

---

[1] Friedberg, *op. cit.* p. 514 *sq.* ; Walter, *op. cit.* p. 719 *sq.* For the opinions of the continental Reformers see particularly L. Richter, *Beiträge zur Geschichte des Ehescheidungsrechts in der evangelischen Kirche* (Berlin, 1858), p. 6 *sqq.*

[2] H. L. von Strampff, *Dr. Martin Luther : Ueber die Ehe* (Berlin, 1857), pp. 381, 393.

[3] *Ibid.* pp. 354, 399.   [4] *Ibid.* p. 394.

[5] See Richter, *op. cit.* p. 31 *sqq.*   [6] *Ibid.* p. 32.

[7] *Ibid.* p. 33 *sq.* ; Friedberg, *op. cit.* p. 514 *sq.*

[8] *Kong Christian den Femtis Danske Lov*, ed. by V. A. Secher (Kjöbenhavn, 1878), iii. 16. 15. 2 *sq.*, iii. 16. 16. 4.

[9] *Sveriges Rikes Lag, till efterlefnad stadfästad år 1736*, ed. by N. W. Lundequist (Stockholm, 1874), Giftermåls-Balk, xiii. 4, xiii. 6, xiii. 8.

[10] G. E. Howard, *A History of Matrimonial Institutions*, ii (Chicago and London, 1904), p. 71 *sqq.*

general revision of the ecclesiastical code, with special attention directed to the law of divorce, was contemplated in the earlier days of the Reformation. A commission of leading ecclesiastics was for this purpose appointed by Henry VIII. and Edward VI. The commissioners drew up the elaborate report known as *Reformatio Legum*, in which they recommended that " divorces from bed and board," which had been rejected by nearly all the English reformers of the sixteenth century as a papist innovation,[1] should be abolished, and in their place complete divorce, with liberty for the innocent party to marry again, should be allowed in cases of adultery, desertion, and cruelty, as also in cases where a husband not guilty of deserting his wife had been for several years absent from her in circumstances which justified her in considering that he was dead, and in cases of such violent hatred as rendered it in the highest degree improbable that the husband and wife would survive their animosities and again love one another. The whole scheme, however, fell to the ground, partly in consequence of King Edward's premature death.[2] Yet the principle represented by it was carried out in practice. In 1548, some years before the commission had completed its report, the new doctrine had been in a measure sustained by the well-known case of Lord Northampton, whose second marriage was declared valid by an Act of Parliament. Under Elizabeth this decision seems to have been deemed good law until 1602, when, in the Foljambe case, it was decided that remarriage after judicial separation was null and void.[3] After the revival of the old canon law, says Jeaffreson, " our ancestors lived for several generations under a matrimonial law of unexampled rigour and narrowness. The gates of exit from true matrimony had all been closed, with the exception of death. Together with the artificial impediments to wedlock, the Reformation had demolished the machinery for annulling marriages on fictitious grounds. Henceforth no man could slip out of matrimonial bondage by swearing that he was his wife's distant cousin, or had loved her sister in his youth, or had before his marriage stood godfather to one of her near spiritual kindred." [4]

In the latter part of the seventeenth century a practice arose

[1] *Ibid.* ii. 73.

[2] J. Macqueen, *A Practical Treatise on the Appellate Jurisdiction of the House of Lords and Privy Council. Together with the Practice on Parliamentary Divorce* (London, 1842), p. 467 ; H. D. Morgan, *The Doctrine and Law of Marriage, Adultery, and Divorce,* ii (Oxford, 1826), p. 227 *sqq.* ; J. C. Jeaffreson, *Brides and Bridals,* ii (London, 1872), p. 319 *sqq.*

[3] Howard, *op. cit.* ii. 79 *sqq.* ; Jeaffreson, *op. cit.* ii. 323 *sq.* ; Morgan, *op. cit.* ii. 229 *sqq.*

[4] Jeaffreson, *op. cit.* ii. 339.

in England which in a small degree mitigated the rigour of the law. While a valid English marriage could not be dissolved by mere judicial authority, it might be so by a special Act of Parliament. Such a parliamentary divorce was granted only for adultery : to a husband whose own conduct had been free from reproach, if he had previously obtained a " divorce from bed and board " in the ecclesiastical court, but to a wife only in aggravated cases, such as incestuous intercourse of her husband with some of her relations.[1] But it was a remedy within the reach of the wealthier classes only : owing to the triple cost of the law action, the ecclesiastical decree, and the legislative proceedings, it could be obtained only through the expenditure of a fortune sometimes amounting to thousands of pounds.[2] As a matter of fact, up to and including the year 1857, no more than 317 divorce bills passed,[3] and the practice had already been in operation for a hundred and thirty years when, in 1801, a married woman for the first time obtained a divorce of this kind.[4]

In the civil divorce law of 1857 the legal principle of the indissolubility of marriage was at last abandoned, though only after stubborn resistance. For the dilatory and expensive proceedings of three tribunals was substituted one inquiry by a court specially constituted to exercise this jurisdiction, a new " Court for Divorce and Matrimonial Causes." On this court was conferred all the authority of the ecclesiastical courts in matrimonial causes, as also power to grant " divorce from the bond of matrimony," as a right, not as a privilege. Such a divorce, however, could only be granted to a husband whose wife had been guilty of adultery and to a wife whose husband had been guilty of incestuous adultery, bigamy with adultery, rape, sodomy, bestiality, or adultery coupled with cruelty or with desertion without reasonable excuse for two years and upwards. " Cruelty " has been defined as " conduct of such a character as to have caused danger to life, limb, or health (bodily or mental), or as to give rise to a reasonable apprehension of such danger."[5] In Scotland the courts began to grant divorces very soon after the Roman connection had been repudiated, and in 1573 a statute

---

[1] W. Blackstone, *The Commentaries on the Laws of England*, ed. by R. M. Kerr, i (London, 1876), p. 416 *sq.* ; Macqueen, *op. cit.* p. 471 *sqq.* ; Morgan, *op. cit.* ii. 237 *sqq.* ; Jeaffreson, *op. cit.* ii. 341 *sqq.*

[2] Howard, *op. cit.* ii. 107 *sq.* ; Blackstone, *op. cit.* i. 417.

[3] W. Burge, *Commentaries on Colonial and Foreign Laws*, iii (London, 1910), p. 862.

[4] Macqueen, *op. cit.* p. 474 *sq.*

[5] Earl of Halsbury, *The Laws of England*, xvi (London, 1911), p. 473 *sq.*

added desertion to adultery of the husband or the wife as a ground for divorce.[1]

On the Continent a fresh impetus to a more liberal legislation on divorce was given in the eighteenth century by the new philosophy with its conceptions of human freedom and natural rights. If marriage is a contract entered into by mutual consent it ought also to be dissolvable if both parties wish to annul the contract. In the Prussian ' Project des Corporis Juris Fridericiani ' of 1749, " founded on reason and the constitutions of the country," it is admitted that married people may demand with common consent the dissolution of their marriage.[2] The ' Project ' never became law ; but in practice divorce was freely granted by Frederick II. *ex gratia principis* at the common request of husband and wife.[3] In the Prussian ' Landrecht ' of 1794 divorce by mutual consent is admitted if the couple have no children and there is no reason to suspect levity, precipitation, or compulsion.[4] In France the new ideas led to the law on divorce of September 20, 1792, previous to which date the Roman canon law had prevailed. In the preamble of the new law it is said that marriage is merely a civil contract, and that facility in obtaining divorce is the natural consequence of the individual's right of freedom, which is lost if engagements are made indissoluble.[5] Divorce is granted on the mutual desire of the two parties,[6] and even at the wish of one party on the ground of incompatibility of temper, subject only to a short period of delay and to the necessity of appearing before a family council who are to endeavour to arrange the dispute.[7] It was said that divorce was instituted in order to preserve in marriage " cette quiétude heureuse qui rend les sentiments plus vifs." [8] Marriage would no longer be a yoke or a chain, but " l'acquit d'une dette agréable que tout citoyen doit à la patrie. . . . Le divorce est le dieu

---

[1] Lord Bryce, *op. cit.* ii. 435 ; J. Erskine of Carnock, *Principles of the Law of Scotland*, ed. by J. Rankine (Edinburgh, 1890), p. 77.

[2] *Project des Corporis Juris Fridericiani* (Halle, 1749), i. 2. 3. 1. 35, p. 56.

[3] E. Roguin, *Traité de droit civil comparé. Le mariage* (Paris, 1904), p. 334.

[4] *Allgemeines Landrecht für die Preussischen Staaten* (Berlin, 1828–32), § 716.

[5] ' Loi sur le divorce, 20 septembre 1792 ' (in *Lois civiles intermédiaires*), i (Paris, 1806), p. 325.

[6] *Ibid.* i. 2, ii. 1 *sqq.* (vol. i. 2), ii. 1 *sqq.* (vol. i. 326 *sqq.*).

[7] *Ibid.* i. 3, ii. 8 *sqq.* (vol. i. 326, 328 *sqq.*).

[8] H. Taine, *Les origines de la France contemporaine*, iii (Paris, 1881), p. 102.

tutélaire de l'hymen. . . . Libres de se séparer, les époux n'en sont que plus unis." [1]

Twelve years later, in 1804, the law of 1792 was superseded by the new provisions in Napoleon's ' Code civil des Français.' Divorce was made more difficult. Mere incompatibility of temper is no longer recognised as a cause for it. Marriage may still be dissolved on the ground of mutual consent, but on certain conditions only : the husband must be at least twenty-five years of age and the wife twenty-one ; they must have been married for at least two years and not more than twenty years, and the wife must not be over forty-five years of age ; the parents or the other living ascendants of both parties must give their approval ; [2] and the mutual and unwavering consent of the married couple must sufficiently prove " that their common life is insupportable to them, and that there exists in reference to them a peremptory cause of divorce." [3] At the Restoration in 1816 divorce was abolished in France ; [4] but it was re-enacted by a law of 1884, the provisions of which were simplified by later laws. The divorce law of the Napoleonic Code was again introduced, but with important changes, one of which was that divorce by mutual consent had disappeared. In the course of the nineteenth century divorce was made legal in several Roman Catholic countries even in the case of marriage between Catholics. [5] In the United States South Carolina stands alone in granting no divorce whatsoever, which is the more remarkable as no state has fewer Roman Catholic citizens. [6] It is the only Protestant community in the world which nowadays holds marriage indissoluble, as result of which it has been necessary for the authorities to enact special legislation concerning the personal and property rights of extra-legal wives and children. [7]

The most general grounds for divorce are offences of some kind or other committed by either husband or wife, and entitling the other party to demand a dissolution of the marriage. In this respect the two spouses are as a rule on a footing of perfect equality ; but there are exceptions to the rule. While any act of adultery in the wife is everywhere a sufficient cause for dis-

---

[1] L. Mortimer-Ternaux, *Histoire de la Terreur 1792–1794*, iv (Paris, 1864), p. 408.

[2] *Code civil des Français* (Code Napoléon) (Paris, An XII.–1804), art. 275 *sqq*.

[3] *Ibid.* art. 233.

[4] E. Glasson, *Le mariage civil et divorce* (Paris, 1880), p. 266.

[5] E. Westermarck, *The History of Human Marriage*, iii (London, 1921), p. 342.

[6] Lord Bryce, *op. cit.* ii. 440.

[7] M. F. Nimkoff, *The Family* (Cambridge, Mass., 1934), p. 456.

solving the marriage, there are still laws that do not allow the wife in all circumstances to demand a divorce from an adulterous husband. Desertion, or " malicious " desertion, or desertion " without just cause or excuse," is very frequently mentioned as a ground of divorce, especially in Protestant law-books. In most countries in which divorce is allowed, ill-treatment of some kind is a sufficient reason for it. An extremely frequent ground of divorce is the condemnation of one of the parties to a certain punishment or his or her being convicted of a certain crime. Some law-books mention as causes for divorce the husband's neglect of the duty to support his wife although he is able to do so (in many jurisdictions of the United States), drunkenness, inveterate gambling habits, or ill-treatment of children. Moreover, certain circumstances are recognised grounds of divorce which do not involve guilt in one of the parties but are supposed to make marriage a burden for the other spouse, such as impotence in the husband or wife, some loathsome disease, and insanity or incurable insanity. The Swiss code contains a provision to the effect that, even though none of the specified causes for divorce exists, a marriage may be dissolved if there are circumstances seriously affecting the maintenance of the conjugal tie.[1]

The English law was until quite recently the only one in Europe that recognised none but sexual reasons for the dissolution of marriage. The Majority Report of the Royal Commission of 1909 recommended that divorce should, in the future, be obtainable for the following reasons : adultery ; wilful desertion for three years and upwards ; cruelty ; incurable insanity after five years' confinement ; habitual drunkenness found to be incurable from the first order for separation ; and imprisonment under commuted sentence of death.[2] These recommendations were deprecated by the Minority Report, which declared, on the one hand, that there was no public demand for any such concessions, and on the other hand, that, as the experience of other countries proved, the granting of the concession was invariably followed by a sudden and serious increase in the number of demands for divorce.[3] The recommendations of the Majority Report were ignored, with the exception of the proposal that in the case of adultery women should be placed on an equality with men,[4] which became law in 1923. " But that," says

---

[1] Westermarck, *op. cit.* iii. 343 *sqq.*
[2] *Royal Commission on Divorce and Matrimonial Causes, Report of the Commissioners*, § 329.
[3] *Ibid. Minority Report.*
[4] *Report of the Commissioners*, § 219.

Dr. Havelock Ellis, " left the law in the highly unsatisfactory condition of only being able to grant the relief of divorce to unhappily married couples when they have agreed to commit either adultery or perjury. In 1936 an extremely temperate Marriage Bill, initiated by Mr. A. P. Herbert, was introduced into the House of Commons ; it was framed in so moderate a spirit in order (as Mr. Herbert put it) ' to secure, for the first time, agreement of the majority of churchmen and to relieve the conscience of the clergy.' . . . Even this Bill, however, was whittled down in its passage through Parliament, but became law in 1937 as the Matrimonial Causes Act." [1]

Legislators are still imbued with the idea that a marriage must inevitably end in a catastrophe, either by the death or some great misfortune of one of the consorts or by the commission of a criminal or immoral act, which is evidently regarded as a more proper ground or excuse for dissolving the marriage than the mutual agreement of both. Divorce by mutual consent, which was recognised by Roman law and for a short time in France at the end of the eighteenth and the beginning of the nineteenth century, is nowadays legal in a few countries only. It remained so in Belgium and Rumania after it was abolished in France, but in both countries the old barriers of the Code Napoléon were preserved, which made it very rare in practice. The civil code of imperial Austria permitted such divorce to Jews—though to no other citizens—in accordance with the principle of the Rabbinic law that the court has no right to interfere when both parties declare that their marriage is a failure and that they desire to dissolve it. In Mexico the marriage may be dissolved, after the observance of certain formalities, by the mutual agreement of the parties when they have been married for at least a year. In Portugal a divorce may be obtained after a separation *de facto* by mutual consent for ten years. In Denmark marriage may be dissolved upon the common application of the parties after living apart for one year and a half, and in Norway and Guatemala after one year's separation in accordance with a decree of separation, and such a decree may itself have been obtained by mutual consent. The laws of Sweden, Finland, Greece, and Costa Rica admit likewise consensual separation ; and a separation may, upon the application of either husband or wife, be converted into a divorce, in Denmark after two years and a half, in Norway, Finland, Greece (apparently), and Costa Rica after two years, and in Sweden after one year. In the Soviet law there are no such restrictions. It goes in fact even further than the French law

[1] Havelock Ellis, *Sex in Relation to Society* (London, 1937), p. 306.

of 1792 by simply stating that " the grounds for divorce may be either the mutual consent of the parties or the desire of one of them." [1]

The unequivocal recent trend of Western legislation has been to increase the legal facilities of divorce, and, as Dr. Ellis remarks, " in no civilised country is there any progressive movement for adding to the legal impediments " ; [2] and there is every reason to believe that this trend will continue in the future. The unreasonable impediments to divorce are only the diluted effects of the Canon Law with its total prohibition of divorce, in conformity with the ascetic spirit of Christianity. In many Catholic countries the Church has already lost her power to enforce this prohibition, and in some of them it has even been succeeded by a remarkably liberal divorce law, owing to the fact that her grounds of divorce have been largely copied from the earlier law relating to judicial separation (a very convenient procedure), which could be obtained more easily than divorce in most Protestant countries. [3] We may take for granted that the canonic dogma of the indissolubility of marriage, in spite of papal protests, will before very long lose its hold on the legislation of the rest of the Catholic world ; and so also the idea that a divorce mostly presupposes a delinquent, which is likewise rooted in the ascetic tendencies of early Christianity, is undoubtedly doomed. The divorce laws of the different Western countries will, no doubt, always vary in details ; but I think one may safely predict that divorce by mutual consent will, sooner or later, be generally recognised by them. It has in recent years been established in an increasing number of countries ; and elsewhere it is strongly advocated by enlightened opinion both in Europe and America.

Some curious objections have been raised to it, besides the general one that it would make divorce too easy and thereby lessen the " sanctity of marriage." In his evidence before the Royal Commission, Lord Gorell argued that divorce by mutual consent would in practice " probably prove to amount to divorce at the will of either party who could make the other's life unbearable in order to force a consent." [4] A similar objection might be made to the chief ground of divorce which is recognised

---

[1] E. Westermarck, *The Future of Marriage in Western Civilisation* (London, 1936), p. 210 *sqq.*

[2] H. Ellis, *Studies in the Psychology of Sex*, vii (Philadelphia, 1928), p. 508.

[3] Westermarck, *The History of Human Marriage*, iii. 357 *sqq.*

[4] *Royal Commission on Divorce and Matrimonial Causes, Minutes of Evidence*, Lord Gorell's Evidence, § 139.

everywhere : it might give rise to the practice of one of the partners hectoring the other by adulterous behaviour with a view to coercing the latter into suing for a divorce. Another argument which has been adduced against divorce by mutual agreement is that it might lead to a precipitated dissolution of the marriage. Mr. Groves asks : " How many of the marriages that have now achieved happiness would have been dissolved in the early days of matrimonial adjustment had there been in the past a social code built upon divorce by mutual consent ? " He answers : " No one knows, but men and women of experience have estimated that it would have been as high as fifty per cent." [1] (Another opponent of divorce by mutual consent writes, on the contrary, that such consent to the dissolution of marriage " is comparatively rare, for it is a matter of human experience that one of the partners very often refuses to release the other.") [2] Precipitation is by no means infrequent when a marriage is dissolved on other grounds ; many divorced couples would perhaps remarry if they did not fear it would make them ridiculous. [3] It is just where divorce is possible on the ground of mutual consent that legislators have taken precautions to prevent a hasty step : they have done so in all modern laws which recognise such a ground for divorce, particularly by requiring previous separation for a certain period, with the single exception of the Soviet law.

On the other hand, the arguments in favour of divorce by mutual consent seem unanswerable. Milton, who was its first protagonist in Christendom, insisted that " marriage is not a mere carnal coition, but a human society " ; [4] that the just ground for divorce is " indisposition, unfitness, or contrariety of mind, arising from a cause in nature unchangeable, hindering and ever likely to hinder, the main benefits of conjugal society, which are solace and peace " ; [5] and that it is a violent, cruel thing " to force the continuing of those together, whom God and nature in the gentlest end of marriage never joined." [6] Dr. Lichtenberger observes that "the dissolution of loveless marriages now is regarded as less immoral than their continuance. The enlightened conscience rebels against compulsion in sex relations, regarding it as a species of rape as revolting within the marriage

[1] E. R. Groves, The Marriage Crisis (New York, etc., 1928), p. 136.
[2] R. De Pomerai, Marriage, Past, Present and Future (London, 1930), p. 258.
[3] Cf. W. J. Robinson, Woman, Her Sex and Love Life (New York, 1928), p. 358.
[4] J. Milton, ' The Doctrine and Discipline of Divorce,' in The Prose Works of, i (London, 1806), p. 373.
[5] Ibid. i. 347 sq.   [6] Ibid. i. 353.

bond as it is without." [1]   Mr. Shaw makes the acute remark :
" To impose marriage on two unmarried people who do not desire
to marry one another would be admittedly an act of enslave-
ment.   But it is no worse than to impose a continuation of
marriage on people who have ceased to desire to be married." [2]

[1] J. P. Lichtenberger, *Divorce* (New York and London, 1931), p.
454 *sq.*
[2] G. B. Shaw, *Getting Married* (London, 1913), p. 167.

CHAPTER XVIII

CHRISTIANITY AND IRREGULAR SEX RELATIONS

IN an earlier chapter I have spoken of abstinence from sexual relationships as the most important form of Christian asceticism, of the high appreciation of virginity, of the obligatory celibacy of the clergy, and of the sinfulness attributed to concupiscence. While the gratification of it in marriage was condoned, all other forms of sexual intercourse were looked upon as mortal sins.

The horror of them found an echo in the secular legislation of the first Christian emperors. Panders were condemned to have molten lead poured down their throats.[1] In the case of forcible seduction both the man and woman, if she consented to the act, were put to death.[2] Even the innocent offspring of illicit intercourse were punished for their parents' sins with ignominy and loss of certain rights which belonged to other, more respectable, members of the Church and the State ; some mediæval lawbooks treated them as almost rightless beings, on a par with robbers and thieves.[3] Persons of different sex who were not united in wedlock were forbidden by the Church to kiss each other ; nay, the sexual desire itself, though unaccompanied by any outward act, was regarded as sinful in the unmarried.[4] Consequently, anything that would tend to arouse a feeling of sexual excitement or a temptation to lust was condemned. The Church prescribed punishment for the writing or reading of lascivious books, singing wanton songs, dancing suggestive dances, wearing improper clothing, bathing in mixed company, frequenting the theatre, or permitting suspected vigils or pernoctations of women in churches under pretence of

[1] W. E. H. Lecky, *History of European Morals from Augustus to Charlemagne*, ii (London, 1890), p. 316.

[2] *Codex Theodosianus*, ix. 24. 1.

[3] *Concilium Claromontanum*, A.D. 1095, can. 11 (Labbe-Mansi, *Sacrorum Conciliorum collectio*, xx. 817 ; H. von Eicken, *Geschichte und System der mittelalterlichen Weltanschauung* (Stuttgart, 1887), p. 573.

[4] " Perit ergo et ipsa mente virginitas." E. Katz, *Ein Grundriss des kanonischen Strafrechts* (Berlin and Leipzig, 1881), p. 114 *sq.* For the subject of kissing see also Thomas Aquinas, *Summa theologica*, ii.-ii. 154. 4.

devotion.[1] In the standard of purity no difference of sex was recognised, the same obligations being imposed upon man and woman.

In this respect there was a fundamental difference between the Christians and the Pagans. In Greece the chastity of an unmarried girl was anxiously guarded.[2] According to Athenian law, the relatives of a maiden who had lost her virtue could with impunity kill the seducer on the spot.[3] Virginity was an object of worship. Chastity was the pre-eminent attribute of sanctity ascribed to Athene and Artemis, and the Parthenon, or virgin's temple, was the noblest religious edifice of Athens. It is true that a certain class of courtesans occupied a remarkably high position in the social life of Greece, being admired and sought after even by the principal men. But they did so on account of their extraordinary beauty or their intellectual superiority ; to the Greek mind the moral standard was by no means the only standard of excellence. The Roman, on the other hand, regarded the courtesan class with much contempt. He encouraged brothels, but only entered them with covered head and face concealed in his cloak. He tolerated the prostitute, but sharply curtailed her privileges. She could go almost naked if she pleased, but might not even wear the *vitta* or the *stola* ; she must not ape the emblems of the respectable Roman matron.[4] The names of prostitutes had to be published on the ædile's list, as Tacitus says, " according to a recognised custom of our ancestors, who considered it a sufficient punishment on unchaste women to have to profess their shame." [5] But both in Rome and Greece pre-nuptial unchastity in men, when it was not excessive,[6] or did not take some especially offensive form, was hardly censured by public opinion. The elder Cato expressly justified it.[7] Cicero says : " If there be any one who thinks that youth is to be wholly interdicted from amours with courtesans, he certainly is very strict indeed. I cannot deny what he says ; but still he is at variance not only with the licence of the present age, but even with the habits of our ancestors, and with what they used to consider allowable. For when was the time that men were not used to act in this manner ? When was such

---

[1] J. Bingham, *Origines Ecclesiasticæ*, vi (London, 1829), p. 386 *sqq.*

[2] J. Denis, *Histoire des théories et des idées morales dans l'antiquité*, i (Paris, 1856), p. 69 *sq.*

[3] L. Schmidt, *Die Ethik der alten Griechen*, ii (Berlin, 1882), p. 193.

[4] H. Ellis, *Sex in Relation to Society* (London, 1937), p. 207.

[5] Tacitus, *Annales*, ii. 85.

[6] Valerius Maximus (*Facta dictaque memorabilia*, ii. 5. 6) praises " frugalitas " as " immoderato Veneris usu aversa."

[7] Horace, *Satiræ*, i. 2. 31 *sq.*

conduct found fault with ? When was it not permitted ?
When, in short, was the time when that which is lawful was not
lawful ? " [1] Epictetus only went a little step further. He said
to his disciples : " Concerning sexual pleasures, it is right to be
pure before marriage, as much as in you lies. But if you indulge
in them, let it be according to what is lawful. But do not in
any case make yourself disagreeable to those who use such
pleasures, nor be fond of reproving them, nor of putting yourself
forward as not using them." [2] Here chastity in men is at all
events recognised as an ideal.

Yet even in pagan antiquity there were a few who enjoined
it as a duty.[3] Musonius Rufus emphatically asserted that no
union of the sexes other than marriage was permissible,[4] and
Dio Chrysostom desired prostitution to be suppressed by law.[5]
Similar views grew up in connection with the Neo-Platonic and
Neo-Pythagorean philosophies, and may be traced back to the
ancient masters themselves. We are told that Pythagoras
inculcated the virtue of chastity so successfully that when ten of
his disciples, being attacked, might have escaped by crossing a
bean-field, they died to a man rather than tread down the beans,
which were supposed to have a mystic affinity with the seat of
impure desires.[6] Plato, again, is in favour of a law to the effect
that " no one shall venture to touch any person of the freeborn
or noble class except his wedded wife, or sow the unconsecrated
and bastard seed among harlots, or in barren and unnatural
lusts." Our citizens, he says, ought not to be worse than birds
and beasts, which live without intercourse, pure and chaste,
until the age for procreation, and afterwards, when they have
arrived at that period and the male has paired with the female
and the female with the male, " live the rest of their lives in
holiness and innocence, abiding firmly in their original com-
pact." [7]

With regard to prostitution, the attitude of the Christians
was not so uniform as might have been anticipated. While it
was denounced as immoral by the more independent and irre-
sponsible divines, others tended reluctantly to justify it as a
means of avoiding greater evils.[8] Foremost among these was

[1] Cicero, *Pro Cœlio*, 20 (48).
[2] Epictetus, *Enchiridion*, xxxiii. 8.
[3] Denis, *op. cit.* ii. 133 *sqq.*
[4] Musonius Rufus, quoted by Stobæus, *Florilegium*, vi. 61.
[5] Denis, *op. cit.* ii. 149 *sqq.*
[6] Jamblichus, *De Pythagorica vita*, 31 (101). *Cf.* F. B. Jevons, in
Plutarch's *Romane Questions* (London, 1892), p. lxxxviii *sq.*
[7] Plato, *Leges*, viii. 840 *sq.* *Cf.* Xenophon, *Memorabilia*, i. 3. 8.
[8] Havelock Ellis, *op. cit.* pp. 207, 235.

Augustine. In a treatise written in 386 to vindicate the divine regulation of the world, we find him declaring that just as the executioner, however repulsive he may be, occupies a necessary place in society, so the prostitute and her like, however sordid and ugly and wicked they may be, are equally necessary; " remove prostitutes from human affairs and you would pollute the world with lust." [1] Christian emperors, like their pagan predecessors, were also willing to derive a tax from prostitution; and when, from time to time, some vigorous ruler sought to repress it by severe enactments these were of no avail. During a thousand years these enactments were repeated again and again in various parts of Europe, and invariably with the same fruitless or worse than fruitless results. [2] In England, in the fourteenth century, prostitution was carried on largely in licensed stews in Southwark, because brothels were forbidden within the city of London, and the bishop of Winchester, who was lord of the manor, had as such jurisdiction over and a profit from the stews, the inmates of which were popularly known as " Winchester Geese." It seemed not to disconcert the bishop or the Church that these women, from whom they profited, were not permitted to receive the rites of the Church while they lived, nor a Christian burial upon their death. There was a cemetery appointed for them far from the parish church, for, as Coke said, brothel-houses were prohibited by the law of God. [3]

As Christianity in its condemnation of unchastity in the unmarried made no distinction between man and woman, it made no distinction between husband and wife in its condemnation of adultery. If continence is a stringent duty for unmarried persons independently of their sex, the observance of the sacred marriage vow must be so in a still higher degree. And in this respect also the Christian view differed essentially from the Pagan one. The Romans defined adultery as sexual intercourse with another man's wife; on the other hand, the intercourse of a married man with an unmarried woman was not regarded as adultery. [4] The ordinary Greek feeling on the subject is expressed in the oration against Neæra, ascribed to Demosthenes, where the licence accorded to husbands is spoken of as a matter of course : " We keep mistresses for our pleasures, concubines for constant attendance, and wives to bear us legiti-

---

[1] Augustine, *De ordine*, ii. 4.
[2] Ellis, *op. cit.* p. 207 *sq.*
[3] G. May, *Social Control and Sex Expression* (London, 1930), p. 105.
[4] A. Vinnius, *In quatuor libros institutionum imperialium commentarius* (Lugduni, 1747), iv. 18. 4, p. 993. *Cf. Digesta*, 1. 16. 101. 1 ; T. Mommsen, *Römisches Strafrecht* (Leipzig, 1899), p. 688 *sq.*

mate children and to be our faithful housekeepers." [1] But at the same time the idea that fidelity in marriage ought to be reciprocal was not entirely unknown in classic antiquity. In a lost chapter of his 'Economics' Aristotle points out that it for various reasons is prudent for a man to be faithful to his wife, but that nothing is so peculiarly the property of a wife as a chaste and hallowed intercourse. [2] Plutarch condemns the man who, lustful and dissolute, goes astray with a courtesan or maid-servant ; though, at the same time, he admonishes the wife not to be vexed or impatient considering that " it is out of respect to her that he bestows upon another all his wanton depravity." [3] Plautus argues that it is unjust of a husband to exact a fidelity which he does not keep himself. [4]

The Christian condemnation of all forms of sexual intercourse outside the marriage relation found a minute expression in the Penitentials, which were catalogues of offences with the exact measure of penance for each offence. Before the conversion of the Anglo-Saxons there had been such codifications of penances made in Ireland and Wales, but it was the second archbishop of Canterbury, Theodore of Tarsus, who gave authority and wide acceptance to a codified penitential. Upon his death in 690 his disciples collected and arranged the decisions he had made in actual cases of penitence that had come before him, for which he had freely used the rules of Church Councils and the teachings of Church Fathers, particularly Basil. The penitential of Theodore was widely applied not only in England but on the Continent, and was followed by some other similar compilations, those of Bede and others, made before the end of the tenth century. But the Penitentials were a part not only of the ecclesiastical discipline, but of the Anglo-Saxon law as well. From the time of its first introduction into England the penitential power included the judicial power. Just as the penance might be prescribed by the priest as a voluntary atonement, so it might be prescribed by the judicial officer as a sort of punishment ; and refusal of the sinner to submit to the judicial sentence was punishable by excommunication. [5]

"The Anglo-Saxon Penitentials," says Dr. May, " placed upon matters of sex more emphasis, both in quantity of regulation and in minuteness of detail, than has, probably, any other general code of conduct." [6] The penance imposed by

---

[1] *Oratio in Neæram*, p. 1386. *Cf.* Schmidt, *op. cit.* ii. 196 *sq.*
[2] Aristotle, *Œconomica*, p. 341. *Cf.* Isocrates, *Nicocles sive Cyprii*, 40.
[3] Plutarch, *Conjugalia præcepta*, 16.
[4] Plautus, *Mercator*, iv. 5.
[5] May, *op. cit.* pp. 60, 61, 67 *sq.*   [6] *Ibid.* p. 61 *sqq.*

Theodore and Bede for simple fornication was generally one year, but this was increased according to the frequency of the act and the age and discretion of the parties. Adultery was a far more serious offence, entailing in some cases only a two-year penance and in others as much as a seven-year fast on bread and water. Penance was ordered even for lustful thoughts with no external expression ; indeed, according to Theodore the atonement for thought was to be as severe as the atonement for the act. The amount of concern with auto-erotism is more marked than with any other form of sexual behaviour. Omitting the chapters of discipline that apply specifically to the clergy, self-abuse was the subject of 25 paragraphs in the Penitentials. With infinite care the varieties of the offence were differentiated, the persons by whom it was committed, their age, their station— lay or clerical—and dignity, the place where it was committed, and the thoughts connected with the commission. For a lay-man the penance ascribed was usually forty days ; for the clergy it was severe according to the rank of the offender. Sodomy and bestiality were considered in at least 22 paragraphs. The divisions of the offences were various, according to the age and position of the one committing them, the one with whom committed, and the method of commission. The penances imposed were severe—as long as twenty-two years or, for some offences, for life.[1]

In the case of extra-matrimonial connections, as in many other points of morals, there has been considerable discrepancy between Christian doctrine and public opinion in Christian countries. The gross and open immorality of the Middle Ages indicates how little the idea of sexual purity entered into the manners and opinions of the people. The influence of the ascetic doctrine of the Church was in fact quite contrary to its aspirations. The institution of clerical celibacy created a large class of people to which illicit love was the only means of gratifying a natural desire. In England, late in the thirteenth century Bracton speaks of the *concubina legitima* as entitled to certain rights and considerations,[2] and among the clergy concubinage prevailed universally, although it was the object of unremitting assault from Councils and prelates.[3] Elsewhere in Europe it had so established itself among the clerical order that even the loftiest prelates shrunk from encountering the risk

---

[1] *Ibid.* p. 61 *sqq.*

[2] H. de Bracton, *De legibus et consuetudinibus Angliæ*, book ii, ch. 30 (vol. i [London, 1878], p. 506) ; book iv, treat. vi (vol. iv [1881], p. 500).

[3] H. C. Lea, *History of Sacerdotal Celibacy in the Christian Church* (London, 1932), p. 244.

attendant upon an attempt to enforce the canons against it. In 1537 the archbishop of Salzburg timidly suggested in a pastoral letter that if the clergy could not restrain their passions, they should at all events indulge them secretly, so that scandal might be avoided and the punishment of their transgressions be left to an avenging God.[1]   In Spain, in the thirteenth and following centuries, all attempts to suppress clerical concubinage were likewise in vain.[2]

During the Middle Ages incontinence was largely an object of ridicule rather than censure, and in the comic literature of that period the clergy are represented as the great corrupters of domestic virtue.[3]   Whether the tenet of chastity laid down by the code of Chivalry was taken more seriously may be fairly doubted.   A knight, it was said, should be abstinent and chaste;[4] he should love only the virtues, talents, and graces of his lady ;[5] and love was defined as the " chaste union of two hearts by virtue wrought." [6]   But while the knight had certain claims as regards the virtue of his lady, while he probably was inclined to draw his sword only for a woman of fair reputation, and while he himself professed to aspire only to her lip or hand, we have reason to believe that the amours in which he indulged with her were of a far less delicate kind.   Sainte-Palaye observes : " Jamais on ne vit les mœurs plus corrompues que du temps de nos Chevaliers, et jamais le règne de la débauche ne fut plus universel." [7]   For a mediæval knight the chief object of life was love ; he who did not understand how to win a lady was but half a man ; and the difference between a lover and a seducer was apparently slight.

The Reformation brought about some change, if in no other respect at least by making marriage lawful for the clergy.   In fits of religious enthusiasm even the secular legislators busied themselves with acts of incontinence in which two unmarried adults of different sex were consenting parties.   In the days of the Commonwealth, in cases of less serious breach of chastity than adultery and incest, each man or woman was for each

[1] Lea, *op. cit.* p. 445 *sq.*

[2] *Ibid.* p. 260 *sq.*

[3] T. Wright, *Essays on Archæological Subjects*, ii (London, 1861), p. 238.

[4] *The Book of the Ordre of Chyualry* (Westminster, 1484 ?), fol. 40.

[5] De la Curne de Sainte-Palaye, *Mémoires sur l'ancienne chevalerie*, ii (Paris, 1781), p. 17.

[6] C. Mills, *The History of Chivalry*, i (London, 1826), p. 214 *sq.*

[7] Sainte-Palaye, *op. cit.* ii. 19.   *Cf.* W. Scott, ' An Essay on Chivalry,' in *Miscellaneous Prose Works*, vi (Edinburgh, 1827), p. 48 *sq.*

offence to be committed to the common gaol for three months, and to find sureties for good behaviour during a whole year afterwards.[1] In Scotland, after the Reformation, fornication was punished with a severity nearly equal to that which attended the infraction of the marriage vow.[2] But the fate of these and similar laws has been either to be repealed or to become inactive.[3] For ordinary acts of incontinence public opinion is, practically at least, the only judge. In the case of female unchastity its sentence is severe enough among the upper ranks of society while, so far as the lower classes are concerned, it varies considerably even in different parts of the same country, and is in many cases mild or acquitting.

Even then the girl may have to pay for her incontinence. Illegitimate childbirth is a frequent cause of prostitution, not only on account of the consequences of the mother's lost virginity, but also for economic reasons. Nowadays she has generally the right to claim support for her child from its father. But there are numbers of cases in which she, for some reason or other, can obtain no support at all, and when she receives some, it is generally quite inadequate from the child's point of view.[4] The illegitimacy of birth affects the offspring even more than the mother. The death-rate for illegitimate infants is very much higher than that for legitimate ones on account of the unmarried mother's inferior economic and social conditions ; and another result of them is the comparatively large number of criminals among the children of unmarried parents, who grow up in so unfavourable circumstances.[5] The way in which they have been treated in the Christian world is a disgrace to its civilisation. In Teutonic countries their position was much better in earlier times than subsequently, when the new religion made its influence felt.[6] And there are still traces left of this

---

[1] L. O. Pike, *A History of Crime in England*, ii (London, 1876), p. 182.

[2] C. Rogers, *Social Life in Scotland*, ii (Edinburgh, 1885), p. 242.

[3] See Pike, *op. cit.* ii. 582 ; D. Hume, *Commentaries on the Law of Scotland*, ii (Edinburgh, 1797), p. 333.

[4] See E. Westermarck, *The Future of Marriage in Western Civilisation* (London, 1936), p. 126 *sq.*

[5] *Ibid.* p. 127 *sq.*

[6] It makes one smile to find that the most radical denial of illegitimate children's rights comes from a great philosopher. Immanuel Kant (*Metaphysische Anfangsgründe der Rechtslehre*, § 49 [*Gesammelte Schriften*, vi (Berlin, 1914), p. 335 *sq.*]) argues that as the infant has been born outside the law, it is not protected by the law ; it has, as it were, crept into the community as contraband (*verbotene Waare*), and as it should not be there at all, the community may ignore both its existence and its destruction. He looks upon this as a dictate of " practical reason " ; but, as I have tried to show in my book *Ethical Relativity*

iniquity.[1] As to incontinence of unmarried men, it seems to me that Christianity has done little more than establish a standard which, though accepted perhaps in theory, is scarcely recognised by the feelings of the large majority of people, or at least of men, in Christian countries. The words which Cicero uttered on behalf of Cœlius might be repeated by any modern advocate who, in defending his client, ventured frankly to express the popular opinion on the subject.

Nor has Christianity in the case of adultery succeeded in eradicating every distinction between husband and wife. Whilst any act of adultery in the wife is everywhere a sufficient cause for dissolving the marriage, there are countries in which adultery on the part of the husband only in certain circumstances gives the wife a right to demand a divorce ; [2] and in Roman Catholic countries where divorce is prohibited we find a similar difference between the infidelity between the husband and that of the wife in the case of judicial separation.[3] But the law may also in other respects make a distinction between them. The French code considers it " excusable " if a husband kills his adulterous wife in the act ; [4] and it makes such a wife liable to imprisonment, while the adultery of a husband is punishable only if he keeps a concubine in the conjugal domicile, and then the punishment is merely a fine.[5] According to the Spanish penal code of 1928, the adultery of a wife is likewise punishable in all circumstances, but that of a husband only if he keeps his accomplice in the house or, otherwise, if his behaviour gives rise to scandal.[6] So also, according to the Italian code of 1930, the adultery of a wife, called *adulterio*, is punishable in any case, but that of a husband, called *concubinato*, only if he keeps his mistress in his home or if he keeps her elsewhere " notoriously." [7] In modern legislation adultery, if punishable at all, is generally an indictable offence, but, as a matter of fact, it is very rarely punished.[8] In England an Act passed in the middle of the

(London, 1932), ch. ix, all his dictates of that mysterious faculty are really only expressions of his emotions ; and in the present case the puritanic influence is obvious.

[1] Westermarck, *The Future of Marriage in Western Civilisation*, p. 128 *sq.*

[2] *Idem.*, *The History of Human Marriage*, iii (London, 1921), pp. 343, 344, 358, 359 n. 11 ; J. K. Folsom, *The Family* (New York, 1934), p. 362 (Texas, Kentucky, North Carolina).

[3] *The History of Human Marriage*, iii. 357 *sq.*

[4] *Code pénal*, art. 324.   [5] *Ibid.* arts. 337, 339.

[6] *Ibid.* art. 620 *sqq.*   [7] *Ibid.* art. 559 *sq.*

[8] Westermarck, *The Future of Marriage in Western Civilisation*, p. 68 *sq.*

seventeenth century made the adultery of a wife (nothing is said of a husband) felony, both for her and her partner in guilt, and therefore punishable by death ; [1] but this Act fell with the fall of the Commonwealth.[2] Parliament has never acted to deprive the Church of her jurisdiction over adultery, but no attempt to make it punishable by the criminal law has succeeded.[3] In the United States, where the Puritan tradition as to sexual offences is dying more slowly than it died in England, there are only two states that have no provision whatsoever for the punishment of adultery, whilst in eighteen other states a single act of adultery is not in itself a criminal offence.[4] The Russian Soviet law takes no notice of adultery.[5]

The early Christians' horror of sodomy has exercised a profounder and more lasting influence upon moral opinion and law than their condemnation of any other form of irregular sex behaviour. It was determined by ancient Hebrew ideas. According to the Old Testament, unnatural sins were not allowed to defile the land of the Lord : whosoever should commit such abominations should be put to death.[6] The enormous abhorrence of them expressed in the law had a very special reason, the Hebrews' hatred of a foreign cult. Unnatural sin was the sin of a people which was not the Lord's people, the Canaanites, who thereby polluted their land, so that He visited their guilt and spued out its inhabitants.[7] We know that sodomy entered as an element in their religion : besides female temple prostitutes there were male prostitutes, *qedēshīm*, attached to their temples.[8] The word *qādēsh*, translated " sodomite," properly denotes a man dedicated to a deity ; [9] and it appears that such men were consecrated to the mother of the gods, the famous Dea Syria, whose priests or devotees they were considered to be.[10] The sodomitic acts committed with these temple prostitutes may, like the connections with priestesses, have had in view to transfer

---

[1] H. Scobell, *A Collection of Acts and Ordinances of General Use, made in the Parliament*, pt. ii (London, 1657), p. 121.

[2] W. Shephard, *A Sure Guide for His Majesties Justices of Peace* (London, 1663), p. 460.

[3] May, *op. cit.* pp. 174, 176. [4] *Ibid.* p. 203.

[5] M. Hindus, *Humanity Uprooted* (London, etc., 1929), p. 88.

[6] *Leviticus* xviii. 22, 24 *sqq.*, xx. 13.

[7] *Ibid.* xviii. 28, xx. 23.

[8] *Deuteronomy* xxiii. 17 ; S. R. Driver, *A Critical and Exegetical Commentary on Deuteronomy* (Edinburgh, 1895), p. 264.

[9] Driver, *op. cit.* p. 264 *sq.* ; J. A. Selbie, ' Sodomite,' in J. Hastings, *A Dictionary of the Bible*, iv (Edinburgh, 1902), p. 559.

[10] Jerome, *In Osee*, i. 4. 14 (Migne, *Patrologiæ cursus*, xxv. 851); F. C. Cook's note to *1 Kings* xiv. 24 in his edition of *The Holy Bible* (London, 1871–81), ii. 571. See also Lucian, *Lucius*, 38.

blessings to the worshippers. In Morocco supernatural benefits are
expected not only from heterosexual, but also from homosexual
intercourse with a holy person.[1] The qedēshīm are alluded to in
the Old Testament, especially in the period of the monarchy,
when rites of foreign origin made their way into both Israel and
Judah.[2] And it is natural that the Yahveh-worshipper should
regard their practices with the utmost horror as forming part of
an idolatrous cult.

When this horror of homosexuality passed into Christianity
the notion that sodomy is a form of sacrilege was here strengthened by the habits of the Gentiles. Paul found the abominations
rampant among the nations who had " changed the truth of God
into a lie, and worshipped and served the creature more than the
Creator " ; he regarded them as the climax of the moral corruption to which God gave over the heathen because of their apostasy
from him.[3] Tertullian says that they are banished " not only
from the threshold, but from all shelter of the church, because
they are not sins, but monstrosities." [4] Basil maintains that
they deserve the same punishment as murder, idolatry, and
witchcraft.[5] According to a decree of the Council of Elvira
those who abuse boys to satisfy their lusts are denied communion
even after their last hour.[6] The Christian emperors Constantius
and Theodosius ordered that sodomites should be punished with
death by the sword or be burnt alive.[7] For ages sodomy remained a religious offence of the first order. It was not only a
" vitium nefandum et super omnia detestandum," [8] but it was
one of the four " clamantia peccata," or crying sins,[9] a " crime
de Majestie, vers le Roy celestre." [10] During the Middle Ages
heretics were accused of it as a matter of course.[11] Indeed, so
closely was it associated with heresy that the same name was
applied to both. In ' La Coutume de Touraine-Anjou ' the

---

[1] E. Westermarck, Ritual and Belief in Morocco, i (London, 1926),
p. 198.
[2] 1 Kings xiv. 24, xv. 12, xxii. 46 ; 2 Kings xxiii. 7 ; Job xxxvi. 14 ;
Driver, op. cit. p. 265.
[3] Romans i. 25 sqq.
[4] Tertullian, De pudicitia, 4.
[5] Basil, quoted by Bingham, op. cit. vi. 432 sq.
[6] Concilium Eliberitanum, ch. 71 (Labbe-Mansi, ii. 17).
[7] Bingham, op. cit. vi. 382 sq.
[8] J. Clarus, Practica criminalis, book v, § Sodomia (Opera omnia, ii
[Genevæ, 1739], p. 151).
[9] E. Coke, The Third Part of the Institutes of the Laws of England
(London, 1680), p. 59.
[10] Mirror, quoted ibid. p. 58.
[11] É. Littré, Dictionnaire de la langue française, i (Paris, 1863), p. 386,
' Bougre ' ; E. S. P. Haynes, Religious Persecution (London, 1904), p. 54.

word *herite*, which is the ancient form of *hérétique*,[1] seems to be used in the sense of " sodomite " ; [2] and the French *bougre* (from the Latin *Bulgarus*, Bulgarian), to which there is an English equivalent, was originally given to a sect of heretics who in the eleventh century came from Bulgaria, and was afterwards applied to other heretics ; but at the same time it became the regular expression for a sodomite.[3] In mediæval laws sodomy was also repeatedly mentioned together with heresy, and the punishment was the same for both.[4] It is interesting to notice that in one other religion, besides Hebrewism and Christianity, it has been looked upon with the same abhorrence, namely, Zoroastrianism, and there also as a practice of infidels, of Turanian shamanists. [5]

In no other point of morals was the contrast between the teachings of Christianity and the habits and opinions of the world over which it spread more radical than in their attitude towards homosexuality. In ancient Greece pederasty in its baser forms was censured, though generally, it seems, with no great severity ; but the universal rule was apparently that when decorum was observed in the friendship between a man and a youth, no inquiries were made into the details of the relationship. And this attachment was not only regarded as permissible, but was praised as the highest form of love, as the offspring of the heavenly Aphrodite, as a path leading to virtue, as a weapon against tyranny, as a safeguard of civic liberty, as a source of national greatness and glory.[6] In Rome there was an old law of unknown date, called Lex Scantinia (or Scatinia), which imposed a mulct on him who committed pederasty with a free person ; [7]

---

[1] Littré, *op. cit.* i. 2010, ' Hérétique.'

[2] *Les Établissements de Saint Louis*, i. 90 ; P. Viollet, in his Introduction to the same work, i (Paris, 1881), p. 254.

[3] Littré, *op. cit.* i. 386, ' Bougre ' ; J. A. H. Murray, *A New English Dictionary*, i (Oxford, 1884), p. 1160, ' Bugger ' ; H. C. Lea, *A History of the Inquisition of the Middle Ages*, i (Philadelphia, 1892), p. 115 n.

[4] Ph. de Beaumanoir, *Les coutumes du Beauvoisis*, xxx. 11, vol. i (Paris, 1842), p. 413 ; Britton [On the Laws of England], i. 10, vol. i (Oxford, 1865), p. 42 ; Montesquieu, *De l'esprit des lois*, xii. 6 (*Œuvres* Paris, 1837], p. 283) ; A. Du Boys, *Histoire du droit criminel de l'Espagne* Paris, 1870), pp. 486, 721.

[5] Westermarck, *The Origin and Development of the Moral Ideas*, ii. 479, 480, 486 *sq.*

[6] *Ibid.* ii. 478 *sq.*

[7] Juvenal, *Satiræ*, ii. 43 *sq.* ; Valerius Maximus, *Facta dictaque memorabilia*, vi. 1. 7 ; Quintilian, *Institutio oratoria*, iv. 2. 69 : " Decem milia, quæ pœna stupratori constituta est, dabit " ; Christ, *Hist. Legis Scatinia*, quoted by J. J. I. Döllinger, *The Gentile and the Jew in the Courts of the Temple of Christ*, ii (London, 1862), p. 274 ; W. Rein, *Das Criminal-*

but this law, of which very little is known, had lain dormant for ages, and the subject had never afterwards attracted the attention of the pagan legislators.[1] But when Christianity became the religion of the Roman Empire, a veritable crusade was opened against it. Constantius and Constans made it a capital crime, punishable with the sword.[2] Valentinian went further still and ordered that those who were found guilty of it should be burned alive in the presence of all the people.[3] Justinian, terrified by certain famines, earthquakes, and pestilences, issued an edict which again condemned persons guilty of unnatural offences to the sword, " lest, as the result of these impious acts, whole cities should perish together with their inhabitants," as we are taught by the Holy Scripture, that through such acts cities have perished with the men in them.[4] " A sentence of death and infamy," says Gibbon, " was often founded on the slight and suspicious evidence of a child or a servant, . . . and pederasty became the crime of those to whom no crime could be imputed." [5]

Throughout the Middle Ages and later, Christian legislators thought that nothing but a painful death in the flames could atone for the sinful act.[6] In England Fleta speaks of the offender being buried alive ; [7] but we are elsewhere told that

recht der Römer (Leipzig, 1844), p. 865 sq. ; Bingham, op. cit. vi. 433 sqq. ; Mommsen, op. cit. p. 703 sq.

[1] Mommsen, op. cit. p. 704 ; Rein, op. cit. p. 866.

[2] Codex Theodosianus, ix. 7. 3 ; Codex Justinianus, ix. 9. 30.

[3] Ibid. ix. 7. 6.

[4] Novellæ, 77. See also ibid. 141, and Institutiones, iv. 18. 4.

[5] E. Gibbon, The History of the Decline and Fall of the Roman Empire, v (London, 1854), p. 323.

[6] Du Boys, op. cit. pp. 93, 403 ; Les Établissements de Saint Louis, i. 90, vol. ii. 147 ; Beaumanoir, op. cit. xxx. 11, vol. i. 413 ; Montesquieu, op. cit. xii. 6 (Œuvres, p. 283) ; Hume, op. cit. ii. 335 ; R. Pitcairn, Criminal Trials in Scotland, ii (Edinburgh, 1838), p. 491 n. 2 ; Clarus, op. cit. book v, Sodomia, 4 (Opera omnia, ii. 151) ; C. E. Jarcke, Handbuch des gemeinen deutschen Strafrechts, iii (Berlin, 1839), p. 172 sqq. ; Charles V., Die Peinliche Gerichtsordnung, art. 116 (Heidelberg, 1842) ; E. Henke, Grundriss einer Geschichte des deutschen peinlichen Rechts und der peinlichen Rechtswissenschaft, i (Sulzbach, 1809), p. 289 ; Numa Prætorius, ' Die strafrechtlichen Bestimmungen gegen den gleichgeschlechtlichen Verkehr,' in Jahrbuch für sexuelle Zwischenstufen, i (Leipzig, 1899), p. 124 sqq. In the beginning of the nineteenth century sodomy was still nominally subject to capital punishment by burning in Bavaria (P. J. A. von Feuerbach, Kritik des Kleinschrodischen Entwurfs zu einem peinlichen Gesetzbuche für die Chur-Pfalz-Bayrischen Staaten, i [Giesen, 1804], p. 13), and in Spain as late as 1843 (Du Boys, op. cit. p. 721).

[7] Fleta, seu Commentarius Juris Anglicani (London, 1735). i. 37 3, p. 84.

burning was the due punishment.[1] As unnatural intercourse, however, was a subject for ecclesiastical cognisance, capital punishment could not be inflicted on the criminal unless the Church relinquished him to the secular arm ; and it seems very doubtful whether she did relinquish him. Pollock and Maitland consider that the statute of 1533, which made sodomy felony, affords an almost sufficient proof that the temporal courts had not punished it, and that no one had been put to death for it for a very long time past.[2] It was said that the punishment for this crime—which the English law, in its very indictments, treats as a crime not fit to be named [3]—was determined to be capital by " the voice of nature and of reason, and the express law of God " ; [4] and it remained so till 1861,[5] although in practice the extreme punishment was not inflicted.[6] In France persons were actually burned for this crime in the middle and latter part of the eighteenth century.[7]

In Christian Europe the rationalistic movement of the eighteenth century brought about a change in the attitude towards homosexual offences. To punish sodomy with death, it was said, is atrocious ; when unconnected with violence, the law ought to take no notice of it at all. It does not violate any other person's right, its influence on society is merely indirect like that of drunkenness and free love ; it is a disgusting vice, but its only punishment is contempt.[8] This view was adopted by the French 'Code pénal,' according to which homosexual practices in private, between two consenting adult parties, whether men or women,[9] are absolutely unpunished. The

---

[1] Britton, *op. cit.* i. 10, vol. i. 42.

[2] F. Pollock and F. W. Maitland, *The History of the English Law before the Time of Edward I.*, ii (Cambridge, 1898), p. 556 *sq.*

[3] Coke, *op. cit.* p. 58 *sq.* ; W. Blackstone, *The Commentaries on the Laws of England*, iv (London, 1876), p. 218.

[4] Blackstone, *op. cit.* iv. 218.

[5] J. F. Stephen, *A History of the Criminal Law of England*, i (London, 1883), p. 475.

[6] Blackstone, *op. cit.* iv. 218.

[7] C. Desmaze, *Les pénalités anciennes* (Paris, 1866), p. 211 ; Havelock Ellis, *Studies in the Psychology of Sex*, ii (Philadelphia, 1915), p. 207.

[8] Note of the Editors of Kehl's edition of Voltaire's ' Prix de la justice et de l'humanité,' in *Œuvres complètes*, v (Paris, 1837), p. 437 n. 2.

[9] For various reasons the sexual abnormalities of women have attracted much less attention than those of men. In Austria, however, they are punished by law ; but a proposal to the same effect which was made in Germany was rejected (Moll, *Die conträre Sexualempfindung* [Berlin, 1891], p. 241 n. ; *Zeitschrift für Sexualwissenschaft*, ii [Bonn, 1915], p. 11 *sq.*, vii [1921], p. 112). Theodore's ' Penitential ' assigned a penance of three years to " a woman fornicating with a woman " i. 2. 12, in F. W. H. Wasserschleben, *Die Bussordnungen der abend-*

homosexual act is treated as a crime only when it implies an outrage on public decency, or when there is violence or absence of consent or when one of the parties is under age or unable to give valid consent.[1] This method of dealing with homosexuality has been followed especially by the legislators of the other Latin countries in Europe and America (except Chile), as well as Russia; [2] and in other countries, where the law treats the act in question *per se* as a penal offence, notably in Germany, a vigorous propaganda in favour of its alteration has been carried on with the support of many men of scientific eminence.

It is argued that the deterring effect of the law must be very slight; this may be inferred not only from the great prevalence of homosexual practices in countries where they are punishable offences,[3] but also from the fact that they are not conspicuously more prevalent in those European countries where the law takes no notice of them; the French call them " le vice allemand." [4] That the punishment could exercise a reformatory influence upon the offender by changing the nature of his sexual desire, is entirely out of the question.[5] Nor is it in the least likely to repress its gratification by engendering moral scruples; the prohibition may on the contrary, as in the case of drink, stimulate the desire.[6] Moreover, when homosexuality is made a legal crime the door is opened wide to blackmailers—a very serious

ländischen Kirche [Halle, 1851], p. 186); but this was much less than that prescribed for male homosexual practices (i. 2. 5, in Wasserschleben, p. 185).

[1] *Code pénal*, art. 330 *sqq*. *Cf.* J. J. Chevalier, *L'inversion sexuelle* (Lyon and Paris, 1893), p. 431 *sqq*.; Ellis, *op. cit.* ii. 347 *sq*.

[2] K. Hiller, ' Recht und sexuelle Minderheiten,' in A. Weil, *Sexual-reform und Sexualwissenschaft* (Stuttgart, 1922), p. 169.

[3] When in England a Church Council in 1102 attempted to root out sodomy by decreeing that any ecclesiastical person found guilty of it was to be degraded, and that profligate, obstinate sodomites were to be struck with anathema, the vice was so widespread that it had to be connived at (May, *op. cit.* p. 101).

[4] Hiller, *loc. cit.* p. 172. According to Ellis (*op. cit.* ii. 350 *sq*.), homosexuality abounds perhaps to a much greater extent in Germany than in France. When Professor W. McDougall, in his book *An Intro-duction to Social Psychology* (London, 1926), p. 357 *sq*., on utilitarian grounds justifies the hardships inflicted upon homosexuals by the present law of England, he must either be ignorant of the frequency of homo-sexuality in this country or assume that if the law were less draconic, it would be even much more prevalent, indeed more prevalent than in any other European country.

[5] A. Moll, *op. cit.* p. 235 *sq*.

[6] C. Müller-Braunschweig, ' Psychoanalyse und Sexualreform,' in Weil, *op. cit.* p. 144. I know a man with homosexual habits who declared that he would be sorry to see the English law changed, as then the practice would lose its charm. Ellis (*op. cit.* p. 351 n. 2) mentions a similar case.

objection.[1] The answer to this criticism has been that " the sound feelings of the people " insist on punishing the offence.[2]

It seems to me obvious that the censure to which homosexual intercourse as such is so frequently subject is, when uninfluenced by any religious considerations, in the first place due to that feeling of aversion or disgust which it tends to call forth in normally constituted adult individuals, whose sexual instincts have developed under normal conditions. This feeling tends to abate or disappear where special circumstances, such as absence of the other sex, the seclusion of women, or other facts, have given rise to widespread homosexual practices ; and in no case seem even the baser forms of homosexuality to have led to anything like those drastic measures that we find where the condemnation of them has been influenced by religious beliefs. There are still to be mentioned other circumstances that have affected the opinion about homosexuality in the Western world. It is popularly supposed to be an abnormality of comparatively few degenerate individuals. Only recent investigations have disclosed the fact that it is found in a very considerable number of people of either sex. In Germany, according to Hirschfeld, the proportion of inverts are somewhat over 2 per cent. and that of bisexual persons 4 per cent.[3] As to the prevalence of homosexuality in France opinions vary, but Dr. Ellis maintains that it seems very doubtful whether inborn inversion is in any considerable degree rarer in France than in Germany. He also thinks we may probably conclude that the proportion of inverts in England is the same as in other related and neighbouring lands, that is to say, slightly over 2 per cent., which would give the homosexual population of Great Britain as somewhere about a million.[4] All these estimates must of course be hazardous, but they are much more likely to be too low than too high ; for homosexuals generally try to conceal their proclivities, and often succeed in keeping them secret from their acquaintances. We have much higher figures in answers given to inquiries in America. Dr. Davis writes : " Slightly over 50 per cent. of a group of 1,200 women college graduates, at least five years out of college, state that they have experienced intense emotional relations with other women, and that in slightly more than half these cases, or 26 per cent. of the entire group, the experience has

[1] See, for example, H. Haustein, 'Strafrecht und Sodomie vor 2 Jahrhunderten,' in *Zeitschrift für Sexualwissenschaft und Sexualpolitik*, xvii (Berlin and Köln, 1930), p. 98 *sq.*

[2] Hiller, *loc. cit.* p. 170.

[3] M. Hirschfeld, *Die Homosexualität* (Berlin, 1920), pp. 485, 493.

[4] Ellis, *op. cit.* ii. 62, 64.

been accompanied by overt physical practices." [1] Of Dr.
Hamilton's group of 100 married men and an equal number of
married women, 17 men and 26 women had indulged in homosexual episodes since the eighteenth year.[2]

Many of those persons may, of course, have been bisexual,
that is, persons attracted to both sexes. Bisexuality may merge
imperceptibly into real inversion, and on the other hand there
may be a bisexual strain in persons who are, or become, normally
heterosexual ; between inversion and normal sexuality there are
all shades of variation. Indeed, scarcely any man is a hundred
per cent. man, scarcely any woman a hundred per cent. woman.
As William James said, inversion is a " kind of sexual appetite of
which very likely most men possess the germinal possibility." [3]
Many physiologists are nowadays of opinion that each sex
contains the latent characters of the other sex—in other words,
is latently hermaphrodite. Among mammals the male possesses
useless nipples, which occasionally even develop into breasts,
and the female possesses a clitoris, which is merely a rudimentary
penis, and may also develop. So, too, a homosexual tendency
may be regarded as simply the psychical manifestation of special
characters of the other sex, susceptible of being evolved under
certain circumstances, such as may occur about the age of
puberty.[4] Thus the sexual instinct of boys and girls shows plain
signs of a homosexual tendency, and is often more or less
undifferentiated.[5] When facts of this kind become more
commonly known, they can scarcely fail to influence public
opinion about homosexuality.

The same may be said of some other findings of modern sex
psychology. Homosexuality is frequently looked upon as a
sign of moral degeneracy of a more general kind, but we now
know that this is not the case. All varieties of moral character
are found among inverts, just as among normal people ; and it
has been pointed out by Dr. Ellis that among great moral
leaders and persons with strong ethical instincts there has been,
and is to this day, in many cases a tendency towards the more

---

[1] Katharine B. Davis, *Factors in the Sex Life of Twenty-two Hundred
Women* (New York and London, 1929), p. 277.

[2] G. V. Hamilton, *A Research in Marriage* (New York, 1929), p. 497.

[3] W. James, *The Principles of Psychology*, ii (London, 1891), p. 439.

[4] F. H. A. Marshall, *The Physiology of Reproduction* (London, 1922),
p. 689 *sqq.*

[5] M. Dessoir, ' Zur Psychologie der Vita sexualis,' in *Allgemeine
Zeitschrift für Psychiatrie und psychisch-gerichtliche Medicin*, v (Berlin,
1894), p. 941 *sqq.* ; Ellis, *op. cit.* ii. 79 *sqq.* ; A. Moll, *The Sexual Life of
the Child* (London, 1912), p. 61 *sqq* ; S. Freud, *Drei Abhandlungen zur
Sexualtheorie* (Leipzig and Wien, 1926), p. 104.

elevated forms of homosexual feeling. This feeling may be just as refined as the heterosexual one. Indeed, for the ancient Greeks true love was nearly always homosexual. Their lyric poets wrote practically no love poems at all to women before Anacreon, and many of them, perhaps all, were only written in old age. They seem to have regarded woman as only an instrument of pleasure and the founder of the family. Theognis compares marriage to cattle-breeding ; Alcman, when he wishes to be complimentary to the Spartan girls, speaks of them as his " female boy-friends." [1] That homosexuality is remarkably common among men of exceptional intellect was long ago noted by Dante, and has often been noted since ; but it is among artists that homosexuality may most strikingly be traced.[2]

While we may assume that a deepened insight into the nature of homosexuality will make people somewhat more tolerant in their attitude towards it, there is another factor that should affect the moral judgment of homosexual practices. When the last residue of the influence of antiquated religious ideas has vanished, normal persons will still feel aversion to those practices, just as genuine inverts often feel aversion to sexual connections with the other sex. But, as I have said elsewhere,[3] owing to the very nature of the moral emotions, aversion cannot be regarded as an adequate cause of moral censure by any one whose judgment is sufficiently discriminate. To be called wrong an act must then be productive of other harm than the mere aversion it causes, provided that the agent has not in an indecent manner shocked any one's feelings. Any moral condemnation of homosexual practices (nobody can, of course, be blamed on account of his abnormal desire) must be founded on an opinion of their hurtfulness, individual or public, whatever they may be. But thoughtful people will be on their guard against the common tendency to seek a rational justification for judgments springing merely from sentimental dislikes.

There is another kind of abnormal sex behaviour to which the public attitude in Christian civilisation has been determined by ancient Hebrew ideas, namely, bestiality. It was a Mosaic ordinance that in the case of sexual intercourse between a man, or woman, and a beast—which was evidently supposed to be productive of offspring—the human offender and the beast as well were to be put to death.[4] In the Christian Penitentials

---

[1] E. F. M. Benecke, *Antimachus of Colophon and the Position of Women in Greek Poetry* (London, 1896), pp. 24 n. 1, 27, 28, 30 ; Ellis, *Sex in Relation to Society*, p. 116.

[2] Ellis, *Studies in the Psychology of Sex*, ii. 26 *sqq.*

[3] *Ethical Relativity*, p. 258. [4] *Leviticus* xx. 15 *sq.*

bestiality was severely condemned—nuns, in particular, were accused of it ; [1] and when in England the temporal law took jurisdiction over certain of the more outspoken sexual vices, it was, like sodomy, made felony by Henry VIII.[2] Moral philosophy has also had something to say on the subject. According to Kant it is a categorical imperative of practical reason that the man whose offence has reduced him to the level of an animal should be expelled from civil society and deprived of human rights, as he is unworthy to be treated as a human being.[3] Kant represents this as a deduction from the general principle of requital (*jus talionis*) which, if the punishment cannot be exactly equivalent to the crime, requires equivalence according to the spirit of the law. That principle, however, has obviously not a rational, but an entirely emotional, foundation ; and the same is the case with the moral condemnation of bestiality, if unaffected by religion or superstition : it is considered immoral because it provokes disgust. It is therefore an opinion which nowadays is gaining ground that it should not be punished at all.[4]

---

[1] May, *op. cit.* p. 101.   [2] *Ibid.* p. 136.
[3] Kant, *Metaphysische Anfangungsgründe der Rechtslehre*, Anhang (*Gesammelte Schriften*, vi [Berlin, 1914], p. 363).
[4] F. Dehnow, ' Sittlichkeitsdelikte und Strafrechtsreform,' in Weil, *op. cit.* p. 165 ; ' Resolution betreffend Sexualstrafreform,' *ibid.* p. 186 ; Haustein, *loc. cit.* p. 98 ; A. Forel, *Die Sexuelle Frage* (München, 1931), p. 428.

CHAPTER XIX

CHRISTIANITY AND THE REGARD FOR THE LOWER ANIMALS

IT has been alleged in a review of a recent book, in which Buddha and Christ are quoted as the highest exemplars of the ideals of love, that " the author betrays either his ignorance of the teaching of Jesus, or his prejudice against Christianity, when he adds : ' In Buddha one finds the more universal sympathy, extending as it does to brute as well as to human life ' ; for even if Jesus did not give specific instructions on the treatment of animals, do not His references to God's care for the flowers of the field and the birds of the air, God's knowledge of the fall of every sparrow, the shepherd's grief at the loss of one sheep, as an analogy of God's love for every sinner ; the lifting of the ox or the ass out of the pit on a Sabbath day, imply that universal sympathy ? " [1] I do not see how these cases can be compared at all with Buddha's rules regarding the treatment of animals. A disciple of his may not knowingly deprive any creature of life, not even a worm or an ant ; he may not drink water in which animal life of any kind whatever is contained, nor pour it out on grass or clay.[2] And the doctrine which forbids the killing of animate beings is not only professed, but in a large measure followed, by the great majority of people in Buddhistic countries. In Siam the tameness of many living creatures which in Europe fly from the presence of man is very striking. Instances have been known in which natives have quitted the service of Europeans on account of their unwillingness to destroy reptiles and vermin, and it is a not uncommon practice for rich Siamese to buy live fish to have the merit of restoring them to the sea.[3] In Burma, though fish is one of the staple foods of the people, the fisherman is despised ; not so much, perhaps, as if he killed other living things, but he is still an outcast from decent

[1] A. E. Garvie, in a review of W. P. Montague's book *Belief Unbound*, in *Philosophy*, vi (London, 1931), p. 258.
[2] H. Oldenberg, *Buddha* (London, 1882), pp. 290 n. *, 351.
[3] J. Bowring, *The Kingdom and People of Siam*, i (London 1857), p. 107.

society, and " will have to suffer great and terrible punishment before he can be cleansed from the sins that he daily commits." [1] The Buddhists of Ceylon are more forbearing : they excuse the fisherman by saying that he does not kill the fish, but only removes it from the water.[2] In Tibet all dumb creatures are treated with humanity, and the taking of animal life is rather strictly prohibited, except in the case of yaks and sheep needed for food. Owing to the coldness of the climate, flesh forms an essential staple of diet ; but the butchers are regarded as professional sinners and are therefore the most despised of all classes in Tibet. Wild animals and even small birds and fish are seldom or never killed, on account of the religious penalties attached to this crime.[3]

Great regard for the lower animal world is also found in other Oriental religions. According to Brahmanism, tenderness towards all creatures is a duty incumbent upon the four castes. It is said that " he who injures innoxious beings from a wish to give himself pleasure, never finds happiness, neither living nor dead." [4] If a blow is struck against an animal in order to give it pain, the judge shall inflict a fine in proportion to the amount of pain caused, just as if the blow had been struck against a man.[5] The killing of various creatures, including fish and snakes, reduces the offender to a mixed caste ; [6] and, according to the ' Vishṅu Puráṅa,' fishermen go after death to the same hell as awaits prisoners, incendiaries, and treacherous friends.[7] To kill a cow is a great crime ; [8] whereas he who unhesitatingly abandons life for the sake of a cow is freed even from the guilt of the murder of a Brâhmana, and so is he who saves the life of a cow.[9] Among many of the Hindus the slaughter of a cow excites more horror than the killing of a man, and is punished with great severity, even with death. [10]

The Jain is even stricter than the Buddhist in his regard for

[1] H. Fielding Hall, The Soul of a People (London, 1902), p. 230.
[2] E. Schmidt, Ceylon (Berlin, 1897), p. 316 sq.
[3] L. A. Waddell, The Buddhism of Tibet (London, 1895), p. 567 sq.
[4] The Laws of Manu, v. 45, in The Sacred Books of the East, xxv (Oxford, 1886).
[5] Ibid. viii. 286.
[6] Ibid. xi. 69.
[7] Vishṅu Puráṅa (London, 1840), p. 208 sq.
[8] The Institutes of Vishnu, 1. 16 sqq., in The Sacred Books of the East, vii (Oxford, 1880) ; Gautama, xxii. 18, ibid. ii (Oxford, 1897) ; Apastamba, i. 26. 1, ibid. ii ; The Laws of Manu, xi. 109 sqq.
[9] The Laws of Manu, xi. 80.
[10] A. Barth, The Religions of India (London, 1882), p. 264 ; J. L. Kipling, Beast and Man in India (London, 1891), p. 118 sq. ; W. Crooke, Things Indian (London, 1906), p. 91.

animal life. He sweeps the ground before him as he goes, lest animate things be destroyed ; he walks veiled, lest he inhale a living organism ; he considers that the evening and night are not times for eating, since one might then swallow a live thing by mistake ; and he rejects not only meat but even honey, together with various fruits that are supposed to contain worms, not because of his distaste for worms but because of his regard for life.[1] Some towns in Western India in which Jains are found have their beast hospitals, where animals are kept and fed. At Surat there was quite recently an establishment of this sort with a house where a host of noxious and offensive vermin, dense as the sands on the seashore, were bred and nurtured ; and at Anjár, in Kutch, about five thousand rats were kept in a certain temple and daily fed with flour, which was procured by a tax on the inhabitants of the town.[2]

According to the ' Thâi-Shang,' one of the books of Taoism, a good man will feel kindly towards all creatures, and refrain from hurting even the insect tribes, grass, and trees ; and he is a bad man who " shoots birds and hunts beasts, unearths the burrowing insects and frightens roosting birds, blocks up the dens of animals and overturns nests, hurts the pregnant womb and breaks eggs." [3] In the book called ' Merits and Errors Scrutinised,' which enjoys great popularity in China, it is said to be meritorious to save animals from death—even insects if the number amounts to a hundred—to relieve a brute that is greatly wearied with work, to purchase and set at liberty animals intended to be slaughtered. On the other hand, to confine birds in a cage, to kill ten insects, to be unsparing of the strength of tired animals, to disturb insects in their holes, to destroy the nests of birds, without great reason to kill and dress animals for food, are all errors of various degrees. And " to be the foremost to encourage the slaughter of animals, or to hinder persons from setting them at liberty," is regarded as an error of the same magnitude as the crime of devising a person's death or of drowning or murdering a child.[4] Kindness to animals is conspicuous in the writings of Confucius and Mencius ; [5] the Master angled but did not use a net, he shot but not at birds perching.[6] Throughout Japan, according to Sir Edward Reed, " the life of

---

[1] E. W. Hopkins, *The Religions of India* (London, 1896), p. 288 ; Barth, *op. cit.* p. 145 ; Kipling, *op. cit.* p. 10 *sq.*

[2] Burnes, ' Notice of a remarkable Hospital for Animals at Surat,' in *Journal of the Royal Asiatic Society*, i (London), p. 96 *sq.*

[3] *Thâi-Shang*, 3 *sq.*, in *The Sacred Books of the East*, xl (Oxford, 1891).

[4] *The Indo-Chinese Gleaner*, iii (Malacca, 1821), pp. 164, 205 *sq.*

[5] Mencius, i. 1. 7, in J. Legge, *The Chinese Classics*, ii (Oxford, 1895).

[6] *Lun Yü*, vii. 26, *ibid.* i (Oxford, 1893).

animals has always been held more or less sacred, . . . neither
Shintoism nor Buddhism requiring or justifying the taking of the
life of any creature for sacrifice."[1]

The regard for the lower animals which is shown by those
Eastern religions and their adherents is to some extent due to
superstitious ideas, similar to those which are found among many
savages.[2] Thus Dr. de Groot observes that in China the virtues
of benevolence and humanity are extended to animals because
these, also, have souls which may work vengeance or bring
reward.[3] The conduct of Orientals towards the brute creation
has further been explained by their belief in the transmigration
of souls. But it seems that the connection between their theory
of metempsychosis and their rules relating to the treatment of
animals is not exclusively, nor even chiefly, one of cause and
effect, but rather one of a common origin. This theory itself
may in some measure be regarded as a result of that intimacy
which prevails in the East between animals and men. Buddhism recognises no fundamental distinction between them, only
an accidental or phenomenal difference ;[4] and the step is not
long from this attitude to the doctrine of metempsychosis.
Captain Forbes maintains that the humanity with which the
Burmans treat dumb animals comes " more from the innate good
nature and easiness of their dispositions than from any effect
over them of this peculiar doctrine " ;[5] and we are told that they
laugh at the suggestion made by Europeans that Buddhists
abstain from taking life because they believe in the transmigration of souls, having never heard of it before. Their motive, says
Fielding Hall, is compassion and *noblesse oblige.*[6] But by its
punishments and rewards, religion has no doubt greatly increased
the natural regard for animal life and welfare, and introduced a
new motive for conduct which originally sprang in the main from
kindly feeling.

In Zoroastrianism we meet with a different attitude towards
the lower animal world. A fundamental distinction is made
between the animals of Ormuzd and those of Ahriman. To kill
one of the former is a heinous sin, to kill one of the latter a pious

[1] E. J. Reed, *Japan*, i (London, 1880), p. 61.

[2] E. Westermarck, *The Origin and Development of the Moral Ideas*, ii
(London, 1917), p. 491 *sqq.*

[3] J. J. M. de Groot, *The Religious System of China*, vol. iv, book ii
(Leyden, 1891), p. 450.

[4] T. W. Rhys Davids, *Hibbert Lectures . . . on some Points in the
History of Indian Buddhism* (London, 1881), p. 214.

[5] C. J. F. S. Forbes, *British Burma and its People* (London, 1878),
p. 321.

[6] Fielding Hall, *op. cit.* p. 237 *sq.*

deed.[1]   Sacred above all other animals is the dog.   The ill-
feeding and maltreatment of dogs are prosecuted as criminal, and
extreme penalties are inflicted on those who venture to kill them.[2]
Nay, if there be in the house of a worshipper of Mazda a mad dog
that has no scent, the worshippers of Mazda " shall attend him
to heal him, in the same manner as they would do for one of the
faithful." [3]   In the eyes of the Parsis, animals are enlisted under
the standards of either Ormuzd or Ahriman according as they are
useful or hurtful to man ; but Darmesteter is of opinion that they
originally belonged to the one or the other not on account of any
such qualities, but according as they chanced to have lent their
forms to either the god or the fiend in the storm tales.   " It was
not animal psychology," he says, " that disguised gods and
fiends as dogs, otters, hedge-hogs, and cocks, or as snakes,
tortoises, frogs, and ants, but the accidents of physical qualities
and the caprice of popular fancy, as both the god and the fiend
might be compared with, and transformed into, any object, the
idea of which was suggested by the uproar of the storm, the
blazing of the lightning, the streaming of the water, or the hue
and shape of the clouds." [4]   This hypothesis seems to attach
excessive importance to mythical fancies, and presupposes an
almost unbounded and capricious allegorism, for which there is
apparently little foundation in fact.   The suggestion that the
animals are referred to either the one or the other category
according as they are useful or obnoxious to man, is at all events
borne out by a few salient features, although in many details the
matter remains obscure.

It appears that among the Zoroastrians, also, the respect for
the life of animals is partly due to superstitious ideas about their
souls and fear of their revenge.   In one of the Pahlavi texts it is
said that people should abstain from unlawfully slaughtering any
species of animals, since otherwise, in punishment for such an
act, each hair of the animal killed becomes like a sharp dagger,
and he who is unlawfully a slaughterer is slain.[5]   But here again
we may assume the co-operating influence of the feeling of
sympathy.   Various passages in the Zoroastrian ' Gathas ' which

[1] J. Darmesteter, *Ormazd et Ahriman* (Paris, 1877), p. 283.
[2] *Vendîdâd*, xiii *sq.*, in *The Sacred Books of the East*, iv (Oxford, 1895) ;
W. Geiger, *Civilization of the Eastern Irānians in Ancient Times*, ii
(London, 1886), p. 36.
[3] *Vendîdâd*, xiii. 35.
[4] Darmesteter, ' Introduction to the Vendîdâd,' in *The Sacred Books
of the East*, iv (Oxford, 1880), p. lxxii. *sq.*   See also *idem, Ormazd et
Ahriman*, p. 283 *sqq.*
[5] *Shâyast Lâ-Shâyast*, x. 8, in *The Sacred Books of the East*, v (Oxford,
1880).

enjoin kindness to domestic animals [1] suggest as their motives not only considerations of utility but genuine tenderness. In a later age Firdausi sang, " Ah ! spare yon emmet rich in hoarded grain : He lives with pleasure, and he dies with pain." [2] Of the modern Persian, Polak says that, " naturally not cruel, he treats animals with more consideration than men." [3] His present religion, too, enjoins kindness to animals as a duty.

According to Islam beasts, birds, fish, insects, are all, like man, the slaves of God, the tools of his will. There is no intrinsic distinction between them and the human species, except what accidental diversity God may have been pleased to make.[4] Mohammed said to his followers : " There is not a beast upon the earth nor a bird that flies with both its wings, but is a nation like to you ; . . . to their Lord shall they be gathered." [5] Mohammedan law prescribes that domestic animals shall be treated with consideration and not to be over-worked ; [6] and in various parts of the Moslem world this law has also been habitually put into practice. The Moslems of India have been represented as kind to animals.[7] In his earlier intercourse with the Egyptians Lane noticed much humanity to beasts.[8] Montaigne said that the Turks gave alms to brutes and had hospitals for them ; [9] and Bosworth Smith is of opinion that beasts of burden and domestic animals are nowhere in Christendom—with the one exception, perhaps, of Norway—treated with such unvarying kindness and consideration as they are in Turkey. " In the East," he adds, " so far as it has not been hardened by the West, there is a real sympathy between man and the domestic animals ; they understand one another." [10]

So also the ancient Greeks were on familiar terms with the animal world. This appears from the frequency with which

---

[1] Darmesteter, in Le Zend-Avesta, i (Paris, 1892), p. cvi.

[2] Firdausi, quoted by W. Jones, ' The Tenth Anniversary Discourse,' in Asiatick Researches, iv (Calcutta, 1795), p. 12.

[3] J. E. Polak, Persien, i (Leipzig, 1865), p. 12.

[4] Cf. W. G. Palgrave, Narrative of a Year's Journey through Central and Eastern Arabia, i (London and Cambridge, 1865), p. 368.

[5] Koran vi. 38.

[6] E. Sachau, Muhammedanisches Recht nach Schafiitischer Lehre (Stuttgart and Berlin, 1897), pp. 18, 103.

[7] J. J. Pool, Studies in Mohammedanism (Westminster, 1892), pp. 176, 177, 247. Cf. R. Heber, Narrative of a Journey through the Upper Provinces of India, ii (London, 1828), p. 131.

[8] E. W. Lane, An Account of the Manners and Customs of the Modern Egyptians (London, 1896), p. 293.

[9] Montaigne, Essais, ii. 11.

[10] R. Bosworth Smith, Mohammed and Mohammedanism (London, 1889), pp. 180, 217.

their poets illustrate human qualities by metaphors drawn from it. And as men were compared with animals, so animals were believed to possess human peculiarities. When a beast was going to be sacrificed it had to give its consent to the act by a nod of the head before it was killed.[1] Animals were held in some measure responsible for their deeds ; they were tried for manslaughter, sentenced, and executed.[2] On the other hand, honours were bestowed upon beasts which had rendered signal services to their masters. The graves of Cimon's mares with which he three times conquered at the Olympic games were still in the days of Plutarch to be seen near his own tomb ; [3] and a certain Xanthippus honoured his dog by burying it on a promontory, since then called " the dog's grave," because when the Athenians were compelled to abandon their city it swam by the side of his galley to Salamis.[4] According to Xenocrates, there were in existence at Eleusis three laws which had been made by an ancient legislator, namely : " Honour your parents," " Sacrifice to the gods from the fruits of the earth," and " Injure not animals." [5] The Areopagites once condemned a boy to death because he had picked out the eyes of some quails.[6] At Athens and in Peloponnesus the slaughter of a labouring ox was prohibited even on penalty of death ; [7] and young animals in particular were believed to be under the protection of the gods.[8] An ancient proverb says that " there are Erinyes even for dogs." [9] This seems to indicate that the Greeks, also, were influenced by the common notion that the soul of an animal may take revenge upon him who killed it, the Erinys of the slain animal being originally its persecuting ghost. Among the Pythagoreans, again, the rule that animals which are not obnoxious to the human race should be neither injured nor killed [10] was connected with their theory of metempsychosis ; [11] and in some cases the prohibition of slaying useful animals may be traced to utilitarian motives.[12] But both in Greece and Rome kindness to brutes was also inculcated for their own sake, on

[1] L. Schmidt, *Die Ethik der alten Griechen*, ii (Berlin, 1882), p. 96 *sq.*
[2] Westermarck, *op. cit.* i (London, 1912), p. 254.
[3] Plutarch, *Cato Major*, v. 6.   [4] *Ibid.* v. 7.
[5] Porphyry, *De abstinentia ab esu animalium*, iv. 22.
[6] Quintilian, *De institutione oratoria*, v. 9. 13.
[7] Varro, *De re rustica*, ii. 5. 3 ; Ælian, *Varia historia*, v. 14.
[8] Æschylus, *Agamemnon*, 48 *sqq.* ; Xenophon, *Cynegeticus*, v. 14.
[9] Schmidt, *op. cit.* ii. 96.
[10] Jamblichus, *De Pythagorica vita*, 21 (98).
[11] Diogenes Laertius, *Vitæ philosophorum*, viii. 2. 12 (77) ; Aristotle, *Rhetorica*, i. 13. 2, p. 1373*b* ; Schmidt, *op. cit.* ii. 94.
[12] Porphyry, *op. cit.* ii. 11, iv. 22.

purely humanitarian grounds. Porphyry says that, as justice pertains to rational beings and animals have been proved to be possessed of reason, it is necessary that we should act justly towards them.[1] He adds that " he who does not restrict harmless conduct to man alone, but extends it to other animals, most closely approaches to divinity ; and if it were possible to extend it to plants, he would preserve this image in a still greater degree." [2] According to Plutarch kindness and beneficence to creatures of every species flow from the breast of a well-natured man as streams that issue from the living fountain. We ought to take care of our dogs and horses not only when they are young, but also when they are old and past service.[3] We ought not to violate or kill anything whatsoever that has life, unless it hurts us first.[4] And if we cannot live unblamably we should at least sin with discretion : when we kill an animal in order to satisfy our hunger we should do so with sorrow and pity, without abusing and tormenting it.[5] Cicero says it is a crime to injure an animal.[6] And Marcus Aurelius enjoins man to make use of brutes with a generous and liberal spirit, since he has reason and they have not.[7]

In the Old Testament we meet with several instances of kindly feeling towards animals.[8] God watches over and controls the sustenance of their life. He sends springs into the valleys which will give drink to every beast of the field. He gives nests to the birds of the heaven, which sing among the branches. He causes grass to grow for the cattle ; and the young lions, roaring after their prey, seek their food from God.[9] While the Jews, as Professor Toy observes, found it hard to conceive of the God of Israel as thinking kindly of its enemies, they had no such feeling of hostility towards beasts and birds.[10] But at the same time various passages which are often quoted as instances of tenderness towards animals allow of another and more natural interpretation ; this is particularly the case with the sabbatarian injunctions referring to domestic animals. Man is the centre of the creation, a being set apart from all other sentient creatures as God's special favourite, for whose sake everything else was

[1] Porphyry, op. cit. iii. 18.　　　　　　　　　　[2] Ibid. iii. 28.
[3] Plutarch, Cato Major, v. 3 sq.
[4] Idem, Quæstiones Romanæ, 75.
[5] Idem, De carnium esu oratio II., i. 3.
[6] Cicero, De republica, iii. 11.
[7] Marcus Aurelius, Commentarii, vi. 23.
[8] See A. Bertholet, Die Stellung der Israeliten und der Juden zu den Fremden (Freiburg i. B. and Leipzig, 1896), p. 14.
[9] Psalms civ. 10–12, 14, 17, 21.
[10] C. H. Toy, Judaism and Christianity (London, 1890), p. 81.

brought into existence. The sun, the moon, and the stars were placed in the firmament of the heaven to give light upon the estate of man.[1] For his sustenance the fruits of the earth were made to grow, and to him was given dominion over the fish of the sea, and over the fowl of the air, and over every living thing that moves upon the earth.[2] And when the earth is to be replenished after the deluge, the same privileges are again granted to him. The fear of man and the dread of man shall be upon all living creatures, into his hand are they all delivered, they shall all be meat for him.[3]

Like the sayings of the Psalmist about the care which God takes of his creatures, those of Jesus likewise express tenderness of feeling. But when he speaks of the sparrows which are not forgotten by God, he does it to comfort his disciples : " Ye are of more value than many sparrows." [4] And when he speaks of the fowls of the air which neither sow nor reap nor gather into barns but are fed by God, he does it as a warning that they shall take no thought for the morrow : " Are ye not much better than they ? " [5] When Jesus asked the Pharisees, " Which of you shall have an ass or an ox fallen into a pit, and will not straight-way pull him out on the sabbath ? " [6] the motive for doing so may not merely be sympathy for the animal. The only occasion on which Jesus is reported to have had anything directly to do with animals was when he was besought by the devils whom he cast out of a man possessed with them to send them into a herd of swine feeding in the neighbourhood. " Forthwith Jesus gave them leave. And the unclean spirits went out, and entered into the swine : and the herd ran violently down a steep place into the sea (they were about two thousand), and were choked in the sea." [7] Nobody could say that this was kind to the swine.

Among the Hebrews the harshness of the anthropocentric doctrine was somewhat mitigated by the sympathy which a simple pastoral and agricultural people naturally feels for its domestic animals. In Christianity, on the other hand, it was further strengthened by the exclusive importance which was attached to the spiritual salvation of man. He was now more than ever separated from the rest of sentient beings. Even his own animal nature was regarded with contempt, the immortality of his soul being the only object of religious interest. " It would seem," says Dr. Arnold, " as if the primitive Christian, by laying so

---

[1] *Genesis* i. 16 *sq.*　　　[2] *Ibid.* i. 28.　　　[3] *Ibid.* ix. 2 *sq.*
[4] *Matthew* x. 29, 31 ; *Luke* xii. 6 *sq.*
[5] *Matthew* vi. 25 *sq.* ; *Luke* xii. 24.
[6] *Luke* xiv. 5. Cf. *Matthew* xii. 11.
[7] *Mark* v. 2–14. See also *Matthew* viii. 28–32 ; *Luke* viii. 27–33.

much stress upon a future life in contradistinction to this life, and placing the lower creatures out of the pale of hope, placed them at the same time out of the pale of sympathy, and thus laid the foundation for this utter disregard of animals in the light of our fellow-creatures." [1] Paul asks with scorn, " Doth God take care for oxen ? " [2]

No creed in Christendom teaches kindness to animals as a dogma of religion.[3] In the Middle Ages various Councils of the Church declared hunting unlawful for the clergy ; [4] but the obvious reason for this prohibition was her horror of bloodshed,[5] not any consideration for the animals. Mr. Mauleverer in Sir Arthur Helps' 'Talk about Animals and their Masters,' says : " Upon a moderate calculation, I think I have heard, in my time, 1,320 sermons ; and I do not recollect that in any one of them I ever heard the slightest allusion made to the conduct of men towards animals." [6] Indeed, " blood-sports " have not only been allowed to pass without any pulpit protest, but evidence appears in the press and on public platforms from time to time of the strong support given to the practice of such sports by ministers of different religious denominations. In a correspondence on the ethics of hunting to which the *Western Mail* some time ago opened its columns, the Rev. J. Price claimed that " man possesses divine authority for killing for sport. . . . Some men and women suffer and die for the life, the welfare, the happiness of others. This law is continually seen in operation. The supreme example of it was shown to the world (I write with reverence) on Calvary (*sic*). Why should animals be exempted from the operation of this law or principle ? " [7] A well-known Christian moralist, Dr. T. Fowler, thinks fox-hunting may be justified on the ground that the amount of suffering inflicted on the fox in addition to that which would be caused by killing it instantaneously is far more than counterbalanced by

[1] Arnold, quoted by E. P. Evans, ' Ethical Relations between Man and Beast,' in *The Popular Science Monthly*, xlv. (New York, 1894), p. 639.

[2] *1 Corinthians* ix. 9.

[3] The Manichæans prohibited all killing of animals (F. Chr. Baur, *Das Manichäische Religionssystem* [Tübingen, 1831], p. 252 *sqq.*) ; but Manichæism did not originate on Christian ground.

[4] P. J. B. Le Grand d'Aussy, *Histoire de la vie privée des François*, i (Paris, 1815), p. 394 *sq.*

[5] Westermarck, *op. cit.* i. 381 *sq.*

[6] A. Helps, *Some Talk about Animals and their Masters* (London, 1883), p. 20. *Cf.* Mrs. Jameson, *A Common-Place Book of Thoughts, Memories, and Fancies* (London, 1877), p. 212.

[7] The National Society for the Abolition of Cruel Sports, *Bulletin* No. 21, June, 1936 (London).

the beneficial effects, in health and enjoyment, to the hunter.[1] We are sometimes told that " the fox enjoys the hunt, too," or that it has "free chances of escape " [2]—which would be an excellent argument if we shared the North American Indian's conviction that an animal can never be killed without its own permission. The kindest words which from a Protestant view have been said about animals seem to have come from sectarians, Quakers and Methodists.[3] Roman Catholic writers have taken pains to show that animals are entirely destitute of rights. Brute beasts, says Father Rickaby, cannot have any rights because they have no understanding and therefore are not persons. We have no duties of any kind to them, as neither to sticks nor stones ; we have only duties *about* them. We must not harm them when they are our neighbour's property, we must not vex and annoy them *for* sport, because it disposes him who does so to inhumanity towards his own species. But there is no shadow of evil resting on the practice of causing pain to brutes *in* sport, where the pain is not the sport itself, but an incidental concomitant of it. Much more in all that conduces to the sustenance of man may we give pain to animals, and we are not " bound to any anxious care to make this pain as little as may be. Brutes are as *things* in our regard : so far as they are useful to us, they exist for us, not for themselves ; and we do right in using them unsparingly for our need and convenience, though not for our wantonness." [4] According to another modern Catholic writer the infliction of suffering upon an animal is not only justifiable, but a duty, " when it confers a certain, a solid good, however small, on the spiritual nature of man." [5] Pope Pius IX. refused a request for permission to form in Rome a Society for Prevention of Cruelty to Animals on the professed ground that it was a theological error to suppose that man owes any duty to an animal.[6]

[1] T. Fowler, *Progressive Morality* (London, 1925), p. 187 *sq.*
[2] F. P. Cobbe, *The Modern Rack* (London, 1889), p. 10.
[3] See J. J. Gurney, *Observations on the Distinguishing Views and Practices of the Society of Friends* (London, 1834), p. 392 *sq.* n. 8 ; L. Richmond, ' A Sermon on the Sin of Cruelty to the Brute Creation,' in *The Methodist Magazine*, xxx (London, 1807), p. 490 *sqq.* ; Chalmers, ' Cruelty to Animals,' in *The Methodist Magazine*, ix (New York, 1826), p. 259 *sqq.*
[4] J. Rickaby, *Moral Philosophy* (London, 1892), p. 248 *sqq.* See also W. E. Addis and T. Arnold, *A Catholic Dictionary* (London, 1903), p. 33 ; R. F. Clarke, ' On Cruelty to Animals in its Moral Aspect,' in *The Month and Catholic Review*, xxv (London, 1875), p. 401 *sqq.* ; J. C. Hedley, ' Dr. Mivart on Faith and Science,' in *The Dublin Review*, ser. iii, vol. xviii (London, 1887), p. 418.
[5] Clarke, *loc. cit.* p. 406.   [6] Cobbe, *op. cit.* p. 6.

It is not only theological moralists that maintain that animals can have no rights, and that abstinence from wanton cruelty is a duty not to the animal but to man. This view has been shared by Kant [1] and by many later philosophers. So also the legal protection of animals has often been vindicated merely on the ground that cruelty to animals might breed cruelty to men or shows a cruel disposition of mind, [2] or that it wounds the sensibilities of other people. [3] In 'Parliamentary History and Review' for 1825–6 it is stated that no reason can be assigned for the interference of the legislator in the protection of animals unless their protection be connected, either directly or remotely, with some advantage to man. [4] The Bill for the abolition of bear-baiting and other cruel practices was expressly propounded on the ground that nothing was more conducive to crime than such sports, that they led the lower orders to gambling, that they educated them for thieves, that they gradually trained them up to bloodshed and murder. [5]

Indifference to animal suffering has been a characteristic of public opinion in Christian Europe up to quite modern times. In his 'Essay on Humanity to Animals,' published in 1798, Thomas Young declared that he was sensible of laying himself open to no small portion of ridicule in offering to the public a book on such a subject. [6] Till the end of the eighteenth century and even later cock-fighting was a very general amusement among the English and Scotch, entering into the occupations of both the old and young. Travellers agreed with coachmen that they were to wait a night if there was a cock-fight in any town through which they passed. Schools had their cock-fights ; on Shrove Tuesday every youth took to the village schoolroom a cock reared for his special use, and the schoolmaster presided at the conflict. [7] Those who felt that the practice required some excuse found it

---

[1] Kant, *Metaphysische Anfangungsgründe der Tugendlehre* (Königsberg, 1903), § 16 *sq.*, pp. 106, 108.

[2] Hommel, quoted by R. von Hippel, *Die Thielquälerei in der Strafgesetzgebung* (Berlin, 1891), p. 110 ; J. Tissot, *Le droit pénal étudié dans ses principes*, i (Paris, 1860), p. 17 ; A. Lasson, *System der Rechtsphilosophie* (Berlin and Leipzig, 1882), p. 548 *sq.*

[3] Lasson, *op. cit.* p. 548 ; von Hippel, *op. cit.* p. 125.

[4] *Parliamentary History and Review*, 1825–6 (London, 1826), p. 761.

[5] *Ibid.* p. 546.

[6] T. Young, *An Essay on Humanity to Animals* (London, 1798), p. 1.

[7] G. Roberts, *The Social History of the People of the Southern Counties of England in the Past Centuries* (London, 1856), p. 421 *sqq.* ; C. Rogers, *Social Life in Scotland*, ii (Edinburgh, 1885), p. 340. In the middle of the last century, when Roberts wrote his book, cock-penance was still paid in some English grammar schools to the master as a perquisite on Shrove Tuesday (*op. cit.* p. 423).

in the idea that the race was to suffer this annual barbarity by way of punishment for St. Peter's crime ; [1] but the number of people who had any scruples about the game cannot have been great considering that even such a strong advocate of humanity to animals as John Lawrence had no decided antipathy to it. [2] Other pastimes indulged in were dog-fighting, bull-baiting, and badger-baiting ; and in the middle of the eighteenth century the bear-garden was described by Lord Kames as one of the chief entertainments of the English, though it was held in abhorrence by the French and " other polite nations," being too savage an amusement to be relished by those of a refined taste. [3] As late as 1824 Sir Robert (then Mr.) Peel argued strongly against the legal prohibition of bull-baiting. [4]

About ten years previously, however, humanity to animals had, for the first time, become a subject of English legislation by the Act which prevented cruel and improper treatment of cattle. [5] This Act was afterwards followed by others which prohibited bear-baiting, cock-fighting, and similar pastimes, as also cruelty to domestic animals in general ; and since 1900 cases of ill-treatment of wild animals in captivity may be dealt with under the Wild Animals in Captivity Protection Act. [6] On the Continent cruelty to animals was first prohibited by criminal law in Saxony, in 1838, [7] and subsequently in most other European states. But in the south of Europe there are still, or have been until lately, countries in which the law is entirely silent on the subject. [8]

Whatever be the professed motives of legislators for preventing cruelty to animals, there can be no doubt that the laws against it are chiefly due to a keener and more generally felt sympathy with their sufferings. The actual feelings of men have been somewhat more tender than the theories of law, philosophy, and religion. The anthropocentric exclusiveness of Christianity was from ancient times to some extent counterbalanced by popular sentiments and beliefs. In the folk-tales of Europe man is not placed in an isolated and unique position in the universe. He lives in intimate and friendly intercourse

---

[1] Roberts, *op. cit.* p. 422.

[2] J. Lawrence, *A Philosophical and Practical Treatise on Horses,* ii (London, 1798), p. 12.

[3] Lord Kames, *Essays on the Principles of Morality and Natural Religion* (Edinburgh, 1751), p. 7.

[4] T. C. Hansard, *The Parliamentary Debates from 1803 to the Present Times,* New Series, x. 491 *sqq.*

[5] *Statutes of the United Kingdom of Great Britain and Ireland,* lxii. 403 *sqq.*

[6] H. J. Stephen, *New Commentaries on the Laws of England,* iv (London, 1903), p. 213 *sqq.*

[7] Von Hippel, *op. cit.* p. 1.   [8] *Ibid.* p. 90 *sq.*

with the animals round him, attributes to them human qualities, and regards them with mercy.[1] Tender feelings towards the brute creation are also displayed in many legends of saints.[2] St. Francis of Assisi talked with the birds and called them " brother birds " or " little sister swallows," and was seen employed in removing worms from the road that they might not be trampled by travellers.[3] John Moschus speaks of a certain abbot who early in the morning not only used to give food to all the dogs in the monastery, but would bring corn to the ants and to the birds on the roof.[4] In the ' Revelations of St. Bridget,' we read : " Let a man fear, above all, me, his God, and so much the gentler will he become towards my creatures and animals, on whom, on account of me, their Creator, he ought to have compassion." [5] Many kind words about animals have come from poets and thinkers. Montaigne says that he never has been able to see without affliction an innocent beast, which is without defence and from which we receive no offence, pursued and killed.[6] Shakespeare points out that " the poor beetle that we tread upon, in corporal sufferance finds a pang as great as when a giant dies." [7] Mandeville thinks that if it was not for that tyranny which custom usurps over us, no men of any tolerable good-nature could ever be reconciled to the killing of so many animals for their daily food, as long as the bountiful earth so plentifully provides them with varieties of vegetable dainties.[8] Towards the end of the eighteenth century Bentham wrote : " Men must be permitted to kill animals ; but they should be forbidden to torment them. Artificial death may be rendered less painful than natural death by simple processes, well worth the trouble of being studied, and of becoming an object of police. Why should the law refuse its protection to any sensitive being ? A time will come when humanity will spread its mantle over everything that breathes. The lot of slaves has begun to excite pity ; we shall end by softening the lot of the animals which

[1] Westermarck, *op. cit.* i. 259 ; W. Schwarz, *Prähistorisch-anthropologische Studien* (Berlin, 1884), p. 203.
[2] La Marquise de Rambures, *L'Église et la pitié envers les animaux* (Paris and Londres, 1908), *passim* ; W. E. H. Lecky, *History of European Morals from Augustus to Charlemagne,* ii (London, 1890), p. 168 *sqq.* ; C. J. Cadoux, *Catholicism and Christianity* (London, 1928), p. 628.
[3] P. Sabatier, *Life of St. Francis of Assisi* (London, 1894), p. 176 *sq.* ; K. H. Digby, *Mores Catholici,* ii (London, 1846), p. 291.
[4] J. Moschus, *Pratum spirituale,* 184 (Migne, *Patrologiæ cursus, Ser. Græca,* lxxxvii. 3056).
[5] St. Bridget, quoted by Helps, *op. cit.* p. 124.
[6] Montaigne, *Essais* ii. 11.
[7] Shakespeare, *Measure for Measure,* iii. 1.
[8] B. de Mandeville, *The Fable of the Bees* (London, 1724), p. 187.

labour for us and supply our wants." [1] In the course of the nineteenth century humanity to animals, from being conspicuous in a few individuals only, became the keynote of a movement gradually increasing in strength.

In an essay on ' The Christian Ideal and some of its Competitors,' Mr. Harvey observes that it is humiliating to recognise how much of the advance towards a more humane attitude to the animal world has been due " not to the direct challenge of any Christian Church, but to the patient educative work of reformers professing no allegiance to Christianity." [2] One reason for this may be the decline of the anthropocentric doctrine and the influence of another theory, which regards man not as an image of the deity separated from the lower animals by a special act of creation, but as a being generally akin to them, and only representing a higher stage in the scale of mental evolution. But apart from any theory as regards human origins, growing reflection has taught men to be more considerate in their treatment of animals by producing a more vivid idea of their sufferings. Human thoughtlessness has been responsible for much needless pain to which they have been subjected. And in spite of some improvement it is so still.

At the same time the movement advocating greater humanity to animals is itself not altogether free from inconsistencies and a certain lack of discrimination. The extreme views on the question, how far the happiness of the lower animals may be justly sacrificed for the benefit of man, may be somewhat modified on the one hand by a more vivid representation of animal suffering, and on the other hand by the recognition of certain facts, often overlooked, which make it unreasonable to regard conduct towards dumb creatures in exactly the same light as conduct towards men. It should especially be remembered that the former have none of those long-protracted anticipations of future misery or death which we have. If they are destined to serve as meat they are not aware of it; whereas many domestic animals never would have come into existence and been able to enjoy what appears a very happy life, but for the purpose of being used as food. But though greater intellectual discrimination may somewhat lessen the divergencies of moral opinion on the subject, nothing like unanimity can be expected, for the simple reason that moral judgments are ultimately based on emotions, and sympathy with the animal world is a feeling which varies extremely in different individuals.

[1] J. Bentham, *Theory of Legislation* (London, 1882), p. 428 *sq.*
[2] G. L. H. Harvey, ' The Christian Ideal and some of its Competitors,' in *Christianity and the Present Moral Unrest* (London, 1926), p. 49 *sq.*

CHAPTER XX

SUMMARY AND CONCLUDING REMARKS

THERE would have been no Paul without Christ, but there would have been no Christianity without Paul. The new faith would, no doubt, have merely remained the religion of a Jewish sect destined to pine away, if Paul had not rescued it for history, and made it a religion of the world. He did this by transforming its character. Jesus had taught, in the Sermon on the Mount, that the salvation of any man depended on his own moral conduct, and that the way which led to the kingdom of God was anything but easy. According to Paul, future life was the result of a divine work of redemption, which prepared the salvation for mankind once for all through the death and resurrection of Christ and faith. Christian theologians often tell us that there is no essential difference between the teaching of Jesus and that of Paul. But from the moral point of view the difference is radical.

I have tried to show that the ethics of Jesus were expressions of his moral emotions, and that these were in general agreement with the nature of such emotions when guided by sufficient sympathy and discrimination. This is proved by the great similarities between the teaching of Jesus and that of the world's other great moralists. Moral emotions are disinterested retributive emotions. Personal anger and vindictiveness are strongly condemned by Jesus ; and the injunctions of forgiveness and kindness to enemies are also found in the Old Testament and other Jewish writings, in the Koran and the Mohammedan traditions, in Brahmanism, Buddhism, and Chinese ethics ; and the principle of forgiveness had advocates in Greece and Rome, as well, the condemnation of anger and resentment being particularly abundant in Stoicism. Quite different from the resentment and retaliation springing from personal motives are moral resentment and the punishment in which it finds expression. These vary indefinitely. The moral indignation of Jesus is often intense, and the future punishment he assigns to unrepentant sinners enormous. This is an unsurmountable stumbling-block for those who insist on the objectivity of the rules of Christian ethics. Nowadays Christians are shocked by

394

the ancient doctrine of hell and make vain attempts to explain it away. But side by side with the doctrine of retribution there is in the gospels the message of forgiveness for the repentant sinner. That repentance is followed by forgiveness is also found in other religions, such as Judaism, Zoroastrianism, Brahmanism, and the Vedic religion. But repentance not only blunts the edge of moral indignation and recommends the offender to mercy : it is also the sole ground on which pardon can be given by a scrupulous judge. When sufficiently guided by deliberation and left to itself without being unduly checked by other emotions, the feeling of moral resentment is apt to last as long as its cause remains unaltered, that is, until the will of the offender has ceased to be offensive ; and it ceases to be so only when he acknowledges his guilt and repents. That moral indignation is appeased by repentance, and that repentance is the only proper ground for forgiveness, however, is due, not to the specifically moral character of such indignation, but to its being a form of resentment. This is confirmed by the fact that an angry and revengeful man is apt to be influenced in a similar way by the sincere repentance of the offender.

ᛒ While Jesus was capable of feeling intense moral indignation, his emotion of moral approval, of which moral praise or reward is the outward manifestation, plays a no less prominent part in his teaching, as is shown by the innumerable cases in which eternal reward is promised for righteousness. Does this imply that Jesus considered hope of reward as an adequate reason for receiving it ? We do not feel the emotion of moral approval or retributive kindliness towards a person if we recognise that he does something merely in the selfish hope of being benefited by it ; and, like all great moralists, Jesus certainly laid stress on the motives of conduct, on inwardness and purity of heart. But there is no inconsistency between benevolence being the immediate spring of action and the hope of reward being an ultimate motive for it : a person may aim at his own happiness as his ultimate end and at the same time aim sincerely at the happiness of his neighbour as a means to that end. The desire to gain divine favour with everything implied in it must certainly have been regarded by Jesus as a right motive for our conduct.

ᛒ While Jesus' doctrine of punishment and reward is an outcome of the retributive character of the moral emotions, his teaching also emphasises that disinterestedness which distinguishes them from other, non-moral, retributive emotions. This he does in his enunciation of " the Golden Rule," which, also, is much older than Christianity and, especially in its negative form, widespread. The disinterestedness of the moral emotions, moreover, partly underlies the rule, " Thou shalt love thy neighbour as thyself," which occurs both in the Old Testament and in the three synoptic gospels. But this maxim contains much more than the disinterestedness of the conception of duty. When a person pronounces an act right or wrong, it implies that it is so, *ceteris paribus*, whether he does it to another or another does it to him ; but this has nothing to do with the particular nature of the act. When my own interests clash with those of my neighbour, I may have the right to prefer my own lesser good to the greater good of another, but only on condition that the other person also, in similar circumstances, is admitted to have the right to prefer his own lesser good to my greater good. No such right to prefer one's own lesser good to the greater good of another is recognised in the precept, " Thou shalt love thy neighbour as thyself " ; but this precept owes its origin to the strength of the altruistic sentiment in him who laid down the rule, and not merely to the disinterestedness of his moral emotions. It is another instance of the relative validity of our moral judgments ; and so are moral rules relating to different groups of neighbours. They vary indefinitely because the altruistic sentiment varies in expanse as well as in strength. The impartiality of my moral emotions does not prevent me from promoting the welfare of my own family or country in preference to that of other families or countries ; but it tells me that I must allow anybody else to show a similar preference for *his* family or country. Among the positive duties resulting from benevolence almsgiving holds a very prominent position in the teaching of Jesus, as it did in Judaism and particularly in the Old Testament apocrypha and in rabbinical literature.

While his ethics were an expression of intense moral emotions in which both the retributive and the altruistic elements came out very prominently, specific religious and eschatological beliefs were blended with the ideas springing from those emotions. Our duties to neighbours were founded upon our submission to the will of God, and their sanctions were rewards or penalties for obedience or disobedience to his commandments. But those beliefs did not essentially alter the contents of those commandments, as is testified by the innumerable parallels between the teaching of Jesus and that of other great moralists. We also find that certain doctrines which had crept into the moral system of the Jews from their religion, but were alien to the emotional origin of morals, were opposed by Jesus, as was the case with his attitude towards the sabbath.

Among the sayings of Jesus there are injunctions which

cannot be meant to be obeyed literally, but are more or less paradoxical, in conformity to the Oriental habit of speaking in proverbs, which stress one side of a case to the exclusion of every other. We must also remember that much of his teaching was conditioned by his belief that the End was at hand ; and least of all must we expect his sayings to be applicable to the circumstances of modern life. It may, moreover, be said that Jesus himself somewhat modified his teaching by recognising the existing institutions of the State. There is no hint that he wanted soldiers to abandon their profession, or that he regarded this profession as wrong ; his attitude towards the centurion whose servant was sick of the palsy was altogether friendly. And when the Pharisees tried to entangle him in his talk, he told them that they should render unto Cæsar the things which were Cæsar's, and unto God the things that were God's. This helped Luther to find a compromise between what we should do as members of the kingdom of God and as members of the kingdom of Cæsar.[1] Roman Catholicism had found another way of softening the severity of the Sermon on the Mount. The harder sayings came to be reckoned as counsels of perfection, the observance of which implied that the performer did more than was required for his own salvation.

While Jesus was a moralist, Paul was in the first place a theologian. Faith is the keystone of his teaching, faith in the redemption through the crucified and risen Christ. He never speaks of Jesus as a teacher or of his teaching, he extremely seldom appeals to any words of Jesus as a moral norm, he never refers to his example in any concrete situation. " A man is justified by faith without the deeds of the law " ; " To him that worketh not, but believeth on him that justifieth the ungodly, his faith is counted for righteousness." Whatever else Paul's conception of faith may imply, it presupposes in the first place the intellectual acceptance of some fact as true ; and such a belief cannot be a proper object of moral judgment. But even if the sin of unbelief, as Thomas Aquinas argues, has its cause in the will because it consists in " contrary opposition to the faith, whereby one stands out against the hearing of the faith," it could not be imputed to anybody who never heard of the faith. Moreover, the faith itself is a gift of God : " God hath dealt to every man the measure of faith." Salvation depends on an " election of grace " : God " hath mercy on whom he will have mercy, and whom he will he hardeneth." Yet there is some reason for his mercy. Those who believe are justified by the

[1] See N. Söderblom, *Jesu bärgspredikan och vår tid* (Stockholm, 1899), p. 56 *sqq.*

grace of God " through the redemption that is in Christ Jesus : whom God hath set forth to be a propitiation through faith in his blood, to declare his righteousness for the remission of sins that are past, through the forbearance of God." Christ " died for all, that they which live should not henceforth live unto themselves, but unto him which died for them, and rose again." " Christ our passover is sacrificed for us." It is thus by the vicarious suffering of Jesus that the wrath of God, aroused by the sin of men, is appeased. " As by one man sin entered into the world, and death by sin," and " as by the offence of one judgment came upon all men to condemnation ; even so by the righteousness of one the free gift came upon all men unto justification of life."

×The idea that all mankind are doomed to death on account of Adam's sin, which Paul had imbibed from his Jewish up-bringing, is explicable by the conception of sin as a kind of material substance or infection which is transplanted by propagation.✝ But the Prophets already broke with the old notions of divine vengeance by declaring that " every one shall die for his own iniquity," and that " the soul that sinneth, it shall die " ; and Ezekiel added that as the wickedness of the wicked shall be upon him, so also " the righteousness of the righteous shall be upon him." This is in agreement with the fact that the moral emotions of disapproval and approval, in their capacity of retributive emotions, are hostile or friendly attitudes of mind towards persons conceived as causes of pain or pleasure. They cannot admit that a person is punished or rewarded on account of another person's behaviour. There cannot be either a guilt or a merit by transfer. It is contrary to the fundamental principles of our moral consciousness.

We find, however, also another line of thought in Paul's epistles. He writes not only that a man is justified by faith without the deeds of the law, but sometimes also that God will show himself as a righteous judge, " who will render to every man according to his deeds," or that " every man shall receive his own reward according to his own labour." In various passages he expresses the idea that faith produces obedience to the law and charity ; and it may be argued that if a person is justified by faith, which is a gift of God, and good deeds are manifestations of it, his " reward " for them is really due to the faith which God has given him, and that the damnation of a person who has done evil is due to the fact that he has not received the gift of faith from God ; whereas if he receives such a gift, and is justified thereby, he will do no evil again. Such a conclusion might be drawn from one of his sayings. But Paul was not a consistent thinker. On the one hand he teaches that justification depends upon faith alone, that faith is a gift of God, that man's work really is God's work, nay that it even was God who gave Israel " the spirit of slumber, eyes that they should not see, and ears that they should not hear " ; but on the other hand he also looks upon the activity of the human will as a factor of importance. When he speaks of the retribution for good and evil deeds, he is evidently moved by his moral consciousness, which repeatedly finds expression without any reference to justification by faith. He refers to " conscience " and speaks of the " witness " it bears, and finds a conscience not only among the Christians, but in every man. " When the Gentiles, which have not the law, do by nature the things contained in the law, these, having not the law, are a law unto themselves : which shew the work of the law written in their hearts."

The antithesis between the moralistic teaching of Jesus as reported in the synoptic gospels and Paul's formula of justification by faith, alternated in the early Church. But through Augustine Paulinism got the upper hand, though a Paulinism modified by popular Catholic elements. To him the object of the faith which is necessary for salvation was the truth guaranteed by the Church, which he regarded as infallible in consequence of its authority as based on apostolicity. But the faith which saves is only the faith that works in love—faith, love, and merit being successive steps in the way to final salvation. This also became the view of the Catholic Church. The conception of merits, which had been current in her from earlier days, was accepted by Augustine, but was reconciled with the doctrine of grace. Faith and love and merits are all God's gifts, and " no one is saved except by undeserved mercy, and no one is condemned except by a deserved judgment." As Paul taught, the elect are saved because God, in virtue of his eternal decree of salvation, has predestinated, chosen, called, justified, sanctified, and preserved them. All men are by nature children of wrath, and are burdened by original sin and their own sins. Therefore a mediator was necessary who should appease that wrath by presenting a unique sacrifice. That this was done constitutes the grace of God through Jesus Christ, who by submitting to death without compulsion became a sacrifice for sin, representing our sin in the flesh in which he was crucified, " that in some way he might die to sin, in dying to the flesh," and from the resurrection might seal our new life.

From the moral point of view the relation between the grace of God and the faith, love, and merit of man in Augustine's doctrine of salvation is an absurdity. If the latter are gifts of

God he rewards man with eternal felicity for what he himself has given him. That God has predestinated some persons to salvation and others to damnation makes moral responsibility impossible, since moral judgments, owing to their very nature, are passed on persons conceived as the cause of a certain mode of conduct which is directly or indirectly attributed to their own will. Nor can Augustine's conception of original sin satisfy even the most elementary moral claim. The punishment for Adam's disobedience was inflicted not only on himself but on his descendants as well; and at the same time they had also to pay for the sin contracted by their parents producing them in sinful lust.

Augustinianism was accepted by the Western Church, though with the secret reservation that it was to be moulded by its own mode of thought when it did not harmonise with the tendencies of the Church. Its greatest and most influential champion was Thomas Aquinas, particularly with regard to its doctrines of God, predestination, sin, and grace. But in spite of his ardent adherence to Augustinianism we find in him a timid revision of it in a moralistic direction. Although he makes an earnest endeavour to assert the sole efficacy of divine grace, his line of statement takes ultimately a different direction. While man cannot merit eternal life without grace, there must for justification co-operate a movement of free will, a movement of faith, and a hatred of sin; in other words, there is an intermingling of grace and self-action, and only then justification takes place. Thus, according to Thomas, the process of grace realises itself with the consent of free will, even though this consent is at the same time the effect of grace. The doctrine that eternal salvation must be merited by good works is common to all the mediæval Schoolmen, and the Council of Trent stamped it with its approval.

This doctrine of grace culminates in the " evangelical counsels." Thomas points out, as others had done before him, that there are both precepts and counsels. A precept is compulsory, whereas a counsel is dependent on the option of him to whom it was given. The observance of precepts is necessary, but also sufficient, for the gaining of eternal life; but there are counsels " regarding those things by which man can attain the appointed end better and more readily." This distinction between command and counsel, between a higher and a lower Christian life, was supported by Paul's saying that the virgin state is superior to the married one, but that he who marries has not sinned. The distinction in question has certainly a solid foundation in our moral consciousness, in so far that a command implies the concept of duty, which is based on the emotion of disapproval, and a counsel implies the concept of goodness, which derives its origin from the emotion of moral approval. It is obvious that if a course of conduct which is not regarded as a duty is held to be meritorious, it is *ipso facto* admitted that a man can do more than his duty. This is denied both by those who derive goodness from duty and consider that what is good is what ought to be done, and by those who derive duty from goodness and consider that everybody ought to do the best he is able to do. Duty, which is the minimum of morality, in so far that it implies that the opposite mode of conduct is wrong, is identified with the supreme moral ideal, which requires the best possible conduct for its realisation. This rigorism may be traced either to the direct or indirect influence of Protestant theology with its denial of all works of supererogation, or to the endeavour of normative moralists to preach the most elevated kind of morality they can conceive. It is certainly not supported by our practical moral judgments, and I do not see how such a doctrine could serve any useful purpose at all. It is nowadays a recognised principle in legislation that a law loses much of its weight if it cannot be enforced. If the realisation of the highest moral ideal is commanded by a moral law, such a law will always remain a dead letter, and morality will gain nothing. It seems to me that far above the anxious effort to fulfil the commandments of duty stands the free and lofty aspiration to live up to an ideal, which, unattainable as it may be, threatens neither with blame nor remorse him who fails to reach its summits.

At the same time there are in the Roman Catholic doctrine of merit certain very objectionable features. It implies that a good deed stands in the same relation to a bad deed as a claim to a debt ; that the claim is made on the same person to whom the debt is due, that is God, even though it only be by his mercy ; and that the debt consequently may be compensated for in the same way as the infliction of a loss or damage may be compensated for by the payment of an indemnity. This doctrine of reparation comes inevitably to attach badness and goodness to external acts rather than to mental facts. No reparation can be given for badness. It can only be forgiven, and moral forgiveness can only be granted on condition that the agent's mind has undergone a radical alteration for the better, that the badness of the will has given way to repentance. This point was certainly not overlooked by the Catholic moralists, but even the most ardent apology cannot explain away the idea of reparation in the Catholic conception of the justification of man. Moreover, the ethical value of the theory of " good works " is much reduced when merit is particularly ascribed to works which our moral consciousness is apt to regard as indifferent or even to disapprove of, namely, ascetic practices, not in the sense of strict self-discipline but of relinquishing worldly pleasures and enjoyments and of deliberate maltreatment of the body. Finally, vicarious efficacy is attributed to good deeds. It is argued that Christ has done more by his suffering than was necessary for redemption, and that also many saints have performed meritorious deeds which God's grace rewards ; and that this surplus merit, or " treasury of supererogatory works," must necessarily fall to the benefit of the Church, since neither Christ nor the saints derive further advantage from it.

The question how Christ's suffering and death can be a means of justification called for an answer. According to Augustine it was a ransom paid to the devil, who has acquired a legal claim on men—a theory which had previously been set forth by Origen—and this explanation was accepted by most of the Western Fathers. It did not, however, exclude the old idea that Christ's suffering and death constituted a sacrifice presented by him to God in order to propitiate him. This has remained the most popular view, although rival explanations have also been suggested, and there is an increasing number of disbelievers. Moral justification is claimed for it. In the recent Report of the Anglican Commission on Christian Doctrine we are told that "the Cross is a satisfaction for sin so far as the moral order of the universe makes it impossible that human souls should be redeemed from sin except at a cost. . . . The redeeming love of God, through the life of Jesus Christ sacrificially offered in death upon the Cross, acted with cleansing power upon a sin-stained world, and so enables us to be cleaned." To me it seems that even the slightest degree of reflection should show how incompatible the infliction of punishment on an innocent person in place of the culprit is with the very nature of our moral consciousness, moral indignation being a hostile attitude of mind towards an individual conceived as a cause of pain.

The Reformation implied an Augustinian reaction and a restoration of Paulinism. It substituted the Bible for the authority of the Church, and to Luther in particular the kernel and marrow of the Bible was the epistles of Paul. We are justified by faith alone. The Schoolmen had developed the hint contained in Paul's expression " faith working by love," and distinguished between an " unformed " faith—a mere intellectual belief—and a " formed " faith, which includes love, and which alone justifies and saves. According to Luther, on the other hand, " we can be saved without charity," but not without pure doctrine and faith. " No good work can profit an unbeliever to justification and salvation ; and, on the other hand, no evil work makes him an evil and condemned person, but that un-belief, which makes the person and the tree bad, makes his works evil and condemned." Luther even denied that we can do any good work at all ; among the famous ninety-five theses which he nailed on the church door of Wittenberg there was the assertion that " the just man sins in every good work." It is true that in his more moderate statements he can declare that the sanctifying grace given after the man has been justified by faith enables him to do good works, nay that good works will necessarily follow his faith ; but then the good works are not really done by him but by God. As Luther grew older, his conception of faith became more and more intellectual, till at last it comprised little beyond the assent of mind to certain articles of an orthodox creed. " One little point of doctrine," he says, " is of more value than heaven and earth ; therefore we do not suffer it (i.e. doctrine) to be injured in the smallest particular. But at errors of life we may very well connive."

Although Luther would not hear of any human merit, he believed in the merit of Christ, who, as the Confession of Augsburg put it, " suffered and died that he might reconcile the Father to us, and be a sacrifice, not only for original guilt, but also for all actual sins of men." Christ's righteousness is imputed to us. Our faith in him makes his piety ours, and makes our sins his. He was the greatest of all sinners, because he assumed in his body the sins we had committed, to make satisfaction for them on the cross ; " he was crucified and died for us, and offered up our sins in his own body." And Christ is represented by Luther as not merely dying instead of us, but also as keeping the law instead of us. " This is the gospel . . . that the law has been fulfilled, that is, by Christ, so that it is not necessary for us to fulfil it, but only to adhere and to be conformed to him who fulfils it." The denial of all human merit in conjunction with the belief in the saving efficacy of the vicarious merit of Christ seems to be the climax of the antimoralism of Christian theology.

The other Reformers were, generally, in substantial agreement with Luther. Zwingli likewise substituted the authority of the Bible for the authority of the Church, and preached the justification by faith alone. But he did not so exclusively as Luther take his gospel from Paul's epistles and then read it into the whole Bible. He was much more than Luther a humanist, and more a moralist as well. He wrote that " it is the part of a Christian man not to talk magnificently of doctrines, but always, with God to do great and hard things." Like Luther, Calvin was an Augustinian in assuming the absolute foreknowledge and determining power of God, the servitude of the human will, the corruption and incapacity of man's nature. But to him the main thing was not the sinner's personal relation to Christ and his appropriation of the Saviour's work, but the awful omnipotence of the divine decree fixing the unalterable succession of events and shutting out all co-operation of the human will. God predestinated certain individuals to salvation from eternity by his gratuitous mercy, and consigned the remainder to eternal damnation, by " a just and irreprehensible, but incomprehensible judgment." To apply earthly standards of justice to his sovereign decrees is meaningless and an insult to his majesty. To assume that human merit and guilt play a part in determining the destiny of men, would be to think of God's absolutely free decrees, which have been settled from eternity, as subject to change by human influence—an impossible contradiction. Yet however useless good works might be as a means of attaining salvation, they are nevertheless indispensable as a sign of election. They are the technical means, not of purchasing salvation, but of getting rid of the fear of damnation.

Reformation was a protest not only against doctrines taught by the Catholic Church, but also against moral abuses practised in its name, such as benefactions being accepted in atonement for flagrant sin, and escape from purgatory being bought in any market-place. But at the same time the Reformers rejected the sound moral principles which were defiled by such corrupt practices, when they denied the value of good deeds however sincere, and the different degrees of sinfulness of which the doctrine of purgatory is an expression. This doctrine, which had been suggested by Augustine and generally accepted by the Schoolmen, had mitigated the monstrosity of the teaching of eternal tortures by intercalating a place between heaven and hell, where those who have been accepted for a blessed state but are only partially prepared for it are subjected to a painful discipline. Its existence had been inferred indirectly from Matthew (xii. 31) and the First Epistle to the Corinthians (iii. 12 *sq.*) ; but the Protestants declared it to be, in the words of the Anglican Article XXII., " a fond thing vainly invented, and grounded upon no warranty of Scripture, but rather repugnant to the word of God." The shocking abuses which were connected with the belief in purgatory—even in the decree of the Council of Trent relating to it there is an allusion to " base gain, scandals, and stumbling-blocks for the faithful "—cannot disguise the fact that the doctrine itself has a moral foundation.

Something similar may be said of the sacrament of penance, the starting-point of which is the contrition, or at any rate attrition, of the penitent, though the real sacrament is the external acts of him and the priest. The satisfaction preceding the absolution, or priestly declaration of forgiveness of sins, became a sheer travesty through the practice of indulgences, which implied the exchange of more arduous penitential acts for very small performances, such as the payment of penance money, with the result that the Church dispensed from the temporal pains of purgatory all, whether living or departed, who either themselves or vicariously performed those ecclesiastical exercises. The practice and theory of indulgences was vehemently attacked by Luther, who substituted repentance alone, which he conceived of as the crushed feeling about sin awakened by faith. But his own doctrine that only such repentance as springs from faith has value before God is also open to criticism, though of a different kind. It alienates repentance widely from the sphere of morality, and is fraught with serious consequences. It makes it as constant as faith. The first of Luther's ninety-five theses runs : " Our Lord and Master Jesus Christ in saying, ' Repent ye,' etc., intended that the whole life of believers should be penitence." Harnack remarks that if men are told that they must constantly repent, and that particular acts of repentance are of no use, there are few who will ever repent.

Whatever importance has been attached either to merits or to faith, the doctrine of salvation has at the same time been influenced by the belief in a mystical efficacy of the sacraments of baptism and the Eucharist, which are common both to Catholics and Protestants. The former is regarded as a bath of regeneration, by which sins are blotted out, and as a necessary means of salvation. According to Thomas Aquinas it is the indispensable medicine for the consequences of the Fall, which abolishes the guilt both of original sin and of all committed sins without exception ; and in the Confession of Augsburg the Lutherans asserted the absolute necessity of baptism quite as emphatically as the Catholics. In Catholicism, however, the notion that unbaptised children will be tormented gradually gave way to a more humane opinion, according to which there is a place, called *limbus*, or *infernus puerorum*, where unbaptised infants will dwell without being subject to torture. But the older view was again set up by the Protestants, who generally maintained that the due punishment of original sin is, in strictness, damnation in hell, although many of them were inclined to think that if a child dies by misfortune before it is baptised, the parents' sincere intention of baptising it, together with their prayers, will be accepted with

God for the deed. The Confession of Augsburg emphatically condemns the doctrine of the Anabaptists that children are saved without baptism. So also the damnation of infants who die unbaptised was an acknowledged belief of Calvinism, although an exception was made for the children of pious parents, provided " there is neither sloth, nor contempt, nor negligence."

The Eucharist, which like the baptism evidently owes its sacramental character to Paul, was looked upon by him as a mystical re-enactment of the death and resurrection of Christ through which the believer participates in his immortality, the bread and wine being an incarnation of his body and blood. Aquinas says of the effects of the Eucharist that it conveys grace, gives aid for eternal life, blots out venial sins but not mortal sins, and guards against future transgressions. Luther maintained that both the Eucharist and baptism, which were the only sacraments recognised by him, work forgiveness of sin and thereby procure life and blessedness, but not without faith ; he insisted that the sacraments do not become efficacious in their being celebrated, but in their being believed in. In any case they are rooted in magical ideas, and the efficacy attributed to them has always retained a magical character. For the supposed saving effect of baptism and the Eucharist there is no moral justification whatever. A righteous God does not forgive a sinner unless he repents, and if he repents he is forgiven without any external rite. Repentance is not much spoken of in connection with those sacraments. In the case of baptism it was formerly expected of converts ; but when infant baptism was introduced it ceased even nominally to be required of him who was going to be baptised.

From this survey of Christian ethics as expressed in theories of salvation and of the agreement or disagreement of these theories with the nature of our moral emotions we now come to the question, how far they may be supposed to have influenced the morality of human conduct. The belief in a god who acts as a guardian of worldly morality undoubtedly gives emphasis to its rules. To the social and legal sanctions a new one is added, which derives particular strength from the super natural power and knowledge of the deity. The divine avenger can punish those who are beyond the reach of human justice and those whose secret wrongs escape the censure of their fellowmen and the righteous god can also reward goodness which receives no other reward. Among the early Christians the hope of future blessedness and especially the fear of eternal punishment must have exercised a powerful effect in connection with their belie in the imminence of the millennium. Fear of divine wrath i often known to have impelled men to conversion.[1] It was an element in the conversion of Paul, and entered into that of Luther, and revivalists like Jonathan Edwards and Wesley often appeal to the emotion of crude fear. Wesley wrote in one of his letters : " My chief motive, to which all the rest are subordinate, is the hope of saving my own soul." [2] William James observes that the " old-fashioned hell-fire Christianity well knew how to extract from fear its full conversion value." As late as the middle of the nineteenth century, General Booth could write : " Nothing moves people like the terrific. They must have hell-fire flashed before their faces, or they will not move." But in that century, at last, a considerable number of Christians began to feel shocked by the ancient doctrine of eternal punishment. Nowadays, according to Dr. Major, the general belief in the English Church is, that " the soul at death passes into the spirit world, and never again has anything to do with its fleshy integument, which has been deposited in the grave " ; and a conviction has grown up that heaven and hell are thought of not as localities but as personal states, and that there is every degree of purgatory between them. Dr. Inge does not think that in our own time at any rate self-regarding motives, based on a calculation of future happiness or misery, have much influence.[3] For those who accept the view expressed in the recent Report of the Commission on Christian Doctrine appointed by the English Archbishops, that the essence of hell is merely exclusion from the fellowship of God, there cannot be much fear of it. At the same time acts which originally were prompted by hope or fear may leave behind habits for which there is no longer any such motive. Moreover, sincere devotion to a divine law-giver may lead to a perfectly unselfish desire to obey his will.

As for the doctrine that a man is justified by faith without the deeds of the law, it may be asserted unhesitatingly that it has proved to exercise an evil influence upon the morality of conduct. While to an ecstatic convert like Paul faith may seem a sufficient source of good deeds as its fruits, the faith of the ordinary believer may fail entirely to produce similar effects. It was already found in the Apostolic age that the formula about salvation by faith alone was taken advantage of as a cloak of laxity ; it was argued that one may have the true faith, although in this case faith remained dead or was combined with immorality. James

[1] A. C. Underwood, Conversion : Christian and Non-Christian (London, 1925), p. 134 sqq.
[2] Wesley, quoted in The Times Literary Supplement, May 21, 1938.
[3] W. R. Inge, Christian Ethics and Moral Problems (London, 1932), p. 74.

evidently saw this danger when he wrote in his epistle : " What doth it profit, my brethren, though a man may say he hath faith, and have not works ? can faith save him ? . . . Faith without works is dead." Ordinary men are not mystics ; and ecstatic converts are dangerous founders of religious creeds. The demoralising effect of the teaching of justification by faith was again testified by its revival at the Reformation. There remain a series of painful confessions of disappointment with the moral results of their work on the part of the Reformers themselves. Sometimes the devil is called in to account for so painful and perplexing a state of things. But it is significant that Luther himself does not altogether acquit the doctrine of justification— though in his view misapprehended—of blame in this matter. It may be worth while to repeat the verdict of Harnack, the great Lutheran theologian : " The holding to the ' faith alone ' (' fides sola ') necessarily resulted in dangerous laxity. What would really have been required here would have been to lead Christians to see that only the ' fides caritate formata ' has a real value before God. . . . If one has persuaded himself that everything that suggests ' good works ' must be dropped out of the religious sequence, there ultimately remains over only the readiness to subject one's self to faith, i.e., to the pure doctrine. . . . The Lutheran Church had to pay dearly for turning away from ' legal righteousness,' ' sacrifice,' and ' satisfactions.' Through having the resolute wish to go back to *religion* and to it alone, it neglected far too much the moral problem, the ' Be ye holy, for I am holy.' " But the faith which is required for salvation may also in another respect be a danger to morality. The Socinians argued that the doctrine of vicarious suffering blunts the conscience and leads easily to moral slackness. And the doctrine of the vicarious merit of Christ may have a similar effect.

But worse things may be said of the doctrine of justification by faith. In Catholicism the faith required is that recognised by the Catholic Church, which is looked upon as the guarantor of the truth of her doctrines ; while the Protestants hold that the faith of their own Church, or at any rate faith in Christ, is neces- sary for salvation. Even in the case of Christians errors in the belief on such subjects as the Trinity, original sin, and pre- destination have been declared to expose the guilty to eternal damnation. This led to those terrific persecutions of heretics which occurred on an enormous scale in Catholicism, but also were advocated and practised by Protestants. Luther's intoler- ance chiefly spends itself in violent words, and he objects to inflicting capital punishment in cases of heresy. Melanchthon was less merciful, and Calvin lays down with great distinctness the duty of repressing heresy by force. And even Zwingli, who once spoke of a heaven in which Christians may expect to meet the wise and good of heathen antiquity, approved of putting false teachers to death. In England Presbyterians, through a long succession of reigns, were imprisoned, branded, mutilated, scourged, and exposed in pillory ; many Catholics under false pretences were tortured and hung ; Anabaptists and Arians were burnt alive. When Reformation triumphed in Scotland, one of its first fruits was a law which declared that whoever either said mass, or was present while it was said, should for the first offence lose his goods, for the second offence be exiled, and for the third offence be put to death.

There has been religious persecution outside Christendom, but then there were mostly political reasons for it.[1] In Christianity, too, such reasons have not been wanting. Another reason was greed ; and an ecclesiastical motive was undoubtedly that the cohesion and power of the Church depended upon a strict adherence to its doctrines. But the principal reason was undoubtedly the doctrine of exclusive justification by faith. Thus Paul, who before his conversion had been persecuting Christians, became afterwards the indirect cause of religious persecution on an infinitely greater scale. It is significant that the reviver of Paulinism, Augustine, also was the spiritual father of persecution.

The persecutions were by no means ineffective. Before operating in any district the inquisitors used to make a proclamation offering pardon under certain conditions to those who confessed and retracted their heresies within thirty or forty days. We are told that when such a proclamation was made on the first establishment of the Inquisition in Andalusia, 17,000 recantations followed. This was presumably regarded as a triumph of truth ; but it was scarcely a triumph of truthfulness. Augustine himself writes that we must avoid the lie, and even when we err in our thought, must always say what we think.

But it is not only by persecutions that the Christian Churches have impaired the spirit of truth. They have also done it by softer means—by inducing the State to make the profession of a certain creed, or at any rate the performance of certain religious rites, a condition of the enjoyment of full civic rights. And this is what even Protestant countries have been doing up to our own

[1] Max Weber, ' Die protestantische Ethik und der Geist des Kapitalismus,' in *Gesammelte Aufsätze zur Religionssoziologie* (Tübingen, 1922), p. 132 n.

time. In the case of the clergy, too, there is considerable inducement to insincerity. Dean Rashdall remarks that the most
deadly result of the doctrine of justification by faith is that it has
fostered the belief that honest thinking is sinful and blind
credulity meritorious. " It deters the clergy from study, from
thought, and from openly teaching what they themselves really
believe."

The highest regard for truth is not to profess it, but to seek
for it. In this respect the Christian Churches have been
lamentably deficient. While the knowledge of religious truth
has been held to be a necessary requirement of salvation, all other
knowledge was for a long time regarded not only as valueless but
even as sinful. " The wisdom of this world," says Paul, " is
foolishness with God " ; and Tertullian expresses the ecclesiastical contempt of scientific knowledge in the famous formula,
" I believe because it is impossible." It has been truly said that
" there is scarcely a disposition that marks the love of abstract
truth, and scarcely a rule which reason teaches as essential for its
attainment, that theologians did not for centuries stigmatise as
offensive to the Almighty." We are told that Europe was at
last rescued from this frightful condition by the intellectual
influences that produced the Reformation. This may be true
in a manner, but it was not the Reformation itself that marked
the change. With Luther reason and faith were deadly enemies :
what Scripture imposes upon us was precisely what reason would
bid us to reject. " All the articles of our Christian faith," he
writes, " which God has revealed to us in his Word are in presence
of reason sheerly impossible " ; and when his natural reason
rebelled against the violence offered to it, the revolt was ascribed
to the direct agency of the devil.

The patient and impartial search after hidden truth, for the
sake of truth alone, which constitutes the essence of scientific
research, is of course the very opposite of that ready acceptance
of a revealed truth for the sake of eternal salvation, which has
been insisted on by the Churches. Nevertheless we are told,
even by highly respectable writers, that the modern world owes
its scientific spirit to the extreme importance which Christianity
assigned to the possession of truth, of *the* truth. This statement
is a curious instance of the common tendency to attribute to the
influence of the Christian religion almost any good which may be
found among Christian peoples. This is particularly prevalent
in the case of morals. It has been claimed that " Christianity
has proved itself the highest ethical force in the history of man " ;
that all virtue and good conduct in mankind owes its origin to the
Christian religion ; that it has been the main source of the moral

development of Europe. I have examined the influence which Christianity has exercised both on morals in general and within various departments of social and moral life, and arrived at different conclusions. It is interesting to note that even a theological writer, like Dr. Inge, says " it is disquieting for Christians to have to admit that the growth of humanity, in the sense of humaneness, does not owe much to the Churches." [1]

My criticism has not been based on any standard of " moral objectivity," because I maintain that there is no such standard, moral judgments being ultimately based upon emotions, which necessarily vary in different individuals. It has been said that Christianity lifts morality out of mere relativity, and that " the Christian point of view gives to conduct an absolute value " ; but, as we have seen, there are in Christianity many different points of view. At the same time there are certain general characteristics which belong to the very nature of our moral consciousness and show a considerable uniformity, especially when the moral judgments are guided by sufficient sympathy and intellectual discernment. These have also within Christianity proved to be important correctives of old dogmas. Professor Sasse writes : " For modern Protestantism, as it has been defined by the Age of Enlightenment, the Lamb of God who bears the sins of the world no longer exists at all. . . . Christ has become merely a new law-giver, a second Moses, who left behind him a moral and religious teaching. And then the salvation or damnation of man depends solely upon the obedience or disobedience to these laws." [2] Yet there are also Protestants who still adhere to Luther's antimoralism.[3] To me it seems that all believers in a righteous God, who has implanted a moral consciousness in the human mind, have to admit that no religious doctrines which conflict with its principles can have a divine revelation as its source.

[1] Inge, *op. cit.* p. 281.
[2] H. Sasse, ' Luther and the Teaching of the Reformation,' in E. G. Selwyn, *History of Christian Thought* (London, 1937), p. 122.
[3] See *supra*, p. 68 ; G. Aulén, ' Kravet på dogmhistorisk revision,' in *Svensk teologisk kvartalskrift*, ix (Lund, 1933).

INDEX OF PERSONS

INDEX OF SUBJECTS